Comparative Politics *OF THE* Global South

FIFTH EDITION

Comparative Politics OF THE Global South

LINKING CONCEPTS & CASES

DECEMBER GREEN
LAURA LUEHRMANN

LYNNE RIENNER PUBLISHERS
BOULDER
LONDON

Published in the United States of America in 2022 by
Lynne Rienner Publishers, Inc.
1800 30th Street, Suite 314, Boulder, Colorado 80301
www.rienner.com

and in the United Kingdom by
Lynne Rienner Publishers, Inc.
Gray's Inn House, 127 Clerkenwell Road, London EC1 5DB
www.eurospanbookstore.com/rienner

Library of Congress Cataloging-in-Publication Data
Names: Green, December, author. | Luehrmann, Laura, 1969– author.
Title: Comparative politics of the Global South : linking concepts and cases / December Green, Laura Luehrmann.
Description: Fifth edition. | Boulder, Colorado : Lynne Rienner Publishers, Inc, 2022. | Includes bibliographical references and index. | Summary: "An innovative blend of theory and empirical material that accessibly introduces the politics of what was once called the 'third world'"—Provided by publisher.
Identifiers: LCCN 2022000118 | ISBN 9781955055550 (paperback)
Subjects: LCSH: Developing countries—Politics and government—Case studies. | Developing countries—Economic policy—Case studies.
Classification: LCC JF60 .G74 2022 | DDC 320.9171/24—dc23/eng/20220318
LC record available at https://lccn.loc.gov/2022000118

British Cataloguing in Publication Data
A Cataloguing in Publication record for this book
is available from the British Library.

Printed and bound in the United States of America

The paper used in this publication meets the requirements of the American National Standard for Permanence of Paper for Printed Library Materials Z39.48-1992.

5 4 3 2 1

To our students—past, present, and future

You inspired this book and you motivate us to continue with it.
Keep asking questions, and go change the world.

Contents

Figures

Preface

The first edition of this text was published in 2003. We wrote it in the wake of September 11, 2001, when the world was coming to grips with one of the most audacious terrorist attacks ever, and the United States was on the precipice of a new era of global engagement. HIV/AIDs was continuing to ravage much of the world, the opaque nature of the emerging war on terrorism was just beginning, and widespread awareness of greenhouse gas emissions and the vast extent of human-made climate change was taking on new importance. In the first edition, there was no discussion of social media, and, even though we discussed the terminological drawbacks to such language, our cases were framed as members of the "third world."

It's simple, but true: much has changed in the twenty years since we began working on this project. The US-led war in Afghanistan ended in disappointment and uncertainty; after an "America First" administration, many openly question the US commitment to global leadership; China's importance is no longer doubted; and the third wave of democracy—despite the initial hopes for a democratic windfall from the Arab Spring—has decidedly crashed. Authoritarianism and populism touch politics in every part of the world, as strong leaders combine the powerful forces of nationalism with technology. The digitization of so many aspects of daily life—from social media communication to classroom instruction and even daily commerce—may increase access to information (although it exposes great gaps), but it also enables the easy surveillance and tracking of even the simplest transactions. And then there's the Covid-19 pandemic. As this book goes to press, yet another highly contagious variant is spreading around the globe, and the wide inequities that animate many of the challenges we discuss in the pages ahead continue to impact countries' abilities to respond to the most significant public health crisis in our lifetimes.

Yet, we contended then, as we do even more strongly now, that the voices of people in what can be called the developing world, third world, majority world, or global south (fighting words that we address in Chapter 1) need to be heard. We also argued then (and argue now) that attention must be paid to the so-called ordinary people—the less visible, yet consequential individuals (sometimes organized in groups, other times not) who rally to either preserve or change the status quo. Whether it is an aggrieved fruit seller in Tunisia, university students in Nigeria, or an inquisitive doctor in China, some of the people who spark change within their societies never (or rarely) make the headlines or rise to the trending-topic ranking on social media. Our hope is to spotlight some of these agents of change—their voices, experiences, struggles, and dreams—to provide a more complete picture of politics, economy, and society in the twenty-first-century world.

* * *

Projects are never solitary; we are fortunate to have a supportive cast of characters who have assisted us along the way. Special thanks to Linda Caron, dean of the College of Liberal Arts at Wright State University, for her support of this project and of our work in general. Our colleagues at Wright State School of Public and International Affairs, and later, the School of the Social Sciences and International Studies have been particularly helpful in the formulation and completion of this book, as well as in creating a supportive environment that fuses excellence in the classroom with active research. It was especially helpful to have designated writing days with two of our colleagues—Lee Hannah and Dan Warshawsky—with whom we shared the triumphs and travails of the writing process, as well as many laughs. We also give special thanks to Shirley Barber for her assistance with many of the figures, as well as to her overall moral support. But it is to our students that we express our greatest admiration; their questions have motivated much of the shape of the book. Their insights, curiosities, and frustrations helped clarify what needed to be included in an introductory text, and they continue to inspire us to ask better questions and try to capture an ever-changing world in terms that are meaningful.

We are also grateful to all the wonderful people at Lynne Rienner Publishers, but particularly to Lynne herself for understanding the need for this book and for going above and beyond, using her experience and expertise to refine it. Her support in carrying this project to a fifth edition is greatly appreciated. We clearly remember connecting with Lynne in the early months of the Covid-19 pandemic, when we were still facing rather strict lockdown measures, to discuss the timetable and scope for the next iteration of this project. Special thanks to Moorea Corrigan; our production editor, Shena Redmond; and our excellent copyeditor, whose diligence has helped us present a clearer, more accurate product.

Between us, we've had three sons grow up with the various editions of this book, and both of our partners have learned to provide that delicate balance of support, encouragement, humor, and distance. To Dave and Joe, we express our love and profound appreciation.

—December Green
Laura Luehrmann

1

Comparing and Defining an Interdependent World

No human culture is inaccessible to someone who makes the effort to understand, to learn, to inhabit another world. —*Henry Louis Gates*[1]

In periods of crisis, some things become clearer. During the Covid PANDEMIC,* we all became acutely conscious of the ways in which even our day-to-day lives and most basic routines can be impacted by things that happen thousands of miles away. Even though analysts have long forecasted that the world was likely due for a pandemic scenario (most notably after the Ebola epidemic in West Africa), it is striking to consider the many ways, both dramatic and subtle, that our world, and our interactions with others, has changed since the March 11, 2020, declaration by the World Health Organization (WHO) that the novel coronavirus labeled Covid-19 was indeed a pandemic.[2] Facing such upheaval, the entire world seemed to change. "Working from home" became the norm in nearly every part of the globe, as all but those deemed "essential" were instructed to "shelter in place" as much as possible to help stop the spread of this highly contagious respiratory virus. Long-used terms like "public health" and "remote learning" stood alongside concepts infused with new meanings, including "social distancing" and "Zoom," as we all tried to figure out the best way to navigate a rapidly moving, seemingly ever-changing landscape. At once, borders and geography seemed both crucial (as countries closed to all but the most essential traffic)[3] and irrelevant (travel blockades were largely impotent against stopping the global advance of the virus and its variants, even if they did slow the spread of the disease).[4] The events of recent years provide a vibrant laboratory from which we can analyze our engagement with the world.

In this book we take a comparative approach to the study of Africa, Asia, Latin America, and the Middle East. How should we refer to this immense collection

---

*Terms appearing in SMALL CAPITAL LETTERS are defined in the Glossary, which begins on p. 493.

of countries, people, and cultures, comprising more than 75 percent of the world's population? As you'll see, we are not the first to struggle with what's in a name. In fact, it was only in the prior edition of this text that we changed the title from *Comparative Politics of the Third World* to *Comparative Politics of the Global South*. Some may argue this change was long overdue. This shift in terminology reflects not only our ongoing discomfort with the "three worlds" terminology, but also a heightened recognition—by scholars, practitioners, citizens, and activists alike—that, despite its drawbacks, the concept of the "global south" is the least offensive and most value-neutral label (despite some obvious geographic inaccuracies).[5] To understand a bit of the controversy, let's begin with a short review of some of the terminology and disputes surrounding characterizations of the majority of the world's population.

There are numerous labels we may employ. One of the most common (and, indeed, the most provocative), is "third world." Why? The term "third world" (tiers monde) was coined by French demographer Alfred Sauvy. In a 1952 article, Sauvy borrowed from eighteenth-century writer Emmanuel Joseph Sieyes to compare relatively poor countries of the world to the "third estate" (the people) at the time of the French Revolution. Sieyes characterized the third estate as ignored, exploited, and scorned. Sauvy characterized the third world similarly, but pointed out that it, like the third estate, has the power to overcome its status.[6]

So what's so off-putting, then, about the term "third world"? First and foremost, it is objectionable for both logical and emotional reasons. Former WORLD BANK president and US deputy secretary of state Robert Zoellick once declared that there is no longer a third world.[7] Not only do critics of the term disdain the concept as unwieldy and obsolete, but they also fault it as distorting reality in attempting to geopolitically and economically classify a diverse group of countries.

And let's face it, the term "third world" can be fighting words. The phrase carries a lot of negative baggage, and is viewed to be antiquated and offensive terminology.[8] Many people cringe at hearing the term and avoid using it because, at the very least, it sounds condescending and quaintly racist. It is not unusual for "third world" to be flung as an insult. For some, the term suggests backwardness. Third world countries are often thought to play a peripheral role in the world, having no voice and little weight or relevance. That is certainly not the case, as this book demonstrates.

The geopolitical use of the term "third world" dates back to the COLD WAR, the period of US-Soviet rivalry from approximately 1947 to 1989, reflecting the ideological conflict that dominated international relations. For decades following World War II the rich, economically advanced, industrialized countries, also known as the "first world," were pitted against the Soviet-led, communist "second world." In this rivalry, each side described what it was doing as self-defense, and both the first and second worlds claimed to be fighting to "save" the planet from the treachery of the other. Much of this battle was over who would control the nonaligned "third world," which served as the theater for many Cold War conflicts and whose countries were treated as pawns in this chess game. Defined simply as the remainder of the planet—being neither first nor second—the concept of the third world has always been unwieldy, often bringing to mind countries that are poor, agricultural, and overpopulated.

Yet, consider the stunning diversity that exists among the countries of every region of the world: surely they cannot all be lumped into a single category and characterized as such today. For example, how do we categorize China? It is clearly led by a communist party (and therefore may be considered second world), but during the Cold War it viewed itself as the leader of the third world. What about Israel? Because of the dramatic disparities within it, the country can be categorized as third world or first, depending on where we look. The same can even be said for the United States. Visit parts of its inner cities, the rural South, or Appalachia, and you will find the so-called third world, or what some even characterize as "fourth world."[9] With the Cold War long over, why aren't the former republics of the Soviet Union included in most studies of the third world? Certainly, the poorest of them are more third world than first.

The fact is, many countries fall between the cracks when we use the three-worlds typology. Some of the countries labeled third world are oil-rich, while others have been industrializing for so long that even the term "newly industrializing countries" (NICs) is dated (it is still used, but has largely been replaced by "emerging economies"). Therefore, in appreciation of the diversity contained within the third world, perhaps it is useful to subdivide it, to allow for specificity by adding more categories. Under this schema, the emerging countries and a few others that are most appropriately termed "emerging and developing countries" are labeled "third world" (e.g., India, South Korea, Brazil, Mexico). "Fourth world" countries could include those states that are not industrializing, but have some resources to sell on the world market (e.g., Nigeria, Afghanistan, and Egypt), or some strategic value that wins them some foreign assistance. The label "less developed country" (LDC) is the best fit in most of these cases since it simply describes their situation and implies little in terms of their prospects for DEVELOPMENT. And finally, we have the "fifth world," which Henry Kissinger once callously characterized as "the basket cases of the world." These are the world's poorest countries. Sometimes known as "least–less developed countries" (LLDCs), they have been under-developed. With little to sell on the world market, they are eclipsed by it. The poorest in the world, with the worst ratings for virtually every marker of human development, these countries are marginalized and utterly dependent on what little foreign assistance they receive.

Today, it is more common to hear the STATES of these regions variously referred to as "developing countries," "less developed countries," or "underdeveloped countries." Currently in vogue are also the stripped-down, minimalist terms "low-income countries" (LICs), "high-income countries" (HICs), and even low- and lower-middle-income countries (LMICs). These are just a few of the labels used to refer to a huge expanse of territories and peoples, and none are entirely satisfactory. First, our subject—comprising four major world regions—is so vast and so heterogeneous that it is difficult to speak of it as a single entity. Second, each name has its own political implications and each insinuates a political message. For example, although some countries contained within these regions are better off than others, only an optimist would label all of them as "developing countries." It is a real stretch to say that some of the countries we'll be looking at are developing. Some are under-developing—losing ground, becoming worse off.[10]

Those who prefer the term "emerging and developing countries" tend to support the idea that the capitalist path of free markets will eventually lead to peace and prosperity for all; it implies a hopeful notion of what is possible. Capitalism is associated with rising prosperity in some countries such as South Korea and Mexico, but even in these countries huge numbers of people have yet to share in many of its benefits. However, the relative term "less developed countries" prompts the question: Less developed than whom—or what? The answer, inevitably, is what we arbitrarily label "developed countries": the rich, industrialized states of Western Europe, Canada, and the United States, also known as "the West" (a term that, interestingly enough, includes Japan but excludes most of the countries of the Western Hemisphere).

Although some are now more careful to say "economically advanced," and people often throw about the terms "advanced," "developed," or "less developed" as a shorthand measure of economic advancement, often such names are resented because they imply that "less developed" countries are somehow lacking in other, broader measures of political, social, or cultural development. Use of the term "developing," or any of these terms for that matter, may sound optimistic, but it suggests that countries can be ranked along a continuum. Such terms can be used to imply that the West is best, that the rest of the world is comparatively "backward," and that the most the citizens of the rest of the world can hope for is to "develop" using the West as a model.

In the 2015 annual letter of the Bill and Melinda Gates Foundation, the famed investors turned philanthropists contended that such terminology has outlived its utility. Why, for example, should Mozambique and Mexico be grouped together?[11] Critics contend that the terminology is intellectually lazy, outdated, and judgmental. The World Bank got rid of the "developing countries" terminology in 2016, in part to highlight measures of economic success, and in part to point out the importance of differences existing within countries themselves.[12] They now classify countries into low-income, lower-middle-income, upper-middle-income, and high-income economies, based on gross national income (GNI) per capita, adjusted annually for inflation. As it phases out the use of "developing or developed" world from within its databases, the World Bank focuses less on general characterization and more on the priority of promoting SUSTAINABLE DEVELOPMENT.

If we look at the issues in terms of sheer numbers, focusing on the size of the populations of the countries we are analyzing, perhaps we should adopt the terminology of "majority world," given that, according to the World Bank, more than 50 percent of the global population may be categorized as either poor (living on less than \$1.90/day) or the higher poverty threshold (\$3.20/day), with a significant increase in the so-called new poor being traced to the negative impacts of Covid.[13] In fact, as we discuss throughout the book, Covid is reversing much of the progress that had been achieved in the years prior to 2020, especially in terms of the growth of the global middle class, most notably in South Asia and sub-Saharan Africa; and the world is risking a "two-speed recovery" of diverging rates for rich, compared to poorer, countries.[14] Demographically, the countries that are included in our "global south" category constitute more than 50 percent of the world's population, lending some credence to this "majority world" label.[15]

Geography is the point of reference for some, including those who argue that the West developed only at the expense of the rest of the world. For these analysts, under-development is no natural event or coincidence. Rather, it is the outcome of hundreds of years of active under-development by today's developed countries. Some have captured this dynamic as the all-inclusive "non-Western world." As others have demonstrated, it is probably more honest to speak of "the West and the rest" if we are to use this kind of term, since there are many non-Wests rather than a single non-Western world.[16] At least "the West and the rest" is blatantly straightforward in its Eurocentric center of reference, dismissing 75 percent of the world's population and treating "the rest" as "other." In the same manner that the term "nonwhite" is demeaning, "non-Western" implies that something is missing. Our subject becomes defined only through its relationship to a more central "West."

Resistance to such treatment, and efforts to change situations, is sometimes referred to as the "North-South conflict," or the war between the haves and the have-nots of the world. The names "North" and "South" are useful because they are seemingly stripped of the value judgments contained within most of the terms already described. However, they are as imprecise as the term "West," since "North" refers to developed countries, which mostly fall north of the equator, and "South" is another name for less developed countries, which mostly fall south of the equator. Similar to any dichotomy, this terminology invites illusions of superiority and "otherness," homogenizing differences and elevating one's own culture or lifestyle.

So, why has the phraseology of global south seemingly come into vogue? Some argue that it has long been the preferred term for what used to be called the third world, even if it must be "used elastically."[17] Used with increasing frequency within the UNITED NATIONS in the 1970s, "global south" has, in many circles, replaced a three worlds construct that became increasingly irrelevant after the collapse of the Soviet Union in 1991.[18] Even if today the metaphor is used to highlight both the empowerment and shared circumstances of many around the world, its origins, traced to the Brandt Commission reports of the early 1980s, are now viewed as patronizing in their call for the financial support of the "north" for modernization efforts undertaken within the "south."[19] Similar to each of the constructs we discussed above, its lines are fuzzy, and we must recognize it for the created construct that it is. To the extent that it helps us grasp some of the common challenges and innovations of people and governments, and how some of these issues are viewed differently than from the vantage point of the developed north, the term "global south" may be useful, albeit imperfect.

Clearly, none of the names we use to describe the countries of Africa, Asia, Latin America, and the Middle East are satisfactory, and any generalization is going to be limited. Even the terms "Latin America" and "Middle East" are problematic. Not all of Latin America is "Latin" in the sense of being Spanish- or Portuguese-speaking. Yet we will use this term as shorthand for the entire region south of the US border, including the Caribbean. And the idea of a region being "Middle East" only makes sense if one's perspective is distinctly European—otherwise, what is it "middle" to? The point is that most of our labels reflect some bias, and none of them are fully satisfactory. These names are all ideologically loaded in one way or another. Because there is no simple, clearly most appropriate identifier available, we use each and all of them as markers of the varying worldviews presented in this text. Ultimately, we leave it to the reader to sift through the material presented here, consider the debates, and decide which arguments—and therefore which terminologies—are most representative of the world and therefore most useful.

What's to Compare?

In this introduction to the COMPARATIVE STUDIES of Africa, Asia, Latin America, and the Middle East, we take a different spin on the traditional approach to discuss much more than politics as it is often narrowly defined. As one of the social sciences, political science has traditionally focused on the study of formal political institutions and behavior. In this book, we choose not to put the spotlight on governments and voting patterns, party politics, and so on. Rather, we turn our attention to all manner of political behavior, which we consider to include just about any aspect of life. Of interest to us is not only how people are governed, but also how they live, how they govern themselves, and what they see as their most urgent concerns.

We employ a political interaction approach. It is an eclectic method that presents ideas from a variety of contemporary thinkers and theories. Our approach is also multidisciplinary. We divide our attention among history, politics, society, and economics to convey more fully the complexity of human experience.[20] Instead of artificially confining ourselves to one narrow discipline, we recognize that each discipline offers another layer or dimension, which adds immeasurably to our understanding of the "essence" of politics.[21]

Comparative politics, then, is much more than simply a subject of study—it is also a means of study. It employs what is known as the comparative method. Through the use of the comparative method, we seek to describe, identify, and explain trends—in some cases, even predict human behavior. Those who adopt this approach, known as comparativists, are interested in identifying relationships and patterns of behavior and interactions between individuals and groups. Focusing on one or more countries, comparativists examine CASE STUDIES alongside one another. They search for similarities and differences between and among the elements selected for comparison. For example, one might compare patterns of female employment and fertility rates in one country in relation to those patterns in other countries. Using the comparative method, analysts make explicit or implicit comparisons, searching for common and contrasting features. Some do a "most similar systems" analysis, looking for differences between cases that appear to have a great deal in common (e.g., Canada and the United States). Others prefer a "most different" approach, looking for commonalities between cases that appear diametrically opposed in experience (e.g., Bolivia and India).[22] What is particularly exciting about this type of analysis is stumbling upon unexpected parallels between ostensibly different cases. Just as satisfying is beginning to understand the significance and consequences of the differences that exist between cases assumed to have much in common.

Most comparative studies textbooks take one of two roads. Either they offer case studies, which provide loads of intricate detail on a handful of states (often the classics: Mexico, Nigeria, China, and India; curiously, the Middle East is frequently ignored), or they provide a CROSS-NATIONAL ANALYSIS that purports to generalize about much larger expanses of territory. Those who take the cross-national approach are interested in getting at the big picture. Texts that employ it focus on theory and concepts to broaden our scope of understanding beyond a handful of cases. They often end up making fairly sweeping generalizations. The authors of these books may reference any number of countries as illustration, but at the loss of detail and context that come only through the use of case studies.

We provide both cross-national analysis and case studies because we don't want to lose the strengths of either approach. We present broad themes and concepts, while including attention to the variations that exist in reality. In adopting this hybrid approach, we have set for ourselves a more ambitious task. However, as teachers, we recognize the need for both approaches to be presented. We have worked hard to show how cross-national analysis and case studies can work in tandem, how each complements the other. By looking at similar phenomena in several contexts (i.e., histories, politics, societies, economics, and international relations of the global south, more generally), we can apply our cases and compare them, illustrating the similarities and differences experienced in different settings.

Therefore, in addition to the cross-national analysis that composes the bulk of each chapter, we offer eight case studies, two from each of the major regions of the third world. For each region, we include the "classics" offered in virtually every text that applies the case method to the non-Western experience: Mexico, Nigeria, China, and Iran. We offer these cases for the same reasons that so many others see fit to include them. However, we go further. To temper the tendency to view these cases as somehow representative of their regions, and to enhance the basis for comparison, we submit alongside the classics other, less predictable case studies from each region. These additional cases are equally interesting and important in their own regard; they are countries that are rarely (if ever) included as case studies in introductory textbooks: Peru, Zimbabwe, Egypt, and Indonesia (see the maps and country profiles in Figures 1.2 to 1.9 at the end of this chapter).

Through detailed case studies, we learn what is distinctive about the many peoples of the world, and get a chance to see the world from a perspective other than our own. We can begin to do comparative analysis by thinking about what makes the people of the world alike and what makes us different. We should ask ourselves how and why such differences exist, and consider the various constraints under which we all operate. We study comparative politics not only to understand the way other people view the world, but also to make better sense of our own understanding of it. We have much to learn from how similar problems are approached by different groups of people. To do this, we must consider the variety of factors that serve as context, to get a better idea of why things happen and why events unfold as they do.[23] The better we get at this, the better idea we will have of what to expect in the future. And we will get a better sense of what works and what doesn't work so well—in the cases under examination, but also in other countries. You may be tempted to compare the cases under review with the situation in your country. And that's to be encouraged, since the study of how others approach problems may offer us ideas on how to improve our own lives. Comparativists argue that drawing from the experience of others is really the only way to understand our own systems. Seeing beyond the experience of developed countries and what is immediately familiar to us expands our minds, allows us to see the wider range of alternatives, and offers new insights into the challenges we face at the local, national, and international levels.

The greatest insight, however, comes with the inclusion of a larger circle of voices—beyond those of the leaders and policymakers. Although you will certainly hear the arguments of leaders in the chapters that follow, you will also hear the voices of those who are not often represented in texts such as this. You will hear stories of domination and the struggle against it. You will hear not only how people have been oppressed, but also how they have liberated themselves.[24] Throughout the following chapters, we have worked to include the standpoints and perspectives of the ostensibly "powerless": the economically poor, youth, and women. Although they are often ignored by their governments, including the US government, hearing their voices is a necessity if we are to fully comprehend the complexity of the challenges all of us face. Until these populations are included and encouraged to participate to their fullest potential, development will be distorted and delayed. Throughout this book, in a variety of ways, we give attention to these groups and their interests within our discussions of history, economics, society, politics, and international relations.

Interdependence: Mutual Vulnerability

As mentioned earlier, we believe that any introductory study of the global south should include both the specificity of case study as well as the breadth of the cross-national approach. Throughout the chapters that follow, we follow a similar pattern: we introduce some of the dominant issues facing the global south, which are approached from a number of angles and serve as a basis for cross-national comparison. For example, not only is it interesting and important to understand the differences in the experience of disease in Zimbabwe as opposed to Iran, it is just as important to understand how religion, poverty, and war may contribute to the perpetuation of public health challenges. Additionally, in trying to understand the impact of climate change throughout the global south, we should be aware of its impact on economic development, how ordinary people are attempting to cope with it, and what they (with or without world leaders) are prepared to do to fight it. After the thematic and conceptual discussion in each unit, we apply these ideas within our eight case studies, as a way to more clearly illustrate these concepts in operation.

Time and again, we return to a recurring theme of INTERDEPENDENCE. By "interdependence," we refer to a relationship of mutual (although not equal) vulnerability and sensitivity that exists between the world's peoples. This shared interdependence has grown out of a rapidly expanding web of interactions that tie us closer together. Most Americans understand that what we do as a nation often affects others—for better or worse. On the other hand, it is more of a stretch to get the average American to understand why we should care and why

Figure 1.1 Global Village of 1,000 People

There are approximately 7.8 billion people living in our world today. It can be difficult to grasp a sense of comparison with this large size. So, instead, imagine that the world is a village of 1,000 people. Who are its inhabitants?

600 Asians
172 Africans
100 Europeans
47 North Americans
81 Latin Americans and residents across the Caribbean

Within this population, a total of 67 have earned a college degree. Within this village, 863 are able to read and write (90 percent of men and 83 percent of women); and 140 are considered illiterate. Approximately half of the village owns or shares a computer, and 801 own a smartphone.

The people of the village have considerable difficulty communicating:
123 speak Mandarin Chinese
60 speak Spanish
51 speak English
51 speak Arabic
35 speak Hindi
33 speak Bengali
30 speak Portuguese
21 speak Russian
17 speak Japanese

And 579 speak other languages as their first language. The six languages recognized as official languages by the United Nations (Arabic, Mandarin Chinese, English, French, Russian, and Spanish) are the first or second language of approximately 45 percent of the world's population, or about 450 of our village of 1,000 people.

In this village of 1,000 there are
310 Christians
250 Muslims
150 Hindus
70 Buddhists

Approximately 60 people believe in other religions, and 160 are not religious or do not identify themselves as being aligned with a particular faith.

One-third of these 1,000 people in the world village are children, and only 100 are over the age of sixty-five. More than half of the population (approximately 57 percent, or 570) lives in cities, with this rate increasing by nearly 2 percent each year. Approximately 10 percent (100) of the village suffers from hunger. Just over half of the women in the village would have access to and use modern contraceptives. With the birth rate outpacing the death rate, the population of the village next year will be 1,011.

In this 1,000-person community, 523 people receive 10 percent of the world's income; another 84 are in the bottom 50 percent share of the income. Even though 900 people in the village have electricity, only 180 people own an automobile (although some of them own more than one automobile). Of the 1,000 people, 260 lack access to safe drinking water, nearly 300 lack basic soap and water, and 323 lack access to safe sanitation.

Of the earth's surface, approximately 30 percent is land (with 71 percent of this being habitable), and just over 70 percent ocean. About 50 percent of the habitable land is used for agriculture, and only 1 percent is used for cities, town, roads, and other forms of infrastructure (despite increasing rates of urbanization).

Due in part to the increasing expansion of educational opportunities in the village, the ratio of students to faculty in our village has been declining; there is now 1 teacher for every 23 students enrolled in primary education. This is not evenly distributed across our global village, though, with 1 teacher for every 42 students in Africa, while there is 1 teacher for every 15 students in North America. Of these teachers, nearly two-thirds of them (64 percent) are women. In our village of 1,000 citizens, there are only 2 doctors.

Sources: Adapted from Donella H. Meadows, "If the World Were a Village of One Thousand People," Sustainability Institute, 2000. Updated using data from the CIA World Factbook, "World" category (www.cia.gov/the-world-factbook/countries/world/) as well as "Our World in Data" (www.ourworldindata.org).

we need to understand what is happening in the world around us—even in far-off "powerless" countries. However, whether we choose to recognize it or not, it is becoming more and more difficult to escape the fact that our relationship with the world is a reciprocal one. What happens on the other side of the planet, even in seemingly less powerful countries, does affect us—whether we like it or not.

Some have used the image of a "butterfly effect" to capture these dynamics. They highlight the possibility of small, simple actions, like the flapping of a butterfly's wings in Brazil, having complex and potentially huge effects far away, like creating a tornado in Texas.[25] Others have taken this concept to apply it to politics, showing how seemingly small actions can have faraway, potentially large, complex impacts.[26] Given events of recent years, this interconnectedness seems to go without saying. Climate change and the Covid pandemic are easily recognizable examples, but there are many others. Perhaps you remember when a single Taiwan-operated mega tanker (the size of the Empire State Building) collided with the banks of the Suez Canal (the transit point for an estimated one-tenth of world trade), blocking the channel for over a week, stranding hundreds of cargo vessels on either side of the blockage. This singular mishap dealt a significant sucker punch to supply chains around the world.[27] Of course, the Covid pandemic had already revealed the many ways in which component parts of critical supplies, including pharmaceuticals, basic safety equipment like face masks, and even computer chips, relied on the smooth operating of a complex web of just-in-time global supply chains that promote specialization and count on the normally efficient worldwide web of trade. Yet, interdependence introduces unpredictable fragilities, and a combination of unforeseen events brought these weaknesses in stark relief.[28]

For example, most are aware that China is the world's supplier for car parts, toys, and many electronics, but few Americans realized that Chinese pharmaceutical companies supply more than 90 percent of antibiotics used in the United States, as well as most acetaminophen, ibuprofen, and even vitamin C.[29] India, the global leader in generic medicine production, depends on China for 80 percent of its active pharmaceutical components, the chemicals that provide medicinal properties to drugs.[30] Business sectors as wide-ranging as the automotive industry and consumer goods (including washing machines and smartphones) have all been impacted by the bottlenecks in component delivery.[31] Multinational corporations (MNCs), government agencies, and municipalities around the world found themselves re-evaluating even their most basic ways of conducting business, which had been based on the rapid "just in time" production and delivery systems of GLOBALIZATION. And none of this is exclusively economic: Freedom House, a NONGOVERNMENTAL ORGANIZATION (NGO) that monitors the status of democracy, political freedoms, and human rights around the world, speaks of the "long arm" of Covid. The global pandemic has exposed previously existing weaknesses in democracy and liberty around the world, irrespective of government type or level of development.[32] In other words, while Covid is not the cause of many of these challenges, it has magnified awareness of many strains that exist around the world. Pressure has been mounting, demanding our attention.

Conclusions: It Depends on Whom You Ask

Let's put it plainly: There will be no simple answers to many of the questions we have raised here or raise throughout the chapters that follow. The best we can do is to present you with a wide range of thinking and alternative perspectives on many of the challenges faced to some degree by all of us. In this book, we look at a series of issues of interdependence, like migration, public health, and climate change, from a number of angles. Before you make up your mind about any of the contending theories we present here, we ask that you judge each on its merits. We firmly believe that reflecting on another's point of view and considering more than one side of any story is the only way to begin to understand the complex social phenomena we now set out to discuss.

Linking Concepts and Cases

The information in this section is provided as a primer for the case studies we discuss throughout the rest of the book. Figures 1.2 through 1.9 should serve as a point of reference as you read about the histories, economies, and politics of the eight case studies introduced here. Throughout the book, we will return to the same countries, applying the ideas introduced in the conceptual chapters to the reality of their experiences.

Now It's Your Turn

From a simple examination of the statistical information that follows, what would you expect to be the key issue, or the most pressing problem each country faces? What can a sketch like this tell you about life in each of these eight countries? Which ones appear most similar, and in what ways? What are some of the most striking differences between these countries? What other information not included here do you consider deserving of attention? Why?

Notes

1. Henry Louis Gates, "'Authenticity,' or the Lesson of Little Tree," *New York Times Review of Books,* November 24, 1991, p. 30.

2. On January 30, 2020, the WHO declared a "public health emergency of international concern," after thousands of new cases were acknowledged within the People's Republic of China. On February 11, the WHO proposed the official name for the disease caused by the novel coronavirus, Covid-19. See Derrick Bryson Taylor, "A Timeline of the Coronavirus Pandemic," *New York Times,* March 17, 2021.

3. According to the COVID Border Accountability Project, 189 of the world's countries, totaling roughly 65 percent of the world's population, closed all land, sea, and air ports of entry to their country; Europe, South Africa, and Asia saw the most closures. See Covidborderaccountability.org.

4. "Border Closures, Pre-travel Tests of Little Use Against COVID-19 Spread: EU Agency," *Reuters*, May 27, 2020; "Countries Slammed Their Borders Shut to Stop Coronavirus. But Is It Doing Any Good?" NPR, May 15, 2020.

5. For some examples of the lively terminological debate, see the special twenty-fifth anniversary issue of the *Third World Quarterly* 25, no. 1 (2004); the special issue of *The Global South* 5, no. 1 (Spring 2011); Marc Silver, "If You Shouldn't Call It the Third

Figure 1.2 Mexico: Profile and Map

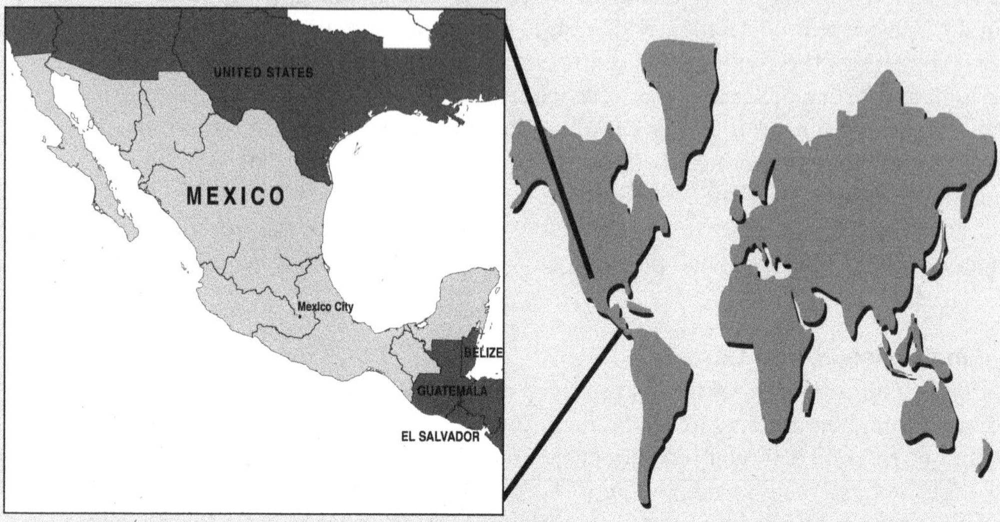

Formal name:	United Mexican States
Area, km²:	1.97 million
Comparative area:	Slightly less than three times the size of Texas
Capital:	Mexico City
Establishment of present state:	September 18, 1810
Population:	130 million
Age under 15 years:	26%
Population growth rate:	0.51%
Fertility rate (children per woman):	2.1
Infant mortality (per 1,000 births):	11
Life expectancy:	77
HIV prevalence (adult):	0.4%
Ethnic groups:	Mestizo 62%, predominantly Amerindian 21%, Amerindian 7%, other 10%
Literacy rate:	95%
Religions:	Roman Catholic 82%, Protestant 8%, other 5%, none 5%
GDP per capita (PPP):	$17,900
GDP growth rate:	–0.3% (2019)
Labor, major sectors:	Services 62%, industrial 24%, agriculture 13%
Population in poverty:	42%
Unemployment rate:	3.5% (with extensive underemployment)
Export commodities:	Cars and vehicle parts, computers, delivery trucks, crude petroleum
External debt:	$456 billion

Source: CIA, *World Factbook 2021.*

Figure 1.3 Peru: Profile and Map

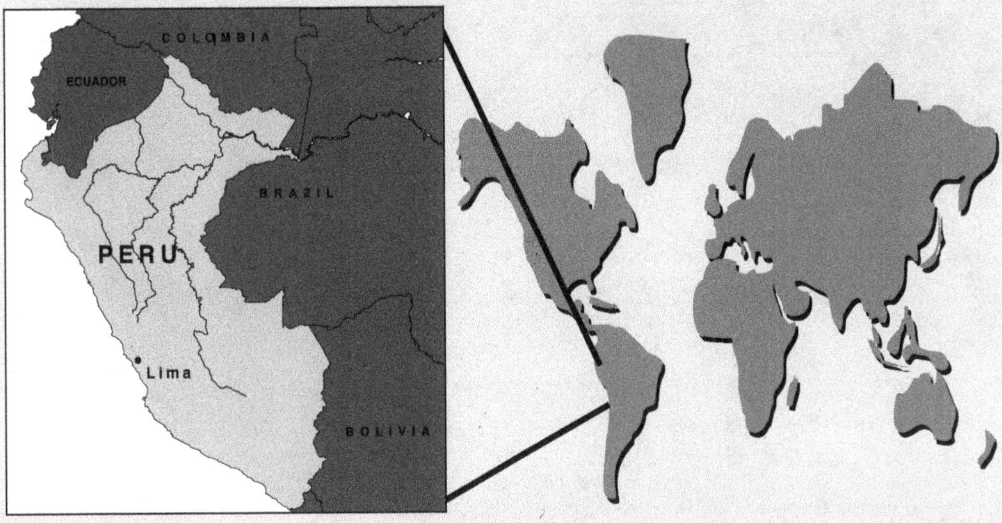

Formal name:	Republic of Peru
Area, km²:	1.28 million
Comparative area:	Almost twice the size of Texas; slightly smaller than Alaska
Capital:	Lima
Establishment of present state:	July 28, 1821
Population:	32 million
Age under 15 years:	25%
Population growth rate:	0.88%
Fertility rate (children per woman):	2
Infant mortality (per 1,000 births):	19
Life expectancy:	75
HIV prevalence (adult):	0.3%
Ethnic groups:	Amerindian 26%, mestizo 60%, white 6%, African descent 4%, other 3.5%
Literacy rate:	95%
Religions:	Roman Catholic 60%, Evangelical 11%, other Christian 3.5%, other 3.5%, none 4%
GDP per capita (PPP):	$11,300
GDP growth rate:	2.1% (2019)
Labor, major sectors:	Services 57%, agricultural 25%, industrial 17%
Population in poverty:	20%
Unemployment rate:	6.5% (data for metropolitan Lima; with extensive underemployment)
Export commodities:	Copper, zinc, gold, refined petroleum, fishmeal, tropical fruits, lead, iron
External debt:	$81 billion

Source: CIA, *World Factbook 2021.*

Figure 1.4 Nigeria: Profile and Map

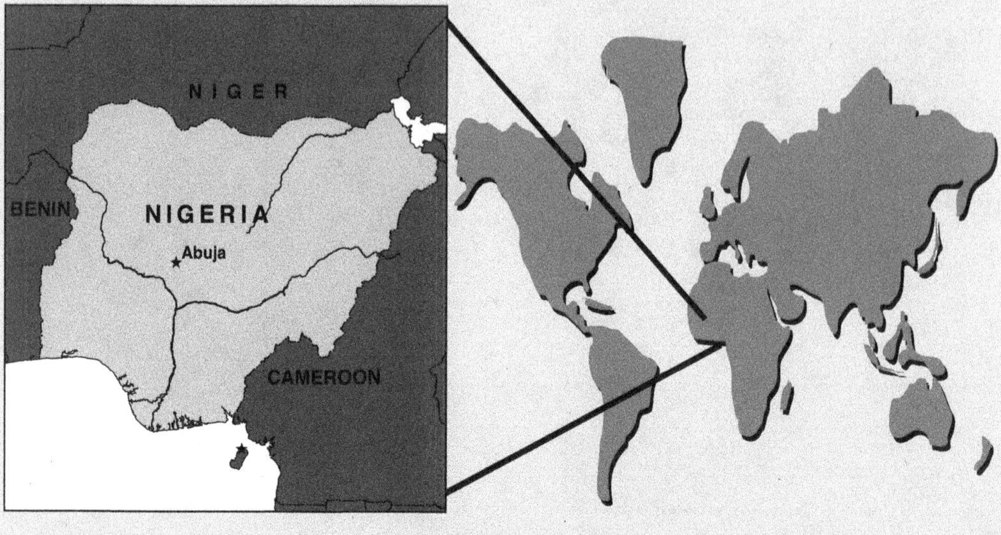

Formal name:	Federal Republic of Nigeria
Area, km^2:	923,768
Comparative area:	About six times the size of Georgia; slightly more than twice the size of California
Capital:	Abuja
Establishment of present state:	October 1, 1960
Population:	219 million
Age under 15 years:	41%
Population growth rate:	2.5%
Fertility rate (children per woman):	4.6
Infant mortality (per 1,000 births):	58
Life expectancy:	60
HIV prevalence (adult):	1.3%
Ethnic groups:	More than 250 groups including Hausa and Fulani 36%, Yoruba 15%, Ibo 15%, Ijaw/Izon 1.8%, Kanuri 2.4%, Ibibio 1.8%, Tiv 2.4%, other 24.7%
Literacy rate:	62%
Religions:	Muslim 53.5%, Christian 46%, other 0.6%
GDP per capita (PPP):	$4,900
GDP growth rate:	0.8% (2017)
Labor, major sectors:	Agriculture 70%, services 20%, industrial 10% (1999)
Population in poverty:	40%
Unemployment rate:	16.5%
Export commodities:	Crude petroleum, natural gas, scrap vessels, cocoa beans
External debt:	$27 billion

Source: CIA, *World Factbook 2021.*

Figure 1.5 Zimbabwe: Profile and Map

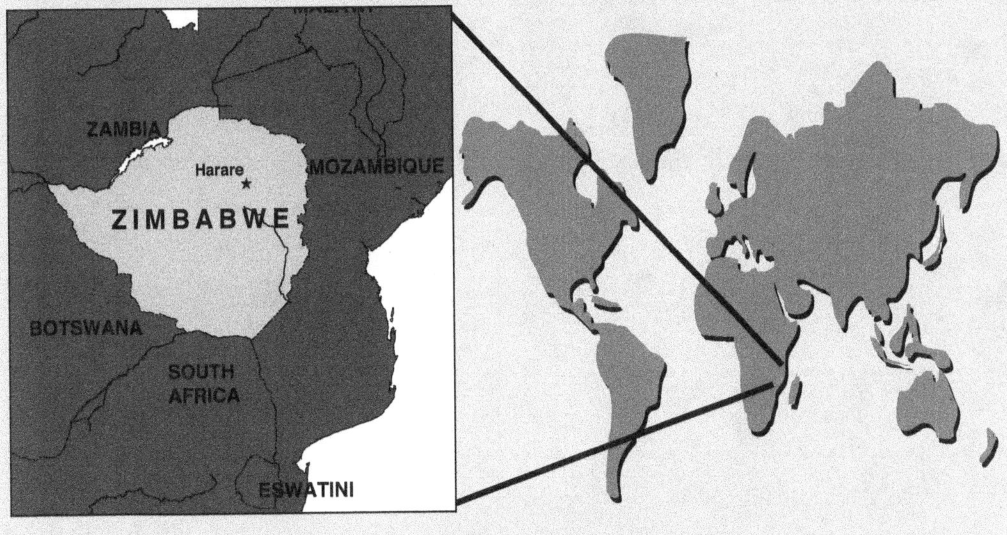

Formal name:	Republic of Zimbabwe
Area, km^2:	390,757
Comparative area:	Slightly larger than Montana
Capital:	Harare
Establishment of present state:	April 18, 1980
Population:	14 million
Age under 15 years:	38%
Population growth rate:	1.9%
Fertility rate (children per woman):	4
Infant mortality (per 1,000 births):	29
Life expectancy:	63
HIV prevalence (adult):	12%
Ethnic groups:	African 99.4% (Shona and Ndebele), other 0.4%, unspecified 0.2%
Literacy rate:	87%
Religions:	Protestant 75%, Roman Catholic 7%, other Christian 5%, Muslim 0.5%, other 0.1%, none 10.5%
GDP per capita (PPP):	$2,700
GDP growth rate:	3.7% (2017)
Labor, major sectors:	Agriculture 66%, services 24%, industrial 10% (1996)
Population in poverty:	38%
Unemployment rate:	11%
Export commodities:	Tobacco, gold, ferroalloys, diamonds
External debt:	$9.3 billion

Source: CIA, *World Factbook 2021.*

Figure 1.6 Egypt: Profile and Map

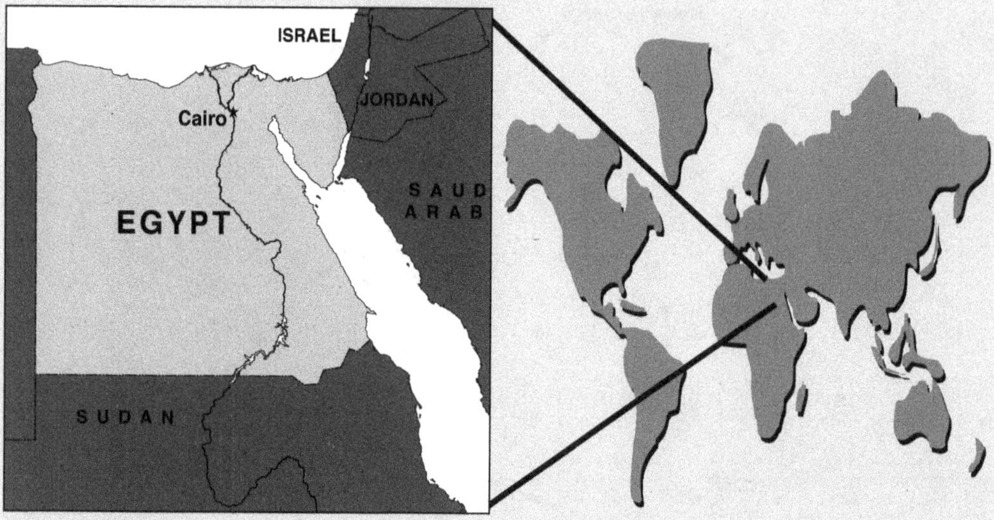

Formal name:	Arab Republic of Egypt
Area, km²:	1 million
Comparative area:	More than eight times the size of Ohio; slightly more than three times the size of New Mexico
Capital:	Cairo
Establishment of present state:	July 23, 1952
Population:	106 million
Age under 15 years:	33%
Population growth rate:	2.1%
Fertility rate (children per woman):	3.2
Infant mortality (per 1,000 births):	18
Life expectancy:	74
HIV prevalence (adult):	0.1%
Ethnic groups:	Egyptian 99.7%, other 0.3%
Literacy rate:	71%
Religions:	Muslim 90%, Christian 10%
GDP per capita (PPP):	$12,000
GDP growth rate:	4.2% (2017)
Labor, major sectors:	Services 49%, agriculture 26%, industrial 25%
Population in poverty:	32.5%
Unemployment rate:	7.8%
Export commodities:	Crude petroleum, refined petroleum, gold, natural gas, fertilizers
External debt:	$109 billion

Source: CIA, *World Factbook 2021.*

Figure 1.7 Iran: Profile and Map

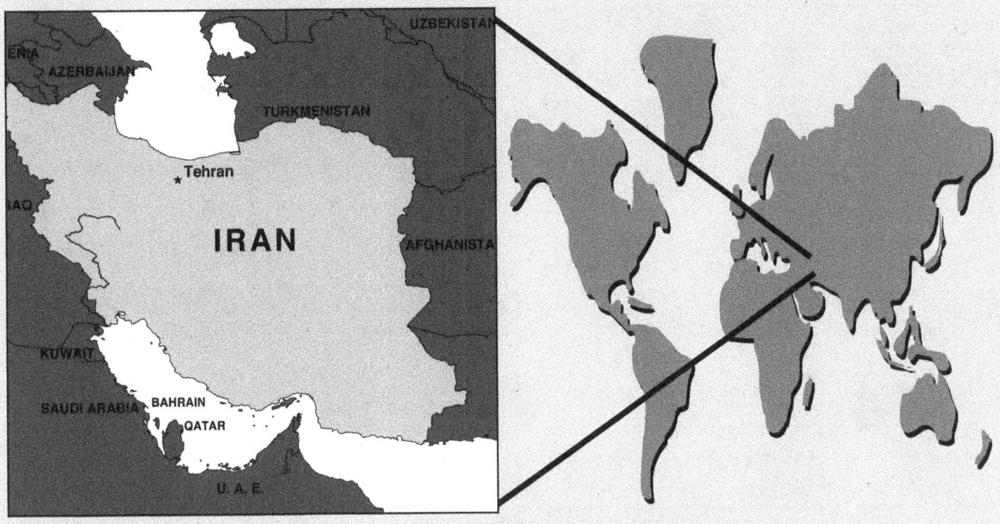

Formal name:	Islamic Republic of Iran
Area, km^2:	1.65 million
Comparative area:	Almost 2.5 times the size of Texas; slightly smaller than Alaska
Capital:	Tehran
Establishment of present state:	April 1, 1979
Population:	85 million
Age under 15 years:	24%
Population growth rate:	1%
Fertility rate (children per woman):	1.9
Infant mortality (per 1,000 births):	15
Life expectancy:	75
HIV prevalence (adult):	0.1%
Ethnic groups:	Persian, Azeri, Kurd, Lur, Baloch, Arab, Turkmen and Turkic tribes
Literacy rate:	85%
Religions:	Shia Muslim 90–95%, Sunni Muslim 5–10%, other 0.3%, unspecified 0.2%
GDP per capita (PPP):	$12,400
GDP growth rate:	3.79% (2017)
Labor, major sectors:	Services 49%, industrial 35%, agriculture 16% (2013)
Population in poverty:	19%
Unemployment rate:	12%
Export commodities:	Crude petroleum, polymers, industrial alcohols, iron, pistachios
External debt:	$8 billion

Source: CIA, *World Factbook 2021.*

Figure 1.8 China: Profile and Map

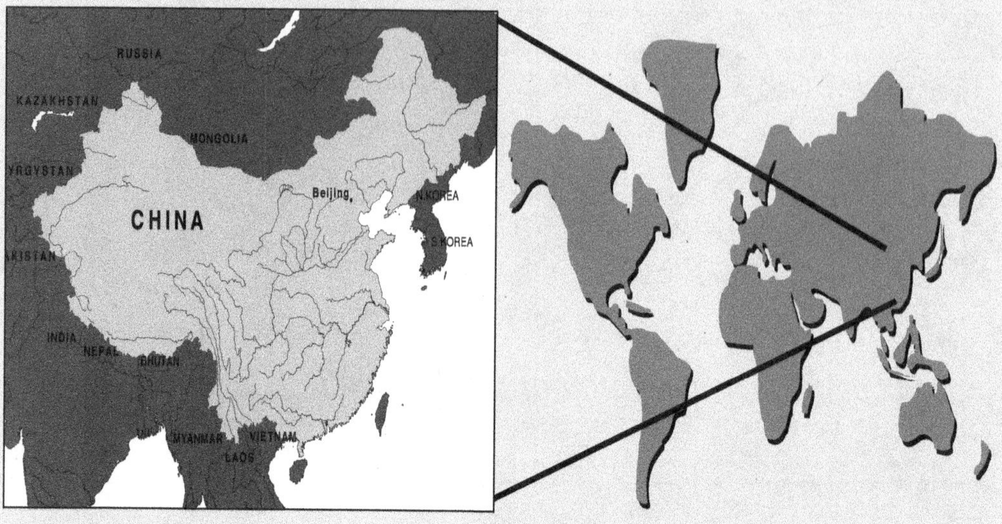

Formal name:	People's Republic of China
Area, km^2:	9.60 million
Comparative area:	Slightly smaller than the United States
Capital:	Beijing
Establishment of present state:	October 1, 1949
Population:	1.39 billion
Age under 15 years:	17%
Population growth rate:	0.26%
Fertility rate (children per woman):	1.6
Infant mortality (per 1,000 births):	11
Life expectancy:	76
HIV prevalence (adult):	not reported
Ethnic groups:	Han 92%, Zhuang 1%, other (including Hui, Manchu, Uighur, Miao, Yi, Tibetan, Mongol, Dong, Buyei, Yao, Bai) 7%
Literacy rate:	97%
Religions:	(Officially atheist), Buddhist 18%, Christian 5%, Muslim 2%, folk religion 22%, other 1%, unaffiliated 52%
GDP per capita (PPP):	$16,400
GDP growth rate:	6.1% (2019)
Labor, major sectors:	Services 43.5%, agriculture 27%, industrial 29%
Population in poverty:	0.6%
Unemployment rate:	3.6% (urban: excludes private enterprises and migrants)
Export commodities:	Broadcasting equipment, computers, integrated circuits, office machinery, phones
External debt:	$2 trillion

Source: CIA, *World Factbook 2021.*

Figure 1.9 Indonesia: Profile and Map

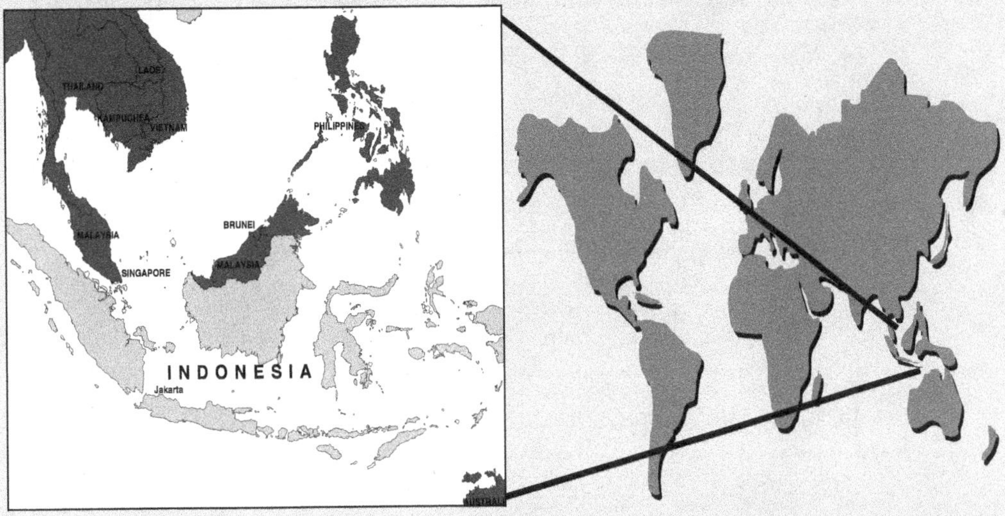

Formal name:	Republic of Indonesia
Area, km²:	1.90 million
Comparative area:	Slightly less than three times the size of Texas
Capital:	Jakarta
Establishment of present state:	August 17, 1945
Population:	275 million
Age under 15 years:	24%
Population growth rate:	0.8%
Fertility rate (children per woman):	2
Infant mortality (per 1,000 births):	20
Life expectancy:	73
HIV prevalence (adult):	0.4%
Ethnic groups:	Javanese 40%, Sundanese 16%, Malay 4%, Batak 4%, Madurese 3%, Betawi 3%, Minangkabau 3%, Buginese 3%, Bantenese 2%, Banjarese 2%, Balinese 2%, Acehnese 1%, Dayak 1%, Sasak 1%, Chinese 1%, other 15% (2010)
Literacy rate:	96%
Religions:	Muslim 87%, Protestant 7%, Roman Catholic 3%, Hindu 2%, other 1.4%
GDP per capita (PPP):	$11,400
GDP growth rate:	5% (2019)
Labor, major sectors:	Services 47%, agriculture 32%, industrial 21% (2012)
Population in poverty:	9.4%
Unemployment rate:	5.3%
Export commodities:	Coal, palm oil, natural gas, cars, gold
External debt:	$393 billion

Source: CIA, *World Factbook 2021.*

World, What Should You Call It?" NPR, January 14, 2015; Dayo Olopade, "The End of the 'Developing World,'" *New York Times,* February 28, 2014.

6. Alfred Sauvy, "Three Worlds, One Planet," *L'Observateur,* August 14, 1952.

7. Lesley Wroughton, "'Third World' Concepts No Longer Relevant," *Reuters,* April 14, 2010.

8. Marc Silver, "Memo to People of Earth: 'Third World' Is an Offensive Term!" NPR, January 8, 2021.

9. Ibid.

10. Andre Gunder Frank, *Capitalism and Underdevelopment in Latin America* (New York: Monthly Review, 1967); United Nations Conference on Trade and Development (UNCTAD), *The Least Developed Countries Report 2021* (New York, 2021).

11. Bill Gates and Melinda Gates, *Our Big Bet for the Future: 2015 Gates Annual Letter,* Bill and Melinda Gates Foundation, 2015.

12. Matthew Lynn, "Why the Title of 'Developing Country' No Longer Exists," *The Telegraph* (London), May 23, 2016.

13. Kay Atanda and Alexandru Cojocaru, "Shocks and Vulnerability to Poverty in Middle-Income Countries," *Let's Talk Development* (World Bank Blogs), March 31, 2021.

14. Nick Cuming-Bruce, "Unequal Vaccine Access Is Widening the Global Economic Gap, a U.N. Agency Says," *New York Times,* October 27, 2021; Rakesh Kochhar, "The Pandemic Stalls Growth in the Global Middle Class, Pushes Poverty Up Sharply," Pew Research Center, March 18, 2021.

15. "COP26: Why a Bad Outcome 'Is the Best We Can Hope For,'" *Euronews,* September 30, 2021; Allessandra Mezzadri, "On the Value of Social Reproduction: Informal Labour, the Majority World and the Need for Inclusive Theories and Politics," *Radical Philosophy* 2, no. 4 (2019), pp. 33–41.

16. Samuel P. Huntington, *The Clash of Civilizations and the Remaking of World Order* (New York: Simon and Schuster, 1996).

17. Jacqueline Anne Braveboy-Wagner, *Institutions of the Global South* (New York: Routledge, 2009), p. 1.

18. Caroline Levander and Walter Mignolo, "Introduction: The Global South and World Dis/Order," *The Global South* 5, no. 1 (Spring 2011), p. 3.

19. Arif Dirlik, "Global South: Predicament and Promise," *The Global South* 5, no. 1 (Spring 2011), pp. 13–14.

20. Naomi Chazan, Peter Lewis, and Robert Mortimer, *Politics and Society in Contemporary Africa* (Boulder: Lynne Rienner, 1999).

21. Frank L. Wilson, *Concepts and Issues in Comparative Politics: An Introduction to Comparative Analysis* (Upper Saddle River, NJ: Prentice Hall, 1996).

22. David J. Elkins and Richard E. B. Simeon, "A Cause in Search of Its Effect, or What Does Political Culture Explain?" *Comparative Politics* 11, no. 2 (January 1979).

23. Monte Palmer, *Comparative Politics: Political Economy, Political Culture, and Political Interdependence* (Itasca, IL: F. E. Peacock, 1997).

24. Colin Leys, *Underdevelopment in Kenya: The Political Economy of Neo-Colonialism, 1964–1971* (London: Heinemann, 1975).

25. In the early 1960s, Edward Lorenz, a meteorology professor at MIT, introduced this idea in his research on what is now known as "chaos theory" (which implies nonlinearity more than randomness). Some scientists rank chaos theory alongside relativity and quantum theory among the great scientific revolutions of the twentieth century. See Peter Dizikes, "When the Butterfly Effect Took Flight," *Technology Review,* February 22, 2011.

26. Catharine A. MacKinnon, *Butterfly Politics* (Cambridge: Harvard University Press, 2017); James Woolsey and Rachel K. Belton, "We Must Face a Connected World's 'Butterfly Effect,'" *Los Angeles Times,* May 5, 2004.

27. Philip Bump, "Why a Ship Stuck in Egypt Threatens the Economy in the United States," *Washington Post,* March 26, 2021; Richard Howells, "How One Ship Can Affect the Global Supply Chain," *Forbes,* March 31, 2021.

28. Peter S. Goodman, "In Suez Canal, Stuck Ship Is a Warning About Excessive Globalization," *New York Times,* March 26, 2021.

29. Ana Swanson, "Coronavirus Spurs U.S. Efforts to End China's Chokehold on Drugs," *New York Times,* March 11, 2020.

30. Chuin-Wei Yap, "Pandemic Lays Bare U.S. Reliance on China for Drugs," *Wall Street Journal,* August 6, 2020, p. A1.

31. Sam Shead, "The Global Chip Shortage Is Starting to Have Major Real-World Consequences," CNBC, May 7, 2021.

32. Sarah Repucci and Amy Slipowitz, "Freedom in the World 2021: Democracy Under Siege," Freedom House, 2021.

Part 1

Historical Legacies

How does one possibly condense thousands of years of the histories of four vast and diverse regions into a few chapters? It is not a simple proposition, but a necessary one. For all their differences, there are some experiences generally shared among these regions, and we will draw your attention to some common patterns. To make this broad sweep of time more comprehensible, we'll be speaking in generalities. We will illustrate with some specific examples throughout the chapters. However, as much as possible, we have attempted to avoid a long list of names and dates. At the risk of leaving out some exceptions to the rule, we believe that it is important to develop a general sense of the history of the global south. It is only with a sense of the full range of experience that one can go on to understand the complex issues that characterize life in the global south today.

The most renowned historians of our time tell us that there is much still unknown about early human history. Dating back over the past 2 million years or so, much of world history is still incomplete, and (with a few exceptions) this is very much the case for the global south. Unfortunately, this lack of information has provided fertile ground for the development of myths, stereotypes, and distortions—many of which continue to be popular today. As you will see, many of these beliefs—that the peoples of the global south made no contributions, had no achievements, had no history—were used by others to justify enslavement, conquest, and domination. Denials of the contributions of the global south and portrayals of their citizens as pagan, barbaric, warlike, or even childlike in some cases, are widely denounced today. For years, historians have worked diligently to repair the damage done by colonial apologists. A more balanced representation of the past is important work for its own sake. But it is also crucial that these histories be reconstructed because so often colonizers did everything they could to destroy all records of them. A greater understanding of the tremendous variety of human experience may not only help to restore the sense of IDENTITY that was taken from colonized peoples—it may also serve as a source of inspiration for Indigenous solutions to some of the problems we must face today.

In their zeal to correct for the wrongs of the past, some historians have overcompensated and ended up providing an equally distorted version of history. Some adopted the values of their colonizers and focused only on the "great civilizations" or EMPIRES of Africa, Asia, Latin America, and the Middle East. They ignored the vast array of smaller (but not lesser) forms of social organization. Yet, the regions we are studying were inhabited for thousands of years by many different groups of people, with different ways of life. Some lived in relative isolation and some had long histories of contact with other peoples across great distances—well before these territories were "discovered" by white men. In fact, much of the global south was integrated on some level into larger regional and even transcontinental networks of trade.

However, in their efforts to correct negative distortions, some historians provided overly romantic views of these empires, extolling only their virtues and portraying the world as it was before the arrival of Europeans as some sort of golden age of peace and plenty. Most analysts today agree that neither portrayal is accurate. There is fairly wide agreement that each extreme oversimplifies. Because humans populated these societies, it is fair to assume that they were neither all good nor all bad. Most historians currently embrace a more balanced approach that seeks to understand these societies in all their complexity. And that complexity includes attention to the vast diversity of societies that existed in the long stretch of history we refer to as "precolonial"—not just empires or small bands of hunter-gatherers, but also everything in between.

2

Precolonial History: What Once Was, and Why It Matters

The past reappears because it is a hidden present. —*Octavio Paz*[1]

One way of conceptualizing the many different ways in which humans organize themselves into groups is to picture a continuum. Large, hierarchical, centralized societies (or EMPIRES lie at one end of this continuum, and much smaller, more egalitarian, decentralized societies are located at the other end, with most societies falling somewhere in between, containing elements of the two more extreme types. Without valuing one form of organization over another, anthropologists often make distinctions between STATE SOCIETIES and STATELESS SOCIETIES. Whereas the great empires have drawn most of the attention of archaeologists and historians, increasingly we are learning about somewhat smaller STATES. Anthropologists tell us that our earliest human ancestors lived in stateless societies. This system of organization has largely disappeared, as its members have been pushed into the most inhospitable environments or absorbed by larger groups. Yet, both state and stateless societies could be found in Africa, Asia, Latin America, and the Middle East at the time of European conquest. Consequently, all these systems deserve attention, as no single type can be considered representative of these vast regions.

Stateless Societies

It is the democratic character of stateless societies that observers frequently find most striking. Relatively speaking, in stateless societies power is shared among the members of the group (often, but not always, both male and female). Also known as ACEPHALOUS SOCIETIES, they have no full-time political leaders, chiefs, presidents, or monarchs. It is not uncommon for elders to guide the affairs of the group. Or a member of the community known for his or her prowess in war or some other talent might serve on a temporary basis to lead communities in a certain function (military, religious, or economic). However, for these groups there is no tradition of a supreme ruler who governs continuously and beyond their immediate area of settlement. Unlike state systems with their courts, retinues, full-time militaries, and so on, in stateless societies people's day-to-day lives are conducted without interference from "government" as we know it.

Yet, no society is truly stateless. Even in these noncentralized societies, there are widely accepted rules that provide a basis for the orderly functioning of the community. Government might appear to be more informal, in that there are no palaces, courthouses, or government buildings of any kind. However, this system is actually highly organized and there are often harsh penalties for violations of the public good. Within stateless societies, a variety of associations (e.g., all-male or all-female secret societies or age grades) are based on kinship, or family relationships. They exist to settle disputes among members, forge unity, and maintain order. These often-complicated arrangements promote cooperation, and time-honored rules allow families to draw on the labor they need in times of hardship. A web of kinship ties forms the basis for this kind of organization. All members of the extended families who make up the community know that the survival of all is based on this system of mutual aid and obligation.[2]

A strong sense of community pervades stateless societies, which exists among small bands or tribal groups of 20–200 people. Stateless societies are renowned for their egalitarianism. Relatively speaking, there are no divides based on CLASS (SOCIAL), no rich and poor. Often working as hunter-gatherers who migrate in seasonal cycles, they rarely establish themselves in one place for long, nor do members produce or accumulate wealth above the bare necessities. Whether primarily composed of hunter-gatherers or small farmers, stateless societies are often associated with subsistence economies. However, the extreme hardship such groups live under today is not traditional—they have been pushed to the most inhospitable environmental margins. Life in such societies was not always tenuous. Many hunter-gatherers preferred what they saw as the good life compared to the hard work and risk involved in food production.[3]

Based on their intimate knowledge of the resources available, the members of stateless societies employed a wide range of techniques to support themselves. Going back at least 3,000 years, statelessness is known to have existed among pastoral populations as well as more settled populations practicing slash-and-burn techniques and shifting cultivation. Some groups, like the Guarani of Brazil, lived off of some combination of these activities. This sense of communalism and egalitarian sharing of resources based on kinship was central to the early success of wet-rice cultivation in Southeast Asia.[4] Stateless societies were identified in the sierras of northern Mexico and in the pampas of South America, as well as in the Amazon Basin.

Small, highly mobile hunter-gatherer populations often lived alongside pastoralists and larger groups of sedentary farmers in symbiotic relationships. There is a great deal of evidence of the interpenetration and complementarity of hunter-gatherer groups by food producers (and vice versa). At times, relations could be described as cooperative, as hunter-gatherer groups, like the San, or the !Kung of southern Africa, traded game and other goods such as wild honey for farm products and implements such as nets or other technologies. Trade was also important for forest farmers, like the Ibo of Nigeria. Through village markets, trading has long been a tradition for women of state and stateless societies in much of western Africa.[5]

However, at other times, relations between these neighbors turned hostile. Conflicts could arise over any number of matters, most notably access to resources. Especially during times of environmental stress, it was not uncommon for settled farmers to come into conflict with pastoralists over land, as herds might destroy a field or farmers might encroach on prime pasture. Like hunter-gatherers, pastoralists did not generally form states, but they did sometimes take them over by conquest. Pastoralists, organized and unified under a strong central regime, were known to raid settled populations. For example, Turkic nomads and other warriors on horses repeatedly swept into India to plunder sedentary societies. Herding populations like the Masai of eastern Africa had a number of advantages, which enabled them, as well as larger, more centrally organized societies like the Zulu (southern Africa), to overwhelm their stateless or less centrally organized neighbors. Similarly, the Aztecs started out as a small group of tough nomads who made alliances to conquer sedentary groups. Often, sedentary societies found it necessary to form larger political groupings, to make alliances and take common action in self-defense. They might erect a walled town at the center of their farmlands to serve as a refuge against raids from their neighbors. The need for defense was one of the most common factors behind the development of states.[6]

State Societies

Historians continue to disagree about the causal relationship between population booms and increased food production. It is still a chicken-or-egg question: Does GROWTH in the production of cereals like rice, millet, and maize contribute to a population boom? Or do population booms necessitate an intensification of agricultural production? Either way, the two factors are clearly associated with the development of state societies. Once production is increased to the point of surplus, time is freed up for some people to work in capacities other than food production, including as full-time political leaders. When this happens, we begin to see more social stratification. There are divisions based on wealth, and clear differences between the rulers and ruled. A merchant class of traders emerges, markets grow, and trade becomes more regularized. In state societies in all regions, the craftwork produced by an artisan class of weavers, potters, and metal- and woodworkers was highly prized. For example, the Chibcha of Colombia were known for their magnificent gold work, recognized as perhaps the finest in the ancient Americas.[7]

At this intermediate level of social organization, clearly a state society but not an empire, government is described as comprising relatively simple small states or chiefdoms. As states grow larger, we see a more centralized political organization and more complex forms of government supported by bureaucracies with increasingly specialized functions like ambassadors, harbor masters, special judges, treasurers, and tax collectors. Commercial city-states dominated the trade in the Southeast Asian archipelago. Often state societies were absorbed into larger empires in their efforts to monopolize trade. The Swahili city-states of the eastern coast of Africa, such as Pemba, Mombasa, and Zanzibar, were autonomous and loosely linked through commercial ties (until they were all brought under the Omani Empire). Similarly, the city-states of Mesopotamia were eventually integrated into a single, powerful entity to ensure the security of trade routes.[8]

States of this size existed long before the conquest of Latin America, especially in the circum-Caribbean area (Panama, Costa Rica, northern Colombia, Venezuela, Puerto Rico, Jamaica, and Cuba). A paramount chief or king arose (in some cases chosen by election, in other cases because of some exceptional talent or charisma, magical powers, skills as a protector, etc.) and was assisted by councils drawn from the heads of the lineages composing the village. At this level of organization, the chief's rule was not absolute. He was limited by his advisers and required to consult the council, although the power of the council varied by state. Often in state societies in Africa and Southeast Asia, decisions were reached by consensus between a king and a council. After lengthy deliberations, the king would pronounce a final decision representing a compromise of views.[9]

In some cases, kings had veto powers and could disregard the consensus of deliberations. Elsewhere, if the council disagreed with the chief's decisions, it could give counter-orders and seek to unseat him. In the Oyo kingdoms of western Africa, a leading minister could command an extremely unpopular king to commit suicide on the basis that the people, the earth, and the gods rejected his rule. There are examples of tyrants in such societies, but generally speaking, rulers still depended on the support of the population. Kings were respected as long as they fulfilled their responsibilities as protectors and providers. There were usually no standing armies to help kings impose their will, and abuses risked reprisals. Therefore, in some states at least, there were traditional checks on the rulers' powers.[10]

Empires

Historians tell us that the differences between chiefdoms and larger, more complex kingdoms or empires are difficult to draw. Certainly empires are distinguished by size of the territories and populations they control. Beyond this, the difference is mostly a matter of degree, as empires are in the simplest sense an expansion and deepening of tendencies found in chiefdoms.[11] The former empires of what is now called the global south greatly resembled more modern empires in terms of size of population or expanse of territory, use of official religions, or conquest of smaller states. Larger kingdoms often developed from these smaller states. Some were very large: historians estimate that the Aztecs controlled a population of nearly 25 million people in the early sixteenth century. Europeans were often surprised at how much the empires they encountered were like the ones at home. In fact, the Aztecs dominated a total area not much smaller than that of Spain. Hernan Cortés wrote that the Aztecs lived much like people in Spain, in terms of harmony and order, and that it was remarkable to see what they had achieved. The Spanish conquerors of Cuzco, the Inca capital, described it as beautiful, with buildings as fine as those in Spain.[12]

The oldest settled communities developed intensive agriculture along rivers, in oases, or in coastal areas. The Nile, the Tigris and Euphrates, the Yellow, and the Niger Rivers were centers of early civilization. The Fertile Crescent of ancient Palestine and Babylon was long accepted as the earliest site for mass cultivation. Yet, there are reports of early kingdoms emerging in coastal and delta regions in other regions as well, such as the Niger Bend of western Africa. In several different parts of the world, over thousands of years, people domesticated wild plants or adopted new ones. It is becoming increasingly clear that, at various times and places, there were also revolutions in food production—and not all of these crops and methods have a Middle Eastern origin. In the Fertile Crescent, as in other food-producing "homelands" like China, the Andes, along the Nile, in Amazonia, and in Mesoamerica, it was common that once a mainstay of the diet was perfected, agriculture spread swiftly across the region, in some cases to other continents.[13]

The Egyptian Empire, one of the preeminent powers in the world for over 2,000 years, was based on the soils of the Nile floodplain. It maximized the benefits of the Nile by building canals, dikes, and embankments. Elsewhere as well, empires developed in the most successful areas of food production. Funan, the first empire in Southeast Asia, became rich off the rice from the Mekong Delta. The Chinese Empire began on the Yellow River plain, and is made up of an uninterrupted succession of two dozen dynasties over 4,000 years. Many other empires were also long-lived; although it influenced and was influenced by Egypt, Kush flourished for over 1,000 years as an original African civilization, and many other empires in the four regions of study survived for hundreds of years. In Latin America, Mesoamerica is often cited as a cradle of civilization. There, the Olmecs, Maya, and Aztecs attained remarkable achievements in a variety of pursuits. The desert coasts of Peru and later its highlands became the economic base for the Inca. Food production increased there, in part, because the Indigenous peoples developed irrigation systems that allowed for higher productivity. Moreover, centralized states could compel the cooperation necessary to extend farmlands. These large states could harness the energy of larger populations through the creation of public works programs. Historians argue that the huge projects that contributed to a boom in production required strong and centralized governments and the extension of authority over larger areas.[14]

The production of surpluses meant an increase in the volume and types of goods available for trade. Increased trade not only created the need for greater political organization, but also financed the increasingly complex activities of evolving states. Whereas the trade of some states was land-based, other emerging empires turned to the seas. Commercial kingdoms situated on the coasts or at the edges of the desert were often based almost exclusively on commerce. Their power depended upon a reliable means of transport (navigable waterways or beasts of burden) and their ability to secure routes. For hundreds of years, a lucrative overland trade was based on cloth and beads, silks, gold, ivory, and enslaved people as caravan routes linked Europe, Africa, the Middle East, and Asia. For example, the trans-Saharan trade lasted for over 1,000 years and financed the great empires of Ghana, Mali, and Songhay in western Africa, whose wealth was based on monopoly control and taxation of the gold passing through their domains.[15]

Seafaring states also amassed great riches. For example, Srivijaya, considered to be the only maritime state among the Southeast Asian classical states, was a commercial power taking revenues from passing trade. Its strategic location

Figure 2.1 Early Empires of the Global South

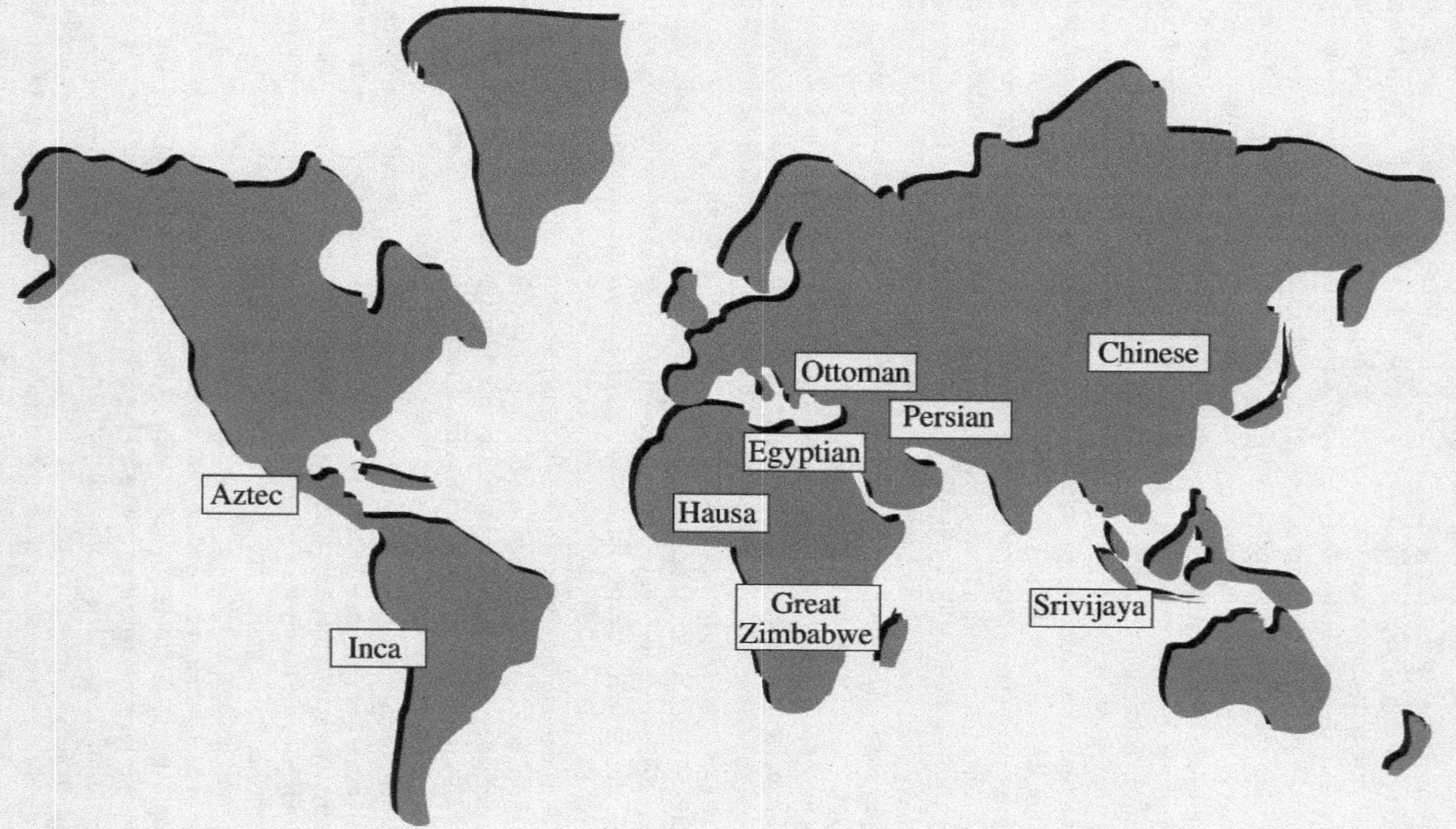

allowed Srivijaya to dominate maritime activity and patrol the archipelago around the Malacca Strait, one of the most significant links in the world trading system. As the dominant power in the area, Srivijaya controlled piracy, provided harbor facilities for shipbuilding and repair, and offered reprovisioning and warehousing services—all in addition to its business in camphor, bird nests, perfumes, pearls, and peppers and spices, among other goods.[16]

Determined to maintain control over this strategically important network of sea-lanes, China and Southeast Asia were pioneers in the development of early naval capacities. Their accomplishments in this area were so substantial that China is considered to have been far ahead of any country in the world in the development of the sailing ship and navigational technology until at least the fifteenth century. Shipbuilding and naval activity were especially common in the Southeast Asian archipelago. Some ships were up to 120 meters long and large enough to carry 500–1,000 people. In the fifteenth century, China sent treasure fleets with hundreds of ships across the Indian Ocean—decades before Christopher Columbus's three ships made their way to the Americas. There is evidence that Indonesians and possibly the Chinese traveled as far west as Madagascar. Some historians believe Asian sailors may have traveled to the Cape of Good Hope, or even around it, long before Europeans did.[17]

However, as early as the second century B.C.E., Arab middlemen conducted much of the trade between East Africa and Asia. From the seventh century through the twelfth the Muslim trade network was vast, and various Muslim empires functioned as free trade areas. Their central position between east and west gave them a decisive advantage in the various long-distance trades at the center of the world economy for hundreds of years. Through their commercial activities, Muslim traders disseminated technological innovations and greatly advanced the areas of navigation, shipbuilding, astronomy, and geography. These coastal merchants visited the Swahili city-states in a sea trade governed by the monsoon winds. Many stayed on and intermarried with African women, forming an ELITE class of merchants on East Africa's coasts.[18]

While a corps of diplomats or ambassadors was key to maintaining stable relations for trade, an interest in protecting or expanding trade and the accumulation of wealth also contributed to the development of another institution common to the world's empires: full-time militaries. Some kingdoms did not have standing armies. Most soldiers were actually farmers or herders who provided their own weapons and provisions. Other states, such as China by the fourth century B.C.E., had professional armies. In western Africa, Mali was renowned for its disciplined cavalry. It had horses and coats of chain mail long before its neighbors. Some Indian kingdoms, such as the Mauryan, had a cavalry of elephants and chariots. Ghana was said to have had an army of 200,000 men, including 40,000 archers. And the Ottoman militaries became regarded as a state within a state, so powerful that they could make and unmake rulers. Similar corps, such as the Mameluks, ruled Egypt for over 200 years.[19]

Where warfare was endemic, its frequency changed the relative importance of the military, which became the core of some states, such as those of the Zulu and the Assyrians. With superior weapons and horses, some groups gained the military power to conquer neighboring groups and expand to collect tribute from subjugated populations or vassal states. As these states grew, they attained larger surpluses by preying on neighboring populations and requiring tribute payments. Warfare between chiefdoms became common, and captives were taken in warfare and enslaved. Stronger groups imposed their wills on weaker groups. The Mongol invasions rearranged politics in India and mainland Southeast Asia. Arab invasions had a similar effect in northern Africa. Tribute could come in the form of material resources or labor. For example, the Akan of western Africa wanted captive labor to mine gold, the basis of the Asante Empire in the eighteenth century. Enslaved people composed a large class in most empires; only slightly better off were subjugated peoples paying tribute.[20]

Therefore, one important part of understanding empires is to see them as a collection of different communities over which there is a centralized government. These kingdoms routinely ruled over vast, sprawling, and varied areas. The Inca Empire ran north to south for over 3,200 kilometers. Such large states required effective political and military institutions to integrate conquered people into the system, and exercised executive, judicial, and legislative authority. They set about enforcing laws, organizing armies, and collecting taxes. Some were better administrators than others. Centralized states such as Persia (Iran) were broken into provinces and run by elaborate bureaucracies. The Inca divided their empire into four quarters, each with a lord (usually a close relative of the emperor). Besides tribute collection and organization of public works, the Inca sought to assimilate conquered peoples by encouraging their use of Quechua, the language of the empire. The imperial government required all those living under its rule to accept the official state religion, but allowed people also to continue worshipping their own gods. Similarly, the Persian Empire imposed uniform laws and used a single language for administration, but was tolerant of local cultures.[21]

Still, the relative egalitarianism found among stateless societies appears to have been unknown at the state level. Rather little is known about women in most early societies, and what we do know is mostly about elite women. Men dominated most state systems. This was not always the case; women sometimes played key political, economic, and religious roles in their communities. But

Figure 2.2 Why Wasn't It China That Conquered the World?

With all of its advantages, why wasn't it China that conquered the world? Historians cite internal divisions within China in the fourteenth and fifteenth centuries. A power struggle between two factions in the Chinese court ended with the ascendance of a group who sought to turn inward. This marked a turning point in China's history, as the empire stopped sending out fleets and dismantled its shipyards. It also abandoned other technologies, in effect stepping back from the verge of its own industrial revolution—about 400 years ahead of Europe. Because it was so centralized politically, under this system China effectively retreated from technological innovation and halted it, just as Europe was rising.

Source: Patricia Buckley Ebrey, *The Cambridge Illustrated History of China* (New York: Cambridge University Press, 2010).

there were only three female leaders in 3,000 years of Egyptian history. Hatshepsut, who ruled as pharaoh starting around 1473 B.C.E., at times chose to reinvent herself as male to gain legitimacy. Aztec women inhabited other realms, and worked as doctors, artisans, merchants, and in temple service. Even in studies of the most famously patriarchal empires, such as those of the Aztecs, Inca, and Zulu—which also tended to be the most militarized, the genders are not described as equal, but as serving complementary functions. Inca noblewomen had access to land, herds, water, and other resources through their mothers, and some historians argue that their activities were viewed as of equal importance to those of men. For the Aztecs, death in childbirth for women was considered the equivalent of death in battle for men—and revered with great honor.[22]

Many of the empires of western Africa also reserved an honored place for women. In fact, women's social position and personal liberty often astonished travelers. Women are known to have served as political leaders of Swahili (Zanzibar was once governed by a Muslim Swahili queen) and Mayan city-states. More often, however, women served at lower levels, as the heads of towns and subregions within empires. Among the Yoruba in Nigeria, the iyalode was a female official with jurisdiction over all women, who spoke on women's issues in the king's council. Similarly, among the Aztecs there were female officials charged with overseeing the affairs of women. Women also served in some imperial armies, and there are examples of all-female regiments led by women (e.g., the Amazons of Dahomey and the Sotho of southern Africa).[23]

Although less commonly found in Latin America, there are examples of empresses and warrior queens in the histories of Asia and Africa. In the Hausa state of Zaria, Queen Amina outfitted her armies with iron helmets and chain mail to successfully wage a series of military campaigns. However, in most cases when women held this kind of power, it was treated as a temporary arrangement. Women served as regents, ruling when the successor to the throne was too young to assume (his) full duties. In matrilineal societies, like the Asante in Ghana, maternal relations were crucial in determining succession, inheritance, and other matters. Here and elsewhere, queen mothers and queen sisters were major power brokers, and often had considerable leverage and influence. An Asante queen mother, Ya Asantewaa, is considered a heroine for leading her kingdom in resistance against British rule in 1900.[24]

The Asante had a relatively large empire. One of the most notable differences between empires and smaller states is that the kinship ties that unite chiefs with commoners in states do not exist in empires. Rather, in empires the ruling group claims separate origins from the MASSES and lives apart from them. A variety of sources tell of the spectacle and luxury of life enjoyed by elites in the empires of the global south. Large retinues of ministers, scholars, and courtiers surrounded emperors. Often imperial courts included harems, as royal polygamy was not uncommon. Kings of large states like Mwene Mutapa (Zimbabwe) distinguished themselves by having 2,000–3,000 royal wives.[25]

Always at the pinnacle of power in this hierarchy was the emperor, who ruled as an absolute monarch. There was little left of the kind of constitutional monarchy described for smaller states, in which a king confers with a council. At the level of empire, the emperor's authority took on a divine status and usually was unquestioned. This far-greater centralization of power was supported by a religious IDEOLOGY that had enormous influence over the population. Every empire was linked with a state religion, and based on some mix of THEOCRACY and royal despotism. As the "son of heaven," the Chinese emperor was considered godlike. Egyptian monarchs were regarded as gods on earth. Rulers often claimed special powers of intercession with God or the gods. As chief religions and philosophies of state, Hinduism and Buddhism helped provide the unity necessary for the first kingdoms of India to become larger political entities. Similarly, Islam created unity among rival Arab clans. It was this unity based in religion that contributed to the rapid growth of the Arab Empire, known as the Caliphate. This empire rivaled Rome at its peak, and controlled an area that stretched from the Mediterranean into Central Asia from the seventh to the eleventh century.[26]

Religious ideologies served the state in other ways as well. In all four regions, emperors were believed necessary for performing important rites. For the Inca, the emperor was responsible for defending the order and existence of the universe. For the Aztecs, the emperor was a renowned warrior, and conquest was necessary to the proper worship of the god Huitzilopochtli—the only assurance that the sun would continue to pass through the sky. Across empires in the global south, it was also common to find that kings and emperors lived lives of ritual seclusion apart from the population. They were often separated from the public behind a screen and communicated only through intermediaries—all based on the belief that the emperor was too holy for common gaze. For example, the Alafin of Oyo, considered to be the incarnation of a chief god, could only be seen through a veil and could never be seen eating. It was not unusual for emperors to be thought to possess supernatural powers.[27] They were often the only ones allowed to transgress the ordinary rules of social life, such as the taboo against incest.

In deference to emperors' unquestioned power, life at imperial courts around the world was immersed in elaborate ritual and ceremony. We know from various sources that the capitals of these empires were often lavish. These were true cities, serving not only as economic but also as cultural centers and populated by tens of thousands, even millions, of people. For example, the Aztec capital Tenochtitlan and the valley of Mexico were home to nearly 1 million people in the early sixteenth century. Described by Spaniards as an "Indian Venice," the city sat on an oval island connected to the mainland by three causeways and interlaced with numerous canals. Chang'an, the capital of the Tang Dynasty of China, was described as magnificent, and was once probably the largest city in the world, with an estimated population of 2 million. Timbuktu and the other capitals of western African empires were described as awash in gold, dripping in opulence, and capable of serving thousands at banquets. The generosity and hospitality of these courts was commented on by visitors of the time. In the tenth century, the emperor of Ghana was known as the richest monarch in the world. The annual revenue of the Mongol emperor in the seventeenth century was said to be ten times that of his contemporary, Louis XIV. When the Mansa of Mali made his pilgrimage to Mecca in 1324–1325, he impressed the world with his wealth and munificence.[28]

Besides feats of monumental architecture, many empires were renowned for their buildings of remarkable beauty and distinctiveness. Many empires also invested in enormous public works projects. The most famous of these is China's Great Wall, a continuous fortification built along its northern frontier. On a similar scale in China is its Grand Canal, a 1,600-kilometer waterway linking north to south. The massive engineering of water systems, such as the use of dams and irrigation, helped the Chinese, the Funan, the Inca, and others increase food production on limited arable land. The Inca produced a surplus in the highlands through agricultural terracing and irrigation. They maintained control over the empire through an impressive system of roads and built suspension bridges to render immense gorges passable. For many lowland Asian empires, wet-rice cultivation required sophisticated water management and regulation to create the higher volume of production necessary to feed larger populations.[29]

As mentioned earlier, the surplus created by such innovations allowed for state patronage of the arts and religion, which contributed to the development of rich material cultures. Empires were known for their production and vast exchange of goods and services, including luxury items. Various empires had specialists in jewelry making and goldsmithing, feather working, silk weaving, and production of other adornments. Empires from all regions are known for their wall paintings and sculpture, such as the Ajanta caves in India, and the cast-bronze portraits of the kings of Ife and Benin in western Africa. Not only did the Gupta kingdom provide for peace and prosperity by reuniting much of northern India, but its two centuries of rule are also described as a period of cultural brilliance, a creative age for the arts and sciences. In the Middle Ages, Muslim society was the scientific center of the world, and Arabic was synonymous with learning and science for over 500 years.[30]

Arab and other non-Western peoples contributed to the development of technologies in several different fields, such as metallurgy. For example, China used coal as metallurgical fuel and for heating houses 700 years before the West.[31] But such feats were by no means confined to Asia. Although little of the global south is considered industrialized today, a variety of industries once flourished throughout these regions. Weaving, which goes back in Egypt and Nubia for a millennium, was once a primary industry in parts of Africa, Asia, the Middle East, and Latin America. The Chinese are credited with technological achievements like the invention of water-powered mills, drought-resistant rice strains, gunpowder, and optical lenses. Some historians argue that China was near its own industrial revolution in the thirteenth century, and world history would be much different today if not for the Mongol invasion and later emperors' failures to resume the Song Dynasty's initiatives.[32]

What we today refer to as the global south was the site of a series of accomplishments in the field of mathematics as well. Arab scholars introduced algebra and the use of zero to the West. Egyptians were the first to use the decimal system. The Chinese are known for their use of geometric equations and trigonometry. Several empires prioritized the study of the sciences, particularly astronomy, through which the Maya are said to have made observations and calculations of astounding complexity. This includes the development of a calendar that is more accurate than the common Western systems in making adjustments in the exact length of a solar year.[33]

The Maya are also known for their complex glyphic writing, which has still not been decoded but is widely considered to be the most advanced in the ancient Americas. Although Sumer is believed to be the first civilization to have created cuneiform writing (about 5,000 years ago), the Egyptians developed writing (about 3200 B.C.E.) and the Chinese have preserved script that dates back as far as the second millennium B.C.E. Instead of lettering, the Inca used mnemonic devices, knotted quipu strings, which were used in recordkeeping and accounting.[34] Yet, there were also highly artistic and prosperous urban civilizations, like the Ife of Nigeria, who did not have writing. Oral cultures there and around the world have produced a large body of myths, legends, and poetry, as well as theater, prose, and philosophy. Griots and other professional historians have transmitted the genealogies and histories of these peoples by memory.[35]

The Assyrians collected their literature in libraries, filled with thousands of stone tablets. The Gupta in India, the Maya, and the Persians are known for their patronage of scholarly activity, including the recording of official histories. In addition to being the center of trade on the Southeast Asian archipelago, Srivijaya was a center of Hindu and Buddhist learning. Correspondingly, Baghdad was such a gathering place for Muslim scholars during the Umayyad Dynasty. Timbuktu, at the time that it was the major hub for the trans-Saharan trade and one of the most celebrated of savanna cities, was also famous for being a city of universities, attracting scholars of international repute. In the third millennium B.C.E., Egypt achieved high intellectual, social, and material standards that compared favorably with most other parts of the world. The Greeks borrowed heavily from the Egyptians in philosophy and the sciences, transmitting to the West many of their accomplishments. Therefore, it is not only the West that has a rich intellectual history. In fact, the West became what it did because of an infusion of knowledge from much of the rest of the world.[36]

For all of their strengths, however, we find a common pattern among empires—authority was inversely related to distance. The larger the area conquered, the more difficult it was to maintain HEGEMONY, or absolute control over the empire. The Songhay Empire in western Africa was almost perpetually engaged against dissidents across its vast frontier, as was the Chinese Empire, which frequently broke down into fiefdoms. Empires tended to overextend themselves and were constantly plagued by problems of administration and succession (one reason Ghana lasted so long is that it stayed relatively small).[37] Whereas smaller groups often unified into larger states under a common cause (e.g., defense against an external threat), after the shared problem was eliminated these larger units tended to break back down into smaller and more local organizations. This was a cycle that repeated itself in all four regions—Africa, Asia, Latin America, and the Middle East—many times before European conquest.

Yet, it is for a variety of reasons (not all of them well understood) that many of the empires described here had long passed from the scene; their capitals were no longer as dazzling and prosperous by the 1500s, when Europeans began arriving in larger numbers. By the time European powers became intent on expansion, many of these empires were showing signs of distress. They were at risk of DISINTEGRATION from infighting and fragmentation.[38] For example, the Mongol Empire was fragmenting when the Europeans arrived. Indian and foreign rivals defeated the Mongols, so that by the time the West began its invasion the empire was vulnerable and divided into many small successor states that were easily played off each other by the French and British. We see this pattern among empires in all four regions. There were the internecine dynastic struggles of China, the civil wars over succession crises of the Inca and Oyo (Nigeria) states, and slave raiding in Africa, which spread firearms throughout the region and contributed to endless wars between various groups.[39] In all of these places, the once-central leadership was weakened, administrative controls broke down, and outlying tributaries attempted to break free of the empire's grasp.

The potential for revolt in these kingdoms was aggravated by heavy taxation and other stresses. These often became more burdensome as empires struggled to survive. For example, just before Spanish conquest, the Aztecs greatly stepped up the pressure on conquered groups. They demanded mass human sacrifices to assuage the gods and prevent a predicted cataclysm. Consequently, tributary and minority groups, long resentful of imperial domination, were eager to ally with the invaders. Europeans benefited enormously from this circumstance and employed a strategy of DIVIDE AND CONQUER.[40]

While it is important to remember that Europeans were not invited guests, there are cases in which people didn't immediately recognize the Europeans as invaders and ended up compromising themselves. There are countless stories of how some societies received the European visitors peacefully—even warmly. Many societies active in the Indian Ocean network of trade accepted the Portuguese enclaves as they had other outsiders for as long as anyone could remember. They gave the Europeans a cautious welcome and sought to profit from their presence. The Aztec emperor Moctezuma at first offered generous gifts to encourage his unearthly looking visitors to leave. When that didn't work, Moctezuma warily welcomed Cortés and his men to Tenochtitlan and treated them as guests.[41]

Once the emperor recognized his error, it was too late. The Aztecs, like most of the other military empires of Africa, Asia, Latin America, and the Middle East, were unprepared to counter European penetration. In some cases, people quickly adapted to the new reality and worked hard to reclaim the advantage. However, many groups fought pitched battles against the invaders and some

Figure 2.3 The Transatlantic Slave Trade

Unique in terms of the enormity of human devastation it caused, the transatlantic slave trade lasted for over 400 years. Although it began on a small scale in the 1400s, by the seventeenth century labor shortages in the Americas had greatly increased the demand for enslaved people. At its height, thousands of men and women in their most productive years were forcibly taken from their communities on an annual basis and sent across the Atlantic on the harrowing trip known as the "Middle Passage." Because so many died along the way, the total number of people enslaved is still unknown, although most historians estimate that at least 12 million Africans served as human cargo in this trade.

Source: J. E. Inikori and Stanley Engerman, *The Atlantic Slave Trade* (Durham: Duke University Press, 1992).

Figure 2.4 The Opium Wars

Those states that were not so open, or that did not receive Europe so warmly, were also forced into the new order—on Europe's terms. As the Middle Kingdom, China believed itself to be at the center of the universe. Largest in size and population, longest in history, untouchable in cultural achievement, the Chinese Empire was in many ways the premier entity when Europeans started arriving in more significant numbers in the sixteenth century. Yet, Europe's appetite for Chinese porcelains, silks, and teas was not reciprocated by Chinese interest in European goods.

As a result, the Europeans (and particularly the British) struggled with their trade deficits until they did find one commodity that the Chinese found habit-forming: opium. This narcotic proved to be a boon to the British economy. Although the Chinese government had recognized the devastation caused by opium addiction and outlawed its sale, the British sold the drug through a smuggling network along the coast. When China attempted to destroy the contraband trade, the British fought what were known as the Opium Wars to force open the country to foreign trade. In decline at the time, the Chinese Empire was easily overwhelmed by the British military. The resulting Treaty of Nanjing in 1842 was the first of several "unequal treaties" that established European dominance in China. The Chinese coast was carved up into five ports open to Westerners. In effect, the emperor was forced to grant concessions at gunpoint—truly a low point in the empire's history. At the mercy of foreigners, China faced a century of humiliation.

Sources: Milton W. Meyer, *Asia: A Concise History* (Lanham: Rowman and Littlefield, 1997); David Landes, *The Wealth and Poverty of Nations: Why Some Are So Rich and Some So Poor* (New York: Norton, 1998); Rhoads Murphey, "The Historical Context," in *Understanding Contemporary China,* ed. Robert E. Gamer (Boulder: Lynne Rienner, 1999); Edward L. Farmer, Gavin R. G. Hambly, Byron K. Marshall, et al., *Comparative History of Civilizations in Asia* (Reading, MA: Addison-Wesley, 1977).

succeeded (at least temporarily). The emperor Menelik drove the Italians out of Ethiopia in the late nineteenth century, and as a result it was one of the few territories never formally colonized. Equipped with European arms his forces had built for themselves through reverse engineering, Samori Touré was able to keep the French out of large parts of western Africa for nearly twenty years. The Inca were able to hold off the Spanish for decades, as resistance was not finally put down until 1572.[42] These are just a few of the examples of Indigenous peoples' fierce resistance to European conquest. But in most cases, it was too late.

Notes

1. Octavio Paz, "Critique of the Pyramid," cited in Ana Carrigan, "Chiapas: The First Postmodern Revolution," in *Our Word Is Our Weapon: Selected Writings of Subcomandante Marcos,* ed. Juana Ponce de Leon (New York: Seven Stories, 2001), p. 428.
2. Roland Oliver, *The African Experience* (Boulder: Westview, 1999); Robert W. July, *A History of the African People* (Prospect Heights, IL: Waveland, 1992).
3. Oliver, *The African Experience.*
4. Milton W. Meyer, *Asia: A Concise History* (Lanham: Rowman and Littlefield, 1997).
5. Oliver, *The African Experience.*
6. Benjamin Keen and Keith Haynes, *A History of Latin America* (Boston: Houghton Mifflin, 2000).
7. Ibid.

8. Jane Burbank and Frederick Cooper, *Empires in World History: Power and the Politics of Difference* (Princeton: Princeton University Press, 2010).
9. Magbaily Fyle, *Introduction to the History of African Civilization* (Lanham: University Press of America, 1999); Meyer, *Asia.*
10. Fyle, *Introduction to the History of African Civilization.*
11. Keen and Haynes, *A History of Latin America.*
12. Ibid.; Peter Bakewell, *A History of Latin America* (Malden, MA: Blackwell, 1997).
13. Peter Bellwood, "Early Agriculturalist Population Diasporas? Farming, Languages, and Genes," *Annual Review of Anthropology* 30 (2001).
14. Bakewell, *A History of Latin America;* Meyer, *Asia;* Douglas J. Brewer and Emily Teeter, *Egypt and the Egyptians* (Cambridge: Cambridge University Press, 2007).
15. Fyle, *Introduction to the History of African Civilization.*
16. Meyer, *Asia.*
17. Ibid.; Rhoads Murphey, "The Historical Context," in *Understanding Contemporary China,* ed. Robert E. Gamer (Boulder: Lynne Rienner, 1999).
18. Fyle, *Introduction to the History of African Civilization.*
19. Ibid.; Brewer and Teeter, *Egypt and the Egyptians.*
20. Ibid.; Bernard Lewis, *The Middle East: A Brief History of the Last 2,000 Years* (New York: Scribner, 1997).
21. Matthew W. Waters, *Ancient Persia: A Concise History of the Achaemenid Empire, 550–330 B.C.E.* (New York: Cambridge University Press, 2014); Irene Silverblatt, *Moon, Sun, and Witches* (Princeton: Princeton University Press, 1987).
22. Silverblatt, *Moon, Sun, and Witches;* Susan Migden Socolow, *The Women of Colonial Latin America* (Cambridge: Cambridge University Press, 2000); Brewer and Teeter, *Egypt and the Egyptians.*
23. Sarah Milledge Nelson, *Ancient Queens: Archaeological Explorations* (Walnut Creek, CA: AltaMira, 2003).
24. July, *A History of the African People.*
25. Oliver, *The African Experience.*
26. Keen and Haynes, *A History of Latin America;* Brewer and Teeter, *Egypt and the Egyptians;* Murphey, "The Historical Context"; Meyer, *Asia;* Lewis, *The Middle East.*
27. Meyer, *Asia;* Laura Laurencich Minelli, *The Inca World* (Norman: University of Oklahoma Press, 2000); Fyle, *Introduction to the History of African Civilization.*
28. Murphey, "The Historical Context"; Oliver, *The African Experience;* Keen and Haynes, *A History of Latin America.*
29. Ibid.
30. Lewis, *The Middle East;* G. Mokhtar, "Conclusion," in *UNESCO General History of Africa: Ancient Civilizations of Africa,* ed. Mokhtar (London: Heinemann, 1981).
31. Murphey, "The Historical Context."
32. Ibid.; Meyer, *Asia.*
33. Keen and Haynes, *The History of Latin America;* Meyer, *Asia;* David Landes, *The Wealth and Poverty of Nations: Why Some Are So Rich and Some So Poor* (New York: Norton, 1998); Murphey, "The Historical Context"; Edward L. Farmer, Gavin R. G. Hambly, Byron K. Marshall et al., *Comparative History of Civilizations in Asia* (Reading, MA: Addison-Wesley, 1977).
34. Minelli, *The Inca World;* David N. Keightley, *The Origins of Chinese Civilization* (Berkeley: University of California Press, 1983); Lewis, *The Middle East.*
35. Oliver, *The African Experience.*
36. Farmer et al., *Comparative History;* Paul Johnson, *The Civilization of Ancient Egypt* (New York: HarperCollins, 1999); Mokhtar, "Conclusion"; Fyle, *Introduction to the History of African Civilization.*
37. Ironically, the largest states were often the most fragile, disintegrating much more easily than smaller states (and even stateless nations), which proved to be more cohesive and durable. Stateless societies on the frontier, like the Chichemecas in northern Mexico or the Araucanians in southern Chile, took the longest to conquer. Small, mobile groups

able to live off the land were hard to suppress—until, in some cases, the Europeans decided that it just wasn't worth it.

38. Oliver, *The African Experience;* Meyer, *Asia;* Minelli, *The Inca World.*

39. Ibid.

40. Maurice Collis, *Cortés and Montezuma* (New York: New Directions, 1999).

41. Ibid.

42. Fyle, *Introduction to the History of African Civilization;* John Hemming, *The Conquest of the Incas* (Boston: Houghton Mifflin Harcourt, 2003).

3

Colonialism and Resistance: Gold, God, and Glory

> Whatever happens we have got / The maxim gun and they have not.
>
> —*Hilaire Belloc*[1]

In most cases, European conquest of what would become the so-called global south did not come overnight. Rather, colonization was the culmination of processes that had begun hundreds of years earlier. The fifteenth and sixteenth centuries represented a turning point for Europe—and for the global south. Most historians agree that until this time, Europe had little on Africa, Asia, the Middle East, or the Americas. It was just another of the world's regions, with its share of accomplishments and failures. In the fifteenth century, few could have dreamed that Europe would dominate the world. How did it all change? How did Europe manage to conquer virtually the entire world? One currently popular view is that Europe simply took advantage of a set of fortuitous circumstances. It was willing to build on the achievements of others (e.g., gunpowder, the compass, and improvements in shipbuilding) and use its military power to take control of the seas and world trade.[2]

What other kinds of generalizations can we make about colonialism? Several, since the main differences between the colonizers were in degree, but not in kind. There are some interesting comparisons to be made in terms of style, but not in terms of substance.[3] Who were the colonizers, who assumed the role of "MOTHER COUNTRY"? The major colonizers in Latin America were the Spanish and the Portuguese, although the British, French, and Dutch took the Guianas and parts of the Caribbean. Spain dominated the Philippines, Puerto Rico, and Cuba until the United States replaced it after the Spanish-American War. The British took much of Asia, including India, Pakistan, Sri Lanka, Burma, and Malaysia. The French claimed Indochina (including Vietnam, Cambodia, and Laos). In Asia the Portuguese had only a few small holdings, and the Dutch controlled the vast archipelago today known as Indonesia.

The British and French were the dominant colonial powers in Africa, with the French taking much of the northern and western regions of the continent, and the British controlling much of the eastern and southern regions. Other colonial powers took pieces of the African cake as well, including the Belgians, Germans, Italians, Portuguese, Spanish, and Dutch.

Although several European powers were interested in the area, the British dominated the waters of the Persian Gulf and influenced surrounding territories from the late nineteenth century until the middle of the twentieth. After the fall of the Ottoman Empire at the end of World War I, much of the Middle East was divided as mandates between the French and British. The Russians continued to dominate Central Asia, and they vied with the British for control of Persia until the two agreed to divide it between themselves into spheres of influence.

Not all of the modern global south was formally claimed and occupied by Europeans, but even territories that were never formally colonized fell under heavy European influence. Because China's coast was carved up between five different alien powers and its emperor was rendered a puppet, it is said to have been "semicolonized" after the Opium Wars of the mid-nineteenth century. Similarly, because they were not insulated from trends ongoing elsewhere, Turkey,

Figure 3.1 How Did Europe Conquer the World?

How did a relative handful of Europeans succeed in conquering these empires? A variety of advantages served the European cause, but the shortest answer is weaponry. Europeans had enormous advantages in military technology throughout the period of conquest. By the seventeenth century, guns were the main weapons favoring Europeans (an early machine gun, the maxim gun, revolutionized violence). Yet, weaponry had made all the difference even hundreds of years earlier.

In Latin America in the early sixteenth century, the Spaniards used steel swords, lanes, small firearms, and artillery, as well as steel body armor and helmets against far greater numbers of Indigenous soldiers with much less effective weaponry and protection. The Inca and Aztecs were equipped only with clubs and axes of wood or stone, slings, bows and arrows, and quilted armor. Brought in on ships from Europe, horses provided the Spaniards with another tremendous advantage in battle. Horses gave the invaders height in combat (which protected riders by giving them a raised fighting platform) and speed in attack. Foot soldiers could never succeed against a cavalry in the open. In addition, the Spaniards unleashed massive dogs in combat. As vicious killers, they terrorized the population. The invaders benefited from other psychological advantages, too. Aztec priests had been predicting the return of the god Quetzalcoatl, as well as the end of the world. The Aztecs had never before seen men with light-colored eyes and hair, let alone horses (which when mounted by Spaniards appeared to be two-headed animals). Combine these advantages with difference in battle tactics (by Aztec standards, the Spanish didn't fight fairly; the Spanish fought to kill, the Aztecs to take prisoners). Add to that the death toll from the diseases Europeans brought with them, and the effect was the literal decimation of populations—not only in Latin America, but in Africa and Asia as well.

Sources: Peter Bakewell, *A History of Latin America* (Malden, MA: Blackwell, 1997); Jared Diamond, *Guns, Germs, and Steel: The Fates of Human Societies* (New York: Norton, 1997); David S. Landes, *The Wealth and Power of Nations: Why Some Are So Rich and Some So Poor* (New York: Norton, 1998).

Thailand, Ethiopia, Liberia, and the handful of STATES that were never officially colonized share many of the legacies of colonialism.

Just as the players involved vary by country, so do the length and period of colonialism. The Spanish and Portuguese were the earliest colonizers, and Latin America was the first region to be colonized. Its era of colonial rule was relatively long, beginning in the early sixteenth century and lasting 300 years or more. Yet, independence came relatively early to Latin America; with a few notable exceptions in the Caribbean and Brazil, most of the region became independent in the 1810s and 1820s.

Compared to Latin America's experience, Western colonialism in most of Africa, Asia, and the Middle East was short-lived. After years of encroaching influence, nearly all of Asia was formally colonized after the 1850s but independent less than a hundred years later, in the 1940s and 1950s. Most of Africa was parceled out to the Europeans at the Conference of Berlin in the 1880s and was (formally) self-governing by the end of the 1960s.

The Middle East's experience is somewhat different. Though the Russians had been encroaching on Central Asia since the sixteenth century, most European powers were more cautious about taking on the Ottoman Empire. During the nineteenth century, when Europe was most active in acquiring colonies, most of the Middle East (with the notable exceptions of Persia, Saudi Arabia, and Yemen) was under Ottoman control. Perhaps because of a long history of mutual antagonism between Christians and Muslims, perhaps because Europeans knew relatively little of the land and overestimated the Muslim powers' military strength, European penetration of the Middle East was delayed (or "veiled," as was the case in Egypt, which the British occupied but over which it had no formal claim). As a result, it was the last major area to fall to the West.

However, by the end of World War I, the Ottoman Empire had bottomed out after a long decline. Despite promises of independence to the Arabs, who had risen up against the Ottomans, Ottoman territories (including former German colonies in Africa and the Pacific) were claimed as protectorates (as did Britain in Egypt) or set aside by the League of Nations as mandates, or wards of the international community. The Western-dominated League granted supervision of the mandates to Britain and France. The French acquired Syria and Lebanon. Control over Iraq, Transjordan, and Palestine passed to Britain. Under this system, the Europeans' primary responsibility was to prepare their wards for eventual self-government. However, many analysts characterize the MANDATORY SYSTEM as a fig leaf for colonialism, as the mandates were treated no differently than colonial possessions elsewhere. Still, the period of mandates was relatively brief. Most of these territories declared their independence in the post–World War II period.[4]

Whether it lasted for one generation or for many generations, most students of the non-Western world agree that colonialism was a formative experience. Although they may disagree about how long-lasting its legacy was, the fact remains that, in one form or another, colonialism is the one experience that virtually every non-Western country has shared. Why did the Europeans conquer the world? What were they after? And what impact did their policies have on the colonized? Analysts disagree in terms of the relative weight they assign the different interests that motivated the Europeans, but most agree that it was based in a mix of what Ali Mazrui characterized as "the three Gs"—gold, God, and glory.[5]

Gold

In many ways, colonialism was the culmination of a process that wrecked Indigenous economies, ruined local industries, and replaced traditional networks of trade with a world system in which Europeans dominated and the rest of the world served. Gold, or the economic motive, was a major if not the major drive behind colonialism. By the beginning of the age of imperialism in the fifteenth century, overland long-distance trade had linked Europe and the non-Western world for over a thousand years. However, it was a technological revolution that would dramatically shift the balance of power—the Europeans' ability to dominate world trade by sea.

From the time of Henry the Navigator, Portugal had led Europe in decades of exploration. Early in the fifteenth century, as the Portuguese began making stops along the coast of Africa, they established plantations in Cape Verde and the Canary Islands. In Africa, the Portuguese were literally seeking gold, but later it was slaving that set in motion a process that would dramatically alter Africa's relationship with Europe. By 1487, the Portuguese had rounded the Cape of Good Hope and entered the bustling Indian Ocean trading network. The newcomers originally sought access to the highly lucrative trade in pepper and spices. They did this by setting up trading posts at strategic bases along the coasts of Africa, Asia, and the Middle East. Over the next hundred years, Portugal practiced a policy of expansionism. Seeking to eliminate the middlemen and gain direct access and control of this trade, Portugal defeated fleets of Egyptians, Arabs, and Persians. Portuguese traders eventually reached as far as China by the early sixteenth century, although the European presence went largely unnoticed by the Chinese emperors until much later.[6]

Meanwhile, seeking another route to the Indies, the Portuguese were joined by the Spanish, who together claimed the Caribbean and much of the Americas as their own. In a papal bull in 1493, Pope Alexander VI randomly determined the line dividing what would become Latin America between the two Iberian powers. This pronouncement formed the basis of the Treaty of Tordesillas in 1494, which formalized their claims. All was decided even before the Portuguese landed in Brazil, but the exclusivity of this relationship would be more or less maintained for another 300 years, until the independence of these territories in the nineteenth century.[7]

The Portuguese weren't as successful at maintaining their interests in Asia. They benefited from a near monopoly in the region for over a hundred years, but were later displaced by the Dutch, French, British, and others, who entered the Indian Ocean trade as competitors in the seventeenth century. The employees of chartered companies, like the Dutch East India Company, were often the first to make contact in these distant territories. Serving as agents of the crown, these companies paved the way for imperialism. Under a royal charter granting him access to much of southern Africa, Cecil Rhodes's British South African Company had the power to conduct warfare and diplomacy and to annex territory on behalf of the British monarch. With enormous resources at their disposal, these companies established EMPIRES in Asia and Africa with a variety of economic interests in mind. They later pushed for concessions and enjoyed monopolies in the Middle Eastern mandates—these profits were also repatriated to Europe. With the exception of the early colonies established by the Spanish and Portuguese, Europeans maintained long relationships in these territories prior to outright colonization.

This was the age of MERCANTILISM, the precapitalist stage marked by the accumulation of capital through trade and plunder on a worldwide scale. Under mercantilism, each power sought commercial expansion to achieve a surplus in its balance of trade. Colonies were developed to suit the mother country's interest, as sources of raw materials and guaranteed markets for its manufactured goods. Colonialism was never about free trade. Rather, in the earliest days it was mercantilist, and through to the end it was protectionist. Whether it was the Spanish in the fifteenth century or the French after World War II, this exclusive arrangement served as the umbilical cord linking the mother country to her colonies.

From the earliest days of colonization, this arrangement simply meant expropriation without compensation. In Spanish America, mining was the principal source of royal revenue. The crown acquired enormous wealth by hauling treasure off in its galleons, creating monopolies, and taxing all wealth produced in the colonies. Under the *quinto,* one-fifth of all gold, silver, and other precious metals belonged to the crown. Innumerable taxes weighed on the Indigenous people, who paid the costs of colonial administration and defense and were expected to produce a surplus for the crown. Such wealth promoted the growth of European industry and subsidized the consolidation of European commercial and military power in Asia and Africa.[8]

With industrialization fully under way in the eighteenth and nineteenth centuries, European economic interests in the non-Western world grew. To ensure the quantity and quality of the raw materials they desired, Europeans yearned to eliminate local middlemen and establish their own monopoly control of production and trade. Eager to sell their newly manufactured wares, the colonizers sought guaranteed markets and set about destroying their Indigenous competitors. They interfered with preexisting regional and long-distance trades. For example, the Spanish colonies were prohibited from producing any goods produced by Spain. In Africa, Asia, the Middle East, and Latin America, self-sufficient economies were destroyed or transformed and subordinated. India and Egypt, which each produced some of the world's finest cotton yarn and textiles, were flooded by cheap, factory-made British fabrics and effectively eliminated as competitors. Millions of artisans were put out of work, with little choice but to turn to farming. Similarly, the Ottoman Empire's handicrafts manufacturing couldn't compete with industrialized production techniques of the West. Colonized peoples were driven out of the most important sectors of their economies, as industrialists, craftsmen, and merchants.[9]

Europe's industrial revolution also demanded reliable access to cheap raw materials. The colonies were established to serve as feeders to the industrial economies of the colonizer, and the result was the development of economies centered on the export of raw materials. Justified by the principle of COMPARATIVE

ADVANTAGE, which holds that efficiency is enhanced by specialization in production, the mother countries decided what their new colonies would produce, based on the colonizer's needs and the particular resources of each territory. Monocultures were created: sugar from Cuba, hides from Argentina, coffee from Kenya, cotton from Egypt. Nigeria and India were unusual in that they exported a handful of different cash crops. The colonies were never to be self-sufficient; instead they were undiversified, vulnerable, and dependent.

To ensure the desired quality and quantity of goods, the mother countries often imposed a system of compulsory crop cultivation. Small farmers were given quotas and obliged by law to produce the assigned cash crops. Those who did not fulfill their quotas could be fined or arrested. In Latin America, Indians were forced to sell their goods at fixed prices usually well below world market value. In addition, they were compelled to buy goods at artificially high prices. Because of the relatively low value of unprocessed goods versus the high cost of imports, colonialism established a fundamental inequality of exchange. The people of the colonies ended up producing what they didn't consume and consuming what they didn't produce.[10] They were in effect marketing raw goods to the West, to repurchase them in finished form.

For all intents and purposes, the resources of one territory were drained to enrich another. The Europeans opened up mines and plantations. Germans and South Africans stripped Namibia of its once-vast diamond wealth. After the Dutch East India Company took Indonesia, all of Java was set aside and parceled into large plantations to grow export crops such as coffee and pepper. Europeans busied themselves obtaining concessions, such as a sixty-year British monopoly to find and develop petroleum and natural gas in most of Persia. Soon foreigners owned the right to control every aspect of this asset, and Persia was the richest known source of petroleum at the time.[11]

Someone had to produce these commodities, and one of the first concerns of every colonial power was how to meet its labor demands in terms of mining, portage, construction, and cultivation. Slavery, tenancy, and debt peonage existed throughout the colonial period. Although King Leopold of Belgium was unrivaled in the barbarism he used to compel labor in Congo, other colonizers used forced labor as well. Under the Spanish system of *repartimiento* (or the *mita*), all adult male Indians had to spend part of their year laboring in Spanish mines, farms, and public works. Barely disguised slavery, the *mita* was an important source of labor for the Spanish until the end of the colonial period. Similar practices, such as land curtailment, or the large-scale appropriation of territory by Europeans, denied the Indigenous people an alternative source of cash income. Once-independent farmers and herders were converted to wage labor. In addition, taxes were imposed at such a rate (and to be paid in the colonizer's currency) that people were left little choice but to seek employment in the colonial economy. Perhaps the most oppressive labor regulations were found in southern Africa, where pass laws and labor contracts created a system of migrant labor that gave employers enormous advantages. To some degree, it continues to this day.[12]

Wherever colonialism existed, no matter who was doing the colonizing, the effect on the colonized was much the same. The demands of the colonial economy often resulted not only in an intensification of the exploitation of labor, but also in a great disruption of community and family. Often men and women were forced to leave their families behind to work as migrant laborers. Overall health and nutrition deteriorated as demands for labor grew. Although most people continued to work as farmers, colonial agriculture was much more extensive than anything known before, demanding more energy and resources to produce commodities for sale in markets. Most Africans, for example, were so busy in their cash-crop farming that there was little time for the production of staples or to supplement their diets with hunting or fishing as before. Often the result was vulnerability to overwork and disease, which spread rapidly with the dislocations associated with an intensification of production and trade volumes. A variety of colonial policies rendered Indigenous populations landless. Under French rule in Vietnam, it is estimated that two-thirds of the population were tenant farmers.[13]

In the worst cases, traditional welfare systems were destroyed. The stress and dislocation of colonialism combined with economic hardship to contribute to a rise in social violence and self-destructive behavior, such as opium addiction in southern China and alcoholism in India and southern Africa. In some places populations actually declined, as death rates rose while fertility rates fell. Forced to produce government crops, Indonesians were left dependent on purchasing rice. But the low contract price for the spices they produced meant that entire regions became impoverished. The commercialization of agriculture left peasants vulnerable, and famine occurred with regularity. It is estimated that 15 million people in India died of famine between 1875 and 1900. During the first forty years of colonial rule, overwork and abuse reduced the population of the Belgian Congo by half. Perhaps the most devastating results occurred in the Valley

Figure 3.2 Did Colonialism Benefit Women?

Colonialism is sometimes argued to have improved the status of women, since the missionaries sought to destroy Indigenous customs and social practices they saw as barbaric, such as female genital cutting, polygamy, and suttee (the practice of burning widows on the funeral pyres of their husbands). However, throughout the precolonial societies of the non-Western world, women's experience varied by race, class, region, age, and other factors. In some communities, non-Western women were much more "liberated" than their Western sisters. Where women had shared political authority or enjoyed economic or sexual autonomy before colonialism, European sexism and colonial policy destroyed such systems and marginalized women. Where patriarchy long predated the arrival of Europeans, colonialism laminated it. Western and non-Western patriarchies joined in an attempt to control women's labor and sexuality, deny them access to education and employment, and deprive them of political power. The colonizers sought to win the allegiance of men by granting them increased authority over women. However, women were not passive victims in this process. In Zimbabwe and elsewhere, some women agitated for a return to the relatively favorable status they had held in their societies before colonialism. In a variety of ways, including the use of so-called weapons of the weak, they asserted their interests. Often, colonial women (both colonizer and colonized) enjoyed more independence than is usually assumed—despite rigorous efforts to keep them "in their place."

Source: Susan Migden Socolow, *The Women of Colonial Latin America* (Cambridge: Cambridge University Press, 2000).

of Mexico, where 90 percent of the population is believed to have died during the first hundred years of colonial rule.[14]

God

Often alongside the conquistadors in Latin America and the traders in Asia and Africa were the missionaries. "God" would be invoked to justify colonialism, and to varying degrees proselytizing was a large part of the colonial effort. Priests came to Latin America on Columbus's second sailing in 1493. The Catholic Church was joined by Protestant missionaries who served as aggressive agents of cultural imperialism as well, to compete for souls in Asia, Africa, and to a lesser extent in the Middle East. Catholic or Protestant, some missionaries saw themselves as protectors of the colonized and were "pro-native" in conflicts with the mother country over their treatment. However, these people of God were colonizers as well, collaborators crucial to the administrative success by helping to bring Indigenous peoples under control. In a massive effort, work was fused with conversion. The "heathens" were gathered together so that they could not only be more easily evangelized, but also taught "Christian virtues" of hard work and unquestioning obedience.

More than any other actor, the missionaries were responsible for compelling colonized peoples to recognize their domination by the invading culture. Missionaries assertively challenged all preexisting belief systems. Their churches were often built on holy grounds, on top of razed temples, to drive home their message. The earliest days of conquest and pacification were often times of violence, dramatic social change, and transformation. For many people colonialism meant the destruction of their world, since Indigenous religions were assaulted by the persistent imposition of European values. Time and again evangelization was conducted with such zeal, and was so heavy-handed, that it amounted to forced conversion. Christianity was imposed with an intolerance that was new in most regions.

Although there were some significant differences in approach (e.g., the Portuguese and Spanish were much more interested in religious conversion than the Dutch), wherever colonialism existed it was based in racism and cultural imperialism. Propounding social Darwinist theories of evolution and survival of the fittest, the Europeans saw themselves as more civilized, cleaner, smarter, and better educated than the people they colonized, who were variously described as devious, lazy, or immoral. The expression of this chauvinism or racism took different forms, depending on the colonizer. For example, whereas the policy of assimilation was based in the French belief in their own cultural superiority, the British were better known for the use of a color bar, based in their sense of racial superiority. However, institutionalized segregation and discrimination was the rule in every colony. Whereas the French were determined that their civilization should be accepted by all living under French rule, the British stressed the differences between themselves and the colonized, and were contemptuous of Indigenous peoples' attempts to adopt the English language and culture.

Yet, in British colonies and all the others, "white man's burden" was about more than just saving souls. It provided a rationale for domination: the fruits of

Western civilization should be shared with the heathen. Again, it was missionaries who took it upon themselves to bear this burden. They were given a virtual monopoly over colonial education. Building schools and clinics was an effective way of evangelizing and advancing the colonial effort. Apologists for colonialism often laud these efforts, which did provide formal education and improved healthcare for some. However, these services were grossly inadequate and unevenly distributed. It is estimated that fewer than 10 percent of Zambian children ever saw the inside of a schoolhouse. Secondary schools were rare in colonial Africa until after World War II. Few universities and technical schools were established; not a single university was built in Brazil during the entire colonial period. There was not one university in Indonesia until 1941. Where schools did exist, often it was only white children or the children of "notable natives" who received these benefits.[15]

In other ways as well, the colonial educational systems existed primarily for the benefit of European settlers and administrators. The schools served as instruments of subjugation. They perpetuated racial inequality by indoctrinating the colonized into permanent subservience and sought to convince Indigenous people of their inferiority. A few professionals were trained, but mostly the colonized were prepared to work as soldiers, clerks, and low-level administrators. The curriculum not only was irrelevant to their needs, but also taught colonized people to disown their birthrights, to give up their traditions, dress, customs, religion, language—in some cases, even their own names. For example, French language, literature, and history were compulsory in colonial Syrian schools, while Arabic language, literature, and history were ignored. The achievements of non-Westerners were disregarded or denied. European institutions were assumed to be innately superior to anything that might have existed before colonialism. In effect, the children who went through these schools were taught to embrace all that was European. These students, who grew up to be the ELITES of their countries, ended up alienated from their own cultures. They were taught to assimilate and adore European culture and to look down on their own as decadent and worthless. The result was an IDENTITY crisis not easily resolved.[16]

Glory

A third factor commonly observed as motivating European efforts to conquer the world was the search for the glory and prestige that comes with recognition as a great power. Nationalistic rivalries for world dominion, in particular the rivalry between the French and the British, compelled the various European powers to claim a share of the cake. Strategic and economic interests combined to raise the stakes in this rivalry. No one wanted to be left out; the colonizers competed fiercely for markets. They also sought control of sea-lanes, access routes, and strategic locations like the Suez Canal, Cape Town, Aden, Ceylon, and Hong Kong to protect their military, logistical, and economic interests. For example, the Suez Canal was considered by the British to be the "lifeline to India," since cutting through it from the Mediterranean to the Red Sea greatly reduced the long journey from Europe around Africa. Not only did this shortcut mean an enormous increase in the volume of trade, but control of India also greatly facilitated the exploitation of China. Therefore, location made Egypt strategically pivotal and the British insisted on maintaining a strong presence there.[17]

Yet, other European powers were just as determined to establish their empires. Out of concern that such intense competition might lead to war, the British, French, Germans, Belgians, and others made agreements for the orderly extension of European influence. Through various meetings, they set out rules for the "legal" appropriation of territories. At the Conference of Berlin in the 1880s, the Europeans divided Africa among themselves. The arbitrary lines they assigned as borders are largely the ones that exist today.

Similarly, the Europeans carved twenty-four nations out of the Ottoman Empire with little knowledge or care as to what they were creating. Often the partitions took place on maps that didn't reflect the interior of the territories. Some of the resulting entities were left landlocked; some were left with little base for economic DEVELOPMENT. Just as devastating in terms of long-term feasibility, the colonizers ignored local factors and drew boundaries between states that cut across religious and ethnic groups.[18] Some groups such as the Kurds became STATELESS NATIONS, spread through Iran, Iraq, and Turkey with no government to call their own. In addition, groups with very different cultures, traditions, and beliefs about government were thrown together to live in MULTINATIONAL STATES. Where divisions are deep, such as in the Sudan, this has meant real problems for the development of national identities. Fearing dominance by larger groups, minorities often maintain their subnational loyalties. Many religious and ethnic groups in Indonesia, Lebanon, and Nigeria, for example, have little sense of national identity. As a result, state SOVEREIGNTY is weak. The existence of multinational states and stateless nations has contributed to innumerable territorial challenges over the years. The result has been attempts at SECESSION (Nigeria, East Timor) as well as IRREDENTIST WARS to redraw boundaries (e.g., those between Israel, Somalia, Iraq, and their neighbors).

In hindsight, it is clear that the borders established by the colonizers would pose long-term problems for the global south. However, in the late nineteenth and early twentieth centuries Europe argued that colonialism was for the Indigenous peoples' own good.[19] Perhaps to satisfy public concerns back home, the colonizers took the paternalistic position that those with a "higher civilization" should be entrusted with the responsibility of tutoring their "little brown brothers" in Western political and social institutions. Westernization was assumed to be synonymous with modernization, and modernization was identified with progress. Colonized peoples were described as childlike or nonadult. The League of Nations determined that this period of guardianship should continue until the peoples of Africa, Asia, and the Middle East were deemed by its largely European members "to be ready" for self-rule.

The role of benevolent father figure was another aspect of the glory Europe was seeking. This self-aggrandizement was clearest in the mandatory system, when the League of Nations authorized France and Britain to govern the territories of the Ottoman Empire. As stewards responsible for the area's welfare, the period of mandate was to be a "sacred trust." While the mandatory system was supposed to prepare the area for independence as soon as possible and be a benefit to its wards, in fact it was foreign occupation.

How much did the guardians do for their wards? How much tutelage in self-rule occurred during colonialism? What kind of lesson in government was colonialism, exactly? Although some historians get caught up in debates over the significance of style and approach, colonial government was overall rigidly hierarchical, lacking democratic forms of ACCOUNTABILITY, autonomy, or decentralization. Although colonialism's reach was concentrated in the cities and dissipated through the hinterland, its rule was authoritarian, and the primary objective of government was the imposition of order.

To this end, the mother countries were abusive. They relied on repression to maintain control. Colonialism created a legacy of military privileges by rewarding soldiers as a special caste with their own set of interests, not subject to civil power.[20] The colonizers created full-time standing armies to crack down on dissent, dissolve parties, and force nationalist leaders like Nelson Mandela underground. Others, such as Sukarno, were sent into exile. Justice was arbitrary; the colonizers imprisoned leaders such as Gandhi and Kenyatta and sometimes used appalling force to put down resistance. It was not uncommon for them to collectively punish entire populations. In one of the worst cases, the Germans fought a war of annihilation against the Herero in South West Africa (Namibia), reducing the population by 85 percent. In many places, the colonizers became quasi-military authorities, reduced to imposing martial law to maintain control.

Not only was Europe determined to hold on to power, but administration was to be on the cheap, with little or no costs to the mother country. To do this, the colonizers relied on the cooperation of Indigenous peoples, and distorted preexisting political systems whenever possible to administer colonial controls. Although there were differences in how much they relied on them, to some degree the British, French, and the others depended on the assistance of "native elites." Known as caciques in Mexico and the Philippines, curacas in the Andes, and mandarins in Indochina, these were Indigenous peoples who either were large landholders or had held traditional power prior to colonization. If no local elites were sufficiently accommodating to colonial interests, the Europeans simply appointed what were called in some areas "warrant chiefs," ambitious men with no traditional claim to power but who had proven themselves loyal to the colonizer.[21] Rewarded with privileges like exemption from taxes or labor service, they served as brokers for the colonial state, charged with overseeing the enforcement of colonial regulations, collecting taxes, and conscripting labor. Under colonialism, corrupt officials often became quite wealthy, administrators embezzled, and offices were bought and sold. In fact, in all four regions it is said that colonialism created a mentality of CORRUPTION. One of its longest-lasting legacies is the notion that government can be manipulated by money, and that political power is the surest route to wealth. Not only was corruption pervasive, but some colonial systems were particularly notorious for their inefficiency and immense bureaucracies.[22]

In effect, then, colonialism destroyed precolonial political systems and delegitimized traditional leaders without providing a viable alternative to AUTHORITARIANISM. Individual rights and freedoms were subordinated to the mother country's desire to hold on to power. Western ideals such as egalitarianism and SELF-DETERMINATION were seldom applied to non-Westerners. The colonial model of government was a small elite maintained in power through reliance on coercion. Despite all its grandiose claims, the colonial state was no DEMOCRACY. Rather, it was government based on intolerance.

Government based on intolerance, alienation from one's own culture, and the creation of economic dependency—this was what colonialism meant to the colonized. Gold, God, and glory all had a role to play in the push for empire. Rather than attributing colonialism to any single factor, it is perhaps best to understand European motivation as based in a mix of these three motives. Certainly, the impact from political, economic, and cultural imperialism is still felt throughout the former colonies. Although it would go too far to blame all of it on colonialism, much of the instability found in so many former colonies should be understood as the logical consequence of this relationship.

The Struggle for Independence

Colonialism was not only a time of dislocation; it was also a time of unrest. There was always resistance to European domination. However, it grew in intensity and complexity over the years. Especially in the cities, ostensibly nonpolitical associations such as study groups, prayer groups, and even dance clubs provided people the opportunity to congregate and discuss grievances. Such associations became nascent political parties advocating various forms of resistance. These groups became nationalist movements as they came together for larger demands such as self-determination.

Groups that usually saw themselves as sharing few interests joined together against the mother country (whether Sunnis and Shiites in Iraq or members of different ethnic groups in Ghana and so on) and were relatively successful in setting aside their differences for their common goals. Yet, multiethnic, multireligious revolts contained the seeds of possible fragmentation, even self-destruction. Nationalist movements in some countries such as Nigeria were always divided by bitter, regional rivalries. Ideological, ethnic, religious, and other divides simmered just under the surface of many of these movements, yet for a while at least, the colonized managed to transcend their differences to unite against the colonizer.[23]

A number of factors combined to promote unity against the colonial powers. In most of Africa, Asia, and the Middle East, the rise and intensification of NATIONALISM corresponded with the period between World War I and World War II. Not only were the colonies expected to sacrifice for the war effort, but the Great Depression hit most of the global south especially hard. An already difficult situation had become intolerable. Asian and African soldiers returning home from the world wars (many of them conscripted) had seen colonial doctrines of white supremacy dramatically challenged. Nationalist movements were emboldened by the Japanese defeat of Russia in 1905, and the near defeat of the Allies in the Pacific in World War II. Supported by international organizations such as the Pan-African Congress, these servicemen were joined by students, workers, professionals, and others who stridently expressed their revulsion toward occupation. If World War II was a struggle against racism and tyranny, then why should colonized peoples everywhere not be granted self-determination?

Beyond these common questions, nationalist movements varied greatly in terms of IDEOLOGY, membership, goals, and strategy. They disagreed over whether peaceful change was possible, or if violence was necessary. And there were serious divides over how much change was necessary, if reform would suffice or if REVOLUTION was a must, and over what kind of government and economic system was preferred.

Although sometimes the split within and between nationalist movements was a matter of rival personalities and ideologies, frequently it was generational—the old versus the new ELITES. The older generation was composed of a relatively privileged CLASS of teachers, religious leaders, and low-level civil servants who resented the restrictions they faced as "nonwhites." Generally social conservatives, they were very class-conscious and tended to distance themselves from the MASSES. The self-titled "civilized natives" in Africa, for example, were calling for more rights primarily for themselves. These were not radical demands; most old-style elites were not asking for independence. Rather, they were seeking better treatment within the system.

Not only were their requests of the colonial government relatively modest, but their tactics were moderate as well. More trusting of the system, the older generation of nationalists played by the rules. During World War I, for example, the Indian National Congress hoped to win favor for its cause by cooperating with the British. These activists undertook letter-writing campaigns and submitted petitions to the colonial powers asking that they end abuses and do more to provide for the welfare of the colonized. Seeking to spur the mother country to take corrective action, they wrote editorials. Some, such as the South African Native National Conference (later known as the African National Congress), used diplomatic means. Egyptians sent a delegation to London to present their case for self-rule. Elite and commoner alike even went to the colonial courts for redress of their grievances.

Figure 3.3 Subversion and Other "Weapons of the Weak"

Although not usually described as "nationalist" resistance per se, people resisted colonial rule for a variety of reasons and in a variety of ways. Tax evasion, desertion, feigning illness, breaking machinery, and other means of subterfuge are known as weapons of the weak. The deployment of these weapons is far more common than revolts and wars, but is not usually covered in history books. In part, this is because some means of resistance were never recognized as such. Escape, for example, can be a weapon of the weak, such as when mass waves of people took flight across regions during the periods of conquest and "pacification" under colonial rule. People sought escape through a variety of other means as well, including alcohol abuse and suicide. Although we generally hear that populations grew under colonialism, in some places birthrates fell because women refused to bring children into the new world of oppression. Abortions and infanticide are believed to have been common in Peru, the Congo, and elsewhere during colonialism. It is important to recognize that what may appear to be individual, private actions may be linked to larger issues as responses to an insufferable situation.

Sources: David S. Landes, *The Wealth and Poverty of Nations: Why Some Are So Rich and Some So Poor* (New York: Norton, 1998); Adam Hochschild, *King Leopold's Ghost* (Boston: Houghton Mifflin, 1998); David M. Davidson, "Negro Slave Control and Resistance in Colonial Mexico," in *People and Issues in Latin American History*, ed. Lewis Hanke and Jane M. Rausch (New York: Markus Wiener, 1993).

On the other hand, the new elite was primarily composed of a later generation of the educated class. Having mostly attended university abroad, the new elites were mobilized by liberal notions of freedom and self-determination. These new elites formed groups like the Nigerian Youth Movement, which were often more militant and more radical in their aims than the older generation of leaders, whom they frequently disdained as accomplices of colonialism. Many once-cautious and genteel groups that had been known for their moderation, such as the Indian National Congress and the African National Congress, were radicalized by colonial refusals to budge. As a newer generation assumed leadership of these movements, it adopted a harder line.[24]

Well organized under charismatic leaders such as Castro, Nkrumah, Gandhi, Sukarno, Nasser, Ho Chi Minh, and Mandela, the nationalist movements gained in membership and strength. Instead of simply ameliorating colonialism, these new nationalists sought to completely uproot it. Their strategy was much more GRASSROOTS-BASED, including previously excluded groups such as women, workers, and youth. Like earlier generations, the new elites used the press and international congresses to make their causes known. But whereas the resistance offered by earlier generations was marked by its politeness and civility, this generation of nationalists organized mass campaigns and were much more confrontational toward those they viewed as their oppressors. Demonstrations, strikes, boycotts, and other forms of mass resistance proliferated in Africa, Asia, and the Middle East after World War I, but boomed after World War II. Starting in the 1920s and 1930s, Latin Americans joined broadly based mass parties seeking more radical change as well. At times, this nationalism took the form of radical mass mobilization. Demonstrations and strikes turned into countless riots and rebellions—and sometimes even revolutions. In the Aba Women's War, one of the most famous events of this period in Nigeria, market women undressed and marched to the Governor's Palace to protest taxes and unfair treatment. In response to the threat to their communities, women also led riots in Mexico and Peru, armed with spears, kitchen knives, and rocks. Men and women turned out into the streets under such circumstances, to let the authorities know that they should listen to their complaints.[25] Often these mass strikes and riots were put down with severe reprisals. In the protests at Amritsar, for example, the British responded savagely, leaving a thousand Indians dead and many more wounded.

Often these movements did attempt to influence the terms of colonialism (or in the case of Latin America, NEOCOLONIALISM). For example, West African farmers sought to alter wage rates and the prices for their crops through cocoa "holdups" of the sale of their produce, refusing to sell until they got a better price. Throughout this period, there were many demonstrations of rural and urban discontent. Colonized people everywhere wanted improvement of health and educational facilities, and equality of economic opportunity. Yet, the movements led by the new elite generally had larger goals in mind. More willing to use violence if necessary, and more revolutionary in their goals than the old-style elites, these nationalists were seeking some form of national self-determination—autonomy, if not independence.

In terms of their vision for the future, many of these groups stressed the positive aspects of Indigenous cultures and the need for a cultural renaissance, to revive the traditional order in the face of the foreign assault. Some favored Western constitutional models for change; some advocated peaceful change, practicing techniques of noncooperation such as civil disobedience and passive resistance. Others adopted and adapted Marxist Leninism, in the belief that capitalism would never lead to DEVELOPMENT and that violent, revolutionary change was the only way independence could be achieved (Algeria, Vietnam, Angola). Others (e.g., the African National Congress in South Africa and the Muslim Brotherhood in Egypt) used a mix of methods. Again, they disagreed not only about how independence should be achieved, but also about the best blueprint for the future.

For many years, the colonizers were able to use the divide between the old and new elites to their advantage. Infighting within and between nationalist movements over goals and strategy no doubt delayed independence. Still, despite the Europeans' best efforts, eventually it became clear that the nationalist movements could not be ignored or written off by the colonizers. The anticolonial struggle was greatly assisted by the fact that, after the world wars, the imperial powers were weakened, impoverished, and exhausted. Public opinion in Europe had turned against unnecessary expenditures, and most of the remaining colonial powers had lost the will to hold on. The colonies were reeling as well; the wars had intensified pressures on them not only for troops, but also for forced labor and supplies. After sacrificing for the war effort, living with shortages, price hikes, and wage freezes for years, the Arabs, Indians, Africans, and others expected rewards for their contribution. They wanted concessions from the mother countries and they expected to be granted more participation in running their own affairs. For example, during World War I in return for their cooperation against the Ottomans, the Allies had made promises to the Arabs for immediate self-government. The Arabs were infuriated when it became clear this was not to be. Why freedom for Czechoslovakia and Yugoslavia and not the peoples of Africa, Asia, and the Middle East?

Figure 3.4 Spiritualism and Nationalist Resistance

Just as religion was used to colonize, spirituality was used in resistance. Because of colonial attempts to co-opt or destroy traditional sources of authority, spiritual leaders were frequently the only ones left with legitimacy. Often denigrated by the colonizers as "witch doctors," these priests and mullahs, prophets, spirit mediums, and healers inspired nationalist movements around the world. Some of these movements were moderate and advocated reconciliation and peaceful change. Others predicted the end of the world and a coming cataclysm for white people. In Southeast Asia, Islamic and Buddhist religious revivals mobilized populations. Pan-Islamism fused religion with nationalism, creating a jihadist tradition that spurred resistance to imperial penetration. Separatist and millenarian churches in Latin America and Africa were often based in ancestral traditions. The common theme across the four regions is that these movements sought to recover their identity and defend the cultural dignity of colonized peoples.

Sources: Ali A. Mazrui, "Seek Ye First the Political Kingdom," in *UNESCO General History of Africa: Africa Since 1935*, ed. Ali A. Mazrui (London: Heinemann, 1993); Edward L. Farmer, Gavin R. G. Hambly, Byron K. Marshall, et al., *Comparative History of Civilizations in Asia* (Reading, MA: Addison-Wesley, 1977).

Figure 3.5 Wars of Liberation

For many countries the road to independence was one of intense conflict and violence, marked by insurgencies and revolts. Where peaceful means didn't work, and where all efforts were met with ruthless suppression, men and women turned to armed struggle. Particularly where there were large numbers of white settlers (e.g., Zimbabwe, Algeria), these conflicts often developed into revolutions and wars for liberation. Contrary to popular perception, both men and women participated in these wars. Women risked their lives to feed and house guerrillas. They performed crucial services, such as moving weapons and information to fighters. In some cases, women served as combatants in Namibia, Zimbabwe, Algeria, and elsewhere. These women became important symbols and rallying points for their nations. For example, Hawa Ismen Ali, who became known as Somalia's "Joan of Arc," was killed while protesting Italian colonialism in 1948.

Source: Ali A. Mazrui, "Seek Ye First the Political Kingdom," in *UNESCO General History of Africa: Africa Since 1935*, ed. Ali A Mazrui (London: Heinemann, 1993).

With some notable exceptions, the United States and the Soviet Union generally supported the nationalists' demands. Whether for altruistic or not-so-altruistic reasons, both new superpowers generally adopted an anticolonial stance and pressured Europe to dismantle its empires. Moreover, in much of the diplomatic language of the times—from the Atlantic Charter, which upheld the right to self-determination, to the charter of the newly established UNITED NATIONS—colonial powers were finding it much more difficult to maintain their LEGITIMACY. Increasingly, in the international arena, they were being held accountable for their actions. The United Nations received complaints from the colonies, and required regular progress reports on how well they were preparing their wards for independence. In effect, a constellation of events, both domestic and international, came together to make the hold of empire less and less tenable. Buoyed by the vacuums created by international events, nationalism throughout the non-Western world was the driving force behind this change. This was as true in the early nineteenth century for Latin America (with the decline of the Iberian powers) as it was by the mid-twentieth century for Africa, Asia, and the Middle East.

The end of colonialism came about at different times and in different ways, but it is fair to say that it mostly came about over the objections of the mother countries. In most colonies, there was little real power-sharing until the very end. The vast majority of colonized peoples were excluded from the rights of citizenship. In much of the global south, all attempts by Indigenous peoples to participate in politics were squelched until after World War II. Although the British and French were more likely than the Belgians, the Dutch, or the Portuguese to allow for an independent press and the right to an associational life, overall the "best" of the colonizers hurt democratization more than they nurtured it. Even those most willing to allow some political opening made often-inadequate and superficial reforms. For every concession granted, there were restrictions that continued to limit political participation.

Yet, these were the lucky ones. Where the colonizers recognized independence as inevitable, and the forcible retention of empire as impracticable and unprofitable, they acted pragmatically. With foresight, they initiated a gradual devolution of power so as to maintain the close ties established under colonialism after independence. While this might have meant problems for the former colonies in terms of continued dependency, a graceful exit by the mother country meant a far greater likelihood that independence would at least begin with some form of democracy.

Others were not so fortunate. For the vast majority of colonized peoples living under Belgian, Dutch, Spanish, or Portuguese rule, there was little preparation for independence or democracy.[26] Even when they left peacefully, as the Belgians and French did from most of their African colonies, they delayed the handover of power until the very end and then left virtually overnight. To punish the colonies for seeking self-determination, the former mother countries cut off aid. There are stories that the French even took the light bulbs with them when they left, and that the Portuguese destroyed water systems. Worse, where strategic interests loomed large or where white settler populations lobbied against independence, the colonizers fought long and bloody wars in a desperate attempt to hold on to power. In countries where class and race conflicts were deepest, independence was achieved with more difficulty and democracy quickly failed. Similarly, where it took a revolution to win liberation, the new government was likely anti-Western, anticapitalist, and based on one-party rule.[27]

Is It "Independence" Only in Name?

However fiercely the colonizers struggled against it, inevitably the period of empire had passed. Although most of Latin America had won its independence more than a hundred years earlier, formal independence in Asia and the Middle East was granted or won in the 1930s, 1940s, and 1950s. The 1960s is the decade most associated with independence in Africa, although several countries were not liberated until later—the last colony to win its freedom was South Africa, in 1994.

For the majority of people living in South Africa and the other former colonies, independence was a time of great optimism and celebration. With the exception of a few elites, most citizens of the global south looked forward to the freedoms associated with self-determination. "Freedom" was variously defined as everything from the end of forced labor, to political autonomy, self-determination, and individual liberty, to the end of colonial monopolies. Finally, it was time for people to control their own resources for their own benefit. Many anticipated a restoration of the dignity taken from them by colonialism, and in these heady days people looked forward to a smooth road ahead. However, too soon it became clear that each newly independent STATE would have its own problems to face. Above all, the nationalists who had brought their countries to independence faced formidable challenges of organizing new governments that would provide the political stability necessary for economic GROWTH.

Conclusions: Independence or In Dependence?

Although we tend to think of the INTERNATIONAL ECONOMIC SYSTEM as a contemporary phenomenon, it existed long before Europeans colonized the world.

Empires in Africa, Asia, and the Middle East had prospered in the world marketplace for over 2,000 years. The Americas were linked in a busy regional trade. Although some areas remained isolated, others played an integral part in the evolving international trade. African, Asian, and Middle Eastern craftsmen and merchants once traded on par with Europeans, as equal partners in the world economy.[28] It is important to understand that before the age of European empire, Europe was just one part of the international economy. A world economy and system of interdependence predates colonialism.

However, that interdependence was fundamentally changed by European imperial expansion. One major effect of this expansionism was that the economic relationship between the West and much of the world shifted substantially over time—to Europe's favor. Whether it lasted for three decades or three centuries, the mercantilist policies associated with colonialism played a decisive role in Europe's rise to power. Noneconomic interests did play a part in motivating this expansionism. But the accumulation of capital created by the transatlantic slave trade, the pillage of foreign lands, and the creation of European monopolies provided the base for Western industrialization and the development of capitalism.

Whereas this early form of GLOBALIZATION meant unprecedented wealth for Europe, for the people to be conquered the European presence was much like an apocalypse. Yes, the history of the world can be described as a series of conquests, and the rise and fall of empires is a recurrent phenomenon in the histories of all regions. This wasn't the first time outsiders had swept through these territories, but it usually involved a relatively marginal disturbance to the underlying continuity of life. The European colonization of Africa, Asia, Latin America, and to a lesser extent the Middle East marked a fundamental, long-term change in institutional structures as a whole and a modification of the network of social norms and beliefs that constituted entire cultural systems. It radically altered people's lives. The effect was often devastating as Indigenous political systems were undermined or destroyed. Social structures were warped, economies were distorted, and cultures disintegrated.[29]

There are analysts who refute such arguments and characterize the effect of European colonialism on the colonized as essentially benign, or even a positive good. They contend that the colonial experience contributed to the overall well-being of Indigenous peoples. Many non-Westerners would remind the defenders of European imperialism that, by and large, colonial rule was established through conquest—it was not something that the colonized ever asked for. It is undeniable that colonial policies resulted in an opening of more international trade routes and an expansion of the volume of trade—but on what basis? The mother countries did introduce new crops and animals, and transfer new tools and techniques to the colonies, but this in no way compensated for the demographic losses and suffering associated with the slave trade and colonialism. The colonizers did bring new ideas and worldviews with them. There was a valuable interchange of ideas, but at what cost—in return for exploitation, pauperization, and humiliation?[30]

Despite all the fanfare, the formal independence of these territories did not fundamentally change the lives of the majority of people living there. Nor did it create the space for the new states' rapid economic development. Rather, colonialism left behind a number of legacies—political, economic, social, and cultural. The former colonizers had put these countries on an unhealthy course from which it has been very difficult to deviate. Much of the global south continues to suffer from neocolonialism in the sense that, since independence, other developed countries have joined the former colonizers to reap the benefits of colonialism without its costs. During the Cold War, the global south was clearly allowed only as much "independence" as the superpowers deemed compatible with their interests.[31]

Now as then, during the various incarnations of globalization, the global world has struggled against its dependent status. The West has regularly intervened to overthrow non-Western governments seeking radical structural changes in class relationships and income distribution. Mohammad Mossadeq in Iran, Jacobo Arbenz Guzmán in Guatemala, Patrice Lumumba in the Republic of Congo—these are just a few of a string of leaders who were eliminated because they dared to challenge the status quo. But it is not just radicals who remember and have hard feelings about these foreign interventions. Ordinary people throughout Africa, Asia, Latin America, and the Middle East resent the fact that they are still not treated as equals. Far less than their counterparts in the West, they control their own destinies, plan their own development, manage their own economies, determine their own strategies and priorities, and generally manage their own affairs. Ironically, non-Westerners are uniquely deprived of a fundamental and inalienable right so lauded by the West—the right to liberty.[32]

Whether it lasted for 60 or 300 years, colonialism was not just a historical blip for many people living in the global south. Rather, it was an extremely important part of their experience, a watershed event they still struggle to overcome. Yet, in recent years, it has become the fashion (even among some living in the global south) to argue that blaming colonialism is an old and tired argument. Those who dwell on its excesses are increasingly accused of beating a dead horse. Is it high time to get over it and move on? Or is it really that simple?

Notes

1. Hilaire Belloc, "The Modern Traveller," cited in Margery Perham II, *Lugard: The Years of Authority, 1899–1945* (London: Collins, 1960), p. 45.

2. David S. Landes, *The Wealth and Poverty of Nations: Why Some Are So Rich and Some So Poor* (New York: Norton, 1998); Jared Diamond, *Guns, Germs, and Steel: The Fate of Human Societies* (New York: Norton, 1997).

3. A. Adu Boahen, "Africa and the Colonial Challenge," in *UNESCO General History of Africa: Africa Under Colonial Domination, 1880–1935,* ed. Boahen (London: Heinemann, 1985).

4. Emory C. Bogle, *The Modern Middle East: From Imperialism to Freedom, 1800–1958* (Upper Saddle River, NJ: Prentice Hall, 1996).

5. This terminology was used by Ali Mazrui in his video series *The Africans* no. 4, 1986.

6. Milton W. Meyer, *Asia: A Concise History* (Lanham: Rowman and Littlefield, 1997).

7. Benjamin Keen and Keith Haynes, *A History of Latin America* (Boston: Houghton Mifflin, 2000).

8. Mark A. Burkholder and Lyman L. Johnson, *Colonial Latin America* (New York: Oxford University Press, 1998).

9. Walter Rodney, "The Colonial Economy," in Boahen, *UNESCO General History of Africa.*

10. Ibid.; Bogle, *The Modern Middle East.*

11. Bogle, *The Modern Middle East.*

12. Keen and Haynes, *A History of Latin America.*

13. Meyer, *Asia.*

14. Edward L. Farmer, Gavin R. G. Hambly, and Byron K. Marshall et al., *Comparative History of Civilizations in Asia* (Reading, MA: Addison-Wesley, 1977).

15. Keen and Haynes, *A History of Latin America.*

16. Boahen, "Africa and the Colonial Challenge"; Farmer et al., *Comparative History of Civilizations in Asia.*

17. Farmer et al., *Comparative History of Civilizations in Asia.*

18. Whereas the colonizers often argued that they had intervened to end anarchy and bring peace to the inhabitants of the territory, in fact the colonizers encouraged fissures and played different groups off each other, to prevent unity and ensure their continued dominance.

19. Not yet democracies themselves until well into the twentieth century, the Spanish and Portuguese certainly never claimed to be promoting self-rule for their colonies in Latin America.

20. Keen and Haynes, *A History of Latin America.*

21. Ibid.; some traditional authorities refused to cooperate with the Europeans. A Peruvian curaca, Jose Gabriel Condorcanqui, opposed Spanish abuses of the Indians and led the largest colonial rebellion in all of Spanish America.

22. Ibid.; Peter Bakewell, *A History of Latin America* (Malden, MA: Blackwell, 1997); Boahen, "Africa and the Colonial Challenge."

23. Mahmood Mamdani, *Citizen and Subject: Contemporary Africa and the Legacy of Late Colonialism* (Princeton: Princeton University Press, 1996).

24. Ibid.

25. Ibid.; Arthur Goldschmidt Jr., *Modern Egypt: The Formation of a Nation-State* (Boulder: Westview, 2004).

26. Farmer et al., *Comparative History of Civilizations in Asia.*

27. Susan Migden Socolow, *The Women of Colonial Latin America* (Cambridge: Cambridge University Press, 2000); Jean Bottaro, *Nationalism and Independence in India* (New York: Cambridge University Press, 2016).

28. Mamdani, *Citizen and Subject.*

29. Bogle, *The Modern Middle East;* Farmer et al., *Comparative History of Civilizations in Asia.*

30. Vrushali Patil, *Negotiating Decolonization in the United Nations* (New York: Routledge, 2008).

31. Burkholder and Johnson, *Colonial Latin America;* Bogle, *The Modern Middle East.*

32. Bogle, *The Modern Middle East.*

4

Linking Concepts and Cases

The past three chapters have outlined in broad strokes some of the history of what would later become known as the global south. To consider some of the legacies of this past, we invite you to explore the patterns described here in greater detail by taking a look at our case studies. Too many people believe that the so-called third world was always "third world," that life in the non-Western world began only during the period of colonization or that the only "civilization" is Western civilization. As you read about the specific histories of these eight case studies, consider the following questions.

How are the precolonial and colonial experiences of these countries similar? How do they differ? What countries colonized them and in what manner were they colonized? How were these countries integrated into the world system before and after colonialism?

What factors, if any, aided the European conquest of these territories? How did these countries attempt to free themselves from Western domination, and why were some struggles less peaceful than others? Did the experiences of those countries that became independent through the use of violence differ dramatically from the experiences of those that became independent through peaceful means? Since independence, what kinds of problems have these countries experienced, and how have they approached these problems? Which experiences since independence have been widely shared, and which have differed?

Case Study: Mexico

Well before it was "discovered" by Europeans, the area once called New Spain had developed a variety of civilizations based on maize surpluses and extensive trade networks. Although archaeologists are still piecing together the region's history, it appears that the Olmecs, dating back to 1200 B.C.E., may be the mother civilization to the empires of Mesoamerica. With their distinctive cities, monumental buildings, art, and sculpture, the Olmecs, and later the Maya (C.E. 250–900), played an important part in shaping the early history of this region.[1]

The Mexica, relative latecomers to the fertile Valley of Mexico in the thirteenth century, were a minor group who eventually built the Aztec Empire around its city-state, Tenochtitlan. At its height, it is estimated that this powerful, complex civilization ruled a population of 25 million. Much of its wealth was based in conquest, as it subjugated its neighbors and took tribute from them. Built on the belief systems of earlier cultures, the Aztec worldview mixed war and religion. The Aztecs believed that conquest was essential to the proper worship of the Sun God. Perhaps the world's leading practitioners of human sacrifice in terms of volume, the Aztecs saw themselves as staving off the end of the world. To ensure the passage of the sun through the sky, they believed it was necessary to feed the Sun God with life—human blood from ritual killing. To satisfy the Sun God's appetites (in one year just before the Spanish invasion, it is estimated that 20,000 people were sacrificed), they warred on their neighbors, taking captives for sacrifice. As you might imagine, the Aztecs had many enemies.[2]

But when a relatively small expedition of Spaniards arrived in 1519, led by the conquistador Hernan Cortés, the existence of local people willing to ally against the Aztecs was only one factor in favor of the foreign adventurers. Though the stage was already set for a strategy of DIVIDE AND CONQUER, just as crucial to the success of the Spanish invasion was a slow and indecisive response by the Aztecs. In part, this was because for ten years prior to the arrival of the Europeans, there had been a series of foreboding omens. The emperor and absolute ruler of the Aztecs, Moctezuma II, had expected a coming cataclysm upon the return of the god-king Quetzalcoatl (the feathered serpent). Quetzalcoatl had been known as a white-skinned deity who took the shape of a man. Understandably, then, the emperor was taken aback by Cortés, with his pale complexion, blue eyes, and red hair. Although still suspicious that the newcomers were men and not gods, Moctezuma initially tried to bribe the mysterious visitors to leave by offering them generous gifts of gold. Yet, this only confirmed the Spaniards' resolve to march on Tenochtitlan, overcome their numerical disadvantage, and quickly decapitate the EMPIRE by taking Moctezuma hostage. Although the Aztecs did rebound and made a last attempt to fight off their attackers, by 1521 they had been devastated by smallpox and were literally starving to death. The empire was destroyed and the rest of central Mexico fell soon thereafter.[3]

Built atop the ruined Aztec capital, Mexico City became the center of the Viceroyalty of New Spain. The territory it covered was immense; it would eventually run from Panama to California, and include a few Caribbean islands as well as the Philippines. For 300 years, New Spain was the most productive and most populous of the Spanish colonies. Although it was eventually silver that produced the most fabulous wealth for Spain, the Spanish crown also encouraged the establishment of haciendas with the encomienda system, which rewarded the conquistadors with land grants and guarantees of plentiful labor. For the Indians this meant their virtual enslavement, as they were now compelled to provide their colonizers with tribute and free labor, in return for the right to live on their own land. Under their agreement with the crown, the encomenderos were supposed to Christianize and assimilate the Indians into a faithful, Spanish-speaking workforce. To help them do this, the Franciscans and other Catholic missionaries arrived early in the sixteenth century and succeeded in making widespread and rapid conversions. However, more than protecting the new converts, the encomienda system and later colonial policies allowed for their exploitation and abuse.[4]

Eventually, it became clear that there simply was not enough labor for the colonial economy to produce the wealth Spain demanded. Living conditions under colonialism were so harsh that the area remained relatively depopulated for some time. To augment the labor force, enslaved Africans were brought in, to share with Indians the lowest rungs of the racist social order. These groups joined mestizos in sporadic rebellions against their mistreatment. However, it was another group—the Creoles, a relatively privileged class—who proved pivotal in Mexico's break from Spain. These second-class citizens within the elite, stigmatized simply because they had been born in the colonies, greatly resented the privileges granted to the immigrant Peninsulars. Moreover, the "Americanos," as they were known, chafed at the fact that the colonial economy was being managed for the benefit of Spain. Instead, the Creoles wanted commercial freedom to trade with countries other than Spain, and to become rich without the crown's interference.[5]

For these reasons, many Creoles initially supported Father Miguel Hidalgo's social revolution in 1810. However, once it was clear that the changes sought by this movement were so far-reaching as to threaten their interests, the Creoles joined the Peninsulars to put down this and later rebellions seeking radical change. The movement for independence was stalled for nearly a decade until, in 1821, in reaction to liberal reforms in Spain, one elite, led by Agustín de Iturbide, displaced the other. Rallying broader support with talk about popular sovereignty, the Creoles claimed power for themselves. Spain was too weak to do much about it, and Mexico became independent with relatively little bloodshed.[6]

In its first fifty years of independence, Mexico continued to suffer from chronic instability. Between 1821 and 1860 the country went through at least fifty different presidencies, each averaging less than one year, and thirty-five of Mexico's presidents during this period were army officers. Government was changed at gunpoint; it was the age of CAUDILLOS, warlords seeking wealth, promising order, and surviving on patronage. Antonio López de Santa Anna was the most notorious of them all—he held the presidency on nine separate occasions. It was also during this period that Mexico suffered its most humiliating experience, enduring several foreign interventions. After a disastrous war with the United States in 1848, Mexico was forced to cede the huge swath of land between Texas and the Pacific (approximately half of Mexico's territory).[7]

For much of the rest of its first hundred years of independence, Mexico was polarized politically, torn apart by the rivalry between liberals and conservatives. In this often-bitter battle, conservatives sought to promote order and defend the Catholic Church, which was by now institutionalized as a wealthy and influential interest group in a firm alliance with elites. On the other hand, liberals were anticlerical and argued that the Church was entirely too powerful—politically and economically—and that reforms were badly needed. The leader of the liberal movement during much of the nineteenth century was Benito Juárez, who as president sought to strip power from both the army and the Church. Conservatives counterattacked and even supported the French, who invaded to collect on Mexico's debt and overthrew the Juárez government in 1864.[8]

The period of French rule under Emperor Maximillian was relatively brief and Juárez was eventually reinstated, but the liberal-conservative divide continued to dominate politics until the rise of the last caudillo, Porfirio Díaz. It can be said that Díaz, who took the post of president through a coup d'état and remained in power for over thirty years (1876–1911), finally provided Mexico with some stability, if nothing else. Associated with the "modernization" of Mexico, Díaz made generous concessions to foreign investors, sold Indian landholdings to private entrepreneurs, and argued that the repression associated with his rule was for a good cause—to modernize Mexico. Considered a loyal friend of the United States, Díaz ensured that any "progress" for Mexicans made on his watch accrued to himself and his cronies.[9]

One lesson of history is that policies that create such widespread misery tend to invite disorder. Francisco Madero, a liberal seeking democratic change in Mexico, ran for president against Díaz in 1910. However, after his suspicions were confirmed that Díaz would not allow himself to be voted out of power, Madero and his followers resorted to more violent means. From all over the country the people answered his call for the overthrow of Díaz, including Emiliano Zapata from the south and Pancho Villa from the north. This was the beginning of the Mexican Revolution; the movement grew rapidly and Díaz, surprisingly weak, stepped down in 1911.[10]

But it was only the beginning of the first major social revolution of the twentieth century. Madero was now president, but he was more of a parliamentarian than a revolutionary. Because the changes he initiated were deemed too little, too late, he was soon confronted by his former compadres. During the most violent phase of the revolution, the country broke down into a brutal civil war that raged until 1917. It was only after disposing of Zapata and Villa that Venustiano Carranza became president, declaring the revolution a success.[11]

The constitution resulting from this revolution was startlingly radical for the times. It set out a framework for significant changes in Mexico's power relationships. Among other things, the constitution (which remains the foundation of Mexico's government today) places significant restrictions on the Church. Far more progressive than labor laws in the United States at the time, the 1917 constitution established the right to strike, the right to a minimum wage, and the right to a safe workplace. As one might expect after years of foreign domination, the document is intensely nationalistic, and places restrictions on foreign ownership. Most significant, perhaps, the constitution gives the government the right to control Mexico's resources and to redistribute land.[12]

The first years of implementation of the revolution's goals were very slow. In part, this was because the government was sidetracked by a civil war in the 1920s when conservative Catholics sought to regain power for the Church. It was also partly due to the fact that the leaders who survived the revolution were not nearly as progressive as its architects. However, by the 1930s, Mexicans had in Lázaro Cárdenas a president determined to reaffirm the revolution's goals. His administration was responsible for distributing 18 million hectares of land, almost twice the amount distributed by all his predecessors combined. Moreover, the Cárdenas government recognized the necessity of providing support services to assist land recipients, whether they lived in the communal system of *ejido*, or on individual family plots.[13]

Although he attempted to steer a middle course, neither too socialist nor too capitalist, Cárdenas was most of all a nationalist, and his attempts to make real the promises of the revolution were perceived by foreign interests—including the United States—as threatening. As late as the 1930s, foreign firms had effectively controlled Mexico's oil reserves. However, invoking the constitutional right of Mexico to control its subsoil resources, Cárdenas expropriated these properties, compensated the companies, and established PEMEX as a state oil monopoly.[14]

Petroleum was only one vital industry in which the state would play a large role. However, the bulk of the Mexican economy continued to be held privately. From the 1940s to the 1960s, Mexico experienced a "miracle" in terms of economic growth, which was nearly unsurpassed, averaging 6 percent per year. Elites were the primary beneficiaries of the so-called miracle. The Mexican middle class grew, but poverty persisted and the gap between rich and poor actually loomed wider. To address this problem and win the support of the poor, the government created a broad system of social assistance. Although it has never amounted to a significant redistribution of income, since the 1940s Mexico has had one of the most progressive social assistance programs in Latin America.[15]

As indicated by its economic policy, Mexican politics since 1917 have been more pragmatic than revolutionary. Soon after the revolution, power was centralized under a single party, which took power in 1928 and controlled the government for seventy years. Known since 1945 as the Institutional Revolutionary Party (PRI), its longevity can be attributed to several, less-than-democratic factors, including its organization. It gradually took control of the military and organized labor, and then welcomed its rivals into the fold. It operated an immense system of patronage, in effect mobilizing the support of the peasantry and buying the loyalty of those who might threaten it.[16]

Under the PRI, Mexico became known as the "perfect dictatorship" because, unlike many of its neighbors to the south, where coups were the norm, Mexico enjoyed remarkable stability. However, it is important to remember that the PRI government was AUTHORITARIAN; as we will see in later chapters, it was not above relying on electoral fraud or even physical coercion to retain power.

Still, compared to many other countries such as Chile and Argentina, such behavior was uncharacteristic of Mexico. As the primary force guiding Mexican politics since the revolution, the PRI was pragmatic ideologically. Although there have always been differences within this large and heterogeneous party, a "pendulum effect" ensuring a tendency toward the center worked for decades to hold all the different elements of the PRI together. For many years, this was the secret of the PRI's success. Until the 1980s, Mexico was effectively a single-party state; the opposition was small and seldom won elections. However, by the early 1980s that had begun to change, as elements within the PRI recognized that the party's survival was incumbent upon its ability to adapt to a variety of changed realities. The split within the PRI became more apparent as Mexico set out on a long road to political liberalization. The modest political opening continued gradually and the PRI appeared to reverse course on several occasions, such as when it claimed victory in the highly disputed presidential elections of 1988. However, prodded by civil society, the PRI managed its internal divisions to allow in 2000 for the freest and fairest elections in Mexico's history.

Case Study: Peru

Although the first Peruvians are believed to have been seminomadic shellfish collectors and fishermen, the earliest known permanent settlements developed with the introduction of maize and the adoption of impressive irrigation systems. The transformation of marginal lands into abundant fields formed the basis of several pre-Inca civilizations, such as the Moche and the Nazca, known for their sophisticated crafts and ceremonial buildings.[17]

However, it is the civilization of the Inca for which Peru is best known. Its empire was immense, running 4,000 kilometers along the spine of the Andes. Heralded for their material well-being and cultural sophistication, the Inca rivaled or even surpassed other great empires in world history. Although there are still debates as to the origins of the Inca, in a relatively short period of a century they were able to subdue and incorporate nearly 12 million people.[18]

At the helm of power was the emperor, who was considered both man and god. Divinely ordained, he enjoyed absolute power and controlled vast material resources. Systems of mutual assistance and expectations of reciprocity were core values of the Inca. Kin groups were allocated shares of land by the state. In return, individuals were expected to work the land, keeping a third of their produce for themselves and turning over a third to support state functions and a third to serve ecclesiastical needs. Subjects were also expected to perform *mita,* or draft labor, through which they helped construct and maintain public works, including a remarkable system of roads and bridges.[19]

Yet, this highly sophisticated, militarized state, defended by tens of thousands of warriors, was unable to stand against 168 Spanish adventurers seeking their fortunes. Clearly, the Spanish had an overwhelming military advantage. Just as crucially, the empire was already factionalized and vulnerable when the foreigners arrived, having just been through a civil war, the result of a succession crisis. The Spanish were able to capitalize on this, using a policy of divide and conquer. Led by the seasoned conquistador Francisco Pizarro, the Spanish ambushed the overconfident Inca and took their ruler, Atahualpa, hostage in 1532. The empire fell soon thereafter.[20]

In the early colonial economy of plunder, Peru became Spain's great treasure house. Lima was constructed as the capital of this seat of Spanish colonial administration, and became known as the Viceroyalty of Peru (1543). Mining overwhelmingly dominated the colonial economy. Little else mattered; as one viceroy famously put it, "If there are no mines, there is no Peru."[21] Silver became the engine for colonial development in Peru, as the demands of the boomtowns created by mining stimulated agricultural production. In addition, Lima became a vibrant center for merchants active in the Atlantic and Pacific trades.[22]

However, because the prosperity of Spain and its settlers was dependent on a reliable source of cheap labor, the Indigenous peoples of Peru were pressed into service. Harassed and humiliated by the Spanish, in the early years of colonial rule many Indians were rendered landless and virtually enslaved under the feudal encomienda system. Under a form of extortion known as the *reparto,* Spanish administrators forced Indians to buy European goods at high prices. Distorting the Inca system of *mita,* the Spanish compelled all adult male Indians to spend part of their year laboring in Spanish mines, farms, and public works (without the state providing anything in reciprocity). Because the silver and mercury mines were such notorious death traps and paid little, the *mita* served as a crucial source of labor for the colonial economy.[23]

Such policies had a devastating impact on the Indigenous population. The *mita* drained off able-bodied workers, contributing to the social disintegration of Indigenous communities. Famine became commonplace, and populations already weakened fell easily to disease. People were demoralized. Abortion, infanticide, and suicide became common forms of escape. Because of the depopulation of Indian communities, significant numbers of Africans were enslaved and brought to Peru to meet the colonial economy's demand for labor.[24]

Although they were treated as less than human by the colonial system, Africans, Indians, and mestizos were by no means passive in their acceptance of this situation. The eighteenth century was an especially tumultuous time in Peru, as over a hundred popular uprisings occurred, some of them seriously threatening the established order. The most significant of these insurgencies was the Great Rebellion of 1780–1781. Led by a curaca who adopted the name of the last Inca king, Túpac Amaru, this revolt was based in Inca NATIONALISM and spread rapidly throughout the southern Andes. Determined to contain the well-organized mass movement, the Spanish set out to reconquer the area, terrorizing villages. Six months later this short but vicious civil war was over, with more than 100,000 dead (nearly 10 percent of the entire population).[25]

The Great Rebellion had the effect of unifying Creoles and Peninsulars against the threat to their privileges. By the early nineteenth century, compared to the rest of Spanish America, the Viceroyalty of Peru was a royalist stronghold. And because the colonial ruling class didn't fracture in Peru as it did elsewhere in Spanish America, it took an intervention of foreign armies to bring independence to the country. With General José de San Martín pressing into Peru from the south, and General Simón Bolívar coming in from the north, Peruvian Creoles reluctantly declared independence in 1821. However, it was not until Bolívar undertook his final campaign against Spain in 1824 that his troops, assisted by Indian GUERRILLA forces, finally defeated the royalists. The republic was established and Simón Bolívar set about the difficult task of establishing the first political institutions of independent Peru.[26]

However, Peruvians were divided over what type of government to pursue, and no constitution lasted for long. Although its constitutions contained liberal guarantees of DEMOCRACY, equality, and respect for human rights, Peru remained a highly stratified society where race and CLASS determined privilege. Power remained dispersed to the countryside as a semifeudal network of Creole landowners controlled vast areas, free from restraint. The 1890–1930 boom in agro-exports accelerated the problem of landlessness for the majority, while the largest haciendas were owned by a group known in Peru as "the forty families." As a result, landholding in Peru remains grossly unequal, and among the most skewed in all of Latin America. During much of the twentieth century, 0.1 percent of farm families controlled 30 percent of the country's land, and more than half of its best soils. This oligarchy, composed of businessmen and landowners, continued for years to dominate Peru. A COMPRADOR class, these elites manipulated politics to serve their own economic interests. For many years this oligarchy was backed by two of the most powerful institutions in the country, the military and the Catholic Church.[27]

In the early years of independence, civilian and military strongmen fought for political power. The country fell into a long period of caudillism. Coups and countercoups were common, particularly in the first thirty years of independence, when there were twenty-four changes of regime. This initial experience established a pattern for Peruvian politics that has persisted, with use of force widely accepted as a means of resolving political conflict.[28]

Just as Peru's politics have swung back and forth between civilian and military rule, its economic fortunes have alternated between boom and bust. After the wars for independence, Peru was in an economic crisis. Silver production had dropped, military spending was high, and the country suffered from chronic deficits. However, by the mid-nineteenth century, guano, or bird droppings, were to have the same effect on the economy that silver once did. Accumulating over thousands of years on the islands off Peru's coast, guano was rich in nitrogen. Once used by Indians as a fertilizer, guano was rediscovered and exported to Europe in the 1840s. For fifty years, the guano boom created great prosperity for the Peruvian oligarchy and the British (who took about half the profits). However, by the 1880s the guano deposits were largely depleted, and Peru was soon unable to pay its bills. Peruvian governments began a tradition of selling off state interests to foreigners, and ended up putting the country's development in the hands of outsiders.

Eventually, Peru managed to move away from its dependence on a single export, and began selling a variety of raw materials to Europe like copper, tin, and rubber. However, because the economy remained focused on production for the international market, not domestic demand, it was more vulnerable to price swings created by forces beyond its control. Adopting a program of export-led growth, Peru continued to experience boom-and-bust cycles. The gap between rich and poor continued to grow. Whenever a government suggested reforms that threatened the interests of traditional elites, the military stepped in.[29]

However, when the military intervened in 1968, "politics as usual" in Peru were dramatically altered. Cuba's Fidel Castro described it "as if a fire had started in the firehouse."[30] The military, which had traditionally repressed all demands for drastic change, initiated a social revolution. At the head of this revolution was General Juan Velasco Alvarado, who as president proclaimed a new economic order that would be based on neither capitalism nor communism. At the heart of this program was sweeping agrarian reform, to rectify the entrenched imbalance in landownership and severe inequalities intensified by economic decline and accompanied by marked growth in population. Military reformers also sought to promote more autonomous development by nationalizing the assets of the foreign corporations that dominated the Peruvian economy, such as the International Petroleum Corporation.[31]

However ambitious the revolution's goals, very little worked as planned, and by 1975 it was over. The reforms were halted and a new government set out once again to calm the oligarchy's fears, embrace a free market approach, and assure foreign capitalists that they were welcome in Peru. However, the economy did not recover. Rather, world prices continued to decline for the country's exports and its foreign debt ballooned. When Alan García Perez was elected president in 1985, he attempted to turn the country around by rejecting the liberal economic strategies of his predecessors. An economic nationalist, García shocked the international community by announcing he would limit Peru's interest payments on its foreign debt to 10 percent of its export earnings. The INTERNATIONAL MONETARY FUND (IMF) responded by declaring Peru ineligible for new credits. The punishment took its toll; Peru was bankrupt and suddenly the world's basket case.[32]

Meanwhile, Peruvians had become caught up in a brutal civil war provoked by the glaring gap between the affluent coast and the desperately poor sierra. The highly secretive Maoist guerrilla group, Shining Path (Sendero Luminoso), called for the creation of an egalitarian utopia. During the 1980s, both Shining Path and the Peruvian military became known worldwide for their use of terror. As the war grew more intense, the rebels seemed unstoppable, taking large portions of the countryside. Civilian governments declared states of emergency, giving the military a free hand in much of the country, and suspended most civil rights. Secret military trials of those suspected of ties to Shining Path landed thousands of innocents in prison. García and his successor, Alberto Fujimori, were both caught in the unenviable position of having to rely on the army against Shining Path. In 1990, after twelve years of uninterrupted civilian rule, Peru's constitution granted excessive powers to the executive, while its democratic institutions were still alarmingly weak.[33]

Elected that year, Fujimori immediately took aggressive steps to deal with the economic and political instability rocking Peru. To jump-start the failing economy, he adopted an extreme policy of neoliberalism and imposed AUSTERITY measures advocated by the IMF. In the war against terror, President Fujimori preferred a similarly draconian approach. In return for cooperation in the US war on drugs, he amassed enough military power to turn loose his security forces on the countryside. When questioned about the iron grip he claimed was a necessity, the democratically elected president of Peru carried out an *autogolpe* (self-coup) in 1992, taking for himself the power to rule by decree. With the help of the military, he closed the congress and the judiciary, suspended the constitution, and proclaimed a state of emergency. Initially, the public overwhelmingly supported the *autogolpe,* primarily because they were desperate for a solution.[34]

Peruvians later reelected Fujimori president, since he was able to provide some semblance of order. Although Fujimori was eventually credited with destroying the terrorists and stabilizing the economy, over time his support dwindled as the population began to question the necessity of his continued authoritarianism. When Fujimori once again attempted to extend his hold on power, ensuring his reelection through whatever means necessary, Peruvians risked clashing with the military and went out into the streets to demand his resignation. After scandals involving videotapes and a manhunt that now seems almost farcical, Fujimori, one of the few dictators left in the region, did finally step down in 2000, paving the way for Peru to make yet another attempt at democratic government and economic development.[35]

Case Study: Nigeria

The country today known as Nigeria contains hundreds of different ethnic groups, each with its own history. Because of the heterogeneity of these peoples, it is impossible to begin to describe all of them here. However, a sketch of the Hausa, Yoruba, and Ibo gives one a sense of the diversity existing in Nigeria. They are the three largest ethnic groups, composing two-thirds of the country's population.

Situated at the edge of the Sahara, the Hausa states of northern Nigeria were kingdoms that rose to prominence based on their location as a major terminus of the trans-Saharan trade. Home not only to fine craftsmen and rich merchants, their kings taxed goods that traveled through their territory on caravans. A strong cavalry-based military ensured the orderly conduct of business, and offered travelers protection from raiders. From the fourteenth century on, Islamic culture and religion gradually spread through northern Nigeria, primarily through commercial networks. Kano was long a famous center of Islamic learning, although Islam did not become a mass religion among the Hausa until an Islamic revolution in the early nineteenth century. A Fulani preacher, Usman dan Fodio, led devout Muslims displeased with corrupt Hausa kings, excessive taxes, and laxity in the practice of Islam in a JIHAD against their rulers. He brought together the discontented into a powerful revival movement that incorporated the Hausa states into a vast theocracy, the Sokoto Caliphate. Conversion was brought with war, as the jihad spread Islam into central and southwestern Nigeria.[36]

One of the groups affected by this expansionist policy in the south were the Yoruba. This powerful empire was based on a confederation of ancient Yoruba kingdoms and known for its remarkable bronzes and terracottas. The most influential of these kingdoms, Oyo, was at its height between the sixteenth and eighteenth centuries. A large and prosperous megastate, it controlled the trade routes to Hausaland and had a formidable military, with overwhelming numbers of bowmen and cavalry. The power of Yoruba kings was limited by a constitutional monarchy that required that kings confer with a council. However, by the late eighteenth century the Oyo king had become increasingly despotic, violating the traditional rights of the population to participate in decisionmaking. This contributed to a series of devastating civil wars that lasted for the next century.[37]

As opposed to the more centralized Hausa and Yoruba governments with their kings and hierarchies, the Ibo lived in relatively egalitarian ministates in which political power was decentralized. There was no empire, no expansionist military; in fact, there were no kings, presidents, or full-time political leaders of any kind. Rather, the Ibo lived in STATELESS SOCIETY. If democracy is largely about the right of political participation, then traditional Ibo politics were extremely democratic. Nearly all Ibo were part of the great assemblies that came together to make important decisions for the group. A council of elders and other age- or gender-based associations enforced these decisions. Although the Ibo traditionally lived in the forests of southeastern Nigeria, they were hardly isolated. As forest farmers, the Ibo produced valuable commodities such as kola nuts (important for ceremonial reasons and one of the few stimulants allowed Muslims) to sell in the long-distance trade that crossed the Sahara.[38]

European demand gradually redirected the caravan-based desert trade toward the coast. Nigeria was located in the heart of what became known as the

Slave Coast. At the peak of the transatlantic slave trade, 20,000 people each year were taken from this area to be sold as slaves. Throughout much of Nigeria, larger military states such as those of the Hausa and Yoruba raided their neighbors for war captives, who were then passed on to African middlemen and sold to Europeans waiting at trading stations on the coast. Although some Africans became wealthy from this trade, it proved devastating for many others. As the slave trade became less profitable, it was replaced by LEGITIMATE TRADE. A number of European countries were by this time rising industrial powers intent on trading their manufactured goods for cheap raw materials. In Nigeria, British trading houses promoted the production of cash crops like palm kernel, which could be used as an industrial lubricant and processed into a variety of products, including soap and candles.[39]

French and German merchants were also interested in this territory, which by the late nineteenth century Britain considered to fall within its sphere of influence. In an effort to eliminate foreign competition of all kinds, African leaders were compelled to sign treaties of protection and free trade (in effect, bypassing Indigenous middlemen and maximizing British profits). The British sent military expeditions to "pacify" those who resisted this encroachment. With conquest still not complete, the British claimed control of the Colony of Lagos and the Protectorate of Southern Nigeria (1900) and the Protectorate of Northern Nigeria (1903). The British conquered these territories separately and they administered them separately, as two very different systems. This policy continued even after the so-called amalgamation of the northern and southern protectorates in 1914.[40]

The architect of this policy was Sir Frederick Lugard, who believed that the north was different from the south and that each should develop autonomously. To overcome shortages of funds and personnel, the British attempted to use a policy known as indirect rule. As opposed to the direct rule associated with the French, which required large numbers of French administrators, indirect rule was much less expensive since it allowed the British to govern through Indigenous rulers. It depended on the cooperation of traditional elites, or "native authorities," who served as intermediaries between the British and the Indigenous MASSES and enforced colonial policy.[41]

Perhaps not surprisingly, in many parts of Nigeria the native authorities were hated by their own people and viewed as corrupt collaborators of colonialism. Although people from all classes found ways to indicate their displeasure with foreign rule, ironically it was the Western, Christian missionaries who educated a new elite of African nationalists. Urban and predominantly southern Nigerian teachers, clerks, doctors, and other professionals asserted themselves as agents of social change. They urged other Nigerians to join across ethnic and regional divides to form trade unions, independent churches, newspapers, and various movements that would become the country's first political parties in the 1920s. Leaders of these early political movements, like Herbert Macaulay (considered by many the father of Nigerian nationalism), often sought reform, not independence. They criticized the colonial government and looked forward to self-rule, but expected the transfer of power to be gradual. On the other hand, radical nationalism experienced an upsurge after the 1930s, as the movement for independence spread beyond Lagos. For example, students organizing the

Nigerian Youth Movement were more militant in their demands, calling for mass education, equal economic opportunities, and a transfer of power to Nigerians.[42]

The British reacted in a variety of ways to the nationalist demands. In some cases they resorted to repressive measures, firing on or jailing nationalists. Eventually the British offered some concessions, including a series of constitutional proposals for self-government. After years of negotiations, the transfer of power began in 1948. Suddenly, Nigerians were to be prepared for the administration and development of their country. The participants agreed that, upon independence, they would establish a parliamentary democracy and continue with a capitalist economic system. The British left peacefully, assured that their vital economic interests would be protected.[43]

As the date of independence neared, the nationalists abandoned the unified, pan-Nigerian approach they had adopted against colonial rule. The major ethnic groups formed regionally based political parties caught up in a three-way struggle: the Action Group (largely Yoruba), the Northern People's Congress (representing the Hausa), and the National Congress of Nigeria and the Cameroons (which drew mostly Ibo support). With the British effectively out of the way, now the enemy was other Nigerians. Perceiving politics to be a ZERO-SUM GAME, there was a polarization of the political process as each group vied for control of the country's resources.[44]

Yet, in 1960 when Nigeria finally became independent, most people were still hopeful about the ability of Nigerians to steer the country toward development. The new government was modeled on British parliamentary democracy. The country was to be administered through a federal system, and was initially divided into three regions: north, west, and east. In the first general elections in 1964, the Northern People's Congress easily established its dominance, controlling enough seats in parliament to name Tafawa Balewa prime minister of Nigeria's First Republic, its first attempt at civilian rule. When Nigeria became a republic, a Nigerian from the east (Nnamdi Azikiwe) replaced the British queen in the ceremonial role of head of state. Obafemi Awolowo of the Action Group was to lead the loyal opposition.[45]

However, almost immediately, all went wrong. Although technically Nigeria had a multiparty system, in each region one large ethnic group dominated all the smaller ones. Even more problematic, the northern region was given twice the area and population of the other two. Given their long history of distrust, there was little prospect of the eastern and western regions ever joining together effectively against the northern region. Tensions mounted. The 1964 parliamentary elections were widely suspected of fraud, and ethnic minorities complained about their lack of representation. Violence broke out in various parts of the country and the government was too weak to contain it. Politics had become a winner-take-all game in which compromise was extremely difficult. Because the country was in constant crisis during its first six years of independence, no one was surprised by (and many Nigerians welcomed) the country's first coup d'état, led by Ibo officers in 1966.[46]

Yet, like the rest of Nigeria the military too has suffered from ethnic, regional, and other divisions. Fear of Ibo dominance contributed to a second coup in 1966, and again northerners controlled the government. The purges and pogrom that followed convinced the Ibo to secede and declare the independent Republic of Biafra. Just seven years after independence, Nigeria was fracturing, consumed by a civil war, the Biafran War, from 1967 to 1970. Determined to maintain the territorial integrity of Nigeria (as well as control over its oil wealth, much of which would have been lost to Biafra), the federal government put up fierce resistance. The fighting was prolonged, as the federal government could not prevail against the forest fighters. In the end, the government resorted to quarantining eastern Nigeria and cutting off food supplies to the Ibo. By the time the Ibo submitted to such tactics and surrendered, an estimated 1 million people had starved to death.[47]

Remarkably, the country remained intact, largely because of a government program of reconciliation and reconstruction. Such a policy was greatly facilitated by the sudden windfall produced by the jump in the price of oil in the 1970s. As a member of the Organization of the Petroleum Exporting Countries (OPEC), Nigeria enjoyed great prosperity in this period. Overnight, it had become one of the wealthiest countries in the world. Unfortunately, since then most of Nigeria's fortune has been stolen or squandered. This was particularly the case during the Second Republic, from 1979 to 1983, when President Shehu Shagari turned politics into a business. The democratic process was subverted as abuse of power occurred on an unprecedented scale. Corruption was so massive and Shagari's government so audacious that fires were set in public buildings to destroy evidence. After a sham vote in which Shagari had himself reelected, the country broke out into open conflict that was only brought to a halt with another coup.

Thus, Nigeria settled into a long period of military rule. During most of the 1980s and 1990s, the generals who ruled Nigeria were more authoritarian and kleptocratic than ever, even as the country slipped into a deep economic decline. After years of overspending and misusing funds, it was now a major debtor. The structural adjustment prescribed by the IMF prioritized debt repayment over basic needs. Nigeria's relations with its creditors improved, but the reforms failed to correct the economy's structural ills.[48]

Meanwhile, the dictatorship was under foreign and domestic pressure to make political as well as economic reforms. After putting off the transfer of power as long as possible, General Ibrahim Babangida offered up his personal design for a Third Republic. When relatively free and fair elections were finally held in 1993, one of Babangida's handpicked candidates, Moshood Abiola, was elected president. As a Muslim Yoruba, he would be the first civilian president from the predominantly Christian south. However, almost immediately Babangida annulled the result, for reasons that are still unclear. Such actions confirmed Yoruba suspicions that the north would never share power or control over the country's oil revenues. Protests shook the country and Babangida stepped down. Within just a few months, one of Babangida's advisers, General Sani Abacha, overturned the weak interim government.[49]

Abacha presided over the most predatory dictatorship Nigeria had ever known. Living standards fell to their lowest point in twenty years. Brazenly corrupt and notoriously cruel, Abacha set about crushing all dissent. For asserting himself to be the legitimate president, Abiola was arrested for treason (a capital offense) and imprisoned until his death, of apparently natural causes, in 1998.

The government became an international pariah for its use of state terrorism against its own people. It is sometimes said that Nigeria became as quiet as a graveyard—until, in what is widely considered a "coup by God," Sani Abacha was found dead in his own bed under somewhat scandalous circumstances.[50]

Abacha's death was celebrated with dancing in the streets. His sudden departure paved the way for another attempt at a transition to civilian rule. The Fourth Republic began with elections in 1999, with all the same problems of its predecessors. This time, it was up to a former military dictator, Olusegun Obasanjo, to lead the country in correcting these problems before the cycle began yet again.

Case Study: Zimbabwe

There was great cultural, political, and economic diversity among the early people of Zimbabwe. Hunter-gatherers long preceded the Shona, Zimbabwe's largest ethnic group, who arrived in the area around C.E. 300. Among the Shona were several subgroups, some of whom lived in empires, and others who preferred stateless societies. Although they are known to have mined and worked with a variety of minerals, most notably iron ore and gold, cattle-keeping was a more important activity for most Shona, who also worked as farmers. Perhaps the wealthiest empire of southern Africa, Great Zimbabwe was an ancient city famous for its stone buildings and vast walls. For reasons that are still unclear, Great Zimbabwe declined and was abandoned in the fifteenth century. On its heels a larger Shona empire was founded in the north, known as Mwene Mutapa (Great Plunderer). Like Great Zimbabwe, it too had an expansionist policy and took tribute from subjugated populations. Though without the cultural and technological achievements of Great Zimbabwe, Mwene Mutapa was also rich in resources and favored by its river access to the main trading centers on the coast. Long before the Portuguese established trading posts nearby, the Shona had been involved in a regional network of trade that connected southern central Africa to coastal trading cities and the Indian Ocean trade.[51]

Most of Zimbabwe continued to be dominated by various Shona kingdoms until the early nineteenth century, when events in South Africa changed the balance of power dramatically. Various South African ethnic groups, including the Ndebele, fled, seeking shelter from the Zulu military onslaught known as the *Mfecane,* or "Great Crushing." By the 1840s the Ndebele had settled in southwestern Zimbabwe, which became known as Matabeleland. Though unable to defend themselves against the overwhelming might of the Zulu, the highly centralized Ndebele kingdom had a professional army and absorbed the resident Shona-speaking inhabitants. The Ndebele also dominated many Shona groups in eastern Zimbabwe, raiding Mashonaland periodically for cattle, grain, and women.[52]

Another raider of sorts, Cecil John Rhodes was one of the biggest empire builders of the nineteenth century. Having come to South Africa from Britain at age seventeen, Rhodes soon became a self-made millionaire as a founder of DeBeers Diamonds. Interested in money for the power it could buy, Rhodes was a British supremacist and advocate of British imperialism. His interest in Zimbabwe was based on rumors of more gold fields to the north of South Africa's enormous Witwatersrand gold reef. Rhodes sent emissaries to Matabeleland to push for concessions. In 1888 the Ndebele king, Lobengula, was deceived into signing an agreement, known as the Rudd Concession, that basically gave the British mineral rights to the entire territory, placing it within the British sphere of influence.[53]

Soon after winning the concession, Rhodes formed the British South Africa Company, and obtained a royal charter to colonize and administer the area north of the Limpopo River on behalf of Britain. Rhodes recruited a "pioneer column" of settlers to invade and occupy Zimbabwe. Upon arrival in Zimbabwe in 1890, the white settlers first established themselves in the predominantly Shona east.[54]

Conditions were ripe for conflict. Disappointed with its luck at striking gold, the British South African Company began looking beyond Mashonaland for new areas to mine. Yet, not only were the Europeans antagonizing the Shona, but the Ndebele considered the east to be their raiding ground and resented the white settlers' presence. When the British attempted to establish a boundary requiring the Ndebele to confine their raids to the western side of the "border," a clash between the settlers and the Ndebele was inevitable. After a series of provocative incidents, the two parties were at war. Although the company's forces were greatly outnumbered, the British, with their modern firearms against the Ndebele's spears, swept into the west. Lobengula died during his escape, and with the Ndebele demoralized, Matabeleland was opened to white settlers. The British forced the Ndebele onto dry and infertile reserves and gave Lobengula's cattle to the settlers. The entire territory was placed under colonial rule in 1895 and became known as Rhodesia. By all appearances, the once-powerful Ndebele were now prostrate, utterly defeated.[55]

So, when a series of uprisings broke out in 1895–1896 and spread over Zimbabwe, the British were taken by surprise. Yet, for the Ndebele and the Shona, colonialism meant not only political oppression and economic exploitation, but also an assault on their way of life. Aggravating their problems were a series of natural disasters. Many Ndebele and Shona believed that these misfortunes were attributable to the presence of white settlers on their land. Traditional religious authorities blamed the settlers for angering God, and warned that Africans must fight to drive them out or they would continue to suffer. Consequently, so many of the Indigenous people responded to the war cry "*Chimurenga!*" that the white settlers, even with their military advantages, found the uprisings difficult to put down.[56]

However, with the help of imperial troops, by 1897 the leaders of what is called the First Chimurenga War had been killed or captured. The British colonial office took over responsibility for Rhodesia, although the white settlers largely administered the country to suit their interests. Africans became second-class citizens in their own land, as racist laws enforced a color bar. Black people were systematically humiliated and exploited. The country was divided into white areas and Black areas. White settlers poured in, taking the best land and establishing large farms. Most Black people were left poor and landless, forced to live in the 31 percent of the territory assigned to them—the wastelands known as reserves. Africans were compelled to work in slave-like conditions. To earn money to pay taxes to the colonial state, young men had little choice but to sign contracts requiring them to leave their families behind on the reserves for a year at a time while they worked in white-owned mines or farms. There discrimination was systematic; the disparity in wages between white and Black workers was enormous. As late as the 1960s, white mine workers earned twelve times as much as Africans—and white farm workers earned twenty times as much as Black workers.[57]

Moreover, the colonial system did everything it could to ensure that African political participation was kept at a minimum. Theoretically, Africans could vote in elections for a legislative council, but since the property and educational qualifications for the franchise were set so high, Black people were legally denied a political voice in this "democracy." This does not mean, however, that they had no political voice. Against the overwhelming force of the colonial military, many Africans turned to WEAPONS OF THE WEAK, adopting postures of noncooperation or "refusal to understand." When possible, workers simply deserted the most abusive bosses and shared "market intelligence," leaving wayside messages like signs carved on trees that alerted others to avoid those employers.[58]

Some Africans submitted to colonial rule, but this does not mean that they accepted it. Rather, to survive, they chose to cooperate and seek some amelioration in their treatment. Still, self-government was a long-term objective for many. By the 1920s, larger numbers of Ndebele had adopted modern forms of political protest. Led by a new elite known for its moderation, they sought change through constitutional means. Black immigrants to Zimbabwe were frequently the initiators of mass-based protest. South Africans founded the Rhodesian Bantu Voters Association, which brought together Zimbabweans from different regions and ethnic backgrounds, and appealed to ordinary people by focusing on the land issue. Churches such as the millenarian Watch Tower movement mobilized grassroots protest.[59] The first African trade union in the colony, the Industrial and Commercial Workers Union, was formed by a Malawian. In response to desperate conditions, Africans led a number of strikes in the first half of the twentieth century. More often than not, such actions were systematically put down by the state.[60]

In their determination not to give in to African demands, the settlers attempted to tighten their control over Africans. One way of doing this was through repression. Under a state of emergency, government was given power to put people in prison without trial. Parties were banned; activists were rounded up, detained, and imprisoned. Another strategy was to ally with traditional elites. Many of these elites, who had long worked for the colonial government as native authorities, were valued for their loyalty and the influence they held in their communities. By co-opting these elites and giving them more power than they traditionally held, including more power over women, white settlers could in effect buy their allegiance and promote a policy of divide and rule, by encouraging tribal consciousness.[61]

A third way of dealing with African nationalism was promoted by white liberals frightened by the Mau Mau killings of British settlers in Kenya. In the 1950s, white voters elected an administration intent upon making Rhodesia appear to be doing something to placate Africans. This government promised land and other reforms (but not "one man, one vote," and franchise qualifications were actually raised). For these reasons, most Black voters rejected these "multiracial" reforms as paternalistic delaying tactics.[62]

Nor did the liberal policy sit too well with white voters for long. The 1962 elections were the end of the liberal experiment, as for the next two decades white voters put into office right-wing extremists led by the Rhodesian Front. In 1965, without consulting Britain (which still had ultimate responsibility for the colony), Prime Minister Ian Smith cut ties with the MOTHER COUNTRY. Through the Unilateral Declaration of Independence (UDI), the settlers displayed their disregard of international opinion and declared Rhodesia an independent, white-run state.[63]

Despite African hopes that the British would use force against the UDI government, they were unwilling to intervene. After diplomatic efforts failed, Britain joined the United Nations in imposing economic sanctions on Rhodesia. Sanctions were not a complete failure, but they had little effect, primarily because the United States and other Western countries broke them. Some characterize this policy as racist, and in part it was, because the West viewed the struggle in Rhodesia through a Cold War lens. For Africans the Second Chimurenga War, which began in 1966, was a war for liberation. Yet, the white government was able to portray the African opposition as communist, and the conflict in Rhodesia as part of the larger East-West struggle. The two parties that dominated the anticolonial effort, the Zimbabwe African People's Union (ZAPU), led by Joshua Nkomo, and the Zimbabwe African National Union (ZANU), led by Robert Mugabe, eventually joined forces toward the end of the war in what was called the Patriotic Front. Both called for a socialist transformation of society. Even more damning, from a Western perspective, they each received military assistance from the Soviet Union and China, as well as neighboring African countries.[64]

Pressure was building on the white government, and despite Smith's claims that majority rule would come "not in a thousand years," by the early 1970s it was becoming increasingly clear that the white government was losing the war. Desperate to hold on to power, Smith tried to preempt the guerrilla victory by promoting a political coalition. Smith was eventually able to win over Bishop Abel Muzorewa, a conservative who had long been associated with the anticolonial cause. Because Muzorewa could not control the guerrillas and because the Patriotic Front was joined by most of the world in denouncing the new government, the internal settlement was not durable. The guerrillas refused to surrender, international sanctions remained in place, and the war intensified and was virtually won by the guerrillas in 1979.[65]

That year the three parties met in London to negotiate a peace settlement brokered by Britain. The resulting Lancaster House Agreement served as the basis for a new constitution based on majority rule, but with protections for minority rights. It established a parliamentary system with a president acting on the advice of the prime minister and set a date for elections. The parliamentary elections, held in 1980, were an extraordinary exercise in democracy, as the three bitterly hostile armies put down their weapons to campaign against each other. Voting did largely break down along ethnic lines, and though there were some irregularities, international observers found the process to be free and fair. An estimated 94 percent of the electorate voted and Robert Mugabe, because his party, ZANU (now known as the Zimbabwe African National Union–Patriotic Front [ZANU-PF]), had won an overall majority in parliament, became the first prime minister of independent Zimbabwe.[66]

As prime minister, Mugabe recognized that Zimbabwe needed stability if it were to develop, and that there could be no stability without a policy of reconciliation. Although there were some hard feelings on all sides, Mugabe did create a coalition government, inviting Nkomo and even a few white people to serve as ministers in his cabinet. However, strains resurfaced by the end of the first year, and the country soon fell into a civil war. After years of peacemaking efforts, the two Patriotic Front rivals sat down at the bargaining table. The Unity Accord was reached in 1987 and ZAPU was absorbed into ZANU-PF.[67]

As mentioned earlier, the government's policy of national reconciliation also applied to white voters, many of whom had panicked after the Lancaster House accords and planned to leave Zimbabwe. Some did go, but Mugabe worked hard to assure them that their property rights would be respected. Although an avowed socialist, Mugabe abided by the Lancaster House restrictions on the redistribution of wealth and adopted an economic pragmatism that surprised many. In fact, the mixed economy continued on much as it had before, with the tiny white minority controlling a disproportionate share of the country's resources. For more than forty years the most crucial issue of all, the land issue, has gone unresolved. So far, at least, many Zimbabweans have found freedom to offer a few material rewards.[68]

Case Study: Egypt

Ancient Egypt's history spans three millennia, but going back a thousand years more or so, to around 7500–5000 B.C.E., most of the occupants of these lands were hunter-gatherers or semi-nomadic herders. As in many other areas of the world, gradually these populations began the shift to agriculture and raising livestock.[69] In Egypt, it appears that this adaptation coincided with climatic changes around 5000 B.C.E. As areas of the country grew increasingly arid, people adopted more permanent dwellings along the Nile and plants and animals were domesticated as a survival strategy. The intense competition between farming and herding groups as rivals for resources over time contributed to the emergence of complex, hierarchical societies with chieftain-kings.[70]

It was in the midst of this process, just before 3000 B.C.E., that the two halves of the country were unified into a centralized state that gradually developed into an empire ruled by thirty-one dynasties. This extremely rich agricultural economy, the most productive in the ancient world at its peak, was based in "the Gift of the Nile," which allowed for the production of surpluses of maize and wheat.[71] Over time this economy diversified into manufacturing, and the Nile, which is like a major highway running through the valley to the delta and the sea, facilitated the development of Egypt's local and long-distance trade.[72]

For twenty centuries, the state's vigorous exploitation of resources sustained rulers and palaces, as well as all manner of artistic achievements and monumental buildings.[73] This system produced large-scale building programs like the pyramids, which are widely recognized as one of the great administrative feats of history. For example, it took 20,000 men 20 years to construct the Great Pyramid of Khufu, which is comprised of 2.5 million limestone blocks with an average weight of 2.5 tons each. This monumental architecture serves as a testimonial to the power and organization of the state, which is believed to have ruled 3–4 million people at its peak.[74]

Most Egyptians lived as peasants in this highly stratified society. Land was the basis for wealth. All land was controlled by the king (or pharaoh) and allocated by him as a reward for services; thus, it was concentrated in the hands of a few.[75] Much of the king's legitimacy was based in the belief that the king was a descendant or the incarnation of the gods. With a dual nature (the divine emanating through his human form), the king was preeminent, an absolute ruler seated at the apex of the political and religious hierarchy.[76]

As elsewhere, class-based inequality coincided and intersected with gender inequality. At times queens ran the country, but they were rarely vested with all the omnipotence of pharaohs. More commonly, as the wives of kings, queens may have had considerable de facto power, but they were not usually considered divine. An exception is Hatshepsut, who ruled a successful and stable regime for fifteen years emphasizing her divine ancestry. She took pains to define her image carefully; in some representations she presents herself as female, and in others as male, with a beard.[77]

Vested with all-pervasive power, the pharaoh was the king of all lands, the intermediary between the world of men and gods. His penultimate duty was to protect order by practicing correct behavior and thought, moderation, and justice. Failure to uphold these norms—or any loss of control—was traditionally read as a sign that the gods had withdrawn their support from him and that it was time for a change. As a result, the sociopolitical structure over Egypt's thirty-one dynasties should be understood as dynamic, evolving in response to changing local and international events. Droughts and other climatic disasters, along with succession crises, subterfuge, and rivalries certainly contributed to the fall of more than one dynasty.[78]

Egypt's pharaonic period is also associated with a growing number of military expeditions and a greater opening to the world. Located at the intersection of many trade routes, Egypt became wealthy off the expansion of the long-distance trade in luxury goods.[79] By the final millennium B.C.E., Egypt was directing more and more of its energy against foreign enemies and had expanded its empire to include Palestine, Syria, and Nubia. Meanwhile, attracted by its strategic importance and extraordinary wealth, Egypt was surrounded and pressured by potentially powerful enemies. Then, the empire began to crumble. The central government faltered, rivals began vying for power, and a wave of foreign invasions commenced.[80]

After thousands of years of preeminence, in 535 B.C.E. Egypt dropped in status from empire to the spoils of empire. It was first conquered by the Persians and later the Greeks as Alexander the Great took control of Egypt in 332 B.C.E. The Graeco-Roman period (332 B.C.E.– C.E. 396) lasted for a millennium and marked a seminal event in Egyptian history: the decay of Egypt's cultural core and transformation of the ancient civilization into something new. Perhaps the best way to sum up the significance of these events is this: most accounts of Egyptian history end with Alexander the Great's conquest.[81]

Now, Egyptians did not passively accept their status as colony; they periodically rose up against corrupt, oppressive, and unjust foreign systems—and they forced the end of more than one foreign occupation.[82] However, for nearly

2,000 years, the country remained a mere province of various larger empires, controlled by Arabs, Europeans (French and British), and the Ottomans. Egyptians found themselves alienated and exploited, second-class citizens in their own land, slaves to foreign rulers.[83]

It was an Albanian soldier serving one of those empires who is said to be the founder of modern Egypt. Ruling the territory from 1805 to 1849, Muhammad Ali, an Ottoman military leader who served as khedive (or viceroy) of Egypt, cut ties to Istanbul and promoted the country's modernization based on a European model. After creating an independent, modern army he transformed Egypt from "provincial Ottoman backwater to expansionist new state," incorporating parts of neighboring lands.[84] However, after his death his successors were unable to sustain these gains and, by the end of the late nineteenth century, many of his achievements were undone. Egypt had fallen heavily into debt and its largest creditor, Britain, had assumed control over the economy and eventually colonized the country.[85]

Clearly, the British occupation of Egypt was driven by economic and strategic interests. The British government shut down Egyptian manufacturers, replacing what was a relatively strong, diversified economy with a monoculture based on cotton (to be sold to British mills). The economy went into shock, stifling inequality grew, and only a tiny minority of landowners and foreigners profited from the cotton economy.[86] Yet, even more essential to British interests was the Suez Canal, a waterway that greatly facilitated transit by connecting the Mediterranean to the Red Sea. The British provided much of the financial backing for its construction and assumed control of what is arguably the most strategic asset in the Middle East.[87]

In a variety of ways (violent and nonviolent), Egyptians resisted British domination. Britain put down the nationalist efforts, sometimes violently, before recognizing Egypt's independence in 1922. Egypt then began a thirty-year liberal experiment with democracy, built around the first comprehensive civic constitution in the Middle East, establishing a constitutional monarchy, the monarch a descendant of Muhammad Ali. It should be noted, however, that there were so many restrictions on this "independence" that for all intents and purposes, the British continued to govern by proxy until 1945, blocking any initiatives or appointments they believed to be contrary to their interests.[88]

After World War II and all the promises of the Atlantic Charter for self-determination, Egyptians were embittered. This "independent country" was still clearly a British dependency.[89] Many Egyptians were disillusioned with parliamentary democracy as a European idea and institution. Some were drawn to Islamic beliefs and values and joined a revolutionary movement, the Society of the Muslim Brothers, which was founded in 1928. Known as the Muslim Brotherhood, the movement rejected political parties, parliaments, and constitutions and, instead, sought to restore what they considered to be the authentic institutions of Islam as the basis of government. For decades the Brothers led huge rallies against the British presence, but they didn't bring down the government. Rather, it was a group of young, educated, middle-class military officers who changed it up on July 23, 1952, with a swift and bloodless coup. Soon after, they dissolved the monarchy and declared Egypt a republic.[90]

One of these officers, Gamal Abdel Nasser, wanted more than just a coup: he wanted a transformation of Egyptian society. The charismatic Nasser, who went on to become the first Egyptian to rule Egypt in over 2,000 years (since Alexander the Great), was a self-declared socialist and POPULIST. Nasser ruled Egypt for sixteen years, giving Egyptians a renewed pride in themselves.[91] Popular because he was anti-imperialist, Nasser reasserted Egypt's standing in the world. He refused to serve as proxy for either side in the Cold War and became a hero in the eyes of many for facing down Britain, France, and Israel in the Suez Crisis in 1956. Not only did Nasser nationalize foreign businesses and seek to diversify the economy and reindustrialize it, he created a welfare state to raise living standards. He is widely adulated by the masses as the only ruler of Egypt who ever did anything for them. But it was in the later years of Nasser's rule that problems became increasingly apparent. The government had become a police state, autocratic and repressive. The bureaucracy was bloated and mediocre and Nasser's grand projects were wasteful. In sum, the Nasser years failed to transform Egypt; his rule turned out to be more populist coup than revolution.[92]

The power vacuum created by Nasser's death in 1970 was filled by his vice president, Anwar Sadat. In the decade that he ruled practically unopposed, Sadat promised a more liberal regime, but proved to be just as dictatorial as his predecessor. But Sadat is best known for breaking with Nasser's policy of nonalignment and opening Egypt to the West by signing the US-brokered Camp David peace accords with Israel. As its reward, Egypt became the second-largest recipient of US aid. The peace deal with Israel caused great upset in Egypt, which had fought (and lost) more than one war against its neighbor. Sadat came to be regarded as a puppet and Egypt fell from grace with the Arab world.[93]

Meanwhile, social and economic conditions failed to improve, and many young people, educated and out of work, gravitated toward militant groups inspired by Iran's Islamic Revolution. Sadat was assassinated by a member of such a group on live TV in 1981, and Hosni Mubarak, his vice president, a former air force general, was immediately sworn in.[94] Like Nasser and Sadat, Mubarak sought the legitimacy conferred by—less than free and fair—elections. He went on to serve five terms (always winning 90 percent or more of the vote). Also like his predecessors, Mubarak ruled as an absolute power. The "Deep State," the security leviathan institutionalized under Nasser, continued to grow to become far more powerful than any single leader, agency, or branch of the government. Bankrolled by the United States at a rate of $2 billion a year, thanks to Egypt's peace deal with Israel, the Mubarak government was able to hold on to power through co-optation and repression for decades.[95] The tipping point finally came when the United States upped the ante, tying continued US aid to pressure for democracy. It was in the 2006 parliamentary elections that for the first time, Mubarak allowed the opposition to participate. And when the Muslim Brotherhood, dogged by Egyptian rulers all these years, won 88 of 444 elected seats, it set off an earthquake—with aftershocks that would pose the greatest challenge yet to what had become a near-pharaonic system of government.[96]

Case Study: Iran

Iran, which was known as Persia until 1935, experienced a dramatic transformation from a vast Persian empire (at one point encompassing nearly 45 percent of the world's population) to an Islamic republic. Grandeur, triumph, invasion, and discord color the historical legacy of this land and people. As a major world empire, Persian culture and civilization endured nearly twenty-five centuries of dynastic rule. It was named for the ancient province Parsa, where the first Iranians settled, and at its height ruled over much of the area we now call the Middle East. The survival of Persian cultural and linguistic traditions provides Iranians a nearly continuous cultural tradition up to the present day.

Modern Iranians go out of their way to emphasize their non-Arab, Aryan heritage. One of the clearest manifestations of this is that the dominant language within Iran is Persian, also known as Farsi, rather than Arabic. While the two languages are based in the same alphabet, they have their origins in separate language families (Arabic in Afro-Asiatic, and Farsi in Indo-European). The adoption of Shia Islam (discussed in Chapter 10) also distinguishes Iranians from Turks and Arabs. As evidence of the continuity of some aspects of pre-Islamic culture, the Zoroastrian tradition of the Nurooz is still celebrated today as the first day of the Iranian calendar, as well as the first day of spring (March 21).

Inhabitants occupied the region now known as Iran as early as the middle paleolithic times, approximately 100,000 years ago, with sedentary cultures as far back as 18,000 to 14,000 years ago. The Elamites were the original inhabitants of southern portions of the Iranian plateau. Their language is believed to be unique, with no discernible connection to any other linguistic group.[97] The Elamites created a regional civilization, which was highlighted in both Akkadian and Babylonian texts. Iran's abundance of mineral resources was known as early as 9000 B.C.E. and copper metallurgy became common in 5000 B.C.E.

The first dynasty of Iran's pre-Islamic phase was the Achaemenid Dynasty (546–334 B.C.E.), founded by Cyrus the Great, who was known for freeing the Jews from Babylonian captivity. The Achaemenians spoke an Indo-European language and believed in Zoroastrianism, a monotheistic religion that rose in Persia before Christianity. In fact, it is believed that the biblical Three Wise Men who visited the Baby Jesus in Nazareth were likely Zoroastrian. A ruler who described his empire as Iranshahr, meaning "land of Aryans," or people who are of pure, noble, and good birth, used the name "Iran" as early as the third century B.C.E.[98] Achaemenid leaders created a hereditary monarchy and empire, which spread throughout the Middle East.

Contemporaneous with the Roman Empire, the Sassanid kings led one of the Persian Empire's grandest dynasties in Mesopotamia and the region now known as Iran. Leadership continued to be hereditary, with a fusion of spiritual and religious power. Sassanid kings imposed Zoroastrianism as the state religion, granting immense powers to members of the clergy. The gradual embrace of Islam began after Persia's wars with the Roman and Byzantine Empires drained the country, increasing discontent within the population. The "golden age" of Islam followed, under rulers known as Abbassids. This 400-year period was marked by tremendous amounts of trade both within the large empire and beyond its borders, widespread public education, scientific developments (especially in medicine and healthcare), and mathematical advances. Although this golden age began to collapse from within—torn apart by internal division and schism—its end was hastened by the European Crusades.

The Mongol invasions of 1258 ended Abbassid rule and divided the Islamic world. A succession of dynasties ruled until 1501, when the Safavid Dynasty—later known for its militarism and conquest—was seated. Safavid rulers battled with the Ottomans, eventually settling on frontier lines roughly equivalent to the modern Iranian-Turkish border.[99] This was also the dynasty that established Shia Islam as the state religion, in a succession dispute that is discussed in Chapter 10.

A new dynasty of Turkish origin, the Qajars, ruled from 1796 to 1925. Similar to what would follow later in Iran, this dynasty struggled to integrate religious authority with modern rule, all the while attempting to return to the glories of the earlier Persian Empire. It was under the Qajars that Tehran became the capital of Persia. Early nineteenth-century educational reforms began to create elites who challenged Iran's relations with the West, fomenting local protests and rebellion and ultimately leading to the first limits on royal power. In 1902, Qajar Shah Muzaffar al-Din,[100] facing the demands of reformers, designed a constitution (based on the Belgian constitution of 1831) that combined a national assembly (Majles) with a constitutional monarchy. The significance of this was only eclipsed by the discovery of oil in 1908.

The religious-secular debate that colors much of Iran's postrevolutionary history is nothing new. In the constitution of 1906, the government officially enshrined religious influence and recognized some rights of religious minorities (especially Zoroastrians, Christians, and Jews) by granting them the right to elect one representative to the Majles. Yet, both legal protections and limits on power were ignored, often at the urging and intervention of imperial powers, especially Britain and Russia, which had divided Persia into spheres of influence as part of their ongoing "Great Game" within the region. (Their influence would continue even after World War II, as Russia continued to occupy the north of the country and Britain controlled most of Iran's oil revenues until nationalization in the early 1950s.) As the constitutional revolution gained fervor, Britain and Russia pressured the Majles to dismiss Morgan Shuster, a US adviser who served as treasurer-general by appointment of the Iranian parliament. Russian forces literally shelled the Majles into submission. As outside influence terminated the hopes of constitutional reformers, the country's independence was essentially nullified.

The Qajar Dynasty gave way to a new era after Reza Khan, a former peasant and military soldier of the Persian Cossack Brigade (commanded by Russia until 1920), staged a coup, dethroned the Qajars, and founded the Pahlavi Dynasty in 1925. In keeping with tradition and alluding to Iran's historical notions of authority, he took the name Reza Shah Pahlavi (Pahlavi was the language of pre-Islamic Iran). He took the Turkish leader Mustafa Kemal Atatürk as his model, promoting secularization and limiting clerical powers. In 1936 he ordered women to unveil, making Iran the first Islamic country to declare veiling illegal (an ironic point to which we will return in Chapter 10). He alienated many groups in Iranian society, but especially the religious clerics. In his modernization plan, Reza Shah attempted to combine retrospective elements of

Iran's pre-Islamic civilization with Western technological achievements. He nominally tried to reduce foreign influence, but his desire to modernize meant he was dependent on Western technology, especially since Britain controlled the Anglo-Persian Oil Company, which financed many development projects and had fueled the British fleet in wartime.

Outside interference in Iranian affairs again became the leading grievance of the people, and ultimately led to the Pahlavi Dynasty's downfall. England viewed Iran as a buffer zone to protect its interests in India and competed with Russia to gain prominent spheres of influence. At the end of World War I, British and Russian troops (again) partitioned Iran. After the Bolshevik Revolution led to the withdrawal of Russian forces, the British attempted to dictate Iran's transformation into a protectorate. The controversial Anglo-Persian Agreement of 1919 provided British "advisers" to Iran—on Iran's bill—as a way to ensure Iran's stability and ultimately its ability to serve as a buffer state protecting India. The agreement was shady at best: Majles deputies never had any opportunity to comment on it, nor was it presented for discussion at the League of Nations.

Iran was again occupied during World War II, even though its leaders had proclaimed neutrality in the conflict. During the war, the Allied powers accused Reza Shah of being pro-German, forcing him to abdicate, board a British ship, and head toward exile in South Africa, where he died in 1944. Even if the Shah himself did not explicitly support the Germans, there was much public sentiment encouraging him to follow the lead of the Ottoman Empire by entering the war on the side of Germany.[101]

The British and the Russians had considered restoring the Qajar monarchy, but decided instead to continue the Pahlavi Dynasty by transferring power to Reza Shah's son, Mohammed Reza Pahlavi, who ruled from 1941 to 1979. He continued the absolute power he inherited from his father, while deepening Iran's controversial ties to the West, in part to ally the country with the West during the Cold War. During his rule, he was significantly challenged by two leaders—both of whom questioned Iran's ties to Western powers. The first was Mohammad Mossadeq, who was considered to be a liberal nationalist. Mossadeq, a Majles deputy educated in Switzerland, became a leading voice in the calls for the nationalization of the oil industry, which England had exclusively controlled. As Mossadeq's popularity increased, the Shah appointed him prime minister in 1953. Yet, even though he was one of the country's leading voices for liberalism, the West vilified the prime minister for leading the changes in Iran's oil dealings. London threatened military force, imposed economic sanctions, and even took Iran to the International Court of Justice in The Hague over oil, to no solution. The final nail in the coffin came when a joint mission between the US Central Intelligence Agency (CIA) and Britain's MI6, in collaboration with the Iranian army, overthrew Mossadeq. As a result of these actions, supported if not encouraged by Pahlavi, the leader lost his domestic legitimacy—already on shaky ground—and was labeled "America's Shah." There was much truth to the charge, as the weakened Shah increasingly relied on Western power games to maintain his own authority as he was vilified at home. Despite objections, the alliance between the Shah and the United States lasted for almost thirty years, as the oil industry was denationalized and the US and British companies raked in the profits.

The second man to challenge the Shah, and ultimately inspire the forces that led to the end of the Pahlavis, was Ayatollah Ruhollah Khomeini, a prominent Shia fundamentalist cleric. Khomeini's first book, *Secrets Revealed,* published in 1941, defended the Persian constitution of 1906. But after police killed theology students in the holy city of Qum, Khomeini declared war on the Shah, which led to Khomeini's arrest and exile. Khomeini was able to capitalize on the festering resentment within Iran as people grew increasingly discontented in the face of prolonged economic crises, humiliating international domination, and attempts to secularize the state. The regime's attempts to marginalize Khomeini—including articles in the official press accusing him of being an anti-Iranian British spy or a homosexual—backfired.[102] Khomeini voiced his criticism of the Shah ever louder, increasing his own support. The Shah's response was to expand the power of his repressive secret service, SAVAK, which went to great extremes in arresting perceived enemies of the regime. Increasingly, the Shah lost control over his own government and, in the face of widespread protests and chaos, he and his family left the country for good in January 1979. Khomeini came in on his heels, declaring the establishment of the Islamic Republic of Iran in April of that year. Rejecting secularism, Khomeini established a Council of Guardians, which institutionalized the role of clerics in interpreting Iranian laws, and ratified himself as the "Supreme Leader" of the state, answering only to God.

Khomeini ruled during an extremely turbulent decade in Iranian life: the country became increasingly isolated from the international community, was devastated by the ten-year war with Iraq, and was fractured along multiple internal divisions that had disappeared during the time of opposition to the corrupt Shah. But people had united around Khomeini and, after his death in June 1989, mourning masses attempting to touch his body caused it to fall from its platform during the funeral march. Defying the Western prediction of the chaos that would follow Khomeini's death, outgoing president Ali Khamenei succeeded Khomeini as Supreme Leader in a relatively seamless transition of power. Ali Akbar Hashemi Rafsanjani, the popular speaker of Iran's Majles, was overwhelmingly elected president, and he served in this capacity for two four-year terms, from 1989 to 1997. Rafsanjani was succeeded by the surprise victory of long-shot Ayatollah Mohammad Khatami, the former minister of culture known for his advocacy of relaxed controls over the media. Khatami served two terms and was succeeded by the populist nationalist Mahmoud Ahmadinejad in 2005. Ahmadinejad's eight-year presidency included international scrutiny of Iran's (resumed) nuclear program, a significantly disputed re-election in 2009, and a terse power struggle between himself and Supreme Leader Khamenei (that included an eleven-day walkout by Ahmadinejad). He was followed by former nuclear negotiator Hassan Rouhani (who had been brutally criticized by the Supreme Leader for his actions), who campaigned as a moderate open to re-calibrating relations between Iran and the rest of the world. The pendulum swung back toward the conservative side with the election of Ebrahim Raisi in 2021.

Case Study: China

It is often said that China is at once over five millennia old and five decades young. This contrast, between one of the world's oldest civilizations and its endurance for more than seventy years as a "People's Republic," captures much of the intrigue that is China today. Ancient China had great influence over its Asian neighbors, especially in the secular rituals derived from Confucian traditions. Today, Chinese civilization is viewed as the world's oldest, charting the relatively continuous existence of human communities for approximately 20,000 years. (Isolated human skeletons have been discovered from much earlier times, contemporaneous with Indonesia's "Java Man.") China's literary tradition is over 3,500 years old, and its written words (known as "characters") can be traced to linguistic precedents dating to approximately 1500 B.C.E.

Similar to many others, Chinese civilization was centered on river systems, especially the Yellow River in the north, where China's earliest recorded history is found, and the Yangtze River in the central and southern regions. It was a region ruled by over a dozen imperial dynasties, marked by fluctuating periods of stability, chaos, conquest, and cultural progress. The leader of each dynasty exercised authority based on the belief that she or he possessed the "Mandate of Heaven," which can best be understood as receiving the favor of one's spiritual ancestors.

China's first documented dynasty, the Shang, began in approximately 1700 B.C.E. Although Chinese records indicate at least one earlier dynasty, the existence of this community through archaeological records is yet to be proven.[103] Evidence of the Shang Dynasty is found in the so-called oracle bones, discovered only in the late 1800s, which were used to receive guidance from the heavens.

China's first unified dynasty, and indeed the source of the Western name "China," was achieved during the Qin Dynasty, which began in 220 B.C.E. Lasting only fifteen years, this was a remarkable dynasty that completed two wonders of the world. The Qin emperor ordered earlier walls used for fortification and defense to be linked literally into one "Long Wall" (known in the West as the "Great Wall"), providing modern Chinese an incredibly important symbol of the endurance of their culture.[104] The second famed creation of this dynasty was the emperor's elaborate tomb, composed of over 8,000 terracotta soldiers and horses buried to protect their identity. This major capital project of the dynasty required extensive resources, including labor power and coercion, and many of the 750,000 workers who planned and constructed the tomb, located in the ancient capital of Xi'an, were killed so they could not reveal its location. China's greatest dynasty, the Han, lasted for four centuries (206 B.C.E.–C.E. 220), and introduced the world's first wheelbarrow, as well as the widespread use of paper and porcelain. It was during this dynasty, contemporaneous with the Roman Empire, that the famed Silk Road, a 7,000-mile trade route from Xi'an to Rome, increased China's interaction with the rest of the world. China's interaction with the West grew steadily after this dynasty and, by the Ming Dynasty (1368–1644), contacts with the Spaniards, Russians, and Dutch were extensive. It was during this time that the Jesuit Mission of Matthew Ricci was begun, launching China's extensive yet troubled relationship with Western religions.[105]

In the midst of this exploration and grandeur, ordinary Chinese citizens lived a difficult life filled with TOTALITARIAN leaders, extensive tax payments to finance imperial projects, and little freedom in either their work or their personal lives, which were mired in poverty. Advancement in Chinese society throughout most of its past was based on academic credentials achieved through a complex examination system that was based primarily on Confucian texts, affording luxury to an extremely small minority of the population (from which women were expressly excluded).

China's relative isolation and size encouraged a "Middle Kingdom" philosophy in which rulers and ordinary citizens alike viewed themselves at the center of world civilization. This attitude manifested itself in China's tributary system of trade, in which foreign powers were required to give gifts to the emperor to show respect or gain favor (and sometimes protection). Additionally, the Chinese viewed anyone outside of their cultural civilization to be "barbarians," little deserving of equal contact or negotiation. Part of the measure, in Chinese eyes, of whether one was civilized or barbarian was one's allegiance to the teachings of a man who lived approximately 2,500 years ago, Kung Fuzi, known in the West as Confucius. His teachings, which may be viewed more as a way of life than a religious tradition, produced a great degree of cultural continuity in Chinese civilization, and even though modern leaders have gone to great lengths to eradicate his impact, it continues today. Confucian thought influenced most of East Asia, well beyond the borders of the Middle Kingdom. Some have claimed that he is "every bit as important to East Asian civilization as Jesus was to the West."[106] Confucius was a traditionalist who reflected, in extremely chaotic times, on solutions to societal problems. He emphasized virtue, tradition, ritual, and the importance of proper relationships. Confucianism emerged as a complex set of doctrines that has been debated and interpreted by leaders for millennia. Confucian thought eventually became required understanding for those who wanted to consider themselves "educated Chinese," and it was officially adopted as the state IDEOLOGY in the second century B.C.E. The Confucian school certainly was not the only worldview during China's past (the Taoists found these teachings authoritarian and restrictive, and the legalists found them too retrospective and lacking in rules), but it certainly was the most important. As a measure of its dominance, the Qing or Manchu Dynasty, China's last, was actually introduced to China by foreigners from the north. The Chinese welcomed them, though, because of their internalization of the Confucian code of conduct and rule.

The Chinese Empire traded extensively with Arabs and Persians for hundreds of years before European contact, under the tributary system discussed above. The Chinese never regarded their trading partners as equals and, indeed, for much of its history China's power was unrivaled, especially on the seas and in its protectorates and colonies throughout Asia, including Vietnam, Burma, and Korea. China's imperial power began to decline, though, in the 1500s, as its leaders turned increasingly inward and encouraged more isolation from the rest of the world. It was the outcome of this turn of events that led, in many ways, to the eventual European conquest of much of China, beginning in the late 1700s. In their desire to increase access to Asia through a Chinese trading point, the British and others established a structure in which foreign citizens would live in China without being subject to Chinese authority, a system known as EXTRATERRITORIALITY. This was the beginning of the erosion of China's sovereignty, as foreigners began living in the country not bound by Chinese laws, but rather by the laws of their home countries. As its trade deficit with China spiraled higher, England goaded China into a series of battles referred to as the Opium Wars (see Chapter 3). China's loss of Hong Kong (and other regions, including Taiwan, Macau, and Shandong) symbolized the imposition of foreign rule over a grand imperial land, rule that was not relinquished until the end of the twentieth century. (Taiwan, which was ceded to the Japanese in 1895, remains an example of contested sovereignty—discussed in Chapter 10.) On a larger scale, to most Chinese these events symbolized the loss of the famed "Mandate of Heaven" and gave birth to a flurry of potential solutions to the crisis. It was a time when many feared that Chinese civilization would fracture endlessly, exacerbated by localized warlord politics or regional military powers.

Shortly after the collapse of the last dynasty in 1911, Beijing University students staged what became known as the first mass demonstration in China's history, on May 4, 1919, to protest the status of Shandong, administered as a German colony since 1898. The warlord-dominated government in Beijing had entered into a secret agreement with the Japanese during World War I. At the Versailles Peace Conference at the end of the war, many Chinese placed great hope in Woodrow Wilson's rhetoric about SELF-DETERMINATION, but their hopes were crushed when they learned that Shandong (the coastal province in which Confucius was born, which is also home to one of China's most sacred mountains) was granted to Japan as part of the Versailles settlement. Protests erupted throughout China and within Chinese communities abroad, and China never did sign the Treaty of Versailles, capping another round of betrayal by the West. Out of this environment of distrust and disappointment, two dominant groups led the way to China's future: the Nationalist Party (KMT), led by Sun Yat-sen, and the Chinese Communist Party (CCP), eventually led by Mao Zedong (even though he was a minor figure for the first years of the party). Both parties focused on rallying different Chinese groups to their cause, and engaged in bitter battles with each other despite two formal attempts to unite for China's future. The final straw was the Japanese invasion of northern China in 1931, after which the CCP was perceived as the aggressive fighter for Chinese interests and for the needs of ordinary people. Following Japan's defeat in World War II and its expulsion from China, all-out civil war ensued between the KMT and the CCP, with the defeated Nationalists eventually exiling themselves to Taiwan. The People's Republic of China (PRC) was declared on October 1, 1949, although its hold on Chinese territory, and on world opinion, was less than complete, which set the stage for a rough ride especially during its first thirty years.

Mao Zedong, affectionately known as "The Chairman," led China for over two and a half decades, from the beginning of the PRC in 1949 until his death in 1976. His legacy remains mixed: he united the country and made the Chinese people proud of their heritage and achievements, while inflicting incredible civil disarray during his attempt to "continue the revolution" from 1966 to 1976, in the period known as the CULTURAL REVOLUTION. Mao was followed by another longtime member of the CCP, Deng Xiaoping, who had been with the party during its rise to power in the 1930s and 1940s. As you will read in Chapter 18, Deng dramatically changed the face of China by opening it to the outside world, promoting the development of political and economic institutions, and attempting to move away from the charismatic rule of his predecessor. Deng, who died in 1997, has also left a mixed legacy: while the lives of ordinary Chinese citizens improved dramatically under his watch, the blood of the Tiananmen Square demonstrations of 1989 is also on his hands. Leaders who followed in his footsteps, including Jiang Zemin and Hu Jintao, faced the difficult task of trying to preserve the Communist Party's monopoly on power while attempting to carefully manage China's re-emergence as a major regional and global player. This balancing act has consumed current CCP General Secretary and President Xi Jinping. Xi, in office since 2012 (and now, thanks to the removal of formal term limits, with an open-ended departure date) leads the country as China's imprint on the region and the world magnifies at the same time its population experiences some of the quickest changes in daily life observed anywhere.

Case Study: Indonesia

Modern Indonesia is an IDENTITY born of trade routes and colonial experience. Despite regional prominence and rich cultural traditions, there was little sense of commonality among the peoples who lived on the thousands of islands in the South Pacific prior to the early nineteenth century. Throughout this book, you should not be surprised to read about the division and tense unity that exist in modern Indonesia in the early twenty-first century, as unity was a concept rarely evidenced in the islands of the archipelago.

The region known today as Indonesia was long populated by humans. You may be familiar with Java Man, the fossilized bones of a hominid that were discovered in 1891. It is believed that this human, known as *Pithecanthropus erectus,* lived over 750,000 years ago and had the capacity for fire building and language. Subsequent archaeological discoveries confirmed populations extending 35,000–40,000 years ago, including Solo Man, named after a river in central Java, and the later Wajak Man, who lived 12,000–13,000 years ago.

Despite the presence of human communities almost 1 million years ago, the majority of today's Indonesians descended from two ethnic groups who immigrated to the islands from the north. These groups include the Melanesian peoples, who are believed to have inhabited the islands approximately 6,000 years ago, and the Austronesians, who migrated to the Indonesian archipelago from Taiwan at approximately the same time.

The Indonesian archipelago was an active player in the early Malay world, with a handful of states and kingdoms that thrived in trading. Early settlements prospered on the main islands, including Ho-Ling in central Java. Chinese records of this civilization report extensive war exploits, labor surpluses, and entertainment based on shadow plays and drums. By the sixth century, major kingdoms developed on Java and Sumatra, highlighted by the Srivijaya kingdom in southern Sumatra. Considered one of the most powerful kingdoms in Southeast Asia, Srivijaya emerged as the chief state and the only maritime state among the classical states in the region. As a commercial state, it began and ended earlier than others. Srivijaya's rulers controlled the critical Straits of Malacca, the preferred travel route between China and India, and its influence reached to southern Vietnam.[107] The exchange of commercial goods was not the only type of trade in this kingdom: it was also viewed as the center both of Hindu and Buddhist studies.[108]

Not surprisingly, due to its location Srivijaya was famous for its navy, financed largely by taxes collected on foreign ships traversing its path. It eventually controlled a vast territory, including most of Sumatra, present-day Malaysia, and Singapore, yet the authority of the king expanded farther, to Borneo and Sri Lanka. The wealth of this kingdom was memorialized in the story that each day the king would toss a gold bar into the sea to acknowledge it as the source of Srivijaya's prosperity. At the end of his reign, the number of gold bars retrieved from the waters quantified the king's power.[109] Yet, because of its export focus, it was a vulnerable state, dependent on the economic situation in India and China.

Even after Srivijaya's decline, Indonesia's prominence in Asian trade continued, and the city port of Malacca rose to prominence in its absence. Asian states (especially China and India) as well as Arab states provided ideal export markets for products abundant on the archipelago, especially spices. The region's abundance of spices, especially cloves, nutmeg, and pepper, were sought by traders around the world. Early Indonesians had established colonies in Madagascar for the transport of spices abroad (especially to the Romans); today, Austronesian languages can still be found there as remnants of this influence.

Increased trade led to heightened cultural interaction between islanders and their mainland Asian neighbors. By the third century, Hindu and Buddhist traditions had filtered into the western islands from India. Neither system was adopted writ large; they were both regionally adapted and made to fit earlier customs, especially animism, a tradition based on the reverence for all living things. Islam did not become a major influence until the thirteenth century, and even then it was often combined with native religious traditions, as well as Hinduism and Buddhism. The Portuguese and the Dutch introduced Christianity much later, in the sixteenth and seventeenth centuries. Another cultural artifact of Indonesia's status as the trading center of Southeast Asia was the adoption of the Malay language by dissimilar people: it became the unifying factor facilitating trade between diverse groups. As Islam spread through the archipelago, the use of Malay became even more predominant.

Accounts of Islam's arrival disagree on the century in which it was introduced, some dating it as early as the seventh century, and others contending it was closer to the thirteenth century.[110] Yet, experts consistently emphasize the influence of the spice-trading route as a major avenue for the spread of Islam. From the start, Islam was interpreted in diverse ways, with *santri* Muslims closely following traditional Islamic rituals, and *abangans* adapting Islamic traditions to their Hindu beliefs. Aceh was one of the first parts of Indonesia to convert to Islam, and to this day Acehnese are known for their relatively strict interpretations of Islamic traditions and for the strength of their convictions.

European influence in the region began in the fifteenth century. The first Portuguese ships sailed into Malacca in 1509, in search of inexpensive spices to preserve meats. The Portuguese eventually took over Malacca, only to hasten its downfall. Throughout the 1600s, Dutch Protestants established the Dutch

East India Company (in search of a monopoly over the spice trade), and gradually increased their territory of control as it fit their economic interests, beginning with the "spice islands" of Maluku and the northwestern coast of Java. They consolidated their rule by expelling other colonial aspirants, including Spain and England (although the English maintained their colonies on Borneo). Even after the collapse of the Dutch East India Company, the Netherlands defeated the English to gain control over their colonies in Southeast Asia by 1816. Despite serious Indigenous challenges to their authority, the Dutch prevailed in establishing control.

As Dutch colonial rule over the archipelago increased, and they began to integrate native Indonesians into their administrative structure, the growing sense of discrimination fostered much discontent. A REVOLUTION OF RISING EXPECTATIONS ensued; those native Indonesians who were afforded the opportunity to pursue higher education and serve in colonial officialdom as physicians, engineers, and other professionals chafed at the rigid subordination they faced compared to their European rulers. Although the nationalist movement was just beginning to form, many voices were calling for change, including the Javanese princess Raden Adjeng Kartini, who championed the emancipation of Indonesian women.[111] As discussed above, this situation of choosing a select few for opportunities produced extremely difficult identity struggles among those selected.

The nationalist independence movement was launched in the early years of the twentieth century, and was given an added spark by ironic celebrations by the Dutch of their own centennial of liberation from Napoleonic rule—which they commemorated in the midst of occupied Indonesia.[112] It all began to come together under the leadership of a young engineer named Sukarno (following the Javanese custom, he had one name). Sukarno founded the Indonesian Nationalist Party in 1927. In response to their independence rhetoric, the Dutch exiled Sukarno, Mohammed Hatta, and other nationalist leaders. World War II provided them an opportunity to return, reorganize, and lead their country to independence.

Indonesia's formal colonial era ended with the Japanese occupation of 1942–1945, during which time the Japanese plundered the region's oil fields to support their imperial navy. Ironic in hindsight, many Indonesians initially welcomed the Japanese, believing they would help in their fight for independence, and that the Japanese would not stay long. Instead, the Japanese sent Indonesians to work as forced laborers in Japan's territories. Those Indonesians who had been recruited and trained by the former Dutch colonial powers were again used as pawns during the Japanese occupation, as they became enforcers of the harshest Japanese policies on their neighbors and compatriots. But it was the Japanese defeat at the end of World War II that spurred Indonesia's independence movement into full gear. Prior to that time, Indonesian nationalists Sukarno and Hatta had begun to campaign for independence. Yet, the movement was hindered by disagreement, rectified mostly by Sukarno's *pancasila* proposal, which emphasized the five principles shared by all Indonesians regardless of ethnic, religious, or political beliefs. These beliefs remain today, enshrined in the preamble to the modern Indonesian constitution.

Indonesia declared its independence in Sukarno's garden the morning of August 17, 1945 (two days after the Japanese surrendered), but struggled with the Netherlands for over four years before the Dutch recognized its independence, only after bloody battles and intense international pressure. Sukarno embarked on a program euphemistically referred to as "guided democracy" for most of his rule, from 1949 to 1965. As a world traveler, Sukarno eloquently espoused the needs of the developing world, especially in the Bandung Conference of Asian and African States in 1955. He was also stridently anti-Western, taking over British and US businesses, expelling Dutch nationals, and withdrawing from the United Nations. A 1965 coup, supposedly masterminded by the Communist Party of Indonesia (PKI), led to much bloodshed. At least 400,000 were killed in fear of communist insurgency in a period that remains one of the country's darkest and least discussed in Indonesia's history.[113]

Out of the ashes of the 1965 coup, the military commander Suharto rose to power. Suharto, who himself had attended a Dutch-run military academy and fought against the Dutch in Indonesia's war of independence, knew well the importance of military strength in maintaining his rule, a principle he applied fiercely throughout his "new order" government, from 1966 to 1998. Although dramatic social improvements were achieved in the first years of his leadership, including declining poverty and increasing literacy rates, his government increasingly became a repressive state, complete with a gulag system used to enforce religious and political oppression. He was forced to resign from power in May 1998, in the face of widespread protests against his handling of the Asian economic crisis and international pressure to resolve the country's economic woes. A caretaker government led by interim president B. J. Habibie, a close associate of Suharto's, was in power for thirteen months before the groundbreaking elections of June 1999, the first free and fair elections to take place in four decades. In this election, the Indonesian Democratic Party–Struggle (PDI-P), led by Megawati Sukarnoputri, scored a resounding majority once the voting results were finally ratified in August 1999. The Indonesian legislature, the People's Consultative Assembly, in October 1999 met and chose Abdurraham Wahid—who was supported by an unprecedented Islamic alliance—as the state's fourth president.[114] Megawati, a critic of Suharto and daughter of Indonesia's founding father, was named vice president. Wahid, the Muslim cleric who was partially blind and in frail health, led the country for approximately twenty months before he was voted out of office by the legislature in July 2001, capping off a six-month impeachment process. Shortly after Wahid agreed to leave the presidential quarters, Megawati took power in a country dizzied by political upheaval, internal violence, and a reeling economy. Susilo Bambang Yudhoyono, popularly known by the acronym SBY, became the country's first directly elected president in 2004. The retired general brought some stability to the country, serving for two terms, yet his decade in office was marked by indecisiveness and a perceived lack of principle. His successor, Joko "Jokowi" Widodo, seemingly ushered in a new era of Indonesian politics, rising as the first president outside of either the military or political elites. A populist former governor of Jakarta known for walking the streets to converse with ordinary people, the former furniture maker and fan of Metallica and Led Zeppelin helped cap a series of transitions in an Indonesian system that has observed much change, at least on the surface.

Now It's Your Turn

As you move on to more contemporary considerations of these eight countries, keep in mind their diverse and rich histories. In what ways can you see their contemporary experience driven by their past? From the brief overviews provided, what traditions or values do you believe should be revitalized or adapted to serve the peoples of these countries? In what ways do you see legacies of Western domination continuing to play out in these countries?

Notes

1. Lynn V. Foster, *A Brief History of Mexico* (New York: Facts on File, 1997).
2. Maurice Collis, *Cortés and Moctezuma* (New York: New Directions, 1999).
3. Peter Bakewell, *A History of Latin America* (Malden, MA: Blackwell, 1997); Benjamin Keen and Keith Haynes, *A History of Latin America* (Boston: Houghton Mifflin, 2000).
4. Ibid.
5. Richard Graham, *Independence in Latin America* (New York: McGraw-Hill, 1994).
6. Ibid.
7. Bakewell, *A History of Latin America;* Keen and Haynes, *A History of Latin America.*
8. Ibid.
9. Ibid.
10. Keen and Haynes, *A History of Latin America.*
11. Ibid.
12. Ibid.
13. Bakewell, *A History of Latin America.*
14. Ibid.
15. Ibid.; Keen and Haynes, *A History of Latin America.*
16. Keen and Haynes, *A History of Latin America.*
17. Bakewell, *A History of Latin America.*
18. Laura Laurencich Minelli, *The Inca World* (Norman: University of Oklahoma Press, 2000).
19. Ibid.
20. Peter Flindell Klaren, *Peru: Society and Nationhood in the Andes* (New York: Oxford University Press, 2000).
21. Ibid., p. 43.
22. Ibid.
23. The Spanish *mita* built on Inca practice, but there were crucial differences. For the Inca, *mita* was part of a larger social contract in which reciprocal benefits linked the community and state. For the Spanish, however, *mita* was purely exploitative, as the state provided no return to the community. Minelli, *The Inca World.*
24. According to Peter Klaren, however, the state did offer some limits on colonial expropriation. For example, Indigenous people could appeal to colonial courts for relief, and some became adept at resorting to Spanish legal institutions to defend their interests. But such policies served as safety valves, effectively strengthening the system against radical or revolutionary challenges. Klaren emphasizes that because the system did sometimes rule on behalf of oppressed groups, this in no way vindicates or balances the colonial legacy, which is overwhelmingly negative. Klaren, *Peru.*
25. Ibid.
26. Ibid.; Mark A. Burkholder and Lyman L. Johnson, *Colonial Latin America* (New York: Oxford University Press, 1998); Graham, *Independence in Latin America.*
27. Cynthia McClintock, *Revolutionary Movements in Latin America* (Washington, DC: United States Institute of Peace Press, 1998).

28. Ibid.
29. Keen and Haynes, *A History of Latin America.*
30. Ibid., p. 43.
31. Ibid.
32. Klaren, *Peru.*
33. Ibid.; Washington Office on Latin America, "Deconstructing Democracy: Peru Under Alberto Fujimori," February 2000.
34. Ibid.
35. Keen and Haynes, *A History of Latin America;* Klaren, *Peru;* Thomas E. Skidmore and Peter H. Smith, *Modern Latin America* (New York: Oxford University Press, 1992).
36. Michael Crowder, *The Story of Nigeria* (London: Faber and Faber, 1978).
37. Robin Law, "The Oyo-Dahomey Wars, 1726–1823: A Military Analysis," in *Warfare and Diplomacy in Precolonial Nigeria,* ed. Toyin Falola and Robin Law (Madison: University of Wisconsin–Madison, 1992).
38. Crowder, *The Story of Nigeria.*
39. Ibid.
40. Ibid.
41. Toyin Falola, *The History of Nigeria* (Westport: Greenwood, 1999).
42. Ibid.
43. Ibid.
44. Peter M. Lewis, Pearl T. Robinson, and Barnett R. Rubin, *Stabilizing Nigeria* (New York: Century Foundation, 1998).
45. Ibid.
46. Ibid.
47. Falola, *The History of Nigeria.*
48. Ibid.
49. Karl Maier, *This House Has Fallen: Midnight in Nigeria* (New York: PublicAffairs, 2000).
50. Ibid.
51. D. E. Needham, E. K. Mashingaidze, and Ngwabi Bhebe, *From Iron Age to Independence: A History of Central Africa* (London: Longman, 1985).
52. Ibid.
53. Ian Phimister, *An Economic and Social History of Zimbabwe, 1890–1948* (London: Longman, 1988); A. J. Wills, *An Introduction to the History of Central Africa: Zambia, Malawi, and Zimbabwe* (New York: Oxford University Press, 1985).
54. Ibid.
55. Wills, *An Introduction to the History of Central Africa.*
56. Ibid.
57. Phimister, *An Economic and Social History of Zimbabwe.*
58. Ibid.
59. In the 1920s the Watch Tower prophesized the Second Coming and claimed that a whirlwind would blow whites and nonbelievers away. Ibid.
60. Ibid.
61. Ibid.
62. Needham, Mashingaidze, and Bhebe, *From Iron Age to Independence.*
63. Victor de Waal, *The Politics of Reconciliation: Zimbabwe's First Decade* (Trenton, NJ: Africa World, 1990).
64. Ibid.
65. Ibid.
66. Ibid.
67. Masipula Sithole, "Zimbabwe: In Search of Stable Democracy," in *Democracy in Developing Countries: Africa,* ed. Larry Diamond, Juan Linz, and Seymour Martin Lipset (Boulder: Lynne Rienner, 1988).
68. Ibid.; Needham, Mashingaidze, and Bhebe, *From Iron Age to Independence;* de Waal, *The Politics of Reconciliation.*

69. Thomas Schneider, *Ancient Egypt in 10 Questions and Answers* (Ithaca: Cornell University Press, 2013).
70. Charles Freeman, *Egypt, Greece, and Rome: Civilizations of the Ancient Mediterranean* (Oxford: Oxford University Press, 2004).
71. Alan B. Lloyd, *Ancient Egypt: State and Society* (New York: Oxford University Press, 2014); Schneider, *Ancient Egypt in 10 Questions and Answers.*
72. Ibid.
73. Douglas J. Brewer and Emily Teeter, *Egypt and the Egyptians* (Cambridge: Cambridge University Press, 2007).
74. Lloyd, *Ancient Egypt;* Freeman, *Egypt, Greece, and Rome.*
75. Brewer and Teeter, *Egypt and the Egyptians;* Schneider, *Ancient Egypt in 10 Questions and Answers.*
76. Lloyd, *Ancient Egypt.*
77. Ibid.; Freeman, *Egypt, Greece, and Rome.*
78. Schneider, *Ancient Egypt in 10 Questions and Answers;* Brewer and Teeter, *Egypt and the Egyptians;* Freeman, *Egypt, Greece, and Rome.*
79. Tarek Osman, *Egypt on the Brink: From Nasser to Mubarak* (New Haven: Yale University Press, 2010); Schneider, *Ancient Egypt in 10 Questions and Answers.*
80. Brewer and Teeter, *Egypt and the Egyptians;* Freeman, *Egypt, Greece, and Rome.*
81. Brewer and Teeter, *Egypt and the Egyptians;* Lloyd, *Ancient Egypt.*
82. Lloyd, *Ancient Egypt.*
83. Arthur Goldschmidt Jr., *Modern Egypt: The Formation of a Nation-State* (Boulder: Westview, 2004); Osman, *Egypt on the Brink.*
84. Osman, *Egypt on the Brink;* Isa Blumi, *Foundations of Modernity: Human Agency and the Imperial State* (New York: Routledge, 2012).
85. Ibid.; Goldschmidt, *Modern Egypt.*
86. "Egypt: A British Protectorate," *American Journal of International Law* 9, no. 1 (January 1915), pp. 202–204; Thanassis Cambanis, *Once upon a Revolution: An Egyptian Story* (New York: Simon and Schuster, 2015).
87. Osman, *Egypt on the Brink.*
88. Goldschmidt, *Modern Egypt;* Osman, *Egypt on the Brink.*
89. Afaf Lutfi al-Sayyid Marsot, *A History of Egypt: From the Arab Conquest to the Present* (Cambridge: Cambridge University Press, 2007); Goldschmidt, *Modern Egypt.*
90. Goldschmidt, *Modern Egypt;* Marsot, *A History of Egypt.*
91. Wael Ghonim, *Revolution 2.0: The Power of the People Is Greater Than the People in Power* (New York: Houghton Mifflin Harcourt, 2012); Goldschmidt, *Modern Egypt.*
92. Osman, *Egypt on the Brink;* Ghonim, *Revolution 2.0;* Goldschmidt, *Modern Egypt.*
93. Goldschmidt, *Modern Egypt.*
94. Cambanis, *Once upon a Revolution.*
95. Ibid.; Ghonim, *Revolution 2.0.*
96. Cambanis, *Once upon a Revolution.*
97. Elton L. Daniel, *The History of Iran* (Westport: Greenwood, 2001).
98. Mike Edwards, "The Adventures of Marco Polo, Part I," *National Geographic,* May 2001; Daniel, *The History of Iran.*
99. Daniel, *The History of Iran.*
100. The title "Shah" reappropriates a pre-Islamic Iranian title for "king."
101. Daniel, *The History of Iran.*
102. Ibid.
103. Lucian W. Pye, *China: An Introduction,* 3rd ed. (Boston: Little, Brown, 1984).
104. Much of the story surrounding the Great Wall is based in legend. While some smaller walls were built prior to the Qin Dynasty, and joined together during the Qin emperor's reign, the bulk of the wall was completed during China's Ming Dynasty (1366–1644), and significantly renovated thereafter. There is evidence to challenge its status as part of China's ancient past. Historian Arthur Waldron has produced extensive research challenging the myth behind the wall, citing, among other points, that even

though Marco Polo traveled extensively throughout the region in the thirteenth century, he made no mention of the structure. Similarly, contrary to popular beliefs, the Great Wall cannot be viewed from space, at least not without significant satellite magnification. Yet, perceptions of the wall's visibility from space predate space travel by humans—*Ripley's Believe It or Not* made the claim as early as 1930. See David C. Wright, *The History of China* (Westport: Greenwood, 2001).

105. Pye, *China.*

106. Michael Schuman, "Reformers Want to Erase Confucius's Influence in Asia: That's a Mistake," *Washington Post,* May 29, 2015.

107. Barney War, "Teaching Indonesia: A World-Systems Perspective," *Education About Asia* 3, no. 3 (Winter 1998).

108. Milton W. Meyer, *Asia: A Concise History* (Lanham: Rowman and Littlefield, 1997); Björn Schelander and Kirsten Brown, *Exploring Indonesia: Past and Present* (Honolulu: Center for Southeast Asian Studies, 2000).

109. Schelander and Brown, *Exploring Indonesia.*

110. Nina Nurmila, "The Indonesian Muslim Feminist Reinterpretation of Inheritance," in *Islam in Indonesia: Contrasting Images and Interpretations,* ed. Jajat Burhanudin and Kees van Dijk (Amsterdam: Amsterdam University Press, 2013), p. 109.

111. Meyer, *Asia.*

112. Robert Cribb and Colin Brown, *Modern Indonesia: A History Since 1945* (New York: Longman, 1995).

113. Sara Schonhardt, "Indonesia Chips Away at the Enforced Silence Around a Dark History," *New York Times,* January 19, 2012, p. A9.

114. Chris Manning and Peter van Diermen, "Recent Developments and Social Aspects of *Reformasi* and Crisis: An Overview," in *Indonesia in Transition: Social Aspects of Reformasi and Crisis,* ed. Chris Manning and Peter van Diermen (Singapore: Institute of Southeast Asian Studies, 2000).

Part 2

Economic Realities

It is an axiom that when the rich sneeze, the poor catch pneumonia. As the global north appeared to be emerging from the PANDEMIC, it is fair to ask how the global south is doing, why a two-track recovery exists, and whether the INTERNATIONAL ECONOMIC SYSTEM is contributing to the development or the underdevelopment of much of the world. With Covid not yet in our rearview mirror, it seems also the time to ask about the structures the pandemic exposed and the processes it sped up. The following chapters focus on INTERNATIONAL POLITICAL ECONOMY (IPE), or the complex economic forces that shape our societies and how economic and political issues interface. As an area of study, IPE's interest in the politics of economics includes a broad array of topics and concerns. In this part of the book we will focus on the gap in wealth and material well-being that exists between high-income countries and low- and lower-middle-income countries—as well as disparities that exist within countries. The existence of such often massive inequality, whether it is due to a combination of GLOBALIZATION, climate instability and transition, technological change, or other factors is a major source of friction. It is the source of what is sometimes referred to as the North-South conflict.

For years, people belonging to two dominant but diametrically opposed schools of thought, NEOLIBERALISM and STRUCTURALISM, have had very different ideas about why this gap exists and how to bridge it. Pro-capitalist neoliberals are highly optimistic about the ability of free trade, deregulation, and small government to work their magic. They believe that the system works; it is just up to individual countries to do better. On the other hand, structuralists are so named because of their focus on structures, or the international economic system as a pattern of social relations with staying power. Much of the global south is dealing with a set of disadvantages that range from their colonial histories to their position in the international economic system. That system is capitalist, which structuralists view as inherently exploitative. For them, under-development and inequality are inherent to the structure of the current international economic system—and those who benefit from it want to maintain the status quo.

To varying degrees, then, structuralists are extremely pessimistic about the possibility of authentic development happening under the existing system. Instead, they call for major changes and the creation of a model that protects people from the painful shifts of capitalism. Many structuralists are abolitionist; they want to replace the system. Others are more pragmatic, offering incrementalist recommendations for how to modify it with new legislation or policies. However, once locked in place, structures are difficult to change. Proponents of this school recognize that it would take a global, highly disruptive event to change the system, such as an economic collapse or simultaneous, sustained protests. So far, they have mostly been able to ameliorate the situation, not fix the problem.[1] Added to the mix are POPULIST, ECONOMIC NATIONALISTS, who share many of the structuralists' criticisms of globalization and neoliberalism, but not necessarily their solutions (though both talk about fair trade over free trade, the need to fight for workers and stand up to corporations that send jobs overseas).

Both structuralists and economic nationalists turn out at antiglobalization protests. They include climate activists, unions and laid-off factory workers, advocates for the rights of Indigenous peoples, feminists, and those demanding vaccine equity as well as ANTI-VAXXERS. Although we recognize the rise of economic nationalism, this story is going to be mostly about the rivalry between neoliberalism and structuralism. As you will see in the following chapters, neoliberals, structuralists, and economic nationalists offer widely divergent answers for the questions we consider: Why does the gap between richer and poorer countries remain, even if it is narrowing? Why are we observing some of the highest levels of global inequality ever recorded? And why, despite some significant gains in recent decades, do so many of the world's countries continue to suffer from under-development? Is this under-development due to poor decisions made by the countries themselves? Or is it due to the position of these countries in the international economic system, a capitalist system that is dominated by rich countries and the organizations working for them?

5

The Global Economy: What the Pandemic Reveals

No More Poor People in a Rich Country

—*Campaign slogan of Pedro Castillo, when he was a candidate for president of Peru*

It seems so long ago now, but in the two decades before the unprecedented crisis set off by the PANDEMIC—the world had accomplished something remarkable. From 1999 to 2020, poverty rates worldwide had dropped by more than 60 percent.[2] That's a notable turnaround, an accomplishment that many of us thought we would never see. But you need more of the backstory to really appreciate this feat: since the 1950s many economists had predicted CONVERGENCE—that incomes in poorer countries would eventually "catch up" economically with richer ones. However, with a few notable exceptions such as China, the twentieth century was not so much about convergence as it was a dreadful period of divergence between the global north and global south. In the 1980s, average annual growth rates were *negative* in 42 percent of low-income countries.[3] The gap in economic growth between the global north and global south was such that many analysts had simply given up on the idea of convergence.

However, in the first two decades of the twenty-first century (for some it dates back to the 1990s), many developing countries started on a growth spurt—in some cases, actually outpacing the global north. As we will see, analysts disagree about its significance, but few countries were left behind: average annual growth rates were negative in only 16 percent of low-income countries in the 2000s and 2010s.[4] Sure, average growth rates had slowed down due to what is called the Great Recession of 2007–2009, but in the years just prior to Covid, something else remarkable happened. As poverty rates declined by 60 percent, over 1 billion people escaped absolute or extreme poverty. Pretty much every region of the world reported declines on this measure (defined as the number of people earning $1.90 or less a day). To put this in perspective, in the early 1980s 44 percent (nearly half) of the world's population lived in extreme poverty. By

2019, that figure had been brought down to 8 percent.[5] As you can see in Figure 5.1, the biggest gains were made in East Asia, but people in most regions benefited. This is a remarkable accomplishment, but it is important to note that two countries—China and India—accounted for much of this improvement. In the years between the Great Recession and the start of the pandemic, some patterns emerged. Many emerging and developing countries initially experienced even faster recoveries than economically advanced economies, which suffered through several years of lackluster growth.[6]

It is no wonder then, that in 2015 the president of the World Bank, Jim Yong Kim, characterized the decline in extreme poverty as "the best story in the world today."[7] The two decades prior to 2020 amounted to what some called "a thrilling epoch in history," as 1 billion people escaping extreme poverty meant historic, enormous progress toward human well-being on multiple fronts.[8] But not everyone was celebrating. For example, due to a slump in oil prices, Nigeria's gross domestic product (GDP) per capita continued to decline for years after 2015.[9] So, yes, although chronic hunger (and in some cases, e.g., Yemen and North Korea, life-threatening food insecurity) remained a serious problem during this period just prior to the pandemic, it had stabilized. By 2020, the world had gone nearly three years since the last famine declared by the United Nations (South Sudan in 2017). In the years before the pandemic, literacy rates

Figure 5.1 Share of People Living on Less Than $1.90 per Day by Region, 2005 vs. 2013 vs. 2020

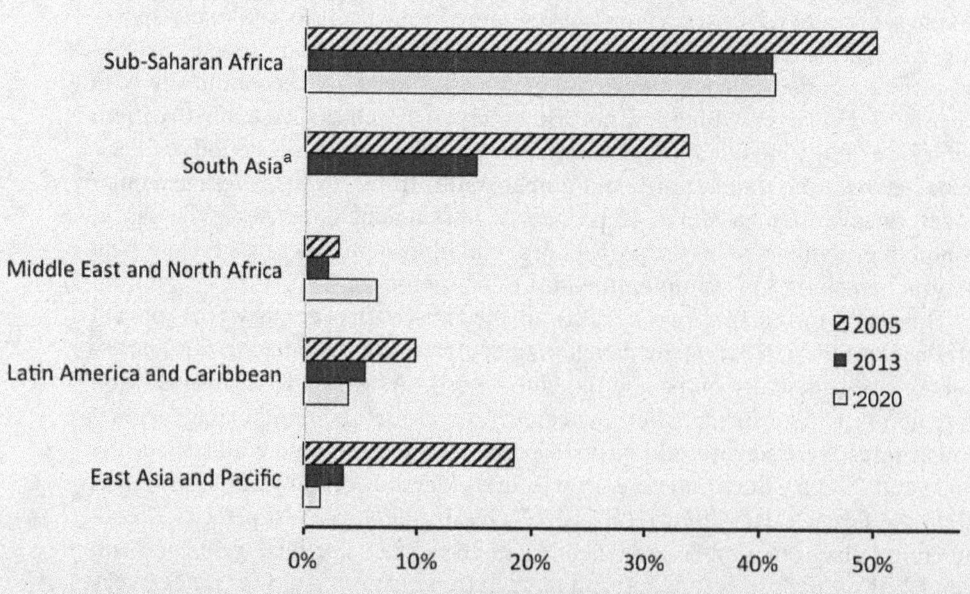

Sources: World Bank, *World Development Indicators 2005;* World Bank, *World Development Indicators 2013;* World Bank, *World Development Indicators 2020.*
Note: a. No data available for 2020.

leapt and life expectancy rose on average globally, from sixty-five years in 1990 to seventy-two in 2017. Polio was eliminated in all but two countries and the death rate from malaria was cut in half. The rates of child marriage and female genital cutting declined and access to contraception increased.[10] Around the world, each and all of these successes were compounding and life-changing.

Yet, Covid, the lockdown of the world economy, and what would become the deepest global recession since World War II wreaked havoc on all this progress as it exposed deeply connected economic, social, and environmental fragilities. You won't be surprised to hear that the speed and magnitude of the collapse in 2020 was unlike any in our lifetimes. For the first time in two decades, the fight against poverty suffered a devastating setback. To paraphrase the World Bank, 2020 was an exceptionally difficult year.[11] It estimated that the number of Covid-induced "new poor" (additional people living in poverty because of the pandemic) rose in 2020 to about 120 million. Keep in mind that the new poor were added to the 700 million who remained in extreme poverty all this time.[12] And don't count on a quick recovery for everyone; economists don't expect that the world will recoup these losses anytime soon.

Rather, what the IMF predicted in 2021 was a two-track recovery with poorer countries left behind richer ones, which would expand rapidly. In other words, in much of the global south the Covid recession contributed to an unprecedented increase in global poverty and inequality that is unlikely to be reversed quickly.[13] It may take decades to recoup, not years. To paraphrase Nicholas Kristof, the indirect effects of Covid have been devastating. Moreover, the coronavirus pandemic diverted the focus away from other diseases and illiteracy, possibly creating a lost generation whose potential is quashed by the epidemic.[14] According to the United Nations, the number of the chronically food insecure increased so that during the first year of the pandemic, a total of between 720 and 811 million people—nearly one in three worldwide—faced hunger. By late 2021, the UN warned of "unprecedented catastrophic levels" of food insecurity, with looming famines in Ethiopia, Yemen, South Sudan, and Madagascar. Afghanistan, northeastern Nigeria, plus several other countries were headed in that direction.[15]

But this reversal of progress is just the tip of the iceberg. And this misery can't be entirely blamed on the pandemic or the lockdown and recession. It is more complicated than that, as we will see, possibly also due to mismanagement, as well as structural factors such as climate change and conflict. And keep this in mind: as much as the growth rates of the early twenty-first century should be celebrated, at that rate it was still going to take the average developing country nearly 170 years to close half the income gap with advanced economies.[16] Despite higher growth rates in many emerging and developing countries just prior to 2020, many of the improvements in poverty reduction, access to healthcare and education, and so forth were due to government investments in these things. Global inequality continued to exist at staggering rates: 1 percent of the world's population owned 46 percent of the world's wealth, whereas the poorest 70 percent owned less than 3 percent. Moreover, even during this period of progress, little was done to reduce the global south's dependence on the north, as the gap in access to vaccines has made clear.[17]

Of course, access to vaccines and uncertainties over new variants of the virus—combined with security and political challenges—will explain a great deal of the variation between countries in the global north and south. Just as there was variation in the disruption this crisis caused, the support countries received, and the policies pursued, the outlook for countries also diverged. As of late 2021, much remained uncertain, but economists expected that the recovery would be unequal, uneven, and in many cases not enough to fix the damage caused by the crisis.[18] Some predicted a two-track recovery (those who were able to control the virus early with vaccines, and those who were unable to do so). As the world's leading INTERNATIONAL FINANCIAL INSTITUTION, the INTERNATIONAL MONETARY FUND, put it, "The degree of expected scarring (or a permanent drop in output caused by the loss of jobs and businesses during the outbreak) varies across countries, depending on the structure of economies and the size of the policy response. Emerging market and developing economies are expected to suffer more scarring than advanced economies."[19] Here's an example of scarring: the pandemic wiped out nearly 114 million jobs in 2020, including 30 million new jobs that would have been created, according to the International Labour Organization. This UN agency predicted that, globally, employment alone would take years to return to pre-pandemic levels.[20]

The Fundamentals: Growth Versus Development

Yet, before we go any further with this discussion of how we are all doing, it is important to become familiar with two concepts fundamental to any discussion of INTERNATIONAL POLITICAL ECONOMY: growth and development. Both things are generally considered to be desirable, and the terms are often used interchangeably to describe economic progress. However, growth and development are actually two very different things. As we will discuss in more detail in the next chapter, proponents of one major school of thought, NEOLIBERALISM, argue that one needs growth to fund development. Its counterpart, STRUCTURALISM, puts the emphasis on equity over growth and points out that it is certainly possible to have growth without development, as has been the case in many LMICs.

Growth refers to an expansion in production, output, and perhaps income. A common indicator of growth is gross national income per capita, which is obtained by dividing GNI by the population. GNI per capita supposedly gives one an idea of how much income the average citizen earns in a year (see Figure 5.2). There's a world of difference between the $1,090 Zimbabweans earned in 2020 versus the $10,610 earned by the average person in China. Similarly, although poverty certainly also exists in HICs, most residents of these countries cannot fathom the hardship found in much of the global south. To put it in perspective, it would take the average resident of Burundi a year and a half to earn what the average American earns in a week.[21] However, keep in mind that income is only one, albeit important, measure of economic well-being, and GNI per capita assumes that income is divided completely equally—a situation that exists nowhere on Earth. In fact, one can assume that in most cases, a few people will earn much more than this figure and the majority will earn far less.

So, whereas growth describes an increase in volume or output, development is generally understood to mean human development and pertains to

Figure 5.2 GNI per Capita, Atlas Method for Rich, Middle-Income, and Poor Countries, 2020 (current US $)

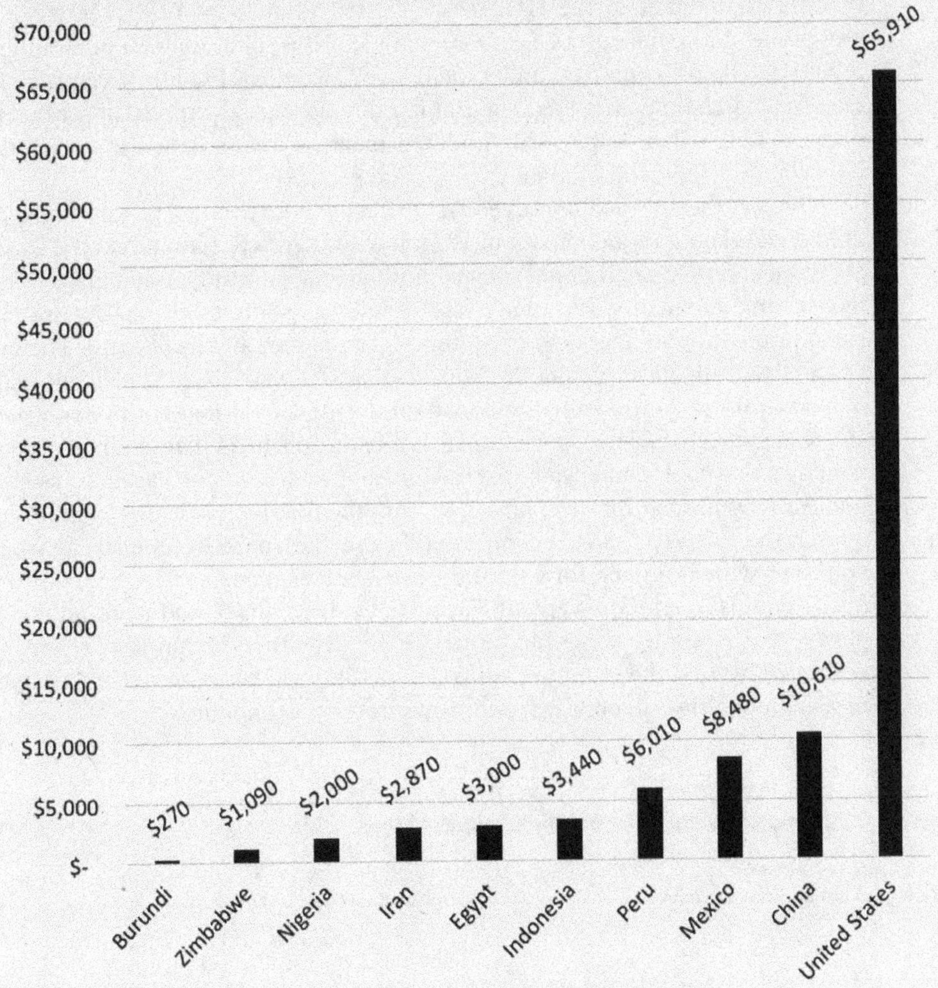

Source: World Bank, *World Development Indicators 2021.*

issues of distribution. Development is a broad concept that is measured by composite indices such as the Human Development Index (HDI) (see Figure 5.3). The Human Development Index was introduced in 1990 as a minimal listing of what was needed for a basic quality of life. Simple and clear, this thirty-year-old index focused on income, education, and health, but did not account for pressures on the planet. However, given the immediate and existential threats that are now unfolding, the HDI has been reoriented and now seeks to advance human development while also accounting for people's interactions with the planet. As a result, the index was adjusted in 2020 to include a new generation of metrics that gives attention to planetary pressures, known as the

PLANETARY PRESSURES–ADJUSTED HUMAN DEVELOPMENT INDEX (PHDI). Some use the term "SUSTAINABLE DEVELOPMENT," or "development that meets the needs of the present without compromising the ability of future generations to meet their own needs."[22] To arrive at the PHDI, the most notable change was that the income component of the HDI was adjusted to account for greenhouse gas emissions, the social costs of carbon, and natural wealth. As with other metrics, the PHDI helps countries understand their progress broadly over time and encourages choices that advance human development while easing planetary pressures. In other words, this updated measure recognizes the connections between development, climate change, and security.[23]

Overall, the new and improved HDI offers a more detailed picture of the economic well-being of a population. We know that growth rates alone tell us little about how people are doing. Perhaps more useful toward that end are measures like income inequality. But increasingly, analysts studying inequality are interested in inequity of access to opportunity, education, and healthcare. The coronavirus put all these inequalities on display. It exposed and, in many cases, increased them. For example, we learned during Covid that entire countries in sub-Saharan Africa have fewer intensive care unit beds than a single average American hospital. Or consider the inequities in accessing the vaccines, as ELITES booked trips abroad for their jabs, and only the relatively wealthy can afford to quarantine, whereas most people don't have the space.[24] As citizens of rich countries were lining up for a third booster shot, as many as 97 percent of those in the poorest countries were still waiting for their first—and were unlikely to get it, at the rate it was going, until 2023.[25] But such inequities existed long before 2020. And the trend overall is a widening gap between richer and poorer in many countries, in both fast and slow-growing economies.

Figure 5.3 Human Development Index, World Rankings, 2019

Very High Human Development		High Human Development	
Norway	1	Lebanon	92
Ireland	2	China	85
Hong Kong	4	Peru	79
Singapore	11	Mexico	75
United Kingdom	13	Iran	70
United States	17	Jamaica	101
		Indonesia	107

Medium Human Development		Low Human Development	
Morocco	121	Nigeria	161
India	131	Afghanistan	169
Zimbabwe	150	Haiti	170
		Niger	189

Source: United Nations Development Programme (UNDP), *Human Development Report 2020.*

Starting at a low base, it isn't unusual for poorer countries to clock the fastest economic growth rates. Sub-Saharan Africa, the world's poorest region, could claim the five fastest-growing economies in 2019. With a growth rate over 6.5 percent Ghana was the star that year; an exporter of cocoa, oil, and gold, it skyrocketed to the fastest-growing economy in the world. However, Ghana and Africa suffered like much of the rest of the world from the Covid recession. Ghana's growth decelerated to just 0.4 percent by 2020 (the regional average was negative 1.7 percent.)[26]

In other words, many of the poorest countries had their worst economic performance in thirty years. Originally, it was predicted that forty-three of the forty-seven poorest would see their GNI per capita drop, affecting the planned 2021 graduation of low-income countries to lower-middle-income countries (those held back include Nepal, Bangladesh, and Myanmar).[27] By late 2021, the International Monetary Fund noted a continuing recovery, with divergences between countries depending largely on vaccine access. They projected continuing uncertainty, but assuming the pandemic subsided sooner than later, global growth would reach 5.9 percent in 2021 before moderating to 4.9 percent in 2022. This would make it the strongest recovery from a recession since 1940, largely driven by Chinese growth and stimulus spending in advanced economies. At 6 percent, US growth rates for 2021 were forecast to rise faster than most of the rest of the world, but not as fast as China (8 percent) or India (9.5 percent) with the poorest countries the farthest behind (sub-Saharan Africa at 3.7 percent).[28]

Speaking of divergences, the pandemic hit the United States harder than China and, as a result, China is expected to pass the United States and become the world's largest economy by 2028, a few years earlier than expected.[29] Even at its still enviable growth rates, it would take another fifty years before average incomes in China would reach the income levels in the United States (according to the IMF, China's GDP per capita was $10,582.10 in 2020, roughly six times smaller than $63,051.40 in the United States).[30] Still, there is no disputing China's rise.

Across the sweeping category known as the global south, there are major differences in the levels of income and economic development. Taiwan, Singapore, Hong Kong, and Israel, sometimes referred to as advanced economies, are relatively wealthy. Of our CASE STUDIES based on 2019 data China, Iran, Peru, Mexico, and Indonesia were considered upper-middle-income countries (with GNIs per capita of $4,046–$12,535). Zimbabwe was reclassified from lower income and joined Egypt and Nigeria as lower-middle-income countries (with GNIs per capita of $1,036–$4,045).[31] China is soon to be considered an advanced economy—and analysts recognize that it is more difficult to make the jump from being a middle-income to a high-income country than it is to transition from one that is low income to one that is middle income.[32]

Although Nigeria is a major oil exporter, by many measures it is a relatively poor country. Indonesia, Iran, Egypt, and Mexico are also dependent on petroleum exports, but to varying degrees. For example, Mexico's economy, spread across the agricultural, industrial, and service sectors, is much more diversified than Nigeria's. With the proliferation of *MAQUILADORAS* or assembly plants over thirty years or so, Mexico's economy has increasingly been based on the export of manufactured goods, as are the economies of China, Indonesia, and others. In the first decades of the twenty-first century, the growth of these economies was largely based on the success of this sector. The economies of all of our case studies are highly export-oriented. Because they are so dependent on sales abroad, they are vulnerable to economic slowdowns in China, the United States, and other high- and upper-middle-income countries (their biggest customers).

As opposed to measures of growth, development indices give us a much clearer idea of people's overall quality of life. Three essential capabilities are commonly associated with development: the abilities to lead a long and healthy life, to be knowledgeable, and to have access to the resources needed for a decent standard of living.[33] Take a look at Figure 5.4. A life expectancy of seventy-five years for Mexico, because it is comparable to the life expectancies of the citizens of many richer countries, suggests that the standard of living for Mexicans is relatively high. On the other hand, that the average Nigerian can expect to live only to fifty-five tells us that something is very wrong.

Speaking of something wrong, due to lack of testing and a likely undercount of fatality rates associated with the disease, Covid taught us all a new measure: "excess death rates," which approximates a more accurate human toll by taking the number of people who die from any cause in a given region and period, and then comparing it with a historical baseline from recent years. This calculation nearly tripled its previous estimated fatality rate for Peru, which by mid-2021, as a proportion of its population, had the highest Covid fatality rates in the world, at 503 per 100,000 people. Bulgaria at 433 per 100,000 and Mexico at 354 rounded out the top three. We knew that of Latin American countries, Peru had been hit particularly hard, with hospitals overflowing and shortages of oxygen. But this measure confirmed that on a per capita basis, Peru had the highest

Figure 5.4 Life Expectancy, 2019

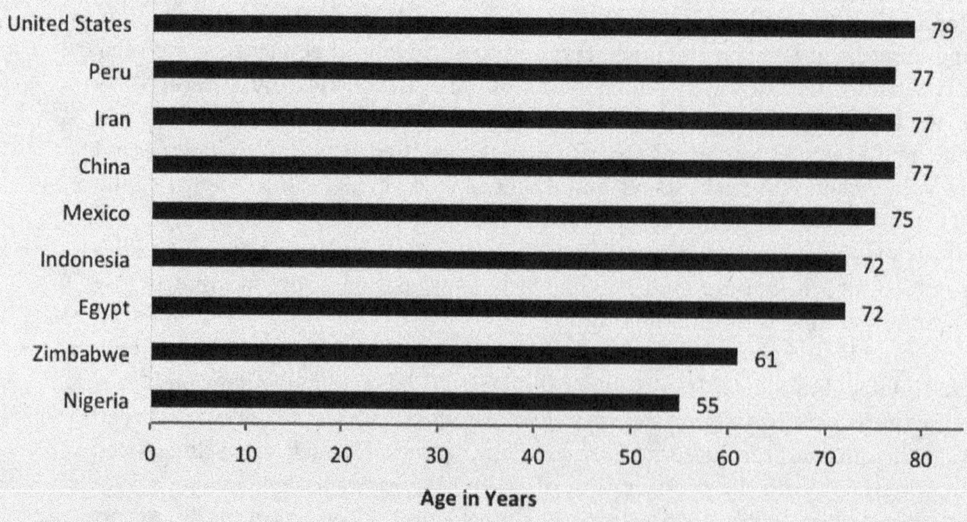

Source: World Bank, *World Development Indicators 2020.*

death toll of any country during the course of the pandemic. Sure, by mid-2021 Brazil had the highest total number of deaths in the region associated with Covid (+450,000), but as a proportion of the population, the toll in Peru more than doubled that of Brazil.[34]

Measures like HDI and similar indicators tell us even more—not only with regard to life expectancy, but also about infant and child morbidity and mortality rates and maternal health, as well as access to social services like healthcare and education (see Figures 5.5 and 5.6). Although there is great variability (within and between LMICs) in how well people are dealing with these problems, the difference between the global south and global north in dealing with maternal and child mortality can be particularly shocking where progress is slow (or nonexistent). Infant and child mortality rates have dropped by 59 percent globally since the 1990s, but still, approximately 5.2 million children under age five died in 2019—most of them from preventable and treatable causes.[35]

This was all accelerated and amplified during the pandemic. For example, more than 3 billion people lacked access to one of the most effective ways of preventing the spread of the virus: basic sanitation, including clean drinking water and handwashing facilities. The future looks even worse. The United Nations estimates that by 2050 over half of the world's population will be at risk due to extremely high stress on the world's water resources.[36] On the other hand, the world has made progress in providing more people with access to improved water sources. From 1990 to 2015, the proportion of the world's population using

Figure 5.5 Infant Mortality Rate, 2019

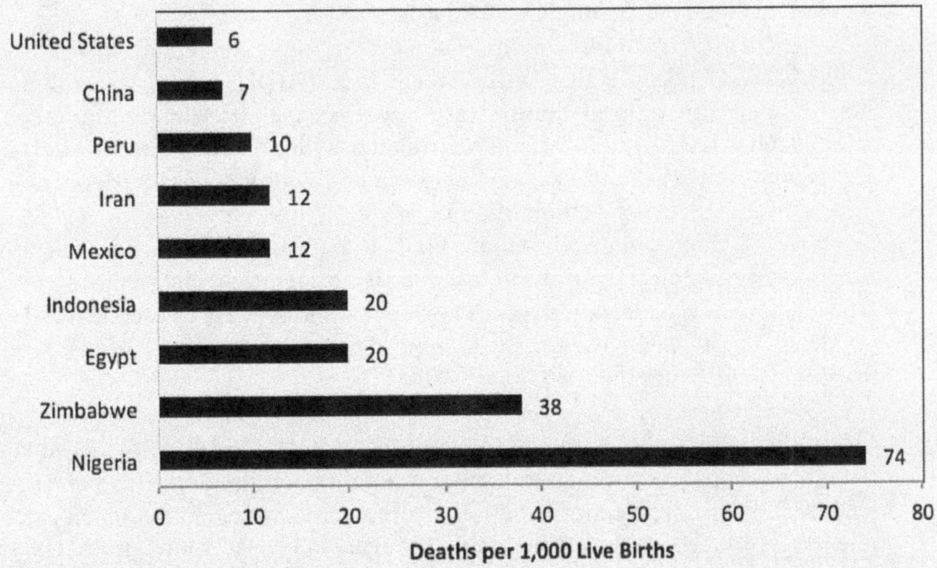

Source: World Bank, *World Development Indicators 2020.*

improved drinking water sources increased from 76 percent to 91 percent. However, that leaves nearly one in ten people (785 million) still lacking access to clean water, including the 144 million who resort to drinking untreated surface water. Similarly, although the proportion of the world's population left with no choice but open defecation has been halved since 2000, 673 million people are left with no other choice.[37]

Prior to Covid, the world had made progress on other fronts, against child marriage and female genital mutilation. But according to the United Nations, over 200 million girls and women alive today (mostly in Africa and the Middle East) have been subjected to female genital mutilation. The economic hardship caused by the pandemic may have reversed years of progress and pushed as many as 13 million more girls into child marriage this decade as families seek to secure their daughters' futures, and forced 2 million more girls to endure genital cutting as campaigns against it have closed down.[38]

Due to Covid shutdowns, it is believed that many individuals have been isolated in unsafe environments and at heightened risk of various forms of domestic and intimate partner violence. Worldwide, nearly one in three women have experienced physical or sexual violence by an intimate partner. Lockdowns and supply chain interruptions also mean lack of access to healthcare services; it is estimated that reduced access to contraception may result in 15 million unintended pregnancies.[39] These problems are related and compounding. Adolescent pregnancies (among females younger than twenty) carry an elevated risk of maternal death and disability. Pregnant girls whose bodies are not fully grown are more likely to develop obstetric fistulas (holes between their bladders and vaginas or rectums and vaginas) as well as other problems; their newborns are more likely to suffer from low birth weights and die in infancy. Although from 1964 to 2019 the global adolescent fertility rate has been cut in half, the numbers remain extremely high in several countries, including Niger, Angola, and Mali.[40]

Another measure offering a closer look at development from a different angle is the Gender-Related Development Index (GDI). Among other things, it tells us that although no country in the world treats its women as well as its men, gender inequality is strongly correlated with poverty. There are certainly differences in the status of women between and within countries, depending on CLASS, regional origin, ethnicity, and other factors. However, in the poorest countries, women and girls are more likely to be illiterate, to earn less than men do, to consume fewer calories, to become sick more often, and to die at younger ages than their male counterparts. They are also less likely to own land, despite evidence that if they have equalized opportunities, women can farm as productively as men, if not more so.[41]

Over the past century, but especially since the 1960s, larger numbers of women in many countries have entered the paid work force. In recent years, however, female participation in the labor force globally has actually declined, from 74 percent in 1990 to 46 percent in 2020. For example, the number of women entering the paid workforce grew tenfold over sixty years in China, from 7 percent in 1949 to over 70 percent in 2014, but dipped to 60 percent by 2019.[42]

A confluence of factors explains the rise and fall of female labor participation, with a different story for every community, as fertility, childcare policies, social norms, structural changes in the economy, and other factors affect female labor force participation. Female participation in the labor force tends to follow a U-shape: it is highest in some of the poorest and richest countries in the world. Yes, it tends to be lowest in countries with incomes in between.[43] For decades, employers worldwide recruited women because they are desperate enough to accept the work and pay that men reject. Even controlling for experience and education, for work of equal value globally women earn 77 cents for every dollar men earn—and women with children earn even less. According to the United Nations, at the current rate of change, it will take 257 years to close the gender wage gap. Although some blame the pay gap on the fact women are more likely than men to work in the INFORMAL SECTOR, with its risks and vulnerabilities, the feminization of poverty can occur even as more women are entering the FORMAL SECTOR. On average worldwide, women carry out two and a half times more household and care labor than men do. Women have a higher incidence of poverty than men, and female poverty tends to be more severe than male poverty, despite the fact that around the world, women often work more hours than men.[44]

Over the past two decades, the world has made progress toward the goal of universal, inclusive, and equitable quality education. With its implications for the individual and society, education plays a crucial role in reducing poverty and promoting development. Just prior to the pandemic, 87 percent of the world's children ages six to eleven were attending primary school and four out of five children who attended primary education completed it. However, 58 million children of primary school age remained out of school; more needs to be done to combat this problem, as the number of children not in school was a problem even before the pandemic.[45]

As it has for other aspects of development, Covid threatens to undo years of hard-won progress made in increased access to education. The coronavirus closed schools around the world in March 2020, but Latin America's schools stayed closed the longest (sixteen months in some places) and was facing an education crisis. Only six countries in the region had reopened schools as of June 2021 and the prolonged school closures are predicted to have long-term consequences. In what has been called "a generational crisis," the World Bank estimates that 77 percent of students in Latin America will end up below the minimum performance for their age, up from 55 percent in 2018. The full toll won't be known until children get back to school, but the fear is that many children will drop out once they realize how behind they have fallen. Even if they only miss ten months of classes, the World Bank predicts that the average student in Latin America could lose the equivalent of $24,000 in earnings over their lifetime.[46]

Of course, this is just another example of how Covid is sharpening inequality as it affects some more than others. Richer children everywhere have advantages that have allowed them to continue their educations through remote learning. Analysts are concerned that dropout rates will rise into the millions. It is estimated that 170,000 Peruvian children dropped out of school, and in Mexico 1.8 million young people are believed to have abandoned their educations in the 2020–2021 school year because of the pandemic or economic hardship. In the global south and north, more are still technically enrolled, but are struggling as many don't have computers, internet, or family to help.[47]

It must come as no surprise that in the global south and global north, before and since the pandemic the majority of children remaining out of school belonged to marginalized groups. However, thanks to important reforms in many countries like the elimination of school fees, literacy rates have improved in several regions. Regional inequities persist, but the gender gap in literacy rates is declining for all regions. As you can see in Figure 5.6, Peru has not closed the gender gap in literacy, but in many Latin American, Caribbean, and Central and East Asian countries, girls' school enrollment is equal to or surpassing that of boys.[48]

Where there are entrenched gender barriers, girls continue to face hurdles in obtaining their education, including all of our cases. It is important to remove these barriers because development workers have known for years that the investment in education for girls pays off in the long run with later marriage, healthier children, and smaller families. Studies suggest that girls who receive an education are more likely to earn increased wages, participate in decisions that affect them, and are less vulnerable to violence.[49] But it is important to stress that economic growth alone will not eliminate inequality; societies must promote the rights of women and girls to reduce gender disparities—and promote development.

Development indices also include attention to virtually all aspects of well-being: caloric intake, access to clean water, and sanitation—access even to cell phones and WiFi. For example, the digital divide (in terms of access to the internet in the north and south) is high, but shrinking overall. As of 2021, there were approximately 4.7 billion active internet users globally, with an estimated 900,000 new users joining daily. That amounts to half the world's population, but there is an access gap: 86 percent, or most of those living in HICs, are online, whereas only 19 percent of the populations in the poorest countries have access to the internet, most of them through mobile devices.[50]

Beyond traditional definitions that emphasize access to goods or services, development has more recently been expanded to include considerations of people's range of choice. This dimension of development includes concerns such as political empowerment and participation, HUMAN SECURITY, and protection of the environment. In this sense, human development clearly includes but goes beyond material needs. This understanding of development recognizes people's need to be creative and productive, to live in dignity, and to enjoy the sense of belonging to a community. Increasingly, human development is being conceptualized as a development of the people, for the people, and by the people. It must therefore be understood as a process as well as an end, a process in which those targeted for development are participants in deciding how they will pursue it. In other words, human development is ultimately about freedom. It is as much about the process of enlarging people's choices as it is about providing people with access to things valuable to their well-being.[51]

The rate of progress in every category of human development varies among and within countries. By some measures, like a sense of community belonging, it could be argued that, generally speaking, the citizens of the global south are far ahead of those living in the global north. There have been some overall improvements in terms of other, more widely recognized, aspects of human development across the world. However, not all have benefited equally from

Figure 5.6 Literacy, 2018

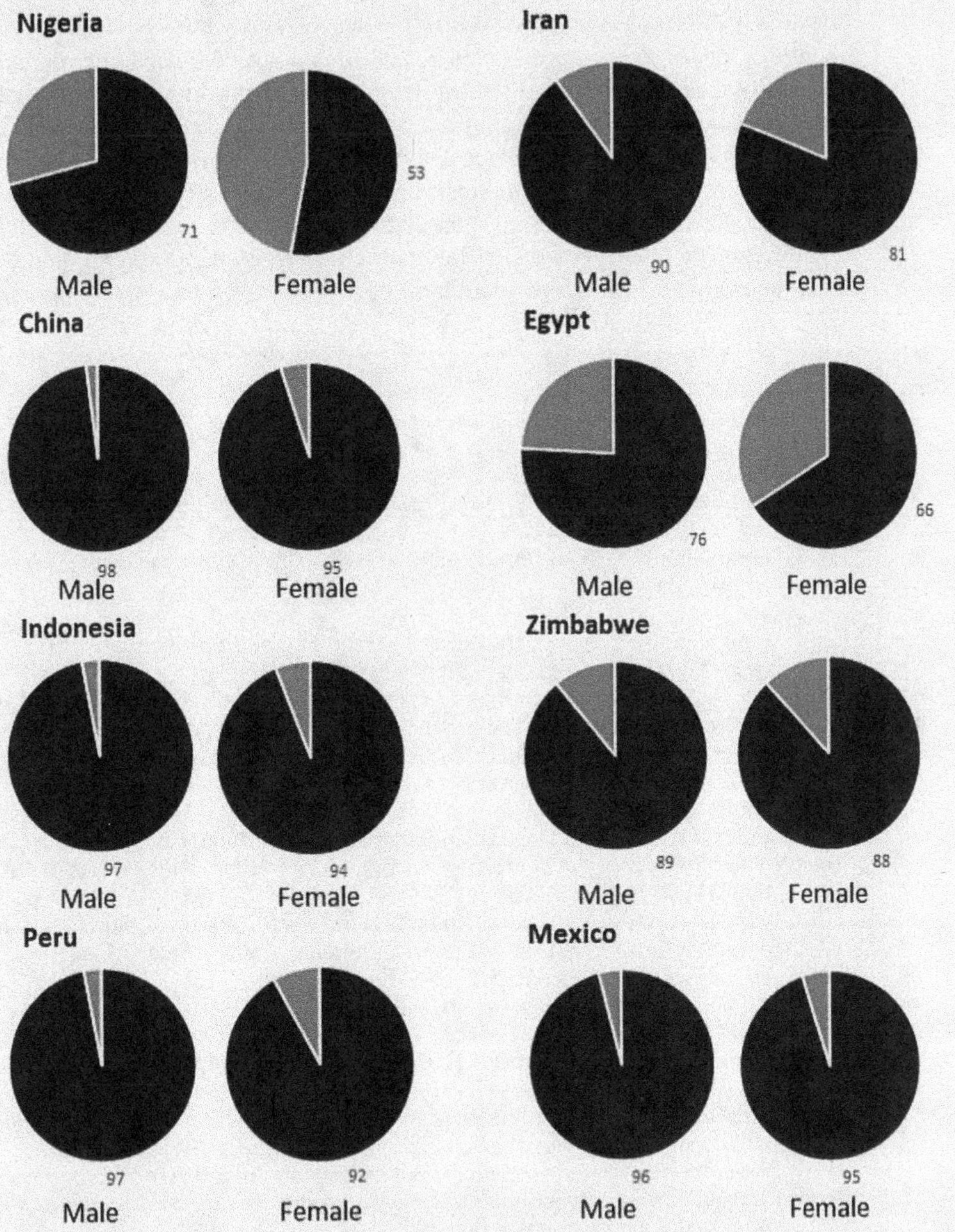

Source: World Bank, *World Development Indicators 2018.* Data for Iran are from 2016; Egypt 2017; Zimbabwe 2014 (latest years available).

Note: Literacy is defined as the percentage of the population older than age fifteen who can read and write.

these improvements (e.g., Peru made significant improvements in its infant mortality rates; Egypt has improved its primary-school enrollment and completion rates for girls). For others, progress is much slower (e.g., in Zimbabwe, where because of HIV/AIDS, life expectancy has actually regressed since independence in 1980, though it improved in recent years to sixty-one after hitting an appalling low of thirty-seven years in 2006). Among LMICs, some are making faster progress on certain aspects of development than others. Why is that and why does under-development continue to exist? Is it due to poor decisions made by governments or some other failure that can only be blamed on the countries themselves? Or is it due to the position of these countries in the international economic system, a capitalist system that is dominated by rich countries and the organizations working for them? Let's now turn to contending explanations of what the problem is and how to address it.

Notes

1. Noel Gross, "Why Do Democrats Keep Saying 'Structural'?" *New York Times,* July 31, 2019; Richard Davies, "When a Factory Relocates to Mexico, What Happens to Its American Workers?" *New York Times,* October 12, 2021.

2. World Bank, "Decline of Global Extreme Poverty Continues but Has Slowed," September 19, 2018.

3. "How Covid-19 Could Imperil the Catch-Up of Poor Countries with Rich Ones," *The Economist,* May 22, 2021.

4. Ibid.

5. Homi Kharas, Kristofer Hamel, and Martin Hofer, "Rethinking Global Poverty Reduction in 2019," Brookings Institution, December 13, 2018.

6. Dev Patel, Justin Sandefur, and Arvind Subramanian, "The New Era of Unconditional Convergence," unpublished paper, Harvard University, April 30, 2021.

7. Gayle E. Smith, "Development Depends on More Than Aid," *Foreign Affairs,* March 1, 2021; World Bank, "World Bank Forecasts Global Poverty to Fall Below 10% for First Time; Major Hurdles Remain in Goal to End Poverty by 2030," October 4, 2015.

8. Smith, "Development Depends on More Than Aid"; John Ruwich, "What China's 'Total Victory' over Extreme Poverty Looks Like in Actuality," NPR, March 5, 2021.

9. "Hard Times: Nigeria's Economy Is Stuck in a Rut," *The Economist,* May 15, 2021.

10. Nicholas Kristof, "Starving Children Don't Cry," *New York Times,* January 2, 2021; George Ingram, "What Every American Should Know About US Foreign Aid," Brookings Institution, October 2, 2019.

11. Christoph Lakner, Nishant Yozan, and Daniel Gerszon et al., "Updated Estimates of the Impact of COVID-19 on Global Poverty: Looking Back at 2020 and the Outlook for 2021," *World Bank Blogs,* January 11, 2021; World Bank, "China Economic Update," July 2020.

12. World Bank, "Understanding Poverty," April 15, 2021; United Nations Children's Fund (UNICEF), "Child Poverty," 2020.

13. Lakner et al., "Updated Estimates of the Impact of COVID-19"; International Monetary Fund, "World Economic Outlook: Managing Divergent Recoveries," April 2021; World Bank, "Understanding Poverty."

14. Kristof, "Starving Children."

15. Ibid.; Food and Agriculture Organization of the United Nations, "The State of Food Security and Nutrition in the World 2021," 2021; "UN Looks to Address 'Unprecedented Catastrophic Levels' of Food Insecurity," *UN News,* October 4, 2021.

16. Maria A. Arias and Yi Wen, "Trapped: Few Developing Countries Can Climb the Economic Ladder or Stay There," Federal Reserve Bank of St. Louis, October 7, 2015.

17. Smith, "Development Depends on More than Aid"; "How Covid-19 Could Imperil the Catch-Up," *The Economist;* Miatta Fahnbulleh, "The Neoliberal Collapse: Markets Are Not the Answer," *Foreign Affairs* 99, no. 1 (January–February 2020).
18. Suttinee Yuvėjwattana, "Thailand Approves $4.5 Billion in Stimulus That Includes Cash Handouts," *Bloomberg,* June 1, 2021.
19. International Monetary Fund, "World Economic Outlook"; "The Transformer: Mexico's President Has Yet to Make People's Lives Better," *The Economist,* February 18, 2021.
20. International Monetary Fund, "World Economic Outlook"; Nick Cummings-Bruce, "Jobs Lost to the Pandemic Will Take Years to Recover, a Labor Organization Says," *New York Times,* June 2, 2021.
21. CIA, *CIA World Factbook,* 2021.
22. "Sustainable Development," United Nations Educational, Scientific and Cultural Organization, August 3, 2015.
23. United Nations Development Programme, *Human Development Report 2020.*
24. Joseph Stiglitz, "Conquering the Great Divide," International Monetary Fund, Fall 2020; Maitreesh Ghatak, Xavier Jaravel, and Jonathan Weigel, "The World Has a $2.5T Problem: Here's How to Solve It," *New York Times,* April 20, 2021; Hannah Beech, "Lavish Parties for the Rich, a Covid Outbreak for the Poor," *New York Times,* June 6, 2021.
25. World Bank, "'Absolutely Unacceptable' COVID-19 Vaccination Rates in Developing Countries | The Development Podcast," August 3, 2021.
26. Jason Mitchell, "IMF: African Economies Are the World's Fastest Growing," *Financial Times,* October 17, 2019; International Monetary Fund, "Recovery During a Pandemic," *World Economic Outlook,* October 2021.
27. United Nations Conference on Trade and Development, "The Least Developed Countries Report 2020: Productive Capacities for the New Decade," December 3, 2020.
28. International Monetary Fund, "Recovery During a Pandemic."
29. "Chinese Economy to Overtake US 'by 2028' Due to Covid," *BBC News,* December 26, 2020.
30. Yen Nee Lee, "The U.S. Will Remain Richer Than China for the Next 50 Years or More, Says Economist," CNBC, March 26, 2021.
31. World Bank, "World Bank Country and Lending Groups," 2021.
32. Barry Eichengreen, Donghyun Park, and Kwanho Shin, "Is Economic Growth in Middle-Income Countries Different from Low-Income Countries?" Brookings Institution, September 25, 2017.
33. United Nations Development Programme, *Human Development Report 2000.*
34. "Covid-19 Data: Tracking Covid-19 Excess Deaths Across Countries," *The Economist,* May 11, 2021; Marco Aquino and Marcelo Rochabrun, "Peru Revises Pandemic Death Toll, Now Worst in the World Per Capita," *Reuters,* June 1, 2021.
35. World Bank, "Under Five Mortality," 2021; World Health Organization, "Children: Improving Survival and Well-Being," September 8, 2020.
36. "Billions Without Clean Water and Sanitation 'a Moral Failure,'" *UN News,* March 18, 2021; World Health Organization, "Fact Sheet: Sanitation," November 2016.
37. United Nations, "Sustainable Development Goals, Goal 6: Ensure Access to Water and Sanitation for All," 2019; World Health Organization, "1 in 3 People Globally Do Not Have Access to Safe Drinking Water," June 18, 2019.
38. United Nations Population Fund, "Child Marriage, Female Genital Mutilation Urgent Priorities as Pandemic Threatens Progress," February 1, 2021; United Nations Department of Economic and Social Affairs, "The World's Women 2020: Trends and Statistics," October 20, 2020.
39. Bhadra Sharma and Jeffrey Gettleman, "In Nepal and Across the World, Child Marriage Is Rising," *New York Times,* March 8, 2021; United Nations Department of Economic and Social Affairs, "The World's Women 2020: Trends and Statistics"; Kristof, "Starving Children."

40. World Bank, "Adolescent Fertility Rate," 2021.

41. Washington Muzari, "Gender Disparities and the Role of Women in Smallholder Agriculture in Sub-Saharan Africa," *International Journal of Science and Research* 5, no. 1 (January 2016).

42. World Bank, "Labor Force Participation Rate, Female," January 29, 2021.

43. Esteban Ortiz-Ospina, Sandra Tzvetkova, and Max Roser, "Women's Employment," OurWorldInData.org, March 2018.

44. Organisation for Economic Co-operation and Development/International Labour Organization, "Tackling Vulnerability in the Informal Economy," 2019; United Nations, "Equal Pay for Work of Equal Value," 2020.

45. UNICEF, "Primary Education," April 2021.

46. "Latin America's Silent Tragedy of Empty Classrooms," *The Economist,* June 4, 2021.

47. Julie Turkewitz, "1+1=4? Latin America Faces a Drop Out Crisis," *New York Times,* June 27, 2021.

48. UNICEF, "Primary Education."

49. Divyanshi Wadhwa, "More Men Than Women Are Literate," *World Bank Blogs,* September 5, 2019; UNICEF, "Girls' Education," 2020.

50. "Digital Around the World," *DataReportal,* April 2021.

51. United Nations Development Programme, "What Is Human Development?" *Human Development Report 2015.*

6

Aid, Trade, and Debt: Contending Views on Development

> The resentment here is that the whole world eats well, and we do not, and nobody remembers us.
> —*Liez Quispe, Peruvian farmer*[1]

> How can it be possible that a garment is cheaper than a sandwich? How can a product that needs to be sown, grown, harvested, combed, spun, knitted, cut and stitched, finished, printed, labeled, packaged and transported cost a couple of euros?
> —*Li Edelkoort, trend forecaster*[2]

Now that you have the backstory on the global economy, let's talk about how it can work better. The answer, of course, differs depending on whom you ask—and this chapter compares and contrasts the major and contending paradigms that claim to have the answers: NEOLIBERALISM, STRUCTURALISM, and (to a lesser degree) ECONOMIC NATIONALISM. First off, it is important to keep in mind that none of these schools of thought is monolithic. Each is a worldview defined by certain core or fundamental beliefs. But there are differences within each school of thought. For example, there are disagreements within each over how far and how fast to go with their recommended changes. Thus, there are moderate and radical divides within each paradigm. Ideologically, neoliberalism includes proponents who run from center to right (moderate liberals to conservatives) on the political spectrum, whereas structuralism runs from the center left (progressives) to the far left. On the other hand, economic nationalism is divided between left- and right-wing variants that disagree about almost everything—except the need to protect domestic producers from foreign competition and what they consider to be unfair trade.

This chapter is about these paradigms, their differing views on GLOBALIZATION, and how we can do better. Elsewhere in this book, globalization is discussed more broadly, in terms of its sociocultural and political aspects, and how it has spilled over to affect just about everything: social relations (including class, race, and gender relations), culture, politics—even climate. In this chapter, we focus on globalization as an economic phenomenon. One thing its fans and critics agree on is that globalization should be understood as the spread of capitalism worldwide, or the exchange of products, services, people, and technology. Globalization is an all-embracing, multidimensional force based in ECONOMIC LIBERALIZATION, or the adoption of capitalist, market-based reforms. Those who subscribe to what has long been the dominant paradigm, neoliberalism, are proponents of this economic liberalization, arguing for free (or open) markets and laissez-faire economics, the French term for "let it be." By this, neoliberals mean that government's proper role is to withdraw from economics as much as possible and to "let economics be"—or allow the "invisible hand" of supply and demand to work. Market forces allowed to operate unimpeded by government interference maximize efficiency, according to these analysts.

Consequently, neoliberals regard globalization as a positive force that helps to further integrate the economies of the world into the INTERNATIONAL ECONOMIC SYSTEM, or the network of world trade based on the remains of a system formed in the post–World War II era. This system is capitalist, and it is underpinned by powerful institutions and organizations, most notably the INTERNATIONAL MONETARY FUND (IMF). Both the IMF and its sister organization, the WORLD BANK, were founded in the years after World War II, initially to assist in the reconstruction of Europe. Each of these multilateral institutions has its own mandate, but over the years their roles have changed and today there is some overlap in their functions. Both organizations are dominated by richer countries, since decisions in these INTERNATIONAL GOVERNMENTAL ORGANIZATIONS (IGOs) are made through weighted voting (i.e., based on each member country's financial contribution).

Whereas the World Bank's stated mission is to provide DEVELOPMENT assistance to the world's poorest countries, the IMF serves in a number of capacities, including the promotion of global economic stability. One way the IMF promotes stability is by serving as the lender of last resort to countries in economic crisis. It distributes loans to countries whose economies are failing.

According to neoliberals, further INTEGRATION into the world economy is exactly what under-developed countries need. LMICs should embrace globalization and raise growth rates by trading more in the international marketplace and competing to attract foreign capital. The WORLD TRADE ORGANIZATION (WTO) works to promote free trade by providing a forum for discussion of the unresolved issues that cause friction between states. Established in 1995, the WTO has significant influence as a referee in trade disputes, since its 164 members account for more than 98 percent of the world's trade.[3] Neoliberals contend that because global capitalism is the best hope for the development of the global south, the WTO provides an invaluable service. Over the past two decades (until Covid), the free flow of technology, capital, and ideas was raising living standards higher, faster, and for more people than at any other time in history.[4] Yet, while middle- and low-income countries are still being encouraged to liberalize their economies, they recognize, in a very real way, their vulnerability to negative trends from the developed world. You know . . . when the rich sneeze, the poor catch pneumonia.

Part of what makes globalization such a fascinating process to study is that it is ambiguous. It can have positive as well as negative effects. It can contribute to increased cooperation and unity while, at the same time, creating conditions for fragmentation and conflict. As Thomas Friedman has pointed out, globalization is everything and its opposite. It can be incredibly empowering and incredibly coercive. Both proponents and critics of globalization agree on its overwhelming force. Neoliberals contend that when it comes to LMICs' absorption into the international economy, the question isn't so much "When?" as it is "How?"[5]

On the other hand, structuralists maintain that the majority of the world's countries already share a common position within the world economy: they are relatively powerless within it. Poorer countries as a whole suffer from a structural disadvantage. They have little influence in setting the agenda or making decisions for the international economic system. Through its enforcement of the existing rules of trade, the World Trade Organization further marginalizes LMICs. Although low- and middle-income countries have joined the WTO, in general it is the richer countries that are much more enthusiastic about the existence of the WTO than are low-income countries, many of which view the organization as just another way for the rich to protect their advantageous position within the existing system.

Structuralists accuse the WTO of selectively dismantling trade barriers in lopsided liberalization that is skewed in favor of industrialized countries and MULTINATIONAL CORPORATIONS (MNCs). In some cases, WTO rules that promote free trade in manufactured goods force LMICs to open up their markets to the products of HICs, while the products of LMICs, especially agricultural goods such as orange juice, often face the highest trade barriers and are effectively shut out of the rich countries' markets.

Together, the world's forty-seven poorest countries (or "emerging and developing," depending on your view) count for less than 1 percent of global trade.[6] Ironically, for all their talk about "free trade," it is the various protectionist measures of advanced economies that have made it hard for much of the global south to earn an honest living through trade. One way that countries boost their own producers while hurting foreign competition is through subsidies, or payments to domestic producers (sometimes small farmers, but often large agribusiness corporations). In 2019, the United States and the European Union (EU) together spent over $150 billion on agricultural subsidies. China spent even more—$185 billion—subsidizing agricultural production to support their own domestic producers' agricultural exports, boosting (over)production and driving down world prices for commodities like sugar, wheat, and rice.[7]

Structuralists characterize this as hypocrisy and call for a different kind of globalization and a renegotiation of the rules of fair trade. However, others argue that the leaders of richer countries should simply practice the free trade they preach. If the governments of the United States and Europe, as well as China and India, cut the billions of dollars each year that they spend protecting their own farmers with agricultural subsidies, it could dramatically improve the welfare of millions of households worldwide. As it is, since these subsidies drive the world market price for their goods so low, farmers elsewhere can't compete; they try to scrape together a living by moving into new areas and overworking the land, causing significant environmental damage.[8]

One turn of events did give many structuralists pause (briefly). In what was called a "historic breakthrough" on cotton, in 2009 Brazil successfully challenged

US agricultural subsidies at the WTO. The WTO found that the US price support program for cotton violated trade agreements. The United States resisted the ruling, but promised to reform its subsidy program and agreed to pay Brazil hundreds of millions of dollars in compensation. At first, the WTO decision appeared to reflect a shift in bargaining power. It showed developing countries that they might have a chance at promoting their rights through the enforcement of free trade rules. However, in the end, the United States only replaced its old subsidies with new ones—and little actually changed.[9]

Structuralists argue that one way or another, the leaders of LMICs are effectively immobilized by the combined influence of richer countries' governments, corporations, and INTERNATIONAL FINANCIAL INSTITUTIONS (IFIs). They maintain that agents of globalization, such as the International Monetary Fund and the World Trade Organization, wield such power over developing countries that they are in effect being recolonized. Though LMICs can bring their complaints to the WTO, they frequently cannot afford costly legal battles. The WTO offers some legal aid, but it is limited. Poor countries can't afford the lawyers and lobbyists that the MNCs and rich countries hire to find loopholes in trade rules and buy the influence they need. In sum, structuralists argue that SOVEREIGNTY is steadily being eroded as governments are forced to give their decisionmaking authority to the IMF, multinational corporations, and richer countries. Yet, others, such as UN Secretary-General António Guterres, recognize the discontent with globalization, but are optimistic about the ability of the system to reform itself. They point to the critical role of trade and call on the international community to commit to "a universal, rules-based, open, non-discriminatory and equitable multilateral trading system under the WTO."[10]

Trade

But is it possible to address the challenges of new economic realities and create a system that protects the vulnerable, while serving the interests of all? As you may have guessed by now, structuralists and economic nationalists doubt it. They argue trenchantly against the economic orthodoxy, while neoliberals accuse their critics on the left of overstating their case and ask what feasible alternative they offer. This is the case for trade as well. According to neoliberals, the best way to jump-start growth rates is to adopt a strategy of trade liberalization or free trade. They maintain that the wealthiest countries have built their success on trade and (okay, with a few notable exceptions) by being open to competition. In fact, neoliberals argue that there is not a single example in modern history of a country successfully developing without trading and integrating with the global economy.[11]

On the other hand, neoliberals point out, it is no coincidence that until recently at least, it's the poorest countries in the world that have been the least open to free trade. The countries that are worst-off have adopted a variety of protectionist policies, artificially "protecting" domestic producers by slapping tariffs on imports. This kind of government interference with trade is notoriously inefficient, argue the neoliberals. Countries that have adopted market reforms and opened their economies, such as Hong Kong, Singapore, and Chile,

Figure 6.1 We Know What They're Against. What Are They For?

Left- and right-wing economic nationalists disagree on almost everything, except their concerns about free trade and globalization. Economic nationalists call for:

- advancing national interests at the expense of foreign interests
- state intervention to promote domestic producers and protect them from foreign competition with tariffs and quotas
- punishing corporations that outsource jobs

Structuralists are more than just critics of neoliberalism. They propose a different kind of globalization and a model of development that is based on principles of social, economic, and environmental justice. They may disagree over how far and how fast to go, but they agree that "another world is possible." The following are a few structuralist recommendations for a new economic system:

- replace the corporate view of economic liberalization with a more democratic and participatory model
- allow developing countries more of a voice in the international organizations that dominate their lives
- adopt grassroots approaches that prioritize sustainable human development and security
- promote public investment with a massive mobilization of resources for a Green New Deal: decarbonize, create green-collar jobs, and raise living standards
- adopt public or state management of the economy (instead of leaving it to market forces)
- end structural violence (extreme poverty) and other forms of economic, social, and environmental degradation
- expand the welfare state: guarantee a decent quality of life for all and fund it through progressive taxation
- diversify economies and trading relationships and promote regional integration
- grant preferential (nonreciprocal) trade preferences to countries in the global south
- establish resource cartels to stabilize (and raise) commodity prices
- regulate multinational corporations and hold them accountable
- promote agrarian reform and transfers of appropriate technology to the global south
- promote equity and pro-poor policies: target investments to benefit low-income groups
- increase foreign aid and put fewer conditions on aid
- forgive debt

Sources: Structuralist recommendations come from a variety of sources, including Miatta Fahnbulleh, "The Neoliberal Collapse," *Foreign Affairs* (January–February 2020); Joseph Stiglitz, *Making Globalization Work* (New York: Norton, 2007); Thomas Piketty, *Time for Socialism: Dispatches from a World on Fire, 2016–2021* (New Haven: Yale University Press, 2021).

have reaped the largest gains in terms of standards of living. Simply put, open economies grow much faster than closed economies. According to neoliberals, the existence of fast-growing economic powerhouses like China and India proves that it is possible to thrive in the current economic system.[12]

As mentioned earlier, neoliberalism's critics include structuralists from the left and economic nationalists, mostly (but not exclusively) from the right. Viewing international institutions and globalization as threats to national sovereignty, economic nationalists are POPULISTS who argue that the neoliberals are hypocrites when it comes to openness. They argue that free markets and openness do not guarantee wealth; a country's wealth depends less on ease of trade than it does on what is being traded.[13]

Yes, economic nationalists feel like the system has failed them. Long dormant but always just beneath the surface, this latest iteration of economic nationalism popped up due to pent-up frustration over the global financial meltdown in 2007 and Great Recession of 2007–2009. In the years leading up to the PANDEMIC, stagnation in economically developed countries fueled economic nationalism—a go-it-alone ideology with the right (i.e., Donald Trump's "Make America Great Again"). Economic nationalism is an ideology and global phenomenon embraced by people around the world, in advanced, emerging, and developing economies. Examples of its leaders include the United Kingdom's prime minister Boris Johnson and Brazil's president Jair Bolsonaro. Also known as economic populism, this camp favors protectionism and state intervention (or STATE CAPITALISM) in the economy to protect a country's economy and its people from the hardships suffered due to neoliberals and a free market. With a focus inward, nationalists largely reject multilateralism as an assault on national sovereignty (e.g., economic nationalism was the idea behind Brexit, or the British exit from the European Union, and President Trump's renegotiation of the North American Free Trade Agreement (NAFTA). Economic nationalists press companies headquartered in their countries to invest in and support workers at home (although only the nativist, right-wing version veers into "exclusionary nationalism," with its hostility toward imported goods and foreign workers—and immigrants).[14]

As populists, those on the right tend to be skeptical of those they regard as governmental and scientific elites. For example, if they're not outright Covid denialists and ANTI-VAXXERS, right-wing economic nationalists are proud vaccine nationalists, putting their own citizens first in line, ahead of more vulnerable populations. In addition, these economic nationalists consider themselves the true patriots and are all about "us versus them." They are critical of multilateral, cooperative efforts to deal with the virus (an example is Trump's withdrawal of the United States from the World Health Organization in the midst of the pandemic).

On the other hand, there are economic nationalists on the left who seek to distance themselves from such views. As we will discuss later, they too are certainly skeptical of Big Pharma and other multinational corporations, but they are far more likely to make the argument that no one is safe until all are (as the longer the virus circulates in populations, there will be new variants, possibly adding new dangers). Like structuralists, they accept many aspects of INTERDEPENDENCE that the people of the world are bound together by an array of mutual vulnerabilities. Left-wing populists reject the nativism of those to their right, but economic nationalists of all stripes share concerns about how globalization outsourced jobs, contributed to inequality, and disproportionately benefited elites. Open to socialist ideals, left-wing economic nationalists also join structuralists in their concern not only about the economic but also about the environmental disasters created by neoliberalism. They blame neoliberalism for failing people and the earth by putting GROWTH above all else, encouraging consumption and the use of fossil fuels.[15]

Structuralists also blame neoliberals for a TOP-DOWN, flawed trade policy that has shipped jobs overseas. They support using the state that works for all—not just the wealthy—to solve these problems (e.g., with progressive taxation and incentivizing or forcing businesses to pay workers a fair wage). As such, left-wing economic nationalists also share many of the structuralists' calls for an alternative, new economic model that adapts socialist ideas to the contemporary era.[16] By taking a BOTTOM-UP APPROACH and prioritizing SUSTAINABLE DEVELOPMENT that includes protection of the natural environment, structuralists differ dramatically from many traditional socialists and the right. However, both ends of the spectrum come together to criticize neoliberalism and call for "fair trade rather than free trade."

Economic nationalists agree that openness involves great risk, and the countries experiencing relative success are few and far between. Not all countries can achieve the success of China, nor should they want to follow the Chinese example, which has embraced globalization but is hardly the model of an open economy. Structuralists agree, and are likely to make the point, that the impetus toward trade liberalization and embrace of globalization is nothing new. In fact, many argue that the reason why so much of the global south is under-developed today is because of the position it was assigned during colonialism. As a result, their economies have been based for years on agricultural goods or minerals.

However, for decades now, the share of agriculture in total employment has been shrinking across all country income groups. Globally, it has contracted by close to a third, from 44 percent in 1991 to 28 percent in 2018.[17] More LMICs are moving in to fill the voids in manufacturing and some, such as China, India, and Indonesia, are moving into the service sectors (based on the provision of services rather than the provision of goods: financial services, hospitality, retail, health, human services, information technology, and education). The textile and steel mills that were once so important to the US, British, and German economies have long since moved south, creating the existing division of labor.

One aspect of this division of labor that is actually not so new is the expansion of regional and product specialization, based in the principle of COMPARATIVE ADVANTAGE. Seeking to increase efficiency through specialization in production, the colonizers created monocultural economies throughout Africa, Asia, Latin America, and the Middle East. This principle, widely revered by liberals for hundreds of years, is based in the assumption that countries differ in their ability to produce certain goods based on their natural resources, labor, and other factors. To maximize wealth, countries should specialize in producing goods for which they have a comparative advantage.

Today, the vast majority of poorer countries continue to produce many of the same goods assigned to them during the days of colonialism—unprocessed primary goods for export. This makes good business sense, according to neoliberals. By concentrating on a few goods for export, LIC economies can become more fully integrated into the world economy. With the hard currency they earn from the sale of their raw materials, LICs can pay their debts and import everything else they need (including food, fuel, and manufactured goods). Moreover, if all countries liberalize their economies and open up to trade, it will mean that businesses will have to work harder to be competitive. The result will be improved and less expensive products—a benefit to all.

Yet, neoliberalism's critics on the left argue that it isn't quite that simple. Although many people are giving up and heading for the cities, 80 percent of the world's poor continue to live in rural areas and work mostly as farmers.[18] During colonialism rural communities were disrupted, many subsistence farmers were forced off the land, and small plots were consolidated into large plantations. This is happening again, but the scale is unprecedented. And it is expected to continue, as rising world food prices have led to a land rush in which private foreign investors and governments are purchasing or leasing millions of hectares of arable land where land rights are weak or unclear. The result is that tens of thousands of farmers are displaced, losing their livelihoods.[19]

Those so far unaffected by such deals farm plots of various sizes; most are smallholders (working tiny plots of two hectares or less) or are landless. The landless often drift around the countryside looking for seasonal work, and are employed as tenant farmers or as migrant laborers on much larger farms or plantations. Smallholders in developed and less developed countries are rapidly being displaced as they find that they can no longer support themselves through farming and are increasingly forced to sell their land to huge agribusinesses. What small farmers had in common is that they once practiced subsistence farming. Farmers ate what they produced and sold the surplus.

However, today the majority of countries have moved away from food production and can no longer be considered subsistence economies. Rather, these are export-based economies, increasingly centered on the production of commodities known as cash crops. Coffee, flowers, sisal, and bananas are just a few examples of cash crops, which are produced for sale abroad (mostly to consumers in developed countries). Mines producing bauxite, copper, and diamonds, and aquaculture and ranches producing salmon and beef, are also sites for the production of cash crops. What these commodities have in common is that they are raw materials, or unprocessed goods that will most likely be sent elsewhere for manufacture into finished goods.

Structuralists argue that as producers of raw materials, LICs are assigned a disadvantageous position in the world economic system, and not only because most raw materials are vulnerable to sometimes dramatic price fluctuations that make it extremely difficult to plan or budget from year to year. It is a rule of economics that labor adds value. Because raw materials are unprocessed, they will always fetch a lower price than they would once processed into a finished good. The prices of exports by higher-middle-income countries (HMICs) (mostly finished goods) have risen. Meanwhile (with the exception of windfall gains from time to time for a few producers due to strong demand for a few commodities like oil, aluminum, and copper), the prices of "soft" commodities (most of Africa's exports) have been falling, suffering a deterioration in the terms of trade.[20]

The "terms of trade," or the overall relationship between the prices of exported and imported goods, are therefore inherently disadvantageous to LICs' economies. Producers of raw materials must struggle to turn out larger volumes just to earn the hard currency to pay for the higher-priced finished goods they must import. The laws of supply and demand simply work against the LICs. For example, Ghanaian farmers can work harder to produce more cocoa for sale on the world market, but the harder they work the less they will earn, since an oversupply of cocoa will drive down its price. In other words, prices are driven down even further as farmers inadvertently add to the problem of oversupply. They produce even more when prices are down, since it takes a bigger crop to scrape by. Meanwhile, because they do not produce the things that they need, these countries are heavily dependent on imports (but without much income to pay for them). The result is that they import more than they export, contributing to a trade imbalance (which they must finance, often by going into debt).

Import dependence, especially within the food and energy sectors, continues to be a very real challenge for many countries in the global south. Only six countries, including the United States and Russia, dominate cereal exports, but cereal imports are spread across a large number of countries in all regions (and China alone accounts for more than 5 percent of total imports). Many feared that governments might respond to the Covid crisis with policies to restrict food exports, or that Covid might contribute to labor or logistical bottlenecks that could raise prices and have a devastating effect on the world food supply (which it did). Because both countries are major food exporters, Russia's attack on Ukraine shocked global commodity markets, exacerbating this trend. Because so many LMICs are heavily dependent on importing food, the concern was that as many as 265 million people across 30 countries could face starvation.[21] But this isn't a new worry; even before the pandemic dependence on food imports posed economic threats that (for better or worse) left countries vulnerable to political instability. For example, street protests in Sudan in 2019, which were initially triggered by an increase in the price of bread, ended up bringing in the coup that took down a long-standing dictatorship (it has since been replaced with another).[22]

There is little that producers of most raw materials can do about this situation as long as their economies remain centered around the production of cash crops for export. No single country can demand higher prices for its goods, since there are many other producers competing for the sale. And demand for most raw materials is relatively elastic. Even if producers of any single raw material could form a producer's club or cartel to obtain a stronger bargaining position (and some have), consumers could turn to substitutes—they could increase their own domestic production of the good, or simply adjust their consumption of it. It is only because demand for oil is relatively inelastic that the oil producers' cartel, the Organization of the Petroleum Exporting Countries, has been able to raise oil prices by slowing down production and restricting oil supplies.

But even oil exporters are not immune; they faced declines in revenue and increases in unrest following a slump in oil prices that continued after 2012 and was worsened by Covid in 2020 before oil prices picked up again in 2021 and shot to record highs in 2022. But the price of oil is affected by several factors, and oil producers can't count on stability in pricing. For example, Iraq's oil revenues declined by 47 percent between 2019 and 2020—their lowest annual level in a decade. The crisis had the potential to further destabilize the already-unstable government. It grated on Iraqis that Iraq, one of the world's largest oil producers, has been unable to provide a reliable supply of electricity to its citizens. Dependent on importing electricity from Iran, it was cut off for nonpayment, leaving large parts of the country in the dark for hours each day.[23]

Therefore, even for oil producers structuralists argue that the world economic system as it currently exists works to reinforce LMICs' dependence and leaves them vulnerable to a variety of problems. Having an undiversified economy is like putting all your eggs in one basket. Chinese manufacturers' appetite for commodities like iron ore, copper, and soybeans helped to raise the price of these goods in 2021, but amounted to a "re-primarization" of the economy and made it harder for countries like Peru to break out of the trap of exporting raw materials and get into the development of value-added manufactured goods and services.[24] When demand remains high, life is good, but then the bottom can fall out. Whenever the world's largest economies slow, the spillover effects hit the rest of the world, especially LMICs dependent on exports. These economies are vulnerable to swings in world market prices for their goods—as well as to blight, drought, and other causes of crop failure.

Moreover, overreliance on the export of one raw material (or a few) has left countries that were once self-sufficient in the production of food crops, like Nigeria, now dependent on food imports. Even worse, some countries with hungry populations produce food crops for export. Brazil, for example, although trying to ensure that its own population is fed, has been tearing down its forests to grow soybeans (a lucrative cash crop) to satisfy Chinese and European demand. Whereas the IMF and neoliberal donor agencies encourage low- and medium-income economies to focus on export-based production as a means of earning revenue, critics maintain that such a focus is unlikely to produce healthy economies that can support their populations.

Most LMICs have had little choice but to accept the neoliberals' advice. And although many countries have attempted to diversify their economies, this is easier said than done. The poorer the country, the more likely its economy is centered on five or fewer products.[25] The economies of many developing countries are dominated by primary commodity dependence on agricultural goods or minerals. As mentioned earlier, this is often associated with heightened vulnerability to external shocks. Economic concentration also undermines the prospects for economic growth and development. Economic diversification, or the export of new products to new markets, helps manage volatility and provide stability. But creating a new export mix requires a structural transformation of their economies. This transformation has often involved a shift from agricultural to nonagricultural sectors, or from manufacturing to services. Moving to a more diverse production and trade structure is a complex process that, among other things, means coordinated policy reforms, a reallocation of resources across industries, and an investment in infrastructure. Although key to economic development and poverty reduction, diversification remains a challenge for most, especially those that are small and landlocked or geographically remote, which also tend to be the world's poorest countries.[26]

But perhaps there are even worse things than a monocultural economy. Some governments are so desperate to earn hard currency that they have joined the booming business of refuse disposal. As citizens worldwide became more interested in recycling and aware of the dangers of pollutants to human health and comfort, an international trade in recycling and refuse removal emerged. Many LICs that found it difficult making ends meet competed to recycle or house the garbage of richer countries, often shipped as second-hand goods from richer to poorer countries or exported illegally or under the guise of being for reuse. The most visible items in this trade are plastics, but they also include e-waste, or electronic waste (discarded computers, televisions, and cell phones) that can be hazardous. In many LICs waste management is left to the INFORMAL SECTOR, known to cause severe health problems for workers as well as children who often live, work, and play in or nearby these dumping grounds.[27]

This is a problem that is only worsening. With continuous upgrades and a growing sense of the disposable nature of these products, one observer stated that "we are facing the onset of an unprecedented tsunami of electronic waste rolling out over the world."[28] This practice of wealthy (predominantly white) populations dumping their (often-poisonous) wastes into poor (predominantly Black or brown) communities is known as environmental racism. Many countries, such as China (which used to accept much of that waste), Malaysia, Vietnam, and the Philippines, have had enough and refuse to accept rich countries' garbage, in some cases shipping so-called recyclables back to Europe and North America.[29]

Yet, accepting rich countries' garbage is only one example of how poorer countries have attempted to cope with their weak position within the international economic system. While some initiatives are best understood simply as coping mechanisms, others aim to change the place of poorer countries within the system. IMPORT SUBSTITUTION INDUSTRIALIZATION is an example of one such effort. In an attempt to follow the developed country path to development through industrialization, many LICs have sought to break out of the mold as exporters of unfinished goods and lessen their dependence on imports. Neoliberals have long pointed to East Asia as evidence that capitalist development worked. The export-driven economies of what were called the FOUR TIGERS—Hong Kong, Singapore, South Korea, and Taiwan, all highly successful emerging markets—were based on the production and export of manufactured goods. For decades, their growth rates regularly exceeded 5 percent per year, and during their boom years it averaged nearly 20 percent (double many LMICs). Per capita income increased more rapidly in these economies than anywhere else in the world. Between 1953 and 2018, for example, GNI per capita in South Korea grew almost 500-fold (from $76 to $33,434)—far surpassing that of Brazil, China, and India. There were similar gains in life expectancy and literacy rates, and an overall reduction in poverty in South Korea and the other industrializing countries.[30]

This is such an astounding success story because coming out of the Korean War (1950–1953), South Korea was one of the poorest countries in the world. Over half the population lived in ABSOLUTE POVERTY in the 1950s. Yet, this number was dramatically reduced over the years to an estimated 2 percent in 2019. Sure, income inequality has grown, and as of 2019 16 percent of the population (mostly the elderly) lived in RELATIVE POVERTY (defined in South Korea as less than half of the median disposable income, or less than $10,500 a year).[31] Thus, even in "success stories" like South Korea and in other advanced economies across the world, millions of young people enter the job market each year, likely to join a permanent underclass not so different than that of those living "down below," as satirized in the 2019 South Korean award-winning film *Parasite.*

Like every country, South Korea has its problems, but neoliberals hold it up as a model for others to emulate. Yet, despite South Korea's successes, analysts have always disagreed about whether the experience of the Four Tigers could be replicated elsewhere. Neoliberals attributed the success of these emerging economies to their openness, embrace of capitalism, and export-oriented approach as well as their well-educated, disciplined, and hardworking labor force. In addition, emerging economies were credited with having an innovative entrepreneurial class, a high rate of savings, and relatively well-developed infrastructures.

Still, it should be noted that the success of these countries was hardly due to *less* state involvement in economies. This was not laissez-faire capitalism at work. Actually, it was economic nationalism. Under the Asian model of state capitalism adopted in the 1950s, governments were heavily involved in nurturing and protecting industries and businesses until they were globally competitive. Although there is some heterogeneity among the East Asian emerging economies, in most cases these states undertook what is called an export offensive. Throughout the region, governments manipulated nationalist interests to promote economic mobilization. Under this policy, the state became a driving force, directing the economy with the aim of improving international competitiveness. The South Korean and Taiwanese governments, and those of other emerging economies like Vietnam, directed economic growth through their allocation of credit to priority sectors. Scarcely a case of the "invisible hand" at work, these governments played an active, catalytic role in guiding investment strategies toward infrastructure and education. They offered incentives and disincentives to prod the economy toward particular exporting industries. Most of these industries were initially light manufacturing and labor-intensive, but gradually became higher-tech. These infant industries were nurtured and protected; the state intervened aggressively and employed protectionist practices to ensure that domestic firms could compete with foreigners.[32]

At the same time that these governments were insulating their infant industries from foreign competition, they avidly sought to attract foreign investment. Decades ago, South Korea and Taiwan successfully lured investors by offering tax incentives, keeping unions weak, and eliminating minimum wage legislation. For many years, these East Asian governments could only be characterized as dictatorships determined to modernize. These AUTHORITARIAN regimes manipulated nationalist identities to mobilize the population to work and sacrifice for the good of the nation. Governments provided little in terms of social welfare. Air and water pollution soared. Political and civil rights were forsaken for economic growth, and governments used repressive mechanisms to resist popular pressure for change.

It is important to note that incomes in Taiwan, South Korea, and the other emerging economies of Asia have gradually improved, as have quality-of-life indicators and (with the notable exception of China, Vietnam, and a few others) respect for political and civil liberties. But it is primarily because of this policy of aggressive government intervention in the economy that the emerging markets were able to capture shares on certain goods. For example, today the East Asian economies make up the world's largest source of electronic components (in 2020, 90 percent of the world's laptops were made in China but, due to rising labor costs, half of them will be manufactured in Vietnam and Thailand by 2030).[33]

These countries base their success on the partnerships that their governments made with businesses to raise productivity and capture an increasing share of the world market. Although this close relationship has been characterized as "crony capitalism" because it is associated with corrupt practices, it has also resulted in the creation of huge economic conglomerates. These economies were so competitive and their performances so strong that, in some cases, they dominated the market in certain goods. For nearly three decades, many of these emerging economies have enjoyed trade surpluses with developed countries. Consequently, the IMF now characterizes Hong Kong, South Korea, and Taiwan as advanced economies. But it is important to remember that, so far, their experience is the exception, not the rule.

Foreign Investment

MNCs in the global south are nothing new; since the days of colonialism (and often predating it) multinational corporations have been active throughout Asia, Africa, the Middle East, and Latin America. In low- and middle-income countries, these businesses have dominated the agriculture and mining sectors. Until a few decades ago, relatively few of the world's manufactured goods were produced in LMICs. However, as mentioned earlier, this has been changing. Some non-Western countries have industrialized (especially East Asia, less so in Africa), and more and more MNCs are looking to lower the costs of production by creating assembly plants overseas. These corporations are highly influential nongovernmental actors in the process of globalization; their investment decisions often mean the difference between whether a country is increasingly drawn into the global economy, or marginalized by it.

Neoliberals and their critics agree that MNCs are extremely powerful economic entities with an enormous scope and range of activities, including banking, pharmaceuticals, industrial goods, oil, foodstuffs, service—virtually any consumer item or need. Coordinating production on a global scale, they are hardly newcomers to the global economy; their precursors, such as the Dutch East India Company, were at the forefront of colonialism. Now as then, as economic units, the largest MNCs (Walmart continued to rank as number 1 in 2020) easily dwarf the vast majority of non-Western economies. As of 2018, of the world's 100 richest economic entities, 69 were corporations, not countries. Apple, Walmart, and Shell each have more cash on hand than relatively rich countries like Russia, Belgium, and Sweden.[34] Analysts have been predicting for years that soon the vast majority of the world's production will be controlled by a handful of powerful MNCs. Such predictions seem to be coming true, as nearly every day one learns of another acquisition, merger, or buyout among these corporate behemoths.

MNCs are headquartered in what we call parent countries and, for many years, these were almost exclusively located in the global north. Until 2020, the United States was home to the largest number of Fortune Global 500 companies, but China has since surpassed the United States as the leading single source of foreign direct investment. Japan was third, followed by France and Germany.[35] It is in parent countries where decisions are made, and to which profits return. Yet, because of their size, some predict that in the not-too-distant future the power of MNCs may overtake that of the NATION-STATE. For decades, sociologists have predicted that our primary IDENTITY may change as we come to view ourselves more as employees of the company for which we work than as citizens of the country in which we live. In many ways, the power of MNCs already rivals that of the nation-state. While MNCs have been accused of being agents of their national governments, the governments of their parent countries are often put to work for the corporation's interests. US interventions to protect MNC interests in Chile, Iran, and Guatemala are just a few examples of political meddling, including the overthrow of LIC governments, when MNCs and developed countries have perceived a government's politics as threatening to the economic status quo.

However, today, it is increasingly common to hear that the once-cozy relationship between corporations and their parent countries is over. Multinational because of their international operations, MNCs are truly stateless entities, not obligated to any particular country. For years, the United States and other countries have bemoaned their inability to force MNCs to comply with their foreign policies (e.g., cooperating with sanctions against Iran).

As you may already be sensing, the role that MNCs play in development is extremely controversial (neoliberals applaud them, structuralists and economic nationalists are more critical of them). However, stripped of all the politics, MNCs are simply for-profit corporations with activities abroad stemming from foreign direct investment. Through their investments these businesses establish subsidiaries or branches in what are known as host countries. New foreign investment worldwide tanked in 2020 due to concerns about Covid but, for years, a high percentage of MNC activity in the global south has been concentrated in Brazil, Singapore, Hong Kong, and India.[36] However, leading the pack is China, which passed the United States as the number one recipient of foreign investment in 2020. There and elsewhere, these corporations argue that they are just managing the production cycle, cutting costs by subcontracting the work. For example, to avoid US tariffs targeting China, Foxconn, the Taiwanese company that manufactures Apple's iPods, shifted their assembly out of China to Vietnam.[37]

As for-profit enterprises, MNCs are constantly seeking to improve their profit margins. Two of the easiest ways of accomplishing this are to lower overhead costs and expand markets. That is precisely what these corporations are doing, whether they are investing in LMICs or in other developed countries. So much foreign investment goes to China because MNCs want access to the potential spending power of the country's 1.3 billion consumers as much as they want the cheap labor. And it was cheap: at the turn of the twenty-first century, some workers in China labored in SWEATSHOPS for as little as 3 cents per hour.[38] Average wages in China have risen over the past few years—manufacturing wages have more than doubled since 2011. Yet, even relatively well-paid Chinese tech workers are known for suffering punishing labor conditions, such as "996" (a 9 A.M. to 9 P.M., 6-day, 72-hour workweek). It was only after several tech workers died that a Chinese court declared 996 illegal. It has since been replaced by "1075," a 10 A.M. to 7 P.M., five-day workweek.[39]

Although it too has been replaced, China's one-child policy has resulted in labor shortages in China. Fewer workers, as well as worker demands for higher wages and improved working and living conditions, have led merchandisers such as H&M, Zara, and Walmart to move production to countries such as Bangladesh, Cambodia, and Vietnam, where wages are even lower. Many Southeast Asian nations are home to large labor pools with low wages (in 2019, a worker earning the average minimum wage in rural China earned $217 a month, compared to $18 a month in Bangladesh and $10 a month in the Philippines).[40] In Myanmar, a low-cost clothing manufacturing hub, clothing exports increased from just under $1 billion in 2011 (10 percent of exports) to more than $6.5 billion in 2019 (30 percent of exports).[41] It is estimated that Covid shutdowns have resulted in the loss of millions of jobs across these industries.[42]

With little hope of employment in the INFORMAL SECTOR, large numbers of city dwellers turn to the underground economy, also known as the informal sector. Although it is the single largest employer in many LMICs, the informal economy is a shadow economy of sorts. Whether they are petty traders, domestic workers, or recyclers, workers in the informal sector often toil in difficult and dangerous conditions, for low pay, and without social protections. Including a wide range of activities, informal sector work is composed of semilegal or illegal activities transacted under the table, and therefore not included in the calculation of a country's gross domestic product. However, it is central to economies throughout the global south, where it is most commonly found. The UN estimates approximately two-thirds of the world's employed population—more than 2 billion people—work in the informal sector. Given its shadowy nature, the estimates range widely, but roughly 85 percent of the labor force in Africa, 68 percent in Asia and the Pacific, 40 percent in the Americas, and 16 percent in HICs are believed to work in the informal sector.[43]

Depending on the circumstances, work in MNC assembly plants can be considered formal or informal sector labor, but pretty much everywhere it is labor intensive and low skilled. In recent years, employers have become notorious for hiring women and paying them too little to live on, with the rationalization (true or not) that because women are supported by male breadwinners, their wages are mere "lipstick money" and need only to be supplemental. In addition, corporations base their preference for female labor on stereotypical ideas about women being "naturally" patient and better suited for the mind-numbing tedious labor demanded by MNCs. Female workers are assumed to be not only more dexterous (important, e.g., for sewing operations and in microprocessing computer chips) but also more docile than men, more accepting of male (managerial) authority, and less likely to join unions.

But factory jobs in particular were already at risk due to the so-called robot revolution that foretells the likely disappearance of low-skilled occupations around the world. Globally, the share of employment in manufacturing declined from 16 percent in 1991 to 14 percent in 2018. The United Nations Conference on Trade and Development (UNCTAD) estimates that two-thirds of jobs in the global south could be at risk of being displaced by automation. In some sectors, the potential losses are even greater. Between 75 and 90 percent of garment and footwear jobs in Cambodia and Vietnam, for example, are in jeopardy due to the introduction of automated assembly lines, known as "sewbots," throughout the industry.[44]

Although structuralists argue that until these workers are paid a decent wage, they are unlikely to become part of the consumer market the MNCs so look forward to, neoliberals urge us to take the long view and consider the presence of MNCs around the world generally as a positive force. They contend that foreign investment is an important agent for growth, generating wealth through the ability to invest freely around the world and the efficient use of the world's resources. According to the pro-MNC argument, when these corporations invest abroad by opening factories, mines, or plantations, they accelerate the development of the host country in a number of ways. MNCs create jobs and, frequently, employees of MNCs earn more than they could elsewhere in the economy. Generally, Chinese suppliers to Western multinationals are said to pay more generous wages and offer better conditions because these suppliers are regularly audited, or monitored for compliance with labor rules. (However, this may just be a way for companies to cover themselves. For example, in what would become a historic industrial accident, auditors had just deemed as safe the Rana Plaza factory building in Bangladesh that collapsed in 2013, killing more than 1,100 people.)[45]

According to the International Labour Organization, 2.3 million women and men around the world die in work-related accidents or from occupational diseases every year (that's over 6,000 each day, about one death every fifteen minutes). Workplace safety in China, which had a terrible rating, has improved a great deal in the past decade, thanks in part to a decline in coal mining accidents and deaths. Deaths on construction sites are, by far, the biggest industrial killer in China now (this is physically demanding and dangerous work in both the global north and south). The vast majority of these deaths involve falls, some kind of structural collapse, or mechanical failure. But the death toll, accident rate, and incidence of occupational disease overall are still relatively high in China. Food delivery workers are also at relatively high risk of death and injury, as traffic accidents in China are a major contributor to deaths and injuries.[46]

Sure, until companies are held accountable to these accidents, we can expect to see more of them. But neoliberals argue that a multinational's presence may mean other benefits for workers. Where Westerners have invested in joint ventures with Chinese firms, workers are said to have more rights, more institutionalized procedures for filing grievances, and so forth.[47] Neoliberals characterize structuralists and economic nationalists who are critical of free trade and foreign investment as "the well-intentioned but ill-informed" being led around by "the ill-intentioned but well-informed (protectionist unions, and anarchists)."[48] They maintain that consumer boycotts of the goods made in these factories are actually hurting workers in LMICs because such boycotts mean a loss of jobs. They offer examples of assembly-line workers in El Salvador, China, and Vietnam who are horrified that Americans would try to "help" them by putting them out of work. The MNCs are the ones "helping" them, by giving them a chance to earn a wage, say the neoliberals.

And neoliberals maintain that by offering people the opportunity to work for a wage, MNCs may be assisting in the development of the community as well. The creation of jobs has a spin-off effect for the larger economy, as MNC workers will spend their earnings on rent, food, and so forth, in the local economy. Furthermore, MNC employees will become skilled workers, familiar with the new technologies the company brings with it when it sets up shop. MNC employees and host countries in general are said to benefit from the corporation's presence, in that by simply being there, MNCs alter "traditional" attitudes. They are said to stimulate the spirit of innovation and entrepreneurship, teach important lessons about competitiveness, and create marketing networks that can extend into and benefit the local economy.[49]

On the other hand, critics of globalization, and of MNCs in particular, contend with virtually every argument the neoliberals put forward. As mentioned earlier, the primary grievance of economic nationalists is that their citizens' jobs are being exported. Meanwhile, structuralists maintain that MNCs, instead of being beacons for change, are actually predatory monopolies that compound an already skewed distribution of wealth. MNC activities widen the growing gap between rich and poor—not only between developed and less developed countries, but also within them. Structuralists maintain that a local ELITE, known as the COMPRADOR class, dominates LMIC economies and political systems, and makes sweetheart deals with these corporations to exploit their own people. For example, in return for kickbacks, a series of Nigerian political leaders and their cronies have nurtured a special relationship with Royal Dutch Shell and other oil companies to join in on the exploitation of the country's riches for the benefit of a few. Theirs is a reciprocal relationship in which compradors work to maintain a climate conducive to MNC interests, and the corporations in turn use their wealth and political clout to help keep local aristocracies in power. If the relationship falls apart, or the population elects a government less compliant and willing to accede to MNC prerogatives, MNCs have been known to "help create" a government more to their liking (as in the 1953 coup that overthrew the democratically elected government of Iran).

Moreover, structuralists and economic nationalists agree that even ordinary citizens of developed countries are at the mercy of these giants, as workers to be displaced in the constant quest for ever-cheaper labor. At the same time, consumers demanding "fast fashion" or goods made for a pittance are part of the problem. As many are starting to realize, "cheap food isn't cheap": a toll is taken on the producers of this food as well as the consumers of it. For decades, MNCs have sought to reduce the costs of overhead even further by setting up shop in thousands of EXPORT PROCESSING ZONES (EPZs) around the world. Corporations are attracted to EPZs because there they pay only minimal taxes. Similar efforts are being made to stop the practice of MNCs investing abroad where they can operate without being held to the environmental standards they would find at home. Emerging and developing as well as developed countries have been accused of taking part in a "race to the bottom," diluting environmental regulations and labor laws to attract investment. And it is working: corporations are finding it profitable to relocate for all of these reasons—especially for guarantees of cheap and controllable labor.

The most egregious examples of cheap and controllable labor involve human trafficking and various forms of modern-day slavery, with an estimated 25 million victims in every region of the world. "Human trafficking" is defined as "the recruitment, transportation, transfer, harboring or receipt of persons, by means of the threat or use of force or other forms of coercion, of abduction, of fraud, of deception, of the abuse of power or of a position of vulnerability or of the giving or receiving of payments or benefits to achieve the consent of a person having control over another person, for the purpose of exploitation."[50] Whether in the form of forced labor, begging, forced marriage, sexual exploitation, the removal

Figure 6.2 Ending the Race to the Bottom?

Viewed by some as a revival of multilateralism, the Group of 7 (G7), a club to promote policy coordination between the world's most advanced economies (Britain, Canada, France, Germany, Italy, Japan, and the United States), is seeking to ensure "the right companies pay the right tax in the right places."[a] In 2021, they were joined by nearly 140 other countries (tentatively including China, and comprising over 90 percent of the world's economies) who agreed to establish a global minimum corporate tax rate of 15 percent. In case you were wondering, the average tax rate for corporations was 23.85 percent in 2020. Advocates argue that setting such a rule is significant: it requires multinational corporations, including some of the largest digital giants like Amazon, Google, and Facebook, to pay taxes where they sell their goods—regardless of where their headquarters are located.[b]

If it goes as planned, a global minimum tax would stop companies from seeking out tax havens and block corporations from moving profits across borders to avoid taxes. However, the plan is likely to face resistance from companies—as well as from many countries, such as Singapore and Ireland that have for years competed for investment in a race to the bottom by offering sweetheart deals to MNCs. Although Ireland eventually relented, it and others pushed back, as did those who argue that 15 percent is far too low (the average global tax rate was 40 percent in 1980). The most enthusiastic proponents of the tax argue that the floor should be at least 25 percent, as 15 percent for corporations is less than the average American pays in state and federal income tax. Skeptics say that this kind of incrementalist reform won't really change things. Rather, it will overwhelmingly benefit richer countries as billions in revenues will flow to the HICs where most of the largest MNCs are headquartered. This will only increase inequality.[c]

Meanwhile, President Joe Biden faces resistance at home including from US Republicans (neoliberals and economic nationalists alike) who promise to oppose it, claiming either that it violates free market principles and hurts business or that the international tax reform amounts to ceding authority to foreign countries. Each country must pass legislation at home to fully activate the agreement by 2023. Thus, this landmark deal remains to be implemented, but it is historic, amounting to the biggest overhaul of corporate tax rules in a century. For some, it signifies an important step toward reshaping the rules of the global economy.[d]

Notes: a. Alan Rappeport, "G7 Finance Leaders Reach a Deal to Curb Offshore Tax Havens," *New York Times,* June 6, 2021.

b. Jeff Stein and Antonia Noori Farzan, "G-7 Countries Reach Agreement on 15 Percent Minimum Global Tax Rate," *Washington Post,* June 5, 2021.

c. Oxfam, "G7 Global Corporate Tax Deal Is Far from Fair: Oxfam," June 5, 2021; Jim Tankersley and Alan Rappeport, "Biden Finds Raising Corporate Tax Rates Easier Abroad Than at Home," *New York Times,* October 30, 2021.

d. "All in the Numbers: Corporate Tax Reform," *The Economist Espresso,* June 4, 2021; Rappeport, "G7 Finance Leaders Reach a Deal to Curb Offshore Tax Havens"; "130 Countries Agree Corporate Tax Minimum," *The Economist Espresso,* July 2, 2021; Alan Rappeport and Liz Alderman, "Global Deal to End Tax Havens Moves Ahead as Nations Back 15% Rate," *New York Times,* October 8, 2021; Tankersley and Rappeport, "Biden Finds Raising Corporate Tax Rates Easier Abroad Than at Home."

and sale of organs or children, and so forth, human trafficking is another problem exacerbated by the epidemic. The virus has aggravated the social and economic inequalities that are at the root of human trafficking. Driven to desperation by the loss of their livelihoods, analysts fear that more people are vulnerable to severe exploitation as they struggle to survive. Analysts believe that traffickers have adapted to take advantage of the pandemic. Meanwhile, government efforts to limit the spread of the disease have often made it easier for traffickers to hide their operations, making victims invisible. This makes identifying those who need help and providing them with that assistance—let alone holding traffickers accountable—all the more challenging.[51]

Children and marginalized groups are particularly vulnerable to exploitation, and often the state is the perpetrator of the abuse. It is estimated that in the *laogai,* or forced labor system in China, 80,000 ethnic Uighurs have been sent to work in factories that are part of an opaque supply chain making goods for brands like H&M and American Girl. The presence of forced labor in supply chains that feed into HICs is extremely common; the industries most affected are computers and mobile phones, clothing, fishing, cocoa, and sugarcane.[52]

There is another class of workers—ones with nimbler fingers who are even more likely to submit to father-like authority. As the rate of extreme poverty fell between 2000 and 2016, child labor is also believed to have declined significantly, by 38 percent. However, there is reason to fear that the desperation caused by Covid reversed the progress made; millions of children are believed to have left school and entered the work force during the pandemic to help their families (a total of 160 million child workers worldwide as of 2021). It is estimated that half of the world's child laborers are engaged in hazardous work under dangerous or difficult conditions that expose them to physical, psychological, or sexual abuse. Most child labor is employed in agriculture and herding, but children are put to work in all sectors, and are uniquely vulnerable to exploitation.[53] Nearly half of the world's child laborers can be found in Africa (72 million), followed by Asia and the Pacific (62 million). The five countries called out by the International Labour Organization recently as making no effort against the worst child labor practices were Afghanistan, Burma, the Democratic Republic of Congo, Eritrea, and South Sudan. On the other hand, some states, like Namibia, Costa Rica, and Peru, have been recognized for having made significant advances to protect children.[54] However, this kind of exploitation is likely to continue to exist as long as corporations seek to remain competitive while increasing profits—and as long as consumers demand ever-cheaper goods.[55]

Another topic of dispute concerns neoliberal claims that MNCs are important in the transmission of values like modernity and entrepreneurship. Many critics are disturbed by such claims because they smack of ethnocentrism. Too often people say "modernity" when they mean "Westernization." By implication then, whatever is non-Western becomes lumped into the category of "backward." Neoliberals clap back, maintaining that modernity is a universally desired goal. However, structuralists point out that what most of the world's people want is an escape from their material poverty. People of the global south may want the comforts and choices many Westerners enjoy, but this doesn't necessarily mean that they want to become Western. Furthermore, structuralists retort that what MNCs are selling isn't modernity—it is the image of modernity. These firms are actually creating dependence by aggressively marketing their products and seeking to alter consumer tastes and attitudes through glossy and often deceptive advertising campaigns.[56]

Structuralists offer a classic example of how MNCs prey on the desperation of the poor: the Nestlé baby formula scandal. In an attempt to create an even more profitable market for its powdered milk products, in the 1970s it came to light that Nestlé had pursued a massive advertising campaign of misinformation. Targeting countries with appallingly high infant mortality rates, the company designed slick advertisements that strongly suggested that its infant formula was better than breast milk. While such claims were patently false on a number of counts, Nestlé was not satisfied with just taking the money of desperate parents. In some countries, it went even further to guarantee itself a market. Ostensibly offered as a welcoming gift, the company went about providing two weeks' worth of baby-formula "samples" to mothers leaving clinics with newborns—without informing them that if they used the formula for two weeks, their breast milk would dry up.[57]

The United Nations General Assembly condemned Nestlé for these actions and there was an international boycott of the Swiss-based company. However, abuses continue as Nestlé (along with Mars and Hershey) in recent years has been accused in courts of using (through their supply chains) thousands of children as slave labor on cocoa plantations in Côte d'Ivoire.[58] Awful but less dramatic forms of abuse by other companies, such as the sale of adulterated baby food, have continued to occur. For example, in 2008 at least six Chinese infants died and 300,000 were sickened because the company making their baby formula had sought to cut costs by lacing it with melamine, an industrial chemical used in plastic that makes the protein content of the formula appear higher than it is.[59]

Closer to home and more recently, in 2021 Gerber/Nestlé and other companies (including makers of "organic" baby foods) were cited after a congressional investigation found that ingredients in many baby foods were contaminated with heavy metals like arsenic, lead, and cadmium at levels that are far higher than those allowed. Other companies involved, including Walmart, refused to cooperate with the investigation, despite the clear risks to infants and toddlers, as exposure to heavy metals has a cumulative effect and been linked to developmental problems, brain damage, and even death.[60]

Under fire for ethical, environmental, and other lapses, many of today's MNCs are fighting negative publicity and working hard to humanize their image by promoting philanthropy, hiring monitors, and adopting a posture of corporate responsibility. However, as mentioned earlier, corporations are increasingly subcontracting parts of the production line to smaller firms that work in greater obscurity. When these abuses are exposed, corporations claim that they have limited power or leverage over these independent contractors or that host governments should be blamed for inadequate labor laws. As long as the neoliberals' staunch advocacy of deregulation prevails, the most that can be expected from MNCs is voluntary compliance with ethical norms and self-monitoring.

MNCs and neoliberals argue that voluntary codes are good enough, since it just isn't good business to misbehave anymore. The oil companies are accused of being some of the worst offenders, of knowingly polluting host countries. Chevron Texaco in Ecuador is one of the most notorious cases, for its spills from 1964 to 1990 that spread into the Amazon groundwater, causing serious illness and death among Indigenous people. Chevron continued to fight and refused to compensate the victims. In response, in 2014 the United Nations Human Rights Council proposed creating a legally binding framework to regulate the activities of multinationals. As of mid-2021, this ambitious effort to promote corporate accountability was still being negotiated.[61]

Whether it is the aggressive promotion and marketing of adulterated baby food or OxyContin, the bad public relations from such misdeeds can be costly, and companies are investing in cleaning up their reputations. But is this just another form of "greenwashing," or deceiving consumers into believing that they are environmentally friendly? Royal Dutch Shell and BP, though once part of an alliance that lobbied hard against taking the threat of global warming seriously, now advertise that they support sustainability and carbon neutrality. They may be forced to put their money where their mouth is. Finding that Shell "helped to drive dangerous climate change," a Netherlands court ordered the MNC to cut its carbon emissions in 2030 by 45 percent from 2019 levels. This "mind-blowing" verdict was huge because it was the first time a court imposed such requirements on a private company, telling it that its pledges and plans weren't enough and that it had to speed up and make sacrifices. Shell promised to appeal.[62]

In response to a newly recognized aspect of consumer preference, some companies have changed the way they do business and are treating workers better than required by often-weak regional laws. Nike makes it known that it has pressed its suppliers to open their factories to independent inspections, to remove child laborers from its lines, and to provide a better environment for its workers. To appeal to a broader clientele, Walmart has been promoting green initiatives in an effort to become the biggest retailer of organic foods. Claiming to be "a strong advocate of the environment," it is also promising to become more energy efficient, and to reduce solid waste. However, the retailer's plastic footprint is estimated to be about a million tons a year. Instead of reducing its footprint, it is being sued for greenwashing, for claiming that its single-use plastics are recyclable or biodegradable. Instead, most plastics are being dumped into landfills and the oceans or burned (for the record: it is estimated that less than one-tenth of all plastic has been recycled).[63]

In another example of how giants react under pressure, after years of resistance, in 2003 the World Trade Organization waived patents and allowed low-income countries to import generic versions of lifesaving anti-AIDS drugs manufactured in Thailand, South Africa, and India.[64] These drugs not only have turned the disease from a death sentence to a chronic illness that can be controlled, but helped to reduce the transmission rate of HIV and thus contain the epidemic. Although the high price of medicines is still a problem for many illnesses, the pharmaceutical industry (also known as Big Pharma) lowered the prices for some of their anti-AIDS drugs in some countries. For example, a common combination of these medicines cost $10,000 per person per year in 2000. A decade later, "the gold standard" in anti-AIDS drugs in Africa cost as little as $75 per person per year. Many chalk up the pharmaceutical corporations' change of heart to competition from cheap generic versions of their drugs. Whatever the reason, the good news is that there has been a dramatic increase in the number of people receiving HIV/AIDS medicines: from 6 million in 2012 to 26 million in 2020. And, contrary to fears that access to medicines would destroy the pharmaceutical industry, they continued to make billions of dollars each year, in one of the most lucrative businesses on Earth.[65]

Figure 6.3 Equitable Access to Vaccines: By Any Means Possible?

Reminiscent of the battle over access to HIV/AIDS medicines is the battle over access to vaccines to protect against Covid. As of late 2021, the gap between richer and poorer nations was glaring: high- and upper-middle-income countries held 85 percent of all purchased coronavirus doses—and were offering booster doses to their citizens. At that point, approximately 60 percent of adults in the United States and 70 percent in the European Union had been fully vaccinated, whereas less than 10 percent of those living in many African and Middle Eastern countries had been. At the rate it was going, many LMICs would be lucky to vaccinate at most 20 percent of their population by the end of the 2021. And that was before the panic over the omicron mutation led to rich country hoarding, instead of delivering on their promises.[a]

Added to that are the problems of vaccine hesitancy and quality. As in the global north, skepticism or hostility to the vaccines is a factor in their rollout, especially where there is deep distrust of government or medical authorities. For some, vaccine resistance may stem from misinformation or Western exploitation and medical abuses dating back to colonialism and since (e.g., Africans were used as guinea pigs for vaccine trials in the 1990s, and for many years, Western pharmaceutical companies refused to make lifesaving medicines affordable while huge numbers of Africans died of AIDS). It is important to be clear that many people in the global south are eager to be vaccinated.[b] But it is not unusual for doses to spoil due to low demand—and it could have something to do with the distances people may have to travel to get a shot, or that they have other, more pressing priorities. However, low demand may also have something to do with the quality of the vaccines made available to them. It is not unusual to hear that the doses delivered by the global north to the global south were dumped on poorer countries close to the end of their shelf-life, and with little advance notice. Of course, not knowing when a shipment is coming makes it all the more difficult to plan and carry out vaccination campaigns. And in more than one case, rich countries delivered vaccines they had decided weren't good enough for their own citizens. Canada donated mostly AstraZeneca to the global south after Canadians determined that vaccine's side effects were too great a risk for Canadians.[c]

Clearly, delivering the vaccine poses a complex set of challenges. But most fundamental is the issue of access. Arguing that "vaccinating a few while neglecting the many is not an effective game plan," advocates for equal access (and soon) called for a variety of additional measures, most notably aimed at sharing raw materials and technical expertise to step up manufacture of the vaccines.[d] Led by South Africa and India, more than sixty countries petitioned the World Trade Organization to allow countries to temporarily override or waive intellectual property rights (which is allowed under international law in emergencies) to increase production of these lifesavers. Currently, the drug companies are protected by patent laws. They set their own prices and choose whether (and on what terms) to establish partnerships. For example, during the pandemic Moderna, which was condemned by treatment access advocates for "behaving as if they have absolutely no responsibility beyond maximizing the return on investment" was earning billions in profits charging poorer countries more than richer ones. For example, the United States paid \$15–\$16.50 per shot while Botswana, Thailand, and Colombia were paying \$27–\$30 per dose of the Moderna vaccine.[e]

The Biden administration surprised many when it joined 100 other countries and the heads of the World Health Organization and World Trade Organization in support of equitable access and a temporary suspension of intellectual property rights (China supported it as well). However, the pharmaceutical MNCs, backed by the EU and Britain, strongly opposed setting aside the patents and sharing their secrets and know-how. They warned that this could disrupt the industry, which we all rely upon, and it would not necessarily speed things up, given the complexity of manufacturing the vaccines.[f] As you might imagine, some characterized the assumptions behind that claim as racist. To narrow the gap between the haves and have-nots, the African Union plans to build five vaccine manufacturing units in Africa over the next fifteen years. The goal is to prepare for a variety of illnesses,

continues

Figure 6.3 Continued

including future pandemics, and to produce 60 percent of the continent's vaccine needs—as opposed to the current 1 percent. Mexico and Argentina are also partnering to produce vaccines for Latin America.[g] Ultimately, it may all be up to the 164 members of the WTO to decide. But even if they get the waiver, the technology transfer, and raw materials (which are in short supply), this effort to expand supplies of the vaccine won't be an immediate solution, as it is estimated that the earliest deliveries from this added capacity won't come until months later. Meanwhile, as the virus keeps mutating, vaccine equity may prove itself to be as much a security issue as it is a trade issue.[h]

Notes: a. Jon Cohen and Kai Kupferschmidt, "Fairer Shares," *Science,* May 26, 2021; "We Need Many More Vaccines," *New York Times,* April 25, 2021; Rebecca Robbins, "Moderna Leaves Poorest Nations Waiting for Shot," *New York Times,* October 10, 2021.

b. Lynsey Chutel and Max Fisher, "Why Only 36 Percent of South African Adults Are Vaccinated," *New York Times,* December 1, 2021; Stephanie Nolan, "Many Obstacles Even as Doses Flow to Africa," *New York Times,* December 13, 2021.

c. Ari Shapiro, "As Omicron Spreads, Vaccine Inequity Risks Creating Further Variants," NPR, December 1, 2021.

d. "Coronavirus Digest: G7 Set to Pledge 1 Billion Vaccine Doses," *Deutsche Welle,* June 11, 2021; Bogolo Kenewendo, "We Need a Better Game Plan to Reach Global Herd Immunity," *Foreign Policy* (June 8, 2021).

e. Robbins, "Moderna Leaves Poorest Nations Waiting for Shot."

f. Peter S. Goodman, Apoorva Mandavilli, Rebecca Robbins, and Matina Stevis-Gridneff, "What Would It Take to Vaccinate the World Against Covid?" *New York Times,* November 27, 2021.

g. Catherine Osborn, "Latin America's Vaccine Stars and Struggles," *Foreign Policy* (May 21, 2021); "African Union Seeks to Boost Vaccine-Making with 5 New Centres," Al Jazeera, April 14, 2021.

h. Goodman et al., "What Would It Take to Vaccinate the World Against Covid?"

Aid and Debt

Although it played a much larger role during the COLD WAR, foreign aid of one form or another is still of critical importance to many countries in the global south. Aid may be directed from government to government, or involve multilateral organizations, including nongovernmental agencies. "Bilateral aid" is commonly defined as the transfer of concessional resources from one government to another. "Multilateral aid" is the transfer of resources from a group of donors (e.g., the United Nations or the Organisation for Economic Co-operation and Development [OECD]) to a recipient. In any case, aid is definitely a tool of diplomacy, used to promote policy objectives and to manipulate the behavior of possible recipients. Aid is used as a carrot to encourage or reward loyalty or desirable behavior. And the withholding of aid can be a stick used to punish those deemed undeserving.

In the ongoing "war on terror," as during the Cold War, US foreign aid has been largely based on strategic calculations. Then as now, the majority of US aid is not humanitarian and does not go to the world's poorest people. After September 11, 2001, the amount the United States spent on foreign aid did increase—particularly for certain emerging and developing countries that have clear strategic value, even though—contrary to popular perceptions—the total remains less than 1 percent of GNI. An economic nationalist who considered it a waste, then president

Trump called for deep reductions in foreign aid. He managed to cut or freeze certain programs, such as those for the Palestinians, but Congress, which sets funding, maintained the existing levels of spending and therefore overall US foreign assistance has remained pretty flat for several years.[66] Although the United States provides aid to nearly 200 countries, a handful of them, including Afghanistan, Israel, Jordan, Egypt, and Iraq, receive the lion's share of all US bilateral assistance. Although these countries also receive economic and development aid, most of this aid comes in the form of military or security assistance and (until recently) went to Afghanistan and the Middle East. That changed after the US pullout of Afghanistan in 2021, but Afghanistan received the most US foreign aid in 2019 ($4.8 billion) by far, followed by Israel ($3.3 billion), Jordan ($1.7 billion), and Egypt ($1.2 billion). A few African countries, such as Ethiopia ($922 million) and Nigeria ($793 million) that are also viewed as important in the war on terror, rounded out the US top ten in 2019.[67]

For years many in and outside the global south have argued that foreign aid may do more harm than good. It invites embezzlement and enriches the well connected, and discourages local initiatives by misdirecting capital to donors' pet projects.[68] Yet, foreign aid has largely been welcomed especially by the poorest countries as a spur to development. With little of value to trade in the world market, many countries have become aid dependent; foreign aid comprised over 55 percent of Tuvalu GNI in 2019, 22 percent of Liberia's, and 31 percent of Central African Republic's.[69] Critics, which include some neoliberals, structuralists, and economic nationalists, maintain that although aid may help in the short run, it can make the long-term situation more precarious as it often casts people living in LICs as passive beneficiaries who need "white saviors." Increasingly, critics are arguing that this top-down system needs to be decolonized. More of the power over aid needs to be put into the hands of the communities it is meant to benefit.[70] In addition, too often much of this aid is stolen or wasted and is not doing much to help countries actually develop.

As with nearly every other topic raised in this chapter, there is a great deal of disagreement about the effectiveness of aid. Both neoliberals and their critics agree that more aid is not necessarily better at promoting development. Nearly everyone, even those who call for increased funding for foreign aid, have problems with the ways in which aid packages have been designed and managed. Some neoliberals contend that aid can promote development if it is used as part of a larger package of reforms. They, such as former UN Secretary-General Kofi Annan, view aid as only one element in a development strategy that can be more effective if it is offered to help recipients run their own economies.[71] Critics to the left argue that aid is too often used to benefit the economic or strategic interests of donor countries, as a tool of capitalism that actually increases dependency and contributes to the further under-development of states. From the right, economic nationalists argue that foreign aid is too often simply a waste of good money and that development can only come from the efforts of private sector entrepreneurs and political reformers.

Foreign assistance comes in a variety of forms: loans, cash, food, clothing, medicine, arms, or just about any other commodity. It can also come in the form of technical or other assistance or services, and can be used to fund programs like those to promote peace and security, democracy and human rights, and education. Contrary to popular American belief, the United States is not a major donor of aid. Most Americans believe that the United States is much more generous, even overly generous, with the aid it offers LICs. Consequently, it is highly unlikely that US politicians will campaign for larger aid budgets. Although the United States does give more in total dollars (it spent over $39.2 billion in FY2019 on aid), it gives less as a share of its GNI (about 0.2 percent) than almost any rich country.[72] Decades ago, in 1970, leaders of the world's rich, industrialized countries set a goal of contributing 0.7 percent of their GNIs to foreign aid.[73] As of 2019, only Norway, Sweden, Luxembourg, Denmark, and the United Kingdom had met (or surpassed) that goal.[74] Although still well short of their commitments (they now average 0.3 percent of GNI), total foreign aid flows increased approximately 200 percent between 2000 and 2019 (from $55 billion to $167 billion); again, more of it was military and security assistance than humanitarian aid.[75]

Sure, the United States gives the most aid in sheer dollars, but the fact that America is, relatively speaking, one of the least generous nations would come as a surprise to many. Poll after poll shows that Americans think that the United States already gives too much aid—they estimate that 25 percent of the federal budget goes to foreign aid—when it is actually closer to 1 percent.[76] But even those who call for the United States and richer countries to be more generous also call for the rich to stop using "poverty porn" to raise money for famine relief. Too often international aid overshadows local efforts to respond to crises and organizations led by people from the global south. Increasingly, even neoliberals are recognizing that the world needs to reinvent foreign aid by shifting money and power closer to the communities that aid is meant to serve. For that matter, even better than aid, structuralists argue, is fairness in lending money and removing barriers to trade.[77]

Moreover, structuralists have argued for years that the United States is the principal beneficiary of the vast majority of its foreign aid to other countries, since so much of this aid is "tied" to guarantee a market for US goods. For example, the United States might extend a loan to Nigeria to buy tractors. This is a loan that the United States fully expects Nigeria to repay with interest, yet Nigeria has no choice but to use that money to buy US tractors, even if Japanese or French tractors are less expensive, or preferred for some other reason. As a result, tied aid is estimated to reduce the value of development assistance by 10–30 percent.[78]

Aid activists point out that such packages should be recognized for what they are: subsidies of donor economies. Low-income countries argue that development should not be a profit-making enterprise for the rich at the expense of the poor. Britain was an early proponent of this argument, and has begun to untie some of the strings attached to the aid it offers. The United States and other HICs have untied some aid, but given hard economic times at home it is increasingly difficult for legislators to persuade their constituents of the need for foreign assistance. Regardless of the reality, politicians find it an easy part of the budget to talk about cutting. Those who seek to sustain or increase aid levels find it politically necessary to show that tied aid offers a reciprocal benefit by creating hundreds of thousands of jobs for the citizens of donor countries.

For many years after the end of the Cold War, the vast majority of foreign assistance offered (to most countries) came not in the form of grants or gifts, but as loans. Although most people's definition of "aid" would seem to call for the concessional terms offered by soft loans, with their low interest rates and long repayment periods, historically a substantial number of these loans are nonconcessional: hard loans, bearing high interest rates and short repayment periods. Moreover, many of these loans have been taken out to service debt (or to make the scheduled payment on the debt accrued from past loans).

Therefore, a great deal of the "assistance" that richer countries offer is in the form of loans meant to pay the interest on an outstanding debt owed to them. This only adds to that debt, which may exist for a variety of reasons. In some cases, the West has lent to allies knowing that the resources would wind up in the hands of irresponsible, wasteful, or kleptocratic governments (some consider this to be "odious debt" and argue that creditors should not expect repayment because they made the loans with full knowledge of how the money was to be used). Or LMICs lost money in failed (but expensive) attempts at industrialization. In other cases, world recessions or unexpected changes in the global economy (e.g., supply chain disruptions and sudden increases in the price of fuel or food, especially if it is imported) have contributed to deficits. The global inflation we saw in 2021 affects all, but hurts the poorest the worst, and puts countries further into debt. For one reason or another, most LMICs have sunk into debt because they have consistently faced shortfalls in their balance of payments (meaning that they are spending more than they are bringing in). Again, structuralists argue this is due to their disadvantageous position in the international economy.

Neoliberals and structuralists agree that often external factors beyond these countries' control have played a large part in creating the crisis. However, to some extent, each country's debt grows out of its own particular combination of problems. Regardless of the source of the debt, it only became a crisis as far as the IMF and donors were concerned in the early 1980s, when Mexico and other debtors declared their inability to pay and threatened a moratorium (or temporary halt) on servicing their debts. Such threats were widely regarded as amounting to an emergency, since banks had eagerly overextended themselves for years, making huge loans to LMICs without worry as to their creditworthiness. Banks and donors feared that if other countries had joined Mexico in the formation of a debtors' cartel, their collective default could have led to the collapse of the international financial system.

Since the debt crisis of the 1980s, INTERNATIONAL FINANCIAL INSTITUTIONS (IFIs) and donors have recognized how vital it is that the vast majority of debtors be willing and able to pay. Donors are working with international financial institutions and are determined to manage the system to better protect it. There have been a variety of attempts to manage developing countries' debt over the years. And the debt burdens of some of these countries have eased, but for others they are still very real. In 1970, total LMIC foreign debt was less than \$100 billion. It rose to \$600 billion by 1980, and to \$1.6 trillion by 1990. As of 2019, the total external debt for all low- and middle-income countries had risen to \$8.1 trillion, or 26 percent of their GNI.[79] Worse, debt has surged under Covid to levels not seen in fifty years, and much of it had to be taken on nonconcessional terms. Much of the increase in debt has been due to the fact that countries had to take out more loans to service (or pay the interest) on their existing debt. In 2019, according to the United Nations Children's Fund (UNICEF), twenty-five countries (most in Africa and South Asia) spent more on debt payments to IFIs in richer countries than they did on education, healthcare, and other social support systems for the poorest. That same year, Lebanon's debt (as a share of its GDP) was 139 percent, Mozambique's was 137 percent, and Jamaica's was 96 percent.[80] These countries are in way over their heads. Many American college students can empathize.

When countries are in this position, just scraping by, making the minimum payments on their bills, there is precious little left over to spend on education, healthcare, or other investments in development.[81] They wind up literally choosing between food and debt, making what has been called "the cruel choice." In the year before the pandemic, sixty-four countries (nearly half of them in sub-Saharan Africa) spent more on servicing their debt than on healthcare. Ethiopia, for example, spent twice as much on its debt than on healthcare. Gambia spent nine times more on debt than healthcare. Some analysts contend that this situation amounts to debt slavery, and is as devastating to a population as war.[82]

The regions hit hardest by debt service often end up paying as much as a third of their entire export earnings to the banks. This debt is as debilitating for the countries with the largest total debts (e.g., Mexico and Brazil) as it is for countries with lower total bills but much smaller economies (e.g., many countries in Africa) (see Figures 6.4 and 6.5). It doesn't take an accountant to see that when the debt burden is this heavy, payment becomes impossible and countries fall into arrears. When this happens, donor responses tend to vary, as it frequently hinges on the donors' political interests. Sometimes the response has been stern: for example, the World Bank suspended disbursements to Zimbabwe in 1999 because it was more than six months' overdue and tens of millions of dollars behind in servicing its debt. Zimbabwe was even threatened with expulsion from the IMF.[83] This was significant because the IMF is so powerful. Most countries do everything that they can to stay in the IMF's good graces. For example, to receive a $12 billion IMF bailout, in 2016 Egypt accepted the IMF's conditions and adopted a series of painful AUSTERITY measures. Egypt allowed its currency to devalue by 48 percent against the dollar, raising prices at the same time that it cut government subsidies of energy and foodstuffs. In return for its efforts, Egypt has been rewarded in subsequent years with more loans (and debt).[84]

The IMF's conditions for aid are based in neoliberalism, in a set of ideas known as the Washington Consensus. Although nearly four decades old, the Washington Consensus still sums up much of the position of the international financial institutions and the donors that dominate them (the United States, Canada, the European Union, and Japan): that under-development is due to the domestic failings of the under-developed countries themselves, specifically their failure to adopt neoliberal economic reforms. In other words, it is argued that struggling economies need internal structural reforms to stabilize. Just as the diagnosis of the problem is universal, so is the cure. A fairly uniform prescription was proposed for dealing with any economy's ills: an embrace of globalization, which includes a liberalization of the economy (or opening) to foreign

Figure 6.4 Total External Debt, 2019

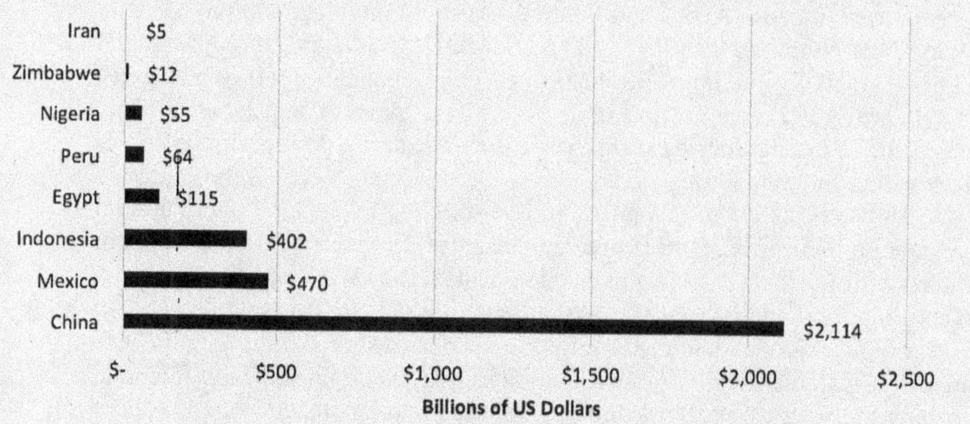

Source: World Bank, *World Development Indicators 2020.*

competition, and the adoption of a series of market-based reforms, including privatization and deregulation. According to the Washington Consensus, economic crises (wherever they occur) should be approached in the same way and treated with a consistent dose of ECONOMIC LIBERALIZATION and fiscal austerity, or belt-tightening. The prognosis for LICs is quite optimistic: if countries will only take their medicine, they will experience healthy growth rates. Healthy growth rates will provide for the growth of a middle class, and then more stable, viable democracies are sure to follow.

It is usually the International Monetary Fund that administers the cure. The IMF plays several highly influential roles in the world economy, and these roles have shifted over time. Increasingly, the IMF's focus is on the promotion of global economic stability (and the prevention and management of financial crises).[85] The IMF monitors economic trends, advises countries on economic policy, and promotes stability by providing technical assistance and serving as the lender of last resort to countries in economic crisis, distributing loans or lines of credit (ideally, concessional loans or credit) to countries whose economies are facing temporary shortfalls. By shortfalls, we are referring to an imbalance in payments, or a situation in which a country is spending more than it is earning. When this occurs, a country is said to be experiencing a deficit, and must find ways to finance or cover this deficit. This is how many countries go into debt: compared to the unpopular alternatives of raising taxes or cutting spending, governments prefer to take out loans to cover the shortfall. When countries run into serious financial trouble, it is often the IMF to which they turn for RESCUE PACKAGES: emergency loans, bailouts, or possibly even debt relief. Again, countries get "rescued" only after they have agreed to the IMF's cure. Obviously, this makes the IMF an extremely powerful institution, with tremendous influence over the decisions of governments.

Figure 6.5 External Debt as a Share of Gross National Income, 2019

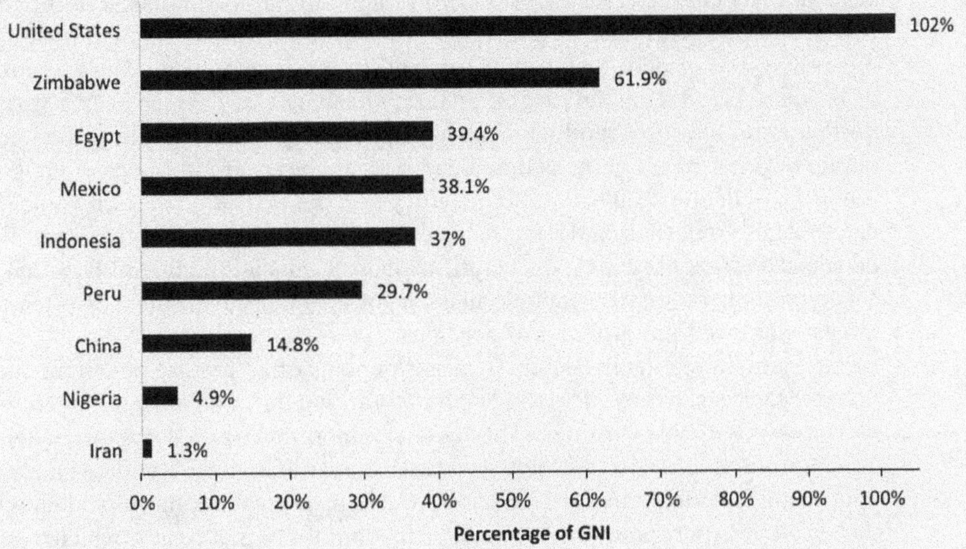

Source: World Bank, *World Development Indicators 2020.*
Note: Data for Iran from 2018; data for the United States from 2020.

So, what is the cure, exactly? What are the conditions attached to the provision of new loans that are so necessary for the servicing of old debt? The first thing to understand is that there is a regimen associated with the cure, known as EXTENDED-CREDIT FACILITIES (ECFs). Also called AUSTERITY PLANS, ECFs are said to allow for more input from the countries they target. According to their proponents, ECFs treat the countries involved more like stakeholders, participating in the design of the plan, and are somewhat less onerous than their predecessor (STRUCTURAL ADJUSTMENT PROGRAMS [SAPs]). ECFs, as opposed to SAPs (which were known as "shock therapy"), are designed to be kinder and gentler. They often include fewer conditions and more emphasis on poverty reduction (as opposed to a singular emphasis on GROWTH). But the IMF's critics contend that the difference between ECFs and SAPs is mostly window dressing—or public relations for the IMF.[86] Like SAPs, these programs are premised on the neoliberal consensus that the world should be run like a business. The IMF argues that its goal is debt reduction. That means getting countries to follow what neoliberals would characterize as more sensible economic policies. According to this view, countries need to adopt multiyear plans based in pro-growth policies and ensure that their revenues exceed their expenditures—to get out of the red. For all the talk about debtor country "participation," there is little dialogue taking place. At its core, any adjustment program is based in the adoption of market reforms, which are believed by neoliberals to lay the basis for future growth. What countries need most is to keep their eyes on the bottom line. In general, short-term consumption should be curtailed to promote long-term investment.

For all of the talk about local ownership and no more "one size fits all," structuralists characterize ECFs as still remarkably uniform, based in the idea that debtor countries need to undergo a series of reforms to promote growth, get themselves out of debt, reduce poverty, and foster development. The first order of business is reducing deficits, or attaining a balance of payments. One way to do this is by cutting spending. Although some argue that the prescribed economic reforms aren't quite as draconian now as they were in the past, the governments of debtor countries, after meeting with the IMF, are to return home and cut the "fat" from their budgets. Most commonly, this involves cutting spending on social welfare programs, on health, sanitation, education, the military, and so forth, but cuts could also include mass layoffs as the government is often the largest employer and provider of pensions.

In addition to cuts in spending, austerity plans often require governments to increase their income by increasing taxes or cracking down on tax evasion, as well as increasing export earnings. The most common means of doing the latter is export promotion, which for most countries means an intensification of the production of raw materials for sale on the world market. Working in tandem with this effort at export promotion is the devaluation of one's currency, which a government undertakes by changing its official exchange rate. A currency devaluation is prescribed because it promises to accomplish two goals at once. It should spur increased export earnings, since one's goods will be cheaper (and therefore more competitive) on the world market. At the same time, devaluation means that because the currency is worth less, the cost of imports will rise, and people will be left with no choice but to buy less—therefore conserving scarce hard currency. As you can imagine, putting consumer goods such as food, fuel, and medicine out of the reach of most of the population doesn't sit well. For example, troops were sent out to put down protests in Lebanon in 2021 after the government allowed a rapid depreciation in the value of the Lebanese pound that worsened already-deteriorating living conditions. Even the World Bank recognized that Lebanon has been going through one of the world's worse financial crises since the mid-nineteenth century. Yet, it has been impatient with government mismanagement and reluctant to provide the assistance the population desperately needs.[87]

However, the shock of Covid appears to have moved these IFIs. In what has been called "a helicopter money drop for those left behind," the IMF is being praised even by some structuralists for quickly providing more than $200 billion in aid to poor countries to help with the Covid recession.[88] But in the bigger picture, the neoliberal goal is to achieve a balance of payments (or even a surplus) where there has been a deficit. According to neoliberals, deep cuts in spending combined with an increase in revenues from export sales will help countries accumulate the hard currency to get out of debt and on the path to prosperity.

The path to prosperity is predicated on the acceptance of some other conditions as well. Here, the emphasis is on the adoption of policies that will enhance productivity and encourage capital flows based on foreign investment rather than aid. The way to accomplish these goals, according to the IMF, is to privatize the economy. Privatization means selling off STATE-OWNED ENTERPRISES

Figure 6.6 Do Exchange Rates Matter?

When we consider "free" and "state run" economies (and the multiple variations in between), one example that illustrates the involvement of governments in economic decisions is the value of the country's currency. The relative weight of currencies compared to each other is known as the exchange rate (e.g., in December 2021, the US dollar was roughly equivalent to twenty-one Mexican pesos). Although it is certainly not the only one to do so, China is an example of a country that has intervened in the markets to control the value of its currency, known as the yuan or renminbi. For nearly two decades, the United States has called on China (and a few other countries as well) to permit their currencies to be traded at more market-oriented rates. Many contended that the Chinese currency was undervalued, which made Chinese exports cheaper and foreign imports (which compete with their products at home) comparatively more expensive. This currency manipulation, it was argued, helped China sell more than it bought abroad, which added to the Chinese trade surplus with the United States.

In an attempt to lend stability to China's emerging economic system, the yuan had long been pegged to the US dollar, a practice that ended only in 2005. After significant pressure from the United States and the International Monetary Fund, Beijing's leaders decided to allow their currency's value to float, or fluctuate, within a small band of value (permitting the daily exchange rate to increase or decrease by 2 percent). While the loosening of control helped deflect foreign complaints, it also strengthened Beijing's case with the IMF that the yuan be named the fifth currency to be included in the Special Drawing Rights basket of important reserve currencies (a milestone that was reached in 2016).

While pressure was on the Chinese to revalue their currency, a common characteristic of structural adjustment programs is the opposite: countries are told to devalue their currency. One of the most striking examples of this was in late 2016 when Egypt allowed its currency, the Egyptian pound, to fall in value by 48 percent, to seal the deal on a $12 billion loan from the IMF. Only a country in crisis would adopt such measures. The immediate effect is pain and panic in the markets as the prices of basic goods suddenly become unaffordable. Governments such as Egypt's are right to worry about a political backlash, but neoliberals counsel that countries must persevere to get back into the black, make their exports more competitive, and attract investment.

Source: Zahraa Akhalisi, "Why Egypt Just Let Its Currency Crash by 48 Percent," *CNN Money,* November 3, 2016.

(SOEs), which are often wasteful and inefficient. Although SOEs were originally created to reduce foreign dominance of LMIC economies, neoliberals argue that these government monopolies over the delivery of public services like water and electricity should be put on the open market and sold to the highest bidder—whether local or foreign. It is not unusual for these state sell-offs to amount to extremely lucrative, high-stakes deals that are less than transparent. Although neoliberals push for privatization because they believe that taking these sectors out of government hands will reduce mismanagement and CORRUPTION, it is commonly said that all that privatization does is to privatize corruption. Another problem is that the privatization of utilities has often meant higher prices for water, electricity, and telephone service, but neoliberals argue that private investors have dramatically improved and expanded services, thereby increasing poor people's access to these services.[89]

Now, let's take a minute here to point out that others are highly skeptical of such claims. They are concerned particularly about privatization of resources such as water, access to which many consider to be a human right. In a famous example from 2000, Bolivians fought a "water war" when the American-owned Bechtel took over the waterworks and nearly doubled the price of water. After days of nationwide, violent protests and a declaration of martial law, the company was forced to leave the country. The community-run waterworks that succeeded it have not been without their problems, but most analysts agree that when it comes to water, the private sector has not been the solution. Too often the private sector has been accused of price-gouging, and has not achieved better success than the public sector in extending services.[90]

Rather, privatization has often reduced access. Yet, the IMF and other IFIs continue to push for privatization as a condition of aid. During the pandemic, due to privatization, many governments in the global south had to intervene to ensure there was sufficient water for handwashing by suspending payments of water bills, temporarily prohibiting disconnections, and reconnecting people to services.[91] However, it is unclear how long the IFIs will be willing to ease up on the rules.

Beyond privatization, neoliberals argue that LIC governments must work harder to attract foreign investment of all kinds. They must make themselves attractive to MULTINATIONAL CORPORATIONS for all the reasons neoliberals have put forward regarding the benefits associated with the presence of MNCs in host countries. According to this view, governments should work aggressively to lure more foreign investment in a variety of ways, including a policy of deregulation (the removal of legal constraints on the operation of businesses, like eliminating health, safety, and environmental regulations).

By the early 1990s, the IMF and donors had added another condition. With the Cold War over, the neoliberals began admonishing LICs to go beyond "getting prices right" and to also work at "getting politics right." Based in the view that DEMOCRACY is a natural complement to capitalism, donors argued that the hardship blamed on austerity and the IFIs' seeming failure to deliver on promises of growth and development were actually due to failures of government, not the model. After years of looking the other way (if the countries involved were their allies or strategically important), the West became convinced that a lack of "good governance" was the problem—not the neoliberal model itself. For more than a decade, Western donors had ignored rampant corruption in Asia and elsewhere as long as governments embraced neoliberal reforms. However, by the late 1990s, corruption, cronyism, and the "incestuous" relationship between government and business in Asia were deplored as the cause of the region's ills. These countries had gotten prices right, but they had suffered from a lack of regulation, supervision, and TRANSPARENCY—in effect, they hadn't "gotten politics right."

The problem, as identified by neoliberals, was one endemic not only to East Asia, but also to much of the global south: political reform had lagged behind economic reform when, from a neoliberal perspective, the success of either reform would be inextricably linked to progress in the other.[92] Structuralists point out that political and economic reforms are at odds with each other. As you can imagine, austerity actually undermines democracies by adding to the strain on them, especially new ones that recently transitioned from dictatorships. In fact, the hardship associated with globalization fuels public distrust and anxieties about economic dislocation. It has been a major driver behind the rise of economic nationalism and helps to explain rising support for populism and authoritarianism in HICs and LMICs alike.[93]

Structuralists doubt the sincerity of neoliberal interest in political reforms aimed at fighting mismanagement and corruption and promoting good governance and democratization, as neoliberals have been willing to overlook less-than-stellar records of certain governments when strategic or other interests have been at play. As a result, the model came under attack—so much so that now it is often said that "there is no consensus on the Washington Consensus."[94] A decade ago when Brazil was booming, one rival to the Washington Consensus was the "Brasilia Consensus" led by former Brazilian president Luiz Inácio Lula da Silva, who put state-led development ahead of growth. The Brasilia Consensus is no more under the conservative Bolsonaro government, but it may make a comeback if Lula makes his own return to power.

Yet, today it is China that is the role model for many and the "Beijing Consensus" that holds more sway, as China has gone from being a recipient of aid to a leading donor. Many countries have turned to China as a source of loans because China makes it a point not to press such conditions. Like other donors, China is looking to enhance its reputation, influence, and standing as a world leader, while promoting its own economic and political interests. Yes, Beijing attaches some of the same strings as the West (access to markets and commodities) as well as some new ones: support for its policy on Taiwan. But China, known as "the rogue donor," certainly isn't going to call on other countries to become more democratic, transparent, or accountable—and some appreciate that.

Instead, China is challenging the United States for dominance on the world stage, and promotes a state-centric economic model rather than the neoliberal model advocated by the West. Since 2013, it has been extending its reach and influence throughout Asia and Africa with a growing collection of investment projects worth hundreds of billions of dollars known as the BELT AND ROAD INITIATIVE (BRI). This initiative is enormous, far surpassing the Marshall Plan. Yet, for all the talk about difference, Chinese aid and investment to build ports, roads, railways, and communications networks also come in the form of loans and, thus, carry the very real risk of adding to the recipients' unsustainable debt loads and dependence on China. And, with Beijing's record at home of turning a blind eye to such things, the Beijing Consensus is blamed for a weakening of environmental and human rights.[95]

Now, to be fair, the West needs to do better on these things as well. But neoliberals maintain that in the long run, perseverance in economic and political liberalization will pay off. It just takes time and patience. They point to a number of countries, like Mexico and South Korea, that have taken this sometimes-harsh medicine in return for emergency loans, and whose growth rates have since recovered. Moreover, Mexico and South Korea underwent extensive political reforms at the same time that they adopted economic reforms. Not that long ago they were authoritarian systems; neither is a model democracy (who is?) but both countries today have made significant progress in their transitions to democracy.

Although the publics of richer countries largely regard poorer countries as deadbeats that are unwilling or unable to meet their obligations, it is important to realize that indebted LMICs are actually net exporters of capital to richer countries. In a widely cited example, Nigeria originally borrowed $5 billion, paid $16 billion on that loan, and years later still owed $32 billion more (this debt was eventually forgiven, but only after Nigeria paid three to four times more than it borrowed in the first place).[96] Economist Susan George contends that the sums that poorer countries have paid to service their debts amount to unprecedented financial assistance from the poor to the rich—an amount George estimated to be equivalent to six Marshall Plans (and that was almost three decades ago). She says that we should not worry about the banks going hungry—they've made back the original principal and more through high interest rates.[97] And the banks continue to make tidy profits from the interest earned on this debt.

In Nigeria and elsewhere, many of the political leaders who accumulated this debt and misappropriated these funds are long gone. However, the citizens of these countries are left holding the bag, responsible for repaying a debt they never asked for, and from which they derived no gain. Eduardo Galeano likens this system to an open artery: so-called emerging and developing countries are not emerging or developing: they are being bled dry. Rather than being healed by the IMF, the veins are kept open for the purpose of drawing more blood—this at a time when much of the global south is facing its worst economic crisis since the Great Depression.[98]

As a result, critics of the neoliberal model don't mince words when they argue that globalization is the new colonialism. Its aims and outcomes are remarkably similar to those of colonialism in that the "development" it promotes is not one that improves the lives of LICs' citizens. Rather, according to the structuralists, free trade and globalization are about ensuring markets for Western goods and retaining poorer countries as a source of cheap labor and raw materials. Sure, under ECFs, the governments of these countries are consulted and allowed to have some input in the decisions that affect the lives of their citizens, but their destiny is still ultimately left in the hands of richer countries (often their former colonizers). The IMF's economic reforms amount to a financial coup d'état in that they undermine the sovereignty of the state and deny people the right to economic SELF-DETERMINATION.

Even if the model one day proves effective in promoting economic development, the IMF has been unwilling to reform itself in any significant way that alters the balance of power between the global north and south (or that reflects the changing reality of the global economy). China has increased its financial contribution to the IMF (and, therefore, its voice), but voting power has so far not shifted to reflect the growing importance of LMICs in the world economy, and IMF and World Bank leaders remain European and American, as has been the custom since the bodies were formed in 1944. The director-general of the World Trade Organization is for the first time a woman and person of African descent, Ngozi Okonjo-Iweala (an American citizen originally from Nigeria), who took office in 2021.[99]

Now, neoliberals maintain that such characterizations are unfair and point to a variety of efforts over the years that the IMF and donors have devised to pull countries out of debt. Yet, this is an offer LMICs cannot resist, since most countries must meet the terms of the IMF or risk being deemed uncreditworthy. For most of them, a bad rating from the IMF can mean economic suicide. Noncompliance risks isolation and severe punishment: the flow of capital in the form of investment, debt relief, or any other type of assistance dries up.

As you would guess, Covid only added to these problems, as governments worldwide, seeking to save their economies from ruin, pursued deficit spending to undertake previously unheard of emergency stimulus measures. Rich countries and even some not so rich, such as Thailand, were desperate to stabilize their economies. They spent billions (Thailand's stimulus equaled about 10 percent of its GDP), borrowing heavily to provide relief programs and save lives. In the short run, it worked: as of mid-2021, governments that put stimulus checks directly in the hands of people appear to have fared better in reducing hardship, supporting their economies, and speeding their recoveries. Because of such spending, in some places, like Thailand, extreme poverty was actually reduced during the outbreak.[100]

Other governments, such as Mexico's, were far less generous with their pandemic-induced stimulus payments and other welfare measures. It surprised many that left-leaning President Andrés Manuel López Obrador was unwilling to increase aid to Mexicans. But having lived through Mexico's debt crisis in the 1980s and 1990s, he was leery of taking on more debt. Mexico spent only 0.7 percent of its GDP to fight the pandemic's economic effects, in contrast with Brazil, which spent 8 percent of GDP, and Argentina 3.8 percent.[101] Although some characterize Mexico's approach as stingy given the crisis posed by the pandemic, ballooning fiscal deficits and debt are legitimate concerns, especially without a credible plan for how to reduce them after these countries recover.

In what might strike some as a role reversal, the IMF's director for Latin America actually encouraged Mexico to spend much more than it did on social protection systems, saying that spending during the pandemic was the right thing to do.[102] The United Nations estimated that $2.5 trillion in aid was needed to respond to the pandemic in the developing world—and recommended it come in the form of grants, not loans. Its report called for a Marshall Plan–like fund to transfer resources immediately to the developing world on a massive scale. The UN warned that Covid is merely one of cascading crises that are coming, and that drive home our interdependence. One of Covid's many lessons is that we (the world) need to be better prepared "next time"—for whatever that is—with a renewed commitment to multilateralism and global solidarity.[103]

So, perhaps it is a sign of just how bad things were during the pandemic that the IMF doubled the amount of money available through loans—not grants—for addressing natural disasters. More than 100 countries requested emergency financing and the IMF had lent over $30 billion to more than 70 of them.[104] In addition, during the pandemic, the donors known as the GROUP OF 20 (G-20) agreed to the DEBT SERVICE SUSPENSION INITIATIVE (DSSI). Aimed at staving off a debt crisis, the DSSI provided temporary debt postponement to seventy-seven of the poorest developing countries, suspending until December 2021 approximately $12 billion in debt repayment due during that period, so that these nations could concentrate on the pandemic. Although this initiative was a balm to many countries, it was not extended to all and it did not cover debt to private creditors.[105]

Meanwhile, Covid exposed long-standing problems and accelerated processes that were well under way long before anyone had heard of the virus.

The aftereffects of the pandemic will be long lasting, as virtually all countries dramatically increased spending to deal with it. As a result, Zambia's debt payments grew from less than 2 percent of its total government revenues in 2011 to nearly 34 percent of its total government revenues in 2021.[106] By 2021, Venezuela, Argentina, and (for the first time in its history) Lebanon had defaulted on their debt obligations and faced lengthy negotiations with creditors to sort it out.[107] Analysts have pointed out that it is not an exaggeration to say that debt threatens to create a global development emergency in much the same way as the pandemic created a global health emergency. With Covid we have moved into unknown territory; the setbacks it is causing could result in social unrest and instability for years to come.[108]

According to the One Campaign, suspending the debt is one of the fastest and simplest ways to support the world's most vulnerable because it allows the money that would have gone to the debt to be spent on emergency needs. This is significant. It adds, though, that DSSI doesn't do anything to actually reduce the debt. And it left out many other vulnerable countries that need this assistance as well, such as South Africa, Egypt, and Morocco. According to the One Campaign, the G-20 should have at least offered to suspend repayment until the pandemic is over. But most importantly, they say, the payments should not just be suspended—for the poorest countries, they should be cancelled.[109]

But debt cancellation wasn't an offer on the table. Moreover, while the pandemic was still raging, the same IMF director who urged governments to borrow more to save their economies warned that it's also right to start thinking about tax and spending reforms. In 2021 Latin America wasn't facing a debt crisis, per se, but it doesn't have to be an emergency for countries to be required to accept IMF demands to cut deficits to be offered some form of debt relief. This may involve debt rescheduling or, more rarely, restructuring or forgiveness.[110] Rescheduling of debt defers payment to a later date; it is a temporary reprieve, allowing for an extension of the period of repayment of the loan. Rescheduling is considered crucial for many countries because it makes their debt burden more bearable.[111]

As opposed to rescheduling, restructuring is an agreed default on part of a debt, whereas forgiveness means reducing or writing it off. While in the past forgiveness was usually the option of last resort, a global campaign from the 1990s to forgive debt was known as Jubilee 2000. It called for forgiveness of debt as part of a biblical mandate (the Book of Leviticus sets down that every fifty years all debts should be canceled, land returned to the dispossessed, and enslaved people set free). The time of liberation was known as "Jubilee," and its namesake movement pressed during the millennium year for a onetime full debt forgiveness for the world's poorest countries. Others characterize debt forgiveness as a long-overdue reparation, paid to the global south by the global north, for the wrongs done during colonialism—and since.

Well, the deadline passed, but the movement and the argument for forgiveness goes on as follows: in countries where most of the population is in poverty, it not only is wrong but also inefficient to require them to spend so much of their revenue paying back their creditors. Perhaps partially in response to such calls, some aid has come in the form of debt relief. However, with a few exceptions (e.g., tens of billions of dollars of forgiveness for Iraq), the closest the IFIs and other donors have ever come to forgiveness for many countries was a debt reduction program initiated in 1996 for HIGHLY INDEBTED POOR COUNTRIES (HIPCs).[112] Highly indebted poor countries were originally defined as having a gross national product (GNP) per capita of less than $675 and "unsustainable" debt (amounting to more than 80 percent of GNP). Under the HIPC program, the IMF, the World Bank, and other multilateral organizations, along with other creditors, promised to expand and accelerate debt relief measures. Relatively speaking, this does not amount to a lot of money, since the HIPC program currently accounts for a small part of the total external debt of LICs. To be considered for the HIPC program, not only must a country be desperately poor, but it also must be willing to divert all the money it would have paid on its debt to programs promoting education, healthcare, and economic development (none of our cases qualified for the program).

Where debt relief has been implemented, it has made a real change in people's lives. For example, within just the first few years of the program, over 1 million Tanzanian children were able to return to school. Zambia was able to hire 4,500 new teachers and abolish school fees as well as offer free healthcare in rural areas. In Niger, the infant mortality rate dropped from 156 to 81 per 1,000 live births, and the percentage of people with access to potable water climbed from 40 to 69 percent.[113] According to the World Bank, in virtually every country that has received debt relief, social spending has increased to five times the amount of debt service spending and social indicators have improved.[114]

Countries that have completed the HIPC program are also eligible for the MULTILATERAL DEBT RELIEF INITIATIVE (MDRI), which promises relief from debt held by four multilateral institutions: the World Bank, the IMF, the African Development Fund, and the Inter-American Development Bank. But to be eligible for either program, one more string is attached: applicants must be willing to faithfully accept all the conditions set for them by the IMF. Only countries that successfully complete key structural reforms are said to have reached the completion point, making them eligible for as much as 100 percent debt reduction. Under HIPC and MDRI programs combined, as of 2021, thirty-seven countries (thirty-one in Africa) had been granted reductions of over $100 billion in debt service relief (three more countries are potentially eligible for the program).[115] HIPC and MDRI helped to reduce public debt among low-income countries from a median debt-to-GDP ratio of close to 100 percent in the early 2000s to a median of just over 30 percent in 2013. But it didn't last; because these programs were not accompanied by structural changes, the HIPC countries' median debt-to-GDP ratio was back up to above 50 percent by 2017.[116]

The debt-to-GDP ratio is a common measure of economic health. Several factors determine how much debt a country can carry before the burden becomes too much. How much debt a country can carry depends on several factors, and that number can change over time. Fragile and conflict-affected states, commodity-dependent countries, and small states are the most vulnerable, but they are not the only ones with unsustainable debt. Countries that have passed the threshold of 70 percent are generally considered to be in debt distress, which means that they are considered at high probability of experiencing difficulties in servicing their debt and going in arrears. And the HIPC countries were not the only ones falling further behind. Even before the coronavirus hit, governments were already paying an increasing proportion of their revenues on the interest payments on their debt and much of it was on nonconcessional terms. According to the IMF, before the pandemic, a quarter of low- and middle-income countries were already in, or at high risk of, debt distress. By 2021, the IMF put that number at half of all LMICs.[117]

Not everyone is in the same boat. Thanks to debt relief, better debt management, and commodity booms, some emerging and developing countries have what the IMF considers "sustainable" debt, whereas many HICs have much higher debt-to-GDP ratios (e.g., Japan, Greece, Portugal, and Italy). In 2021, Japan had the world's highest debt as a percentage of GDP, at 256 percent. In case you were wondering, that same year US debt was 132 percent of its GDP (yes, the United States had the world's largest debt at $29 trillion in December 2021).[118] The US debt, which grew significantly after the 2007–2009 financial crisis and again in response to Covid, is expected to rise to levels not seen since World War II. The mounting debt for advanced economies is no doubt concerning, but HICs like the United States and Japan have traditionally been considered safer bets in that they hold the world's reserve currencies, allowing them to carry debt more cheaply than other countries. And they can more easily manage debt, in part because they have better credit ratings and can therefore pay lower interest rates. However, economists disagree about how sustainable this is, or whether the United States will eventually have to face the consequences.[119]

Clearly, the global debt movement recognizes that not all countries need or want debt cancellation (as this could affect their access to credit in the future). However, advocates for debt relief maintain that the current situation is not sustainable and they ask us to consider (as consumers) our own complicity in the system. Moreover, they argue that debt restructuring must be combined with other, more comprehensive and far-reaching change, such as regulating lenders and lessening LMICs' dependence on cheap commodity exports.[120] In other words, forgiveness is only a first step toward offering debt-burdened countries the new beginning they desperately need.

Conclusions: Is There No Alternative?

In this section of the book we discussed the global south's position in the international economic system and challenges that are at least partially attributable to globalization and the Washington Consensus. According to IMF, "There is much to cheer in the neoliberal agenda . . . there are aspects of the neoliberal agenda that have not delivered as expected."[121] In response, neoliberals have moderated their position, putting forward a variety of "post-Consensus" reforms that still operate within the existing system, but show more concern about environmental sustainability and broadening development than past iterations. For example, as part of a Green Climate Fund to help countries mitigate and adapt to the ruinous effects of climate change, HICs promised a decade ago over $100 billion a year in climate financing to LMICs. However, as of late 2021, these pledges had not been met in full and were insufficient anyway. Many African countries were already spending much more than they had received to mitigate a climate crisis they did not create.[122]

Although some old-school neoliberals say that post-Consensus reforms amount to an overreaction and structuralists say they are not enough, we are repeatedly reminded by old and new school neoliberals that "there is no alternative" to neoliberalism.[123] In the global north and south, we see rising support for structuralist and economic nationalist solutions, but globalization can seem unstoppable. Neoliberals insist that this is a good thing and point to such gains as those made in reducing extreme poverty in the years before the pandemic.

On the other hand, structuralists point out that the progress made was ephemeral, easily reversed by Covid because structural changes in the international economic system are needed. The proof that nothing really changed is the continued existence of massive inequality. For example, the post-Covid recovery is two-track. Countries that have access to vaccines (the richer countries of the global north) are simply going to recover faster than those that do not (the poorer countries of the global south). Since the pandemic started, most of these countries still struggle to achieve growth and development because of their dependent, disadvantageous position in the international economic system that dates back to colonialism. Structuralists contend that reparations are due. Although richer countries struggle as well, the rules are simply not the same for the rich and poor. With a total national debt of nearly $29 trillion as of December 2021, the United States has several times the combined debt of all of the developing world.[124] However, for better or worse, the world's largest debtor is unlikely to ever be held to the rules it expects others to follow.

So, what do you think? Why does the enormous gap between the richest and poorest countries remain, even if it is narrowing? Why are we observing some of the highest levels of global inequality ever recorded? And why, despite some significant gains in the years just prior to the pandemic, do so many of the world's countries continue to suffer from under-development? Is this under-development due to poor decisions made by the countries themselves? Or is it due to the position of these countries in the international economic system, a capitalist system that is dominated by rich countries and the organizations working for them?

Notes

1. "The Whole World Eats Well, and We Do Not," *Washington Post,* July 14, 2021.
2. Imran Amed, "How Can a Garment Be Cheaper Than a Sandwich?" *New York Times,* December 10, 2020.
3. World Trade Organization, "The WTO," 2021.
4. "What Is Globalization?" Peterson Institute for International Economics, October 29, 2019.
5. Thomas L. Friedman, *The Lexus and the Olive Tree* (New York: Farrar, Straus and Giroux, 1999).
6. Gayle Smith, "Development Depends on More Than Aid," *Foreign Affairs,* March 1, 2021.
7. Organisation for Economic Co-operation and Development, "Agricultural Policy Monitoring and Evaluation 2020," 2020.
8. Daniel A. Sumner, "Congress Needs to Cut Ties with the Cotton Lobby," *US News,* January 28, 2016.
9. Samuel T. Ledermann and William G. Moseley, "The WTO's Doha Round and Cotton," *African Geographical Review* 26, no. 1 (April 27, 2012); Sewell Chan, "US and Brazil Reach Agreement on Cotton Dispute," *New York Times,* April 6, 2010.

10. United Nations, "Poor Countries Biggest Losers When Trade Tensions Escalate, Secretary-General Tells World Body's Special General Council, Warning 'There Are No Winners,'" May 10, 2019.

11. Thomas L. Friedman, "Protesting for Whom?" *New York Times,* April 24, 2001.

12. Daniel Griswold, "The Blessings and Challenges of Globalization," Cato Institute, September 1, 2000.

13. Jackie Smith and Timothy Patrick Moran, "WTO 101: Myths About the World Trade Organization," in *Annual Editions: Developing World 01/02,* ed. Robert J. Griffiths (Guilford, CT: McGraw-Hill/Dushkin, 2001).

14. Ian Gladding, "Rise of Economic Nationalism and Its Implications," *Lewis University Experts Blog,* April 25, 2018; Monica de Bolle, "The Rise of Economic Nationalism Threatens Global Cooperation," Peterson Institute for International Economics, September 4, 2019; Thomas B. Edsall, "Trumpism Without Borders," *New York Times,* June 16, 2021.

15. Miatta Fahnbulleh, "The Neoliberal Collapse," *Foreign Affairs* (January–February 2020).

16. Ibid.

17. Organisation for Economic Co-operation and Development (OECD) and the World Trade Organization, "Aid for Trade at a Glance 2019: Economic Diversification and Empowerment," 2019.

18. World Bank, "Agriculture and Food," September 30, 2020.

19. Landesa, "The Global Land Rush," 2021.

20. World Bank, "Sub-Saharan Africa's Growth Will Slow in 2015 amid Falling Commodity Price," *Africa's Pulse,* no. 11 (April 2015); Larry Elliott, "Economics: Poor Nations Ride High on Commodity Boom," *The Guardian,* May 10, 2006.

21. Pamela Coke Hamilton and Janvier Nkurunziza, "COVID-19 and Food Security in Vulnerable Countries," United Nations Conference on Trade and Development, April 14, 2020; Martin Armstrong, "Coronavirus Crisis: Where Reliance on Imports Is Highest," Statista, April 29, 2020; "Food Security and COVID-19," World Bank, February 28, 2022.

22. "Sudan Crisis: What You Need to Know," *BBC News,* August 16, 2019.

23. International Energy Agency, "Energy Market Turmoil Deepens Challenges for Many Major Oil and Gas Exporters," 2020; Jane Arraf, "Iraq, Struggling to Pay Debts and Salaries, Plunges into Economic Crisis," *New York Times,* January 4, 2021.

24. Evelyn Cheng, "China Is Growing More Worried About How Surging Commodity Prices Will Affect Business Profits," CNBC, May 27, 2021; Alexei Barrionuevo, "A Mine of Riches and an Economic Sinkhole," *New York Times,* September 11, 2010.

25. United Nations Conference on Trade and Development, "Commodity Dependence and the Sustainable Development Goals," August 3, 2017.

26. OECD and the World Trade Organization, "Aid for Trade at a Glance 2019"; Cecile Fruman, "Economic Diversification: A Priority for Action, Now More Than Ever," *World Bank Blogs,* March 1, 2017.

27. Will Nichols, "Up to 90% of World's Electronic Waste Is Illegally Dumped, Says UN," *The Guardian,* May 12, 2015.

28. Vanessa Forti, Cornelis Peter Baldé, Ruediger Kuehr, and Garam Bel, "The Global E-Waste Monitor 2020," United Nations University, 2020.

29. "Why Some Countries Are Shipping Back Plastic Waste," *BBC News,* June 2, 2019.

30. Jung Min-kyung, "S. Korea's GNI per Capita Surges 500-Fold Since Korean War," *Korea Herald,* December 19, 2019; Kongdan Oh, "Korea's Path from Poverty to Philanthropy," Brookings Institution, June 14, 2010; Ruchir Sharma, "Is Vietnam the Next 'Asian Miracle'?" *New York Times,* October 13, 2020.

31. Min-kyung, "S. Korea's GNI per Capita Surges 500-Fold Since Korean War"; Oh, "Korea's Path from Poverty to Philanthropy"; OECD Better Life Index, "Korea," 2021.

32. Andrew Walker and Xiaoke Zhang, "Debating East Asian Capitalism: Issues and Themes," in *East Asian Capitalism: Diversity, Continuity, and Change,* ed. Andrew Walter and Xiaoke Zhang (New York: Oxford University Press, 2012).

33. Yu Nakamura, "Southeast Asia to Be World's Top Laptop Producer, Surpassing China," *Nikkei Asia,* September 26, 2020.
34. Global Justice Now, "69 of the Richest 100 Entities on the Planet Are Corporations, Not Governments, Figures Show," October 17, 2018.
35. Brandon Pizzola, Robert J. Carroll, and James Mackey, "The Changing Headquarters Landscape for Fortune Global 500 Companies," *Bloomberg Tax,* November 17, 2020.
36. United Nations Conference on Trade and Development, *World Investment Report 2020: International Production Beyond the Pandemic* (Geneva, 2020).
37. Tucker Higgins, "China Surpasses U.S. as Largest Recipient of Foreign Direct Investment During Covid Pandemic," CNBC, January 24, 2021; Yimou Lee, "Exclusive: Foxconn to Shift Some Apple Production to Vietnam to Minimize China Risk," *Reuters,* November 26, 2020.
38. Kathleen Schalch, "Study Finds American Firms Doing Business in China Are Not Improving Conditions for Chinese Workers," NPR, May 5, 2000.
39. C. Textor, "Minimum Wage per Hour in China as of March 2020, by Region," Statista, April 12, 2021; Lily Kuo, "TikTok Owner ByteDance Shortens China Work Hours, Discouraging Notorious '996' Routine," *Washington Post,* November 1, 2021.
40. International Labour Organization, "Statistics on Wages," May 14, 2021.
41. Chen Lin, John Geddie, "Myanmar Crisis Sounds Death Knell for Garment Industry, Jobs and Hope," *Reuters,* April 8, 2021; Oxfam International, "COVID-19 Cost Women Globally Over $800 Billion in Lost Income in One Year," April 29, 2021.
42. Ibid.
43. "Nearly Two-Thirds of Global Workforce in the 'Informal' Economy—UN Study," *UN News,* April 30, 2018; World Bank, "As COVID-19 Wreaks Havoc on Service Workers, Is the Informal Sector Increasing Global Inequality?" May 24, 2021.
44. OECD and the World Trade Organization, "Aid for Trade at a Glance 2019"; Tansy Hoskins, "Robot Factories Could Threaten Jobs of Millions of Garment Workers," *The Guardian,* July 16, 2016; Federico Guerrini, "Robots Could Take Away Two Thirds of Jobs in Developing Countries, the UNCTAD Says," *Forbes,* November 18, 2016; Adam Minter, "So Long to the Asian Sweatshop," *Bloomberg,* September 4, 2016.
45. Amelia Pang, *Made in China: A Prisoner, an SOS Letter, and the Hidden Cost of America's Cheap Goods* (Chapel Hill: Algonquin Books, 2021); Rachel Abrams, "Retailers Like H&M and Walmart Fall Short of Pledge to Overseas Workers," *New York Times,* May 31, 2016.
46. International Labour Organization, "World Statistics," 2021; "Work Accidents and Deaths in China Fall but Familiar Failings Remain," *China Labour Bulletin,* October 30, 2019.
47. Paul Mozur, "Apple Puts Key Contractor on Probation over Labor Abuses in China," *New York Times,* November 9, 2020.
48. Friedman, "Protesting for Whom?"
49. Jon C. Pevehouse and Joshua S. Goldstein, *International Relations* (New York: Pearson, 2020).
50. United Nations, *Protocol to Prevent, Suppress, and Punish Trafficking in Persons, Especially Women and Children, Supplementing the United Nations Convention Against Transnational Organized Crime,* Article 3, 2000.
51. United Nations Office on Drugs and Crime, "Impact of the Covid-19 Pandemic on Trafficking in Persons," 2021.
52. "Supply Chains Based on Modern Slavery May Reach into the West," *The Economist,* July 19, 2018.
53. International Labour Organization, "Child Labour Rises to 160 Million—First Increase in Two Decades," June 10, 2021; International Labour Organization, "Child Labour, 2021: International Year for the Elimination of Child Labour," January 15, 2021.
54. Richard Pérez-Peña, "Futures in Peril: The Rise of Child Labor in the Pandemic," *New York Times,* September 27, 2020; International Labour Organization, "Child Labour, 2021."

55. Bureau of International Labor Affairs, "Child Labor and Forced Labor Reports: Peru," 2019.

56. Beatrice Newbery, "Labouring Under Illusions," in Griffiths, *Annual Editions.*

57. Prakash S. Sethi, *Multinational Corporations and the Impact of Public Advocacy on Corporate Strategy: Nestle and the Infant Formula Controversy* (Boston: Kluwer Academic, 1994).

58. Oliver Balch, "Mars, Nestlé and Hershey to Face Child Slavery Lawsuit in US," *The Guardian,* February 12, 2021.

59. Yanzhong Huang, "The 2008 Milk Scandal Revisited," *Forbes,* July 16, 2014.

60. Aislinn Simpson, "Baby Formula Recall in China After Infant Death," *London Telegraph,* September 13, 2008; Roni Caryn Rabin, "Some Baby Food May Contain Toxic Metals, U.S. Reports," *New York Times,* February 4, 2021.

61. Chloé Maurel, "Will There Be a UN Treaty to Punish the Abuses Committed by Multinationals?" *Equal Times,* July 26, 2018; Elin Hofverberg, "Reflecting on 10 Years of the United Nations Guiding Principles on Business and Human Rights," Law Librarians of Congress, June 28, 2021.

62. Kalina Oroschakoff, Eline Shaart, and America Hernandez, "Shell Ordered to Slash Emissions in 'Mind-Blowing' Dutch Verdict," *Politico,* May 26, 2021.

63. Marc Gunter, "Wal-Mart Sees Green," *Fortune,* July 26, 2006; Irena Ivanova, "Greenpeace Sues Walmart, Claiming It Lies About Plastic Being Recyclable," *CBS News,* December 21, 2020.

64. Peter S. Goodman, Apoorva Mandavilli, Rebecca Robbins, and Matina Stevis-Gridneff, "What Would It Take to Vaccinate the World Against Covid?" *New York Times,* May 15, 2021.

65. Joint United Nations Programme on HIV/AIDS (UNAIDS), "HIV Treatment Now Reaching More Than 6 Million People in Sub-Saharan Africa," July 6, 2012; Tina Rosenburg, "H.I.V. Drugs Cost $75 in Africa, $39,000 in the U.S. Does It Matter?" *New York Times,* September 18, 2018; Smith, "Development Depends on More Than Aid"; Goodman et al., "What Would It Take to Vaccinate the World Against Covid?"; Rosie McCall, "Big Pharma Companies Earn More Profits Than Most Other Industries, Study Suggests," *Newsweek,* March 4, 2020.

66. James McBride, "How Does the U.S. Spend Its Foreign Aid?" Council on Foreign Relations, October 1, 2019; George Ingram, "What Every American Should Know About US Foreign Aid," Brookings Institution, October 15, 2019.

67. Katharina Buchholz," Where U.S. Foreign Aid Is Going," Statista, December 23, 2020; McBride, "How Does the U.S. Spend Its Foreign Aid?"

68. Brett Stephens, "To Help Haiti, Stop Trying to Save It," *New York Times,* July 12, 2021.

69. World Bank, "Net ODA Received (% of GNI)," 2021.

70. "Foreign Aid Is Having a Reckoning," *New York Times,* February 14, 2021.

71. Kofi A. Annan, "Trade and Aid in a Changed World," *New York Times,* March 19, 2002.

72. Ingram, "What Every American Should Know."

73. OECD, "The .7% ODA/GNI Target—A History," June 2010.

74. Ingram, "What Every American Should Know."

75. Ibid.; World Bank, "New Official Development Assistance and Official Aid Received (Current US $)," 2021.

76. McBride, "How Does the U.S. Spend Its Foreign Aid?"; Ingram, "What Every American Should Know."

77. "Foreign Aid Is Having a Reckoning," *New York Times,* February 13, 2021.

78. Polly Meeks, "A Knotty Problem: Turning Words into Action on Tied Aid," Network on Debt and Development, February 20, 2018.

79. "International Debt Statistics 2021: Debt Accumulation of Low- and Middle-Income Countries Surpassed $8 Trillion at End-2019," *World Bank Blogs,* October 12, 2020.

80. Homi Kharas and Meagan Dooley, "COVID-19's Legacy of Debt and Debt Service in Developing Countries," Brookings Institution, December 2020; United Nations Children's Fund (UNICEF), "COVID-19 and the Looming Debt Crisis," April 2021.

81. Jubilee USA Network, "Debt Slavery Is Foreign Aid in Reverse," 2016.

82. Abiy Ahmed, "Why the Global Debt of Poor Nations Must Be Cancelled," *New York Times,* April 30, 2020; The One Campaign, "Why the G20's Decision to Suspend Debt Repayments Matters During COVID-19," April 15, 2020.

83. World Bank, "Zimbabwe: Overview," October 4, 2016; International Monetary Fund, "Statement by the IMF on Zimbabwe," October 21, 2016.

84. Merritt Kennedy, "IMF Approves $12 Billion Bailout for Egypt After Austerity Measures," NPR, November 11, 2016; Zahraa Alkhalisi, "Why Egypt Just Let Its Currency Crash by 48%," *CNN Money,* November 3, 2016.

85. International Monetary Fund, "How the IMF Promotes Global Economic Stability," March 8, 2021.

86. International Monetary Fund, "IMF Extended Credit Facility (ECF)," April 2, 2021; "Mission: Possible," *The Economist,* April 11, 2009.

87. "Several Injured in Lebanon Protests over Plunging Currency," Al Jazeera, June 27, 2021; "Mired in Crisis, Lebanon Begs for Foreign Assistance," *The Economist,* July 10, 2021.

88. Alan Rappeport, "IMF Board Backs $650 Billion Aid Plan to Help Poor Countries," *New York Times,* July 9, 2021.

89. Nancy Birdsall, "Managing Inequality in the Developing World," in Griffiths, *Annual Editions.*

90. Tom Evans, "'Water Justice' Advocate: Don't Privatize," CNN.com, January 8, 2010; Juan Forero, "Who Will Bring Water to the Bolivian Poor?" *New York Times,* December 15, 2005.

91. Léo Heller, "Privatization and the Human Right to Water and Sanitation," United Nations Human Rights Office of the High Commissioner, July 21, 2020.

92. This is ironic since of the least-liberalized countries in the region, the People's Republic of China was also the emerging economy least affected by the Asian economic crisis. In a remarkable exception to neoliberal rules, China has not been subjected to an austerity plan and, in the meantime, it soaks up the largest amount of the world's foreign investment.

93. Edsall, "Trumpism Without Borders."

94. Stephen Grenville, "No Consensus on the Washington Consensus," Lowy Institute, June 7, 2017.

95. Salvador Santino F. Regilme Jr. and Obert Hodzi, "Comparing US and Chinese Foreign Aid in the Era of Rising Powers," *Italian Journal of International Affairs* 56, no. 2 (January 18, 2021); Kristen A. Cordell, "The Evolving Relationship Between the International Development Architecture and China's Belt and Road," Brookings Institution, October 2020; David E. Sanger and Mark Landler, "Biden Urges G7 to Act to Limit Reach of China," *New York Times,* June 13, 2021.

96. Jubilee USA Network, "Why Drop the Debt?"; "Ending the Cycle of Debt," *New York Times,* October 1, 2004.

97. Susan George, *Ill Fares the Land* (New York: Penguin, 1990).

98. Eduardo Galeano, *Open Veins of Latin America* (New York: Monthly Review, 1973).

99. Sewell Chan, "Perils Remain Despite Recovery's Pace, IMF Head Says," *New York Times,* April 25, 2010; "Mission: Possible," *The Economist.*

100. Stella Kaendera and Lamin Leigh, "Five Things to Know About Thailand's Economy and COVID-19," *IMF News,* June 23, 2021.

101. "A Long Way Down: Why Latin America's Economy Has Been So Badly Hurt by Covid-19," *The Economist,* May 15, 2021; "Where the Pandemic Clobbered Economies Hardest," *The Economist,* January 1, 2021.

102. "How Will Latin America's Covid-19 Bill Be Paid?" *The Economist,* May 1, 2021; "Where the Pandemic Clobbered Economies Hardest," *The Economist.*

103. Maitreesh Ghatak, Xavier Jaravel, and Jonathan Weigel, "The World Has a $2.5T Problem," *New York Times,* April 20, 2020.

104. Jonathan Masters and Andrew Chatsky, "The IMF: The World's Controversial Financial Firefighter," Council on Foreign Relations, August 20, 2020.

105. Peter S. Goodman and Alan Rappeport, "This Is the Plan to Rescue Poor Countries from the Pandemic," *New York Times,* June 24, 2021.

106. Ibid.; International Monetary Fund, "Low Interest Rates and High Debt Will Shape the Years Ahead."

107. Ibid.

108. Homi Kharas, "What to Do About the Coming Debt Crisis in Developing Countries," Brookings Institution, April 13, 2020.

109. Ahmed, "Why the Global Debt of Poor Nations Must Be Cancelled"; The One Campaign, "Why the G20's Decision to Suspend Debt Repayments Matters During COVID-19"; World Bank, "COVID 19: Debt Service Suspension Initiative," June 4, 2021.

110. "How Will Latin America's Covid-19 Bill Be Paid?" *The Economist.*

111. Jubilee USA Network, "Debt Slavery Is Foreign Aid in Reverse."

112. "Debt Relief Lifts Aid to Record Highs in 2005—OECD," *Business Recorder,* April 5, 2006; Esther Pan, "Iraq: The Regime's Debt," Council on Foreign Relations, February 16, 2005.

113. Emilio Sacerdoti and Philippe Callier, "Debt Relief Yields Results in Niger," *IMF Survey Magazine,* January 25, 2008.

114. "Oxfam Applauds Zambia's Free Health Care," *The Ottawa Citizen,* April 1, 2006; Jubilee USA,"Debt, Poverty, and the MDGs," 2007; IMF, "Debt Relief Under the Heavily Indebted Poor Countries (HIPC) Initiative," March 23, 2021.

115. IMF, "Debt Relief Under the Heavily Indebted Poor Countries (HIPC) Initiative"; World Bank, "Debt Relief," 2021; Jubilee USA Network, "HIPC: Understanding the Heavily Indebted Poor Country Initiative (HIPC)," 2021.

116. Patrick Kirby, Sinem Kilic Celik, Sebastian Essl, and Andre Proite, "Debt in Low-Income Countries: A Rising Vulnerability," *World Bank Blogs,* January 25, 2019.

117. Kimberly Amadeo, "What Is the Debt-to-GDP Ratio?" *The Balance,* May 28, 2021; International Monetary Fund, "Joint World Bank-IMF Debt Sustainability Framework for Low-Income Countries," March 17, 2021.

118. International Monetary Fund, "Global Debt Database," 2021; US National Debt Clock, December 1, 2021.

119. James McBride, Andrew Chatzky, and Anshu Siripurapu, "The National Debt Dilemma," Council on Foreign Relations, September 9, 2020.

120. Jubilee Debt Campaign, "The New Developing World Debt Crisis," November 2, 2016; The One Campaign, "Why the G20's Decision to Suspend Debt Repayments Matters During COVID-19."

121. Jonathan D. Ostry, Prakash Loungani, and Davide Furceri, "Neoliberalism Oversold?" *Finance and Development* 53, no. 2 (June 2016), p. 38.

122. Ellen Johnson Sirleaf, "This Is What Africa Needs Right Now," *New York Times,* November 6, 2021.

123. Jon Stone, "Neoliberalism Is Increasing Inequality and Stunting Economic Growth, IMF Says," *The Independent,* May 27, 2016.

124. David Ransom, "The Dictatorship of Debt," *New Internationalist,* no. 312 (May 1999); US National Debt Clock, December 1, 2021.

7

Linking Concepts and Cases

As we turn now to a discussion of how our eight case studies are faring in the INTERNATIONAL ECONOMIC SYSTEM, think about the years just prior to the pandemic and since. Identify some of the various ways in which these countries are coping with the economic pressures on them.

How are our cases doing in terms of GROWTH and DEVELOPMENT? Have there been any significant changes in their economic fortunes since this book was published? Which countries do you consider to be better off? Which are performing the worst? Why have some countries been more successful in their adoption of NEOLIBERALISM than others? How do you define "success"? In which countries has the pursuit of economic growth meant environmental devastation? How dependent is each of these countries on the export of raw materials? How diversified are their economies? Is it appropriate to characterize all (or any) of these countries as "emerging and developing," or "under-developing"? Why?

Case Study: Mexico

Mexico today is in many ways considered by the West to be a model of neoliberal economic reform. However, thirty years ago the country was at the epicenter of a debt crisis. The government had borrowed far beyond its means, was being charged exorbitant interest rates, and could not keep up with its payments.[1] After Mexico rocked the international financial system by threatening to default on its debt, the country was compelled to adopt a series of AUSTERITY PLANS. However, Mexico's economic problems continued and its debt piled up. By 1994, to win US support for Mexico's membership in the North American Free Trade Agreement, Mexico agreed to the terms of another round of economic reforms. Mexico had little choice but to faithfully meet the conditions outlined by the INTERNATIONAL MONETARY FUND. These included a series of measures, including a 40 percent devaluation of the peso that went into effect literally overnight. The combined effect of the reforms proved a shock to the system.

Known as the Tequila Crisis, growth rates plunged into the negative digits. Inflation and interest rates soared. The effect was like that of a financial neutron bomb: it destroyed the population, leaving only the real estate standing.[2]

The gravity of this crisis spurred the IMF to provide Mexico with a $40 billion emergency bailout package—at the time, the largest rescue ever. Growth rates since then have been up and down from 1993 to 2021, but averaging just 0.53 percent. However, in 2020 Covid contributed to Mexico's worst growth rates in nearly 100 years: *negative* 8.3 percent. By 2021, Mexico was experiencing a recovery, albeit a slow one, with 0.8 percent growth.[3] However, Mexico's experience illustrates both the benefits and the risks of GLOBALIZATION. Economic contraction in its neighbor to the north dramatically affects demand for Mexican goods. It should come as no surprise that analysts make their forecasts for Mexico based on the status of the United States and its recovery.

Since the establishment of the North American Free Trade Agreement (NAFTA), a free trade zone established between the United States, Canada, and Mexico in 1994, trade between the parties has grown exponentially. Because goods produced in Mexico can be exported duty-free to either of its NAFTA partners, and because of Mexico's low wages and lax enforcement of environmental regulations, MULTINATIONAL CORPORATIONS eagerly set up shop in the country. Since the passage of NAFTA (and now with the US-Mexico-Canada Agreement [USMCA], which reformed and replaced NAFTA in 2020), trade between the United States and Mexico has taken off, from $104 billion in 1994 to a high of $614 billion in 2019. For imports and exports, Mexico is the second most important US trading partner. On the other hand, the United States is by far Mexico's most important trading partner, as 80 percent of Mexico's exports go to the United States.[4]

Mexico mostly exports automobiles, electronics, and their parts to the United States, and *MAQUILADORAS* in Mexico have mushroomed and created millions of jobs, but with devastating results for rivers, which are now rank with industrial by-products and raw sewage. Many Mexicans farming on small plots have had a hard time holding on after NAFTA eliminated tariffs and opened up Mexico to competition against US and Canadian agribusinesses, which could sell their cheaper foodstuffs in Mexico duty-free. Yet, by other measures the free trade agreement has been a boon for the Mexican economy, which is the second largest in Latin America.[5]

Before the pandemic, extreme poverty had declined in this upper-middle-income country, but just barely. The richest 1 percent owned almost a quarter of the country's wealth.[6] Yes, since NAFTA there are more Mexican billionaires than ever and the middle class has grown and amounts to nearly half the population. Mexico has one of the lowest unemployment rates in Latin America, but over half of the Mexican population works in the informal sector. And the wage convergence promised to come with NAFTA has yet to appear. In 1994, when NAFTA went into effect, autoworkers in the United States made more than five times as much as Mexicans in similar positions. In 2016, US workers were making nine times more. Wages have risen so slowly that the average Mexican autoworker earns just $3.14 an hour. Still, this is much better than the minimum wage in Mexico, which was raised to $7.10 a day in 2021.[7]

For over thirty years, every Mexican president pursued the neoliberal model, without the promised benefits for the majority. This explains why so many voters were willing to give a proud leftist a resounding victory in 2018. Andrés Manuel López Obrador (known as AMLO) rose to power calling for fundamental political and economic changes, a "fourth revolution" that will empower the majority. The plan was to pay for his ambitious infrastructure and antipoverty programs through the elimination of corruption, estimated to cost the country $50 billion each year.[8]

But AMLO took office during a recession, and a year later, the pandemic, which hit Mexico harder economically than anything in the past century, has dominated much of his time in office. At one point, Mexico had one of the highest death tolls in the world from the virus. It is estimated as many as 10 million Mexicans fell back into poverty due to Covid lockdowns and as of 2021 more than half the population (70 million people) lived below the poverty line.[9] People who had never considered themselves poor now had nothing to eat. However, arguing that going into more debt would only make the country more dependent, the president responded with an austerity package rather than an influx of Covid aid and stimulus measures. Talk about trading places: in the midst of the crisis, the IMF begged the government to provide more of a safety net, while Mexico's leftist president adopted the fiscally conservative policies he had always railed against.[10]

Case Study: Peru

Since independence, Peru has struggled through fifty-year cycles of debt, dependence, and default.[11] It has been dependent on the sale of agricultural goods and mineral products for much of the past hundred years. Here is a country where the gap between rich and poor was only recently beginning to show signs of narrowing, but much of that progress has been lost with Covid. As discussed in Chapter 4, a tiny ELITE of landowners and merchants has long controlled the country's wealth.

Fifty years ago, prices for Peru's exports plummeted while its expenditures rose, and the country fell deeply into debt. By the 1980s, its creditors were demanding that the country pay half of all the hard currency it earned each year to service its debt of $16 billion. Unable to keep up with its payments, Peru fell $1 billion into arrears. In what has been described as a "brave but dumb" strategy, then president Alan García declared a moratorium on servicing its debt, limiting payments to 10 percent of its export earnings. The international financial community responded by making Peru ineligible for credit. Peru became a pariah—desperate for cash, forced to dramatically cut imports, and living day to day.[12]

By the end of García's term, many Peruvians were frantic for another approach. With the backing of business elites, President Alberto Fujimori undertook one of the most ambitious neoliberal reforms in Latin America and opened Peru to foreign investment. The reforms, which included drastic cuts in social spending, were likened to a form of shock therapy (so named for the invasive psychiatric procedure in which the patient is nearly killed to be saved). This policy became known in Peru as "Fujishock."

In this case, the patient reacted by going into a deep recession. The sudden lack of government services, including sanitation and potable water, paved the way for a reappearance of cholera, a poverty-related disease that had been unknown in Peru since the 1800s. Some parts of Peru had never before known such economic distress. Yet, because Fujimori was willing to push through the reforms, Peru was able to resuscitate its relationship with the IMF and obtain debt relief. By the mid-1990s, foreign investment was up and the country was registering impressive growth rates. Most important for Peruvians, inflation was brought down to the lowest levels in forty years. Despite the hardship associated with Fujishock, the end to hyperinflation bought the president enormous goodwill.[13]

Fujimori's successors continued with neoliberal reforms and for the past two decades, in macroeconomic terms at least, under neoliberal, pro-business leadership, the Peruvian economy appeared to be one of the most vibrant in the region, often characterized as thriving. Although they weren't as exuberant as they had been in most of the decade from 2000 to 2009, in the 2010s Peru's economic growth rates were healthy, ranging from 2 to 8 percent. Much of Peru's economic expansion was based on growing Asian (especially Chinese) demand and higher prices for its minerals.[14]

The generally stable, healthy growth since the Great Recession has translated into some improvements in the lives of more Peruvians. GNI per capita grew steadily, from $1,900 in 2001 to $7,060 in 2019.[15] Poverty rates came down, as the percentage of the Peruvian population earning less than $2 a day was cut from 55 percent to about 20 percent between 2005 and 2019.[16]

Just prior to the pandemic, Peru became widely known as a success story in the region. But growth was prioritized over development, and the pandemic and the economic shutdown undid many of those gains. When the pandemic hit, Peru only had 13 doctors per 10,000 people, one of the worst rates in Latin America. Although the government at first tried to cover up the death toll, the per capita mortality rate from the virus in Peru turned out to be much higher than had been previously reported—one of the highest in the world.[17]

During the 2020 slowdown, GDP declined by more than 11 percent and employment fell by 20 percent.[18] Despite what is said to be the most generous government effort in Latin America to aid the population (an emergency payment of $220 to over 6.5 million households), it wasn't enough to offset the damage. The Covid recession threw 2 million people back into poverty, amounting to nearly 30 percent of the population. Similarly, whereas Peru had cut its debt in 2017 to almost half of what it had been twenty years earlier, by the end of 2020 much of that ground was lost, as Peru's debt reached 35 percent of GDP.[19]

Most economists expected that Peru's economy would bounce back strongly in 2021, by 10 percent or more, based on recovered domestic demand and external demand for key commodities. Yet, much of this depends on how soon the pandemic is brought under control and if Peru can manage its multiple political crises.[20] The presidential race in 2016 was between two business-friendly neoliberals. However, by the time of the Covid recession there was a clear shift; by 2021, neoliberalism was widely viewed as broken. The population was angry, which enabled Pedro Castillo, a little-known left-wing union leader calling for structural change, to narrowly beat Keiko Fujimori, a right-wing neoliberal, in the presidential elections. Although the new president has been accused of being a communist and vague about how he would use Peru's resources to benefit Peruvians, his sentiment was clear. As Castillo said, "The people have woken up. We can take this country back!"[21] It remains to be seen if this political newcomer will survive long enough to make good on his claims.

Case Study: Nigeria

Although in recent years it has dropped from being the sixth to the world's fifteenth largest exporter of oil, Nigeria would seem to be the envy of much of the developing world. However, Nigeria is also one of the world's poorest countries. Forty percent of the population lives below the official poverty line.[22] Oil hasn't meant development for Nigeria; it is often said to be a curse. Part of the problem is that Nigeria is known as being "fantastically corrupt." One Nigerian government after another has stolen or wasted a large portion of the hundreds of billions of dollars in revenue generated by oil.

But before all the blame goes to corrupt or incompetent policymakers, however, a word needs to be said about the role of MNCs in Nigeria, especially Shell Oil, the region's biggest operator, which for years carried on with little or no government oversight.[23] As a result, the Niger Delta, site of most of the country's onshore petroleum and natural gas reserves, is an environmental basket case. It is estimated that 13 million barrels of oil have been spilled in Nigeria's wetlands, which is equivalent to an *Exxon Valdez* disaster every year for the past fifty years. These companies resist taking responsibility for the devastation, however, blaming most of the spills from pipelines on oil pirates, pipeline sabotage, and illegal refining.[24] It is true that oil theft by cartels is a big business in the Niger Delta. It is also true that little of the wealth created by the extraction of oil has been returned to residents.[25]

But that poverty is hardly restricted to Nigeria's southeast. Nigeria's rank on almost any level of human development is especially tragic given the country's tremendous potential. Its vast resources could provide a diversified economic base; its huge population could create an economy of scale. President Muhammadu Buhari has talked enthusiastically about his plan to diversify. But Nigeria is a classic monocultural economy. Approximately 90 percent of its foreign exchange is earned from the sale of petroleum and petroleum-based products, an industry that fails to employ many Nigerians (in 2020, it was estimated that youth unemployment was over 50 percent).[26] Because of the state of disrepair of its refineries, Nigeria actually has to import nearly all of its fuel needs; power outages that go on for days and long lines at gas stations are routine.[27]

Back in 1999, Nigerian citizens turned out at the polls hoping that after years of dictatorship a civilian-run government might be able to straighten out the country's economic mess. But the treasury was empty and the country was in arrears in repayment of a nearly $30 billion debt that exceeded 75 percent of the country's GDP.[28] Desperate for debt relief, Nigeria accepted neoliberal reforms. Nigerian leaders have attempted to raise revenues by increasing Nigeria's output of oil and by attracting foreign investment. They accepted austerity plans that (among other things) meant cutting government subsidies of food, which resulted in higher prices for basics.[29] And because it accepted the IMF's conditions, Nigeria was able to make a deal with the United Kingdom, France, and other creditors in 2005 to reduce its debt by $30 billion.[30]

Although some of this money was to go toward meeting basic human needs, Nigeria has had mixed results. For example, it has reduced maternal mortality rates and made progress against diseases such as polio and HIV/AIDS. But it has not done much to increase the percentage of women in wage employment or in parliament, and it has largely failed to provide sanitation or deal with environmental challenges associated with climate change.[31] Life expectancy has lengthened, but only from 47 to 55 years. Infant mortality has been reduced more substantially (but is still high) at 74 deaths per 1,000 live births (compared to 6 infant deaths per 1,000 live births in the United States).[32]

Moreover, after nearly two decades of civilian rule in Nigeria, severe inequality persists. In the years just prior to the pandemic, economic growth rates were relatively low but steady, averaging just over 2 percent. But due to Covid restrictions, Nigeria slid into a recession with a *negative* 6 percent growth rate in 2020. Before Covid, 80 million of the population of 200 million lived on less than $1.90 a day. The World Bank estimates that thanks to Covid and high population growth, the number of Nigerians living in absolute poverty will rise to 100 million by 2023.[33]

By late 2021, the economy was bouncing back as oil prices recovered after years of decline. But even when business is good in Nigeria, income inequality persists.[34] As in many other parts of the world, inflation rose dramatically in Nigeria—to the highest rates in decades. Higher prices meant devastation, as people already living in or on the edge of poverty simply can't obtain basic needs. Worse, in the northeast, where the insurgent terrorist group Boko Haram has devastated food production, there is a looming humanitarian disaster leaving over 12 million people needing aid.[35] As one economist put it, it's like the country has been hit by a macro-hurricane.[36]

Case Study: Zimbabwe

With what was once its comparatively diverse resource base, Zimbabwe's economy should be better off than that of many other African countries. At independence, it was relatively more industrialized than much of Africa, with its sugar refineries and textile industry. It sold (and still sells) tobacco, gold, and other minerals on the world market. A few decades ago, it was able not only to feed its population, but also to export its surplus foodstuffs. Back then, under President Robert Mugabe and the government of the Zimbabwe African National Union–Patriotic Front (ZANU-PF), a liberation movement turned political party, Zimbabwe was making significant strides in human development with an antipoverty campaign as a priority. The new government invested heavily in schools and healthcare, undoing the years of mistreatment and neglect that had been policy under white minority rule. Such programs succeeded in attaining for Zimbabweans one of the highest literacy rates on the continent.

However, Zimbabwe was dependent on the export of raw materials and fell deeply in debt, given the terms of trade. The Mugabe government had little choice but to accept the terms of a STRUCTURAL ADJUSTMENT PROGRAM (SAP) in 1991. Because of the budget cuts required by the IMF, the government had to reduce its investment in development and the country lost the impressive gains it had made in terms of infant and child mortality and literacy rates. In much of Zimbabwe the SAP came to stand for "Suffering for African People."[37]

The Mugabe government blamed several years of drought and the IFIs for the country's economic shambles. The World Bank and Western donors blamed the Mugabe government's CORRUPTION and mismanagement for the country's woes. In 1999, Mugabe defaulted on Zimbabwe's debt, became a pariah to the IFIs, and struck out on his own. He appealed to the 70 percent of the population who live in rural areas, resurrecting the long-neglected issue of land reform and seizing white-owned farms (which dated back to the days of Rhodesia's apartheid).[38]

Thousands of poor Black farmers were supposed to get the land, but they received only small plots; the best land went to high-ranking ZANU officials. Not only did the confiscation of large farms mean the loss of jobs for hundreds of thousands of farm laborers, but business confidence was in tatters, investors were scared off, and tourism ground to a halt. The effect on the economy was clear. By 2006, harvests were cut in half.[39] Zimbabwe's GDP growth rate hit a record low of *negative* 17.6 percent in 2008.[40] People found that they could not afford basic necessities as inflation grew at one point in 2008 to an unprecedented, estimated annual rate of 500 billion percent (the highest rate on the planet).[41] As a snapshot of how bad it was for the average Zimbabwean, by 2004 life expectancy had dropped from sixty-one years two decades earlier to forty-three—the shortest in the world.[42]

After years of resisting neoliberal reforms, in 2017 Zimbabwe changed course under new leadership. It had no choice. By late 2018, Zimbabwe's debt-to-GDP ratio was 77 percent. This was down from its record high of 248 percent in 2005. But the current debt is still considered unsustainable and the country is in debt distress, in arrears for most of its debt.[43] Consequently, President Emmerson Mnangagwa wants to normalize relations with creditors to access the aid his country needs. However, restructuring Zimbabwe's $8.8 billion debt is contingent on substantive political and economic reforms, including agreeing to IMF monitoring. But the government is walking a tightrope, trying to meet the IMF's demands without pushing the country into an ever-graver crisis. For example, a 150 percent increase in fuel prices kicked off massive protests in 2019.[44] And this was before the pandemic.

Many hoped that Zimbabwe's economic situation would improve in Mugabe's absence. However, Covid has taken a toll there as elsewhere. Growth rates in 2019 and 2020 were *negative* 8 percent and nearly half the population was living in extreme poverty.[45] In 2020, it was estimated that nearly half of Zimbabwe's population (7 million people, including 3.2 million children) was facing food shortages and in urgent need of assistance. The unemployment rate that year was 80 percent and consumers were angry, grappling with (at its peak) nearly 1,000 percent inflation.[46] Chronic cash shortages (we mean literally: the ATMs often run out of currency) are the norm. One might not have expected it in one of the world's poorest countries, but years ago Zimbabwe was one of the first to go to a cashless economy—in the cities, everyone uses plastic (in the countryside, bartering made a comeback).[47]

One bit of good news is that as of 2019, life expectancy in Zimbabwe had increased to fifty-nine years. The country no longer had the lowest life expectancy in the world (in 2020 Central African Republic took that title, with a life expectancy of fifty-three).[48] However, analysts predict that even after Covid presents less of a threat, Zimbabwe will continue to face serious challenges. Recurrent droughts and floods associated with climate change have ravaged Zimbabwe (and much of southern Africa) in recent years, and more is expected to come. Only 23 percent of rural dwellers have access to clean water and sanitation, which also increases the risk of other deadly diseases such as cholera and typhoid.[49] It's clearly an intolerable situation. Neoliberals may say that Zimbabwe is finally headed in the right direction, but combined with other pressures, the pain of IMF reforms may contribute to the political instability that makes democratization impossible.

Case Study: Egypt

President Abdel Fattah al-Sisi may face many of the same economic challenges his predecessors did, but it looks like he has not learned from their mistakes. Like them, he is grappling with a variety of intersecting problems: a resource-poor country (although there have been some recent offshore gas discoveries), a bloated and inefficient bureaucracy where the military's needs come first, a huge budget gap and rapid population growth, along with endemic unemployment and underemployment.[50] Egypt suffers from all these problems, not to mention leadership that emphasizes growth over development, resulting in subpar educational and healthcare systems. Covid made all these problems painfully clear. And Egypt's leaders are not preparing for the challenges already posed by climate change, such as water scarcity, which is already affecting Egyptian agriculture and is likely to get worse.[51]

To be fair, there has been some progress in some areas. Prior to the 1990s, Egypt was considered an impoverished country. Today, it is considered a lower-middle-income country. In the years just prior to the pandemic, Egypt ranked in the high human development category, having made significant strides in GNI per capita, life expectancy, school enrollment, and literacy rates between 1990 and 2019. However, the World Bank characterizes Egypt's economic growth over this period as "moderate and uneven."[52] Unemployment has hovered around 10 percent for the past several years. Sure, other places have it worse, but many people, especially the young, among whom the jobless rate in 2019 was more like 26 percent, have nowhere to turn but to informal sector jobs, which account for 68 percent of new jobs. This is especially problematic given that over half the population is under age thirty.[53]

Other problems are festering as well. For years, government spending has continued to far outpace revenue, and Egypt's economy simply does not produce and sell enough goods and services to keep up with its debt. Egypt's debt-to-GDP ratio improved in recent years, but it is high—it was 90 percent in 2020.[54] And the debt is a heavy burden on Egypt: nearly one-third of government expenditures goes to servicing this debt.[55] Desperate to receive a $12 billion bailout from the

IMF, the al-Sisi government has adopted neoliberal reforms. For example, in 2016 it devalued the Egyptian pound by 48 percent—leading to a currency crash and inflation. President al-Sisi has also cut subsidies for fuel, resulting in higher transport and, therefore, food prices. Meanwhile, the government has lacked a credible plan to promote the development that would create equitable growth.[56]

Analysts agree that far-reaching structural reforms are needed to transform Egypt's economy into a dynamic system that can reduce poverty, create productive employment opportunities, and maintain social and political stability. Instead, al-Sisi keeps the military happy by splurging on prestigious fighter jets and tanks—it was the world's third largest importer of weapons from 2015 to 2019. According to analysts, Egypt is pursuing a largely state-driven, military-led strategy centered on megaprojects such as $58 billion to build a new capital in the desert outside Cairo. Meanwhile, corruption continues to run rampant. This is nothing new. Rather, the only difference between today and the Mubarak years is that now the military has come from behind the curtain to show itself as a leading economic actor.[57]

As an example of misplaced priorities, the state (under both Mubarak and al-Sisi) simply disengaged from its social obligations. As a result, Egypt has periodically experienced shortages of essential goods. The government has cut the welfare system, pensions, and key subsidies. According to the World Bank, the al-Sisi government's acceptance of austerity stabilized the economy, but any progress made was undermined by the pandemic. Under the stress of Covid, the education and healthcare systems crumbled.[58] For example, the number of people living in poverty rose from 21 percent in 2009 to nearly 30 percent by 2020.[59] Key sectors of the economy have been seriously impacted by Covid. These include Suez Canal fees, tourism, and oil, as well as remittances from workers abroad. In the years before the pandemic, tourism had already taken a hit (especially since the terrorist attack on a Russian passenger plane in 2015). The number of foreign visitors had been cut in half since the 2011 uprising, but tourism dropped by 70 percent more in 2020 due to the pandemic.[60]

Growth in tourism and overall began to recover with the easing of curfews and social distancing in 2021, but in Egypt a combination of unfavorable domestic and external factors continue to work against development or equitable growth.[61] For example, the government's historical pattern of enacting a measure—testing the public's response and amending its policies accordingly—has often resulted in simply putting off painful but necessary reforms. That strategy can't last forever; Egypt is aid dependent. The IMF for now, at least, appears to be calling the shots.[62] President al-Sisi, mindful of the fate of his predecessors, does not hesitate to rely on repression to deal with his critics. But he has also been careful to calibrate reforms so as not to provoke massive protests. As one analyst put it, in what has become an all-too-familiar tale in Egypt, the strongman finds himself on a tightrope, facing countervailing winds. He must choose his steps carefully, or lose the fragile stability upon which his rule rests.[63]

Case Study: Iran

Economic issues have long plagued the Islamic Republic of Iran. The system combines central planning, state ownership of key industries, village farming, and small-scale private industries. Leaders try to balance economic well-being, self-sufficiency, and the proper role of the government, while facing challenging regional and international constraints. The founder of the Islamic state and first Supreme Leader, Ayatollah Ruhollah Khomeini, famously promised, "We will build real estate, make water and power free, and make buses free." This revolutionary pledge, among others, has yet to be realized.[64]

Iran's financial problems have intensified in recent decades—impacted by domestic mismanagement and external sanctions. Yet, even after most international sanctions were lifted in 2016, years of US sanctions and a long-lasting trade embargo worsened economic contraction: the Iranian economy's last growth was in 2017, and inflation has measured above 30 percent since 2018.[65] Pressure from the United States is not new: Washington has imposed some form of restriction on activities with Iran since the seizure of the US embassy in Tehran in 1979. Yet, the "maximum pressure" sanctions imposed by the Donald Trump administration in 2018–2019 are believed to have exacted more damage to the Iranian economy than any other single action in 2020, even if they did not precipitate the collapse of the Iranian economy, as some had expected.[66]

A central issue is Iran's economic dependence on other countries, especially trade in oil. Referred to as "black gold," oil has dominated life in Iran since its discovery in the early 1900s. Iranian leaders have worked to diversity the economy beyond oil. Continued US sanctions—especially after 2017—decreased this reliance; Iran's share of oil income among total state revenue is now one of the lowest of all net oil-exporting countries.[67] Estimates are that oil provided roughly 9 percent of government revenues in 2020, a decrease of 29 percent from 2019.[68]

Iran is the largest economy remaining outside of the WORLD TRADE ORGANIZATION (WTO). Even though it submitted an initial membership application in 1996, it became an observer state only in 2005, and further steps in the accession process are likely to be rocky at best. (The WTO's rules on consensus mean that opposition from a single influential member—the United States in this instance—can block a case.)

Economic challenges have led to widespread protests, often met with brutal repression. The 2019 protests, for example, widely viewed as the bloodiest since the 1979 revolution, were sparked by the state's surprise announcement of huge increases in gasoline prices.[69] Even though Iranians enjoy some of the cheapest fuel prices in the world, the sudden increase (in the middle of the night) impacted the cost of basic items. Local leaders reported protests in as many as 70 percent of provinces.[70] Some have argued that Iranians, even prior to the Covid pandemic, have been anxious about their very survival.[71]

As an Islamic state, Iran has attempted to integrate the teachings of the Quran into all aspects of life, including the financial sector. Iran is viewed as one of the "pioneers" of Islamic finance, offering SHARIA-compliant products since 1983 (even if Iran's Islamic banking is grounded in Shia, rather than Sunni, jurisprudence).[72] Iran is the only country besides Sudan where the entire financial industry is obliged to be consistent with the principles of sharia law,[73] although other countries, including Turkey, Malaysia, Afghanistan, Pakistan, and Kuwait, offer Islamic banks as an option to conventional, interest-bearing banks.[74] Yet, a combination of plentiful nonperforming loans, as well as competing interpretations of sharia by Shia and Sunnis, limits the strength of Iran's financial structures.

Unemployment is a persistent challenge, especially among the youth. Attempts to privatize nationally owned companies threaten to further increase unemployment, and plans to decrease state subsidies on critical items, including basic foods, medical goods, gasoline, and utilities, are met with fear and sometimes violence. Poverty remains endemic for large swaths of the population (with more than 60 percent of society living in RELATIVE POVERTY), and millions have been relegated to extreme poverty in one year alone (2020–2021).[75] Slums are increasing at an alarming rate, with somewhere between 10 and 13 million citizens "entirely excluded" from health, labor, or unemployment insurance or benefits.[76] While women are increasingly integrated into the work force, they tend to dominate in traditional areas like education and healthcare, and their employment can be curtailed by the wishes of their husbands.

President Hassan Rouhani's failure to deliver on economic expectations dealt a serious blow to Iranian moderates, and economic issues fared prominently in the 2021 presidential race. Rouhani's embrace of a more globally engaged Iran was not always welcomed by the Supreme Leader, who called for a revitalization of Iran's "resistance economy" that focuses on self-sufficiency over interdependence.[77] Upon assuming the presidency in 2021, conservative Ebrahim Raisi inherited a broken financial system and a country drowning in "economic misery."[78]

For much of the pandemic Iran was the worst Covid-impacted state in the region,[79] exacerbated by an economic contraction of 12 percent in the years prior to Covid.[80] Losses in the informal sector and high-contact services were more extreme, and tanking oil revenues due to the crash in global demand for oil, in addition to health and social assistance needs, took a huge toll on the country's fiscal deficit and public debt.

On the surface, the economy should be one of the greatest strengths of the Islamic Republic of Iran. With a relatively diverse economic structure and significant reserves of natural resources, in addition to a highly educated, urban population of youth, Iran has much going for it. Yet, economic underperformance and discontent have been the norm. The state's response to the Covid pandemic has increased government debt as well as public frustration, at the same time that inflation and other pressures mount. Political, religious, and external barriers continue to limit Iran's economic achievements.

Case Study: China

Students are often surprised to find China included in a text on the global south. It is perhaps ironic that a state that prided itself on autarky and self-sufficiency (in the 1950s and 1960s) is now one of the most interconnected economies in the world. In a matter of decades, China transitioned from isolation to integration, increasing both wealth and inequality within its borders.[81] Chinese markets weathered the Great Recession better than the developed economies, and, even during Covid, maneuvered through the mind-boggling disruptions better than nearly all world economies. In 2020, the People's Republic of China (PRC) was the only major world economy to report growth (even if it was a forty-four-year low at 2.3 percent).[82] This shrinkage ended a nearly half-century run on growth during which China's GDP increased at an annual average of 9.5 percent.[83]

Chinese leaders have adopted multiple economic models, some disastrous and some successful. In the late 1950s, Mao Zedong launched the Great Leap Forward as a way to modernize the country and catch up with the West. Through intense agricultural and industrial programs that included encouraging farmers to construct "backyard burners" to melt down pots and pans to make steel, Mao proclaimed that the Chinese people could surpass Western production totals in less than fifteen years. The results were devastating: as many as 30 million people are believed to have died (many from starvation) because of the misguided agricultural and ideological policies of the period (archival research estimates this total could be as high as 45 million).[84] Mao's successor, Deng Xiaoping, made economic growth his primary goal. Touting such non-Marxist phrases as "to get rich is glorious" and "it is all right for some to get rich first," Deng launched an economic revolution. Ordinary people could start their own companies and trade their agricultural products with local governments, and even foreign firms such as Coca-Cola were invited to produce and sell their products on the mainland—matters that were beyond imagination during the Mao years.

The Chinese economy embodies stark contrasts. Chinese banks were once prototypes of inefficient bureaucracies; now the Industrial and Commercial Bank of China is the largest public company in the world and the major "big four" state banks are commanding an increasing presence on the international scene.[85] China has more billionaires than the United States and India combined, yet nearly 600 million people earn less than $150 monthly.[86] Even though the Chinese Communist Party (CCP) pledges a rhetorical commitment to gender equality, women have fared worse as the economy improved—the reverse of what was observed in Brazil, India, Mexico, Thailand, and elsewhere.[87] Inflation (hovering around 2 percent) and producer price index increases (approximately 13 percent) present big challenges, and unemployment threatens to derail the newfound wealth. While the overall unemployment rate is approximately 5 percent, the rate for youth (ages sixteen to twenty-four years) vacillates between 15 and 16 percent.[88] Jobs are plentiful for blue-collar workers, but in short supply for college graduates.[89]

China's economic drivers continue to be exports and infrastructure. Every major city is connected by the world's longest high-speed railway lines (enough to stretch across the continental United States seven times), with new routes being added to smaller cities, and construction crews working twenty-four hours a day.[90] With the Asian Infrastructure Investment Bank (AIIB) and the BELT AND ROAD INITIATIVE (BRI)—a major investment in ports, rail lines, roads, infrastructure—Beijing's economic wingspan is vast. Since its launch in 2013, more than 150 states and international organizations have endorsed the massive effort. To date, other multinational efforts to rival Beijing's "project of the century" have fallen flat, even as opposition to Chinese investment (and rising debt burdens borne by recipient countries) increases.[91] The potential for a Beijing Consensus to rival the laissez-faire orthodoxy of the Washington Consensus is growing, especially as democracy faces global challenges and China fills in gaps left by a perceived US retreat. Covid politics are at work here, too, as Beijing attempts (with mixed success) to provide effective prevention to the pandemic.[92]

To continue its economic gains, Beijing needs to stimulate domestic consumption rather than remaining reliant on exports. Yet, market bubbles and continued irregularities open the Chinese economy up to volatile risks, evidenced recently by the crisis surrounding the real estate developer and wealth management company Evergrande, owned by the man who was once Asia's richest person. After the company failed to make payments on hundreds of billions in loans, fears of potential ripple effects and threats to other sectors of the economy were palpable.[93]

Demography presents another challenge. The aging population decreases the labor supply at the same time that demands for healthcare and social services are skyrocketing. China faces a dwindling labor supply of sixteen- to twenty-four-year-olds, the age bracket that once packed factories and fueled the country's export-driven success. CCP leaders continue to attempt policy levers—including further manipulation of its planned birth policies to permit three children per family—to overcome demographic shortages. China's retirement age is one of the lowest in the world (sixty for most men; fifty for women).[94]

Beijing connects its political legitimacy to positive economic performance. It may be a risky proposition, as much is beyond the control of policymakers. Yet, Covid actually made the world more dependent on Chinese exports, which experienced sturdy growth in 2021 compared to 2020.[95] Now that the yuan holds special drawing rights as one of the five major world currencies within the IMF, Beijing is increasingly recognized as the major world economy that it long aspired to be. Surviving both the trade war with the United States and (at least to date) coronavirus shock, Beijing's confidence is increasing. Whether this confidence is warranted remains to be seen.

Case Study: Indonesia

As the largest economy in Southeast Asia, Indonesia was once hailed as one of the "Little Tigers" of Southeast Asia. Although challenges remain, Indonesia is now one of the best-performing emerging market economies, with the IMF assessing that it "has the firepower to boost its economic recovery" to be a significant regional player.[96]

Indonesia has long searched for a viable economic model. Even after its political break from the Dutch, the Indonesian economy depended on primary crops introduced by the Netherlands. Sukarno nationalized all plantations, leading to widespread stagnation and capital flight. Inflation and poverty were widespread after the government defaulted on its foreign debt; most external assistance ceased. Indonesia's second president, Suharto, attempted to turn the economy around, especially by mending ties with other countries. As a staunch anticommunist, Suharto received much aid from Western countries. His model was a familiar one in Asia: promote industrial and business growth with government support, while limiting dissent.

After Indonesia's oil boom, Suharto shied away from the so-called Berkeley Mafia free market advice of the 1960s (Indonesia's own version of the Washington Consensus).[97] The oil collapse in the mid-1980s wreaked havoc, as prices tanked. In response, the "Mafia" advised an increase in exports. Corruption and patronage were rampant even as Indonesia's market successes received much praise.

All gains came to a screeching halt with the crisis of 1997; no Asian country fared worse. The economy contracted nearly 14 percent. Inflation topped 65 percent and the national currency lost 70 percent of its value, producing what the World Bank referred to as one of the most dramatic reversals of fortune ever.[98] After the crisis, many Indonesians looked to the Chinese model of state-supported economic growth, the so-called Beijing Consensus, to replace the neoliberal Washington Consensus, which many blamed for the economic crises.[99]

Indonesia was rocked by the demands of lending institutions. IMF conditions for the $45 million aid package required leaders to redirect funds away from assistance programs and social spending, sparking a fury of unrest. Initial runs on banks led to street riots; the economy shrank. Demonstrations against Suharto, viewed as impotent in the face of outsider demands, eventually toppled him. Indonesia experienced limited debt forgiveness (including a $3 billion restructuring plan following the 2004 tsunami), and a gradual restoration of assistance programs. Corruption and poor governance curtailed monies from multilateral institutions. Yet, the tables were turned in 2012, when Indonesian leaders confirmed a $1 billion contribution to the IMF's European bailout reserves—money drawn from precisely the same foreign exchange reserves that leaders amassed in case they faced more demands from the IMF.[100]

When he became Indonesia's seventh president in 2014, Joko Widodo (popularly known as Jokowi) inherited a strong but struggling economy. Jokowi's humble background influenced his populist approach: while growing up, his family was evicted from their illegally built shacks three times, and he began working jobs to support his family at the age of twelve. One journalist referred to his background as "Indonesia's version of Abraham Lincoln's log cabin in the woods."[101] Under Jokowi, Indonesia joined the exclusive club of 1-trillion-dollar economies in 2017, and formally transitioned into middle-income status in 2020.[102]

Yet, even prior to Covid, Jokowi faced many challenges. Overreliance on state-owned enterprises, interregional disparities (including a widening Gini coefficient), and youth unemployment each threaten progress.[103] Economic growth has been accompanied by a widening gap between rich and poor. Penned by local media as the "infrastructure president," Jokowi has emphasized prestige projects: more than 27 million Indonesians watched the unveiling of the country's longest bridge on Instagram.[104] As it pursues one of the most rapid urbanization experiences in the world, Indonesia trails behind neighbors in providing access to safe drinking water and modern sanitation systems.[105] Of the four main causes of death for children under five, two of them (diarrhea and typhoid) are fecal-borne illnesses connected to inadequate water supply and sanitation.[106]

Jokowi pursued an "economy first" approach to Covid, initially downplaying the severity of the virus. The president contended that a strict lockdown might be an option for wealthier countries, but would lead to chaos and collapse in Indonesia.[107] Along with the Philippines, Indonesia had the worst Covid outbreak in Southeast Asia. The World Bank estimates that years of progress in poverty reduction were lost to the pandemic.[108]

In 2016, the World Bank characterized Indonesia as "a confident middle-income country," having made enormous gains in poverty reduction even in the face of slowing growth rates.[109] By 2020, the World Bank called Indonesia's development trajectory over prior decades "remarkable," albeit highlighting significant gaps that may imperil these gains.[110] To be able to demonstrate its prowess, and achieve Jokowi's stated goal of transforming Indonesia into one of the world's top five economies by 2036, Jakarta must adequately address these holes in an otherwise promising economic situation.

Now It's Your Turn

Perhaps as the neoliberals tell us, the experience of a handful of countries should be a lesson to all the rest. However, after two decades of sacrifice and deteriorating conditions for the majority, is it right for developed countries to continue to insist that the neoliberal model is the only feasible path to development? Are neoliberals correct that there really is no alternative?

Should the leaders of less developed countries simply press for a more flexible approach to further integration into the international economic system as it currently exists? Will the managers of the system (Western donors and the international organizations they control) allow alternative paths to be forged? Or can a combination of strategies utilize non-Western experience and culture to create a system more beneficial for all? What does "independence" mean in a globalized world economy?

Notes

1. James Nelson Goodsell, "Mexico's New President Takes Office—with $80 Billion Debt," *Christian Science Monitor,* December 1, 1982.
2. Alejandro Nadal, "The Microeconomic Impact of IMF Structural Adjustment Policies in Mexico," in *The All-Too-Visible Hand: A Five Country Look at the Long and Destructive Reach of the IMF,* ed. Friends of the Earth and The Development Gap (Washington, DC: Friends of the Earth, April 1999).
3. "Mexico's GDP Growth Rate," *Trading Economics,* 2021.
4. Ioan Grillo, "Forget Trump's Wall: For Mexico, the Election Is About Nafta," *New York Times,* September 23, 2016; M. Angeles Villarreal, "U.S.-Mexico Trade Relations," Congressional Research Service, April 26, 2021.
5. Vanda Felbab-Brown, "The Ills and Cures of Mexico's Democracy," Brookings Institution, March 2019; Elisabeth Malkin, "Nafta's Promise, Unfulfilled," *New York Times,* March 24, 2009.
6. Jude Webber, "Wealthy Mexicans Find They Can Buy Comfort but Not Protection," *Financial Times,* June 21, 2020; Felbab-Brown, "The Ills and Cures of Mexico's Democracy."
7. T. K. McDonald, "The Economics of Mexico's Middle Class," *Investopedia,* February 28, 2021; "Informal Employment in Mexico Hits New Record," *Mexico Today,* November 15, 2019; Carrie Khan, "Will NAFTA 2.0 Really Boost Mexican Wages?" NPR, October 17, 2018; Pietro Straulino-Rodríguez, Nora M. Villalpando Badillo, and Iván Andrade Castelán, "Mexico Approves Increases to Daily Minimum Wages for 2021," *National Law Review,* December 24, 2020.
8. Felbab-Brown, "The Ills and Cures of Mexico's Democracy."
9. Mariana Campero and Ryan C. Berg, "Mexico's Midterm Elections Matter to the United States," Center for Strategic and International Studies, June 2, 2021.
10. Azam Ahmed, "Mexico's Leftist Leader Rejects Big Spending to Ease Virus's Sting," *New York Times,* June 8, 2020; Azam Ahmed, "In the Epicenter of Mexico's Epicenter, Feeling Like a 'Trapped Animal,'" *New York Times,* September 23, 2020.

11. Cynthia McClintock, *Revolutionary Movements in Latin America* (Washington, DC: United States Institute of Peace Press, 1998).

12. Susan George, *The Debt Boomerang: How Third World Debt Harms Us All* (Boulder: Westview, 1992); McClintock, *Revolutionary Movements in Latin America.*

13. George, *The Debt Boomerang.*

14. "GDP Growth (Annual %)—Peru," World Bank, 2021; "The World Bank in Peru," World Bank, April 9, 2021.

15. "Peru," World Bank, 2016; "Peru Economic Outlook," *FocusEconomics,* 2021.

16. "Peru—Poverty Headcount Ratio at National Poverty Line," *World Data Atlas* (New York: Knoema, 2019).

17. "Self-Medication Increases Pandemic's Deaths in Peru," *The Economist,* October 3, 2020; Mitra Taj and Julie Turkewitz, "Left and Right Clash in Peru's Election, with an Economic Model at Stake," *New York Times,* June 6, 2021.

18. "Peru Overview," World Bank, October 1, 2021.

19. "Peru," World Bank, 2016; "The World Bank in Peru," World Bank, April 9, 2021; "Peru Is Heading Towards a Dangerous New Populism," *The Economist,* July 25, 2020.

20. "The World Bank in Peru," World Bank, April 9, 2021; "The Man with the Straw Hat: Pedro Castillo Is on the Verge of Becoming Peru's President," *The Economist,* June 12, 2021.

21. Dan Collyns, "Leftist Teacher Takes on Dictator's Daughter as Peru Picks New President," *The Guardian,* June 3, 2021; Taj and Turkewitz, "Left and Right Clash in Peru Election."

22. "Oil Production in the Leading Oil-Producing Countries Worldwide in 2020*," Statista, 2021; "The World Factbook," Central Intelligence Agency, 2021.

23. "How Nigeria Is Fighting Corruption," *The Economist,* July 26, 2016.

24. Stanley Reed, "Shell and Nigerian Partner Are Sued in Britain over Spills," *New York Times,* March 2, 2016.

25. "Crude Oil Disruptions in Nigeria Increase as a Result of Militant Attacks," US Energy Information Administration, August 18, 2016; "The Economist Explains How Nigeria Is Fighting Corruption," *The Economist,* July 26, 2016.

26. Chijioke Ohuocha and Libby George, "Nigeria's Central Bank Ends Dollar Sales to Exchange Bureaus," *Reuters,* July 27, 2021; "Youth Unemployment Rate in Nigeria in Selected Quarters Between the 1st Quarter of 2018 and the 4th Quarter of 2020," Statista, 2021.

27. Ruth Olurounbi and William Clowes, "Nigeria Fuel Subsidies Near $300 Million a Month, NNPC Says," *Bloomberg,* March 25, 2021.

28. Douglas Farah, "Nigerian Leader Pushes for Debt Relief," *Washington Post,* October 30, 1999.

29. Jean Herskovits, "Politics in Nigeria Have 'Ground to a Halt,'" Council on Foreign Relations, March 25, 2009.

30. "Nigeria Settles Paris Club Debt," *BBC News,* April 21, 2006.

31. "Nigeria 2015: Millennium Development Goals: End-Point Report," Office of the Senior Special Assistant to the President on Millennium Development Goals (MDGs), 2015.

32. "Life Expectancy at Birth," World Bank, 2021; "Mortality Rate, Infant," World Bank, 2021.

33. "Overview: The World Bank in Nigeria," World Bank, November 3, 2020; "Nigeria's Economy Is Stuck in a Rut," *The Economist,* May 15, 2021.

34. "Exchange Rate in Nigeria," *Focus Economics,* 2021; "Nigeria: Foreign Investment," *Santander,* September 2021.

35. Alonso Soto, "Surging Inflation in Nigeria Fuels Crime Wave, Says World Bank," Al Jazeera, June 15, 2020; "Nigeria Emergency," United Nations High Commissioner for Refugees (UNHCR), 2021.

36. "Nigeria's Economy Is Stuck in a Rut," *The Economist;* Dawn Kissi, "Nigeria Goes from Powerhouse to Pariah as 'Hurricane' Hits Economy," CNBC, May 8, 2016.

37. Julius E. Nyang'oro and Timothy M. Shaw, "The African State in the Global Economic Context," in *The African State at a Critical Juncture: Between Disintegration and Reconfiguration,* ed. Julius E. Nyang'oro and Timothy M. Shaw (Boulder: Lynne Rienner, 1998); Robert I. Rotberg, "Africa's Mess, Mugabe's Mayhem," *Foreign Affairs* 79, no. 5 (September–October 2000).

38. Rachel L. Swarns, "Zimbabwe Starts Arresting White Farmers Defying Eviction," *New York Times,* August 17, 2002; "From Breadbasket to Basket Case," *The Economist,* June 29, 2002.

39. Daniel Pepper, "Zimbabwe's Army Takes Over Black Farms," *Christian Science Monitor,* June 5, 2006; Norimitsu Onishi, "'No One Is Safe': Zimbabwe Threatens to Seize Farms of Party Defectors," *New York Times,* August 24, 2016.

40. "GDP Growth (Annual %)—Zimbabwe," World Bank, 2020.

41. Greg Mills and Jeffrey Herbst, "Bring Zimbabwe in from the Cold," *New York Times,* May 28, 2009; "IMF Country Report No. 09/139," International Monetary Fund, May 2009.

42. Celia W. Dugger, "Zimbabwe Health Care, Paid with Peanuts," *New York Times,* December 19, 2010; "Zimbabweans Have 'Shortest Lives,'" *BBC News,* April 8, 2006.

43. "Zimbabwe: External Debt to GDP," *Trading Economics,* 2021; "Zimbabwe: Joint World Bank–IMF Debt Sustainability Analysis," International Development Association and World Bank, February 2020.

44. "Seeking to Change Deadbeat Image, Zimbabwe Pays Debt," *France24,* September 12, 2021; "Implement Substantive Reforms, Paris Club Creditors Tell Zimbabwe," *Reuters,* July 8, 2020; Elliot Smith, "Zimbabwe in 'Economic and Humanitarian Crisis' as IMF Sounds Alarm," CNBC, March 3, 2020; "Freedom in the World: Zimbabwe 2020," Freedom House, 2020.

45. "Zimbabwe GDP Growth Rate 1961–2021," World Bank, 2021; Kudzai Chimhangwa, "Zimbabwe's Odious Debts," OpenDemocracy, November 18, 2020.

46. "Implement Substantive Reforms, Paris Club Creditors Tell Zimbabwe," *Reuters*; "Zimbabwe UNICEF Zimbabwe Humanitarian Situation Report—January–December 2020," United Nations Children's Fund (UNICEF), March 12, 2021.

47. Jeffrey Moyo and Norimitsu Onishi, "A Cashless Economy in Zimbabwe? With Little Cash, There's Little Choice," *New York Times,* November 3, 2016.

48. "Life Expectancy at Birth: Total (Years) Zimbabwe," World Bank, 2021.

49. "Drought and Decline: Zimbabwe," International Rescue Committee, 2021.

50. Julia Goldman, "Egypt's Economy Stuck in the 'Doldrums,'" Atlantic Council, June 16, 2016.

51. "Thinking Big," *The Economist,* March 21, 2015; Tamara Cofman Wittes, "Egypt: Trends, Politics, and Human Rights," Brookings Institution, September 9, 2020.

52. "About Egypt," United Nations Development Programme, 2016; United Nations Development Programme, "Egypt," *Human Development Report 2020.*

53. "Unemployment Total: Egypt, Arab Republic," World Bank, June 15, 2021; "Egypt: Youth Unemployment Rate from 1999 to 2019," Statista, June 30, 2021; Mohammed Soliman, "Egypt's Informal Economy: An Ongoing Cause of Unrest," *Columbia Journal of International Affairs,* October 29, 2020; "Egypt Population 2021," *World Population Review,* 2021.

54. "Egypt Government Debt to GDP," *Trading Economics,* 2021.

55. Maged Mandour, "Sisi's War on the Poor," Carnegie Endowment for International Peace, September 23, 2020.

56. "Egypt Averts Economic Collapse, for Now," *New York Times,* November 5, 2016; "Egypt: Inflation Rate from 1986 to 2026," Statista, 2021; Emad El-Din Shahin, "Egypt's Revolution Turned on Its Head," *Current History,* December 2015.

57. "Egypt: Overview," World Bank; Abigail Hauslohner, "Egypt's Military Expands Its Power over the Economy," *Washington Post,* March 17, 2014; Declan Walsh, "Sisi Promised Egypt Better Health Care: Virus Exposed His True Priority," *New York Times,* November 11, 2020.

58. Walsh, "Sisi Promised Egypt Better Health"; Tarek Osman, *Egypt on the Brink: From Nasser to Mubarak* (New Haven: Yale University Press, 2010).

59. "Poverty and Equity Brief: Arab Republic of Egypt," World Bank, April 2020.

60. Mustansir Barma, "Struggles for Egypt's Tourism Sector," Carnegie Endowment for International Peace, December 17, 2015; "Egypt Eyes Slow Return for Tourism After Revenues Dive in 2020," *Reuters*, January 4, 2021; United Nations Development Programme, *Human Development Report 2020,* 2020.

61. "Egypt Economic Outlook," *FocusEconomics;* "The World Bank in Egypt," World Bank, April 5, 2021.

62. "A Dollar Crisis Threatens Egypt's Economy," Stratfor, March 10, 2016; "The World Bank in Egypt," World Bank.

63. Declan Walsh, "Where's My Mercedes? Egypt's Financial Crisis Hits the Rich," *New York Times,* March 10, 2016.

64. Quoted in Robert F. Worth, "Iran's Plan to Phase Out Subsidies Brings Frenzied Debate," *New York Times,* December 2, 2009.

65. Abigail Ng, "These 6 Charts Show How Sanctions Are Crushing Iran's Economy," CNBC, March 22, 2021.

66. Jackie Northam, "Why Iran's Economy Has Not Collapsed amid U.S. Sanctions and 'Maximum Pressure,'" NPR, January 16, 2020; Henry Rome, "Iran's Economy in 2020," Eurasia Group, December 16, 2020.

67. Parisa Hafezi and Davide Barbuscia, "Iran Says It Will Fare Better Than Others After Oil Crash amid Battered Economy," *Reuters,* April 22, 2020.

68. Ibid.

69. Farnaz Fassihi and Rick Gladstone, "With Brutal Crackdown, Iran Is Convulsed by Worst Unrest in 40 Years," *New York Times,* December 1, 2019; Daphne Psaledakis and Humeyra Pamuk, "U.S. Imposes Sweeping Sanctions on Iran, Targets Khamenei-Linked Foundation," *Reuters*, November 18, 2020.

70. Ali Fathollah-Nejad, "Why Iranians Are Revolting Again," Brookings Institution, November 19, 2019.

71. Masoud Mostajabi, "Iran's Botched Handling of the Coronavirus May Impact June Election," Atlantic Council, March 15, 2021.

72. Jacopo Dettoni, "Iran and the Islamic Finance Crown," *The Diplomat,* June 16, 2015.

73. Ibid.

74. "Global Islamic Finance Forecast to Grow as Main Markets Recover—S&P," *Reuters,* May 3, 2021.

75. Najmeh Bozorgmehr, "Spiralling Poverty in Iran Adds to Pressure on Regime," *Financial Times,* January 25, 2021.

76. Ali Fathollah-Nejad, "Four Decades Later, Did the Iranian Revolution Fulfill Its Promises?" Brookings Institution, July 11, 2019.

77. Djavad Salehi-Isfahani, "The Dilemma of Iran's Resistance Economy," *Foreign Affairs,* March 17, 2021.

78. Vivan Yee, "Iranian Hard-Liner Ebrahim Raisi Wins Presidential Vote," *New York Times,* June 19, 2021.

79. Masoud Mostajabi, "Iran's Botched Handling of the Coronavirus May Impact June Election," Atlantic Council, March 15, 2021; Parisa Hafezi and Davide Barbuscia, "Iran Says It Will Fare Better Than Others After Oil Crash amid Battered Economy," *Reuters*, April 22, 2020.

80. "World Bank Overview: Islamic Republic of Iran," World Bank, March 30, 2021.

81. Virginia Harrison and Daniele Palumbo, "China Anniversary: How the Country Became the World's 'Economic Miracle,'" *BBC News,* October 1, 2019.

82. Johnathan Cheng, "China Is the Only Major Economy to Report Economic Growth for 2020," *Wall Street Journal,* January 18, 2021.

83. Keith Bradsher, "China's Economy Shrinks, Ending a Nearly Half-Century of Growth," *New York Times,* April 16, 2020; Lucy Tompkins, "Extreme Poverty Has Been Sharply Cut. What Has Changed?" *New York Times,* December 2, 2021.

84. Frank Dikötter, *Mao's Great Famine: The History of China's Most Devastating Catastrophe, 1958–1962* (New York: Walker, 2010); Louisa Lim, "A Grim Chronicle of China's Great Famine," NPR, November 10, 2012.

85. Jason Bisnoff, "The World's Largest Banks 2021: Banks Grew Larger During the Pandemic, with U.S. and Chinese Banks Dominant," *Forbes,* May 13, 2021; Elmar Hellendoorn, "Geopolitical Change and the Emergence of Chinese Banking," Atlantic Council, October 6, 2021.

86. Li Yuan, "Why China Turned Against Jack Ma," *New York Times,* December 24, 2020.

87. Mariya Brussevich, Era Dabla-Norris, and Bin Grace Li, "China's Rebalancing and Gender Inequality," Working Paper no. 21 (Washington, DC: International Monetary Fund, May 2021), p. 138.

88. John Liu, Lin Zhu, Yujing Liu, and Bihan Chen, "China's Youth Unemployment Spikes as Students Graduate," *Bloomberg News,* August 16, 2021.

89. Keith Bradsher, "Most Major Economies Are Shrinking. Not China's," *New York Times,* January 17, 2021.

90. Ibid.; Adi Ignatius, "Americans Don't Know How Capitalist China Is," *Harvard Business Review,* May–June 2021.

91. Michael Peel and Sam Fleming, "West and Allies Relaunch Push for Own Version of China's Belt and Road," *Financial Times,* May 2, 2021; David Stanway, "China's Belt and Road Plans Losing Momentum as Opposition, Debt Mount—Study," *Reuters,* September 29, 2021.

92. Sui-Lee Wee and Steven Lee Myers, "As Chinese Vaccines Stumble, U.S. Finds New Opening in Asia," *New York Times,* August 20, 2021.

93. "China: What Is Evergrande and Is It Too Big to Fail?" *BBC News,* November 5, 2021.

94. Keith Zhai, "China to Allow Families Three Children," *Wall Street Journal,* June 1, 2021.

95. Ignatius, "Americans Don't Know."

96. Minsuk Kim and Robin Koepke, "Indonesia Has an Opportunity to Boost Growth," *IMF Country Focus,* March 3, 2021.

97. For more on this group and their impact on Indonesian economic policy, see Karl Schoenberger, "Berkeley-Trained Group Plays Key Role," *Los Angeles Times,* June 1, 1992. After independence, Indonesia had only one Indigenous economist, who faced many challenges in the virulently anti-capitalist climate promoted by President Sukarno. With financial support from the Ford Foundation, in the late 1950s Dutch-trained Professor Sumitro Djojohadikusumo was able to send six of his students to the University of California, Berkeley, for advanced studies in classic economics. When they returned with their degrees, their mentor had been ousted from Sukarno's cabinet. Shortly after the coup that brought Suharto to power, this so-called Berkeley Mafia, some of whom had taught part time at the Army Staff College (where Suharto was a student), later rose to become economic advisers to the so-called New Order administration under Suharto.

98. Sadanand Dhume, "Indonesia's Promise," *Wall Street Journal,* November 20, 2006.

99. Andrew Higgins, "Some in Indonesia Praise, Seek to Replicate China's Fight Against the United States," *Washington Post,* March 29, 2010, p. A09.

100. Peter Alford, "Fifteen Years After Humiliation, Indonesia Turns the Tables on the IMF," *The Australian,* July 11, 2012.

101. Michael Bachelard, "Joko Widodo: Man with a Mission," *Sydney Morning Herald,* June 14, 2014.

102. Marcus Mietzner, "Economic Capacity, Regime Type, or Policy Decisions? Indonesia's Struggle with COVID-19," *Taiwan Journal of Democracy* 16, no. 2 (December 2020), p. 11.

103. Jemma Purdey, Antje Missbach, and Dave McRae, *Indonesia: State and Society in Transition* (Boulder: Lynne Rienner, 2020); Trissia Wijaya and Samuel Nursamsu, "The Trouble with Indonesia's Infrastructure Obsession," *The Diplomat,* January 9, 2020.

104. Wijaya and Nursamsu, "The Trouble with Indonesia's Infrastructure Obsession."
105. "Chapter 12: Water Supply and Sanitation," in *Indonesia Public Expenditure Review* (World Bank, 2020), p. 269.
106. "Clean Water for Millions: How Indonesia Met the Challenge," World Bank, May 29, 2020.
107. Mietzner, "Economic Capacity, Regime Type, or Policy Decisions?" pp. 28–29. Jokowi stated that Indonesia's economic contraction (5.3 percent in the second quarter of 2020), could have been much worse (as high as 17 percent) if they had implemented a lockdown. His controversial health minister also speculated early on that Indonesia had no Covid cases because its citizens prayed so much, while another health official suggested that Indonesians were immune to the virus because of their Malay race (Mietzner, pp. 6–8).
108. "The World Bank in Indonesia," World Bank, April 6, 2021; Minsuk Kim and Robin Koepke, "Indonesia Has an Opportunity to Boost Growth," *IMF Country Focus,* March 3, 2021.
109. "Indonesia: Overview," World Bank, April 5, 2016.
110. "Indonesia Public Expenditure Review: Spending for Better Results," World Bank, June 22, 2020.

Part 3
Politics and Political Change

Ideas are powerful. To realize the ability of ideas to change the world, individuals get together with similarly minded people to take the next step(s), transforming values into action. All people hold opinions and viewpoints about the world around them. Should income be equally distributed? Should political leaders provide moral and religious guidance? How should citizens respond to perceived CORRUPTION and abuse of power? Thoughts about authority, society, gender relations, economic resources, the environment, and other priorities help shape the general perspectives that people hold about their role in the world. Ideas about the way things should be often impel people into action, sometimes in violent ways. This will be the subject of the chapters that follow.

In this part of the book, we also consider the impact of ideas and their translation into action in terms of the "waves" of democratization, which hit much of the world toward the end of the COLD WAR. (The "first wave" of DEMOCRATIC TRANSITIONS is commonly identified with the expansion of democracy in the United States and Western Europe [1820s–1926]. The "second wave" [1945–1962] is associated with independence and the experimentation with democracy in much of Asia and Africa. The "third wave" began in the 1970s and stretched through the late 1990s, impacting STATES in Europe, sub-Saharan Africa, Asia, and Latin America.) After the so-called Arab Spring began in 2011, the push for renewed political transitions grew strong, even as these transformations hardly led to the types of lasting changes envisioned by many who participated in the widespread protests and social movements of the era. Yet, it is now clear that this wave has crashed, with freedom and democracy experiencing consistent years of decline (even among many of the consolidated democracies in the world). In the chapters that follow, we explore the various ways in which different governments have handled the crises that bubbled up during this period, even before the Covid PANDEMIC made things more challenging.

8

Civil Society Takes on the State

Finally, the gates are open to us. —*Iranian soccer fan after women were permitted to attend soccer matches for the first time since 1981*[1]

Sometimes decades pass and nothing happens; and then sometimes weeks pass and decades happen. —*attributed to Vladimir Lenin*

Politics is about agreement and disagreement, consensus and discord. It all starts with an idea. In this chapter, we explore the ranges of perspectives held by ordinary citizens, activists, and leaders. These viewpoints derive from many sources, including history (both ancient and recent), practical experiences of daily life and policy, and leadership cues and demands. Additionally, worldviews are framed by a combination of more seemingly subtle influences, as varied as educational systems, entertainment opportunities and institutions, and basic information sources that are made available to the public. We examine belief systems that both unite and divide people, and focus on ideas as sources of conflict and cooperation. Passion is a major part of the story. Yet, our emphasis goes beyond simply the beliefs that people hold: we examine the forums in which these views are expressed, the ways that other groups attempt to curtail people's ability to express opinions, and how crafty activists subvert limits on expression.

Ideas merge theoretical, often-fuzzy concepts of the way the world "should be" with the necessarily concrete actions that people take on a day-to-day basis to try to bring their visions to life. The sheer multiplicity of ideas invites controversy: When one person's or group's ideas conflict with those of others, how can these differences be reconciled? Why do some people's ideas seem to count, at least in the public realm, more than those of others, and how is this negotiated (or not)? We often think of leaders as holding a monopoly on creating the ideas that make their way to policy, but this is not always the case. When groups of people begin to identify with a value or idea system different from that of their leaders, they may organize and challenge the status quo. Sometimes they succeed, and sometimes their efforts result in painful failure.

Ideologies

Ideas that are free floating, unattached to a more general perspective or value system, are not very likely to have tremendous impact. Yet, when connections between sets of values and perspectives are recognized as interconnected, and when these views impel people to action, they literally have a force that may change the world.

When people share similar ideas linked to programs for action, we refer to this idea set as an "IDEOLOGY," literally the "science of ideas" (although such beliefs are hardly described with scientific precision). At their most fundamental level, ideologies are sets of ideas that describe the world or current state of affairs, help people understand their role within society, and arouse people to take an action, either to preserve or to change the existing situation. Ideologies consist of loosely connected systems of ideas: few traditions propose a strict laundry list of beliefs one must hold to subscribe to a given ideology. Rather, people notice common tendencies in beliefs, and often unite together with others who share similar perspectives.

Ideologies attempt to simplify complex problems and point toward potential solutions. They tend to be the foundation of most policies and actions, even if they are not identified as such. Most of the major systems of ideas that have been at the forefront of the global south were formulated in response to experiences with colonialism and dependence, especially the economic struggle to survive. Leaders and ordinary citizens alike turn to ideologies to help them cope with civil unrest, crushing poverty, and international humiliation. Ideologies often provide deceptively clear-cut answers to complicated realities, especially during times of instability. Frequently, groups of people who share an ideological worldview get together to form a political party as a way to implement the ideas that they feel are important. Political parties serve as mechanisms to recruit like-minded members to lobby and govern. While political parties appear and disappear, and quite often adopt varying and misleading names, political ideologies endure.

Common in discussions about ideologies are the terms "conservative" and "liberal." These concepts represent two major schools of ideological thought. They are relative terms, meaning that what is seen as conservative in one country or social situation might not be so seen in another. Liberalism, which developed throughout European societies in the early 1800s, is often considered the first coherent political ideology. Liberals emphasize the freedom of the individual, limits on governmental interference, and the equality of all human beings. The belief that all people possess inalienable rights to life, liberty, and the pursuit of property, for example, is a classical liberal idea derived from the writings of John Locke. Liberals hold optimistic beliefs about what individuals and groups can achieve, and they often fight for progressive (forward-moving) changes.

Because of liberalism's high value on freedom, this ideology had a tremendous impact on the wars of liberation discussed in Chapter 3. If all people are created equal, as liberalism contends, then individuals should be able to rule themselves, rather than having decisions made for them by colonial leaders in a faraway land. Liberal beliefs encouraged the fight for self-governing peoples who had been subjugated to foreign rule, some for centuries. This movement was particularly pronounced in the post–World War II environment. The outcome of many of these wars of national liberation, however, was the perpetuation of political control and limits on freedom. Liberalism also has influenced the desire by some ethnic groups to pursue their own homeland, often distinct from the government in which they live. Yet, the desire for cultural representation and self-expression does not always lead to the fight for a new state. Owing to the influence of liberalism, some ethnic groups have staked a claim to greater public expression of their culture and ways of life, achieving rights to use their native language, educate their children about their history and culture in public schools, and demand greater representation in public life.

Liberal ideas have also been responsible for many revolutions throughout the world, especially popular movements to overthrow monarchies, dynasties, and other forms of hereditary rule that precluded individuals from power. Some liberal revolutions attempted to redistribute land and economic resources that had been taken away from people. One example is found in President Benito Juarez's La Reforma program in Mexico in the mid-1800s, which stripped the Catholic Church of much of its property and power and formally granted civil rights to Indigenous peoples. Juarez's liberal program was also popular for its staunch resistance to French invaders. Other liberal movements fought to bring voting rights and other participatory freedoms to groups, including women, minorities, and youth. Liberal proponents today in the global south attempt to advance greater respect for human rights and individual freedoms, and they often lead the vocal charge toward democratic institutions. Fundamentally, liberals agree that the power of government needs to be limited, although they disagree over the fine lines of state involvement, especially in the realm of economics.

If liberals agree that governmental power should be limited and that individuals should have a say in decisions that are made about their lives, there is disagreement about matters of degree. Debates about the role of government in people's lives have led to two major types of liberals. One group, often called positive liberals, arguing that government ought to shoulder some level of responsibility for people's lives, calls for diminishing the inequality among groups, fostering greater participation, and in general promoting the well-being of citizens. Positive liberals are often the strongest supporters of welfare-state policies, including childcare, healthcare, education, unemployment insurance, and pensions. People often assume that welfare policies are designed only for the needy in society, but actually many welfare programs, including public education and public pensions, are distributed to all citizens, irrespective of need, and are present in most states of the world. In contrast, negative liberals believe that there should be minimal government involvement in the economy, arguing that the market, regulated by the forces of supply and demand, should be allowed to operate freely. This group argues that government involvement often has the unintended consequence of limiting individual freedom by creating patterns of dependence and perpetuating cycles of poverty. These debates can become quite heated. Yet, in the global south, the degree of governmental assistance is often framed not by ideological but rather by economic concerns.

Ideas do not exist in a vacuum. They are usually formulated, expressed, and modified in response to other views of the world. This explains the development of the other major school of thought, conservatism. Conservatives are known for attempting to preserve the status quo, and sometimes for encouraging a return to values and traditions of the past. As conservatism began to develop, it challenged each of the major premises of the liberal way of viewing the world.

Traditional conservatives emphasize an organic view of society, in which the needs of the whole society, the so-called social fabric, are more important than individual freedom. In contrast to the liberals' emphasis on the equality of all people, conservatives emphasize that every person is born with natural inequalities, thereby contradicting the liberal notion of the fundamental equality of all people. Conservatives emphasize the talents and skills that some people have at birth but others do not. They advocate a slower approach to change, highlighting the utility of existing institutions and patterns of behavior and reviling the dangerous passions and actions of revolutionaries. They lament the liberals' promotion of rapid change, and believe that revolutions tend to bring about more harm than good because they damage key traditions and hierarchical structures that serve as the basis for social traditions and IDENTITY. Many conservatives prefer familiar patterns of relations, rather than the uncertainty that comes from progressive change. It is from this belief that we tend to associate conservatives with the status quo; in fact, the label "conservativism" derives from the Latin word *conservare,* which means "to save or preserve." Conservative parties and groups today, while they often support democratic institutions, urge caution in the pace of transitions and cast a wary eye toward liberal causes.

One modern manifestation of conservative ideas is found in religious fundamentalism, including Christian and Islamic variants, the adherents of which promote the value of religious institutions and authority, often placing great emphasis on traditional family structures and gender roles. Much of the debate surrounding fundamentalists and their detractors relates to the adaptations of religious institutions to the modern world. Adherents to fundamental traditions often promote a stricter, sometimes-literal interpretation of religious texts, whether they be the Torah, Bible, or Quran.

Islamist movements, also discussed in this chapter, have often been motivated by the perceived encroachment of Westernization, concomitant with the rise of individualism and SECULARISM, which are viewed as threatening to traditional lifestyles. After the Soviet withdrawal from Afghanistan in 1989, civil war ensued. One group that emerged from the ashes was the Taliban, an Islamist political group that ruled the country from 1996 until late 2001, when they were ousted by US and allied forces who invaded Afghanistan in retaliation for their support of another Islamist group, al-Qaeda. The Taliban is an antimodern group that grew out of the mujahidin who fought the Soviets during their occupation of Afghanistan from 1981 to 1989. The Taliban have long promoted a rigidly conservative approach to Islamic religious beliefs that includes strict gender segregation based on a belief that men and women are fundamentally unequal. Their ideas are couched in the refutation of Western, secular standards of behavior. While

Figure 8.1 Do All Muslims Agree?

In the early decades of the twenty-first century, followers of the Muslim faith are second in number only to Christians. While estimates vary, most agree that Muslims compose nearly 25 percent of the world's population, and that Islam is the fastest growing faith tradition in the world. With so many adherents, it is logical to assume that there are varying levels of agreement and disagreement among the Muslim faithful. The biggest source of lasting division originated in a succession struggle launched after the prophet Muhammad's death in 632. Today, the majority of Muslims, approximately 90 percent, characterize themselves as Sunni Muslims. The name "Sunni" derives from Sunna, meaning "the tradition of the prophet Muhammad." The primary schism is Shia Islam, meaning the "Party of Ali."

Upon Muhammad's death in 632, his cousin and son-in-law, Ali, claimed to be the leader of all Muslims. But most believers followed Abu Bakr, who was reputed to be the first outside of Muhammad's family to convert to Islam. Abu Bakr became the first of the four caliphs, or successors, in the Sunni tradition. Twenty-three years after Muhammad's death, Ali was named the caliph. His rise to leadership was controversial and not recognized by many; Syria's leader, among others, refused to recognize Ali, who ruled from Kufah, Iraq, facing much dissention.

A series of succession crises, including the murder and torture of disputed leaders, led to the creation of Shia Islam, the first major schism within Islam. Sunnis today continue to outnumber Shiites, although Iran, Iraq, Azerbaijan, and Bahrain are majority-Shiite states. The Shiites replaced the caliphate with imams, claiming that their leadership was hereditary from Muhammad. After the schism, Shiites were persecuted and acted in secret, during which time they devised their own teachings on the implementation of the word of Muhammad. One change was the designation of an authoritative figure to interpret divine will, rather than placing the onus on the community of believers, as Sunnis taught.[a] The Shiites believe that imams, as religious leaders, possess knowledge of which the masses are incapable. This view complicated the challenges of rival successors, since imams were viewed as infallible leaders. Although most Turks are Sunnis, the Shiite minority in Turkey is known as Alvis.

The major Shia sect is the "Twelvers," named for the twelve imams following Muhammad. Twelver Shia Islam is the state religion in Iran. Developed in the sixteenth century, this sect highlights the twelve legitimate imams, beginning with Ali and ending with the twelfth or "hidden" imam, who went into concealment in 941, but who will reappear someday in the future to finish the triumph of Shia Islam. Between the sixteenth and eighteenth centuries, Twelver Shia Islam merged with Persian tradition, forging a tight bond with the development of Iranian identity and nationalism.[b]

The Iraq War had a lasting impact on Shiite communities, even though Shiites, like their Sunni counterparts, remain a greatly diverse and amorphous sect who are not united under a single leader. As Vali Nasr, author of *The Shia Revival* argues, "The Middle East that will emerge from the crucible of the Iraq war may not be more democratic, but it will definitely be more Shiite."[c] Despite the sectarian bloodshed that has marked much of the Iraq War and the conflicts that have followed, the two major sects of Muslim believers lived mostly in peace throughout the centuries.

In the eighth century, the mystical movement of Sufism developed, in protest to the formalism of Islam. The title comes from the Arabic word suf, meaning "wool." Many Sufis wore coarse woolen clothes, imitating the Christians from Syria. Although both Sunni and Shiite fundamentalists reject it, Sufism has appeal among those who are frustrated with the power-seeking *ulamas,* or clerics. Sufism views Islam as a religious experience rather than a call to political action.[d]

Notes: a. Sandra Mackey, *The Iranians: Persia, Islam, and the Soul of a Nation* (New York: Penguin, 1996).

b. Ibid.

c. Vali Nasr, "When the Shiites Rise," *Foreign Affairs* 85, no. 4 (July–August 2006), p. 59.

d. Mackey, *The Iranians.*

their resurgence since the departure of US and allied forces from the country in 2021 has been problematic for nearly all Afghanis, it has been especially disastrous for women. During their first time in power (in the 1990s), women were only permitted in public if escorted by a male relative, and they were banned from educational facilities; they were beaten for any violations. For two decades after their ouster, the educational system was rebuilt, fortified by more than a billion dollars in aid, only to collapse within weeks of the Taliban's return, when women at public universities and schools were barred from leading programs, teaching, or even attending classes, often replaced by male religious purists who, in many cases, hold minimal academic experience.[2] Many fear the return of violence, including honor killings, public executions, and other forms of punishment supported by extremist leaders. Even before the Taliban's return, Afghanistan ranked poorly in its protections for women: more than half of all Afghan women reported physical abuse, 17 percent reported sexual violence, and nearly 60 percent stated they were in forced marriages. Women who turned to shelters after receiving grisly injuries, including broken bones or internal injuries from severe beatings, literally feared for their lives as the men who perpetrated the crimes against them were released from prisons after the Taliban returned.[3]

Christian fundamentalists express hostility toward individualism and secularism, objecting to the liberal separation of church and state that made religious values and practices a private rather than a public matter. Conservative evangelical Christians have been active in many parts of the global south, including Latin America (especially Guatemala and Brazil), Africa (including South Africa and Zimbabwe), and some Asian states (notably the Philippines). While there is great variation among followers, in general evangelical Christian churches advocate conservative sexual and gender mores, economic discipline, as well as a greater role for some newer church institutions. In Brazil, for example, evangelical leaders in government have publicly contested the role of the Catholic Church in society. In Guatemala, fundamentalist Protestant groups rally in opposition to unions and against LIBERATION THEOLOGY, a left-leaning perspective on Catholicism discussed later in this chapter. Many of the fundamentalist traditions in Africa trace their origins to anticolonial movements. Surveys indicate that Pentecostals make up just over 25 percent of all the world's Christians, comprising approximately half of all Christians in Zimbabwe, Brazil, Guatemala, and South Africa.[4] Disparate groups of fundamentalist Christians in Africa, believed to number in the tens of millions, have joined together in opposition to abortion, feminism, and the rights of homosexuals, and some conservative religious leaders have also dangerously undermined public health and human rights initiatives, even in the face of the Covid pandemic.[5]

Conservatism and liberalism are only two of many traditions of like-minded ideas. The other major world ideologies that have affected social, political, and economic life include socialism, communism, fascism, and anarchism. Each of these ideological systems developed in response to liberal views of the world, and promotes its own ideas about the value of individualism, governmental involvement in the economy, and the structure of society. It is important to understand the basic definitions of each of these distinct ideologies. But it is also necessary to keep in mind that the underlying components of any ideological system are changed, adapted, and even manipulated by people to fit their particular circumstances and to match their goals. Nonetheless, an understanding of the common characteristics of these views provides an important starting place for this inquiry of the role of ideology in the global south.

Socialism is an ideological tradition that has had tremendous impact throughout the entire world, either in its application or in its opposition. Because of the centrality of economic matters, socialism, in multiple variants, has been a particularly important ideology in the global south. Historically, socialism was critical of private property and the uneven distribution of wealth. It is an idea that significantly predates one of its most famous adherents, Karl Marx, who adapted early socialist ideals and melded them onto a revolutionary framework. Marxist socialists argued that fundamentally there are two types of people in the world, making up the dominant CLASSES of society. First are the few who own property and therefore exert much influence in economic, political, and social affairs. They are known as the BOURGEOISIE. Yet, the bourgeoisie could not exist without the MASSES, who in a Marxist framework are forced to work at the mercy of the powerful, and labor tirelessly without proper compensation or protection against abuse. This second class, which always outnumbers the first, is known as the PROLETARIAT. Writing in the midst of the European industrial revolution of the mid-1800s, Marx argued that once the workers of the world were made aware of their uneven plight caused by the powerful property owners, inevitably they would rise up in anger and overthrow their oppressors. Marx predicted that after the revolution, which was likely to be violent, proletarians would rule in their self-interest, attempting to eliminate the bourgeoisie. During this stage of initial socialism, economic inequalities would persist, but they would be eradicated in the final stage of the revolution, when communism would be achieved.

While Marx's ideas may seem particularly appropriate for individuals living and working in the countries of the global south, it was really only after the innovations of another revolutionary activist that his ideas were applied in the effort to promote wide-scale change. In imperial Russia, the activist later known as Vladimir Lenin, hardly a paragon of the industrial battlefield that Marx predicted would bring his revolutions to life, took up the ideas articulated by Marx and his collaborator, Friedrich Engels, and from them crafted a plan to implement a Marxist revolution by a group of ELITES, a highly disciplined VANGUARD PARTY. This Leninist party would not wait around for electoral victories that Lenin believed would never come. Rather, it would seize state power and implement a Marxist revolution from above. Revolutionary hopefuls throughout the developing world found a solution in Lenin's model, which ran counter to Marx's initial focus on worker-led mass revolutions. Lenin's ideas on the connection between imperialism and capitalism seemed especially relevant to many at a time when capitalism was rapidly becoming a global movement. Lenin taught that richer capitalist countries used the poorer countries of the world to finance their own GROWTH and prosperity. Capitalism, by definition, would promote uneven DEVELOPMENT, as the rich countries would get richer on the backs of cheaper labor in the non-Western world, which was becoming increasingly dependent on trade with the imperialist powers. These ideas strongly resonated with citizens in the global south who recognized their exploitation, especially in countries with formal imperialist governing structures. Communist movements, following the Leninist model, were integral in independence movements in Vietnam, Indonesia, Angola, Mozambique, and Guinea-Bissau.

Even though Karl Marx believed that communist revolutions would be conducted in the advanced, industrialized countries of Europe and North America, his ideas were most vigorously applied to countries in the global south. In fact, some would argue that the perceived failures of communism since 1989 were predictable from the beginning: a Marxist revolution simply was not tailored to a global south, nonindustrial country. Chairman Mao Zedong's application of Marxist communism in a nonindustrialized setting spawned similar revolutionary movements in other countries, including Peru, Vietnam, Nepal, and Cambodia. In countries where full-fledged Marxist-Leninist revolutions have been undertaken, however, the leadership has never moved beyond the stage of initial socialism, during which time a single party can rule, theoretically, in the name of achieving final communism. It is because of this connection—some would say deviation—of Marxist socialism that many people associate socialism with one-party rule. This correlation, however, is not wholly accurate.

Democratic forms of socialism have also influenced SOCIAL MOVEMENTS in the countries we are studying. Fabian socialists argue that the original goal of socialists has been distorted by its revolutionary application by Marx and his adherents. They argue that democratic, peaceful means are the only viable way to promote the socialist cause. These democratic socialists attempt to promote greater equality (especially economic equality) among citizens, and advocate a strong role for government in promoting the needs of society. Democratic socialism was especially influential during the African wars of independence of the 1970s, when leaders encouraged governments to be proactive in citizens' lives, especially in the areas of literacy and education. From the mid-1960s until the recession of the 1970s, President Julius Nyerere of Tanzania, for example, promoted a socialist model of economic development under the *ujamma* model, a Kiswahili word that means, roughly, "familyhood" or "pulling together." Nyerere not only collectivized agriculture and factories, but also, under the leadership of a single party, mandated major investments in primary schools and social services. In general, socialist leaders are critical of unbridled capitalism, pointing to often-disastrous effects of the market on the environment, family and social relations, and culture. They tend to be the people leading the charge against international economic institutions such as the WORLD BANK and the INTERNATIONAL MONETARY FUND, although they are certainly not alone in their critiques. Socialism in the non-Western world, though, emphasizes NATIONALISM and local traditions, rather than the international and universal working-class identity promoted by initial socialist activists.

If liberalism emphasized people as individuals, conservatives urged a focus on society and its traditions, and socialists viewed the world in the framework of classes. In response to each of these ideologies, another combination of ideas—fascism—was formed that found fault with each of the preceding characterizations of the world. Similar to the other ideologies, its basis was found in historical tradition, including linguistic interpretations of history, so-called scientific understandings of race and racial identity, and an elitist prescription for political power and governance. Ideas that would form the core of fascism existed long before the ideology was named. Fascism emphasizes that which unites people as a way of segregating individuals into homogeneous groups to promote unity and strength. Because of its opposition to most of the systems of ideas that developed before it, and because of its negative proscriptions on life in general, it may be argued that it is clearer to understand what fascists are against than what they are for.[6]

Fascists believe that the class focus of socialism is too divisive, especially because it emphasizes status as either a worker or an owner over a person's national heritage. The term "fascism," first coined in Italy, comes from the Latin word *fasces,* alluding to a set of reeds tightly bound together. Fascist leaders emphasize the importance of race and nationality, promoting in many cases a racially pure community of individuals who work together without division. Fascism also teaches that it is necessary to have a strong leader who will provide guidance and direction to the masses, and that the all-powerful leader understands the needs and the interests of the people better than they themselves do. In this sense, fascism is clearly an elitist ideology, which openly concentrates the majority of the power among a small minority of seemingly qualified individuals.

Fascists emphasize the fundamental inequality of humans and promote a clear hierarchy, often based on biological conceptions of race, of "superior" and "lesser" peoples. While fascists are not the only group to deny the universal equality of all people, they go further, openly advocating the use of violence for handling contradictions that exist between people. While the most destructive fascist dictatorships were promoted in the European countries of Italy (under Benito Mussolini) and Germany (under Adolf Hitler), fascist AUTHORITARIAN movements have also been strong in the global south as well, especially in Chile under Augusto Pinochet. Fascism is an authoritarian ideology of exclusion, and regimes that adhere to it promote division and hierarchy, violating the fundamental human rights of those deemed inferior and preventing individual liberties for all except the few deemed worthy of holding power. Fascists deny the desirability of a multicultural society, arguing to violent extremes that multiple ethnic groups cannot coexist within a single society. This ideology calls for a strong government that organizes and leads the masses, as well as a developed propaganda system that educates and motivates them into action.

In recent years, groups adhering to neofascist beliefs have gained prominence in many parts of the world, especially in economically troubled regions where immigrants, refugees, migrant workers, and other groups seen as outsiders can be scapegoated for a wide range of social and economic problems. Neofascist violence is aimed at particular ethnic communities. Neo-Nazi attacks in Germany, for example, have targeted the immigrant Turkish, African, and Vietnamese populations with firebombs and other violent attacks. Similar to their ideological predecessors, these activists condone the use of violence and segregation to promote the cause of their own, self-defined group.

Ideologies develop as a way to capture the relationship between leaders in government and ordinary citizens. Anarchists challenge the desirability of hierarchical power structures, emphasizing voluntary cooperation and free association over power and control. Anarchism is difficult to characterize as a single school of thought, as its adherents' beliefs straddle many points along the ideological spectrum. Noam Chomsky frames anarchism as a historical tendency rather than an ideology per se.[7] Anarchists are often known for their acts of disobedience. They share a concern about the concentration of power, whether governmental power over ordinary citizens, patriarchal power of men over women, or global corporate power exercised by business conglomerates. Most anarchists promote the values of democratic participation, decentralization, and opposition to bureaucracy. While some anarchist groups condone the use of violence to further their cause, this is a point of disagreement among those adhering to this ideological perspective.

Anarchist movements have been particularly popular among youth. In Mexico, for example, anarchists are especially focused on environmental causes, railing against capitalism, and supporting animal liberation. Conscientious objectors of required military service have also aligned with antimilitarist anarchist youth groups. Anarchists claim that no one should have authority or control over another. In this, they often challenge basic rules of behavior. Puerto Rican feminist and labor activist, Luisa Capetillo, is perhaps Latin America's best-known anarchist; she gained notoriety by becoming the first woman to wear pants in public in Puerto Rico. Through her work to encourage labor unionization in Puerto Rico, she worked to redefine women's freedom. The 1994 Zapatista uprising in Mexico and student strikes were particularly influenced by anarchism, challenging especially the power of government over minority ethnic groups. This movement, which was viciously repressed by authorities, sparked Indigenous activists across Latin America and in other regions as well. Nevertheless, the Zapatistas, who long dismissed Mexican elections as corrupt, put forward an independent, Indigenous, female candidate, Maria de Jesus Patricio Martinez, for president in 2018, although by late 2021 they were warning that the region was on the verge of civil war.[8]

Because of their disdain for governing structures, anarchist movements tend to reach across borders and geographic limitations to embrace a global audience. The environmental movement Earth First! confronts government and corporate behavior, especially its disregard for ecological concerns and its anthropocentric, or human-centered, bias. Additionally, diverse movements against transnational corporations and seemingly supranational organizations like the WORLD TRADE ORGANIZATION, the IMF, and the GROUP OF 20 have mobilized activists of all stripes to challenge the authority and actions of large bureaucracies. Protests organized to disrupt such meetings unite environmentalists, farmers, students, intellectuals, feminists, and union activists. Although not all of the participants are necessarily anarchists, the focus on the negative aspects of global capitalism goes right to the core beliefs of anarchism. Many terrorist groups, discussed in Chapter 10, base their actions in the ideology of anarchism as well.

While it is clear that a variety of ideological systems exist, true understanding of the power of these worldviews can only be found in comparison. To examine systems of ideas, it is helpful to visually align beliefs on the POLITICAL SPECTRUM. We commonly use the terminology of "left, right, and center" to place beliefs in comparison with each other. The terminology we use comes from seating arrangements in the National Assembly of France during the revolution of the late 1700s. Moderates sat in the center, those who favored DEMOCRACY and rapid change congregated on the left side (or wing), and those who supported the monarch and the Catholic Church, arguing against change, sat on the right. We continue to use this linear system today to compare belief systems, although it is helpful only as a general guideline. People and groups cannot be placed on the spectrum with clear precision (few of us hold completely consistent views and opinions), and all discussions about the spectrum in a particular country or society must be understood as relative to particular circumstances.

To aid the comparison of beliefs, ideas are placed along the political spectrum according to views on the importance and desired direction of change, the role of government in the economy, and the perceived value of religious institutions. To the left of center, beliefs focus on the positive value of change (especially forward-moving developments), a larger role of government in economic matters, including the promotion of greater equality, and a smaller public role for religious institutions in the lives of people. To the right of center, church and religious institutions serve a more important role in government and society. Advocates of right-wing ideologies are more suspicious of change, and prefer that government be less involved in economic affairs generally. To the right of center, people tend to emphasize the decline of society and advocate a reevaluation of social, political, and economic structures, and often a return to values of an earlier period. Because anarchist beliefs usually complement other ideological traditions, and because of the great variety of perspectives embodied within anarchism, it is difficult to clearly place it on one side of the spectrum or the other. As the language of this explanation suggests, there are few absolutes in the characterization of ideologies, but these general patterns capture the most important ideas. Keep in mind that an understanding of the dominant ideological leanings in a particular society or governing administration will provide only limited information about the policies of the regime. For example, although we have highlighted the role of government involvement as a point distinguishing some ideological traditions, state interventionist economic programs have been used by regimes characterized as rightist (Juan Perón's Argentina) as well as by those characterized as leftist (Salvador Allende's Chile).

How and why do people develop particular opinions and views? We are all products of a lifelong process generally referred to as "socialization," through which individuals acquire their beliefs and values. Some of this socialization is accidental. Other aspects of socialization are deliberate attempts to pass on values and belief systems from generation to generation. Beliefs about government, politics, economics, and the role of the military are all influenced by some of our earliest life experiences. Educational and religious institutions, the media, peer groups, and family each influence the development of beliefs. While much of the process of acquiring attitudes about society is implicit and somewhat taken for granted, such as family relationships between women and men, governments and social groups may also explicitly influence people's sense of values, especially as they relate to the governing system. Institutions of the media are often overlooked as sources of socialization, yet news organizations, television programs, and official social media can be important sources of information about civic and political life.

The media both inform and persuade. Recognizing the power implicit in controlling access to information, many governments exercise some level of control over communications media, often through a monopoly over news and publishing outlets. Sometimes two versions of media are produced, an official version for public consumption, which downplays the tensions existing in society, and a version meant only for viewing by government leaders, which expresses a more accurate account of pressures and hot spots. Government regulation of the media, which makes the expression of unofficial opinions problematic and even dangerous, often forces dissident groups to publish their opposition views underground. These unofficial communication avenues, which straddle the permissible and the forbidden, have been especially lucrative in environments where entrepreneurship and risk-taking are encouraged. In China, for example, simply stamping a book "for internal consumption only" means that there will be a huge market on the side for bootlegged copies. Arguments over media control also fare prominently in Iran, where, despite the proliferation of media sources, both print and electronic, boundaries are enforced by the powerful Council of Guardians, and national and localized shutdowns of the internet have been noted. Editors who challenge the boundary of the permissible have been jailed, flogged, and even executed by hanging.[9]

The importance of digital communication can hardly be overstated; our reliance on the internet of course only increased during Covid shutdowns and quarantines. The six-hour global outage of Facebook and related applications, including Instagram and WhatsApp, in late 2021, highlighted how vital even just a few platforms have become. In Haiti, people rely on WhatsApp to notify each other about gang violence in particular neighborhoods; in Syria, where years of war have destroyed the traditional telecommunications infrastructure, doctors and emergency workers rely on social media apps to monitor the coronavirus, including critical delivery communications about oxygen suppliers needing to move from camp to camp.[10] In addition to reliance on Facebook and its related apps for phone service and texting (e.g., WhatsApp is installed on 99 percent of all smartphones in Brazil), small companies known for providing medical communication on social media content lost critical sales during even a short outage, demonstrating their vulnerability to glitches or changes.[11] Such tools present two pronounced areas of challenge for life in the global south: access and censorship. Globally, approximately two-thirds of the world's school-aged children (ages three to seventeen years old) lack internet connections in their homes, according to UNICEF and the International Telecommunication Union (ITU), leading UNICEF's executive director to proclaim this "more than a digital gap—it is a digital canyon."[12] Not surprisingly, regional disparities are stark, with 95 percent of school-aged children in sub-Saharan Africa unconnected at home, 88 percent in South Asia, and 49 percent in Latin America and the Caribbean.[13]

The digitization of communication invites novel means by which a government can spy on its population. For over two decades, Chinese leaders have operated a so-called Great Firewall to block access to perceived sensitive sites and information, especially references to dissident movements and views. Iran has some of the most sophisticated means of controlling and censoring information on the internet, even as the country boasts an internet penetration rate of approximately 85 percent.[14] Egypt, too, has a history of shuttering access to information to serve government interests. In 2011, after Facebook posts sharing images of police brutality drew people into the streets in protest, the Hosni Mubarak government tried to cut off all internet access in Egypt. In more recent years, the government has mastered digital tools to block websites and surveil users, especially targeting and imprisoning female TikTok influencers for "violating family values and principles" on social media channels.[15] Nigerian leaders banned Twitter, which is used by millions of its citizens, after the microblogging site deleted a tweet by President Muhammadu Buhari, threatening secessionist groups allegedly responsible for attacks on government offices and harkening back to the Biafran War, during which Buhari served as a Nigerian armed forces commander. Ironically, the ban was announced on the Nigerian government's Ministry of Information account—on Twitter.[16]

In the face of such repression, cyber-duels ensue, and crafty netizens find ways around limits. In many countries, users attempt to use a virtual private network (VPN) to circumvent censorship by way of a secure connection through a different country, browsing as if they were in that country. Increasingly, governments are banning more VPN tools, which then invites others to find more ways around them. The NONGOVERNMENTAL ORGANIZATION Reporters Without Borders (RSF) refers to journalism as "the vaccine against disinformation," and notes that, in 2021, free journalism was curtailed in more than 130 countries, including being totally blocked or seriously impeded in 73 of the 180 countries ranked by the organization.[17] Not only are vital sets of information channels being increasingly squeezed, overall public mistrust of journalists and their work is reaching disturbing levels, with nearly 60 percent of respondents expressing doubt in the media—exacerbated in many cases by the Covid pandemic and some leaders' promotion of medically unproven remedies.[18]

Looking at the world around us, we observe similarities and differences among groups of people. It is often difficult to articulate the source of differences, when they exist. Much of it is related to the processes of socialization. When we compare political attitudes across multiple societies, people commonly speak of a POLITICAL CULTURE that exists among a defined group of people such as "Mexican political culture" or "Egyptian political culture." This concept was developed to capture the commonly shared understandings and basic assumptions that people in a common experience tend to exhibit.

To say that a group of people shares a particular political culture does not mean that they agree on all of the important issues of politics and governance. Rather, it means that they are likely to share some common perspectives about their public surroundings, including their political leaders, governmental structure, and the enduring symbols and values of public life.[19] Political culture includes citizens' general feelings toward government, including their desire (or lack thereof) to participate in political issues. It also captures a sense of people's understanding of the decisionmaking process, including attitudes about its merits. Understanding that people have social, political, and economic experiences different from our own helps us avoid assumptions that the way relationships and institutions operate in one setting is the way that they exist elsewhere. The concept of political culture helps us recognize the long-term impact of social, historical, and economic circumstances.

Figure 8.2 "Antisocial Media"

The internet provides some novel opportunities for social organization and the expression of citizen voice. Yet, many of the same characteristics that make these technologies useful can make them dangerous as well: the forum is quick, ripe with information that its users provide (including sensitive contact information and personal details); it crosses national borders, making the legal terrain more complicated; and the (at least temporary) anonymity it can provide makes accountability more difficult to establish. In some societies, "internet mobbing" and "virtual lynchings" have arisen, sometimes with grim consequences. *The Economist* quipped that "antisocial media" are developing, providing opportunities to target individuals for revenge or retribution.[a] Lists of targeted teenagers appeared on Facebook in southern Colombia, with three of the sixty-nine people named on the hit list killed within less than two weeks (police originally viewed the lists as a hoax, even though just a month earlier, a university student in Bogotá was imprisoned for allegedly creating a Facebook page calling for the assassination of the Colombian president's son). In China, a woman was dubbed the "stiletto kitten killer" for crushing a kitten's skull with her high heels, and a nationwide hunt began. She was tracked down five days after her personal contact information was posted on QQ, China's wildly popular, free instant messaging service.[b] Chinese internet forums, dubbed "human-flesh search engines," are creating a "cyberposse" of sorts[c]—eager netizens hunt down presumed violators of an unwritten moral code, forcing individuals to take cover to attempt to evade the branders of local justice. Uncivil society meets the information age.

Another darker aspect of social media is its role in promoting misinformation (false information that is shared, regardless of intent) and disinformation (deliberately misleading information that is spread to mislead or manipulate).[d] Even prior to the era of social media, we have been aware of the powerful role mass communication has in spreading hate and inciting violence—the role of hate propaganda disseminated by radio programs in the Rwandan genocide of 1994, for example, is well documented.[e]

According to so-called Facebook Papers disclosed to the US Securities and Exchange Commission by a company whistleblower, the social media giant's efforts to monitor and respond to disinformation are woefully impotent throughout much of the world beyond the United States, especially in the global south. For example, even though the United States comprises less than 10 percent of Facebook's daily users, Facebook allocates 84 percent of its budget set aside to respond to disinformation.[f] The impact of social media hate speech fueled by coordinated social media disinformation campaigns has been documented, including in India, where tensions against minority Muslims have been inflamed by posts on Facebook and WhatsApp, and where many were killed in riots that were fed by complex propaganda campaigns.[g] Even when platforms create rules against "coordinated inauthentic behavior," and after reports from civil society groups (including the Next Billion Network, a collaborative that focuses on the negative impact of social media in the global south), implementation is weak and sometimes completely nonexistent. Some of the challenge is made worse by the paucity of language experts able to quickly sift through the nuances of sometimes hundreds of local languages that can be common on social media, as well as the bureaucracies of reporting, verifying, and blocking online discourse. But it invites a critical eye toward the ability of communication platforms to promote both civil and uncivil society.

Notes: a. "Antisocial Media," *The Economist,* August 25, 2010.

b. Richard Spencer, "Just Who Is the Glamorous Kitten Killer of Hangzhou?" *The Telegraph* (London), March 4, 2006.

c. Brydon Brancart, "After More Than a Decade, the Human Flesh Search Engine Is Still Raging Across Chinese Social Media," *Whats on Weibo,* February 6, 2018; Tom Downey, "China's Cyberposse," *New York Times,* March 3, 2010.

d. Valerie Strauss, "Word of the Year: Misinformation. Here's Why," *Washington Post,* December 10, 2018.

e. Pierre-Antoine Pluquet, "From Hate Speech to Genocide, Lessons from the 1994 Genocide Against the Tutsi in Rwanda," United Nations Educational, Scientific and Cultural Organization (UNESCO), July 4, 2021.

f. Regine Cabato, "How Facebook Neglected the Rest of the World, Fueling Hate Speech and Violence in India," *Washington Post,* October 24, 2021.

g. Ibid.

A classic study on political culture attempted to use these ideas to compare cultures throughout the world. The Civic Culture study of the 1950s and early 1960s, based on survey research, was conducted by a group of leading US political scientists.[20] It identified three dominant types of political culture. First, Gabriel Almond and Sidney Verba classified a "participant culture," in which most people exhibit pride toward their country's political system, feel that they should participate in it, and have a sense that their participation makes a difference. They also generally understand the way the system works. Second, the study identified a "subject culture," in which people tend to discount their ability to participate in and change politics; rather, they view themselves as obedient subordinates of the government. People in these societies tend to be aware of the operations of the political system, but overall are cautious about participating in it. Finally, the study identified a "parochial culture," in which people tend to identify almost exclusively with their immediate locality, feeling that national political issues have little to do with them. In such cultures, people tend to speak little about political affairs because in their viewpoint such matters rarely touch their lives.

What did Almond and Verba conclude about political culture from their study? The only one of our cases that was included in this original study was Mexico, which was characterized as the prototypical parochial culture. Although recognizing that each country contains people with a mix of views, Almond and Verba generalized about each society as a whole. This was a pivotal attempt to make broad statements about many countries at once, in a comparative framework.

Yet, there are serious limitations to such an approach. For one, it invites the potential for discriminatory assumptions or even establishing a hierarchy of favored characteristics. It was clear by the way the findings were presented that a participatory, aware, and active population should be the ultimate goal for each society. Yet, there was little recognition that the standards for the study were based on Western traditions and cultures, which promote civic duty and activism as a virtue. The Civic Culture study and others that have followed in its footsteps are indicative of the wide-eyed optimism of many Americans in the late 1950s and 1960s. The implicit hope was that Western-style democracies were going to flourish around the world, and that there was a single model of the so-called developed, democratic state. In fact, the guiding assumption of the Civic Culture study was that the participant culture is a precondition to stable democracy.

In addition to being ethnocentric, this approach tended to emphasize the changes that were not taking place, presumably because people did not exhibit characteristics found in other Western cultures, rather than the realm of the possible, or what could take place. Also, such an aggregated view of single political cultures oversimplifies complex societies. The assumptions of national culture make grandiose claims that are difficult to substantiate. For example, in a state like Nigeria, with over 250 different ethnic groups, does it really make sense to talk of a singular "Nigerian" political culture? There is also a problem of cross-cultural translation: concepts such as EFFICACY, duty, and participation do not always translate across languages and cultures very clearly, and people have differing images in their minds as to their precise meaning. Political culture is useful to explain differences among groups, but it is less helpful when used to explain so-called national traits, as David Elkins and E. B. Simeon identified.[21] While it is clear that culture is important, it is less clear how to measure it. At best, the concept of political culture is useful for understanding general orientations, but it is important that we not make assumptions much beyond this.

Identities

When individuals assess the world around them, they make decisions based on a self-perception of who they are, or their identity. Increasingly, we understand that people's self-perception influences their behavior and attitudes. It affects whom we define as potential collaborators or competitors, and it impacts the outcome that we seek. The traditional ideologies discussed earlier are largely devoid of an explicit awareness of self-identity: they aim to provide an outlook based on larger issues often irrespective of individual attributes. Yet, a growing trend in social thought and action revolves around identity issues that fundamentally get at the question of who we are. They tend to be personal ideologies that encourage people to fight for recognition of the joint needs and preferences of particular groups, often those that have been denied expression in the past. Identities are extremely complex concepts. For one thing, we each have multiple individual characteristics: one individual may embody the identities of friend, daughter, Asian, worker. We choose to emphasize a particular trait based on the context in which we are involved. For example, at a sporting event, people are usually defined as either athletes or spectators. At an international sporting event, it becomes even more complex, with the characteristic of national identity becoming important. Yet, at other gatherings, like some religious meetings, one's categorization as a woman or a man, or as a believer or a nonbeliever, can be the defining characteristic.

Individual and group identities are quite closely related; in addition to describing themselves individually, people group with others. This involves the development of a collective, or shared, identity. Groups of ordinary people mobilize around a common self-definition, usually as a way to achieve a common goal. Additionally, leaders attempt to rally their citizens around an identity related to their own power. Officials who are defensive about their own ability to maintain power are particularly adept at rallying people around a shared sense of belonging, often making promises to varied groups as a way to lock in their support. Such POPULIST attempts can be particularly strong in countries undergoing dislocation as well as in societies where significant class inequality exists. The Peronists in Argentina exemplified populism by forming coalitions of the urban poor and parts of the organized working and middle classes, promising greater economic equality and independence (especially economic) from foreign countries. The 1979 Iranian Revolution was a populist movement that rallied the common people against the West, personified in opposition to the Shah. Populist movements are fundamentally about identity and pride: they attempt to rally groups to action in the name of a narrowly described "people." This careful categorization can be especially potent when framed as a uniting force of "the people" against a powerful and hated enemy. In the case of Iran, for example, deep-seated anger toward the United States serves as fertile soil from which contemporary populist rhetoric may grow, especially given the more combative policies of the Donald Trump administration after the United States withdrew from the Joint Comprehensive Plan of Action (JCPOA) regulating Iran's nuclear developments, placing Tehran again under punitive sanctions. Even during the terms of very differently styled presidents, Mahmoud Ahmadinejad (2005–2013) and Hassan Rouhani (2013–2021), populism remained a powerful political tool, in large part because of the ability to mobilize citizens around very real external threats to the regime.[22] Indonesian leader Joko Widodo (Jokowi), president since 2014, has also turned to populist techniques to shore up his appeal, highlighting his humble origins as well as his status as a relative political outsider. As Indonesia reeled during the Covid pandemic, he turned to well-known populist techniques to sow doubt against rumors, fake news, and the rhetoric of those who doubted him, framing them as enemies of the people.[23]

Populist movements may be left or right in orientation, but their motivation is nearly the same. The difficulty with populism on its own, however, is that "the people" rarely fit into one category. Populism is usually combined with other movements. Nationalist movements, for example, have been common bedfellows for populist leaders.

For over 200 years, the idea of nationalism has been used to promote the interests and needs of a particular nation, or group of people. Usually, nations are identified as sharing a common history, culture, language, ethnicity, or religion, although the actual components of national identity can vary widely. Nationalist movements have been a potent uniting (and dividing) force throughout many of the countries that we are studying. The initial struggle faced by many of these countries was to establish a common identity after the colonial period. National identities were therefore defined more in opposition to the colonial rulers than in composition of shared characteristics. The concept of "Indonesia," for example, was a novel identity for the disparate ethnic groups who had operated a vast trading network from the islands of Java and Sumatra for centuries. Yet, especially between the two world wars, the notion of a single, independent Indonesia was created and promoted, mostly by students and young professionals, in opposition to Dutch rule. It is an identity still waiting to be wholly crafted and accepted by all who live under the government of the republic.

Throughout the global south, Indigenous nationalist movements developed as a way to honor unique local traditions and ethnic identities. After a sense of identity was mobilized against the occupying powers, nationalist movements sometimes turned to violence as a means of expelling foreign influence, as in Vietnam, Algeria, Indonesia, Zimbabwe, Mozambique, and Angola. Some nationalist leaders propelled their movements with socialist ideology, such as Ho Chi Minh in the Vietnamese struggle against France and later the United States. Other nationalist leaders turned to socialist policies to help reconstruct their countries after achieving independence, including Algeria, India, Mozambique, and Angola. In its opposition to capitalism, socialism presented a means for national self-sufficiency and economic independence.[24]

Today, nationalist movements of identity are on the rise, but they certainly are not new—as discussed in our study of wars of national liberation in Chapter 3. We identify two types of nationalist mobilization: one calls for independence from larger political units that attempt to incorporate multiple national groups, and the other tries to bring attention to their identity in the face of global homogenization. Most of the countries that we are studying are richly multinational, made up of people with diverse linguistic, religious, historical, and cultural traditions. For some, this has not been an issue of great division, either because the leadership suppresses such discussion (as in the case of Tibetan identity in China), or because the groups themselves fail to see a need to challenge the status quo. For others, the expression of diverse national identities can be dangerous business. For example, the Kurdish people, many of whom identify as a nation with a common language and culture, have increasingly challenged their incorporation within the political entity of Turkey. Turkish leaders have defined the "Kurdish question" as a terrorist threat, and have until recently outlawed any independent expression of Kurdish identity, including their native language. The arrest of Kurdish leader Abdullah Öcalan lessened separatist tensions somewhat, but the potential for aggression, in both separatist action and state response, remains. We return to the question of the role of violence in irredentist movements in Chapter 10.

In addition, with increasing economic INTERDEPENDENCE and trade, the rise of GLOBALIZATION motivates some national groups to emphasize their unique characteristics in the face of the commercial and cultural homogeneity. While there are many positive aspects of a global economy and the conveniences it brings, many believe that it inhibits Indigenous cultures and traditions in the name of modernity. In response to the perceived growth of Western values and goods, many groups increase their expression of microidentities. Some of this has been in response to global corporate developments. For example, there was much resistance in China when Seattle-based Starbucks opened a coffee shop in the cherished Palace Museum, the former residence of the emperors and empresses known outside China as the Forbidden City. Many Islamic groups decry the pervasiveness of Western standards in areas of fashion, gender relations, and entertainment. One scholar, Benjamin Barber, framed this tension "Jihad vs. McWorld."[25] Since September 11, 2001, though, Barber and others have quickly cautioned us not to make the easy and inaccurate assumptions that the world can so neatly be characterized in a binary fashion, grouping people in tight categories as either in favor of Western-style modernization, or not. Rather, the image that Barber attempted to convey in the provocative title of his study is more accurately viewed as a means of capturing the diverse opposition that has formed to the proliferation of mass markets, technology, and Western-dominated popular culture.[26] For many groups on the receiving end of this new culture, it forces a reevaluation of their fundamental identity.

People also emphasize their class identity, which is based on their status within the economic structure. For example, people who consider themselves "working class" tend to identify with others who receive hourly wages for their labor. Although the origins of class awareness are largely Marxist, people who speak of a class identity are not necessarily Marxist revolutionaries. Income is unevenly distributed in every society. Guillermo O'Donnell and others have argued that a middle class, who are without the extremist tendencies of either wealth or dire poverty, is critical in transitions to democracy, as we discuss in Chapter 12. But especially in societies where there is a sharp divide between the rich and the poor, such as Peru, identity as a member of the working class or the upper class is extremely

Figure 8.3 Tibet and the Tibetan People

Located in southwestern China, Tibet is a great example of a region in which people exercise multiple identities. Living on the world's highest plateau, the Tibetan people have fought against conquest by many peoples, including the Mongols, the imperial Chinese, and the British. Shortly after the declaration of the People's Republic of China in 1949, troops of the Chinese Communist Party marched into Tibet, attempting to enlarge their rule over the important border region. Suppression of the Tibetan uprising was fierce: thousands of Tibetans were killed and hundreds of sacred monasteries were destroyed. While the Chinese Communist Party was nominally successful at establishing its rule, many, including the main spiritual leader of the Tibetan people, the Dalai Lama, fled to India in 1959, where the government-in-exile remains today.

Buddhism was declared the official religion of Tibet in the eighth century. Yet, Tibetan Buddhists are not all unified in their expression of religious tenets or doctrine—in fact, a fierce rivalry has long existed between two groups, the "Yellow Hat" sect (known as the Gelugpa) and the "Black Hat" sect (the Kagyupa). Until the 1600s the Black Hats, led by the Karmapa Lama, dominated Tibetan affairs, but for the past four centuries the Yellow Hats, under the leadership of the Dalai Lama, have persevered. The current Dalai Lama, believed to be the fourteenth reincarnation of the spiritual leader, received the Nobel Peace Prize in 1989 for his advocacy of peace and environmental concerns. Not all Tibetan Buddhists, though, share his passion for nonviolence.

Residents of Tibet today include native inhabitants of the region, as well as Chinese migrants from other regions of the country—including many of the Han Chinese majority, who moved to Tibet in search of economic opportunities promoted by the government in Beijing. Many native residents of the territory fear they are losing their Indigenous culture, religious traditions, and way of life, which are challenged not only by Han migration to the region but also by the modernizing ways of young Tibetan residents. Changes are likely to accelerate now that the world's highest railway route has opened between Beijing and Lhasa (a forty-eight-hour trek). Additionally, the current Dalai Lama is not going to be around forever (he was born in 1935)—the search for his successor is likely to be fierce.

important, a lesson that feminist mobilizers took some time to learn. Class identity has been an often-cited rallying cry to stand in opposition to the status quo.

Another source of identity that is often masked by the dominance of the government is a regional identity. This shared identity among residents of a particular region, such as a north-south distinction, or the type of region, such as urban or rural, is heightened when governments pursue economic reforms that promote regional disparities. For example, regions in Mexico may be differentiated by the prevalence of export industrialization in the north, leading to relative prosperity as compared to destitution in the south, where the economy is more dependent on domestic sales. Since independence, northern Nigeria, which is predominantly Muslim, has dominated political power and decisionmaking, but most of the oil is found in the southern, predominantly Christian and animist parts of the country. Indonesia is another country with pronounced regional differences, compounded by linguistic and religious differences that are geographically concentrated. The westernmost province of Aceh, deemed the most "Islamic" of any region in the state, is sometimes called "the front porch of Mecca" because it points toward Saudi Arabia. It also has great natural wealth in its possession of liquefied natural gas, which distinguishes it from other provinces.

In many countries of the global south, a majority of the population lives in the countryside, often making their living off of the land. Contrary to popular belief, rural dwellers are not necessarily conservative in their political views, nor are they passive recipients of the status quo. In some cases, peasants may be the forerunners to progressive change. For example, African scholars have long highlighted a rural bias, noting, in some cases, higher voter turnout in African rural areas compared to cities, as well as increased access to education and improved public health outcomes for rural children as a result of the close engagement with rural voters.[27] Peasants around the world are known as crafty political entrepreneurs who know how to work the system to their maximum advantage. Throughout the global south, we see rural residents rallying for their rights, whether it is protesting the loss of land to the state, advocating for education and safe drinking water, or standing up to corruption, among other issues. But the picture is complex, and clientelism, or the maintenance of PATRON-CLIENT RELATIONSHIPS that reinforce the status quo, can persist in rural areas. Mexico's Institutional Revolutionary Party (PRI) relied on rural support for years, and rural dwellers fearful of change were a crucial base of support for the Mugabe regime in Zimbabwe.

Throughout the world, religious affiliations also serve as an important sense of identity. It is not surprising that one's basic values and assumptions about human beings, morality, and justice color opinions on issues of politics, economics, and culture. In the United States, a separation of church and state tends to be promoted, meaning that religion is often viewed as a personal matter, and that religious beliefs should not become too closely involved in matters of politics and governance, although the dividing line is often challenged. The separation of church and state is a contested concept in many regions and within many spiritual traditions of the world. In fact, in some of the countries that we are studying, a greater fusion of religion and politics is desired not only by the political elites, but by some ordinary citizens as well. The declining rate of affiliation with formal church organizations in the United States (as well as Western Europe) does not mimic trends found in the global south, as rates of formal religious identity continue to increase, due in part to religious conversions, but even more so to powerful demographic trends. Pew reports that restrictions on religious expression (by the government as well as social actors) in many of the most populous countries of the world, including China, Egypt, Indonesia, Iran, Nigeria, and Pakistan, are at the highest levels since tracking began in 2007.[28]

When contemplating religious issues and their importance in politics and governance, many think of the Middle East, the birthplace of the world's three major monotheistic religions: Islam, Judaism, and Christianity. While religious issues are indeed important in this region, religious values and beliefs are difficult to separate from events in other parts of the world as well. Two predominantly Muslim countries present an interesting paradox. In Turkey, where the population is 99 percent Muslim, until very recently the government has fiercely upheld SECULARISM, established at the beginning of the modern republic in 1923 (President Recep Tayyip Erdoğan in 2022 appeared to promote the more open expression of religious identity, rattling many). The Islamic Republic of Iran, however, established by the revolution in 1979, is a formal THEOCRACY. For example, Iran's highest institution of authority, the Council of Guardians, bases its decisions on the sacred

Muslim text, the Quran, rather than the country's 1979 constitution. Attempts to develop political and religious pluralism face fierce opposition from religious clerics, who hold much of the power within the country.

Another source of the controversy is related to the connection between those who use Islam as a source for their political ideology and those who undertake violence in the name of Islam. Most Muslims view jihad, often translated from the Arabic as "struggle," as an individual struggle to overcome temptations and submit to the will of God, or Allah (the term "Islam" means "submission to God"). It is true that some, a minority within the faith, view jihad as struggle against enemies of Islam. These individuals and the groups they support may accurately be characterized as advocates of militant Islam, just as we have discussed regarding adherents of more aggressive forms of other traditions above. And extremists who claim that their faith inspires violent acts usually lose the support of others in their faith community.

As we have discussed, the labeling of any action or group is fraught with difficulty, especially from the perspective of the people being discussed. This controversy has become particularly acute as analysts try to characterize so-called political Islam. Many terms have been coined to capture the ideology and political program that some derive from their Islamic faith, with "Islamism" becoming a commonly used term by advocates and detractors alike. As we find with almost any label, as much is obscured as is understood—not all politically active Christians see the world through the same lens, for example, so why should it be assumed that all Muslims do? Because of these terminological debates, trying to characterize the numbers is difficult.

The intellectual roots of Islamism as an ideology can be traced to Sayyid Abul Ala Maududi, an Indian journalist who fought in the anti-imperial struggle and then moved to Pakistan to build a more pure Islamic state, later founding the Islamist party Jamaat-e-Islami (JEI) in 1941 to counter the secularism and

Figure 8.4 Are All Arabs Muslim? Are All Muslims Arab?

Despite the fact that the terms are often used interchangeably, there are important differences in meaning between "Arab" and "Muslim." Generally, Arabs are viewed as a community defined either linguistically (countries in which the dominant language is Arabic, which is a member of the Semitic family of languages), politically (citizens of a country that is a member of the Arab League, an organization of twenty-two states that is headquartered in Cairo, Egypt), or genealogically (families who trace their ancestry to the Arabian Peninsula or Syrian desert). Any categorization has exceptions—Somalia, for example, is a non-Arab country that is a member of the Arab League, and many people who speak Arabic do not consider themselves to be Arab.

Arabs identify with many different religious traditions. The majority of Arabs are Muslim, but there are also Arab Christians (concentrated in Lebanon, Egypt, Palestine, Jordan, Sudan, and Syria), and Arab Jews (in Morocco and Tunisia). Not all Muslim-majority states are Arab. For example, the Islamic Republic of Iran, is Persian, and not Arab.

Muslims are adherents of Islam. Muslims come from many different ethnic groups, and are connected by their belief in Islam. Less than a quarter of the world's Muslims are Arab—the world's most populous Muslim countries are in Asia: Indonesia, Pakistan, Bangladesh, and India.

Westernization of Pakistan. He emphasized personal transformation and the grounding of all human activity in faith. Another source of Islamist views was Sayyid Qutb, an Egyptian civil servant who, after graduate study in the United States, rejected Western values as corrupt and immoral. Returning to Egypt, he vocally criticized what he perceived to be his government's replication of Western decadence. Qutb eventually became a leader of the oldest Islamist party, Egypt's Muslim Brotherhood. As an activist, his outspoken ways landed him in jail (where he refined his ideas), and ultimately he was hanged by the Egyptian government.

Some Islamists have been emboldened by what they perceive as the corrupt, HEGEMONIC ways of Western governments, most notoriously the United States. They have taken great exception to, since 1991, the stationing of US troops in Saudi Arabia, the land that is home to Mecca and Medina, the two most sacred sites of Islam. (Even though US troops were formally withdrawn from Saudi Arabia in 2003, several thousand troops, jet fighters, and other weaponry, including a drone base, remain, and the Trump administration authorized new US troops to Saudi Arabia to counter a perceived threat from Iran.[29]) Islamists hold views in varying levels and degrees, some arguing that the greatest threat to peace is internal (e.g., believers who are not faithful), and others targeting external threats (e.g., the United States). Cartoons depicting the prophet Muhammad insult Muslims (whether Islamist or not) around the world to varying degrees, and contribute to the sense that, as a faith community, Muslims remain poorly understood by many non-Muslims. Pew data reflect a lack of factual knowledge about Islam by many Americans, with nearly half stating that they do not personally know a Muslim. A global survey also highlighted negative views (including greedy, fanatic, violent, and immoral) that Muslims and non-Muslim Westerners have of each other.[30]

The role of formal Catholic Church institutions has been an intense issue in Mexican politics since as far back as the mid-1800s. Mexicans have fought two civil wars to decide the Church's role. The country is overwhelmingly Roman Catholic, but fiercely anticlerical. The 1917 revolution sought to limit the Church's involvement in politics. Religious schools were closed, and church property was seized. Priests were prohibited from voting or wearing the collar in public. But the election of the socially conservative National Action Party (PAN) in 2000 emboldened the Church and reignited a number of controversies about the role of religion in Mexican public life.

In some countries, governments construct a specific doctrine to explain the proper place of religion in politics and society. Political and military leaders in Indonesia, for example, long promoted the importance of the *pancasila,* literally the "five principles." These pillars of Indonesian life are monotheism, national unity, humanitarianism, representative democracy by consensus, and social justice. Sukarno, the first president of Indonesia, created the *pancasila* creed as a way to unite the diverse peoples of Indonesia. Although the meaning of the *pancasila* doctrine is debated today, it remains an important symbol of leaders' aspirations to create unity out of diversity, even as a "hot button" issue.[31]

Another example of the importance of religious identity in the global south comes from a Christian tradition. Liberation theology is a movement that started within the Catholic Church, and it has had an especially powerful impact in

Latin America. In Brazil, the world's most populous Roman Catholic state, the impact of this theology continues in the lay communities focused on social justice.[32] It is by definition an action-oriented ideology that calls on its followers to promote a preferential option for the most economically poor members of society. As a system of thought, it is intriguing because of its combination of Marxist revolutionary ideas (which are explicitly hostile toward organized religions) with Christian teachings. While its origins were within Roman Catholicism, it is increasingly becoming an ecumenical movement, including other Christian churches and institutions. And although many of its leaders received training in European religious institutions, liberation theology is increasingly becoming an Indigenous intellectual and ideological movement, with native theologians addressing the social ills plaguing the less developed world.

In 1971, Peruvian theologian Gustavo Gutiérrez published *A Theology of Liberation,* considered by many to be the definitive statement.[33] In it he stressed social praxis (practice), with a commitment to critical reflection and a renewed dedication on the part of the universal church to the disenfranchised poor and destitute. Gutiérrez argued that too many Christians, especially Catholics, focus on the orthodoxy (correct teachings) rather than on the orthopraxis (correct practice) of a Christian life. Liberation theology maintains that people need to move beyond doctrine to focus on the economic, political, and social issues that affect ordinary people on a daily basis. Advocates of this approach contend that poverty is caused by structures (e.g., the INTERNATIONAL ECONOMIC SYSTEM) rather than individual, idiosyncratic characteristics, including laziness, bad luck, or other sources of blame. Therefore, the "liberation" of the poor is more than an act of individual charity; it is a demand for a new social and economic order to promote the universal humanity of all peoples. Second is the idea of collective sin, articulated by Brazilian theologian Leonardo Boff, who argued that people who support unjust regimes, even if they themselves do not personally exploit the poor, are collectively responsible for the result.[34] Boff's statements implicated not only leaders and citizens in the Western, developed world, but citizens of poorer countries as well. Liberation theology has impacted many of the countries we are studying here. A 2000 pastoral letter in Mexico, for example, criticized political and economic systems as "poverty-generating structures," and called on people to fight to build a more just society. The South African Council of Churches applied the principles of liberation theology, through Black theology, to end apartheid. Several ecumenical organizations, including the Zimbabwean Catholic Bishops Conference and the Zimbabwe Council of Churches, played important roles in the struggle against white minority rule, and continue to condemn human rights abuses. They argue that poverty is due to oppressive structures and call for activism, primarily through the development of base Christian communities that work to educate, evangelize, and empower the economically poor. Movements inspired by liberation theology have met with harsh repression by governments (backed by military force) and institutional churches as well, especially in El Salvador and Guatemala. This has provoked an increase in violence by adherents.

Mobilization around issues of gender has been particularly strong throughout the non-Western world, especially since 1975, when the UNITED NATIONS held its first international women's conference in Mexico City. Similar to other groups, women have mobilized in response to repression, exclusion, and other crises, on their own behalf and in the interest of others, especially children. As we discuss below, there is no single brand of feminism, but rather many different viewpoints commonly united around the desire to advance the voice of women in today's world. Feminism includes a rich history of advocacy and engagement throughout the global south.[35]

Feminism is a complex worldview that includes many perspectives, and there are vigorous debates about what defines a "feminist." One school of thought distinguishes feminists who work primarily for civil equality that recognizes the fundamental equality between women and men. Such groups, often called liberal feminists, have been at the forefront of suffrage movements as well as civil rights movements that fight for gains in equality before the law. This view is contrasted with another school of thought that emphasizes the differences that exist between women and men. Commonly known as radical feminists, they argue that liberal feminists fail to recognize the unspoken assumption that women should perform the same as men. In contrast, radical feminists fight for the equal recognition of women's standards as well as men's; they argue that women's ways need to be recognized for their inherent contributions as well. It is a question of standards and assumptions; while radical feminists agree that men and women are equal, they contend that stopping there fails to challenge the continued dominance of a male-centric society.

Feminists have actively challenged notions of "correct" female (and by association, male) behavior that are rooted in custom and tradition. In a related fashion, many women openly confront the notion that politics is the exclusive domain of men. Mexico, for example, has a long history of feminist activism, so much so that it may be argued that Mexico, not the United States, has been the cradle for feminism in the Western Hemisphere. Sor Juana Inéz de la Cruz, who lived in the 1600s, is said to be the first feminist of the Americas. In large numbers, Mexican women joined the revolutionary armies of Pancho Villa and Emiliano Zapata. Benita Galeana led the first land takeovers by squatters during the Great Depression. She was arrested sixty times and lost her eyesight while on a hunger strike fighting for women's suffrage. Since the 1980s, *MAQUILADORA* workers have claimed an unusual degree of freedom for themselves, despite the low pay and sexual harassment they continue to face in the factories. Mexican feminists today are fighting for reproductive rights, for better working conditions, and to have violence against women (especially sexual assault and wife battery) taken more seriously.

Similar to other sets of activists, groups working to further women's causes disagree about the point of focus for their actions. Some groups accuse others of reinforcing gender distinctions by focusing on issues of family, motherhood, and children, replicating traditional political roles. Engaging in so-called motherist activism (discussed below), groups in Latin America, for example, were challenged by radical feminist leaders because their work focused on practical interests, such as providing meals to deprived children, rather than on more "strategic" issues, including sexual freedom and domestic violence.[36] Yet, the mothers' groups, in their emphasis on seemingly practical needs, rallied tens of thousands of activists against military regimes, revealing that the emperor had no clothes.

Some argue that women are uniquely placed to fight for the interests of their children, and indeed women have potently harnessed this connection to challenge state norms and policies.

Another debate centers on the relationship between culture and feminism. This has definitely been a theme of contention and division among Latin American, African, and Islamic feminists. Women who work within the system, or within the structure of prevailing religious norms, are accused by others of replicating traditional views that subordinate women, rather than challenging the status quo.

Non-Western variants of feminism have argued that "practical" concerns, including providing meals and healthcare to families, can be just as feminist as the political concerns of other feminists, like demanding access to political decisionmaking. Adherents to the latter focus, which is considered to be more "strategic" than practical, claim to be working for larger structural changes that would ultimately transform gender relations. But non-Western women do not hold a monopoly on this desire: in Latin America, for example, feminism was central to the effort to delegitimize military rule and re-create CIVIL SOCIETY.[37] Yet other feminist groups, in the face of the same struggles, adopted an explicitly human rights character to their activism. Economic crises and the imposition of austerity programs impelled women to organize and demand relief, filling in the gaps of what government could not (or would not) provide. Maybe some viewed this as practical and too "traditional," but to the women who were organizing, it was feminism at its best.

To be successful, people plan their strategies within existing contexts—sometimes this means radically challenging the system, and other times it means reforming it along the edges. Patriarchy and social conservatism are so pervasive, for example, that many women in northern Nigeria believe that reform within Islamic law is the only hope for promoting gender equality. The issue of modest clothing associated with some interpretations of Islamic customs captures some of this controversy. Many Westerners associate the traditional headscarf or veil with women's oppression and submission to male authority. Yet, for many Muslim women, the decision to wear a headscarf is a conscious choice; the wearing of a veil, or *purdah* (literally, "curtain"), provides them an avenue of expression and even opposition. For some, veiling literally creates a wall that allows women to move through the male world of school and work; it allows a quiet insubordination. For others, it is liberating to be listened to, rather than looked at. In Tunisia, donning a religious veil was forbidden until after the Arab Spring revolution of 2011, selecting the *niqab,* a full Muslim veil that leaves only the eyes showing, as a welcome expression of religious devotion. Yet, in 2019, citing security reasons, it was again outlawed.[38]

Clearly, not all women are feminists. In fact, some ardently oppose mobilization and action in the name of equality or women's causes. Some groups, self-proclaimed antifeminists, reject the importance of feminist issues and often agree with gender segregation and clearly defined family roles. They frequently advocate a culturally conservative position, reaffirming the notion of a predetermined place for women at home, rearing the family, rather than in the marketplace or

Figure 8.5 LGBTQIA Rights in the Global South

One of the most personal aspects of identity can also be the most dangerous. Advocates for the rights of lesbian, gay, bisexual, transgender, queer/questioning, intersex, and asexual/aromantic/agender individuals point out that throughout many countries of the global south, individuals lack the basic freedom to express gender identity or sexual orientation. As of 2021, sixty-nine countries around the world have laws that criminalize or harass people on the basis of their sexual orientation or identity, including states in which the death penalty can be applied for cases of consensual homosexual conduct (Brunei, Iran, Mauritania, Saudi Arabia, Somalia, South Sudan, Yemen, and in the northern states of Nigeria where sharia law is applied).[a] Even in states where homosexuality is not criminal, discrimination persists. Invasive (and blatantly illegal) practices to "undo" one's sexual orientation or gender identity persist in countries lacking either the state capacity or will to enforce rights, and transgender individuals have been especially vulnerable.[b] As we have observed in so many issue areas, Covid exposed already existing inequalities; in multiple states (reaching beyond the global south), anti-LGBTQIA bias was apparent as individuals were targeted for perceived violations of public health safeguards related to the pandemic.[c]

The record on rights is not all negative, however. Some strides have been made in marriage equality. Argentina became the first Latin American state to legalize same-sex marriage (in 2010), and courts in Mexico and Brazil have more recently conferred the right to equal unions as well (although, in Mexico, the legal right can vary by state). Chilean lawmakers legalized same-sex marriage in 2021, in what many viewed as a "landmark victory" that marked an emerging norm in Latin America.[d] Discrimination safeguards have been developed in Angola, Mauritius, and South Africa—the only African state where gay marriage is legal.

Notes: a. Noor Zainab Hussain, "Legal Hurdles Faced by LGBT+ People in Africa," Reuters, October 27, 2020; "Homosexuality: The Countries Where It Is Illegal to Be Gay," BBC News, May 12, 2021.

b. Paul J. Angelo and Dominic Bocci, "The Changing Landscape of Global LGBTQ+ Rights," Council on Foreign Relations, January 29, 2021.

c. Graeme Reid, "Global Trends in LGBT Rights During the Covid-19 Pandemic," Human Rights Watch, February 24, 2021.

d. Pascale Bonnefoy and Ernesto Londoño, "Chile Legalizes Same-Sex Marriage at Fraught Political Moment," *New York Times,* December 7, 2021.

other public domains of men. Key issues of antifeminists include opposition to abortion and women's employment outside the home.

Each of these approaches, and the actions they inspire, arouse debate about cultural values and standards. Are there universal norms, applicable to all people irrespective of culture, level of development, or social system, or is there merit in an approach referred to as CULTURAL RELATIVISM, in which standards are dependent on relative circumstances?

Elites, Masses, and Legitimacy

It has been implicit in our discussion to this point that power is distributed unequally. Usually in public life, some people hold power and other people are influenced by it. In this chapter, we have emphasized that all people possess ideas about the world around them. It is obvious that in many areas of life, the ideas of some matter more than the ideas of others. In every society around the world, people can be divided into two categories, either the elites (possessing power and influence) or the masses (lacking power and influence relative to the elites). There are always more of the latter. Even though the so-called elites may exercise more influence and authority in economics, politics, culture, or other areas, they are not able to maintain this status indefinitely.

An important term that conveys one of the most fundamental political relationships between elites and masses is LEGITIMACY, sometimes viewed simply as rightfulness. All leaders, no matter their level, need to be concerned about their legitimacy. It can be viewed as a sense that an individual or group who has power, holds such power properly. Individuals or groups can possess power or influence, but if the people over whom they have influence do not view them as legitimate, their power and influence will likely be short-lived.

Sociologist Max Weber identified three primary sources of legitimacy: tradition, charisma, and legality. Traditional legitimacy is based on cultural precedents established for recognizing authority and power. A tribal chief, for example, bases his legitimacy on this source. Hereditary monarchies, in which some people receive their influence because of membership in particular families, are other sources of traditional legitimacy. The "Mandate of Heaven," possessed by members of the Chinese imperial leadership, is another example of legitimacy that is traditional in nature. Charismatic sources of legitimacy are based on personal attributes that command attention, respect, and often obedience. Charisma is something that people are said to exhibit, as well as something given to them in the eyes of ordinary people. For example, Ayatollah Ruhollah Khomeini, the former religious leader of the Iranian Revolution, was viewed as a mythical hero to many. Before the 1979 revolution, while he was living in exile (mostly in Turkey, Iraq, and France), people in Iran insisted that they could see his face in the moon.[39] The third source of legitimacy, according to Weber, is legality: establishing seemingly impersonal rules and procedures to determine the recipients of leadership and authority. In this example, elections and laws transfer a sense of legitimacy to individuals and groups.

Legitimacy is what makes political systems last. It transforms raw power into a sense of authority. Without legitimacy, rulers' mandates are enforced out of a sense of fear, rather than a sense of duty or obligation. A lack of legitimacy can cause a government to crumble. In some cultural traditions, there would be signs from the ancestors or the spirits that a leader had lost his or her legitimacy. In imperial China, for example, natural disasters were perceived to be signs that the emperor had lost the legitimacy to rule. In many modern democracies today, legitimacy is based on the popular mandate. Although elections are increasingly being viewed as the legitimizing tool of modern leaders, this has not always been the case, nor do many leaders maintain their legitimacy based on legal means alone.

Do powerful elites really need to be concerned about their legitimacy? They do. It is difficult to survive on coercion alone, and leaders need authority to accomplish the day-to-day tasks of governing. Coercion and the violence it entails are costly, not only in a crude financial sense, but in terms of morale as well. Certainly, some authoritarian leaders have made extensive use of threats and coercion as a means of maintaining their power. But it is extremely difficult (although not impossible) to maintain power in this manner for long. Leaders in all areas of public life need to develop connections with the masses, and must be able to foster a sense that they are legitimately empowered to make decisions. When citizens no longer believe that the leadership has legitimacy, they are often impelled to act. Ordinary citizens, even in the face of dire constraints on their behavior and threats of coercive responses from leaders, attempt to challenge circumstances that they feel are unjust and illegitimate. While some of these attempts face anguishing defeats, others are successful at challenging the state of affairs and bringing about desired change.

Leaders maintain their legitimacy in a variety of different ways. Ideology plays a key role, as members of the elite attempt to craft views and actions to their liking. The manipulation of ideologies by leaders is particularly acute in TOTALITARIAN systems, in which the government has control over most aspects of people's lives. The use of important symbols, like buildings, images, linguistic phrases, and historical heroes, is another means by which leaders attempt to promote and increase their legitimacy. In societies that have experienced revolutions, or have had a recent history of revered leaders, paying homage to and noting a lineage from these leaders can be a powerful source of legitimacy, especially in uncertain times. On the seventieth anniversary of the founding of the Chinese Communist Party in 2021, for example, President and General Secretary Xi Jinping ordered large pictures of himself to be carried on high behind the traditional posters of Mao Zedong and Deng Xiaoping.[40] This rather obvious demonstration of the lineage of his authority is not unlike other public relations campaigns in which leaders engage. In examining legitimacy, one must be careful to avoid connections between legitimacy, stability, and popular content. Just because a pronounced sense of legitimacy may seem to be present in a particular country does not mean that citizens agree with actions that their government takes.

Leaders may also promote their legitimacy by providing material gains to the population. Indonesia's former president Suharto based much of his legitimacy, especially in the later years of his rule, on promises to the people that their economic lives would improve. When the futility of this promise was painfully realized in the spring of 1998, however, his legitimacy plummeted, and he was forced from office. This example provides another lesson about the importance of stability. When leaders are successful at maintaining it, for the most part life is stable. When they fail, it can often lead to popular mobilization or other forms of participation, a topic to which we now turn our attention.

Ideas in Action

If they are not acted upon, ideas remain a possibility, rather than an expression of will. In the remainder of this chapter, we examine the next step: when individuals and groups decide to take action based upon their beliefs. We examine forms of "political participation," which we define simply as efforts by ordinary people to influence the actions of their leaders.[41] Sometimes activists work within the bounds of legal activity, although oftentimes they attempt to change or break the conventional rules. While in some systems, especially totalitarian regimes, citizens are forced to participate in governmentally sponsored demonstrations, rallies, or protests, for our purposes we examine only participation that is voluntary. Fundamentally, political participation is about communicating preferences to the people who have power and influence (elites).

Participation is a choice, and one that is only exercised by a portion of any population. One important characteristic that participants tend to exhibit is a sense of efficacy, which is a sense that one's participation can make a difference. If you believe that by writing a letter to an elected official you are likely to influence her or his point of view, you have a strong sense of efficacy. On the other hand, if you do not vote because you are of the mind that it does not make a difference, you have a low sense of efficacy. Oftentimes, a sense of efficacy also correlates with level of education, as well as socioeconomic security.[42] It takes time to be active and engaged in public life, and few people can afford to take time off from work or be away from family to speak at a neighborhood assembly or picket against an unjust action.

How do people participate in their political, social, and economic world? We often think of voting in elections as the primary means of political participation, but in fact this is just one of four primary ways that people can participate in public life: (1) explicit communication, spoken and written; (2) regime action, including voting and joining political parties or legal organizations; (3) mobilizational action, including demonstrating in social movements or rallies or participating in boycotts or other forms of group resistance; and (4) inaction, refusing to vote or obey authority, or utilizing the so-called WEAPONS OF THE WEAK. These categories are not necessarily mutually exclusive. In fact, individuals and groups who feel dissatisfied with one type of action, such as normal constituent communication, often decide to pursue another strategy, like joining a protest.

Spoken and Written Communication

Many citizens decide to communicate with their public leaders, often using simple means such as social media, online petitions, telephone calls, letters to officials or to the media, speeches, and public signs. Most officials establish some form of channel to foster communication between themselves and their constituents. Some leaders embrace this digital diplomacy. Argentine president Mauricio Macri (who led from 2015 to 2019) was branded the master of Snapchat, and longtime autocratic leader of Cambodia, Hun Sen, also turns to Facebook to craft his popular image.[43] Throughout the Covid pandemic, many African leaders and governments, including Zimbabwe's Emmerson Mnangagwa, and the governments of Malawi and South Africa, used the platform to inform citizens of public health regulations and updates on their handling of the virus.[44]

Letters to the media can be an extremely useful way to communicate dissatisfaction with a leader or policy. Even in the most totalitarian systems, government-controlled newspapers—print and online—are designated as receiving points for citizen letters and complaints. Even if the letters themselves are not published in the "official" media, they are often collected and distributed for the leadership to read. Petitions, usually put forward by groups of people, provide another open channel, although not without risk.

Regime Action

The second major category of participation is regime action, or participation that is overtly designed to support the functioning of the larger political, social, or economic system. This is the type of participation with which most people are likely familiar. In many countries, democratic and nondemocratic alike, citizens are called on to elect representatives to make decisions in their name. The difference in nondemocratic systems, though, is that there is little if any choice of candidates, or the candidates who are elected fail to exercise power or influence. Citizens are also called on to vote in a referendum, a direct vote in which the entire electorate is asked to accept or reject a proposal. Recent referenda have taken place in Kyrgyzstan, Thailand, and Colombia, in which citizens narrowly defeated the landmark peace agreement with FARC rebels.

Political parties stand out as one of the most common vehicles of participation. They develop as groups of similarly minded individuals and organize so that they can influence policy decisions. Parties help individuals identify with issues in public life, and they organize people into action. They also promote a common identity among participants, in some cases helping to bridge ethnic or cultural divides. In democratic and nondemocratic systems alike, political parties form so that the elites can appeal to ordinary citizens. In some countries, until recently a single party dominated public life, and citizens have had few choices but to belong to the ruling party. In others, a meaningful PARTY SYSTEM has developed in which competing groups of people openly vie for attention and power. Parties often rename themselves, craft new coalitions (with other parties as well as constituent groups), and shift power balances, all in the attempt to maintain dynamic links between elites and masses.

Maurice Duverger classified three main types of political parties, based on their style of organization and operation.[45] The first is the CADRE PARTY, in which PERSONALIST REGIMES, often based on friendships and favors, together with factional groupings comprising people with similar approaches who try to stick together, dominate the relatively small group of elites involved in political matters. Often in systems where cadre parties prevail, the right to vote is limited, meaning that political parties do not face the need to justify their ideological positions or policies beyond the groups already possessing power or influence. A second type is the MASS PARTY, which attempts to reach out beyond the walls of power to appeal to less politically engaged individuals and groups. Mass parties have open membership, but their leaders often target specific segments of the population to whom they plan to pitch their ideological appeal: factory workers, intellectuals, peasants, or other groups. To maintain their interest and support, mass parties develop local branch offices that provide services and information to their likely constituents. Duverger's third type is the DEVOTEE PARTY, which is dominated by a charismatic leader and a small elite united in forging a revolutionary path. The Chinese Communist Party during Mao's leadership is an exemplar of such an elitist party, even if its rhetoric attempted to cater to a mass audience.

How important are political parties within the global south? In single-party states, like the PRC, they are the primary venue through which the elites exercise their power. In transforming states, such as Indonesia, the nascent political party system is dominated by personalities and crowded with minute factions. In other countries, including Peru, traditional parties have become virtually extinct. Many leaders sense they are better off without a party than with one. In states where personal relations continue to dominate politics, elections tend to be centered on candidates rather than parties. These systems are marked by extreme electoral volatility, and can easily open the door for populist antisystem candidates who have few qualms about dissolving democratic institutions once they capture the seats of power.

Another type of institution that facilitates the participation of ordinary citizens is the employment organization or union. Independent unions attempt to provide a collective voice to workers. They attempt to promote workers' rights and interests, including sick leave, access to healthcare, and the right to strike, which is restricted in many areas of the world. Unions played an important role in civil rights movements in South Korea and South Africa. In some countries, unions work closely with elites; left-leaning political parties tend to develop strong ties with labor and trade unions. Unions may also serve as the launching pad for oppositional movements and parties. The Movement for Democratic Change (MDC) in Zimbabwe, for example, which has posed the greatest challenge that the ruling Zimbabwe African National Union–Patriotic Front has ever faced, grew out of labor unions. In other countries, governments attempt to co-opt independent expression through the establishment of official, state-sponsored unions. The famous big box stores in China are the only location in the world where Walmart employees may form a union—one that is under the firm supervision of the Communist Party organization (local offices are usually directed by someone from company management). In fact, independent unionization is a dangerous business throughout the global south—not that this prevents some activists from trying.[46]

In countries reliant on exports, including Nicaragua, El Salvador, Guatemala, Mexico, and Honduras, independent trade unionists face many restrictions on their ability to strike. Labor repression is also common in many African countries, where arrests for union activities are common. Throughout the Middle East, independent trade unions are virtually nonexistent. In this region, the situation is particularly bleak for foreign workers, who make up approximately two-thirds of the labor force in many countries. In most countries in the region, foreign workers are not permitted to join or form any type of workers' union.

Union organizing can also be found among the youth. Children's labor unions, whose origins are found in the New York newsboy strikes against Joseph Pulitzer and William Hearst at the turn of the twentieth century, are vying for a stronger voice in national and international debates about child labor. According to the International Labour Organization (ILO), there are more than 218 million children workers worldwide—many full time.[47] Labor organizing for youth can be tough, yet Brazilian street children formed the first modern children's labor union in 1985.[48] Similar groups can be found throughout Africa, Southeast Asia, and India. Children's labor unions are becoming increasingly organized (some now hold international meetings), and they are united in the voice that child labor should not be abolished, but rather reformed.

Mobilizational Action

The third category of participation is mobilizational action, which includes social movements and other forms of collective action by aggrieved groups of people. By definition, this form of participation involves more than one person. People around the world understand the strength that can be found in numbers.

When a group of like-minded individuals forms to influence the turn of events around them, they are said to have formed a social movement. We often think of participants in social movements as attempting to change the status quo and bring about a new state of affairs, but in fact many participants in social movements are fighting instead to maintain the current state of life. Social movements form when there are grievances, either because people sense that they are being unfairly singled out or that they are not doing as well as other groups (RELATIVE DEPRIVATION), because they feel that promises, either implicit or explicit, have not been kept (rising expectations), or because they perceive a threat of some sort. There is also a sense that "time is ripe" for change, providing an opportunity structure for action. There are seemingly favorable times for groups of people to engage in collective action, often because of a political or economic transition, unexpected access to power, divisions among leaders, or a decreased likelihood of repression.[49] Changes in the international environment and movements with "spillover effects" also inspire action. Savvy activists develop expectations of the likelihood of repression, and act accordingly.

Social movements can be defined by an issue, such as civil rights or environmental protection, by a core group, such as women's movements or students' movements, or by a common target, such as antiglobalization protests or antimilitary demonstrations. One of the most common characteristics of social movements is that they often begin with a narrowly defined issue, and then rather quickly blossom to include other complaints and interests, broadening their appeal to a greater number of groups. Rarely are social movements confined to a single issue, and alliances between sets of activists are common. A group of students begins a protest ostensibly about economic corruption. Then, they are joined by unemployed workers angered by layoffs, and state employees frustrated at the inattention of their government-controlled union. The widespread protests then attract others who are at odds with the regime, including mothers who are confined to the home because of factory cutbacks, migrant peasants who cannot find work for more than a week at a time, and high school dropouts who want to get in on the action. This situation was part of the story of the widespread demonstrations in China in the spring of 1989.

University students wanting to pay homage to a fallen leader sparked the movement. After other groups joined the students in Beijing and 300 other cities, and after the international media picked up on the unlikely protests, a prodemocracy movement formed. As participants multiplied, the task of the protest organizers increased exponentially. Disagreements about tactics increased, like whether protesters should stage a hunger strike, whether they should openly confront the regime by blocking Tiananmen Square during an international summit, and whether they should negotiate with other protesting groups. We now know, thanks to extensive documentation and interviews with exiled protest leaders, that a serious factional split developed early on in the movement. Disagreement among movement leaders is common after a protest gets off the ground.

Participants in social movements often disagree about the scope of their protest actions. Do they want to provide a wake-up call to the regime and then return to life as usual, or do they want to bring regime leaders to their knees, attempting to cripple the economic and diplomatic base of the state? Some protesters view dialogue (especially with governments) as "selling out," while others view it as a strategic tactic. Some activists want to forge alliances with other organized social groups, uniting in their common cause of increasing regime TRANSPARENCY and accountability. Movements to extend political freedom and promote environmental protection are often linked, either in formal coalitions or because activists cross lines. Concern for the survival of Indigenous peoples is often linked to environmental concerns, as in Nigeria with the Movement for the Survival of the Ogoni People (MOSOP), and in Mexico with the Zapatistas. In China, many of the same activists who supported the movements in 1989 have been among the harshest critics of the Three Gorges Dam and other similar megaprojects.

Economic concerns have been a major mobilizing force throughout the global south. For many years, people unable to cope with AUSTERITY PLANS (discussed in Chapter 6) have protested against EXTENDED-CREDIT FACILITIES, most visibly in what has come to be known as an "IMF riot." These riots, which often involve looting and burning, are a form of protest that has broken out in India, Jamaica, Egypt, Indonesia, Greece, and Argentina as people have found that they can no longer manage with such devastating hardship. Less dramatic, but sometimes more deadly, versions of IMF riots take the form of mass demonstrations, such as those in Bolivia motivated by fatigue over fifteen years of structural adjustment.

In addition to achieving a desired goal, social movements are important because they provide a sense of identity and belonging to participants. In her studies of Peruvian women's movements, Maruja Barrig argues that by participating in democratically organized programs like communal kitchens and milk distribution programs, women develop a sense of solidarity and model behavior that could be extended to other areas of life.[50] To better understand the organization and impact of social movements, we examine two subtypes: women's movements and youth mobilization.

People often think of women's movements being involved in suffrage, or the right to vote. Women's mobilization, though, has gone well beyond the vote, and women activists have refused to be held back by the absence of the right to vote. For example, even though Mexico had some of the most vibrant and developed women's networks throughout Latin America as early as the 1930s, it was among the last countries in the Southern Hemisphere to grant women suffrage.[51] Women's movements, especially in the third world, have been particularly strong at demonstrating that personal issues are indeed political issues. NEOLIBERALISM has contributed to crises and poverty, and women have been channeled disproportionately into low-paid and transitory work. This has led many women to seek participation in community-based and neighborhood organizations to survive as they struggle to fill the gaps created when the state cuts services. Already struggling to support a family, these women face a huge burden without social services to rely on. Yet, it sometimes seems that the most burdened and desperate people can mobilize to accomplish huge tasks. For example, women spearheaded the Madres de Plaza de Mayo movement in Argentina, which brought attention to the "disappeared" husbands and sons of the participants, ignited human rights protests, and launched similar movements throughout Latin America. Another example of motherist activism can be found in China following the crackdown on the students in Tiananmen Square. Ding Zilin, whose son was killed on the last evening of the demonstrations as he attempted to vacate the square, and other mothers have staged an international movement to publicize the plight of their children and the brutality of the Chinese government. Although mothers go to the front lines for defense of family and morality, often they are subjected to STATE-SPONSORED TERRORISM, sexual abuse, and humiliation. They face similar discrimination within other participatory channels, including parties and unions that co-opt women into auxiliary chapters. Whether in traditional parties or social movements, women must prove themselves against visible and invisible obstacles. Women in many countries form their own organizations because their demands for equality and justice are viewed as divisive or frivolous.

Women throughout Latin America, especially in Peru and Chile, have established communal dining programs to pool resources and feed the economically poor. Some of these programs are decades long and have been used as models for others to copy. During the mid-1980s, one of the largest social movements in Latin America was the Vaso de Leche, or Municipal Milk, program. Based in Lima, Peru, its participants distributed at least a single serving of milk a day to millions of children and pregnant women. Popular social programs initiated and led by women incorporated new groups into public affairs. These activities are important not only for the services they provided to needy people, but also for the linkages they established between women's groups. They help many women feel a sense of belonging and empowerment, which helps promote active involvement in public affairs that otherwise seem "off limits," developing leadership skills and independence.[52]

Additionally, college and university students are often at the forefront of protests and social movements. Students tend to be skeptical of the norms of government and society, yet optimistic about their ability to make a difference. Many Latin American youth argue that their role is to offer sorely needed answers for the new situations their countries are facing. The traditional model of the party is exhausted; the youth need new organizations capable of responding to demands for a new, more participatory, and flexible political culture. Students tend to be risk-takers, willing to sacrifice time, money, and sometimes their lives to make a point. Some have noted a correlation between presence of major universities and presence of social movements, especially in capital cities (Tehran, Mexico City, Beijing). University campuses also can be ideal locales for communication networks. The national university of Peru, San Cristóbal de Huamanga, for example, served as the launching pad for one of the most violent movements in Latin America, Sendero Luminoso. Some student movements to unseat leaders have been successful, such as in Indonesia in 1998 and Iran in 1979, while others have been painfully unsuccessful, notably in Mexico in 1968 and China in 1989.

University students also have a history of political activism in Iran. In November 1979, in the early days of the Islamic Revolution, students were one of the groups leading the seizure of the US embassy in Tehran when fifty-two American hostages were captured. Twenty years later, in July 1999, student-led demonstrations for press reform broke out at Tehran University, spreading to eighteen cities. Sensing an open opportunity caused by widened rifts between Iran's conservative Supreme Leader, Ayatollah Sayyid Ali Khamenei, and the popularly elected but lower-ranking president, Mohammad Khatami, students staged five successive days of protest for democratic reform and press freedom. Students mobilized after the legislature passed a restrictive press law and after conservative leaders ordered the closure of a popular left-leaning Islamic newspaper, *Salam.*

In response, police forces raided the university dorms while students were sleeping, pushing some from multistory windows. In response, even more students joined the protest, using updated twists of slogans from the 1979 revolution. The chant "Independence, Freedom, Islamic Republic," was altered to "Independence, Freedom, Iranian Republic." Most accounts claim that the police killed one student, and approximately twenty more were seriously injured. In addition, nearly a thousand students were arrested for participating in the unrest, and at least four people were sentenced to death, in secret trials, for inciting violence.[53]

During the summer of 2009, a daring movement played out throughout Iran and the global blogosphere as millions of Iranians took to the streets to demonstrate against the announced results of a presidential election that had been ceded to the incumbent, Mahmoud Ahmadinejad. Protesters from many walks of life challenged the legitimacy of his reelection in what was termed a "Twitter Revolution": activists engaged in unprecedented use of information communication technologies to gather protesters, adopt last-minute strategies in response to government repression, and spread brutally explicit evidence of the government crackdown around the world. The most haunting image of the movement was that of Neda Agha-Soltan, a young woman who was shot to death during the protests. A witness captured the image on his mobile phone, which was eventually transferred to YouTube (outside of Iran), after which the clip of the dying woman went viral. The day after the election, the state shut down the internet entirely for half an hour while the authorities struggled to gain control. The regime responded with blunt force. One eighty-year-old woman lamented, "They have killed so many of the young and the well intentioned. Even the shah did not kill like this."[54]

Weapons of the Weak

The final type of participation is powerful in its ability to cause disruption through inaction or (on the surface) seemingly inconsequential acts of individual resistance. If the traditional spaces to which people can turn are denied (unions, political parties, media, protest channels), they learn to turn elsewhere to express their sentiments, especially their grievances. Anthropologist James C. Scott identified weapons of the weak as a way to categorize concealed, disguised, individual resistance. These actions, which he viewed as part of a larger category of everyday forms of resistance, include seemingly small acts like concealing a pig from state officials or falsifying income records. They may not garner the same amount of attention as a revolt in the national capital, but they can be extremely effective tools against injustice nonetheless. People pursue less obvious and less explicitly confrontational forms of resistance when open challenge to authority is too risky. In varied contexts, Scott and others draw our attention to these forms of resistance pursued by dominated groups, such as women, peasants, or other disenfranchised individuals. As discussed in Chapter

3, some of these tactics were common forms of resistance in struggles for national liberation.

Some analysts have sought to explain why women and other repressed groups in some parts of the world appear to be aloof from politics and less likely to participate in democratic struggles. They argue that, in many cases, women's political power and participation have declined since the precolonial period. Women's initial response to being politically marginalized during colonialism was resistance. However, this resistance often proved ineffective and was followed by a disengagement from formal politics or withdrawal into a consciously apolitical stance. Instead, women have come to favor private, extralegal channels and institutions including families, secret societies, spirit cults or prayer groups, and traditional women's associations. Additionally, women tend to be more active with regard to socioeconomic issues at the local rather than the national level.

But part of the reason why some groups appear complacent to outsiders is that observers fail to recognize acts of resistance that do not utilize more conventionally recognized channels of protest. Many actors employ weapons of the weak in the face of power, accomplishing in subtle acts what might never be achieved in more traditional routes. Individuals feign support for a cause, while subtly putting a cog in the wheel to block it. Actors can drag their feet, pretend compliance, and organize others to break rules through acts of civil disobedience. As Célestin Monga argues, outsiders often lament the absence of civic participation in African societies because they overlook the long tradition of Indigenous activism, what he terms the "anthropology of anger."[55] People get angry when systematically oppressed, and they develop ways of escaping repression. They pretend to accept the rules imposed by authoritarian groups, and are constantly adjusting to escape domination and circumvent coercive strictures. Such participation is GRASSROOTS-BASED and highly creative. Activists subvert the rules by not confronting power directly. These informal methods of participation and protest may be what truly pushes change.

Subversive music is a common form of political expression. For example, one of Africa's most famous Afrobeat musicians, Fela Anikulapo-Kuti, considered music a weapon. While praise-singing is a tradition associated with greats such as King Sunny Adé, Fela invented a new art: abuse-singing. In the late 1970s, Fela took on then president Olusegun Obasanjo, the military dictator of Nigeria, arguing that Afrobeat was the only music through which people could say what they felt and tell the government what they thought. Fela was beaten and jailed. His seventy-eight-year-old mother was thrown from a second-story window and later died of her injuries. He is followed in these pursuits by his son, Femi Kuti, whose Afrobeat songs attack corrupt politicians and warn about AIDS. Punk bands in China, which emerged on the scene after rock bands were significantly censored for their connections to protest movements, draw small crowds, which helps them evade censors and the police. They perform their most anti-establishment lyrics—including tributes to the Tiananmen mothers and others associated with the movements in 1989—in broken English. In this way, they reach their audience and express their disillusionment, without being hauled away.[56] Even though rock music is illegal in Iran, some daring groups have flourished in the underground rock scene in their refusal to conform to the regime.[57]

Another highly influential political forum for dealing with real-life issues like corruption, drug trafficking, AIDS, and sexism is the *telenovela,* or soap opera, a favorite form of entertainment for millions in Latin America. The *telenovela* is much more influential than the newspaper in Mexico; it is said that writers are using this art form the way Thomas Paine used the pamphlet. As dictatorships have been retired, a flourishing independent medium is taking advantage of the political openness to tackle once-taboo subjects.

Weapons of the weak are seemingly invisible and unthreatening, yet they convey a strong message about the grievances and power of dominated people. Mass abstention can be another weapon of last resort. In expectation of massively fraudulent elections in Peru, the main opposition party encouraged people to stay away from the polls, to spoil the ballots, or to write "no to fraud" on them. Mexican voters employed a similar strategy by writing "null and void" on their ballots. Dissidents might slip an encrypted missive into a newspaper article, the true meaning of which becomes clear when the last word of each sentence is read vertically up and down the column. In the middle of a photograph portraying an abundant harvest, "down with dictatorship" is subtly carved in the wheat. By the time these tricks are discovered, it is too late for authorities to pull thousands of magazines or newspapers from the shelves. Another example is found among the women of Iran, who boldly challenge traditional Islamic customs of modesty by turning to a Facebook page ("Stealthy Freedoms of Iranian Women") and posting photos of themselves flaunting their hair in public (without hijab). Resisting the "morality policy" these women frame their actions, which include posing at major tourist attractions, or letting a scarf slip while driving on the highway, as "small acts of rebellion." Sometimes, a male family member joins in the picture, as a sign of approval and as an attempt to ward off criticism.[58] While these actions may not seem forceful, or overtly political, each is an expression of voice and power in its own right.

Some find their situation so egregious that they perceive their only option to be that of "exit."[59] Increasingly, analysts recognize suicide as an explicit political choice by individuals who feel they have no other option. Women who feel trapped in arranged marriages, or torn between the modern world of the city and their desire to return to more traditional patterns in their rural homes, gain a sense of control over their fate through suicide that they cannot find in life. While suicide is usually conducted in private, these cases are often unique in their public display. Since the early 2010s, a spate of highly public suicides at factories in China served as a wake-up call to the conditions within some Chinese factories, including at Foxconn, the world's largest contract electronics supplier. Interpretations of these so-called weapons of the weak, which also included employees simply walking off the factory floor, varied, including sociologists' claims that they were signs of a generation rejecting the regimentation of their predecessors who served as the "cheap labor army" responsible for China's economic reemergence and a response to the prevailing toxic work culture.[60] The spark that ignited the Arab Spring—when Mohammad Bouazizi, a vegetable salesman in Tunisia, set himself on fire after a policewoman confiscated his unlicensed cart, slapped him, and spat in his face—demonstrates how one act can serve as a contagion across great distances. His protest and painful death (he lay in the hospital for nearly ten days before he died), sparked protests that toppled the government of Tunisian president Zine el Abidine Ben Ali, spreading to much of the Arab world.

The management of information is another classic form of everyday resistance. For example, rumor is especially popular and effective in Africa, where oral traditions are highly valued. Rumor has been described as a potent brew of what is not known in the here and now, linked to what may or may not be known by those able to manipulate the supernatural. Rumors are hypotheses; in places where there is no authoritative news or information source, rumors don't just titillate, they are currency.[61] In the last days of Mobutu Sésé Seko's reign in Zaire, rumors about prophecies of his impending doom greatly undermined what was left of the regime's credibility and contributed to its ultimate demise.

Conclusions: Civil or Uncivil Society?

To what can such varied forms of citizen participation and activism lead? Some speak of the potential emergence of a civil society in which citizens are able to enjoy some level of autonomy, or independence, from the government, and a multiplicity of voluntary associations are permitted to form. The belief is that if citizens are able to seek membership in independent associations, absent of government control or influence, this promotes an actively engaged citizenry that will adopt a moral sense of obligation to participate in civic causes. With a multiplicity of groups and voluntary associations, people have an increased opportunity to express themselves as well as to hear competing viewpoints and perspectives. This leads many to connect civil society with democracy. This straightforward connection is misleading.

In many regions of the world, the development of an independent merchant class is viewed as part of a nascent civil society. If people have an area in their life over which the government has no influence or control, this is said to foster an independent, civic identity above political divisions. For example, after the 1985 Mexico City earthquake, the urban poor worked through neighborhood organizations to force the government and the World Bank to alter their recovery plans. Similar civic action groups have formed to fight crime and corruption in Mexico and South Africa. The combination of high crime rates and distrust of police competence contributed to the phenomenal growth of one South African vigilante group that has morphed into a private security business, Mapogo a Mathamaga, which is infamous for its use of corporal punishment. This form of mob justice is popular; Mapogo has branches throughout the country and boasts of thousands of members, even if their version of extralegal justice is starting to wear thin on leaders and citizens alike.[62]

High literacy rates and access to independent media promote an independent sense of society, as citizens can educate themselves about alternative ideas and approaches to issues. The digital revolution, spawned by changes in communication technology, has also dramatically changed people's sense of self, state, and society. These changes are important not only for the options they make available for citizens, but also for the increase in accountability they can foster. Some view the development of an increasing space for civil society as a potential birthing ground for democracy, since it promotes the existence of diverse competing groups and encourages citizens to take an interest in and participate in government.

Yet, citizens with access to information and freedom to organize will not automatically be more benign, democratic, or inclusive. Given the increased space for organization and mobilization, it is just as likely for antidemocratic groups to form. This is especially, although not exclusively, the case in regimes with a recent history of political and social violence in which individuals were socialized into accepting coercion and repression as a regular mode of behavior. The existence of competing groups is not a silver bullet against repression. Leigh Payne refers to the proliferation of "uncivil movements," paramilitary groups, death squads, and the like that promote exclusion and violence as a means of competing and gaining power within a democratic system.[63] Such groups are common in a variety of countries, with or without past experiences of authoritarianism. They gain influence through the use of threats, legitimating myths, and coalition formation, and no system is immune. Exclusionary movements are capable of securing their demands within the democratic system, so they face no pressing need to overthrow it. But these groups provide an insidious threat to an inclusionary democratic society. They use democratic language, institutions, and strategies toward their own uncivil ends. They can transform themselves into political parties with undemocratic goals. The Oodua People's Congress in Nigeria, a Yoruba militia that once played a big part in the prodemocracy movement, transformed its message into a hard-line ethnic supremacist agenda. Given the elitist, antipeasant rhetoric common among student demonstration leaders in China, many wonder whether the 1989 movements, had they been successful, would have resulted in a more or a less democratic outcome than exists today.

The presence of these "uncivil" groups and behaviors highlights the value-laden approach to the civil society debate. David Rieff argues that many have used the concept of a civil society, correlated with increased tolerance, expression, and diversity, to welcome groups we approve of.[64] Yet, if civil society merely refers to groups that are able to operate independent of the reach of the state, their ideology about mode of action or inclusion of minority groups has nothing to do with it. In this estimation, war criminals fall into the same category as human rights leaders. The US National Rifle Association, which the United Nations has refused to admit as a legitimate nongovernmental organization, is as much an agent of civil society as is the International Campaign to Ban Landmines, which has received considerable international financial and emotional support. Rieff, Payne, and others cause us to question the mere proliferation of organizations as a desirable consequence linked to the weakening of political power. As Alison Brysk reminds us, constituents participating in free and competitive elections have returned authoritarian leaders to power in many countries—and not only in the global south.[65] It is possible that, in some circumstances, citizens can be the individuals and groups who most repress other citizens.

Notes

1. Quoted in Tariq Panja, "Iranian Women Allowed to Attend Soccer Game for First Time Since 1981," *New York Times,* October 10, 2019.

2. Cora Engelbrecht and Sharif Hassan, "New Taliban Chancellor Bars Women from Kabul University," *New York Times,* September 27, 2021.

3. Alissa J. Rubin, "Threats and Fear Cause Afghan Women's Protections to Vanish Overnight," *New York Times,* September 4, 2021.

4. "Have Pentecostals Outgrown Their Name?" *Christianity Today,* May 29, 2020.

5. John Campbell, "The Pervasive Influence of Nigeria's Religious Leaders," *Africa in Transition* (blog), Council on Foreign Relations, February 3, 2021.

6. Roger Eatwell, *Fascism: A History* (New York: Penguin, 1997).

7. Noam Chomsky, *On Anarchism* (New York: New Press, 2013).

8. "Indigenous Woman Registers to Run for Mexican Presidency in 2018," *Reuters,* October 7, 2017; "Zapatistas Warn That Chiapas Is on Verge of Civil War, Accuse State of Kidnapping," *Mexico News Daily,* September 21, 2021.

9. "Iran: Freedom on the Net 2021," Freedom House, September 21, 2021.

10. Mae Anderson, "Outage Highlights How Vital Facebook Has Become Worldwide," *AP,* October 5, 2021.

11. Ibid.

12. "Two Thirds of the World's School-Age Children Have No Internet Access at Home, New UNICEF-ITU Report Says," United Nations Children's Fund (UNICEF), November 30, 2020.

13. Ibid.

14. "Iran: Freedom on the Net 2021."

15. "Egypt: Freedom on the Net 2021," Freedom House, September 20, 2021.

16. Ruth Maclean, "Nigeria Bans Twitter After President's Tweet Is Deleted," *New York Times,* June 5, 2021.

17. "2021 World Press Freedom Index: Journalism, the Vaccine Against Disinformation, Blocked in More Than 130 Countries," Reporters Without Borders, 2022.

18. Ibid.

19. This definition is based on the classic perspective on political culture that was developed in the 1950s and 1960s. Its most common source is Sidney Verba, "Comparative Political Culture," in *Political Culture and Political Development,* ed. Sidney Verba and Lucian Pye (Princeton: Princeton University Press, 1965).

20. Gabriel A. Almond and Sidney Verba, eds., *Civic Culture: Political Attitudes and Democracy in Five Nations* (Princeton: Princeton University Press, 1963).

21. David J. Elkins and E. B. Simeon, "A Cause in Search of Its Effect, or What Does Political Culture Explain?" *Comparative Politics* (January 1979).

22. Mahmood Monshipouri and Manochehr Dorraj, "The Resilience of Populism in Iranian Politics: A Closer Look at the Nexus Between Internal and External Factors," *Middle East Journal* 75, no. 2 (Summer 2021), pp. 201–221.

23. Thomas Pepinsky, "COVID-19 and Democracy in Indonesia: Short-Term Stability and Long-Term Threats," *Order from Chaos,* Brookings Institution, January 26, 2021.

24. Roberta Garner, *Contemporary Movements and Ideologies* (New York: McGraw-Hill, 1996).

25. Benjamin R. Barber, *Jihad vs. McWorld* (New York: Times Books, 1995).

26. See Benjamin R. Barber, "Beyond Jihad vs. McWorld," *The Nation,* January 21, 2002.

27. Robin Harding, *Rural Democracy: Elections and Development in Africa* (Oxford: Oxford University Press, 2020); Célestin Monga, *The Anthropology of Anger: Civil Society and Democracy in Africa,* trans. Linda L. Fleck and Célestin Monga (Boulder: Lynne Rienner, 1996).

28. Samirah Majumdar, "Key Findings About Restrictions on Religion Around the World," Pew Research Center, September 30, 2021.

29. Gordon Lubold, "U.S. Forces Expand Reach in Saudi Arabia," *Wall Street Journal,* January 25, 2021.

30. Michael Lipka, "Muslims and Islam: Key Findings in the U.S. and Around the World," *Fact Tank,* July 22, 2016.

31. Joe Cochrane, "Indonesia's Ancient Beliefs Win in Court, but Devotees Still Feel Ostracized," *New York Times,* April 14, 2018.

32. Eduardo Campos Lima, "To Understand Our Battles over Critical Race Theory and Liberation Theology, Look to Brazil's Fight over Paulo Freire's Legacy," *America Magazine,* November 22, 2021; Larry Rohter, "As Pope Heads to Brazil, a Rival Theology Persists," *New York Times,* May 7, 2007.

33. Gustavo Gutíerrez, *A Theology of Liberation: History, Politics and Salvation* (Maryknoll, NY: Orbis, 1971). Other key events in the development of liberation theology included the 1968–1969 Second General Conference on Latin American Bishops, in Medellín, Colombia, which met to discuss the implications of the Second Vatican Council (also known as Vatican II) for Latin America; the 1979 meeting of the Council of Latin American Bishops, in Puebla, Mexico, and the 1967 publication of "A Letter to the Peoples of the Third World"; see Third World Bishops, "A Letter to the Peoples of the Third World" (August 15, 1967) in *Liberation Theology: A Documentary History,* edited by Alfred T. Hennelly (Ossining: Orbis Books, 1990).

34. While some of these ideas were and continue to be extremely popular at the grassroots levels in many countries, the institutional Catholic Church has responded with harsh criticism. Leonardo Boff, for example, was required to spend a year in "obedient silence" from 1985 to 1986 because of opposition from Rome toward some of his writings. He was eventually forced out of the priesthood for mixing politics and religion too much.

35. There have been many books (including novels) and edited collections that focus on non-Western views of feminism. For a sampling, see Kumari Jayawardena, *Feminism and Nationalism in the Third World* (London: Zed, 1986); Jane Jaquette, ed., *The Women's Movement in Latin America: Participation and Democracy* (Boulder: Westview, 1994); Bernardine Evaristo, *Girl, Woman, Other* (New York: Black Cat, 2019); Lucy Delap, *Feminisms: A Global History* (Chicago: University of Chicago Press, 2020).

36. Jaquette, *The Women's Movement in Latin America.*

37. Jane Jaquette, "Introduction: From Transition to Participation: Women's Movements and Democratic Politics," in Jaquette, *The Women's Movement in Latin America.*

38. "Tunisia Bans Niqab in Government Buildings," *BBC News,* July 5, 2019.

39. Bager Moin, *Khomeini: Life of the Ayatollah* (New York: St. Martin's, 2000).

40. Jun Mai, "Xi Jinping to Outline His Vision of a Strong China in Grand National Day Celebration," *South China Morning Post,* October 1, 2019.

41. This definition is based on the pioneering work on this subject conducted by Sidney Verba, Victor H. Nie, and Jae-on Kim, *Participation and Political Equality: A Seven-Nation Comparison* (New York: Cambridge University Press, 1978).

42. Ysesnia Alvarez Padilla, Mary E. Hylton, and Jennifer Lau Sims, "Promoting Civic Knowledge and Political Efficacy Among Low-Income Youth Through Applied Political Participation," *Journal of Engagement and Scholarship* 12, no. 2 (January 2020).

43. Denise Hruby, "Meet the True Kings and Queens of Facebook and Snapchat," *BBC Capital,* May 20, 2016.

44. Luke Tyburski, "African Leaders Respond to Coronavirus . . . on Twitter," Atlantic Council, March 24, 2020.

45. Maurice Duverger, *Political Parties: Their Organization and Activity in the Modern State* (New York: Wiley, 1963).

46. Javier C. Hernández, "Across China, Walmart Faces Labor Unrest as Authorities Stand Aside," *New York Times,* November 16, 2016.

47. "World Day Against Child Labour—Background," United Nations, June 12, 2021.

48. Sarah Bachman, "Underage Unions: Child Laborers Speak Up," *Mother Jones* (November–December 2000).

49. Sidney Tarrow, *Power in Movement: Social Movements and Contentious Politics* (New York: Cambridge University Press, 1998); William A. Gamson, "The Social Psychology of Collective Action," in *Frontiers in Social Movement Theory,* ed. Aldon D. Morris and Carol McClurg Mueller (New Haven: Yale University Press, 1992).

50. Maruja Barrig, "The Difficult Equilibrium Between Bread and Roses: Women's Organizations and Democracy in Peru," in Jaquette, *The Women's Movement in Latin America.*

51. Ibid.

52. Monica Gu, "Lima Women Use Community Kitchens to Feed the Poor," *New York Minute Magazine,* August 17, 2017.

53. In July 2000 a military court acquitted the Tehran police chief blamed for leading the charge to violence the year before, inciting a muted but audible outcry from many in Iran and abroad.

54. Will Yong and Michael Slackman, "Across Iran, Anger Lies Behind Face of Calm," *New York Times,* June 11, 2010.

55. Monga, *The Anthropology of Anger.*

56. Julien Girault, "Anarchy in the People's Republic of China, According to Chinese Punks," *Japan Times,* October 12, 2014.

57. Jai Brodie, "Iran's Rock Stars and Their Underground Scene," *The Guardian,* June 4, 2014.

58. Fernaz Fassihi, "Iranian Women Find New Platform for Personal Freedom Push," *Wall Street Journal,* May 13, 2014.

59. See Albert O. Hirschman, *Exit, Voice, and Loyalty; Responses to Decline in Firms, Organizations, and States* (Cambridge: Harvard University Press, 1970).

60. David Barboza, "After Suicides, Scrutiny of China's Grim Factories," *New York Times,* June 7, 2010, p. A3; Jack Kelly, "China's Toxic Work Culture Results in Deaths and Suicide," *Forbes,* January 12, 2021.

61. Anastasiya Astapova, *Humor and Rumor in the Post-Soviet Authoritarian State* (Lanham: Lexington Books, 2021); Stephen Ellis, "Tuning In to Pavement Radio," *African Affairs* 88, no. 352 (July 1989).

62. Christopher Clark, "South Africans Are Taking the Law into Their Own Hands," *Foreign Policy,* November 29, 2018.

63. Leigh A. Payne, *Uncivil Movements: The Armed Right Wing and Democracy in Latin America* (Baltimore: Johns Hopkins University Press, 2000).

64. David Rieff, "The False Dawn of Civil Society," *The Nation,* February 22, 1999.

65. Alison Brysk, "Democratizing Civil Society in Latin America," *Journal of Democracy* 11, no. 3 (July 2000).

9

Linking Concepts and Cases

Now that you have a sense of the variety of views and actions that are taken in the global south, we present you with evidence from our eight CASE STUDIES so that you can explore these ideas further. As you look at issues of voice and participation in these countries, try to observe patterns of similarity and difference between and among them. What is the impact of history on the development of POLITICAL CULTURE? To what do you attribute differences in the frequency and volatility of expression? In which of these cases can you see generational-based clashes, and what is their source? Which countries have more mobilized civil societies, and which cases appear to be less vibrant? Why do you think this may be so?

Case Study: Mexico

Seventy years ago, poet Octavio Paz described Mexico as trapped in a labyrinth—with a political culture of cynicism and suspicion deeply rooted in the country's history.[1] Part of the explanation for this is that for decades under the Institutional Revolutionary Party, the Mexican government actively sought to preempt all meaningful citizen participation. Through its use of CORPORATISM, the government attempted to incorporate or co-opt all potentially influential groups in society. But Mexicans (arguably identified simplistically as "parochial" in classic civic culture studies) agitated for change and exercised their democratic rights in a variety of ways. Thanks to the efforts of citizen groups, Mexico made the transition. But CIVIL SOCIETY is still fighting to change old ways and let Mexico's leaders know that it should be society that dictates and the government that obeys.

It was in 2000 when, for the first time in over seventy years, in free and fair elections Mexicans voted into power a party other than the PRI. That election ushered into government the National Action Party, the party of Presidents Vicente Fox (2000–2006) and Felipe Calderón (2006–2012). The PAN is a conservative, pro-business party that long opposed the PRI. It has a religious agenda and is socially conservative. It is most popular in Mexico's northern states and its supporters believe that GLOBALIZATION is the best way to promote economic GROWTH, along with free market, neoliberal reforms. However, as we discuss in later chapters, after twelve years in power it struggled to deal with a range of political and economic challenges and its popularity flagged. By the 2012 elections, many Mexicans were feeling that the PAN was as equally corrupt as the PRI. But they appreciated the relative stability offered by the PRI during the long years of the dictatorship and elected it back into power as the PRI branded itself as the party that could make deals and govern Mexico out of the economic and security crises it faced.[2] At the time the PRI was considered center-left, although during its long years in power its IDEOLOGY fluctuated over time, swinging from left to center to right and back again in what is described as the "pendulum effect."[3]

By 2018 people were disenchanted with the largest parties and upset by the recession, the lack of security in the country, and their sense that corruption was as bad as ever.[4] The National Regeneration Movement, known as MORENA, a relative newcomer party that was created in 2014, swept the elections just four years later, winning the presidency and a majority of seats in Congress. Led by veteran politician Andres Manuel López Obrador (AMLO), a big part of its brand was that it is an outside party, something entirely new and disruptive. MORENA sought to create a "big tent" coalition of traditional leftists, breakaway elites from the PAN and the PRI, and evangelical social conservatives. It drew these disparate groups together by tapping into citizen demands that their government continue evolving, moving toward finally realizing the core ideals of the Mexican Revolution.[5]

MORENA, which ran as the incumbent party in the 2021 midterm elections, lost its supermajority in Congress, but managed to maintain a simple majority. It is social democratic and populist, and it campaigned promising a change: a cleaner, transformational government that would prioritize the fight against poverty and corruption. However, making good on that promise is easier said than done and, by 2021, it was already having a hard time managing expectations and was suffering from internal divides. In that election, MORENA as an incumbent party continued to appeal to working-class voters, although it appeared to have lost support among many of the young people who helped it come to power in 2018. Analysts wonder if the party can go on without its creator, since presidents in Mexico are prohibited from running for re-election. The good news for MORENA is that the main opposition parties, the PAN and PRI, which did the unthinkable and joined forces against AMLO, were in even worse shape, unable to offer credible alternatives.[6]

Some analysts suggest that Mexico's party system could decompose, replaced by an increased personalization of politics. That is certainly a possibility—and a risk to democracy. As people's expectations of democracy continue to go unmet, it could open the door to authoritarians.[7] Some say it already has, with AMLO. Yet, a positive sign for democracy is that citizens have sought to hold their political representatives accountable in other ways besides elections. Despite the danger, Mexican civil society has remained highly active and demonstrations are common. According to Freedom House, environmental activists and representatives of Indigenous groups protesting large-scale infrastructure projects have been targeted for violence and some activists have been murdered.[8]

Citizens have also turned out in recent years in a series of large demonstrations to protest the lack of government response to rising rates of gender-based violence in Mexico. It is estimated that over 40 percent of Mexican women have been victims of sexual assault and an average of eleven women are killed every day in Mexico.[9] Sexual abuse, including sexual harassment and domestic violence, is common and the government is accused of acts of omission and commission. Police have been accused of rape, and, for agents of the state as well as everyone else, impunity is the norm, as perpetrators are rarely punished. Local, state, and federal governments, including AMLO's, have responded by unveiling plans, but often fail to implement them. Worse, AMLO has minimized violence against women, claiming (without evidence) that 90 percent of all calls reporting domestic violence are fake. Moreover, he has dismissed such concerns as politically motivated and cut funding for government services like women's shelters. In response, a growing feminist movement in Mexico is demanding the transformative change that the president promised in his campaign.[10]

Mexicans have been galvanized to action because, even in this democracy, institutional channels are still not responding to people's needs.[11] It doesn't always work out this way, but there are examples from Mexico of how citizen engagement can effectively push for change. Tax evasion and tax privileges in Mexico have long been known to be a serious problem. In 2019, following a landmark legal case to release tax data, the government was forced to publish information on tax rebates issued to Mexico's wealthiest. In response, outraged citizens flooded social media with images of the recipients' lavish lifestyles. These images were much more impactful than any report. There was such a public outcry that within a month, in a victory for accountability and TRANSPARENCY, the Mexican Congress passed a bill nullifying all tax rebates going forward.[12]

Civil society in Mexico seeks to engage the state in other, less legalistic ways as well. Teachers' strikes, including work stoppages and even blockading railways, are frequent in Mexico, often over pay disputes and education reforms. In 2019, nearly 100,000 university employees went on strike when the federal government, as part of an austerity plan, forced the closure of several universities.[13] These protests have sometimes ended in clashes with security forces and deaths. But most protesters are practicing civil disobedience precisely because they believe in democracy. And they will use whatever tactics are necessary to demand that the system work for them.

Case Study: Peru

It is often said that Peruvians, traditionally identified as having a strong civil society and a weak state, value decisive leadership over institutional checks and balances.[14] Some analysts suggest that this tendency to favor authoritarians goes back to the days of the Inca Empire and centralized rule. Such traditions continued under colonialism—as did militarism, which has been a constant in Peru.

There is a long tradition of military intervention in Peruvian politics; most of the country's nearly 200-year history has been spent under military rule. During much of the 1990s, large numbers of Peruvians supported President Alberto Fujimori's growing authoritarianism as a necessity in the country's wars against TERRORISM and inflation. However, by the end of the decade, this justification no longer rang true for most people. Peruvians became increasingly divided over what they valued more highly—security or freedom. Although Fujimori still had his supporters, Peruvians were becoming impatient with his excesses. They resisted Fujimori's efforts to overturn the constitution and destroy the integrity of the electoral process. Because of the groundswell of activism that brought Fujimori down, observers argued that the 2001 elections showed that it could no longer be said that civil society in Peru was weak or antidemocratic.[15] It was primarily an urban, middle-class civil society that rallied to prevent *continuismo,* the open-ended continuation in office desired by Fujimori. Fifteen years later, tens of thousands turned out in 2016 to protest against Fujimori's daughter's possible election to the presidency, chanting "Fujimori Never Again." (However, Keiko Fujimori lost that election by only less than 1 percent of the vote.) Still, Keiko is the object of *antifujimorismo,* said to be Peru's most enduring political movement of the past twenty years.[16]

Hundreds of mostly young people took to the streets in Lima and across Peru again in record numbers in November 2020, this time rocked by epic corruption scandals and the mismanagement of the devastating PANDEMIC resulting in one of the highest death rates in the world. They were also protesting—after years of high economic growth rates—Peru's deepest economic decline on record.[17] The culmination of events, which has left people disillusioned with the system, not knowing whom to trust, has proven catastrophic to the public's faith in democratic institutions. Citizens were "incandescently angry" about what many called a congressional coup: Congress's impeachment of Martín Vizcarra, a president popular for taking on corruption (but who himself was accused of corruption). Protesters clashed with riot police and forced the dissolution of the widely disliked Congress for pursuing petty political disputes rather than focusing on national crises. You should know that, at the time, half of the members of Congress (including Keiko Fujimori, who was again running for president) were under investigation for corruption themselves. But as lawmakers, they enjoyed immunity from prosecution. As you can imagine, this left Peru headed for more instability as it tried to grapple with and recover from the pandemic.[18]

The mostly peaceful protests of November 2020—which were met by heavy police use of tear gas and rubber bullets at close range—were the largest of this century in Peru, the largest since the pro-democracy movement that brought down the authoritarian Fujimori government. Yet, these demonstrations, led mostly by young people in Lima, the Amazon, and the Andes, were remarkable for condemning the entire political system, and aimed at bringing down the shambles of a democracy. Even before the pandemic threw the country into a tailspin, support for democracy had declined in Peru to some of the lowest levels in Latin America. According to a 2018–2019 survey, Peruvians identified the military of all institutions as the most trustworthy.[19]

Until the 2020 protests, the most vocal protest in Peru had been focused on land rights and the use of resources, where extraction companies operate in 70 percent of the rainforest. Such companies often ignore clauses in their contracts about respecting local people. They didn't have to worry about accountability since, historically, Indigenous movements in Peru have been weaker than in neighboring countries.[20] However, in recent years Indigenous movements have emerged bigger and more powerful than ever. In response to economic liberalization, over fifty native groups, comprising as many as 300,000 people, have forged broad coalitions that cut across class and the urban-rural divide to challenge the extractive economy. Utilizing noninstitutionalized forms of collective action, they are proving capable of disrupting politics as usual and face down presidents intent on pushing economic growth by opening up land in the Amazon that has traditionally been respected as off-limits.[21]

More visible and better organized than they have been in the past, communicating across the jungle to isolated communities via radio, Amazonian Indigenous groups have turned out in the thousands, successfully calling general strikes and closing down roads and rivers to traffic for weeks at a time. They have even threatened to cut off the supply of oil and natural gas to the capital. These activists insist that the land is theirs and that if the government opens it up to mining, oil, and natural gas companies, a variety of problems will follow, including destruction of the environment and loss of their way of life. It was also in this period that we saw a long-elusive alliance forming between Amazonian and Andean Indigenous peoples (who together comprise 26 percent of the population and who also know racism, marginalization, and the negative impact of extractive industries). From their point of view, this is a life-or-death struggle. They have dug in for a protracted battle—and it is the most serious challenge to state authority that recent governments have had to face.[22]

Some Peruvian administrations have taken a harder stance than others on "clashing visions of progress," but the general response has been that economic interests need to come first. Peru's political elite has argued that those who seek to keep the Amazon for themselves are selfish and are sitting on resources that the state owns the right to by law—untouched resources that could be used to modernize and develop the entire country.[23] In 2009, after sixty-five days of civil disobedience against an oil project in the Amazon, the government suspended civil liberties, criminalized peaceful social protest, and sent the police in to stop the demonstrations with intimidation, often with excessive use of force. Tensions flared and, in what is known as the Bagua massacre, a violent altercation broke out between police and protesters in which thirty-three died and hundreds were injured.[24] Then president Alan García defended his actions, characterizing the activists as "wild," "savage," and "terrorists." Such amped-up rhetoric is always concerning, as it is more likely to be followed by the government giving security forces and vested interests who oppose the protesters carte blanche to resort to extreme measures. That should be changing under President Pedro Castillo, who is from the mountains and may be the most pro-Indigenous leader Peru has ever had. But Peru is believed to be one of the deadliest countries in the world for an environmentalist or land defender. Between 2013 and 2020, at least twenty such activists were murdered in Peru, including Arbildo Meléndez Grandes and Gonzalo Pío Flores, both Indigenous leaders and environmental defenders.[25] Clearly, the Peruvian tradition of a strong civil society that stands up to the state continues.

Case Study: Nigeria

Often described as a "conglomerate society," Nigeria is composed of more than 250 different ethnic groups whose divisions are complicated by regional, religious, and linguistic identities. The "Big Three," which together comprise more than half of Nigeria's population, are the Hausa-Fulani (mostly Muslim, traditionally from the North), the Yoruba (a mix of Muslim, Christian, or adherents of traditional African religions from the South West), and Ibo (mostly Christian or adherents of traditional African religions from the South East). For most of the years since independence in 1960 (until 1999), political power, both civilian and military, had been largely under the control of northern Muslims, who dominated the military and resented the southern domination of commerce that dates back to colonialism. Until 1999, only northern Muslims had served as president (elected or not) and many southerners felt that they had never had a government that represented their interests.

Even since the transition to democracy in 1999, in this oil-rich country, where political power translates into access to economic resources, politics is viewed as a winner-take-all gamble. Politicians from all regions have propagated myths of irreconcilable differences, while working hard to blur the glaring disparity between rich and poor. This explains why elections in Nigeria, as in many other countries, are fought as mortal combat.[26]

It is often said that Nigeria's political leaders fear being usurped by each other more than by a popular revolt. Through backroom deals, identity politics have certainly been at play in all the elections since the return to civilian rule in 1999 (when, for the first time in Nigeria's history, a Yoruba Christian from the South West won the elections and was inaugurated president). Something that had the potential to touch off instability is actually an arrangement worked out years ago to promote stability: a "power shift" or "rotation" guaranteeing that presidential candidates from the major regions get a turn (or two) at the presidency.[27] Here's the deal: back in 2007, as retirement neared for the first democratically elected president (Olusegun Obasanjo), Nigeria's power brokers agreed that after two terms of the southwesterner's presidency, it was time for someone different. To send a signal that no single group would monopolize power and thus strengthen the democracy's legitimacy, they decided that the next president would be a Muslim northerner—although those from the South and South East pointed out that they had never had a turn.[28]

To make this long story shorter, a Muslim northerner (Umaru Yar'Adua) won the 2007 election and Nigeria witnessed the first civilian-to-civilian transfer of power in its history. However, this crowning achievement was followed by crisis. In 2010, Yar'Adua died rather suddenly of health problems and the vice president, Goodluck Jonathan (a Christian from the South) was inaugurated as president, despite protests from northerners who claimed that they hadn't finished their turn at the presidency.[29] Jonathan ended up finishing the northerner's term, won the 2011 election, and served a term in office before losing in a 2015 reelection bid to Muhammadu Buhari, a northern Muslim. Until this point, Nigeria appeared to have become a dominant party democracy, as every president and the majority of seats in Congress had belonged to the center-right People's Democratic Party (PDP). But in what some argue was a good thing for the democracy, the PDP split. Buhari was the candidate of the All Progressives Congress (APC), founded as an alternative to the PDP. It is to the left of the PDP, calls itself social democratic, and campaigned promising change.[30]

Thus, the 2015 election marked a turning point for the country. It was the first major PDP loss since the return to democracy and the first time in Nigerian history that an incumbent seeking reelection had to turn over power to his opponent. Some were worried that Jonathan and his supporters might dispute the election results and not follow through with the alternation in power, but Jonathan stepped aside graciously. However, the APC, which includes a variety of personalities and interests, is in disarray, divided into factions. Buhari was reelected and the APC managed to hold on to power in 2019, mostly because voters were willing to give it another try. The PDP also suffers from infighting. As of 2021, although other parties existed, none had the finances and organizational skills to pose a threat in the 2023 elections. Analysts predict that it will be a battle between the PDP and APC—unless an independent candidate with crossover appeal and the ability to rally voters appears out of the blue.[31]

But there's more to civil society in Nigeria than political parties. Citizens engage the state in a variety of ways and with a variety of goals in mind. In one of the biggest demonstrations in a generation, in October 2020 young protesters organized via social media with the hashtag #EndSARS to rise up and march peacefully in cities across the country. After a video showing the unprovoked killing of a man by Special Anti-Robbery Squad (SARS) officers went viral, citizens raised hundreds of thousands of dollars through crowd-funding to support the protesters, demanding that the government eliminate the notorious SARS police unit, known for its brutality.[32] Echoing the protests over the murder of George Floyd and much like the Black Lives Matter movement, with its horizontal organization and no central leader, this youth-led protest faced down military and police violence and extortion. It also demanded police accountability, grew out of frustration over the government's inept response to Covid, and developed into a larger protest about bad government generally, calling attention to gender inequality, corruption, and the way the democracy wasn't working. Influential figures such as Nollywood actors and other artists, including Afrobeats musician Davido, brought global attention to the protests. President Buhari sought to quiet the protesters by promising to disband SARS and committing to police reform, but the officers were just redeployed elsewhere. Meanwhile, police killed more than a dozen unarmed protesters and the government banned demonstrations and censored social media. The protests eventually quieted down, but the authorities, accustomed to being in control, were shook: Nigeria's young people discovered their potential power to mobilize—and half the population is under the age of nineteen.[33]

A civil society group that recently has had some success is comprised of the residents of the Niger Delta, once abundant with life, now one of the most polluted places on the planet. Tens of millions of barrels of oil have been spilled since the companies started production in the 1950s—quadruple the amount spilled in BP's disaster in the Gulf of Mexico in 2010.[34] Residents have for years sought to hold multinational corporations, especially Royal Dutch Shell, accountable for oil spills that contaminated the waters, causing the loss of livelihoods, illness, and death. The oil companies have blamed the damage on the sabotage of pipelines and oil theft, and Nigerians knew that they did not have much of a chance of winning in Nigerian courts. But, in what has been described as "a watershed moment in the accountability of multinational corporations," Britain's Supreme Court ruled that a group of 50,000 Nigerian farmers and fishermen could bring a case against Royal Dutch Shell. That same year, a Dutch court ruled that the company was liable for allowing the leaks to occur and ordered it to perform clean up and compensate the residents.[35] Although the decision can be appealed, this could be the first sign that companies—which have made billions in profits in these creeks and marshes—will no longer be able to operate with impunity.[36]

Case Study: Zimbabwe

Although it appears to go quiet from time to time, Zimbabwe has a flourishing rural and urban civil society. Its urban civil society had largely come together to challenge the Zimbabwe African National Union–Patriotic Front and the monopoly on power it has held for more than four decades. The grievances that contributed to the opposition's rise had been festering for years. Economic hardship has turned many people who didn't normally think of themselves as political into activists. In the 2000s, almost all Zimbabweans disapproved of the government's handling of the economy, and three-quarters of those surveyed wanted then president Robert Mugabe to resign.[37] In 2005, a new party, the Movement for Democratic Change, capitalized on this sentiment with its election slogan "Change Everything, Everything Changes." With a focus on political and civil rights, this liberal party called for ending government corruption and increasing transparency, reducing poverty, and strengthening the RULE OF LAW. It was joined by a variety of others, converging on Mugabe from all directions.

The multiracial MDC has splintered and been weakened by infighting (something the government has encouraged). However, it still enjoys a remarkably broad base of support. Although the party grew out of Zimbabwe's trade unions, which are male-dominant, it included a feminist plank in its campaign.[38] The MDC's core supporters are the young urban dwellers (the so-called Born Frees) who were either children at independence or born soon after. Mugabe's appeals to Black nationalism fell flat with much of this younger generation, who are too young to remember the humiliation and suffering that Black people experienced under white rule.[39] Interestingly, voting is based not so much on ethnicity as on an urban-rural split (the MDC is popular in predominantly Ndebele Matabeleland, whereas due to years of scorching repression, the pro-Shona ZANU-PF has never been well liked there).

Regarding civil society, Zimbabwe is a story of the state leading society as much as it is about society leading the state. And what happened in Zimbabwe is a good example to the world of what happens when crucial questions are left unresolved for decades. For many activists, land has sacred and cultural value, as well as productive potential. The effort to reclaim the land is for them not just a development issue, but also a restitution and justice issue.[40] While some analysts accused Mugabe of having cynically used the land reform movement to hang on to power, it is important not to forget the very real needs asserted by this social struggle and to recognize that the anger stems from past injustices and deprivation. The reconciliation model promoted by the West has not resulted in justice or reparation. From the point of view of many rural people in Zimbabwe, the neoliberal, laissez-faire approach to land reform had to be challenged.[41]

The MDC did not oppose the idea of land reform, but criticized the government for how it went about it. Because the MDC had been supported by the West, the government was able to portray it as the lackey of white farmers and Britain. For decades in Zimbabwe, tensions have run high, as critics of the government are targeted for harassment and abuse. The MDC's Morgan Tsvangirai once said that he wouldn't call the massive street protests for fear of a bloodbath. It very nearly came to that in 2008, when Mugabe came closer than ever to losing power in a runoff election, as hundreds of MDC supporters were beaten, arrested, and murdered. To stop the bloodshed, Tsvangirai dropped out of the race and tried to bring the crisis to a "soft landing" by entering into a coalition government to promote power-sharing, stabilize the country, and avoid catastrophe.[42]

For his part, it appears that Mugabe entered into this unity government only to co-opt or demobilize his opposition. Mugabe certainly succeeded in frustrating his opponents and outlasting them. In 2016, in the biggest turnouts in nearly a decade, a sea of red appeared in major cities as thousands of MDC supporters, wearing the color of the party, protested economic conditions.[43] Given Mugabe's hold on security forces, the opposition chose not to encourage a popular uprising; rather, they only went as far as to call for a "dignified exit"—not an overthrow of Mugabe.[44] These efforts, however, were met with violence as police fired tear gas and water cannons at the crowds. With a crackdown on social media, the new movement had a hard time maintaining momentum.[45] In the end, it was not this broadly based opposition that ended Mugabe's nearly forty-year rule—it was his own military.

Yet, Mugabe's exit in 2017 has not meant happily ever after. Politically, not much has changed. Combine that with Covid and a worsening economy, and we see that individuals and civil society organizations, traditional actors as well as new voices have mobilized—all calling for political and economic reforms. For example, in the face of an inept government response to the pandemic, civil society repurposed itself. Not only have there been strikes and labor protests, citizens have stepped up to act as watchdogs, providing community support and public goods the state has failed to provide. Various groups, including artists and musicians, as well as some Christian churches have brought attention to corruption and called for government accountability. They have monitored government policy and misuse of funds, demanded personal protective equipment for frontline workers, distributed masks to citizens, and supported the rights of citizens against police abuse. They have also stood up for journalists who are being harassed for reporting on the pandemic. Yet, citizens exercising their rights to protest is still dangerous business in Zimbabwe. Women's groups, in particular, have been targeted for violence by security forces. As a result, more protest is now done online, through social media, replacing public rallies and debates. Inspired by the Black Lives Matter movement, #Zimbabwean Lives Matter has drawn global attention to its cause, drawing nearly 1 million tweets in its first three days.[46]

However, the reality is that digital activism leaves in place the old rural/urban divide, as cyber-activism cannot reach the many Zimbabweans who do not have access to the internet. Meanwhile, the government has used Covid as an excuse to declare a state of emergency and lockdowns as a means for cracking down on civil society. According to one estimate, the government has arrested more people than it has tested for the virus. It is consolidating its autocratic rule and considers social media a battleground. Offline it launches violent reprisals against its critics, which it characterizes as terrorists.[47] Yet, citizens have fostered fresh partnerships and have rallied, responding by finding new ways to collaborate and demonstrate in a widespread campaign against corruption and human rights abuses. Organizing in the face of repression is nothing new in Zimbabwe, but as civil society is adapting to manage the pandemic and push back against the state, it is establishing the legitimacy of civic leadership and a resilience that may last long after the pandemic.[48]

Case Study: Egypt

Egypt's national identity is based in its greatest claim to exceptionalism: a history that spans millenniums. Central to Egyptian political culture is the ancient concept of *maat,* which defines acceptable behavior as recognizing one's place in society, respecting authority, and acknowledging and respecting the will of God—as opposed to being excitable, argumentative, and insistent in demands. Clearly, such a system places a premium on obedience and conformity.[49] The old religions (and new) closely tie the subject to the state, and political obedience has long been considered an important part of each individual's religious duty. Therefore, *maat* explains much of the abiding authoritarianism found in Egyptian political culture.[50]

Given that the culture puts a premium on obedience to authority, it can't be surprising to hear that the Egyptian people are said to be easy to govern. But this worldview does not prescribe blind obedience to the ruler. The king too was answerable to *maat;* he did not stand above the order but was a part of it. When the incompetence of elites exhausted people's patience, uprisings against rulers who fail to maintain *maat* were deemed necessary to restore balance.[51]

It is easy to see how this pattern unfolded in recent years. For decades under Hosni Mubarak and his predecessors, Egyptians had fulfilled their part of the bargain with the state. Citizens had been taught to "walk next to the wall," to keep their heads down and not to get involved in politics. They raised their children to fear politics and the state, to choose safety over activism.[52] Some obeyed authority because it was habit, or they were cynical about the possibilities for change. In addition, many Egyptians' political competence is said to be low, the average person's factual knowledge of politics limited.[53] So, depending on the individual, there were a variety of reasons for Egyptians not to tangle with the state.

But Mubarak's failures with regard to *maat* were legion by 2011, and recognition of this fact culminated in the massive, unprecedented mobilizations at Tahrir Square. Because the ruler was unable to maintain the social contract, the nature of his relationship with the governed changed unequivocally. And, in a change without precedent in Egypt, people felt entitled to decide who ruled them and pushed out three regimes in three years (first President Mubarak, then an interim military administration, and, finally, President Mohamed Morsi). Egypt's revolution fueled uprisings across the Arab world and shook authoritarian regimes in China and Russia.[54]

What was particularly shocking about the uprising in Egypt was that compared to its neighbors, Egypt has never seemed vulnerable to falling apart. But there are divides over identity and ideology, which are widely characterized as radically polarized. Within Egyptian civil society, we see traditions of both secular nationalism and religious radicalism. Consequently, those who live there disagree vehemently over central questions regarding the best form of government, the role that religion should play in public life, the role of the military in politics, and the status of women. On these questions, there is little consensus seeking or attempt at negotiation—and dictators have made the most of it, playing groups off each other. As a result, Egypt is said to have a fragmented political culture.[55]

This fragmentation has been aggravated by the state-dominated media, which played (and continue to play) a game of divide and rule that serves the state's interests. Under Mubarak, citizens had virtually no opportunity for critical engagement or debate. It was not until "liberation technology" (social networking sites and new media) that people were able to circumvent control by elites and make use of unconventional means of public expression and participation. Abdel Fattah al-Sisi has used his powers to crack down on this; his government harasses and arrests its critics. It is estimated that his jails are filled with tens of thousands of political prisoners. The government tightly controls not only the traditional media; it passed a cybercrime law to regulate social media, which it has accused of violating "Egyptian family values." For example, it has sought to make examples of several TikTok stars (all women), who have been tried and sentenced to years in prison for flaunting their sexuality.[56]

As elsewhere, social media, which is designed to favor posts over dialogue, has also intensified polarization and undermined the democratic transition in Egypt.[57] New media has facilitated the spread of misinformation and hate speech. But perhaps no other political movement in Egypt is more polarizing than the Muslim Brotherhood, the one opposition party the various dictatorships feared (and fear) most.[58] Even though it has spent most of history banned and its members persecuted, the Brotherhood has proven to be the best organized and most enduring opposition group Egypt has ever known. Founded in 1928, this mainstream Islamist group became known for its religious activism and simple message: "Islam is the solution."[59] Over the years, the Brotherhood became known for its members' self-discipline and for its violent and nonviolent tactics: it could turn out huge crowds in demonstrations and provide the schools and clinics that the government did not. It could also inspire the most brazen terrorist acts—most notably the 1981 assassination of President Anwar Sadat.[60]

However, starting in the 1980s—while still banned—the Brotherhood shifted away from the use of violence to engage in democratic politics by running candidates as independents. Eventually, it was successful, winning a sizable number of parliamentary seats in 2005 and 2011–2012, as well as the presidency in 2012. But the Brotherhood had significantly less success in the actual operation of government. One of its leaders, Mohamed Morsi, was elected to and then ousted from power—and the group was outlawed again in 2013. Despite the fact that it has been banned and (with the support of President Donald Trump) designated a terrorist group, persecuted, stripped of assets, driven underground and into exile, the Brotherhood has persevered, using new media to convey its message. Although diminished, it still resonates, as the Brotherhood has the support of hundreds of thousands (perhaps 1 million) Muslims—not only in Egypt, but throughout the world.[61]

Since overthrowing Morsi's elected government, first general and now President al-Sisi has tried to replace Islamism with another perennial favorite in

Egypt, ultranationalism, and to distract citizens by blaming scapegoats and stoking fears of foreign plots.[62] He is counting on Egyptians' deep love of the military and comfort with authoritarianism—and that their fear of sliding into civil war like their neighbors will keep Egyptians walking next to the wall. As of late 2021, al-Sisi's hard-line approach appeared to have worked: Egypt pretended to have a democratic process, but this was one-man rule. New electoral laws favored the "party of the president," which mobilized the economically stressed population with handouts. The resulting parliament was compliant, dominated by pro-Sisi parties. Interest in politics was declining, as was electoral turnout. It seemed that the only Egyptians not walking next to the wall were more or less divided into two partisan camps—those who want a religious dictatorship and those who want a military dictatorship.[63] This left things looking pretty dim to those who had rooted for those young Tahrir protesters now sidelined—secular and Islamist liberals alike—who once stood for democracy.

Case Study: Iran

Iranian civil society has, since the revolution of 1979, reflected (and sometimes magnified) the structural tensions created by the dual system within the Islamic Republic: the coexistence of elections for parliamentary and executive leaders, alongside a Supreme Leader, appointed for life, at the helm of the system. Yet, as some analysts put it, given the "highly securitized setting" within which Iranian civil society operates, it is paradoxical that it has "managed not just to survive, but in some ways, even to thrive."[64] Iran is known to encompass a broad political spectrum of ideas, often in conflict with each other.

Iran's political culture is deeply impacted by its status as a theocracy. Ayatollah Ruhollah Khomeini often declared that "politics and religion are one" and that Iran's theocracy is "God's government." The implication of this conception puts dissenters in a dangerous space: opposition to the government is de facto opposition to God. Since 1979, the Islamic Republic has had only two men occupy this position: Khomeini and Sayyid Ali Khamenei. The Supreme Leader possesses "ultimate power" on nearly all public (and many private) matters.[65] Khamenei's leadership has not always been unquestioned, nor has it been smooth. While some of this tension is between reformist leaders and the Supreme Leader, at other times gaps between religious scholars and Khamenei have surfaced. With the increased talk of Khamenei's successor, this structure faces great pressure. As Supreme Leader, Khamenei exerts huge influence over the two institutions (the Assembly of Experts and the Guardian Council), who will select his successor after his passing. With the election of President Ebrahim Raisi in 2021, viewed as "groomed for this moment"—many believe he is there to "seal" the system by ascending to the post after his mentor, Khamenei, passes on.[66]

Conservatives in Iran today take issue with the accusation that they are trying to go backward. They state that they, too, are interested in reform, just not Western-style reform. In their view, changes in Iran must fit within the context of "Islamic-style" democracy, in which clerics still hold political power befitting an Islamic and not a liberal republic. In the eyes of conservatives, liberalism is too risky, and is seen as a genuine threat to the status quo. There are many within Iran—including some religious clerics—who are pushing discussion about the ways in which an active faith life can thrive in a more open society.

Mobilized by the revolution, but then quickly shuttered, civil society within Iran has vacillated under the presidencies of attempted reformists (Presidents Ali Akbar Hashemi Rafsanjani, Ayatollah Mohammad Khatami, and Hasssan Rouhani) and conservatives (Mahmoud Ahmadinejad and Ebrahim Raisi). Iranian civil society is fueled by an internal struggle between groups that want to forge a uniquely Islamist path to a modern state and society, and those who envision a modern Iran less hostile to secular demands and more open to Western traditions.[67] One observer even claims that Iranian society is "a culture at war with itself."[68]

Of the many groups pushing for greater change in Iranian politics and society, women and youth stand out. Women were prominent during Iran's constitutional revolution of 1906–1911, and, in 1963, they were afforded the right to vote and to run for office. Even though women were extremely prominent voices during the 1979 Islamic Revolution, their voices have been less prevalent in national politics. Since 1997, women have submitted their names as presidential candidates to the Council of Guardians, challenging the orthodox interpretation of Article 115 of the Iranian constitution, which states that "the president should be elected from among spiritual and political men" (the original language may be interpreted as either "men" or "figures"). To date, no women have been approved as candidates (and the right of women to run for the presidency was affirmed in October 2020).[69] Women serve as cabinet ministers, members of parliament, ambassadors, and provincial directors. Former president Rouhani tapped a woman, Masoumeh Ebtekar, to serve as one of the country's twelve vice presidents (a former spokesperson for the students who seized the US embassy in 1979, she had previously served as vice president for environmental affairs under President Khatami).[70] For well over a decade, female students have outnumbered male students at universities, and curtains no longer divide men and women within classrooms.

Yet, this advancement has created both opportunities and dilemmas—it is problematic, for example, for women with degrees to find husbands with the same level of education, and married women still require their husband's permission to work outside the home or travel internationally.[71] Until recently, Iranian women were even forbidden from attending men's sporting events. Leaders in Tehran succumbed to domestic pressure (including a former national team captain who called for a boycott of all soccer games until the ban on women in stadiums was relaxed) as well as encouragement from the International Federation of Association Football (FIFA), although the relaxation extended to only international events, and attendees were supervised by female security personnel in black chadors.[72] Some have referred to the first match open to women (a World Cup qualifying 14–0 romp by the Iranian team against Cambodia) as "among the most consequential sporting events to be played in years."[73] The decision was announced shortly after a soccer fan, twenty-nine-year-old Sahar Khodayari, died after setting herself on fire to protest the six-month prison sentence she received for attending a club soccer game earlier in the year.[74] Exercising WEAPONS OF THE WEAK, other women have evaded the informal ban (which is an unwritten rule) by disguising themselves as men.[75]

As we observe elsewhere, Iranian women are not a solid ideological bloc; some promote gender segregation and the withdrawal from UN bodies and agreements that are deemed too feminist or un-Islamic. And it was the vice president for women and family affairs, Masoumeh Ebtekar, who supported the limitation on women's international travel without her husband's permission, stating that it would be up to a judge to rule that the travel is "necessary," and characterizing such an exemption as traveling "on bail."[76] In its 2020 Global Gender Gap Report, the World Economic Forum ranked Iran 148 out of 153 countries surveyed, highlighting gender-based disparities in economic participation, educational attainment, health, and political empowerment.[77]

Younger citizens, especially university students, have a long history of activism in Iranian politics. Their role is significant, as more than 50 percent of the Iranian population is under thirty-five years of age. This is the segment of the population most adept at using social media and other advances in information communication technologies, and they continue to use them to angle their case. The Islamic Republic is experiencing a significant brain drain, losing an estimated $150 billion per year as young Iranians vote with their feet and leave their home country.[78] Youth have been the backbone of nearly every mass demonstration or movement since the late 1970s, and they continue to take to the streets to demand change, incurring the wrath of the administration and its security apparatus. They are likely to continue to demand a voice in the increasingly crowded public arena of the Islamic Republic of Iran and may likely form the backbone of Iran's sometimes wary, yet always resilient, civil society.

Case Study: China

Despite prior decades of gains for civil society organizations and relatively independent expression, the figurative space for Chinese citizens to express their preferences has been significantly shrinking under the leadership of Xi Jinping.[79] The government has targeted journalists, academics, and anyone perceived to be an activist, with especially harsh punishments for religious and ethnic minorities. Government actions include demotions, censorship, travel restrictions, and imprisonment—all for expressing viewpoints that may be perceived as critical of CCP governance.[80]

The expression of ideas within modern China is limited by the dominance of the Chinese Communist Party. Even though alternative parties exist—they constitute the so-called loyal nonopposition—decisions within China today need the approval of CCP officials. The CCP abides by the Leninist principle of mandating a singular, elitist, unchallenged party, with harsh penalties for perceived violations. Perhaps the most well-known Chinese dissident imprisoned for his views is Liu Xiaobo, a former literature professor and activist who was in and out of detention and labor camps since 1989 and who, despite receiving the 2010 Nobel Peace Prize, remained largely unknown within China (thanks to government censorship). Nevertheless, after his death in 2017 (while still in captivity), the government not only blocked references to his name but also, for the first time, filtered images in private one-on-one chats using social media platforms.[81]

Despite the risks, there is a strong tradition of dissent within China, dating back to the first student demonstrations against the government in the May 4th

Movement of 1919. Ironically, some of the same leaders who denounced the Chinese government then were responsible for violently ending demonstrations in the nation's capital in 1989, in the largest civil unrest the CCP faced since its founding in 1921. University students and citizens from all walks of life gathered in Tiananmen Square and hundreds of Chinese cities to protest inflation, corruption, and the absence of political reform. As the world's media captured the dynamic situation, the government sent tanks to crush the movement. Even to this day, awareness of these events within China is limited by aggressive detection and content blocking tools—now mostly automated by artificial intelligence software—throughout Chinese internet searches.[82]

As we see elsewhere, often, as limits increase, so does the courage of some individuals. For example, author Yang Jisheng, who wrote an investigation of the Great Leap Forward (for which he was honored by Harvard, but unable to leave China to attend the ceremony), published a more recent book about the Chinese Cultural Revolution, *The World Turned Upside Down*. Yang, who is in his eighties, initially delayed the publication of the English edition of his book for fear that his grandson's college applications could be placed in jeopardy. In the end, though, it was the culture of repression that convinced him of the urgency of an honest assessment of history.[83]

Freedom of religious belief is prescribed within the Chinese constitution. Explicit, state-sanctioned congregations exist, in addition to underground associations of believers, who often congregate at great risk. Formal regulations on religious affairs, in effect since 2018, permit some activities by state-registered religious organizations and monitor online religious activity as well as restrict the timing and locations of religious celebrations and amount of permissible donations.[84] The most egregious aspect of Beijing's limitations is the incarceration of more than a million Uighurs and other Turkic Muslims in the PRC's northwest province of Xinjiang. The Chinese government does not deny this reality of mass internment camps—they defend it as "lawful" and necessary responses to extremism.[85] This crackdown, which includes Kazakhs and other minorities, is a systematic, government-organized campaign to constrain the voice of significant portions of Chinese society, and is believed to have included at least 1 million detainees.[86] There are reasons to believe the clampdown is expanding, geographically and in terms of targets. In Inner Mongolia, where the dominant ethnic group has been framed as a "model minority," recent campaigns to enforce Mandarin-only language in schools, as well as strict nationwide limitations on hours for videogame availability, suggest widening attempts at controlling citizen behavior.[87] Chinese Christians, especially those affiliated with unregistered "house churches," are facing increasing hostility and limitations—the CCP even produced a state-approved Bible with significant modifications to dull any potential activism by believers.[88]

The effects of development on gender in China have been uneven. Communist leaders inherited a dismal record of attention to women in 1949. Although the situation has improved greatly (baby girls, e.g., are no longer forced to have their toes broken to create a small foot through binding), women in China today continue to face many struggles. Traditional attitudes toward girls have been reinforced with population planning policies implemented since the 1980s (although couples are now permitted to have up to three children, until 2016 most married couples were limited to one child). Since 2021, laws have changed so that all married couples may have as many as three children, a stark recognition of the social and economic dilemmas exacerbated by decades of population planning that have created a rapidly aging society.[89]

If we measure civil society in terms of independent organizations, it's not a promising picture. Most organizational life is corporatist, and groups need permission from local authorities to form and gather. Some have created a new term to capture the reality of NONGOVERNMENTAL ORGANIZATIONS in China, calling them "government-organized nongovernmental organizations."[90] Under Xi, undoubtedly the strongest leader since Mao Zedong, NGOs operate with much less latitude, and a particular pall was cast when a registration law for foreign NGOs was passed in 2016.[91] Even within international governmental organizations such as the UNITED NATIONS, Beijing attempts to silence NGOs that may challenge their priorities, most notably targeting organizations that do not parrot Beijing's official line on the status of Taiwan.[92]

The corporatist nature of China's state-society relations was clear during Covid, as state-run organizations, online groups, and big business worked in concert with government agencies to respond to the pandemic, an example of what may be called a "state-mobilized movement."[93] Volunteers donning vests and red armbands reminiscent of Maoist campaigns delivered essential supplies, assisted with household monitoring of symptoms, and served medical professionals as needed. Online organizing for fund-raising and the distribution of critical supplies was wildly successful.[94] Again, this mobilization highlights the state-led aspect of Chinese civil society, including silencing those whose voices most need to be heard. For example, one of the first doctors to attempt to sound the alarm about Covid before it had a name was Dr. Li Wenliang, who raised concerns about the virus with some of his medical school classmates in online chat rooms. In early January 2020, he was summoned by his medical directors as well as police and forced to sign a statement that denounced his warnings as "an unfounded and illegal rumor."[95]

In today's China, any independent or grassroots mobilizing that includes even a vague suggestion of priorities other than the CCP is quickly repressed. While this silences many, it empowers others. Outspoken entrepreneur Ren Zhiqiang published an essay criticizing the government's handling of Covid, calling Xi "a clown who desires power"—he was sentenced to eighteen years in prison.[96] Another brave individual, after reading of the rapid cremation and government-supervised burial at sea for Liu Xiaobo, used a pseudonym to post an ominous message suggesting the futility of censorship by the regime: "Scared of the living, scared of the dead, and even more scared of the dead who are immortal."[97] Civil society, against all odds, continues to take on the Chinese state.

Case Study: Indonesia

Indonesia is a country rich in diversity (which should not be surprising, given its geography of more than 10,000 islands). Rather than viewing linguistic, cultural, and religious diversity as strengths, however, Indonesian leaders and to some extent ordinary citizens sometimes view them as threats. Especially during the thirty-two-year reign of General Suharto, Indonesia's second president, any identity that contradicted national unity was squelched. The two biggest offenders were expression of religious division and communism.

In this environment, citizens tend toward compliance rather than confrontation. Yet, after Suharto's dramatic resignation in 1998 (following the mass protests ignited by the Asian financial crisis), a plethora of voices flooded Indonesia's major cities. Newly emboldened demonstrators faced a dilemma familiar to others protesting authoritarian rule: since organized opposition had been illegal for so long, there were few available networks through which opposition groups could mobilize. Today, while members of civil society have more freedoms to associate and spread their message, civil society remains fragmented and often weak.

During Suharto's "New Order" (1966–1998), the only viable electoral force—not technically a political party at the time—was Golkar, a federation of functional associations and trade unions that served as an umbrella for anticommunist associations and a government-fabricated identity. Opposition parties existed, but their acceptance was always at the discretion of government leaders. Truly competitive political parties were not permitted until 1999, and Golkar remains as a viable parliamentary force, although in a crowded arena (sixteen parties competed in the 2019 elections, with nine passing the 4 percent threshold to take a seat in the People's Consultative Assembly, Indonesia's bicameral legislature).[98]

As the world's largest Muslim majority state (approximately 87 percent of citizens identify as Muslim, primarily Sunni), religion has long been an important identity. Although religious expression is more common today, Indonesia's political institutions are secular, designed to help mediate potential fissures along religious lines. Yet, religious intolerance is becoming increasingly common. The highly publicized and contentious trial of the former Jakarta governor, Basuki Tjahaja Purnama, commonly known by his nickname, Ahok, brought these tensions to the surface. The first non-Muslim governor of Jakarta since 1965, Ahok, a Christian of Chinese descent, was an extremely popular political independent known for improving public transportation and cracking down on corruption. He was imprisoned for two years for blasphemy, convicted of insulting Islam by challenging some of his contenders' claims that faithful Muslims should not support non-Muslim politicians. Ahok's casual comment (that a particular verse in the Quran was being misused to discourage Muslims from supporting him) was made as Muslim supporters enthusiastically cheered for him during a campaign rally. The off-the-cuff comment was edited online to sound dismissive of Muslim holy texts, which angered many conservative groups. In an explosion of "faith politics" in Indonesia, some even called for an Islamic caliphate to replace Indonesia's secular system.[99] At the least, this incident activated a previously latent political divide between pluralists and Islamists.[100] During his trial in 2016–2017, Jakarta endured months of marches, mostly calling for Ahok's downfall, and the case was widely viewed as a litmus test of religious tolerance.[101]

Religious identities (and resulting cleavages) in Indonesia are not new, even as some characterize a growing "born-again Islamic movement" within the country.[102] Formerly, the most serious religious-based conflict had been within

Islam, between parties with varying adherence to Islamic law. Violence between Indonesia's Christians, who make up the second-largest group of religious believers (but still constitute less than 10 percent of the population), and Muslims, has been less commonplace, although activist representatives of many faiths have been calling on the government to uphold the secular constitution and guarantee the right to freely practice their faith.

Indonesian civil society includes a variety of groups, although they remain fragmented and often have a close connection to core political elites. Citizens are actively engaged in political discussions, especially online. Some have even called Indonesia the "social media capital of the world."[103] Favorable demographics, cheap data plans, and relatively inexpensive smartphones combine to promote Indonesia as the world's most addicted smartphone users, with "prolific" use of social media.[104] Internet users are known to be critical of government and society, and they play an outsized role in elections, with campaign staff members using WhatsApp groups to communicate. In many ways, current president Jokowi Widodo owes his rise to social media: his staff developed and distributed a wildly popular adaptation of "Angry Birds," with the candidate throwing exploding tomatoes at corrupt officials.[105] His campaign also released a remake of the popular One Direction song ("What Makes You Beautiful"), highlighting the traffic, corruption, and flooding problems that people hoped Jokowi could fix.[106] But, as we discussed, social media can take on a decidedly uncivil tone as well. Within Indonesia, analysts have noted the enabling of religious intolerance, as well as its weaponization.[107]

Since the landmark 2005 peace agreement that granted Aceh unprecedented autonomy within the republic (the province of Aceh is seen as the birthplace of Islam in Indonesia), formal Islamic courts organized on the principles of Islamic religious law, or sharia, have been established throughout the province, which is long known for its orthodox views. Since their implementation in 2006, the sharia courts have received mixed reviews, with flogging—even of non-Muslims—becoming more frequent (although non-Muslims may usually choose to be prosecuted under either national or religious laws).[108] Jokowi has called for an end to public caning.[109] Some groups report the increased harassment of women as well as detainment of male and female foreign aid workers for meeting with a person of the opposite sex in ways considered inappropriate by the sharia police. Others praise the changes, viewing sharia courts as proof of the province's autonomy and as demonstrating that it is possible to be both Muslim and modern.[110] As an increasing number of women are being charged for morality crimes, an all-female flogging squad was inaugurated in 2020.[111]

Indonesian identity is an extremely sensitive topic, and debates over inclusion rage. One region that has faced simmering discontent and discord is West Papua, Indonesia's least-populous province, which prior to 2007 was known as West Irian Jaya. Activists in this heavily militarized region have been subject to abuse at the hands of the Indonesian military in response to separatist demands by some Papuans, whose physical appearance, more Melanesian than Asian, is distinct from other Indonesians. Individuals continue to be imprisoned displaying the outlawed Papuan flag, the Morning Star—a treasonous act in the eyes of Indonesian authorities.[112] The challenges in Papua follow the pattern of coinciding cleavages: in addition to differences in ethnicity and socioeconomic opportunities, a significant religious cleavage exists. Locals are mostly Christian or animist and clash with the newer, predominantly Muslim residents of the region, whose migration to the island has been encouraged by Jakarta. It is also a region rich in natural resources, namely gold and copper, and deforestation is a huge concern. Movement toward a possible UN-sponsored referendum, modeled after the one held in Timor-Leste in 1999, goes in fits and starts, although Jakarta continues to oppose such a step. Plans to extend the 2001 Special Autonomy Law, which expired in 2021, gave rise to large protests, as many believed the extension is being used to repress Papua's independence movement.[113]

Indonesia's population is diverse and dynamic, and in recent years has engaged in civil and uncivil activism. This Southeast Asian giant continues to grapple with contending meanings of citizenship, nationality, and voice.

Now It's Your Turn

Why do you think people turn to political ideologies to achieve their causes? How can ordinary citizens and leaders alike be manipulated by ideologies? Why do you think youth are attracted to particular movements? After reading about some of the forms of activism and expression discussed in this chapter, do you view any actions, such as wearing an Islamic headscarf, differently than you did before? Why or why not? What are some of the seemingly unusual ways in which people are making their concerns known? Why do they choose these methods? How do economic, political, and cultural factors contribute to activism (or lack thereof)?

Notes

1. Octavio Paz, "Latin America and Democracy," in *Democracy and Dictatorship in Latin America: A Special Publication Devoted Entirely to the Voice and Opinions of Writers from Latin America,* ed. Octavio Paz, Jorge Edwards, Carlos Franqui, et al. (New York: Foundation for the Independent Study of Social Ideas, 1982).

2. Katherine E. Bliss, "Party Politics in Mexico's Midterm Elections," *Hemisphere Focus* (Center for Strategic and International Studies) 17, no. 3 (July 9, 2009).

3. James C. McKinley Jr., "Mexico Faces Its Own Red-Blue Standoff," *New York Times,* July 9, 2006; "Mexico's Midterm Elections and the Future of Democracy," Wilson Center, July 10, 2009.

4. Marc Lacey, "Disgruntled Mexicans Plan an Election Message to Politicians: We Prefer Nobody," *New York Times,* June 21, 2009; Malcolm Bleith, "Mexico's Blast from the Past," *Newsweek,* July 2, 2009.

5. Kenneth F. Greene and Mariano Sánchez-Talanquer, "Latin America's Shifting Politics: Mexico's Party System Under Stress," *Journal of Democracy* 29, 4 (October 2018).

6. Chase Harrison and Carin Zissis, "Explainer: Making Sense of Mexico's Massive Midterms," Americas Society/Council of the Americas, June 2, 2021; Maria Verza, "Party Chaos Threatens Mexican President's Administration," *AP News,* October 13, 2020; Greene and Sánchez-Talanquer, "Latin America's Shifting Politics."

7. Greene and Sánchez-Talanquer, "Latin America's Shifting Politics."

8. "Freedom in the World: Mexico," Freedom House, 2020.

9. Viridiana Rios, "Mexican Women Are Fed Up and Lopez Obrador Doesn't Get It," *New York Times,* March 4, 2021; Maria Abi-Habib and Natalie Kitroeff, "Rape Allegations Have Divided Mexico's Governing Party," *New York Times,* March 2, 2021.

10. "Freedom in the World: Mexico," Freedom House; Abi-Habib and Kitroeff, "Rape Allegations Have Divided Mexico's Governing Party."

11. "As You Were," *The Economist,* July 5, 2010; "Taking It to the Streets," *Houston Chronicle,* November 4, 2006.

12. Paul von Chamier, "How Civil Society Action Led to Fairer Taxation in Mexico," Center on International Cooperation, February 6, 2020.

13. "Teacher Strikes Have Cost Oaxaca Students Two Years of Classes," *Mexico News Daily,* April 11, 2019; Feliks Garcia, "Mexico Teachers Protest: 6 Killed and 100 Injured in Oaxaca After Clashes with Police," *The Independent* (UK), June 20, 2016.

14. Francisco Durand, "The New Right and Political Change in Peru," in *The Right and Democracy in Latin America,* ed. Douglas A. Chalmers, Maria do Carmo Campello de Souza, and Atilio A. Borón (New York: Praeger, 1992); Ernesto García Calderón, "Peru's Decade of Living Dangerously," *Journal of Democracy* 12, no. 2 (April 2001).

15. Moises Arce, "The Persistence of the Two Perus," *Current History,* February 2014.

16. Dan Collyns, "Thousands Protest Against Presidential Bid by Daughter of Corrupt Former Peru Leader," *The Guardian,* April 6, 2016; Dan Collyns, "Leftist Teacher Takes on Dictator's Daughter as Peru Picks New President," *The Guardian,* June 3, 2021.

17. Patricio Navia, "Peru's Problem Is Bigger Than Not Having a President," *Americas Quarterly,* November 16, 2020.

18. Mitra Taj and Anatoly Kurmanaev, "Peru's Surprise New Leader Stokes Anger, Fear in a Traumatized Country," *New York Times,* November 10, 2020.

19. Anatoly Kurmanaev and Mitra Taj, "Peru's President Steps Down After Just 6 Days, Leaving Country Adrift," *New York Times,* November 15, 2020; Mitra Taj, "In Peru's Presidential Election, the Most Popular Choice Is No One," *New York Times,* April 11, 2021.

20. Alex Emery, "Peru's Farmers Fight Police over Southern Copper Mine," *Bloomberg Businessweek,* April 15, 2010; Joseph Zárate, *Wars of the Interior* (London: Granta, 2021).

21. Arce, "The Persistence of the Two Perus"; Kristina Aiello,"Peru's 'Cold War' Against Indigenous Peoples," North American Congress on Latin America (NACLA), July 15, 2009.

22. Simon Romero, "Protesters Gird for Long Fight over Opening Peru's Amazon," *New York Times,* July 11, 2009; Laura Fano Morrisey, "The Rise of Ethnic Politics: Indigenous Movements in the Andean Region," *Development* 52, no. 4 (2009); Gerardo Rénique, "Law of the Jungle in Peru: Indigenous Amazonian Uprising Against Neoliberalism," *Socialism and Democracy* 23, no. 3 (November 2009); Zárate, *Wars of the Interior.*

23. Rénique, "Law of the Jungle in Peru."

24. "Blood in the Jungle," *The Economist,* June 13, 2009; Stephanie Boyd, "The Ticking Time Bomb," *New Internationalist,* no. 427 (November 2009); "To the Barricades," *The Economist,* December 6, 2008; "Documentary About Peru's Bagua Massacre Wins Award in Madrid," *Telesur,* May 7, 2016.

25. Juan Carlos Riveros, "Climate Justice for the Indigenous People of Peru," World Wildlife Fund, December 15, 2014; Marisol de la Cadena, "Indigenous Cosmopolitics in the Andes," *Cultural Anthropology* 25, no. 2 (May 2010); Simon Romero, "Protesters Gird for Long Fight over Opening Peru's Amazon," *New York Times,* July 11, 2009; Andrew C. Revkin, "Peru Prepares to Host Climate Talks as Its Indigenous Forest Defenders Die," *New York Times,* November 17, 2014; "World Report: Peru," Human Rights Watch, 2021.

26. Funso Afolayan, "Nigeria: A Political Entity and a Society," in *Dilemmas of Democracy in Nigeria,* ed. Paul A. Beckett and Crawford Young (Rochester: University of Rochester Press, 1997).

27. "The Candidates to Be Nigeria's Leader," *BBC News,* December 4, 2006.

28. "Profile: Umaru Yar'Adua," *BBC News,* December 17, 2006.

29. Ernest Aryeetey, "Can Nigeria Fail?" Brookings Institution, June 24, 2010.

30. Chris Stein, "Nigeria's Ruling All Progressives Congress Dealt Setback," *VOA,* June 10, 2015; Nicholas Ibekwe, "Nigeria: How Progressive Is the APC?" *New African,* February 10, 2015.

31. Brandon Kendhammer, "Nigeria's New Democratic Dawn?" *Current History* 114, no. 772 (May 2015); Tayo Oke, "APC, PDP in Disarray; Is There an Alternative?" *Punch,* August 10, 2021.

32. Ruth Maclean, "In Nigeria, 'Feminist' Was a Common Insult. Then Came the Feminist Coalition," *New York Times,* March 12, 2021.

33. "Nigeria Erupts as Lagos Comes to a Standstill," *Foreign Policy* (October 20, 2020); Melinda Fakuade, "Davido on the Power of Afrobeats Music and Nigeria's #End-SARS Movement," *Rolling Stone,* November 5, 2020; Rick Gladstone and Megan Specia, "Nigeria's Police Brutality Crisis: What's Happening Now," *New York Times,* November 14, 2020.

34. Ruth Maclean, "Taking on Big Oil, and a Dirty Legacy, in Nigeria," *New York Times,* July 25, 2021.

35. Stanley Reed, "UK High Court Says Nigerians Can Sue Shell in Britain over Oil Spills," *New York Times,* February 12, 2021.

36. Elian Peltier and Clair Moses, "A Victory over Big Oil for 4 Nigerian Farmers," *New York Times,* January 31, 2021; Maclean, "Taking on Big Oil, and a Dirty Legacy, in Nigeria."

37. "Zimbabwe's Tighter Belts, and Shorter Tempers," *The Economist,* October 28, 2000.

38. Not all women are MDC supporters. Older, rural women with less formal education are some of ZANU-PF's staunchest supporters, and many of them fear the uncertainty that would come with a new government.

39. "Freedom in the World: Zimbabwe," Freedom House, 2021; Douglas Rogers, "Zimbabwe's Accidental Triumph," *New York Times,* April 15, 2010.

40. Sam Moyo, "The Land Occupation Movement and Democratization in Zimbabwe: Contradictions of Neoliberalism," *Millennium* 30, no. 2 (June 1, 2001).

41. Ibid.; Douglas Rogers, "Zimbabwe's Accidental Triumph," *New York Times,* April 15, 2010.

42. Greg Mills and Jeffrey Herbst, "Bring Zimbabwe in from the Cold," *New York Times,* May 28, 2009.

43. "Zimbabwe Anti-Mugabe Protest: Police Fire Tear Gas," *BBC News,* August 26, 2016.

44. "Zimbabwe Holds Largest Anti-Mugabe Protest in Years," *Agence France-Presse,* April 14, 2016.

45. "Letter from Africa: Zimbabwe's Flag Fury," *BBC News,* June 1, 2016; Jeffrey Moyo and Norimitsu Onishi, "Mugabe Mocked the Internet, Then Discovered Threat in Online Pastor," *New York Times,* October 3, 2016.

46. Andrew Harding, "Rappers and Actors Push Zimbabwe Hashtag Viral," *BBC News,* August 6, 2020.

47. Maureen Kademaunga and Otto Saki, "Reclaiming Civil Society Legitimacy in Zimbabwe," Carnegie Europe, December 7, 2020; "Coronavirus: Zimbabwe Arrests 100,000 for 'Violations' of Measures," *BBC News,* July 19, 2020.

48. Kademaunga and Saki, "Reclaiming Civil Society Legitimacy in Zimbabwe."

49. Alan B. Lloyd, *Ancient Egypt: State and Society* (New York: Oxford University Press, 2014).

50. Thomas Schneider, *Ancient Egypt in 10 Questions and Answers* (Ithaca: Cornell University Press, 2013).

51. Arthur Goldschmidt Jr., *Modern Egypt: The Formation of a Nation-State* (Boulder: Westview, 2004).

52. Ashraf Khalil, *Liberation Square: Inside the Egyptian Revolution and the Rebirth of a Nation* (New York: St. Martin's Press, 2011); Wael Ghonim, *Revolution 2.0: The Power of the People Is Greater Than the People in Power* (New York: Houghton Mifflin Harcourt, 2012).

53. Jakob Erle, Jakob Mathias Wichmann, and Alexander Kjaerum, "Political Culture in Egypt: The Political Values and Norms of the Voters," Danish Egyptian Dialogue Institute, 2012.

54. Thanassis Cambanis, *Once upon a Revolution: An Egyptian Story* (New York: Simon and Schuster, 2015).

55. Hanan Badr, "Public Sphere, New Media and Political Culture in Post-Revolutionary Egypt," in *Media Culture in Transformation: Political Communication, Social Networking, and Transition in Egypt,* ed. Hanan Badr (Bonn: Max Weber Stiftung, 2016).

56. Marc Lynch, "The Rise and Fall of the New Arab Public Sphere," *Current History,* December 2015; Badr, "Public Sphere, New Media and Political Culture in Post-Revolutionary Egypt"; Philip Loft, "Egypt in 2021: Politics, Human Rights and International Relations," House of Commons Library, April 8, 2021; Declan Walsh, "Egypt Sentences Women to 2 Years in Prison for TikTok Videos," *New York Times,* July 28, 2020.

57. Lynch, "The Rise and Fall of the New Arab Public Sphere"; Thomas L. Friedman, "Social Media: Destroyer or Creator?" *New York Times,* February 3, 2016.

58. Ghonim, *Revolution 2.0.*

59. Cambanis, *Once upon a Revolution;* Tarek Osman, *Egypt on the Brink: From Nasser to Mubarak* (New Haven: Yale University Press, 2010).

60. Osman, *Egypt on the Brink.*

61. Cambanis, *Once upon a Revolution;* Zachary Laub, "Backgrounder: Egypt's Muslim Brotherhood," Council on Foreign Relations, August 15, 2019; Steve Holland and Arshad Mohammed, "Trump Weighs Labeling Muslim Brotherhood a Terrorist Group," *Reuters,* April 30, 2019.

62. Mona Eltahawy, "Sisi's War on Reporters," *New York Times,* November 23, 2015.

63. Michael J. Totten, "The Muslim Brotherhood Takes Off Its Mask," *World Affairs,* May 21, 2015; Elizabeth R. Nugent, "Op-Ed: How Polarization Shattered Egypt's Democratic Experiment," *Los Angeles Times,* January 21, 2021.

64. Paulo Rivetti and Mohsen Moheimany, "Upgrading Civil Society in Iran: Dynamics of Adaptation," Middle East Institute, September 17, 2015.

65. Rana Rahimpour, "Iran's Supreme Leader: Who Might Succeed Ali Khamenei?" *BBC News,* December 11, 2020.

66. Reuel Marc Gerecht, "In Ebrahim Raisi, Iran's Clerics Have Groomed and Promoted Their Ruthless Enforcer," *Washington Post,* June 25, 2021.

67. In her book, *Honeymoon in Tehran: Two Years of Love and Danger in Iran* (New York: Random House, 2009), Azadeh Moaveni highlights this divide between religious militants and those preferring a more private interpretation of their faith.

68. Reza Afshari, "A Historic Moment in Iran," *Human Rights Quarterly* 31, no. 4 (November 2009), p. 840.

69. Many believe this announcement was designed to help improve voter turnout, especially after legislative elections in early 2021 reported the lowest turnout of any post-1979 elections in the state. See Kourosh Ziabari, "Iran Clears Path for Women to Run for President," *Asia Times,* October 16, 2020.

70. Andrew Hanna, "Profiles of Women Politicians, Activists," *Iran Primer,* United States Institute of Peace, March 8, 2021.

71. David Blair, "Iran's Big Woman Problem: All of the Things Iranian Women Aren't Allowed to Do," *The Telegraph,* September 21, 2015; Jon Haworth, "Social Media Fight Spreads in Iran as Women Seek to Regain International Travel Rights," *ABC News,* February 27, 2021.

72. This source highlights that even Saudi Arabia had recently permitted women to see athletic events. See Amir Vahdat and Mehdi Fattahi, "Iran Women Attend FIFA Soccer Game for First Time in Decades," *AP,* October 10, 2019.

73. Tariq Panja, "Iranian Women Allowed to Attend Soccer Game for First Time Since 1981," *New York Times,* October 10, 2019.

74. Farnaz Fassihi, "Iran's 'Blue Girl' Wanted to Watch a Soccer Match. She Died Pursuing Her Dream," *New York Times,* September 10, 2019.

75. Panja, "Iranian Women Allowed to Attend Soccer Game."

76. Haworth, "Social Media Fight Spreads in Iran."
77. Kourosh Ziabari, "Iran Clears Path for Women to Run for President," *Asia Times,* October 16, 2020.
78. "Four Decades After Its Revolution, Iran Is Still Stuck in the Past," *The Economist,* February 9, 2019.
79. Barbara Demick, "Uncovering the Cultural Revolution's Awful Truths," *The Atlantic,* January–February 2021.
80. "China: Freedom in the World 2021," Freedom House, 2021.
81. Amy Qin, "Liu Xiaobo's Death Pushes China's Censors into Overdrive," *New York Times,* July 17, 2017.
82. Cate Cadell, "China's Robot Censors Crank Up as Tiananmen Anniversary Nears," *Reuters,* May 26, 2019.
83. Demick, "Uncovering the Cultural Revolution's Awful Truths."
84. Eleanor Albert and Lindsay Maizland, "Backgrounder: Religion in China," Council on Foreign Relations, September 25, 2020.
85. John Sudworth, "China Defends Detention of Uighur Model in Xinjiang," *BBC News,* August 18, 2020.
86. Ben Mauk, "Inside Xinjiang's Prison State," *New Yorker,* February 26, 2021; Austin Ramzy and Chris Buckley, "'Absolutely No Mercy': Leaked Files Expose How China Organized Mass Detentions of Muslims," *New York Times,* November 16, 2019.
87. James Palmer, "Why China Is Cracking Down on Video Games," *Foreign Policy* (September 1, 2021).
88. Walter Russell Mead, "Beijing's Collision with Christians," *Wall Street Journal,* December 22, 2020.
89. Keith Zhai, "China to Allow Families Three Children," *Wall Street Journal,* June 1, 2021.
90. Matt Schiavenza, "The Uncertain Future of Civil Society in China," *Asia Society,* January 29, 2018.
91. Edward Wong, "Clampdown in China Restricts 7,000 Foreign Organizations," *New York Times,* April 28, 2016.
92. Rana Siu Inboden, "China Is Choking Civil Society at the United Nations," *Foreign Policy* (September 27, 2021).
93. Grzegorz Ekiert, Elizabeth J. Perry, and Xiaojun Yan, eds., *Ruling by Other Means: State-Mobilized Movements* (Cambridge: Cambridge University Press, 2020).
94. Diana Fu, "How the Chinese State Mobilized Civil Society to Fight COVID-19," Brookings Institution, February 9, 2021.
95. Chris Buckley, "Chinese Doctor, Silenced After Warning of Outbreak, Dies from Coronavirus," *New York Times,* February 6, 2020.
96. Chris Buckley, "China's 'Big Cannon' Blasted Xi. Now He's Been Jailed for 18 Years." *New York Times,* September 22, 2020.
97. Qin, "Liu Xiaobo's Death."
98. Indonesia's legislative branch, the People's Consultative Assembly, is a bicameral system, with 550 members in the People's Representative Council and 130 members of the Regional Representative Council, elected by the twenty-six provincial parliaments and sixty-five members appointed from various societal groups.
99. Hannah Beech, "Christian Politician in Indonesia Is Freed After Blasphemy Prison Term," *New York Times,* January 23, 2019; Hannah Beech and Muktita Suhartono, "Faith Politics on the Rise as Indonesian Islam Takes a Hard-Line Path," *New York Times,* April 15, 2019.
100. Eve Warburton, "Deepening Polarization and Democratic Decline in Indonesia," in *Political Polarization in South and Southeast Asia: Old Divisions, New Dangers,* ed. Thomas Carothers and Andrew O'Donohue (Washington, DC: Carnegie Endowment for International Peace, 2020), pp. 25–41.
101. Kikue Hamayotsu, "Indonesia in 2014: The Year of Electing the 'People's President,'" *Asian Survey* 55, no. 1 (January–February 2015), pp. 174–183; "Indonesia Blasphemy Case: Emotional Scenes as Ahok Trial Begins," *BBC News,* December 13, 2016;

"Jokowi Blames 'Political Actors' for Violence at Indonesia Rally," *Bloomberg News,* November 4, 2016; Yenni Kwok, "The Blasphemy Trial of Jakarta's Governor Puts Indonesian Secularism in a Shockingly Poor Light," *Time,* December 12, 2016.

102. Richard C. Paddock, "The 'Niqab Squad' Wants Women to Be Seen Differently," *New York Times,* March 23, 2020.

103. Karishma Vaswani, "Indonesia's Love Affair with Social Media," *BBC News,* February 16, 2012; Tony Starr, "Indonesia's Social Media Savvy Moves It onto the Movember Map," *PRI's The World,* November 5, 2013; Sam Bollier, "Voting in the 'World's Social Media Capital,'" *Al Jazeera,* July 2, 2014.

104. Thomas Paterson, "Indonesian Cyberspace Expansion: A Double-Edged Sword," *Journal of Cyber Policy* 4, no. 2 (2019), p. 218.

105. Sam Bollier, "Voting in the 'World's Social Media Capital,'" *Al Jazeera,* July 2, 2014.

106. Ibid.

107. Paterson, "Indonesian Cyberspace Expansion," p. 217.

108. "Aceh Flogs 13 Young People for Breaking Its Strict Islamic Laws," *Agence France-Presse,* October 17, 2016; "Two Christians Publicly Flogged in Indonesia for Drinking, Gambling," *The Straits Times,* February 8, 2021.

109. "In Indonesia's Aceh, Two Christians Choose Flogging over Jail for Drinking, Gambling," *Agence France-Presse,* February 9, 2021.

110. Karishma Vaswani, "On Patrol with Aceh's Sharia Police," *BBC News,* February 2, 2010.

111. Haeril Halim, "Aceh Unveils New Female Flogging Squad," *Agence France-Presse,* January 28, 2020.

112. "Freedom in the World 2021: Indonesia," Freedom House, 2022.

113. Johnny Blades, "West Papua: The Issue That Won't Go Away for Melanesia," Lowy Institute, May 1, 2020; "Protests Flare in Papua as Students Demand Independence Referendum," *The Guardian,* September 29, 2020.

10

Violence: The Call to Arms

This regime has pushed people toward violence . . . the more they repress, the more aggressive and angry people get. —*Twenty-nine-year-old Iranian political activist who emigrated to the Netherlands, on the 2019 protests throughout Iran*[1]

The people of Afghanistan—we were born in war and we grew up in war and we are still in war. We don't know about our future, and what happens next. Maybe it's worse. —*"Layla" (pseudonym), former Afghan defense lawyer and legal adviser who emigrated to the United States in 2016, reflecting on her home country after the return of the Taliban in 2021*[2]

Crises are rarely isolated events. The global Covid PANDEMIC unleashed a public health crisis of proportions none of us had ever seen before. The concomitant economic challenges were accompanied by civil and social unrest the world over. In its 2021 Global Peace Index, the Institute for Economics and Peace reports a deterioration of peace for a ninth consecutive year, caused by ongoing conflicts, increasing militarization, and a widening gap between the world's most peaceful and least peaceful countries. Globally, violence (or the threat of violence) is one of the most pressing issues facing citizens, even as deaths from terrorism have been decreasing for the past six years.[3]

Violence is expressed in a variety of ways. For example, on September 11, 2001, Americans faced violence in a way that most in this country had never experienced. When planes were crashed into the towers of the World Trade Center in New York City, the Pentagon just outside Washington, D.C., and a field in rural Pennsylvania, the power of organized violence jolted the country's sense of security in a way most had never experienced. As the United States and the world struggled to understand the reasons for these actions, we contemplated a force that has long been employed by individuals and groups. In Chapter 8, we discussed people's option of "voice," focusing on ideologies and participation. In this chapter, we investigate participation that engages the use of violence. We examine a variety of means of violent expression, highlighting the individuals and groups behind the actions and emphasizing the role of governments and militaries, terrorists and revolutionaries. The World Bank now estimates that violence is becoming the primary cause of poverty in the world, noting that poverty rates are 20 percent higher in countries impacted by cycles of violence, and forecasts that by 2030, up to two-thirds of the world's extreme poor will live in countries characterized by fragility, conflict, and violence.[4]

Some view violence as the breakdown of politics, but we encourage you to view it instead as a tool used by actors to accomplish their goals. Violence is a powerful weapon, used by terrorists, governments, GUERRILLAS, militaries, militias, and activists canvassing the whole gamut of ideological persuasion. While many commonly view the use of violence as a means of gaining territory, such tactics are also often used to exact responses like fear, intimidation, surrender, and subjugation, as we will see in this chapter. The psychological force of violence (or the threat thereof) is perhaps the greatest source of its potency.

Violence can take many forms, and its perpetrators justify it in a variety of ways. Behind violent acts are myriad motivations, aspirations, and justifications—all open to competing interpretations. As students of the global south, we attempt to classify types of actions taken by ordinary people and political ELITES alike, but these labels are often reductionist (overly simplified) and may imply judgment. Take TERRORISM, for example. Analysts work to come up with a clearcut definition of what is meant by the term—it involves purposeful acts against innocent civilians in order to provoke fear and insecurity. Clearly, some individuals and groups engage in these acts in ways consistent with this view, and they take action without apology—priding themselves as among the world's most renowned terrorists. Yet, other times, the term is used as a political label to characterize a seemingly unjustifiable action by a group of people. In discussions of this topic, watch carefully the labels that are tossed around; tagging a group as "terrorist" can often fulfill a political agenda to delegitimize a group's perspective. Classifying acts of political deviance is a subjective enterprise.

Terrorist violence is used in many different types of conflict and by many activists of all stripes. Here, we will observe terrorism at work, including during warfare, revolutions, and times of peace. The designation of terrorist acts can sometimes be a puzzle; dependent upon one's perspective, the task of defining what exactly "terrorism" is has befuddled many social scientists. As linguist, activist, and political commentator Noam Chomsky once stated, "What is terrorism to some is heroism to others."[5] Sometimes, the fiery debate has taken on the language of "freedom fighters" versus "terrorists"—it should not be surprising that groups of people using violence believe that the ends justify the means.

Rather than trying to argue for or against a particular definition, we highlight key components: terrorism is a deliberate organized act, with the goal of inspiring fear. Usually, innocents are victimized, although the definition of who is "innocent" can be manipulated. Terrorists have shown devastating flexibility in their targets and their tactics, which include bombings, kidnappings, hijackings, and the threats of such actions. They want to gain an audience—attention, even negative attention, is what they seek—to publicize their causes. They seek to alter opinion and policy. Contrary to popular belief, they're not all after land or material resources. Rather, they sometimes fight bigger, more seemingly abstract issues such as GLOBALIZATION. Since attention is what these groups are after, the proliferation of nonstop news reports on television, radio, and the internet has become an accessible platform. Terror tactics evolve based on the response of societies and governments. In a scenario that seems almost quaint by today's standards, planes used to be commandeered by hijackers to go to Cuba. Nowadays, groups are creating weapons of mass destruction out of airplanes. Why? The flexibility of terrorism requires relatively few people to pull it off, and in the twenty-first century it is easier to acquire adequate materials to invoke terror. Maybe the world has become jaded and it takes more to get our attention—which is precisely what advocates of terror and other forms of violence desire.

As we discuss various manifestations of violent expression, watch for the use of threats by perpetrators and for the use of labels by victims, and try to understand the motivations behind competing sides of the issues.

Conflict and War

Why do people, especially in groups, turn to aggressive acts of defiance? There have been many theories to explain when and why people turn to violent means.[6] To some, resorting to violence is a way of dealing with their dissatisfaction over a state of affairs. When facing frustration and unmet expectations, it is argued, people are likely to turn to aggression. Conflict is also likely in societies that experience great change, whether political, economic, or cultural. This can be especially true if that change is uneven, as the fits and starts of life often are. Promises of dramatic improvement are often unfulfilled, leaving some, particularly those who believe they made the most sacrifice in the name of the cause, feeling betrayed. People who believe they have limited options to make their voices heard try to challenge each aspect of security and comfort.

Another explanation, known as the RESOURCE MOBILIZATION approach, emphasizes agents' ability to put together effective leadership and political opportunities for expression. In this view, collective action is taken when the time is right and when the necessary connections between resources and people can be crafted. Because of the power of human agency, though, no single approach can be used to help explain the rise of violent action.

Significant differences, also known as CLEAVAGES, can almost always be found in societies and groups of people. These are based on a variety of factors, including the myriad identities discussed in Chapter 8, as well as perceptions of well-being and fair treatment. Yet, these differences are not always viewed as relevant, and they may remain latent for long periods of time. What sparks the change? In other words, what are some of the factors that make cleavages important enough for people to act on, even in violent ways?

One of the issues that alters a situation from low to high priority is the perceived extent of differentiation between and among groups. Many argue that the perception of stark differences between the rich and the poor in a given region or society can often be a source of violence. In the literature on SOCIAL MOVEMENTS and mobilization, this view is referred to as RELATIVE DEPRIVATION. It is one thing if everyone is poor, but if some people are poor and others are very rich by comparison, the likelihood for action is much greater. If there is a strongly held perception that the difference between those who have benefited from a particular policy or program is great, a sense of indignity may impel people to act. As we saw earlier, the general state of the economy is an important factor that influences individuals' and groups' perception of their well-being and their decisions about action or inaction. In times of economic hardship, especially if policies are perceived as unevenly harming some groups of people, we have observed that some groups will turn to crime, violence, and other disruptive forms of behavior.

Expectations about changes in lifestyle are also important. If people have little reason to hope for anything from society or government, they often remain passive and largely inactive. But if they are given reason to anticipate more, especially through sacrifice, their hopes increase. Expectations sometimes end up going dangerously unfulfilled. Sometimes, there is an ASPIRATION GAP between what one expects and what one can actually achieve or acquire. Exposure to international media that portray a variety of lifestyles and norms, increased interaction with other members of society who live in different circumstances, and, especially, elite cues about that way of life can all help create circumstances that widen this chasm. A related idea is the REVOLUTION OF RISING EXPECTATIONS, which people experience as they begin to believe in the possibility and likelihood of positive change, for either themselves or their families. People naturally develop expectations about their future life. For example, many students attend college with the expectation that they will be able to get a good job to support themselves after graduation. Expectations often have a way of increasing in scope, and it is common for people to believe that with hard work and effort, life will get better. If this cycle is broken, and quality of life decreases rather than improves, it can be followed by frustration and disappointment.

Yet, the motivation for action is not always as it appears, and people sometimes use unexpected public forums like sports events and funerals to vent their frustration. Sporting events have long been fertile ground for the expression of discontent. In what was dubbed the "Soccer War," 6,000 people were killed and 12,000 were injured during the 1969 World Cup qualifying game between El Salvador and Honduras.[7] Frustrated by the perceived lack of fairness of referees during a match in the Democratic Republic of Congo (DRC) after the Congolese lost a World Cup qualifying match to the Italians, fans took to the streets, attacking Chinese businesses because they misperceived that the referee was Chinese (he was from Japan). Chanting "Chinese go home," many used the event to protest Chinese investment in the copper-mining industry throughout the DRC.[8] Funerals have also been known to spark protests and sometimes riots, especially if mourners seek retribution because they perceive that their loved one was targeted.

Others, led by political scientist Arend Lijphart, have assigned importance to the patterns of division existing within society, distinguishing between coinciding and crosscutting cleavages.[9] These expressions are used to characterize whether or not the significant conflicts and areas of difference in society are diffused among varying groups, or are concentrated among particular sectors of society. For example, if the economically poor in a given country also tend to be the religious minority, employees in the service sector of the economy, and predominantly women, this would be an example of coinciding cleavages. In all aspects of differentiation, a particular group of people seem to be getting the short end of the stick. Coinciding cleavages are more volatile, as all of the conflicts are stacked up into tidy groups and it is clear who does not agree with whom. In contrast, crosscutting lines of division help defuse the conflict: the significant points of difference are spread among multiple groups in society, keeping any one group from perceiving any tremendous amount of injustice. Although real life never conforms to neatly crafted categories, Nigeria is often cited as an example of coinciding cleavages, where differences in religion, ethnicity, and region line up. Yet, not all Yoruba are Christian and, of course, the regions are not entirely homogeneous. Some Ibo, for example, live in the north. Another example can be found in Mexico, since the south is much poorer, less industrial, and more Amerindian than the rest of Mexico. Again, it is an imperfect categorization, since the southern region of Chiapas contains some divisions between Indians who are Protestant and those who are Catholic. The point remains, though: more pronounced divisions can invite greater potential for conflict along these lines. They certainly invite an "us versus them" distinction that can significantly hinder consensus building.

Another factor that influences the potential for violent action relates to the availability of meaningful avenues of expression. Protests and riots are sometimes designed to be turbulent from the outset, but other times they turn violent when participants feel they are being ignored or that it is only through destructive action that their voices will be heard. Yet, violence is not always an act of desperation. Ironically, some groups have engaged in violent tactics just as they were about to achieve their goals.[10]

In our discussion of the relevance of differences, we have concentrated mostly on groups smaller than governments and STATES. We now turn to a discussion of types of war, which is usually one of the first categories of violent conflict that comes to mind. Since the eighteenth century, "war" has been defined as violence between states or between organized groups, with the explicit goals of gaining territory, seeking revenge, or conquering recalcitrant groups of people. The twentieth century has been called the "century of war" because of the dominance of hostile conflict—three times as many people died in war during this century than during all of the prior centuries combined.[11] Wars produce scarred soldiers, lonely widows, traumatized victims of torture and rape, and political prisoners. Increasingly, the casualties of war are civilians rather than combatants.

There are many different types of wars, and an increasing variety of conflicts are now categorized as such, or as warlike situations, including "nonconventional" wars such as the war on terrorism. Some of the main types of warfare include interstate, civil, GUERRILLA, and PROXY WARS, as well as wars of liberation waged by ethnonationalists.

Interstate and Separatist Wars

Interstate wars are the most conventional type of modern warfare, even if today they are no longer in the majority. Wars between states mostly involve traditional militaries, and commonly occur over border disputes, contested landholdings, and perceived threats to security. The legacies of colonialism have often been the source of wars in the global south, with conflicts over borders that fail to recognize significant historical, ethnic, and cultural continuities, and the creation of MULTINATIONAL STATES and stateless peoples. China, for example, has fought border wars with India (1962) and the Soviet Union (1969–1978), and has invaded Vietnam (1979).

One extremely volatile border situation can be found between two South Asian giants, Pakistan and India, in the region called Kashmir. It has been a point of conflict since the departure of the British in 1947; in two full-scale wars and other outbreaks of violence, tens of thousands of people have died on what is viewed as the highest battlefield on Earth. A United Nations cease-fire in 1949 provided both India and Pakistan a portion of the Kashmir region, which is rich in resources and historical connections, but this compromise barely held—and it is rarely viewed as little more than a temporary solution. The territory controlled by New Delhi, India's only Muslim-majority state, is referred to as Jammu Kashmir, while the Pakistani-controlled territory, also predominantly Muslim, is named Azad (Free) Kashmir. In addition, ever since Pakistan ceded a small tract of land to China in the 1950s, Beijing has occupied the northernmost part of the territory (Aksai Chin), even building a road linking Tibet and Xinjiang. Part of the reason for the enduring conflict in the region is that inhabitants themselves are not united in their desire for the future, a common dilemma in border wars. Plans to hold elections in 1995—with the hope of resolving the dispute—were abandoned after an attack on a Muslim mosque. Nuclear tests by Pakistan and India in 1998 escalated tensions even further, an attack on the Indian parliament in December 2001 brought these two Asian states to the brink of war, and tensions flared among a troop and paramilitary buildup in 2019 as well. Multiple peace talks have taken place to attempt to resolve the Kashmir conflict, although it is disputed who can legitimately represent the multiple sides involved, and violence—carried out by protesters and by paramilitary forces sent in to quell them—accompanies any effort to resolve the long-running standoff.

One of the most devastating interstate wars in the global south was the eight-year war between two Middle Eastern giants, Iran and Iraq. Claiming over 500,000 lives, it was one of the longest wars in the recent history of the Middle East. Although the conflict began when Saddam Hussein ordered Iraqi forces to invade Iran during a perceived time of weakness for the young Islamic Republic, its origins can be found in historical, territorial, and ideological differences. Even though Iraq initially welcomed the Islamic Revolution of February 1979, it broke relations with the Iranian regime in October of that year, branding it "non-Islamic" for inciting Shiite communities throughout the Gulf to rebel against their regimes.[12] Hussein and many Iraqis feared that the Islamic Revolution would embolden Iran to challenge contested waterway claims and the Gulf region in general. At one point during the war, Iran demanded Hussein's ouster as a precondition for peace talks, flaming internal opposition within Iraq. Iraq's capture of Kharg Island, Iran's principal Gulf oil terminal, in December 1985, quieted anti-Hussein movements within the country.

The war itself was one of the most brutal in the region, as Iran launched so-called human-wave attacks in which hundreds of thousands of civilians, including boys as young as nine years old, were sent to their death in assaults on Iraqi artillery positions. (This has been a strategy used by combatants with large populations, such as China in the Korean War and by both sides of the Ethiopia-Eritrea conflict.) Religiously motivated troops joined the war in their attempt to seek martyrdom; some were even given symbolic keys to a paradise that was promised to martyrs. Iraq responded with mustard and nerve gas agents. Iraq was surprised that Tehran didn't crumble during the initial attacks, and by 1982 began to seek peace. Iran refused these initiatives and attacked across the border, significantly weakening the Iranian military and leading to a long standoff with Iraq. After a prolonged war of attrition, the UN-brokered cease-fire was accepted in 1988. The only border crossing between Iran and Iraq was reopened in 1999 to allow Iranian pilgrims to visit Shia holy sites in Iraq.

Figure 10.1 The Kurds

Another important example of separatist conflict can be found in the diverse Kurdish population, who are considered the largest group of stateless people (approximately 25–35 million) in the Middle East. At least one-fifth of the Kurds live in Turkey, with significant populations also found in Iran, Iraq, Syria, Lebanon, Armenia, and Azerbaijan. Facing widespread persecution since the late 1980s, many Kurds have immigrated to Germany (where they have faced much neo-Nazi violence) and the Netherlands. Contrary to popular perception, the Kurds are not a single, homogeneous group. Kurdish people speak several different, often mutually indecipherable, languages and espouse different forms of Islam (although most are Sunni Muslims). Even in a similar fight for autonomy and the creation of an independent Kurdistan (not to be confused with the Iranian province of Kurdistan), rivalries dominate, and thousands of Kurds have died at the hands of other Kurds.

Turkey is the Kurds' main path to the West. Yet, depending on the mood in Ankara, one can be sent to jail for broadcasting in Kurdish, running a political campaign on the basis of ethnicity, or too openly advocating a sense of Kurdish pride, which is viewed as a separatist act by some, a terrorist act by others. Since 1984, war between the Turkish government and some Kurds has claimed at least 40,000 lives and driven several million Kurds from their homes. Common interpretations of Turkish law hold the promotion of "hatred between ethnic groups" to include any mention of Kurdish identity. Approximately 1.4 million Kurds live in Iran's remote northwestern province of Kurdistan; about twice that live elsewhere in Iran. As Sunni Muslims, many Iranian Kurds face oppression from the Shiite regime in Tehran, and Iran's Kurdish Nationalist Movement has been driven into Iraq. Even though Kurds in Iran enjoy relative autonomy, protests have turned more urgent, especially after five Iranian Kurds were hanged in Tehran, accused of belonging to a political party viewed by the Iranian government as a terrorist organization.[a]

The Kurdish challenge has been particularly acute in Iraq. Following the 1991 Gulf War, most Iraqi Kurds (approximately 2.5 million) moved into a semiautonomous northern district, protected by a no-fly zone enforced by the United States and Great Britain. Violence against them, though, began long before the Gulf War. US intelligence estimates that from 1987 to 1988, Saddam Hussein's government used chemical agents to gas to death 50,000–100,000 Kurds.[b] Many actions by Iraqi Kurds have helped spur Kurdish pride in other areas of the Middle East, especially after Iraqi Kurds overwhelmingly voted for independence (93 percent "yes") in a regional referendum in 2017—even if their aspirations received no international backing.[c]

Kurds have also been deeply impacted by the war in Syria where, since 2013, they carved out some autonomy during the civil war. In

continues

Figure 10.1 Continued

Kurdish-controlled areas of northern Syria, the drive for gender equality was successful, cementing a role for separate women's militia units, institutionalizing gender representation in government, and establishing "Women's Houses" for dispute settlement.[d] After the rise of the Islamic State, Kurdish forces in Iraq and Syria fought its advance, receiving significant backing and material support from the United States in this effort. This support became complicated as Turkey increased its formal intervention in the Syrian conflict in late 2016, even as the United States increased its support for Syrian Kurds against the Islamic State. Turkish-backed forces in northeast Syria were accused of committing war crimes, including murder, torture, and arbitrary detention of Kurdish residents, as well as the recruitment of children.[e] Former US president Donald Trump pulled most US forces out of the region as Turkey launched a new offensive against the Kurds in 2019, essentially abandoning Kurdish forces that had been trained and backed by the United States, even as the Kurds had demonstrated themselves to be "America's most able partners" in the fight with the Islamic State.[f] The surprise move, which Kurdish leaders viewed as a "stab in the back," was the latest example, in the eyes of many Kurds, of broken promises to their people.[g]

Notes: a. Kawe Qoraishy, "Iran's Kurdish Question," *Foreign Policy* (May 17, 2010).

b. Barbara Crossette, "Iraq Is Forcing Kurds from Their Homes, the UN Reports," *New York Times,* December 11, 2000.

c. David Zucchino, "After the Vote, Does the Kurdish Dream of Independence Have a Chance?" *New York Times,* September 30, 2017.

d. Rod Nordland, "Women Are Free, and Armed, in Kurdish-Controlled Northern Syria," *New York Times,* February 24, 2018.

e. Jiyar Gol, "Syria Conflict: The 'War Crimes' Caught in Brutal Phone Footage," *BBC News,* November 3, 2019.

f. Julian E. Barnes and Eric Schmitt, "Trump Orders Withdrawal of U.S. Troops from Northern Syria," *New York Times,* October 16, 2019.

g. "Turkey-Syria Border: Kurds Bitter as US Troops Withdraw," *BBC News,* October 7, 2019.

Wars are also fought over contested definitions of states and the "stateness" of people—questioning what amount of territory should be included within internationally recognized borders. Earlier, we introduced the notion of the NATION-STATE and the existence of areas of tensions in some, although by no means all, multinational states. The preservation of borders and territorial integrity is an ESSENTIAL FUNCTION of states. Yet, the modern state has "deterritorialized" many national groups, sometimes because of the artificial demarcation of boundaries, often at the hands of imperial powers. Groups challenge their incorporation into a particular state for a variety of reasons, often relating to issues such as religious expression, ethnic disputes, or pressures relating to natural resources. Of course, few of these issues stand alone. Some Indigenous groups, like the Dayaks and Igorots in Southeast Asia, seek to maintain a traditional, nonindustrial, nonurban life that conflicts with national economic DEVELOPMENT plans of many states. Other groups take issue not with the industrial or economic goals of the government, but rather want to have their own homeland or government. This phenomenon is also known as SECESSION. For most, the goal is either to achieve national liberation from political occupation or to create a new political state. For others, the struggle is for humane treatment, more autonomy, and the right to the free expression of their cultural traditions. Sometimes—though not always—this can lead to violent conflict, either in the suppression of the movement (e.g., China's response to the expression of an independent Tibetan identity), or in the expression of the need for a new identity. The Sikh community in Punjab, India, seeks a homeland called Khalistan, the "Land of the Pure." To date, India has been hostile to calls for this homeland, which geographically stands at the strategic intersection of India, the People's Republic of China, and Pakistan.

Indonesia has also faced much secessionist conflict grounded in aims of SELF-DETERMINATION. The state leadership vigorously pushed national assimilation policies that emboldened resistance. Aceh, a northwestern province on the island of Sumatra with a population of 4 million, was home to the longest-running and most violent separatist conflict in Indonesia, with nearly thirty years of conflict claiming between 15,000 and 30,000 lives, including many civilians. The Acehnese are considered to be more orthodox Islamic than residents in other regions of Indonesia. After receiving some degree of autonomy, Aceh's leaders opened the first provincial SHARIA court in 2003, although there already had been local religious courts to handle family matters.[13] The region is also a major oil and gas producer, and many Acehnese long held that Jakarta robbed them of a large share of their deserved revenue.[14] Following the 2004 tsunami in the Indian Ocean (Aceh was the land closest to the epicenter of the underwater earthquake), new life was breathed into the peace negotiations, and a formal peace agreement between Free Aceh and the Indonesian government was signed in 2005, although it is a peace without justice, in the eyes of many.[15] This accord led to legislation granting considerable autonomy to Aceh province, and in 2006 direct elections for provincial and district leaders were held as the former armed insurgency movement attempted to morph into a mainstream political player. It remains true that more groups of people are actively fighting today for new forms of political independence and expression than in decades or centuries past. Yet, some caution should be taken against viewing these conflicts as rooted in "ancient tribal" or even distinctly religious rivalries.[16] Such conflict, rather, has been stoked by modern power plays or by rivalries that were introduced by external, often colonial powers.

The results of these disputes can be disastrous, including displacement, ethnic cleansing, and genocide. The global south is riddled with the tragedies of such conflict, including the murder of Armenians by Turks (1915), of Kurds by the Iraqis (1984–1991), of Hutu and Tutsi in Burundi (1993–1998), of Tutsi and moderate Hutu in Rwanda (1994), of Hmong by Laotians and the Chinese (1975–1979), and of Africans by Arabs in Darfur (since 2003). More recently, tens of thousands of Rohingya Muslims in Myanmar have been killed, and hundreds of thousands more displaced, by the Burmese military since 2017.[17] Ethnic cleansing at the hands of Ethiopian leaders now backed by Eritrea has been documented in Ethiopia's Tigray region since November 2020, the result of simmering tensions over power-sharing in Ethiopia's fragile democracy.[18] The civil war erupted after leaders in the northern Tigray region defied the prime minister's order to delay regional parliamentary elections (due to the Covid pandemic), after which the government declared a state of emergency, restricting communications and launching a military offensive. The war has since devolved into battles between rival military factions, with the government calling on citizens to arm themselves to defend the capital from rebel forces, with significant atrocities in the northern Tigray region raising the specter not only of famine, but also the possibility of the entire erasure of whole villages.[19] Ethiopian authorities have arrested many high-profile Tigrayans, including a bank CEO, priests, and UN staff members, accusing them of supporting rebels.[20] Events in Myanmar and Ethiopia share an uncomfortable commonality in that leaders of both states, personally accused of masterminding the systematic targeting of their own citizens, are prior recipients of the Nobel Peace Prize: Myanmar's state counselor Aung San Suu Kyi (1991) and Ethiopia's prime minister Abiy Ahmed (2019).

In another region of the world, since at least 2017, authorities within China have been systematically rounding up perceived militants, mostly members of the ethnic Uighur minority within the country's northwest Xinjiang province, imprisoning them in massive camps. While Beijing's leaders have acknowledged the existence of what they term "re-education camps," established, in their words, to combat Islamic extremism and separatism, they state that most prisoners have been released and they deny allegations of any human rights abuses.[21] Yet, Amnesty International and others have detailed systemic state-organized "mass imprisonment, torture and persecution" against not only Muslim Uighurs but also ethnic Kazakhs and other minorities, and the United Nations contends that up to 1.5 million Uighurs remain in internment camps throughout the PRC.[22] The United States, the European Union, Canada, and the United Kingdom have each imposed sanctions against China over the situation in Xinjiang, which has included the documentation of the systematic detention of minority populations, forced sterilizations, and mandatory birth control, all part of what observers are referring to as the "largest incarceration of an ethnoreligious minority since the Holocaust."[23] The evidence includes firsthand accounts from individuals who have survived imprisonment and torture, as well as hundreds of pages of internal Chinese government documents that detail not only the mass imprisonment of perceived "extremists," but also how to respond to questions from family members, emphasizing cultivation of "gratitude" toward the Chinese Communist Party for responding efficiently to the "virus" of Islamic radicalism that threatens the country.[24] In January 2021, the US government officially declared the actions a genocide, followed shortly thereafter by Canada and the United Kingdom, among others.[25] Yet, to date, these pronouncements have done little to alter Beijing's policies in the region.

Civil Wars

Although interstate conflicts are obviously important, an increasing number of battles in the world today are internal. Even some of the major cross-border wars, including those between India and Pakistan, and Eritrea and Ethiopia, trace much of their origins to civil conflict. The global south has been beleaguered by civil wars, including conflicts in Algeria, Angola, Cambodia, Côte d'Ivoire, Ethiopia, Laos, Nicaragua, Somalia, Sudan, Syria, Uganda, and Yemen—just to name a few. Civil wars, which occur within a single country, are known to be among the most brutal and damaging types of conflict, inflicting particularly heavy tolls on civilian populations. Families are often separated in civil wars, either by the outcome of the war or along lines of allegiance. Because of the brutality involved, ill will and the scars of war often continue after the official conflict has ended. Sometimes, the estrangement can last for decades or longer.

Civil wars are fought for a variety of reasons. Some researchers are challenging the assumption that the existence of multiple ethnic groups makes a country more prone to civil war. In their study of 127 civil wars from 1945 to 1999, James D. Fearon and David D. Laitin found that irrespective of the ethnic mix, the probability of civil war declines as countries get richer.[26] If these findings hold true, they turn the table on past explanations of conflict and suggest that efforts to promote good government, economic development, and capacity building, including policing, could be successful strategies in war-torn countries. These findings also remove the aura of inevitability that tends to cloud some views of conflict.

Oftentimes, battles rage over which leader or group should rule a country. Such was the nature of the Chinese civil war from 1945 to 1949, which ended with Nationalist Party (Kuomintang [KMT]) forces fleeing to the island of Taiwan and the Chinese Communist Party proclaiming the People's Republic of China. Other civil wars are fought between rival leaders or groups. Colombia is a country that was torn apart by civil wars throughout much of the nineteenth century, waged between rival Liberal and Conservative Party leaders, guerrillas, drug traffickers, and other entrenched interests. The war in Colombia was launched in the mid-twentieth century by a conflict now referred to as La Violencia. This war initially started out as a street riot in Bogotá, following the assassination of a Liberal Party leader and candidate for president. It has worsened as Colombia's problems have mounted; there has been continued elite conflict over the future direction of the country, the deepening and professionalization of the drug trade and the concomitant development of a police force that rivals the military in many ways, and the development of paramilitary groups throughout the country. A war that began between two rival political parties has devolved into an ideological struggle including more than one group of Marxist-Leninist guerrillas, the military, narcotraffickers, and militias, with significant regional and international involvement. Colombia endured the longest-running insurgency in Latin America. Exhausted, the government and FARC finally struck a peace deal in 2016. Yet, to the surprise of many observers, a narrow majority of citizens voted down the peace agreement in a plebiscite, objecting to the leniency with which the accord treated the rebels. Colombia's president, Juan Manuel Santos (who was awarded the 2016 Nobel Peace Prize for his efforts), refused to give up on the deal. He renegotiated it to win additional concessions from FARC and sent it to Congress, which approved the deal. A historic domestic court, known as the Special Jurisdiction for Peace, began operating in 2018, revealing "explosive" findings that dramatically increase the victim counts from the conflict, assigning blame not only to FARC rebels but also to the Colombian military.[27]

From 1967 to 1970, a civil war was fought in Nigeria in which more than 1 million people died. The declaration of war was the culmination of a series of events, most immediately a pogrom directed against Ibos in the north. Led by Odumwegwu Ojukwu, the Ibo sought to create "Biafra," an independent and sovereign state carved out of their traditional home in Nigeria's southeast. However, for a variety of reasons, including concern over the loss of the substantial oil revenues coming from the region, the north and west combined forces to resist secession by all conceivable means. Biafra became Africa's most internationalized war in the 1960s, as the countries of the world lined up on one side or the other. When the much larger and better-equipped federal army found that it could not prevail against the Ibo forest fighters, it resorted to a policy aimed at starving the Ibo into submission. The blockade had devastating consequences, particularly on women and children. Although they eventually lost the war, the Ibo won international sympathy, as the Biafra conflict was considered by many to be a genocide led by the largely Islamic north against the Christian southeast.[28]

Guerrilla Warfare

The term "guerrilla," deriving from the Spanish word for "little war," refers to troops operating independently of state militaries, and often in opposition to them, following a relatively loose set of methods designed to deceive enemy forces and overcome deficiencies in equipment, force size, and location. In their attempt to damage the LEGITIMACY of a government, guerrilla forces target civilian populations for recruitment. Women soldiers have participated in this form of combat more than other types of warfare.[29] Additionally, there is often an extensive effort, through propaganda, terror, and policies, to win the support and fighting power of peasant populations. Guerrilla groups are known for setting up successful pilot projects, including schools and clinics, to provide services to groups often ignored by the state and to win their support.

In guerrilla warfare, conventional rules of engagement, especially concerning noncombatants, are largely ignored. Policies, both psychological and concrete, are designed to exhaust and demoralize the enemy while recruiting civilians through either fear or persuasion. Battles tend to center around long, protracted campaigns, often from a rural base. Guerrilla tactics are mobile, necessitated by their smaller troop sizes, and often rely on the element of surprise. Guerrilla fighters can often face a difficult transition in posture from rebel resister to governing decisionmaker or even legitimate soldier, as many Taliban fighters in the long-standing war in Afghanistan realized. After the withdrawal of US forces in the fall of 2021, guerrilla fighters within the Taliban missed the fighting, including the opportunity for martyrdom.[30]

Guerrilla tactics are often adopted by revolutionaries who perceive the unorthodox methods of fighting to be their only shot at victory. Examples include the Chinese civil war and revolution, Fidel Castro's 1959 revolution in Cuba, and Ho Chi Minh's battles against the Japanese, French, and later US troops in Vietnam. The modern Chinese state was founded largely upon the principles of guerrilla violence. Mao Zedong, the leader of China's 1949 revolution and one of the modern world's leading revolutionaries, was a man of contradictions. He was a poet and librarian, which is how he first encountered Marxist and Leninist theories about revolution. Mao came of age in a China that was on the brink of collapse, worn down by the imperial wars of the late 1800s, the infighting of the warlord period following the collapse of the Qing Dynasty, as well as the economic misery and political uncertainties that follow the end of an

Figure 10.2 Taiwan: "Renegade Province" or Independent State?

The controversy surrounding the status of Taiwan, just off the southeastern coast of China, demonstrates that in some ways the Chinese civil war of the 1940s still rages. After the Chinese Communists defeated the Chinese Nationalists in the fall of 1949, Chiang Kaishek and his supporters completed their transfer to Taiwan, much to the chagrin of the Indigenous population. (An uprising in 1947, prior to the complete arrival by the Nationalists, is believed to have claimed over 20,000 lives.) From their base in Taipei, the Nationalists pledged to "retake" mainland China, up until the death of Generalissimo Chiang in 1975. Major combat was averted largely by the positioning of the US Seventh Fleet in the Taiwan Straits, which separate the two lands. Owing to anticommunist sentiment in the 1950s and 1960s, most of the world, with the exception of France and later Great Britain, refused to recognize the newly minted Communist Party regime as the legitimate government of China—they recognized the Nationalist regime on Taiwan instead. This continued until the early 1970s, when Taiwan left the United Nations and most countries of the world completed normalization of relations with the People's Republic of China.

Both groups involved in the dispute purported at one time to support "one China," but the Nationalists and the Chinese Communist Party each viewed themselves as the legitimate government of all Chinese people. Taiwan currently maintains formal diplomatic ties with fourteen small states—half the number it held in the 1990s—and lacks formal representation in the United Nations.[a] Recent Taiwanese leaders, including the first directly elected president, Lee Teng-hui, and the two presidents from the pro-independence Democratic Progressive Party, Chen Shui-bian and Tsai Ing-wen, have challenged the traditional interpretation of "one China," in careful, but very intentional ways, much to the consternation of Beijing. Even during the strongest periods of cross-strait disagreement, however, trade links between China and Taiwan flourished: China is Taipei's largest trading partner. Public opinion is difficult to gauge, but most Taiwanese support maintaining the status quo, with only a fraction supporting unification of Taiwan with China (especially as Beijing increasingly curtails Hong Kong's liberties).[b]

From the perspective of Beijing, Taiwan's eventual reunification with the motherland remains a top priority, and CCP leaders have increased the sense of urgency in the region, as Xi Jinping declared Beijing's "unshakeable commitment" to reunification with Taiwan.[c] Many credit the maintenance of peace and stability in the region to the so-called strategic ambiguity that has persisted since the late 1970s; the United States provides Taiwan with defensive weapons, but leaves the question of whether it would formally defend Taiwan less clear. Others openly express concern that this era is rapidly coming to an end, and that the so-called Taiwan Temptation may tip the balance toward the CCP's favor.[d] US military leaders have warned that Beijing is increasing its threats to employ a "military option" against Taiwan, with one former Indo-Pacific commander stating that China could attempt to seize Taiwan by force by 2027.[e]

Notes: a. After the United Nations resolution expelling the Taiwanese delegation passed, George H. W. Bush, then the US ambassador to the United Nations, warned that the UN "crossed a very dangerous bridge" and expressed concern that the international body had made "a very serious mistake." Quoted in Shannon Tiezzi, "Taiwan and the UN: On the Outside Looking In," *The Diplomat,* October 25, 2021, pp. 55–61.

b. Lindsay Maizland, "Why China-Taiwan Relations Are So Tense," Council on Foreign Relations, May 10, 2021.

c. "CCP 100: Xi Warns China Will Not Be 'Oppressed' in Anniversary Speech," *BBC News,* July 1, 2021.

d. Oriana Skylar Mastro, "The Taiwan Temptation: Why Beijing Might Resort to Force," *Foreign Affairs* (July–August 2021).

e. Max Boot, "The Risk of a War over Taiwan Is Growing. Here's How to Deter Beijing," *Washington Post,* July 21, 2021.

EMPIRE. Although Mao was a relatively insignificant participant in the founding of the Chinese Communist Party in Shanghai in 1921, he grew to lead it throughout the revolutionary war with KMT forces, and was the man who proclaimed the beginning of the PRC in Tiananmen Square on October 1, 1949. Throughout the revolutionary war and in wars that followed the establishment of the PRC, Mao advocated a type of warfare known as "people's war," which combined guerrilla tactics with Mao's emphasis on China's "human factors," highlighting the importance of the MASSES and the need to motivate and organize them. Mao often stated that "if our hearts are pure, we will fight with the strength of 10,000 men." The so-called people's war of 1927 to 1949 combined elements of social revolution with a war for national SOVEREIGNTY. From its base in China's northern rural areas, the CCP successfully employed guerrilla tactics to conquer cities, win the support of the population, and reign victorious.

Proxy Wars

Another type of conflict, sometimes referred to as "warfare by substitutes," involves surrogate fighters who are recruited to fight battles that other, often more powerful groups do not want to get involved in directly. Such proxy wars, when outside actors advance their agenda by using local fighters, were especially common during the COLD WAR, when the United States and the Soviet Union acted as patrons for wars that were in their interest. The United States propped up anticommunist governments, including Indonesia, South Korea, South Vietnam, and Chile, while the Soviet Union did what it could to support Marxist-Leninist regimes throughout the world, including China (initially), North Korea, and North Vietnam. Recognizing that even the most powerful states or richest groups cannot afford to be in constant war with their enemies, these countries chose instead to support dissenters, separatists, and other potential clients of a rival to avoid mutual assured destruction. During the Cold War, proxy conflicts were used to avoid direct opposition between the superpowers.

The goal of this type of conflict is to wear down the enemy, weakening it by encouraging the waste of resources, without expending a tremendous amount of one's own resources or energy. Surrogate conflict can also include the assassination of political leaders or individuals. It often includes direct sabotage. In the early 1980s, for example, the United States "unofficially" provided support, buttressed by a special operations manual of the Central Intelligence Agency, to Nicaraguan Contra rebels who were fighting the leftist Sandinista government. Similar efforts were taken by the Soviet Union to encourage North Korea to attack South Korea in 1950.

Some turn to this substitute conflict as a way of improving their own image and to place some distance between themselves and the seemingly unsavory battles at hand. It has been argued that a group known as Islamic Jihad, an offshoot of the military wing of Hamas, was used as a proxy to carry out executions on behalf of the government of Iran, which attempted to improve its international image following its isolation during the 1980s.[31] In proxy conflict, nationals are involved usually in training and support, employing private armies in a country to put down revolutionary movements, assassinate critics of the regime, and maintain control. Fidel Castro's Cuba was relatively unusual in sending large numbers of soldiers abroad; since many of the fighters were nonwhite, they were welcomed in places that the Soviets and the East Europeans were not, including Ethiopia, Mozambique, and Angola.

Proxy wars permit the sponsoring agent to focus on "big picture" events and strategy, while others do the "grunt work" on the ground. For example, the early stages of the US-led war in Afghanistan in 2001 were viewed by many as a form of proxy war, using Northern Alliance and other anti-Taliban forces to do the dirty work, while the United States led the air campaign and provided intelligence. The long elusiveness of Osama bin Laden (who was captured and killed in May of 2011) was attributed to the use of Afghan, Pakistani, and other ground forces who likely succumbed to bribes from bin Laden's associates to permit him to escape the country. In a majority of proxy wars, there are often very real regional conflicts or domestic divisions at the heart, which are greatly amplified by the patronage of outsiders. As is discussed in Figure 10.3, the involvement of numerous external forces—many with conflicting agendas—has greatly amplified the nature of the ongoing conflict in Syria. Libya is another contemporary conflict with proxy elements involving Russia, Turkey, the United Kingdom, and the United States, among other external players.[32]

Behind the Disruption

So who is responsible for acts of violence? As you might imagine, there is great diversity in the types of individuals and groups who believe their use of destructive means is justified. In this section, we discuss some of the major types of groups involved in belligerent activities. The faces behind the disruption can be as diverse as the forms of violence that are employed. For example, even though men make up the majority of individuals who engage in terrorism, women have frequently joined terrorist groups. Some argue that participation in violent groups provides women a rare outlet for gender equality, an argument that is used to explain women's participation in terrorist organizations and revolutions.[33] Women also avoid detection, sometimes making the most of their status as privileged noncombatants. Other explanations include shaming men into action, increasing fear (by making both men and women suspects), and the need for greater numbers of participants, as the number of men in detention or under surveillance increases.[34]

In Peru's Shining Path (Sendero Luminoso), large numbers of women participated as equals in the group's apparatus, overcoming the subordinate role and status historically ascribed to them in Peruvian society. And some made it to top positions in the regional command and the National Central Committee, including Abimael Guzmán Reynoso's first wife, Augusta la Torre, who served as the second in command in the organization. (Guzmán's second wife, Elena Iparraguirre—known as Comrade Miriam—also exercised significant influence over the movement, for which she received a life sentence.) Women have served as suicide bombers for Boko Haram in Nigeria, and as combatants for the Kurdistan Workers Party (PKK) in Turkey, the Palestinian uprising (INTIFADA), and the Liberation Tigers of Tamil Eelam, along with an increasing number of other movements. It is believed that as many as one-fourth of Russian revolutionaries

Figure 10.3 Wars in Syria and Afghanistan

The Syrian civil war started as a protest movement in 2011, as part of the Arab Spring that swept North Africa and the Middle East. A number of grievances also contributed to the conflict, including the government's repressive response to what started as a peaceful protest, in addition to a record-setting drought that made preexisting challenges worse. Within months, a rebel army had formed with the intention of overthrowing the government led by Bashar al-Assad. The al-Assad family favored cronies mostly drawn from their own minority Alawite (a sect affiliated with Shia Islam) community. Meanwhile, the majority Sunni population, including the Kurds, were largely excluded from political and economic power. The al-Assad regime, intensely paranoid about what might happen if they ever lost power, refused significant reforms, relying instead on repression to put down challenges to their rule.

Just keeping tabs of who is fighting whom can be dizzying. The rebels, with different identities and ideologies, fractured into hundreds of competing groups, some moderate and others more extreme, including the Islamic State (see Figure 10.7) and affiliates of al-Qaeda. What started out as a civil war quickly descended into a multidimensional proxy war, with external actors picking sides and fighting out their own conflicts. US administrations claimed to support moderate rebels, but remained cautious about providing them with the lethal assistance they needed to fight al-Assad, over fears that the weaponry might fall into hands of jihadists. Meanwhile, Russia, Iran, and the Shiite militia Hezbollah came to the assistance of al-Assad with air strikes and ground troops. As al-Assad attempted to show the world a choice between his secular rule and a violent jihadi alternative, he released hundreds of convicted Islamist militants from prisons.[a]

Fearing that this was part of a larger Shia conspiracy, the Saudis and Gulf states came in to aid the Sunni rebels. So, Syria became a replay of the Cold War, with the United States and Russia backing opposite sides. Syria is also a battle for Islam, with Sunnis (Saudis) and Shia (Iran) facing each other down. Add Turkey to the mix; given its dislike of al-Assad, it supported the rebels (as long as they weren't Kurdish, given Turkey's own "Kurdish problem"). When former president Donald Trump ordered the surprise removal of 1,000 US troops supporting Kurdish fighters on the Syria-Turkey border in 2019, Turkey increased their military operation to create a "buffer zone," forcing hundreds of thousands of additional people to leave.[b] Adding to the mix, there's the Islamic State, whom everyone claims to be fighting. Even after most US troops withdrew, nearly 500 soldiers remain to protect eastern Syrian oil fields from falling into the hands of the Islamic State.

The result is what UN officials have called "a complete meltdown of humanity."[c] A formal cease-fire was signed in 2020, which has decreased violence in parts of Syria, but low-level conflict and turmoil remain. As of late 2021, the death toll is estimated at well over 500,000, and analysts were projecting years of instability.[d] More than half of Syria's population of 22 million has been forced from their homes, 6 million of them refugees. Those who remain live in a country that is divided and largely devastated.

Another conflict that existed formally for more than two decades—but, in actuality, closer to four—is Afghanistan. Launched in October 2001, in retaliation for the September 11 terrorist attacks, formal conflict spanned four US presidencies and became the longest war in American history. Former president George W. Bush initiated war against the Taliban, who had been leading the country since the Soviet withdrawal in 1989 after their failed nine-year occupation. Intelligence supported the claim that the Taliban, an Islamist movement and military organization funded largely through profits from illegal trade and trafficking, were harboring al-Qaeda leader Osama bin Laden, the main individual responsible for the September 11 terrorist attacks.[e] Bin Laden, who had aided Afghan mujahidin during the Soviet occupation, moved to Afghanistan after being expelled from Sudan in 1996—he was killed by US Navy SEALs in Pakistan in May 2011.

Even after the shift was made from conflict to reconstruction, way back in 2002, Afghanistan remained divided and insecure. "Major combat activity" was declared over in 2003,[f] yet the Tal-

continues

Figure 10.3 Continued

iban reemerged in 2006. Facing an increasingly unstable situation in 2009, President Barack Obama committed 17,000 US troops to Afghanistan, to complement the US and NATO forces in the country. Pledges by multiple US presidents to withdraw all troops were complicated by increasing attacks by terrorist organizations. Even as further attacks and air strikes continued, President Trump signed a peace agreement with the Taliban in February 2020, ensuring a full withdrawal of US and NATO troops in exchange for the promise of security from further attacks. The final evacuation of most troops and Western civilians, under President Joe Biden, was complicated by the unexpectedly rapid advance of Taliban forces across the country, with the final weeks of a formal Western presence on the ground chaotic, uncoordinated, and dangerous. The chaotic scenes were reminiscent of the US departure from Saigon a generation earlier.

It is estimated that approximately 171,000 Afghanis, including security forces, militants, and civilians, died in the NATO-led conflict that spanned two decades, along with more than 2,500 allied soldiers.[g] The UN reports that 6 million Afghanis have been displaced by the war and other sources of conflict and instability.[h] As this book goes to press, the Taliban are in control, but the situation is uneasy and unstable. Increasingly isolated, crises (political, economic, and social) are piling up, the Islamic State Khorasan is proving to be a formidable adversary, and the Taliban are out of money. As one observer put it, "The Taliban won the war in Afghanistan, and an economic crisis may be their prize," as they have lost nearly every source of funding available to them.[i]

The two wars, despite important differences, exhibit some challenging similarities. Even if Afghanistan lacks the chemical weapons attacks of Syria, both are proxy wars involving outside powers. The instability from these fragile states has fueled the largest migrant and refugee crisis facing the world. Both have shown the dangers of poor governance, corruption, and foreign entanglement, especially on the rise of insurgency and extremism. They have also demonstrated that wars may be easier to start than to end.

Notes: a. Rania Abouzeid, "The Jihad Next Door: The Syrian Roots of Iraq's Newest Civil War," *Politico,* June 23, 2014.

b. Zachary Laub, "Syria's Civil War: The Descent into Horror," Council on Foreign Relations, March 17, 2021.

c. Anne Barnard, "Battle over Aleppo Is Over, Russia Says, as Evacuation Deal Reached," *New York Times,* December 13, 2016.

d. "Why Has the Syrian War Lasted 10 Years?" *BBC News,* March 12, 2021.

e. Former president Bill Clinton ordered cruise missile strikes on al-Qaeda bases in Afghanistan and Sudan in August 1998, in retaliation for al-Qaeda attacks on US embassies in Kenya and Tanzania earlier that month. In February 1998, Osama bin Laden, Ayman al-Zawahiri, and other Islamist leaders had issued a *fatwa* condemning the stationing of US troops in Saudi Arabia, as well as US support for Israel.

f. Hannah Bloch, "A Look at Afghanistan's 40 Years of Crisis—from the Soviet War to Taliban Recapture," NPR, August 31, 2021.

g. Keith D. McGrew, "Afghanistan War," History.com, August 20, 2021.

h. "Afghanistan Refugee Crisis Explained," United Nations High Commission for Refugees (UNHCR), August 16, 2021.

i. Alexandra Stevenson, "Short on Money, Legal and Otherwise, the Taliban Face a Crisis," *New York Times,* September 2, 2021.

in 1917 were women.[35] It was a woman who was sent to assassinate India's prime minister, Rajiv Gandhi, in 1991. In 1970 one female Palestinian refugee, Leila Khaled, almost single-handedly hijacked a commercial plane, evacuating all passengers before she blew it up. Even in the famously patriarchal al-Qaeda, the glass ceiling was shattered when a woman dressed as a man sauntered into a meeting of military recruits and launched an explosion that killed five men and wounded at least thirty—thwarting the profile used by antiterrorist forces

Figure 10.4 Legality as a Tool of State Terror

Governments possess many means to craft seemingly "legal" means by which they can impose their will and limit opposition voices. Perceived troublemakers, for example, are often forced into exile: either to remote parts of the country, or outside of the state altogether. In China some dissidents have been released from prison, but they are provided a one-way ticket out of the country and often depart without being able to send notice to their families. Other countries place activists under house arrest in remote areas as a way of keeping them out of trouble. Iran, for example, confined former presidential candidates (and Green Movement leader) Mehdi Karroubi, Mir Hossein Mousavi, and Zahra Rahnavard, Mousavi's wife, to house arrest for more than a decade.[a]

Police brutality is another overt form of state violence; in Egypt, the police are widely detested as the country's worst human rights abusers. But Egyptian police are not unique; state actors in many countries brutalize populations with torture, disappearances, and extrajudicial executions as part of routine public policy. Amnesty International reports that in Rio de Janeiro in 2019, police killed 1,810 people, averaging 5 per day.[b]

Another formalized method of state violence is capital punishment. Although official statistics are lacking, it is believed that China annually executes more people than all of the rest of the world combined. As a supposed deterrent, many executions in China occur in public arenas, following sentencing rallies that are broadcast on television. Excluding China, nearly 90 percent of all executions in 2020 occurred in just four countries: Iran, Egypt, Iraq, and Saudi Arabia. Even during the Covid pandemic, Egypt tripled its report of annual executions (from 32 to at least 107) in 2020.[c] But half the world (108 countries) has abolished the death penalty.

Notes: a. "Iran's Rouhani Years: From Euphoria to Disappointment," *Agence France-Presse,* June 14, 2021.

b. Amnesty International, "Police Violence," n.d.

c. Amnesty International, "Death Penalty in 2020: Facts and Figures," April 21, 2021.

around the world to identify perpetrators.[36] The participation and leadership of women cannot be reduced to ideology or level of restrictions imposed on them. Observers note that some of the women emerging as jihadists throughout Europe are different than their predecessors who worked under the careful supervision of men—they are even a more "feminist type of jihadist," oftentimes converts who were turned back from attempts to enter Syria.[37]

Young people have also long been attracted to violence—often drawn to the idea of belonging to a meaningful group that provides direction and identity. Shining Path, born in a university setting, appealed especially to students. The most violent stages of China's Cultural Revolution employed the use of middle- and high school–aged "Red Guards" to terrorize those labeled enemies of the CCP and to foment revolutionary fervor throughout the country. In Zimbabwe, both the Zimbabwe African National Union (ZANU) and the Zimbabwe African People's Union (ZAPU) mobilized entire classrooms of children, who left with their teachers to train as guerrillas. Children—with an increasing focus on girls—are used as agents to carry out suicide attacks, including by Boko Haram and the Islamic State (and affiliates) in Nigeria, Indonesia, and throughout the Lake Chad basin.[38] Participants in the Palestinian intifada are believed to be particularly young (nearly 70 percent of Palestinians are under the age of

Figure 10.5 Exporting Repression

Throughout this book, we have attempted to highlight the positive and the negative impacts of globalization. One aspect of easier access to information and borders that highlights the underbelly of interdependence is the ease with which leaders can reach beyond their borders to capture individuals who challenge their regime or who have been accused of crimes, often perceived crimes against powerful leaders. While the practice of hiring agents to capture or kill enemies of the regime in other countries is not at all new, the scale with which some countries are employing these tactics is definitely picking up, in part aided by the internet and artificial intelligence tools that assist with long-distance surveillance, as well as an international climate that seems to facilitate these breeches. Some of the most egregious examples of harassment, detention, and even assassination have been the murder and dismemberment of journalist Jamal Khashoggi by Saudi agents in Istanbul, Russia's lethal poison attack against Alexander Litvinenko, and the sophisticated use of international networks to extradite enemies of the Chinese Communist Party back to Beijing.[a] The list of perpetrators is vast, including Turkey, Rwanda, Iran, and Egypt, in addition to Saudi Arabia and Russia.[b] According to Freedom House, the People's Republic of China is marked as the world's worst offender, with an elaborate and seemingly comprehensive global campaign of transnational repression, assisted by loopholes in international law and practice, in addition to changes in its own legal framework that cast a wider net over perceived violations of Chinese law beyond Chinese territory.[c] The Institute for Economics and Peace reports that the number of weapons imports per capita increased in 2021 in ninety-two countries, adding fuel to an already raging fire.[d]

Notes: a. "China: Transnational Repression Case Study," Freedom House, 2021.

b. "Repression Without Borders," *New York Times,* August 28, 2021.

c. Nate Schenkkan and Isabel Linzer, *Out of Sight, Not Out of Reach: Understanding Transnational Repression* (Washington, DC: Freedom House, February 2021).

d. Institute for Economics and Peace, *Global Peace Index 2021,* June 4, 2021, p. 12.

twenty-nine).[39] In Boko Haram, suicide bombers have been as young as seven years old, and it is estimated that roughly 20 percent of activists recruited by Boko Haram are children.[40] Youth have been active in arson attacks, hand-to-hand combat, sabotage, and suicide missions. Some postulate that their involvement can be explained by the lack of outside commitments that would limit their availability for activities, while others point to youths' propensity for risk-taking, their passion for causes, and their mobility.

Militaries and Militias

In any discussion of the major groups that sponsor violence as a means to achieve goals, we would be remiss if we excluded governments themselves. As sociologist Max Weber highlighted in his classic definition of the "state," one of the greatest powers of governments is their monopoly over the right to use force. This does not mean, of course, that states are the only groups that hold coercive power, nor does it imply that all use of government force is proper or legitimate, but it does accurately imply that governments tend to have the most organized, well-financed, and effective means of making their preferences known. By engaging forces in wartime combat, adopting domestic policies that include executions and punishment, and supporting abductions, assassinations, and forced relocations, it is clear that governments all around the world use violent means to achieve their ends.

As an institution of government, the state military wields tremendous power. Militaries consist of disciplined, organized, and well-funded groups of people with great influence: official armed units are used to implement key directives of governments, often using force. Militaries are found in almost every country of the world. The major exception is Costa Rica, which dissolved its military in the 1950s, even though it still has a small paramilitary force.

Young men under the age of twenty-six nearly exclusively carry out military acts. In World War I, women first donned military uniforms and received military ranking. Yet, today in Israel, Eritrea, North Korea, and Norway, both sexes are formally required to enroll in military service, and increasingly women participate in noncompulsory military training and combat as well. Kurdish militias in Syria have separate Women's Protection Units, known as the Y.P.J., that serve as equal partners with men's units in combat.[41] Just as it is wrong to assume that all women are mothers, it is also a mistake to think that all mothers are peaceniks and opposed to the use of violence to effect change. African women trained with men and fought alongside them in Zimbabwe's war for liberation. In the mid-1970s approximately one-third of the soldiers fighting for ZANU were women, and some of these women held positions of authority over men. In addition, civilian women provided assistance to the guerrillas as their way of fighting. They cooked for the rebels, and because for a while at least women could better avoid the attention of Rhodesian soldiers, they sometimes disguised their bundles as babies and smuggled supplies to guerrilla bases. Just as women participated in the war effort in various ways, so too did they have different expectations about what the coming change should mean for them.

Although it is notoriously difficult to measure and verify, trends seem to indicate an increased toll of warfare on noncombatants.[42] The Costs of War Project at Brown University estimates the toll to be particularly high in Iraq, where they report 68 percent of total deaths as civilian, with 36 percent each in Pakistan and Syria.[43] Some of this can be attributed to the "civilianization" of war and the rising use of improvised explosive devices, as noncombatants are increasingly targeted for attack or are innocently caught in the cross fire. In Afghanistan, the civilian death toll skyrocketed by nearly 50 percent in the first months of 2021, as more women and children were killed and wounded than at any other time since systematic reporting began in 2009, according to a UN report.[44] Counting deaths in the war in Syria has been riddled with difficulties, so much so that the UN officially stopped counting deaths in the conflict in 2014—it resumed counting in 2021 only after the United Nations Human Rights Council requested it.[45] The use of both drones and cluster bombs—which have been under an international ban since 2010 for the indiscriminate nature of killing—tell only part of the story.[46] Suicide attacks on hospitals, schools, and other civilian targets add to the misery of these (literal and figurative) battles.[47]

Another development of modern warfare is the inclusion of large numbers of children as active protagonists of warfare, formally and informally. Although difficult to track, the UN estimates that between 2005 and 2020, more than 93,000 children (defined as any person under eighteen years of age) were parties to conflict, although they also state that the true number of "child soldiers" is much higher.[48] The trend is alarming: the number of children formally recruited by armed forces rose from just over 600 in 2018 to nearly 8,000 in 2019, with over 3,100 children recruited in the Democratic Republic of Congo alone.[49] Most child soldiers are between the ages of fifteen and eighteen; some have been as young as six.[50] One expert on the topic claims that child soldiers serve in almost 75 percent of the world's conflicts.[51] The presence of children in combat has become a critical problem in Africa and Asia, although youth are used as soldiers, porters, cooks, messengers, checkpoint guards, sexual slaves, and spies throughout the world. Because of their agility and fearlessness, children have also been employed to do much of the more dangerous work in battle zones, including mine-clearing operations. Not surprisingly, poverty and perpetual cycles of conflict are viewed as some of the main conditions affecting the increase of child soldiers, although the influence of teachers, family, friends, local politics, and culture all play a role as well.[52] The largest numbers of child soldiers are found in the DRC, Somalia, Syria, and Yemen.[53]

Even if they are not formal "soldiers" per se, children have been combatants in some of the world's bloodiest conflicts. In the Palestinian uprising, for example, children have been active agitators against Israeli forces, throwing stones and sabotaging units, and they have paid dearly, often with their lives. Some children are forced to take up arms, but others are given little choice in the face of poverty, discrimination, and the pressure to conscript. Pregnancy, often the outcome of gang rape by comrade or enemy soldiers, isn't enough to keep young girls out of combat, either. Young girls have been used as suicide bombers in Sri Lanka and Lebanon, and many girls are allocated to soldiers as rewards, as "wives." In Uganda, children have been forced to brutally beat other children to death, their victims lying face down on the ground, with arms and legs restrained.[54]

Young soldiers receive little or no training. In warfare, children are also subjected to severe punishment, sometimes even harsher than what adults would receive. There have also been reports of widespread juvenile disappearance, extrajudicial execution, and torture. Perhaps because they have a less developed sense of right and wrong, children (in some places known as the "lost generation") are said to commit the worst atrocities. Drugs are also used to make children effective killers. Children want approval, and sometimes they find acceptance in the most violent groups. Often, child soldiers are orphans, who together with street children are particularly vulnerable to recruitment and desperately eager to please adults (even if the adult is responsible for them being orphaned). Most have been traumatized themselves, as witnesses to murder of their families, and are sometimes even forced to participate in ritualized killings. The Revolutionary United Front (RUF) in Sierra Leone, for example, trained its child soldiers by ordering them to kill other children, or even their own parents, or someone they knew so that they wouldn't fear death or try to escape.

Not surprisingly, the insecurities of the Covid pandemic have worsened the reality for many children around the world, increasing the likelihood that children will be recruited to join armed forces and militia groups, as well as worsening the chances of prior child soldiers being able to participate in reintegration programs or other forms of systematic support as they leave combat.[55]

In Figure 10.6, we present comparative data on militaries in the global south. While we believe this information is a useful starting point, we urge you to consider that countries are notorious for underreporting the size of their formal military force strength, as well as the amount of budgetary resources committed to the military. One way that governments get around full reporting of their troop strength is by creating paramilitaries and other semimilitary units that are not counted in the official troop total. For example, the PRC, which has undertaken dramatic formal troop reductions since the mid-1990s, does not include the approximately 1.5 million members of the People's Armed Police (PAP) in its official troop count. After the foundation of the Islamic Republic of Iran in 1979, clerical leaders called for a standard military to protect the country's borders and maintain internal order, as well as a separate Revolutionary Guard, known as the Pasdaran, to protect the Islamic character of the system. The Revolutionary Guard has fewer troops compared to the regular military, yet is considered the dominant military force and the backbone of major operations. It controls the paramilitary Basij Resistance force, a volunteer military of approximately 90,000 men and women who, as loyalists to the 1979 revolution, are used to brutally dispel dissent. This ambiguity is one reason why the CIA, in its World Factbook, reports the portion of the population available for military service and the portion fit for military service, rather than actual troop numbers.

Figure 10.6 Militaries in the Global South, 2019

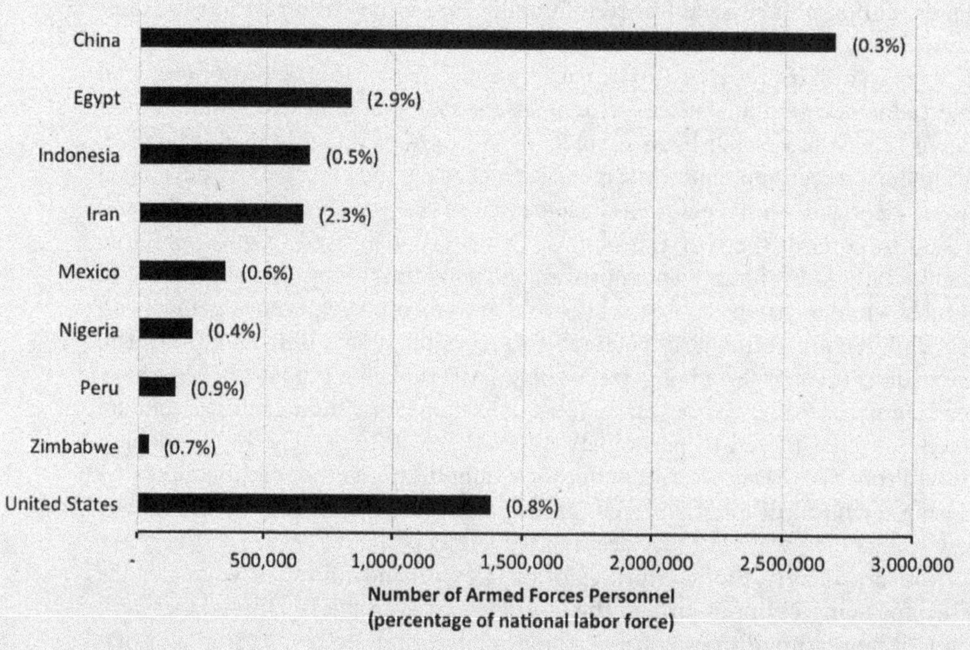

Source: World Bank, *DataBank*, 2021.

As you can see, despite the fact that China has the world's largest standing army by far, its official military accounts for only a fraction of the labor force, whereas Egypt and Iran each show a larger percentage of the overall labor force enlisted in the armed forces.

Despite relatively generous expenditures for militaries—when compared to spending for healthcare and education, for example—soldiers in the global south tend to be compensated poorly. It is common for soldiers to seek second or third jobs to support themselves. As a result, it is common for groups to turn to extortion at roadblocks, kidnapping, bribery, and other malfeasance to supplement their income. In Lebanon, where the army faced intense criticism for its handling of citizen protests, soldiers often leave the military to join independently armed paramilitary groups that offer better pay and benefits.[56] Nigerian police have their hands full attempting to rein in Boko Haram, for example, yet their official military pay, held low by decades of underfunding, renders many soldiers homeless.[57] These realities leave soldiers open to bribery or desertion, and do not help promote stability within the armed forces.

The declared goal of the modern military is to provide defense and security for a country. Civilian leadership over the military is recognized as a common value in the world today. In this model, the military is simply one of many interest groups lobbying for its own priorities. This norm is known as civilian rule, which has been violated in many countries, and not only in the global south. So-called professional militaries act on the authority of governments and possess restricted powers to challenge civilian political leadership. They develop particularized areas of expertise, such as challenging external enemies, and keep out of areas beyond their purview, such as political infighting. No military is completely professional in this sense, but we can observe varying degrees of professionalism using this metric.

The polar opposite of this civil-military duality—military rule—often begins when elements within the military sense a crisis. The manifestations of this perceived crisis are varied, but can include societal cleavages, leadership controversies, economic malaise, tensions within the military itself, defeat in war, contagion effects from neighboring countries, external intervention, personality conflicts between the military leadership and political leaders, or simply an easy power grab.[58] In the interest of providing stability, the argument goes, a disciplined, professional military would often be the best candidate to lead an interim transition. Unfortunately, in many situations the perceived "crisis" lasts longer than most civilian leaders originally envision and the so-called transition becomes standard operating procedure. Chile, for example, experienced military rule for eighteen years; Nigeria operated as a military dictatorship from 1966 to 1999 (with a brief break from 1979 to 1983). Military rule is often precipitated by a government overthrow, or a coup d'état, when the governmental leader or part of the leadership is replaced by violence or threat. After a coup, which is usually quick, the military government is often referred to as a junta, or council. Military commanders have then been known to take control of schools, train new soldiers in their own doctrine, and take elaborate measures to silence the masses.

Military coups and military rule have been a common occurrence in the global south. In Iran, the 1921 coup ushered in a "new order," only to be followed by another coup in 1935. Sometimes coups are initially welcomed by the population, like the Nigerian coup against corruption, fraud, and economic mismanagement in 1983. Many people applauded the military as saviors of the country. Some coups appear to be contagious, following one after the other. Nigeria experienced several military coups postindependence. Myanmar experienced a coup of its democratically elected leadership in early 2021, just as a newly elected parliament was preparing to be seated, in what US Secretary of State Antony Blinken called a "reign of terror."[59] Coups are not necessarily violent—in fact many are bloodless, although a particularly brutal coup occurred in Chile in 1973, in which at least 2,000 people died. Nearly 300 died in a failed coup in Turkey in 2016 and thousands have been detained, accused of supporting it.

Even in the absence of outright military rule, there are circumstances when militaries wield a tremendous amount of influence, even in the selection of the prime minister or other executives of government. Such persuasion is often made in threats not to support or protect a leader if she or he violates the wishes of the military. The term PRAETORIANISM is used to characterize states where civilian authorities face such intimidation. Some more simply call it blackmail. The concept derives from the praetorian guards who protected the Roman emperor. Often they would threaten to withdraw their crucial support if they did not get to choose who would be in power. Similarly, through their threats of vetoes and departure, militaries can shape policy.

Unlike most of its neighbors, Mexico has succeeded in establishing an unwritten deal between civilian and military leaders, as long as the military polices itself for human rights abuses and stays out of politics. This reality has held true even as the politicization and expanded power of the Mexican military, begun under former President Felipe Calderón, continues to deepen.[60] However, Mexico had a long tradition of military intervention in politics; much of the nineteenth century was known as the age of *CAUDILLOS*. After the Mexican Revolution, several military figures vied for power. From 1917 through the 1930s, citizen-soldiers ruled, as all of Mexico's presidents during that period had started their careers as officers in the revolutionary army. The military continued to play an important role in the Institutional Revolutionary Party (PRI) and, therefore, the government throughout the 1930s. In the early 1940s, President Lázaro Cárdenas began to demilitarize politics by dramatically reducing military expenditures and limiting the military's representation in the party. Since 1943, candidates for president have been automatically disqualified if they have a military background. Over time, the military has largely stayed in the barracks in Mexico and, unlike armed forces elsewhere, the Mexican military has not exploited periods of crisis to expand its influence. Although it has grown in power in recent years, until recently most analysts have not considered the military in Mexico to be an independent political "wild card" in the way that it is in other countries. Even given their increased visibility and enhanced role in domestic security, few fear a military coup—but an outright coup may not be necessary to hold power.[61]

In many countries of the global south, militaries have a mixed record of achievements and failures. They have been good at providing order and economic growth. Yet, they have also racked up a miserable record of human rights protection, especially in circumstances where they rule outright or where they are temporarily installed as an interim government. Some military regimes are characterized as caretaker governments, preoccupied with law and order and less concerned with implementing social changes. Corrective military regimes attempt to create a national identity and promote orderly economic development. Revolutionary military regimes promote the most radical changes of all, highlighting dramatic land reform that is never fully implemented.

Rape has been used as a deliberate military tactic, especially within the strategy of ethnic cleansing, but in other forms of violent warfare as well. It has been common in the wars in Syria, Ethiopia, South Sudan, and Colombia, among other countries. Women and girls are frequently victims of gang rape committed by soldiers and militias. The Khomeini regime in Iran set up so-called residential units to suppress female dissidents. The elite Revolutionary Guard used these outposts to continuously rape women who refused to submit to the regime.[62] Thousands of women and young girls were violated in what was once known as "the rape capital of the world," the Democratic Republic of Congo; years later, the international NONGOVERNMENTAL ORGANIZATION Doctors Without Borders (MSF) contends that thousands still need "serious care" in response to the systematic violence they face.[63] In Ethiopia, women and girls in refugee camps have been particularly targeted, while others report violent assaults in exchange for basic supplies in the midst of a debilitating civil war.[64] Others have documented being held captive for days or weeks, while being assaulted by multiple men (often soldiers) at a time, some with nails, gravel, and shrapnel being inserted into their body parts.[65] In many conflicts around the world, rape has also been used as a form of genocide, as male soldiers and paramilitaries have been ordered to impregnate "enemy" women. Sexual assault has long been part of a purposive strategy, as in Syria, to sever women's ties to the community and to strip them of their dignity and pride. It often leads to the complete ostracism of these women. In China's detention camps in Xinjiang province, Uighur women have experienced not only forced sterilization and torture, but also repeated, systematically organized gang rape (by police as well as paying citizens) while in confinement.[66] These trends highlight the sexualization of war (or conflict in general) in the modern world, including the development of sexual terrorism.

In some countries, regular military units are declining in numbers, prestige, and the support they receive. Some cannot escape their tarnished reputation; others appear to be bureaucratic beasts lumbering over sick economies. They are being replaced, especially in areas of conflict, by paramilitary units—relatively autonomous armed groups often in charge of security for an individual person, political party, or institution. To avoid the stigma of the appearance of military rule, some governments are turning to civilian militias to handle their security tasks. These can sometimes be virtual death squads, as we have seen in Rwanda, East Timor, and elsewhere. Their funding comes from the government (although often through covert channels) and they usually report directly to military officials. In some cases, including Colombia, paramilitaries comprise off-duty soldiers and police hoping to pocket some extra cash. Paramilitary units are often launched in an attempt by governments to wash their hands of violent acts. In Mexico, anti-crime self-defense forces started forming in 2011 in response to the violence unleashed by the cartels and the government's war on drugs. The militias act as vigilantes and are known for arresting people they accuse of working for criminal groups, holding their own court trials, and meting out sentences. In recent years many of them have expanded and become known for increasingly questionable behavior, such as extortion as well as kidnapping and brutalizing police and soldiers and seizing police stations and weapons. The government has attempted to fold them into the police structures, but it has not been able to control the militias, or enforce the rules, thus the militias further weaken the rule of law in Mexico.[67] Other militias work more closely with the government. In the early 1980s, China created the People's Armed Police, a unit that surged in growth after the crackdown on students in Tiananmen Square in 1989. The PAP, unlike the regular police force in China, is fully armed—it guards government offices, patrols borders, and quells riots and uprisings.

The point is that the power of military units can become extremely dangerous in transitional circumstances, such as after the fall of powerful leaders or a change in power, as rogue groups, still possessing weaponry and the desire for influence, attempt to maintain their power and voice. In Indonesia, a paramilitary group formed from former police cadets who failed the four-year officer course. Some believe that this unit—named Gunung Tidur—was responsible for a fatal series of fires during the May 1998 riots that led to Suharto's downfall.[68] Similar episodes have been reported in Tajikistan, Nigeria, and elsewhere. The Islamic Republic of Iran supports a variety of militia groups that help expand its influence throughout the region.[69]

In addition to traditional government militaries and militia groups, privately employed soldiers play an important role in wars in the global south. Mercenaries are as old as war itself, but in today's world their recruitment, deployment, and action involve a multimillion-dollar business. Often, these soldiers-for-hire travel from country to country to earn a financial profit. For example, Serb and Ukrainian soldiers trained fighters in the Democratic Republic of Congo. In fact, foreign mercenaries fueled both sides of the conflict in the DRC. There and in Angola, over eighty companies were used to funnel soldiers into the battlefield. The most famous is the South African–based company Executive Outcomes, which was resurrected in 2020, that grew famous for providing fighters in Angola and Sierra Leone to guard mines that were the source of so-called conflict diamonds (illegally mined jewels used to funnel profits to militia groups). In Colombia, British Petroleum hired a battalion of soldiers to protect its interests, and mercenaries have been hired to protect Firestone's rubber plants as well. The Wagner Group, affiliated with the Russian government, emerged first in Ukraine and has since been active in Syria, Mozambique, Sudan, and Central African Republic; it is known for its secrecy as well as its flagrant disregard for international norms of conflict.[70] Mercenary conflict is widespread in Libya, Yemen, Nigeria, Ukraine, Syria, and Iraq. One analyst contends that "the Middle East is awash in mercenaries" from Kurdistan to the United Arab Emirates.[71] Hardened soldiers from around the world sell their services to the highest bidder, fighting not for patriotism, but for profit. Soldiers are hired by legitimate governments, terrorist cells, and even nongovernmental organizations.[72]

Governments may possess a monopoly over the right to use force—which states use to change circumstances and to promote the status quo—but by no means are they the only promoters of violent change. We now turn our attention to some other groups that advocate or promote aggression to achieve their cause.

Terrorists

Who are terrorists? In the mid-1970s, terrorist expert Frederick Hacker argued that terrorists are usually characterized as criminals, crazies, or crusaders, and that sometimes they are characterized as all three.[73] As discussed at the beginning of this chapter, labeling individuals or groups as "terrorists" can be fraught with difficulty and inaccuracies. Why do people turn to tactics that target civilians? Some trace it to feelings of hopelessness, or the belief that there is no other avenue through which people can express their opinions. Terrorism often involves groups who are struggling for resources. In fact, it has been argued that terrorism takes place because modern war, which requires large militaries, advanced weaponry, and the like, has become a luxury tool of rich countries. All in all, terrorism can be a monetarily cheaper alternative to conventional warfare and, yet, due to its ability to foster fear and insecurity, it can be extremely effective in achieving political objectives. Many different types of terrorist groups can be identified. Terrorists may be associated with political revolutionary movements (including the famed "Carlos the Jackal"), national liberation (or separatist) causes (e.g., the Philippines' Abu Sayyaf and Sri Lanka's Tamil Tigers), or single-issue campaigns (e.g., the Animal Liberation Front). Such groups are found along all points of the ideological spectrum, but tend to congregate especially on the extreme left (e.g., Peru's Shining Path) and the extreme right (e.g., al-Qaeda).

Terrorist violence is used in many kinds of political activity. Some distinguish forms of terror by categorizing the targets of such activity. Domestic terrorism involves acts that are based in a single country without significant support from outside sources. Actions by the Free Aceh movement in Indonesia would qualify as ethnonationalist domestic terrorism. The Philippines has several domestic Islamist groups that are especially active in the southern regions of the country, including Abu Sayyaf, famous for kidnappings, bombings, and even a plot to assassinate a sitting president.

In contrast, international terrorism includes terror activity that is not limited to one state. For example, an extremely well-coordinated and sophisticated attack in Mumbai in November 2008 left at least 160 people dead, with more than 300 injured. This attack, a siege throughout India's second-largest city that lasted three days, was coordinated by Lashkar-e-Taiba, one of the largest Islamist terrorist organizations in southern Asia, based in Pakistan. The attackers, most of whom were in their early twenties, arrived in Mumbai on inflatable speedboats, armed with Kalashnikovs, hand grenades, and bombs, and proceeded to launch attacks in restaurants, taxis, luxury hotels, a train station, and a Jewish center in Mumbai. The attacks were surprising in their scope and their preparation: planners used Google Earth to orchestrate their carnage, which was documented in terrifying detail via social networking sites around the world.[74] One gunman had been instructed by his handler: "Everything is being recorded by the media. Inflict maximum damage. Keep fighting. Don't be taken alive."[75] Only one gunman, Ajmal Kasab, survived, and he was sentenced to death in May 2010.

Figure 10.7 Islamic State

Born of war, feeding off of conflict, and aiming to usher in apocalyptic "end times," the Islamic State has become one of the most violent and visible terrorist groups to develop in recent years. As a jihadist extremist Sunni group known for devastating brutality (including mass killings and public beheadings, the images of which are then splashed over the internet), the Islamic State grew out of the war in Iraq (2003–2011), when an al-Qaeda branch in Iraq formed an umbrella organization known as the Islamic State in Iraq and al-Sham,[a] also known as ISIS. In 2013, its activists joined the rebellion against Bashar al-Assad in Syria and a year later, after successfully overrunning Mosul in northern Iraq, its leaders declared a caliphate (or, a state governed by sharia law that is led by a caliph, or "God's deputy on earth"),[b] announcing the formation of the Islamic State. With access to substantial wealth, the Islamic State terrorized its perceived enemies—Muslim and non-Muslim alike. This caused it to lose much support, even from other committed terrorists, including al-Qaeda leaders who disavowed the Islamic State in February of 2014 over its attacks against other Muslims.[c]

In 2015, another branch of the Islamic State formed, again out of war—this time, the allied war in Afghanistan that was launched in October 2001 as retaliation for the September 11 attacks. This group, formally known as Islamic State Khorasan (IS-K), consisted initially of disaffected Taliban members from Pakistan, who believed the Taliban were too moderate in their actions. IS-K claimed responsibility for the horrific suicide bombing at Kabul airport as US forces were withdrawing from Afghanistan in the fall of 2021, killing 170 Afghan civilians and 13 US troops. Shortly after the Taliban takeover of Kabul in August 2021, IS-K denounced the Taliban for being insufficiently hard-line (and were especially critical of their negotiations with former US president Donald Trump).[d] IS-K accused Taliban leaders of apostacy for their perceived abandoning of jihad, a branding that makes their killing lawful under Islamic State Khorasan's interpretation of Islamic law.[e] Colin Kahl, US undersecretary of defense for policy, has described IS-K as a "mortal enemy" of the Taliban.[f] Their mere existence, let alone growth, raises the specter of Afghanistan once again becoming a safe haven for terrorists.

A powerful IS affiliate has formed in Nigeria as well. The Islamic State West Africa Province (ISWAP), concentrated in northeast Nigeria near Lake Chad and in border zones of Niger and Cameroon, has captured multiple military bases and built its arsenal by forcibly taxing local residents. Analysts contend it has surpassed Boko Haram, both in numbers and capacity, and is now viewed as the strongest jihadist group in Nigeria as well as one of the Islamic State's most active affiliates.[g]

Notes: a. Bilad al-Sham roughly translates as "land on the left hand," referring to an area sometimes known as "Greater Syria."

b. "What Is 'Islamic State'?" *BBC News,* December 2, 2015.

c. Ibid.

d. Azi Paybarah, "What Is Islamic State Khorasan, a.k.a. ISIS-K?" *New York Times,* August 27, 2021.

e. Frank Gardner, "Afghanistan: Who Are Islamic State Khorasan Province Militants?" *BBC News,* October 11, 2021.

f. Karen DeYoung, "Defense Officials, Lacking a Base Near Afghanistan, Warn of Terrorist Threat," *Washington Post,* October 27, 2021.

g. Tomás F. Husted, "Boko Haram and the Islamic State's West Africa Province," Congressional Research Service, March 26, 2021; "Nigeria Says Iswap Leader Abu Musab al-Barnawi Is Dead," *BBC News,* October 14, 2021.

The deep pockets of international terror networks reach into many different societies as a way of evading detection—transferring funds through the use of promissory notes or other underground methods that require minimal paperwork and are therefore difficult to trace. But it's not all about unmarked Swiss bank accounts. One arrangement is a centuries-old system known as *hawala*—which is Hindi for "in trust." This system allows people working in one country to deposit payments (often in currency or gold) at a local office so that a third party can have virtually instantaneous access to the money in another country in a paperless transaction conducted through phone calls and emails. Some have described this as the Western Union of the non-Western world, updated to include social media networks like WhatsApp to facilitate transactions.[76] Originating in South Asia, *hawala* offices are found throughout the Middle East, northern Africa, and Asia, and they are the primary transmission source for sending and receiving remittances. Even though the vast majority of *hawala* transactions are completely legitimate, some banks operating under this system have been accused of funneling profits from customers' fees to terrorist leaders, including Osama bin Laden and other high-ranking members of al-Qaeda, even though the 9/11 Commission confirmed in the latter case that funds were transferred by interbank wire rather than through the *hawala* system.[77] In fact, *hawala* networks have been extremely important in providing financial services and humanitarian aid through nongovernmental organizations in Afghanistan, as less than one in six Afghans have bank accounts (one in twenty-five women) and formal banks are sparse at best.[78]

Another source of creative financing for illicit activities draws on the relationship between drug cartels and terrorist organizations, dating back to the 1970s. Terrorist groups rely on the sale of illicit drugs, especially opium, to finance their operations.[79] Terrorist groups throughout Latin America offer protection to local peasants and coca growers, particularly in certain remote regions where coca production can go largely undetected. Taxes on coca growers and levies on traffickers' flights out of the region, as well as unauthorized sales of timber and gold mining, can be lucrative sources of revenue.

Prior to September 2001, few Americans had heard of al-Qaeda (meaning "The Base"), even though many were familiar with the name of its leader, Saudi fugitive Osama bin Laden. Al-Qaeda, formed in 1988, is a deeply embedded international network of terrorists based in many countries; it supports extremist Sunni Muslim fighters in conflicts around the world, including Chechnya, Tajikistan, Kashmir, and Yemen. But as we have learned, many al-Qaeda operatives live and work elsewhere. Some of the stated goals of this network include the overthrow of nearly all conservative Muslim governments, to be replaced by a more virulent form of Islamic governance, and the expulsion of Western influence from the Muslim world, especially the US presence in Saudi Arabia. Even though al-Qaeda members often mention freedom for the Palestinians in their rhetoric, this seems to always take a back seat to their other concerns. In addition to funding its own terrorist activities, al-Qaeda is believed to be the premier funding source for Islamic extremist activities in the world. In 1996, bin Laden publicly issued his "Declaration of War" against the United States, which he and other members of al-Qaeda view as the chief obstacle to change in Muslim societies. The organization wavered after bin Laden's death at the hands of US Navy SEALs in May 2011, and, even as it is likely to continue to present challenges to the Taliban as they attempt to govern Afghanistan, most analysts contend that it is "no longer the force it once was," with the likelihood of it returning to "global prominence as an Afghanistan-based terrorist movement far from guaranteed."[80] Even if al-Qaeda's stature remains unsure, insecurities in

Syria, Iraq, and elsewhere provide oxygen to terrorist organizations—large and small—to regroup and act.

Terrorist groups combine multiple grievances to craft their own unique expression of rage against the status quo. These groups often present a combination of ideologies and demands and then fit their actions to their strengths and circumstances. For example, for years Uganda's Lord's Resistance Army (LRA), formed in the 1980s, was the deadliest militia in Africa. The group was initially led by Alice Lakwena, and later by her cousin, Joseph Kony, a former Catholic choirboy who is said to be possessed by spirits. LRA leaders promoted the proliferation of gangs, murderers, rapists, and sheer terror, especially in northern Uganda, recruiting thousands of child soldiers for their terror. For nearly two decades, from 1987 to 2006, they fought the Ugandan army, telling young recruits to smear botanical shea butter on their bodies to repel bullets and to sing Christian hymns as they marched straight toward the enemy. After suppression by the Ugandan army, Lakwena fled to Kenya, where she died in 2007. The LRA aimed to re-create the Kingdom of God and establish a state based on the Ten Commandments. In addition to Christian precepts, the group incorporated aspects of Indigenous religions and minor tenets of Islam—Kony announced that Fridays would be a second sabbath, largely as a way to appease his financial sponsors in Khartoum, Sudan (a majority Muslim state where Friday is observed as the sabbath day). This sponsorship was largely designed to counter Uganda's support of separatists in southern Sudan. Some of the LRA's more unusual tenets, though, including bans on eating the meat of white-feathered chickens and riding bicycles—a primary form of transportation in Uganda—cannot accurately be traced to any of these belief systems. Kony claims that he is instructed by God, and that the LRA is strict about enforcement: one man was killed for violating the bicycle ban, and LRA soldiers forced the dead man's wife to eat one of his feet or be killed. LRA agents are famous for abducting young teens—as many as 25,000 young girls and boys, according to the United Nations.[81] In 2005 the International Criminal Court (ICC) issued arrest warrants, on charges including twelve counts of crimes against humanity, for Joseph Kony and four LRA associates. These were the first warrants issued by the ICC since its establishment (in 2002). As of early 2022, Kony remains at large, with the United States and Uganda having called off the search for the fugitive warlord.

Even though terrorism by independent groups is most common, terrorist methods are also advocated by clandestine agents of governments, through government-sponsored or -supported groups designed to intimidate and repress individuals and groups within society. They often use death squads to threaten and eliminate their enemies. Although states risk being ostracized by the international community by engaging in terrorist acts, this is a gamble that some are willing to take. Increasingly, even if groups are not acting on the orders of a government, they are acting with its support (ideologically and often financially), giving rise to the term "state-sponsored terrorism." Because of the passion that groups are able to incite for their causes, attempts to isolate state-sponsored terrorists have been incomplete at best.

There is a growing list of known governments that are active in supporting groups beyond their shores: the usual suspects include Iran, Cuba, North Korea,

Figure 10.8 The Israeli-Palestinian Conflict

Perhaps few struggles are more enduring than the ongoing conflict between Arab Palestinians and the Israeli government. This dispute has been the source of five major wars, and has contributed to numerous other regional upheavals, claiming thousands of lives—including children, teenagers, and entire families. The outbreak of conflict, especially following the 1967 Six-Day War, has displaced millions of Palestinians, scattering them across multiple states and refugee centers in the region. Terrorist violence has marred all sides in this clash, rife with border disputes, intense religious symbolism, and security concerns. It seems that no one's hands are clean—but each side claims it has been provoked by the other, and both the Israeli government and the Palestinian Authority claim that the injustices of the situation make it difficult for them to control those under their rule. In fact, one of the dangerous turns in the dispute has been the willingness of individuals to take actions into their own hands, sometimes wrapping themselves in nail-studded explosives and taking their own lives—along with the lives of many others—in crowded urban areas. In 2002, Wafa Idris, a volunteer medic with the Palestine Red Crescent Society, was identified as the first female suicide bomber to attack Israel within its borders (she has since been followed by several more). While police attacks and the bulldozing of homes have been commonplace on the Israeli side, suicide bombings have proven to be a weapon of choice for some Palestinians.

Shortly after the death of former Palestinian Authority leader Yasser Arafat in 2004, Mahmoud Abbas was elected president of the Palestinian Authority. As the Palestinian Authority increased its level of institutionalization, a surprise parliamentary victory was won by Hamas, the Palestinian Sunni Islamist organization famous for its comprehensive Palestinian welfare programs, as well as its controversial charter that calls for the destruction of the state of Israel. Following its victory, the United States, the European Union, and Israel imposed an economically crippling response that cut all fund transfers and tax receipts. The controversy only emboldened Hamas and its supporters and made many question the West's hypocritical response to a democratically elected government. Following a World Bank report that documented the devastating effects of these measures, monies were again channeled to the Palestinian people through elaborate means that bypassed the Palestinian Authority. Yet, a significant schism between President Abbas (whose base is in the West Bank) and Hamas (who remain in control of the Gaza Strip) has presented an impasse for international negotiations, which remain deadlocked over the fundamental issues of borders, security, settlements, and the status of Jerusalem, the city claimed as a holy city to three major world religions: Christianity, Islam, and Judaism. After years without significant conflict, an Israeli raid on the Al-Aqsa Mosque at the beginning of the Muslim holy month of Ramadan in 2021 reignited conflict that was born of years of blockades, occupation, and discrimination.[a]

Note: a. Patrick Kingsley, "After Years of Quiet, Israeli-Palestinian Conflict Exploded. Why Now?" *New York Times,* May 15, 2021.

and Syria. Cuba, Yemen, and North Korea have been accused of providing safe haven to hunted terrorists. With the insecurity that follows in the wake of terror attacks, it is tempting to divide the world in two, placing countries that cooperate with the US-led global war on terrorism on one side and those that do not on the other. As we discuss in Chapter 17, the BUSH DOCTRINE implicated any country that supports terrorists as being terrorists themselves. Such seeming clarity, though, can be misleading. True, there are some countries that invoke sovereignty—the right to control what happens within one's borders—and argue that they will not cooperate in this war on terror, which they claim is just another attempt by the United States to impose its will on others. Yet, there are other countries, including the

Philippines and Somalia, plagued by weak governments that struggle to control their own territory.

Iran has long been viewed as a large-scale sponsor of terrorist violence—a charge that leaders in Tehran vehemently deny. The Islamic Republic is accused of having committed or sponsored assassinations in northern Iraq, attacks against the Kurdish Democratic Party of Iran, and other policies of liquidating the regime's opponents who live outside the country. Iran also stirs the coals with neighboring Iraq by providing safe haven to Kurdish operatives. Following the attacks of September 11, the United States argued that it would welcome Iran's support in the war on terror if it withdrew support from perceived terror groups. In fact, the United States needed the support of Iran to help forge ties with the Northern Alliance in Afghanistan. Iran had assisted the Northern Alliance and other anti-Taliban groups through the 1990s, and some viewed their mediation as "essential" to convincing the factions of mujahidin fighters in Afghanistan to work with the United States to topple the Taliban regime.[82] Iran's continued support to militias and movements in Bahrain, Lebanon, Syria, Yemen, Iraq, and elsewhere provide crucial support to terrorist operations far beyond their border.[83]

Libya also was long branded an active sponsor of terror. Once behind the wheel of government in 1969, Colonel Muammar Qaddafi sought to launch an Arab-Islamic revolution, for which he trained thousands of foreign terrorists each year in Libyan camps. Among the most famous was Carlos Ramirez Santos, also known as "Carlos the Jackal," who operated on behalf of Libya, Syria, and Iraq until his extradition from Sudan and deportation to France in 1997. By 2003, though, building on the improved relations he experienced after agreeing to turn over the Libyans accused of planting the bomb on Pan Am Flight 103, which killed 207 people, Qaddafi formally declared the existence of his chemical and nuclear weapons programs and invited international inspectors into Libya. (Although some claim his announcement was in response to the US-led war in Iraq, he had made similar offers, to no avail, beginning in the late 1990s.)[84] After the weapons programs were destroyed, the French government followed through on pledges to help Libya build a peaceful nuclear power program, and in 2006 the United States restored diplomatic relations with Libya, removing it from the list of countries believed to be officially sponsoring terrorism.

Another way to categorize types of terrorism is by focusing on the tools used to provoke fear or cause damage. While nuclear weapons and their delivery tend to be cost-prohibitive and technologically problematic for many countries of the world, bioterrorism is more within their reach. This leads some to refer to biological and chemical weapons as the "poor man's nuclear bomb" and "great equalizer." Biological weapons, including anthrax, the plague, and smallpox, are viewed as an ideal tool for many terrorists today because their effects take days to appear, making an elusive escape more likely. Yet, it can be extremely difficult to contain any outbreak resulting from a biological attack, meaning that the perpetrators may themselves be harmed as well. Such weapons remain dangerous because of their availability and potency: small amounts can wreak havoc on large groups of people. They have already been used as weapons of mass destruction—most notoriously by Saddam Hussein's forces against the Kurds in

Iraq, killing thousands and causing lifelong damage to an estimated 200,000 more.[85] The United Nations has accused Bashar al-Assad's government in Damascus of using chemical weapons against its own civilians seventeen times, highlighting material evidence that the Syrian regime continues to stockpile and produce such weapons, in violations of multiple international agreements.[86]

Chemical weapons, in the form of mustard gas, chlorine, sarin, phosgene, VX, and other agents, are believed to be the easiest-made weapons of mass destruction and are viewed as particularly horrendous because of their invisible and insidious stealth nature.[87] Their ingredients, including pesticides and fertilizers, are readily available. The main obstacle to their effective deployment comes in the difficulty of producing large quantities, as well as a delivery method, because in most cases they must be miniaturized to be potently dispensed. As of early 2022, three of the countries included on the US State Department's list of state sponsors of international terrorism (Iran, Syria, and Sudan) are known to possess chemical weapons. After the al-Assad government in Syria used sarin to kill more than 1,000 civilians in 2013, it was pressured to give up its chemical arsenal. However, the government's use of chemical warfare has not ended; rather, only the type of weapon has changed. There is much evidence suggesting that al-Assad has used chlorine gas (which remains legal as a widely available industrial chemical) strategically, to displace civilians from rebel-held areas. Despite its other, mundane uses, chlorine is a terrifying weapon; it is a choking agent that dissolves the lungs and there's no sheltering from it, as there is from other bombs, as it seeps into basements. Another state sponsor of terrorism, Sudan, is accused of using blister agents against civilians in Darfur in 2016.[88] The United States and Russia possess the two largest stockpiles of chemical and biological weapons in the world and, despite some progress, have yet to destroy their stockpiles as agreed to in the Chemical Weapons Convention (CWC) of 1993. In fact, less than six months after the Russian Federation declared, in 2017, that it had fulfilled its obligations and destroyed its remaining chemical weapons, operatives deployed by Moscow poisoned one of Vladimir Putin's political foes in England and, two years later, used a similar chemical agent to poison Putin's rival, Aleksei Navalny.[89]

Even if conventional nuclear weapons may be out of reach for many states, some believe the world faces an increased threat of nuclear terrorism due to the quantity of materials relatively unaccounted for—including plutonium and highly enriched uranium—as well as the increased number of nuclear-capable states. Even if an individual cannot piece together enough material to build a nuclear bomb, it is believed that a group could still build such a device—widely referred to as a "dirty bomb"—to spread radiological contamination. Widespread destruction can be achieved by wrapping radioactive material (including spent fuel rods) around conventional explosives. Once detonated, in the form of a car bomb, suitcase nuke, or other device, the intense radiation will be far more destructive than the blast itself. As of yet, there are unconfirmed suspicions that Iran received or smuggled nuclear materials out of the former Soviet Union. It is extremely difficult to know the extent to which terrorist groups have access to such materials, although it is highly plausible.

Revolutionaries

One of China's great revolutionaries, Mao Zedong, once emphasized the violence and uprootedness of revolutions in his famous observation that a REVOLUTION "is not a dinner party. . . . A revolution is an insurrection, an act of violence by which one class overthrows another."[90] To elaborate on Mao's prose, a "revolution" may be defined as a change in regime with the desire to achieve extensive, relatively quick, and often concurrent changes in economic, political, and social structures. Even though many countries claim to hold a revolutionary heritage, if we adopt the conventional definition of revolutions as fundamental transformations in the everyday way of life, they are actually fairly rare events. The classic revolutionary states, in which such dramatic changes were implemented, are China, France, and Russia.[91] Revolutions such as these are unlike other changes of power because their goal is to destroy the existing system, often through the use of charisma and violence. In the Chinese and French Revolutions, for example, people even changed their names and ways of referring to others. Following China's 1949 revolution, it was common for people to refer to each other by the egalitarian moniker "comrade" rather than by surname or title.

Yet, there have been many attempts to promote revolutions and revolutionary change beyond the three traditional "grand" revolutions. Many countries in the global south claim a revolutionary heritage, including Iran, Mexico, Turkey, Cuba, Vietnam, and Zimbabwe. Revolutions are often launched from remote regions where governmental groups have less control, and their leaders build their power base through ideological persuasion. Those at the forefront of the revolutionary effort often employ guerrilla tactics, especially the element of surprise, such as when the Zapatistas unexpectedly marched into the city of San Cristobal de las Casas on New Year's Day in 1994. In a nutshell, revolutions are about change.

Revolutions bring new people to power, incorporating groups like peasants and workers who had otherwise been left out of the process. In this sense, they attempt to "liberate" people—a term that is commonly associated with revolutionary endeavors. Many revolutions are class based, arising from structural changes that pit one group of people against another. Revolutions can also be born of crises manifested in territorial expansion, economic reorganization, international dislocation, or population expansion. Situations ripe for revolution include those involving widespread misery, oppression, and injustice, combined with either a weak government that is unable to solve the problems facing it or a significant crisis. In these situations, when "push comes to shove," groups who perceive themselves on the losing end of the bargain concentrate their resources and attempt to overthrow the oppressive system. In revolutionary situations, groups demand some role in decisionmaking, whether facing down military rulers (e.g., in Mexico, Bolivia, or Cuba), colonial regimes (e.g., in Vietnam and Algeria), or monarchies (e.g., in imperial China and Russia). In each of these cases, the entrenched elite was unable (or unwilling) to incorporate the new voices without a fight. Revolutions can also follow the collapse of an empire or regime, as happened with the collapse of the Qing Dynasty in China, the Ottoman Empire in Turkey, and the Qajar Empire in Iran (then known as Persia). A crisis situation unites otherwise disconnected groups to rebel against the status quo and claim power. Successful revolutions often coalesce around a single leader (or small group of leaders) who is able to harness discord into a potent political force.

Sometimes leaders of revolutions are (or become) military leaders as well, including Turkey's Mustafa Kemal Atatürk, Burkina Faso's Thomas Sankara, and Algeria's Houari Boumedienne. Yet, not all revolutionary leaders have a military background: Iran's Ayatollah Khomeini was a religious leader, China's Mao Zedong was a librarian, Guinea-Bissau's Amilcar Cabral was a census taker, and most people believe that the Zapatistas' Subcomandante Marcos was once a professor. Revolutionary leaders tend to have charisma and come from the relatively privileged classes—many are leaders of the intelligentsia, among the most educated members of society and accustomed to having their say. Yet, the harbingers of revolutionary movements often suffer some sort of major setback, experiencing failed expectations, or from an aspiration gap, as discussed earlier in the chapter. Many leaders of revolutions face a tumultuous history in their own countries—difficulties they often rectify with a vengeance against their former suppressers.

For example, Khomeini was exiled to Iraq from 1964 to 1968 for criticizing the Shah and allegedly sparking riots. He was later evicted from the Shia holy city of An Najaf by Saddam Hussein. Khomeini viewed himself as uniquely fit to avenge the problems of the West, especially the humiliations wrought on Muslims in the Middle East. Following his victorious return to Iran in 1979—after mass protests against the Shah's regime had long festered—he quickly acted on these ambitions, transforming the Iranian Revolution into an Islamic Revolution.[92] Mustafa Kemal Atatürk, leader of the 1919 Turkish Revolution, also viewed himself as distinctively able to lead his country down a new path. The difference between their approaches was the role of religion in their revolutions: Khomeini believed that an orthodox version of Islam and a rejection of all things Western were the best corrective to Iran's problems, while Atatürk prescribed an unyielding form of secularism to overcome Turkey's challenges. Both rode the rising wave of nationalism in their respective societies.

Another revolutionary who capitalized on nationalist themes was Ho Chi Minh, leader of the modern revolution in Vietnam, whose name means "Bringer of Light." At the end of World War I, when he was a student in France, Ho approached President Woodrow Wilson with the hope that Wilson's doctrine of self-determination would be applied to Vietnam. Wilson turned Ho away. Ho later founded the Viet Minh (whose name is an acronym for the Vietnam Independence League), but died before his dream of a unified North and South Vietnam could be realized, at tremendous cost. Affectionately known by many Vietnamese as "Uncle Ho," he repelled French attempts to regain an Asian empire in the 1950s, and later frustrated US attempts to defeat them in the 1960s and 1970s.

Some revolutionary leaders are already incumbent rulers who overthrow their fellow leaders to establish a new governing system. The Turkish Revolution of 1919 is one such example. Some have called it an ELITE REVOLUTION, or a revolution from above—defined by the swift overthrow of the elite by other members of the elite, limited mass participation, and limited violence.[93] Ellen Trimberger argues that the specific characteristics of elite revolutions, especially their restrictions on the involvement of the masses, can lead to situations in which the military may regularly intervene, which certainly holds true for the coup-riddled experience of Turkey.[94] The Peruvian Revolution (by coup), led by General Juan Velasco Alvarado, may also be described as a revolution from above. Despite these examples of elite revolutions, it is important to note that most are made "from below," incorporating the masses or other disenfranchised groups in an overthrow of the power structure. In fact, the Velasco revolution failed in part because it did not incorporate the participation of other groups, including the people it meant to serve—the peasants.

Women have been active participants in revolutionary struggles and wars: harboring rebels, moving weapons and intelligence through war zones, staffing health organizations, and carrying rifles. Women served key roles in revolutions in Nicaragua, Palestine, South Africa, Zimbabwe, Mexico, and the Philippines. In the Philippine Revolution of 1896–1902, known as the first anticolonial independence movement in Asia, women gained prominence. In one example, Teresa Magbanua was known as the Filipina "Joan of Arc" for her battles against the Spaniards in the late 1800s. In the Mexican Revolution, Emiliano Zapata's and Pancho Villa's armies included women revolutionaries, called *soldaderas*. They were originally camp followers who fed soldiers and provided services that the government did not. Gertrudis Bocanegra organized an army of women during the Mexican War of Independence in 1810; she died in 1817 after being arrested and tortured. Women often organized their own units, armed themselves, and fought as soldiers equal to the men. In unprecedented numbers, women participated in every aspect of the anti-Somoza effort in Nicaragua; in fact, they made up 30 percent of the Sandinista army and occupied important leadership positions, commanding full battalions. They were mostly young women, and the men with whom they shared units appeared for the most part to accept them. But after the revolution, women were largely ignored, even betrayed, by the Sandinistas.[95] And although there were female soldiers in Namibia, women never rose to officer status. In Namibia and Zimbabwe, female soldiers were often stigmatized after the war for being "mannish" by carrying guns. When Sam Nujoma thanked the Namibian people for their contribution to the country's liberation, he mentioned women specifically but did not recognize them as fighters.

Despite proclamations of great change, revolutions fade away—they are difficult to sustain. Revolutions require resources (personnel, coercion, money), energy (charismatic leaders and committed followers), and a level of ideological zeal and commitment that few societies can maintain for very long, much to the chagrin of those who led the revolution and those who suffered losses during it. China's Cultural Revolution is the best example of one leader's attempt to literally "continue the revolution" and maintain its legacy.

Terror often plays a large role in revolutions and revolutionary societies. Because revolutions attempt to achieve dramatic changes, there is little room for dissent or discussion. As with much violent conflict, clear sides are chosen by combatants and bystanders alike. Individuals and groups who are viewed to be against the regime are labeled "counterrevolutionaries," a charge that carries great danger, often tantamount to a death sentence. Especially after it is perceived that there has been some setback to revolutionary progress, terror methods, including torture, isolation, and forced labor, are commonly employed as means of holding on to power and keeping the revolution alive.

One of the most problematic legacies of revolutions is the selection of leadership beyond the revolutionary generation. Succession is an issue in many countries of the non-Western world, but especially in those with a revolutionary heritage. Leadership transition in nondemocratic states is rarely orderly. Leaders tend to seek to rule for life, and few mechanisms are put in place to choose their replacements until a crisis precipitates change—which means that leadership turnover happens during times of instability. Plato hypothesized that such circumstances, often deriving from chaotic mass rule, produce authoritarian despots. Deng Xiaoping's death in 1997 passed with barely a hiccup, because Jiang Zemin had been given almost eight years at the helm under Deng's steady hand and continued hold on (informal) power. The formal transfer of power from Jiang Zemin to Hu Jintao in 2002–2003 was similar in some ways, masking the fact that Jiang still controlled the reins, albeit from behind the scenes. Even after the titles of power were conferred to Hu Jintao, the leader of China's so-called fourth generation, Jiang and his protégés continued to exercise power for at least a year afterward. The groundwork for the transition to the fifth generation of CCP leaders (which took place throughout 2012–2013) was set by mid-2010, when Xi Jinping and Li Keqiang had each received promotions to key military and party posts. In Cuba, for years many expressed uncertainty about life after Fidel Castro, an uncertainty that was already apparent even when Fidel's less charismatic brother Raul assumed control during an ongoing "temporary" transfer of power after one of Fidel's health crises in July 2006. Since his death in late 2016, in part due to the prolonged transition time since his brother's assumption of power, little has changed. In South Africa, even though there was plenty of worry as Nelson Mandela neared retirement, his protégé, Thabo Mbeki, was able to provide a sense of continuity. However, since then tensions have grown, as Mbeki's second term was cut short due to party infighting. Today, under Mbeki's successor, Jacob Zuma, many find the party of Mandela to be unrecognizable. And in North Korea, in the months surrounding the elevation of one of reclusive leader Kim Jong-Il's sons, Kim Jong-Un, tensions in the region were significantly heightened, especially after North Korea launched artillery attacks against a South Korean island along the disputed maritime border. Some observers believe the actions, part of a larger pattern of North Korean aggression, demonstrated a less than enthusiastic embrace by the Korean military of Kim Jong-Il's designated successor.[96]

Do revolutions often accomplish what their leaders set out to achieve? Since revolutions claim to promote fundamental transformations in power relations, it is important to assess their gains. Few revolutions are total failures, but only few accomplish most of their explicit goals. In the early years of a revolution, it is common to observe significant attempts at land distribution and social change, employing at least the rhetoric, if not the reality, of equality. Fidel Castro, for example, appeared to be confronting machismo with laws requiring men to help with domestic responsibilities, but the laws were rarely enforced. Most revolutions also produce at least some form of leadership change, although one tyrant may simply be replaced by another, or by someone even more despotic.[97] The ruling groups in power after the revolution rarely deliver on the grand pledges they used to mobilize people to join in the first place.

Social stratification is rarely decreased in postrevolutionary societies—rather, the bureaucratic malaise and the expansion of state power that tend to follow revolutionary conflict often increase the gap between rich and poor.[98] Revolutions in the global south have an especially poor record of promoting equality and increased freedom, even if some redistribution of wealth or land reform actually takes place, such as in China and Cuba. In China, Cuba, and Nicaragua, one form of inequality was simply replaced by another, as the former landlords became poor and party leaders became more comfortable. Pledges to promote sexual equality, as well, are often relegated to lower status after the revolution is won, leading many to argue that promises of gender equality are formulated only to secure support of women during the revolutionary fight. In Namibia and Zimbabwe, promises of gender equality were "postponed" to appease still-powerful traditional (patriarchal) interests that the vulnerable revolutionary governments needed as allies. In the dangerous attempt to create "new" societies and new cultural foundations, and to do this quickly, huge groups of people often get caught in the cross fire. Although the statistics remain hotly debated, it is estimated that 2–3 million people died during Pol Pot's disastrous communist revolution in Cambodia, and at least 1 million died during the revolutionary fervor in Vietnam. Mao Zedong went to the grave with many deaths on his shoulders: some estimate that as many as 60 million people died in China as a result of his rule.[99]

Due to these broken promises, postrevolutionary societies often face great difficulty dealing with the revolutionary heritage they inherit, and governing groups in these societies tend to be defensive and reactionary. For example, in Iran in 1981, two years after the Islamic Revolution, the government crushed the so-called Marxist mujahidin after they purportedly bombed the Islamic Republic's office in Tehran. The mujahidin had been part of the coalition that overthrew the Shah in the first place, but they quickly fell out of favor with Khomeini and his supporters. The new government executed 6,000 of its members and supporters, and thousands of ordinary people answered the virulent call to attack the "enemies" of Islam. Training camps were established, including one camp in Tehran that was reserved for women trainees only.[100] In Mexico, Cuba, and China, the complex legacy of revolutionary leaders has proved a formidable challenge to the ruling regime that follows it, especially when groups ruling in the name of a revolutionary heritage seem to abandon prior goals and pledges.

To conclude our discussion of revolutions and revolutionary heritage, we compare two revolutions that continue to shape life in the global south. Both the 1979 Iranian Revolution and the 1949 Chinese Revolution were extremely popular with the population. In China, this support was sustained, for the most part, until the crackdown on the students in 1989. In Iran, the "grand coalition" quickly collapsed. Even though it was estimated that approximately one-fifth of the Iranian population demonstrated against the regime of Mohammad Reza Shah Pahlavi in December 1979, the euphoria ended shortly after it toppled the Shah's regime.[101]

The execution of the 1979 Iranian Revolution was rapid, while the Chinese Revolution was drawn out over twenty-two years of warfare before the PRC was established in 1949. Both revolutions took time to consolidate. In fact, most issues in both societies today emanate from the struggle of trying to be "modern" and relatively integrated without losing the hard-fought gains of the past. Both revolutions replaced imperial eras, even if there was a thirty-eight-year interim period in the case of China. The Iranian Revolution rid society of an unpopular monarch who had already once been deposed, ending 2,500 years of dynastic rule. In China, the Qing Dynasty had collapsed in 1911, but rival groups and factions, including political parties, warlords, and millennial cults, sparred over the country's future throughout most of the transition.

In their attempt to shoot for the moon, revolutionaries sometimes create new problems for themselves and those who follow them. Leaders in Iran and China, for example, realized that their calls for "revolutionary" families to have many children as a way of prolonging the revolutionary spoils soon created a painful drain on public resources. Mao encouraged population growth throughout the 1960s and early 1970s, yet mandated limits on family size in the late 1970s. In the 1980s, Iran's population jumped from 34 million to more than 50 million. As a result, Iran has introduced one of the world's most comprehensive family-planning programs, making every form of birth control available free of charge and requiring couples to pass a family-planning course before they can legally marry. This initiative prompted the health ministry to send officials door-to-door, with clerics issuing FATWAS to approve intrauterine devices and vasectomies.[102]

Both postrevolutionary societies are now evaluating the modernization of their regimes and the ways that they can continue revolutionary rhetoric while reaching out to other countries. The Iranian Revolution is undergoing an "Islamic Reformation"—defining the proper relationship between Islam and the modern world.[103] Iran leads the Islamic world in this debate, publicly challenging precepts everywhere from the courtroom and editorial pages to the cinemas and blogs. And clerics convicted of taking the debate too far have become celebrities among the ordinary population, especially since the Green Movement of 2009. Ever since the death of Mao Zedong in 1976, Chinese leaders have rethought their revolutionary saga, once even stating that Mao was 80 percent correct and 20 percent wrong in his handling of Chinese affairs. After Deng Xiaoping pushed China to open its doors to the outside world, Chinese began to question their revolutionary rhetoric more than ever. Few communist cadres had considered rehearsing their memorization of Mao's quotations while sitting at a Starbucks or Kentucky Fried Chicken.

What was accomplished by these two revolutions, grand in scale if not in achievement? In both China and Iran, literacy rates increased dramatically, especially among the youth. Between 1970 and 1990, literacy in Iran topped 90 percent, even as the population itself had doubled.[104] China also achieved dramatic improvements in literacy and healthcare between the 1940s and the 1970s, especially in the countryside. Revolutions in both countries provoked fearful responses from nearby states. Turkey blames the rise of PKK terrorism and separatist claims on the Iranian Revolution, and many of China's Southeast Asian neighbors, led by Indonesia, formed the Association of Southeast Asian Nations (ASEAN) as a way of combating a possible domino effect of communism throughout the region. Obviously, new cadres of leadership entered the ranks in both countries as a result of their revolutions. As the postrevolutionary generation gives way to the post-postrevolutionary leadership, the combination of pragmatism and revolutionary legacy that is used to justify their rule may become increasingly difficult.

Conclusions: Whither Violence?

Is the world more violent today than in the past? Those who argue that it is point to the end of the largest military buildup the world has ever seen, the Cold War, and the resulting widespread availability of weapons—to governments, individuals, and nonstate actors as well. They also find evidence in the renewal of latent issues, such as separatist movements and ethnic violence that were suppressed by prior regimes—as we have witnessed in Yugoslavia, Rwanda, Nigeria, and Indonesia. There are also those who maintain that the world today is no more violent than in the past. They point to current moves toward strengthening regional and international norms against violence, despite the violent nature of governments throughout time and the ongoing determination of violent revolutionaries and terrorists. However the question is answered, it is up to you to weigh the evidence and decide.

As we have shown in this chapter, the use of violence as a means of implementing change is not always ideologically, religiously, or culturally based. Nor is it always the usual suspects (the "criminals, crazies, or crusaders") who are the perpetrators of violence. State-sponsored violence, domestically and internationally, makes up a large proportion of violence in the world today. Our discussion has also highlighted that it is not only so-called extremists who engage in violent acts. Some groups and individuals feel that it is only through hostility and aggression that they can get the respect, attention, and credence they deserve.

It is tempting when looking at these issues and actors to be reductionist: to claim that the tactics of revolutionaries, terrorists, and government fighters are evil, that actions are always based in fanaticism, or that violence is always irrational. One does not have to condone the use of violence to evaluate such actors on their own terms and attempt to understand why they take the actions they do.

While many see violence as the only way to resolve a situation, it is difficult to make the transition beyond violence. The use of violence is often, although by no means always, self-perpetuating. People are forced to take sides, defining "enemy" groups and dehumanizing neighbors, colleagues, and fellow citizens. Following times of discord and disruption and attempts to move beyond them, there is a great sense that past "scores" need to be settled.

Notes

1. Quoted in Farnaz Fassihi and Rick Gladstone, "With Brutal Crackdown, Iran Is Convulsed by Worst Unrest in 40 Years," *New York Times,* December 1, 2019.

2. Quoted in Alisha Haridasani Gupta and Francesca Donner, "'Lost Between Borders': Afghan Women on the Lives They Left Behind," *New York Times,* September 14, 2021.

3. Institute for Economics and Peace, *Global Peace Index 2021: Measuring Peace in a Complex World* (Sydney: Institute for Economics and Peace, 2021), pp. 3, 6.

4. "World Bank Group Strategy for Fragility, Conflict and Violence 2020–2025," World Bank, February 26, 2020.

5. Noam Chomsky, *Pirates and Emperors: International Terrorism in the Real World* (New York: Claremont, 1986).

6. For a concise summary of approaches to violence in the literature, see Jack A. Goldstone, ed., *Revolutions: Theoretical, Comparative, and Historical Studies,* 2nd ed. (New York: Harcourt Brace, 1994).
7. Toby Luckhurst, "Honduras v El Salvador: The Football Match That Kicked Off a War," *BBC News,* June 27, 2019.
8. "Unrest in DR Congo After TP Mazembe Lose to Inter Milan," *BBC News,* December 18, 2010.
9. Arend Lijphart, *Democracy in Plural Societies: A Comparative Exploration* (New Haven: Yale University Press, 1977).
10. Charles Euchner, *Extraordinary Politics: How Protest and Dissent Are Changing American Democracy* (Boulder: Westview, 1996).
11. Michael Renner, "How to Abolish War," *The Humanist,* July–August 1999.
12. Daniel C. Diller, ed., *The Middle East,* 8th ed. (Washington, DC: Congressional Quarterly, 1994).
13. "Aceh's Sharia Court Opens," *BBC News,* March 4, 2003.
14. Amy Chew, "Aceh Independence Call Triggers Fears of Renewed Conflict in Indonesia's Restive Province," *South China Morning Post,* June 1, 2019.
15. Usman Hamid, "13 Years of Peace Without Justice or Truth in Aceh," *The Diplomat,* August 15, 2018; Julia Suryakusuma, "Aceh 14 Years On: Peace by Fiat?" *Jakarta Post,* August 21, 2019.
16. Yahya Sadowski, "Ethnic Conflict," *Foreign Policy* 111 (Summer 1998).
17. Chris Wilson, "Military Anxiety and Genocide: Explaining Campaigns of Annihilation (and Their Absence)," *Journal of Genocide Research* 21, no. 2 (2019), pp. 178–200.
18. Declan Walsh, "Ethiopia's War Leads to Ethnic Cleansing in Tigray Region, U.S. Report Says," *New York Times,* February 26, 2021; "Ethiopia's Tigray War: The Short, Medium and Long Story," *BBC News,* June 29, 2021.
19. Walsh, "Ethiopia's War Leads to Ethnic Cleansing"; Declan Walsh and Abdi Latif Dahir, "Why Is Ethiopia at War with Itself?" *New York Times,* November 5, 2021.
20. "Ethiopia Rounds Up High-Profile Tigrayans, U.N. Staff," *Reuters,* November 10, 2021.
21. "Who Are the Uighurs and Why Is China Being Accused of Genocide?" *BBC News,* June 21, 2021.
22. Alisa Chang, Anna Sirianni, and Patrick Jarenwattananon, "New Report Details Firsthand Accounts of Torture from Uighur Muslims in China," NPR, June 10, 2021.
23. Scott Simon, "China Suppression of Uighur Minorities Meets U.N. Definition of Genocide, Report Says," NPR, July 4, 2020.
24. Austin Ramzy and Chris Buckley, "'Absolutely No Mercy': Leaked Files Expose How China Organized Mass Detentions of Muslims," *New York Times,* November 16, 2019.
25. Edward Wong and Chris Buckley, "U.S. Says China's Repression of Uighurs Is 'Genocide,'" *New York Times,* January 19, 2021.
26. Cited in Gary J. Bass, "What Really Causes Civil War?" *New York Times Magazine,* August 13, 2006.
27. Julie Turkewitz, "Colombia Seeks Justice for War Atrocities via New Court," *New York Times,* March 6, 2021.
28. Toyin Falola, *The History of Nigeria* (Westport: Greenwood, 1999).
29. Eleanor O'Gorman, "Writing Women's Wars: Foucaldian Strategies of Engagement," in *Women, Culture, and International Relations,* ed. Vivienne Jabri and Eleanor O'Gorman (Boulder: Lynne Rienner, 1999).
30. Susannah George, "After 20 Years of Waging Religious Guerrilla Warfare, Taliban Fighters in Kabul Say They Miss the Battle," *Washington Post,* September 19, 2021.
31. Walter Laqueur, *The New Terrorism: Fanaticism and the Arms of Mass Destruction* (New York: Oxford University Press, 1999).
32. Alia Brahimi, "Libya Has a Mercenaries Problem: It's Time for the International Community to Step Up," Atlantic Council, May 21, 2021.

33. Amy Caiazza, "Why Gender Matters in Understanding September 11: Women, Militarism, and Violence," *Institute for Women's Policy Research,* no. 1908 (November 2001); Jakana L. Thomas, "Wolves in Sheep's Clothing: Assessing the Effect of Gender Norms on the Lethality of Female Suicide Terrorism," *International Organization* 75, no. 3 (March, 2021), pp. 769–802.

34. Alissa J. Rubin and Aurelien Breeden, "Women's Emergence as Terrorists in France Points to Shift in ISIS Gender Roles," *New York Times,* October 1, 2016.

35. Amy Knight, "Female Terrorists in the Russian Socialist Revolutionary Party," *Russian Review,* no. 38 (1979); Laqueur, *The New Terrorism.*

36. Christopher Dickey, "Women of Al Qaeda," *Newsweek,* December 12, 2005, pp. 27–36.

37. Rubin and Breeden, "Women's Emergence as Terrorists in France."

38. "Afghanistan War: Child Used in Suicide Attack," *BBC News,* July 12, 2019; "Indonesian Mother Forgives Teen Suicide Bombers Who Killed Her Sons," *South China Morning Post,* September 12, 2021; Joel Parkinson and Drew Hinshaw, "'Please, Save My Life.' A Bomb Specialist Defuses Explosives Strapped to Children," *Wall Street Journal,* July 26, 2019.

39. Taylor Luck and Fatima Abdulkarim, "Can a New Generation Change Palestinian Politics?" *Christian Science Monitor,* February 22, 2021.

40. Jessica Trisko Darden, *Tackling Terrorists' Exploitation of Youth* (Washington, DC: American Enterprise Institute, 2019), p. 6.

41. Rod Nordland, "Women Are Free, and Armed, in Kurdish-Controlled Northern Syria," *New York Times,* February 24, 2018.

42. Valerie Epps, "Civilian Casualties in Modern Warfare: The Death of the Collateral Damage Rule," *Georgia Journal of International and Comparative Law* 41, no. 2 (2013), pp. 307–355.

43. Devon Haynie, "The Long-Reaching Human Toll of Sept. 11, by the Numbers," *U.S. News and World Report,* September 10, 2021.

44. "As U.S. Withdraws, Civilian Casualties in Afghanistan Reach a Record High," *AP,* July 26, 2021.

45. "Syria War: UN Calculates New Death Toll," *BBC News,* September 24, 2021.

46. Rick Gladstone, "Casualties from Banned Cluster Bombs Nearly Doubled in 2019, Mostly in Syria," *New York Times,* November 25, 2020.

47. "Afghanistan: Record Number of Women and Children Killed or Wounded," *UN News,* July 26, 2021; "Six Grave Violations Against Children in Times of War," United Nations Children's Fund (UNICEF), August 26, 2021.

48. "Children Recruited by Armed Forces," UNICEF, August 27, 2021.

49. "On Average 25 Children Killed or Injured in Conflicts Every Day for the Past Decade: New Report," Save the Children, November 19, 2020.

50. Emeline Wuilbercq, "Children as Young as 6 Forced to Become Child Soldiers Due to COVID-19 Poverty," *Reuters,* February 12, 2021.

51. "Child Soldiers," *Talk of the Nation,* NPR, February 16, 2005. See also P. W. Singer, *Children at War* (New York: Pantheon, 2005).

52. Rachel Brett and Irma Specht, *Young Soldiers: Why They Choose to Fight* (Boulder: Lynne Rienner, 2004), pp. 9–36.

53. Emeline Wuilbercq, "Factbox: Ten Facts About Child Soldiers Around the World," *Reuters,* February 12, 2021.

54. "Uganda LRA Rebels 'on Massive Forced Recruitment Drive,'" *BBC News,* August 12, 2010.

55. "COVID Fuelling Risk of Recruitment and Use of Children in Conflict, UN and EU Warn on International Day," *UN News,* February 12, 2021.

56. Emma Graham, "Lebanon's Army Needs $100 Million Immediately for Soldiers' Basic Needs, General Says," CNBC, July 15, 2021.

57. Max Siollun, "Nigeria's Military Is Part of the Problem. It's Also the Solution," *Foreign Policy* (June 7, 2021).

58. Isawa Elaigwu, "Nation-Building and Changing Political Structures," in *UNESCO General History of Africa: Africa Since 1935,* ed. Ali A. Mazrui (London: Heinemann, 1993).
59. Alex Cuddy, "Myanmar Coup: What Is Happening and Why?" *BBC News,* April 1, 2021.
60. Mary Beth Sheridan, "As Mexico's Security Deteriorates, the Power of the Military Grows," *Washington Post,* December 17, 2020.
61. Ibid.; Stephanie Brewer, "Militarized Mexico: A Lost War That Has Not Brought Peace," Washington Office on Latin America, May 12, 2021.
62. Sorayya Shahri, "Women in Command: A Successful Experience in the National Liberation Army of Iran," in *Frontline Feminisms: Women, War, and Resistance,* ed. Marguerite R. Waller and Jennifer Rycenga (New York: Garland, 2000).
63. Preethi Nallu, "Rape Is Being Used to Terrorise the Population, Says DRC Gynaecologist," *The Guardian,* May 22, 2015; "Thousands of Survivors of Sexual Violence in Serious Need of Care in DRC," Doctors Without Borders, July 15, 2021.
64. Michael Georgy, "'Choose—I Kill You or Rape You': Abuse Accusations Surge in Ethiopia's War," *Reuters,* January 23, 2021.
65. "Ethiopian Forces Are Using Rape as a Weapon of War in Tigray, Amnesty Says," *AP,* August 11, 2021.
66. Matthew Hill, David Campanele, and Joel Gunter, "'Their Goal Is to Destroy Everyone': Uighur Camp Detainees Allege Systematic Rape," *BBC News,* February 2, 2021.
67. Vanda Felbab-Brown, "Militias in Mexico: Citizens' Security or Further Conflict Escalation?" *Insight Crime,* December 22, 2015.
68. John McBeth, "Bombs, the Army, and Suharto," *Far Eastern Economic Review* 164, no. 4 (February 1, 2001).
69. Sune Engel Rasmussen and Amira El Fekki, "Shadow Network of Militias Backs Iran," *Wall Street Journal,* February 26, 2021.
70. Ilya Barabanov and Nader Ibrahim, "Wagner: Scale of Russian Mercenary Mission in Libya Exposed," *BBC News,* August 11, 2021; Declan Walsh, "Russian Mercenaries Are Driving War Crimes in Africa, U.N. Says," *New York Times,* June 27, 2021.
71. Sean McFate, *Mercenaries and War: Understanding Private Armies Today* (Washington, DC: National Defense University Press, 2019), p. 2.
72. Ibid., p. 4.
73. Frederick J. Hacker, *Crusaders, Criminals, Crazies: Terror and Terrorism in Our Time* (New York: Norton, 1976).
74. Rahul Bedi, "Mumbai Attacks: Indian Suit Against Google Earth over Image Use by Terrorists," *The Telegraph,* December 9, 2008.
75. Vikas Bajaj and Lydia Polgreen, "Suspect Stirs Mumbai Court by Confessing," *New York Times,* July 20, 2009.
76. Mike Crawley, "Somali Banking Under Scrutiny," *Christian Science Monitor,* November 28, 2001; "Hawala Traders Are Being Squeezed by Regulators and Covid-19," *The Economist,* November 20, 2020.
77. *The 9/11 Commission Report: Final Report on the National Commission on Terrorist Attacks upon the United States* (New York: Norton, 2004), pp. 169–172.
78. Alex Zerden, "Rassessing Counter Terrorism Financing in a Taliban-Controlled Afghanistan," *Just Security,* September 17, 2021.
79. Laqueur, *The New Terrorism.*
80. Joby Warrick, "As Opportunity Beckons in Afghanistan, al-Qaeda's Leader Squabbles and Writes 'Comically Boring' Books," *Washington Post,* September 22, 2021.
81. "Former LRA Leader, Ex-Child Soldier, Sentenced to 25 Years in Prison," *UN News,* May 6, 2021.
82. Ray Takeyh, *Hidden Iran: Paradox and Power in the Islamic Republic* (New York: Henry Holt, 2006), pp. 122–123.
83. Ashley Lane, "Iran's Islamist Proxies in the Middle East," Wilson Center, May 20, 2021.

84. Flynt Leverett, "Why Libya Gave Up on the Bomb," *New York Times,* January 23, 2004, p. 23.

85. "Iraqi Kurds Mark 25 Years Since Halabja Gas Attack," *BBC News,* March 16, 2013.

86. Edith M. Lederer, "Watchdog: Syria Has Likely Used Chemical Weapons 17 Times," *AP,* June 4, 2021.

87. "A History of Chemical Weapons," *Talk of the Nation,* NPR, May 8, 2006.

88. "Sudan Government Accused of Using Chemical Weapons in Darfur," *BBC News,* September 29, 2016.

89. Michael Schwirtz, "Nerve Agent Was Used to Poison Navalny, Chemical Weapons Body Confirms," *New York Times,* October 6, 2020.

90. Mao Zedong, "Report on an Investigation of the Peasant Movement in Hunan: March 1927," in *Selected Readings from the Works of Mao Tsetung* (Peking: Foreign Languages Press, 1971), p. 30.

91. See Goldstone, *Revolutions;* Theda Skocpol, *States and Social Revolution: A Comparative Analysis of France, Russia, and China* (New York: Cambridge University Press, 1979).

92. Elton L. Daniel, *The History of Iran* (Westport: Greenwood, 2001).

93. Ellen Kay Trimberger, "A Theory of Elite Revolutions," *Studies in Comparative International Development* 7 (1972).

94. Ibid. Trimberger also included the Meiji Restoration of 1868 as an example of this specific type of revolution. This point explicitly challenges the theories of Huntington and others who argued against the inclusion of mass mobilization because of its potentially destabilizing outcomes.

95. Margaret Randall, *Sandino's Daughters: Testimonies of Nicaraguan Women in Struggle* (New Brunswick: Rutgers University Press, 1995).

96. "North Korea Firing: Why Now?" *BBC News,* November 23, 2010.

97. Jack A. Goldstone, "The Outcomes of Revolutions," in Goldstone, *Revolutions.*

98. Ibid.

99. Stéphane Courtois, Nicolas Werth, Jean-Louis Panné, et al., *The Black Book of Communism: Crimes, Terror, and Repression,* ed. Mark Kramer, trans. Jonathan Murphy (Cambridge: Harvard University Press, 1999). In his study of the Great Leap Forward, Frank Dikőtter estimates that this movement alone was responsible for at least 45 million deaths. See Frank Dikőtter, *Mao's Great Famine: The History of China's Most Devastating Catastrophe, 1958–1962* (New York: Walker, 2010).

100. Donna M. Schlagheck, *International Terrorism: An Introduction to the Concepts and Actors* (Lexington: Lexington Books, 1988).

101. Dariush Zahedi, *The Iranian Revolution Then and Now: Indicators of Regime Instability* (Boulder: Westview, 2000).

102. Robin Wright, "Iran's New Revolution," *Foreign Affairs* 79, no. 1 (January–February 2000).

103. Ibid.

104. Ibid.

11

Linking Concepts and Cases

Violence can be powerful, and, as we have discussed, it can take many different forms and derive from many different motivations. In what ways is conflict expressed differently in the countries that we are studying? What are the main sources of discord and how are they expressed? Do you observe any significant differences between the STATES that were established via revolutionary or liberation wars and those that were not? How do the power and role of the military in each of these states impact the operation of government or the expression of dissenting opinion? What legacies of past conflict can you observe in these states? Based on what you already know about our cases, what type of situation do you expect to find in each of these countries? For example, given what you learned about CIVIL SOCIETY in Chapter 8, what expectations do you hold for the expression of violence in each of these states?

Case Study: Mexico

Mexico belongs to a small, select club: it is one of the few countries in Latin America that hasn't had a coup in nearly a century. Years ago, in a quid pro quo deal struck in 1946 to promote stability, Mexican officers agreed to stay out of politics as long as the security forces were given near total autonomy and placed beyond scrutiny. As a result, the Mexican military has been unique in its willingness to obey the president as the commander-in-chief and let civilians rule. Admittedly, this is a less than perfect arrangement, which is complicated by as well as complicates the greatest threat the country is facing: a drug war.[1]

It is not unusual today to hear that Mexico is facing its greatest crisis since its revolution due to the violence unleashed by organized crime. The Mexican drug trade has grown exponentially in recent decades. Fifty percent of the cocaine entering the United States came through Mexico in 1990—as of 2017, over 90 percent of it did. Mexico now supplies most of the heroin and methamphetamine brought into the United States. And Mexico and China are the biggest suppliers of fentanyl, an opioid many times more potent than heroin. Over the years Mexican drug sales to the United States have become more lucrative (Americans spend an estimated $150 billion each year on cocaine, heroin, marijuana, and methamphetamines), and the trade has become more competitive, and bloodier.[2]

The situation had gotten out of control when in 2006 President Felipe Calderón declared a war on drugs. In an attempt to decapitate the cartels, he launched a militarized campaign that resulted in a number of high-profile drug seizures, arrests, and extraditions.[3] However, Calderón's war had an unintended effect: as a kingpin was removed, intergroup competition soared as his lieutenants fought to succeed him.[4]

The stakes were (and are) high because, as Calderón put it, Mexico is next door to the biggest drug addict in the world.[5] As the cartels have splintered and continued their infighting, they have become increasingly brazen and gruesome in their attacks, assassinating each other and terrorizing ordinary people (including uploading videos of mutilations, beheadings, and the like to YouTube). During Calderón's presidency, the homicide rate more than doubled in just five years, growing from 9 per 100,000 in 2006 to 22 per 100,000 in 2011.[6] As of 2020, several Mexican cities (Los Cabos, Acapulco, Tijuana) have some of the highest murder rates in the world. Between 2006 and 2021, the drug war killed an estimated 300,000 people (many of them innocents caught in the cross fire).[7]

As a result, more than one analyst has characterized Mexico as a failed state, at risk of rapid and sudden collapse.[8] Although what Mexico is facing is not a political insurgency, these mafias (which have diversified their operations to include kidnapping, extortion, money laundering, and human trafficking) also mean to influence politics. Mexico's transition to democracy disrupted the long-established understanding between organized crime and the government that defined the rules of the game in a way that allowed business as usual to go on with limited government interference. After 2006, the compact was broken; because the government—now democratic—was taking on the cartels, the drug lords decided to undermine the democracy.[9]

In fact, the cartels have hijacked the democratic process. To get their candidates into power they are bombing campaign offices, threatening and assassinating candidates and government officials, and scaring voters away from the polls. Over 100 people were killed in the lead-up to the 2021 elections, which were some of the most violent. Meanwhile, politicians use these mafias to fund their campaigns and, once in power, to enrich themselves. In addition, the cartels have spread into people's everyday lives, providing services the state does not. In many parts of the country they serve as the authority, punishing thieves and rapists, and even enforcing quarantines during the PANDEMIC.[10]

But the drug trade could not exist as it does without the cooperation of the state. Local and state officials are coerced or co-opted by the offer *plata o plomo* (silver or lead)—faced with the choice of cash or a bullet. Officials are often too weak to confront criminals or eager to work with them, which leaves criminals free to operate with impunity. The vast majority of crimes go unreported because people don't trust the police. It is estimated that no one is held accountable in nine out of ten murders.[11]

Andrés Manuel López Obrador was brought to power promising change. With his "hugs, not bullets" approach, AMLO proposed fighting the cartels by fighting poverty, decriminalizing drugs, offering amnesty to low-level cartel members, going after corruption, and disrupting cartel finances. But his efforts have not coalesced into a clear policy. Instead, AMLO has expanded on the practices of his predecessors and relied more than ever on the armed forces, which now have an almost untouchable status, to fight the cartels. Meanwhile, the number of homicides (by state and nonstate actors) in Mexico reached record highs. There were over 35,000 murders in Mexico in 2019—that's about six times the rate in the United States.[12]

Case Study: Peru

Forty years ago, a horrendous civil war was heating up at the time that Peru was transitioning from dictatorship to democracy. Just as civilians were resuming power, a leftist insurgency movement, Sendero Luminoso (Shining Path), began its attacks.[13] Sometime earlier, in the impoverished region of Ayacucho, an obscure philosophy professor, Abimael Guzmán Reynoso, had begun to command a following. A personality cult developed around Guzmán. To his followers, this philosopher king was incredibly charismatic. What became a fanatical GUERRILLA movement was in many ways more a religion than a political entity; Guzmán's followers were true believers, remarkably devoted to the cause.[14]

Although the Shining Path's IDEOLOGY drew from Marxist philosophy, this was unlike other Latin American revolutions in that Guzmán disdained the Cuban model and rejected Soviet assistance.[15] According to Guzmán, Peru's social order had to be destroyed to make way for a new one, and this required killing 10 percent of the civilian population. The more violence the better, argued the rebels; it was only after purification through bloodshed that Peru would become a Maoist utopia. It is estimated that, in twenty years of terror, the government forces (including militias) and the guerrillas killed almost 70,000 Peruvians. The Shining Path was responsible for about 54 percent of the fatalities.[16]

But the military did its part to add to the death toll as well. The newly democratic Peruvian governments adopted similar responses to the insurgency. They declared states of emergency, suspended constitutional guarantees, and to varying degrees turned the war over to the military. In its zeal, the military committed gross human rights violations against anyone suspected of being a member of the Shining Path. Most Peruvian leaders equivocated, unable to decide whether to fight a ruthless, dirty war, or to pursue a developmentalist solution to root out the fundamental causes of the insurgency and win over the population.[17]

President Alberto Fujimori (1990–2000) had no such qualms. This president favored a no-holds-barred, draconian approach. In return for its loyalty, Fujimori gave the military absolute control over the counterinsurgency program. As a result, in 1992 Peru was identified as having the highest rate of disappearances of any country in the world.[18] But it was this free rein that Fujimori credited with his victory over TERRORISM. In September 1992 not only was Guzmán captured in a hideout above a Lima dance studio, but so were the master computer files for the entire organization. This amounted to a bonanza; police rounded up more than a thousand suspects within a few weeks. Yet, even more crucial, the government succeeded in totally destroying Guzmán's mystique. Placed in a cage and dressed in a striped prison uniform, "President Gonzalo" was revealed on television as a meek, paunchy, middle-aged man with thick glasses.[19] Because so much of the Shining Path's power was based in the personality cult centered on Guzmán, this dramatic change in persona proved devastating to the movement.

With the war over, Peruvians were left to pick up the pieces. In 2003 a Peruvian TRUTH COMMISSION report found that there were more than 70,000 victims of the war that lasted from 1980 to 2000, most of them low-income peasants. According to the report, the Shining Path was responsible for the majority of deaths and disappearances, but 37 percent of these crimes were perpetrated by state security forces and paramilitaries.[20] Although the commission called for trials of the members of the armed forces accused of atrocities, only a few officers have been held accountable for their actions during the war (although former president Fujimori was found guilty in 2009 and sentenced to twenty-five years in prison for ordering death squad killings and kidnappings).[21]

Meanwhile, the Shining Path is back. It has reorganized and split into two factions. They reportedly have less revolutionary zeal than their forebears and appear to have reinvented themselves as part insurgents and part drug traffickers. The rebels provide security for drug gangs, which supply them with money and weapons. Otherwise, relatively little is known about members of the new Shining Path.[22] They are a danger, though not an existential threat to the state. For example, they have threatened a gas pipeline that supplies approximately 40 percent of Peru's electricity. Rebels have attacked military caravans, and, in one of the worst atrocities in decades, fourteen people (men, women, and children) were massacred in a remote, mountainous area of Peru known for coca production, just days before the 2021 elections. Pamphlets of a dissident wing of the Shining Path were found on the bodies, warning people not to vote. This only inflamed the narrative that the runoff election in 2021 was a choice between Keiko Fujimori (and a return to dictatorship—Alberto is her dad) or Pedro Castillo (and an embrace of Marxist radicals).[23]

Castillo narrowly won these elections and has been hounded by allegations that his closest advisers are closet terrorists. The military has enjoyed impunity even since the return to democracy because civilians like President Castillo have been reluctant to assert strong control over the military. In Peru, any encroachment on military autonomy or even mild criticism of the military is taboo—out of fear that it might provoke a coup.[24] Meanwhile, the few hundred guerrillas are more of a threat to Peru's war on drugs than they are a terrorist threat. But if you ask them, Peruvians will tell you that it is neither drugs nor terrorism that keeps them up at night: it's Peru's crime rates, which are among the highest in Latin America.[25]

Case Study: Nigeria

Nigeria suffers from myriad social and economic divisions, which are too numerous to discuss here.[26] Nigeria's various divides have on more than one occasion resulted in open conflicts. When the Ibo, the largest ethnic group indigenous to the southeast, declared their intent to secede and create their own independent country—Biafra—Nigeria descended into a civil war that raged from 1967 to 1970. More than 1 million Ibo died in this civil war before it was over—most of them civilians, many of them women and children. Although in the end the military government prevailed, Nigeria had come very close to breaking up.

Such a threat remains a possibility in Nigeria, and the military would argue that what some might call its outsize role is actually a necessity, given that the country is battling two major insurgencies at the same time. Most Nigerians would agree that the wars, one in the North East and one in the South East, threaten the state. Until 2021 the challenge in the North East was posed by Boko Haram, whose members initially took up arms in several northern cities in 2002 because they were poor, unemployed, and sick of government corruption. They offered political Islam as a solution and seek to transform Nigeria into an Islamic state. Boko Haram, a Hausa expression of disgust with Western education, has decimated education in some areas and tested the capacity of the democratic government. It posed such a security challenge that the 2015 elections had to be delayed so that people could vote. And Boko Haram inspires great fear; it has come to be known for its use of child (often female) suicide bombers on soft targets such as crowded markets.[27] It was Boko Haram who most famously kidnapped 278 Chibok schoolgirls in 2014, setting off an international social media campaign. They terrorized the entire region for a decade. By 2021, a total of more than 30,000 people had been killed and millions internally displaced across four countries, due to clashes between government forces and these militants. In 2019, Nigeria was second only to Afghanistan in a select group of five countries (including Iraq, Somalia, and Syria), which together accounted for 62 percent of the world's deaths from terrorism.[28]

By 2021, due to the death of Boko Haram's leader, its rival, Islamic State West Africa Province (ISWAP) appeared to be replacing Boko Haram as the leading jihadi threat in Nigeria. ISWAP is, as its name suggests, an Islamic State affiliate, one of many in Africa where it is finding the bases lost in the Middle East. It is unclear how ISWAP's ascendance will affect the humanitarian crisis in Nigeria. Boko Haram was known for its harsh treatment of Muslim civilians, which ISWAP found to be counterproductive. ISWAP focuses on government targets and says it seeks to win over hearts and minds. It is said to pose an even greater threat than Boko Haram to the Nigerian military, which has been accused of committing war crimes of its own and has been so unable to protect civilians that they have left people to save themselves, adopted a defensive strategy, and retreated to garrison towns.[29]

Meanwhile, the longer-standing crisis is in the South East and South, including the Niger Delta, which comprises 70,000 square kilometers of mostly marsh and creeks. Its inhabitants contend that this environment has been ruined by the oil industry and the oil wealth taken to bankroll the rest of the country. Some have taken up arms. Various guerrilla armies, militias, and gangsters are participants in this unconventional war, carrying out kidnappings, pipeline bombings, and piracy. This multidimensional war has run intermittently; at its peak in mid-2016, the conflict had reduced Nigeria's oil output by 25 percent, to a twenty-year low.[30]

Given the country's dependence on oil exports, the Niger Delta conflict poses a mortal threat to Nigeria's economy. Nigeria's governments have struggled to gain control over the region. They have resorted to scorched-earth tactics and, when that failed, turned to a radically different approach. Conceding that many of the militants' demands were justified, the government offered up a cease-fire and AMNESTY, and promised to pay fighters who were willing to lay down their weapons ($13 a day) and provide them with job training. It is estimated that approximately 30,000 fighters took the deal, which did bring a semblance of peace for a while.[31]

Since then, a number of different groups seeking change have come and gone. Some are more peaceful than others but, as of 2021, the most notable was the Indigenous People of Biafra (IPOB). Its armed wing, the Eastern Security Network (ESN) has "returned to the creeks," resumed the war on the oil industry, and is invoking Biafra, calling for secession. The government has characterized the ESN as a terrorist group, cut the amnesty program, and sent troops to the area.[32] President Muhammadu Buhari threatened to treat the pro-Biafra militants like Boko Haram (a comparison that many in the Delta reject).[33]

Instead of addressing the roots of the problem, the democratic government's heavy-handed reprisals could turn the conflict in the South East into all-out civil war. As one analyst put it, "Nigeria's military is ironically the cause of, and the solution to, many of the country's security problems."[34] In the end, it's the Nigerian population that suffers, caught between the insurgents and Nigeria's murderous military.

Case Study: Zimbabwe

Chimurenga is a Shona word that has great salience for all Zimbabweans. It has a number of meanings, but it generally refers to revolution, war, struggle, and resistance. In the First Chimurenga War, in the 1890s, the Shona and Ndebele fought against the loss of their land to white settlers. The Second Chimurenga War, which started in the 1960s and ran until 1979, also about the reclamation of land, was what most people consider to be Zimbabwe's war for liberation. It was revolutionary in its aims, although not necessarily in its outcome.

Two nationalist movements led this liberation war, the Zimbabwe African People's Union (ZAPU) and the Zimbabwe African National Union (ZANU), an offshoot of ZAPU formed in opposition to it. In 1963 the armed wing of ZANU sent its first group of soldiers to China for guerrilla training. China continued to support ZANU throughout the liberation war, and the Soviet Union provided assistance to ZAPU's armed forces. Meanwhile, the West for years largely stood behind the white governments—in effect, leaving Africans little choice but to turn to the communists. This was perfect for white Rhodesians, who joined white South Africans in portraying themselves as the last bulwarks against Black communism. Consequently, with the involvement of external actors, Zimbabwe's struggle became for many outsiders a COLD WAR PROXY WAR.

Justified as a necessary response to the "communist threat," the white government put the country under a state of emergency that would last fifteen years. ZAPU and ZANU were banned, and their leaders, including ZANU's Robert Mugabe (a teacher turned guerrilla fighter), were held in detention for nearly a decade. While ZANU and ZAPU had their disagreements, both armies were led by nationalists who appealed to Africans as Zimbabweans rather than as Shona- or Ndebele-speakers. Neither liberation army was ethnically homogeneous, but because they tended to recruit from their different areas of operation, they became identified in that way—ZANU as primarily Shona, ZAPU as Ndebele.[35] Despite the rivalry between them, in 1976 the two parties joined forces in an uneasy alliance known as the Patriotic Front (PF).[36] By 1979, the white government was so weakened that it was forced to negotiate a peace. The Patriotic Front was ready for an end to the carnage as well; although approximately 1,000 whites died defending Rhodesia, it is estimated that some 30,000–80,000 Blacks died in the war for liberation.[37]

However, not long after independence Zimbabwe was back at war; this time the struggle was between the victors. For years there had been tensions between ZANU-PF and PF-ZAPU, but relations became hostile after the 1980 elections, when Mugabe was elected president in Zimbabwe's first democratic elections. Although each blamed the other for provoking the violence, the four-year civil war that followed clearly had an ethnic dimension. The Fifth Brigade, an entirely ZANU and Shona-speaking elite military unit, was set loose to find dissidents in Matabeleland, a heavily pro-ZAPU region. The countryside was ravaged as the military used scorched-earth tactics. By the time a unity accord was brokered in 1987, between 8,000 and 30,000 more people had been killed, most of them Ndebele civilians.[38]

Since the late 1990s, it has been their own government that has posed the greatest threat of violence to Zimbabweans. Faced with the strong democratic challenge posed by the Movement for Democratic Change, the Mugabe regime resorted to a variety of tactics. The government's Operation Murambatsvina (Operation Drive Out Filth) in 2005 bulldozed the homes and businesses of more than 700,000 people in Harare and other cities. Although the government says it was cracking down on illegal activities and promoting public order, others contend that this mass eviction was ZANU-PF's effort to stave off a possible uprising by dispersing the political opposition, mostly the urban poor.[39] Activists have been attacked, kidnapped, arrested, tortured, and murdered. The biggest strikes since 2007 were met with the worst violence in two decades.[40]

What has the military had to say about all of this? Although in many ways it remains a revolutionary army, Zimbabwe's military was for years considered relatively professional. However, as the government has become increasingly desperate to hold on to power, it became more politicized. Members of the military hold powerful positions not only in ZANU-PF, but also in the cabinet, parliament, and state agencies. After soldiers rioted in late 2008 over low pay and high inflation, the Mugabe government decided to secure the army's loyalty by giving it the right to plunder. One example is the cash cow known as the Marange diamond fields. Characterized by one expert as "a freak of nature," the Marange fields contained one of the highest concentrations of diamonds in the world. With the blessing of the ruling party, the military moved in, clearing the area by attacking illegal miners, and killing hundreds of them.[41] Despite attempts through the Kimberley Process and other mechanisms to characterize this loot as "blood diamonds" (and prohibit its sale), the Zimbabwean government fought hard and won the right to export millions of carats of these gems on the world market each month—it is estimated that Zimbabwe could triple production and earn $12 billion annually from the sale of diamonds.[42]

Since rumors of a coup plot in 2001, President Mugabe consistently favored officers with the highest-ranking posts within the party. Moreover, the president had promised to crush any who dared to oppose him.[43] But in the end, even Mugabe couldn't outmaneuver the military, which played the role of kingmaker. Vice President Emmerson Mnangagwa had the support of the military, and when Mugabe sought to remove Mnangagwa from the line of succession in favor of his wife, the military put an end to Mugabe's rule with a palace coup.

Although many had looked forward to this day, Mugabe was never held to account for his crimes, and human rights groups say that repression has only increased under Mugabe's successor, Mnangagwa. The new government has no problem with using lethal force to disperse protesters. Masked and unidentified men—including a death squad known as "the Ferret Team," comprised of intelligence operatives, the military, and police—abduct, torture, and terrorize government opposition leaders and activists. The Mnangagwa government has even used Covid to justify its crackdown on human rights.[44] President Mugabe always said that he would rule for 100 years, and in many ways it appears that his successor regime is Mugabe's reincarnated.

Case Study: Egypt

It's hard to imagine now, but for many years, Egypt was a beacon of tranquility, its society a model of peacefulness and tolerance. Yet, this country, which hadn't had a civil war in more than 7,000 years, has turned into a breeding ground of violence. It's a chicken and egg problem: Egypt is widely considered the birthplace of modern jihadism and is the incubator of several terrorist groups.[45] Meanwhile, the authorities have perennially cracked down not only on radical Islamists but on all dissent. Like Mubarak, President Abdel Fattah al-Sisi has no tolerance for criticism. But he is taking it further than Mubarak ever did; for those (of any stripe) who dare to criticize this illiberal government, life is increasingly harsh and brutal.[46] This included not only anyone suspected of supporting the Muslim Brotherhood or any of the opposition, but journalists as well. It was estimated in 2019 that Egypt was holding approximately 60,000 political prisoners.[47] Now, the regime claims that this crackdown is necessary to defend the country, but others argue that it is in fact the government that is the main perpetrator of violence, using the guise of fighting terrorism but only creating more terrorists. And so we must consider the perennial question: Is state violence a necessary response to terrorism? Or is it stoking terror?

Interestingly, after the Egyptian revolution of 2011 that took down Mubarak, many Egyptians welcomed the military back into power in 2013 because they desperately wanted Egypt to avoid becoming another Syria or Iraq.[48] Yet, since then, violence and crime disrupt daily life in Egypt at significantly higher levels than they did even under previous dictators. Crime rates seemed to spin out of control after the 2011 protests, and many Egyptians became increasingly anxious about carjackings, robberies, and violent crimes. President al-Sisi has brought relative stability, but through heavy-handed repression and fearmongering, threatening that without him, Egypt could go the way of its neighbors. As a result, Egyptians are even less free than they were under Mubarak. Egypt does face multiple, internal threats from different and even competing jihadists. None of them currently pose an existential threat to the government, but its hands are full.[49]

Of the multiple terrorist groups currently operating in Egypt, the most active and capable is the jihadist Sinai Province, now known as the Islamic State in Iraq and al-Sham–Sinai Province (ISIS-SP).[50] This homegrown organization pledged allegiance to the Islamic State in 2014, declaring its intention to turn the Sinai Peninsula into part of an Islamic State caliphate.[51] ISIS-SP, which first emerged after the Egyptian revolution of 2011, is based in the northern Sinai desert, a vast and mostly arid expanse. Largely unpopulated, impoverished, neglected by the government, the Sinai has for years been a security vacuum, a perfect breeding ground for criminals and extremists.[52]

Despite its relatively small army of 800–1,200, ISIS-SP has inflicted a large number of casualties. It has made some spectacular raids, killing hundreds of soldiers and police. It singled out soft targets (civilians, particularly Copts, tourists, and foreign workers) and claimed responsibility for the downing of a Russian passenger jet in 2015. Imitating the Islamic State's trademark punishment, the beheading of a Croatian engineer signaled that ISIS-SP has moved away from its prior restraint. And there is growing concern that as attacks by ISIS-SP and others increase in sophistication, they will target the Suez Canal, vitally important to global commerce.[53]

Analysts agree that ISIS-SP is a dangerous, sophisticated terrorist group capable of skillfully planning, coordinating, and executing complex attacks. Yet, the Egyptian military, the largest standing military in the Arab world, is known to be more oriented toward fighting interstate warfare rather than asymmetric conflicts. Although it undertook a massive counterinsurgency effort in 2018, extending a state of emergency, brutalizing civilians and displacing thousands, the Egyptian army has struggled against this twenty-first-century threat, resulting in a relentless, brutal, and ineffective counterinsurgency campaign in the Sinai.[54] Rather than addressing the root of the crisis, the regime has blamed foreign conspiracies for its problems. But the war at home is against anyone the military government might view as its remaining political opposition—which includes all opponents, both secular and Islamist. For example, on August 14, 2013, in an attack on Muslim Brotherhood sit-in at a mosque, Egyptian security forces perpetrated the Rabaa massacre: "one of the world's largest killings of demonstrators in a single day in recent history," with nearly 1,000 casualties.[55]

Is the al-Sisi government's policy—which includes classifying the Muslim Brotherhood as a terrorist group—actually becoming a self-fulfilling prophecy? Thousands of the group's members (including former president Morsi, who died in detention) have been jailed and a generational schism appears to be deepening. Younger people blame their elders for the Brotherhood's recent failures and threaten to transform the movement into one seeking the violent overthrow of the government.[56] Analysts say that the regime's misdeeds could result in wider unrest or even civil war, but that it would be premature to characterize this shift as imminent. In fact, some analysts characterize Islamists in Egypt as still traumatized by Mohamed Morsi's overthrow and the Muslim Brotherhood's loss of power, as diminished, in hibernation. Yet, by capitalizing on the terrorist threat, President al-Sisi has moved the story away from being about democracy to one focused on security.[57] And so far, many Egyptians have been willing to let him do so, if it will save them from the fates of their neighbors.

Case Study: Iran

Coups, revolution, internal security forces, state-supported violence, and PRAETORIANISM: each may be found within the Islamic Republic of Iran. Periods of major strife and unrest have been fueled by opposition to leaders as well as resentment toward the intrusion of foreign powers. Building on their revolutionary heritage and status as a THEOCRACY, Iran's Supreme Leaders pursue three "core" objectives: exporting the Islamic Revolution, supporting Islamist (especially anti-Western) movements, and eradicating Israel.[58]

The Iranian military has always been a patron to the powerful. In 1925, after the fall of the Qajar Dynasty, Reza Khan took the historical title for Iranian kings—"Shah"—adopting the name Reza Shah Pahlavi. He and his son, Mohammad Reza Pahlavi, relied on the military to suppress any threats to their power. The Shah's demise was hastened by his appeal for assistance from the West, and the quick collapse of his own military. Because the system was corrupt to the core, it fell apart easily. What followed was nearly a spontaneous revolution that included many diverse groups from Iranian society. Women wore the veil (which the Shah declared illegal in 1936) to protest the prior regime and the debauchery of the West. It was an unusual revolution in several ways, being urban in origin, involving relatively little bloodshed, and resulting in the creation of a rightist theocracy that was retrogressive in nature.

A key figure in Iran's revolution was Sayyed Ruhollah Moosavi Khomeini—a cleric whose given name means "Inspired of God." The Pahlavi government had published an article ridiculing the cleric in January 1978. Religious demonstrations in the holy city of Qum followed, and the government's violent response left many demonstrators dead, launching a cycle of demonstrations every forty days, as customary in Shia Islam.[59] The continuation of demonstrations, a major movie theater fire exacerbated by a slow state response, and Khomeini's inflammatory speeches (from abroad) coincided to lead the country toward revolution. In November 1978, the Shah—who at this time was very ill—placed Iran under military rule.

One of the biggest surprises of 1979 was the departure of the Pahlavi military after the Shah left for the United States to receive medical care. Islamic revolutionaries provided airport security to allow the exiled Khomeini to return from Paris. Khomeini capitalized on popular discontent—especially among the youth—and successfully coaxed the military to desert the monarch. The Ayatollah purged monarchists loyal to the Shah by dismissing 12,000 personnel, most of whom were officers, in an attempt to "Islamicize" the military.[60] He then created the Islamic Revolutionary Guard Corps (IRGC), also known as Pasdaran, and later the Basij Resistance Force, a paramilitary group commanded by the IRGC that was behind the "human wave" attacks during the war with Iraq. Members of the Basij (also known as the "Mobilization of the Oppressed") remain the regime's chief enforcers, called on to put down protests.

The IRGC was created in 1979 to protect the Islamic character of the system; Ayatollah Khomeini deeply distrusted the loyalty of the conventional military. An elite force, much smaller than the regular military (yet with its own army, navy, and air force), the IRGC is tightly connected to the Supreme Leader, providing regular advice.[61] As a former defense minister, Supreme Leader Sayyid Ali Hosseini Khamenei helped organize the IRGC, and it remains one of his primary backers, as well as the likely force Khamenei has empowered to protect the regime after he is gone.[62] The IRGC fulfills many roles, overseeing aspects of the economy (including housing, dam and road construction, food, and even cultural and educational activities), and creating a praetorian system that some refer to as the "Iranian deep state."[63] Former president Hassan Rouhani has even publicly criticized the business role of the IRGC, calling it a "government with a gun."[64]

Iran's sponsorship of international terrorism strains relations with others. Iranian support for Hezbollah (Party of God), a radical Shiite Muslim group based in Lebanon responsible for attacks against the United States (notably the attack on the Marine barracks in Beirut in 1983), is a point of great contention. Hezbollah aspires for a state akin to Iran's Shiite theocracy, and leaders maintain close contact with the Iranian Supreme Leader, who serves as a spiritual and political mentor, as well as the IRGC. Iran also has significant financial and military ties with Hamas (Islamic Resistance Movement), a Sunni Islamist group that receives major funding from Tehran. The IRGC is closely connected to conflicts in Syria, Iraq, Yemen, and Bahrain—exporting weapons, providing military training—and even has a known presence in Latin America (focused on economic and humanitarian projects).[65]

Because of Iran's theocratic rule, enemies of the regime are defined to be enemies of God. One of the Iranian regime's most famous pronouncements of decided enemies was Khomeini's 1989 *fatwa* (religious injunction) against Salman Rushdie, author of the seemingly sacrilegious *The Satanic Verses*. This decree provided a sum of over $2 million (plus expenses) for efforts to kill Rushdie. Even though Iranian leaders distanced themselves from the decree in 1998, and attempts on Rushdie's life have failed, attacks on his collaborators have had mixed success; a suicide bomber sent to London accidentally blew himself up in a hotel room, the book's Japanese translator was stabbed to death, and attempts on the lives of the publishers were made as well. Other enemies include political dissidents, such as Shapour Bakhtiar, the last prime minister under the Shah, who was murdered (on orders from the Iranian government) in Paris in 1991. As many as 360 émigrés are believed to have been abducted and later executed, from many countries around the world.[66] Expatriates have been targeted as well. Since Iran does not recognize dual citizenship, those who are arrested are treated as Iranian citizens and are not afforded consular privileges. The case of abducted *Washington Post* reporter Jason Rezaian, held by the Iranian government for 544 days (much of that time in solitary confinement), is one noted example.

Violence played an integral role both in the collapse of the Pahlavi Dynasty and in the creation of the Islamic Republic. As cleavages deepen, and Iran searches for a more active stage in regional and world affairs, the possibilities for political disruption remain.

Case Study: China

Similar to many of the countries we have studied, China has had multiple revolutions rather than a single revolutionary moment. Yet, strangely enough, especially for their fervently anti-imperial character, both of China's major revolutions incorporated Western ideas, only later adapting "Chinese characteristics." The first revolution took place in 1912, after the last dynasty of China, the Qing, collapsed. Sun Yat-sen, a Christian medical doctor known as the father of modern China, planned the revolution from Tokyo, Honolulu, Vancouver, and London. Yet, the revolution, led by the Nationalist Party, failed to consolidate. Warlords, individuals who had accrued military and political power during the unrest that accompanied the collapse of the dynastic period, engaged in violent attempts to regain control over their fiefdoms. Out of this, another Nationalist leader, Chiang Kaishek, rose to the fore. Twice the KMT worked together with the younger, inexperienced, and ill-equipped Chinese Communist Party, and twice the alliance collapsed. In the second United Front, as their alliances were called, the KMT and the CCP worked together, some would say in a half-hearted manner, to expel the Japanese, who had invaded the north of China. It was during this conflict—in which the Nationalists gained the reputation as a corrupt band of soldiers who would quickly flee from the advancing Japanese—that the CCP gained the support of many of China's ordinary people. This was especially true in the countryside, the main recruiting ground for the fledgling CCP. Even though Mao Zedong was a backseat member at the first party meetings in Shanghai in 1921, by the late 1920s he had begun to emerge as a revolutionary hero and cultural icon who would impact China like no other person.

Yet, victory over the Nationalists in China's civil war (1945–1949) was not enough. In Mao's attempt to "continue the revolution," he launched the country into a state of virtual civil war during his so-called CULTURAL REVOLUTION. Even though the main campaigns of the ten-year movement, designed to promote absolute equality and cleanse China of foreign and Confucian influence, were primarily confined to China's major cities, the period is referred to as "the ten dark years," which no Chinese living on the mainland escaped. This decade of unrest—a "planned revolution" of sorts—was rife with purges, public denunciations, propaganda, and ideological fervor. It is now believed that at least 1.5 million people were killed, and approximately 16 million teenagers and young adults were dispatched to the Chinese countryside to engage in hard labor and "learn from the peasants."[67]

The People's Liberation Army (PLA), as the joint military forces of the PRC are called, is closely intertwined with the CCP. In fact, the PLA, founded in 1927 as a guerrilla force, follows in a long line of military involvement in politics: military commanders established many Chinese dynasties. It is common to hear that the CCP commands the gun, meaning that the PLA is subordinated to the party. Mao himself argued in 1927 that "all political power grows out of the barrel of a gun," and later that "the party commands the gun, while the gun shall never be or must never be allowed to command the party." The PLA is a "party-military," designed to protect the CCP at all costs. One of the clearest examples of this was when Deng Xiaoping, as chair of the Central Military Commission, effectively utilized PLA units to clear Tiananmen Square in 1989. Following the examples of his predecessors, President Xi Jinping concurrently holds the posts of general secretary, chairman of the Central Military Commission, and president.

China's PLA is a mighty force sworn to protect the CCP—a major part of which includes safeguarding the territorial integrity of the state. Covert and overt forces check any perceived separatist activity, with noted sensitivity focused on Tibet, Xinjiang, and Inner Mongolia. It goes far beyond a visibly increased military presence, as CCP officials are assigned to live with ethnic minorities in their own homes, and even the slightest personal decision (e.g., skipping a shave or an off-the-cuff remark) can result in detention.[68] Inside China's northeastern border province of Inner Mongolia, schools are phasing out Mongolian language instruction and authorities circulate images captured from protests, offering financial incentives for neighbors and friends to provide information on participants. No images of the Tibetan spiritual leader Dalai Lama are visible any longer, replaced with murals propagating Xi's "China Dream."[69] From the perspective of Beijing, Taiwan's growing presence on the world stage is viewed as separatism as well. As we discussed in Chapter 10, tensions surrounding Taiwan's political status and identity are increasing, as Xi highlights the need to "fulfill reunification" as part of the Chinese people's "glorious tradition" of opposing separatism.[70]

Restructuring processes since 2019 aim to professionalize the ranks, including linking promotions to advanced graduate study, aspiring to transform the PLA, the world's largest military force, into a "world class outfit" by the centennial anniversary of the PRC in 2049.[71] Some observers contend that China used the Covid pandemic as a distraction and an enticer to develop its capabilities and strategic relationships, expanding its reach through the Belt and Road Initiative as well as attempts at "vaccine diplomacy" with other global south states. This includes increasing the construction of silos for intercontinental ballistic missiles (ICBMs) by tenfold, increasing its nuclear arsenal, as well as its successful testing of a hypersonic weapon built to evade existing missile defense systems. A nuclear power since 1964, Beijing's leaders have balked at joining any arms control talks, spotlighting the fact that the United States and Russia each have five times the nuclear warheads that China holds.[72] The future of the global arms race will include cyberweapons, space arms, and hypersonic weaponry, significantly changing conventional deterrence calculations.[73] By emphasizing intensive improvements in its strategic nuclear arsenal, naval capabilities, reach in outer space, and launch of a hypersonic weapon capable of evading American defenses, the Chinese military is realistically approaching (and possibly surpassing) parity with the United States. General Mark A. Milley, the chairman of the US Joint Chiefs of Staff, refers to China as the "No. 1" nation-state military challenger to the United States.[74] Beijing's claims to disputed territories within the East China and South China Seas, including the militarization of some of the islands, increase tensions over the control of the military and civilian presence in one of the busiest sets of shipping lanes in the world.[75]

Case Study: Indonesia

Indonesia has faced considerable turmoil, including economic crises, ethnic and religious conflict, territorial loss, and devastating natural disasters. Violence has seeped into many of these challenges.

Prior to the 2000s, military involvement was formally included in the bureaucracy at every level of civil government. The Indonesian armed forces have traditionally filled in when there was a vacuum of civilian leadership (including building roads and linking regions to electrical grids), only withdrawing formally from politics in 2004. Yet, their influence has grown during Jokowi Widodo's presidency.[76]

President Jokowi is wrestling with growing antiminority sentiment, terrorist organizations, and continued separatist leanings. Under such pressure, Jokowi forged closer ties with military commanders. Heads turned when Jokowi appointed Wiranto, a former military chief with a deeply tarnished record of human rights violations, to two ministerial posts.[77] Tensions flared after Jokowi's second inaugural, when Wiranto was stabbed by a purported radical with ties to a group boasting loyalty to the Islamic State, leading to a heightened military presence.[78] With other Jokowi appointments, second-generation family members of military elite from prior regimes are gaining influence, returning to what some term the "dual function" role of the military (adding politics and business to their security role).[79]

Jokowi's appointment of his two-time electoral rival Prabowo Subianto as defense minister was especially troubling. Prabowo, Suharto's former son-in-law, was implicated in the illegal abduction of pro-democracy activists from his time as commander of the Indonesian army's Special Forces.[80] For nearly twenty years, Prabowo was a pariah in international affairs, prohibited from visiting the United States due to atrocities committed under his leadership.[81] A perennial candidate, Prabowo is likely to run for president in 2024.

Despite promises to reckon with Indonesia's violent past, Jokowi favors the military's version of internal threats, highlighting communism and separatism as risks demanding vigilance. It's working. Societal attitudes, measured in recent Asian Barometer Surveys, indicate that nearly 40 percent of Indonesians surveyed "strongly agree" or "agree" that the army should have a role in helping to govern the country, second only (regionally) to Thailand.[82] During Covid, the Indonesian military held leading positions on the state's public health task forces, and members were deployed to promote public health and enforce social distancing mandates—moves that were criticized by civil society organizations.[83] The fragile ethnic and religious balance in many regions is under strain, as identity becomes increasingly politicized. Always latent under the surface, the Covid pandemic has also heightened anti-Chinese sentiment, leading to an increase in attacks on the country's ethnic Chinese community, who are often scapegoated during times of crisis.[84]

Religious extremism is also surging. One prominent Islamist group, Jemaah Islamiah (Islamic Organization [JI]), was implicated in the October 2002 attack on a nightclub in a resort area of Bali, which left nearly 200 people dead. This group, known for its desire to establish an Islamic state combining Malaysia,

Indonesia, Singapore, and parts of the Philippines, is purported to have links to al-Qaeda, a charge its leaders deny. After appearing dormant for much of the 2010s, JI is growing again, raising funds (under the guise of promoting social welfare functions) and sending members to Syria for combat experience and training.[85] Analysts also point to smaller group efforts, sometimes referred to as "lone wolf" attacks, including the involvement of women in terrorist activities.

Indonesia's highest profile terrorist is the JI leader Riduan Isamuddin (known as "Hambali")—described as the Osama bin Laden of Southeast Asia. A veteran of Soviet-era Afghanistan, he is accused of helping plan or finance much of JI's activity, including devastating church and school bombings. He was captured in Thailand and kept in an undisclosed location before being transferred to Guantánamo—where he was held as a "high value" detainee for eighteen years without charge.[86] Indonesian officials have repeatedly requested the United States to retain him, placing him among the so-called forever prisoners of Guantánamo.[87] He and two accomplices were formally charged in August 2021 but, as this book goes to press, no trial date has been set.[88]

Separatism is another threat. Pressure focuses on insurgent strife in Western Papua (known until 2007 as West Irian Jaya), on the Indonesian half of Papua New Guinea. Although the province, home to the world's largest copper and gold mines, was incorporated by the Dutch, many Indigenous Papuans believed they would achieve their independence after the Dutch left, having been promised self-rule. The Dutch formally transferred control of Papua to the United Nations, and then to Indonesia, with an agreement that Indigenous Papuans would decide, within six years, whether or not to remain part of Indonesia.[89] Indonesian military forces occupied the land in 1963, and the referendum on independence has—to date—never taken place. An autonomy law was promulgated in 2001 that earmarked some relevant government posts for native Papuans and guaranteed that up to 80 percent of the mineral wealth from the region would be returned to it. Yet, the extension of the Special Autonomy Law seems to be yet another attempt to repress the movement.[90] Tensions flared when a brigadier general was ambushed and killed in Papua's central highlands (the first general to die in action in the republic's history), prompting calls for a "strong response" from Jakarta.[91] This and other flash points across Indonesia are likely to continue to challenge political, military, and civil society leaders for years to come.

Now It's Your Turn

What has been the effect of catastrophic violence in the countries that have experienced it? What do you think it takes to become a revolutionary leader? Why are some leaders more successful than others at rallying people to implement change? Do any of our country case studies seem ripe for revolution? How would you compare the various responses of these governments to revolutionaries or perceived insurgents? Why do you think some people believe that violence is the only solution to their dilemmas? What would it take for you to adopt violent means of expression?

Notes

1. "Human Rights in Mexico: Untouchable?" *The Economist,* November 3, 2001; Kevin Sullivan and Mary Jordan, "Fox Takes Steps to End Army's Rights Abuses," *Washington Post,* November 11, 2001; Kevin Sullivan, "Memories of Massacre in Mexico," *Washington Post,* February 14, 2002; Azam Ahmed and Eric Schmitt, "Mexican Military Runs Up Body Count in Drug War," *New York Times,* May 26, 2016.

2. Council on Foreign Relations, "Mexico's Long War: Drugs, Crime, and the Cartels," February 26, 2021; Adam Isacson, "Four Common Misconceptions About U.S.-Bound Drug Flows Through Mexico and Central America," Washington Office on Latin America, June 20, 2017; US Drug Enforcement Agency, "2020 National Drug Threat Assessment," March 2021.

3. Shannon K. O'Neil, "Mexican-US Relations: What's Next?" *Americas Quarterly,* Spring 2010.

4. "Special Report: Mexico's Cartels Will Continue to Erode in 2016," Stratfor Analysis, January 25, 2016.

5. Michele Norris, "Tackling America's Drug Addiction," NPR, June 18, 2010; Enrique Krauze, "The Mexican Evolution," *New York Times,* March 24, 2009.

6. Beatriz Magaloni and Zaira Razu, "Mexico in the Grip of Violence," *Current History,* February 2016.

7. Rebecca Gordon, "The Failed War on Drugs in Mexico (and the United States)," BillMoyers.com, March 27, 2015; Council on Foreign Relations, "Mexico's Long War"; "Ranking of the Most Dangerous Cities in the World in 2020," Statista, 2021.

8. Frank James, "Obama Rejects Hillary Clinton's Mexico-Colombia Comparison," NPR, September 9, 2010; Rory Carroll, "Hillary Clinton: Mexican Drug War Is Colombia-Style Insurgency," *The Guardian,* September 9, 2010.

9. Shannon O'Neil, "The Real War in Mexico," *Foreign Affairs* 88, no. 4 (July–August 2008); Mariana Campero and Ryan C. Berg, "Mexico's Midterm Elections Matter to the United States," Center for Strategic and International Studies, June 2, 2021.

10. Marc Lacey, "Mexican Democracy, Even Under Siege," *New York Times,* July 5, 2010; "Freedom in the World: Mexico," Freedom House, 2020; Oscar Lopez, "'We're Living in Hell': Inside Mexico's Most Terrified City," *New York Times,* August 3, 2021; Ioan Grillo, "How Mexico's Drug Cartels Profit in the Pandemic," *New York Times,* July 7, 2020.

11. Magaloni and Razu, "Mexico in the Grip of Violence"; Grillo, "How Mexico's Drug Cartels Profit in the Pandemic"; "Freedom in the World: Mexico," Freedom House.

12. "The Transformer: Mexico's President Has Yet to Make People's Lives Better," *The Economist,* February 18, 2021; Council on Foreign Relations, "Mexico's Long War"; Campero and Berg, "Mexico's Midterm Elections Matter to the United States"; "Sergeant Lopez Obrador: Mexico's President Is Giving the Armed Forces New Powers," *The Economist,* May 1, 2021.

13. The name "Shining Path" comes from one of Peru's most prominent authors, José Carlos Mariátegui, who stated that "Marxist-Leninism is the shining path of the future." See "Abimael Guzmán: Peru's Shining Path Guerrilla Leader Dies at 86," *BBC News,* September 11, 2021.

14. M. Elaine Mar, "Violence in Peru: Shining Path Women," *Harvard Magazine* (May–June 1996); Cynthia McClintock, *Revolutionary Movements in Latin America* (Washington, DC: United States Institute of Peace Press, 1998).

15. Carlos Ivan Degregori, "After the Fall of Abimael Guzmán: The Limits of Sendero Luminoso," in *The Peruvian Labyrinth,* ed. Maxwell A. Cameron and Philip Mauceri (University Park: Pennsylvania State University Press, 1997).

16. Peter Flindell Klaren, *Peru: Society and Nationhood in the Andes* (New York: Oxford University Press, 2000); Ramiro Escobar, "Rights—Peru: Reparations Near for Victims of Civil War," Inter Press Service, May 2, 2006.

17. Klaren, *Peru.*

18. Human Rights Watch, "Peru: Torture and Political Persecution in Peru," December 1997; US Department of State, *Country Reports on Human Rights, 2000* (Washington, DC: US Government Printing Office, 2000); Escobar, "Rights—Peru."

19. Degregori, "After the Fall of Abimael Guzmán"; McClintock, *Revolutionary Movements in Latin America.*

20. William Aviles, "Despite Insurgency: Reducing Military Prerogatives in Colombia and Peru," *Latin American Politics and Society* 51, no. 1 (Spring 2009).

21. "Fujimori Gets Lengthy Jail Term," *BBC News,* April 7, 2009.

22. Simon Romero, "Cocaine Trade Helps Rebels Reignite War in Peru," *New York Times,* March 17, 2009; US Department of State, "Peru 2016 Crime & Safety Report," Overseas Security Advisory Council, March 14, 2016.

23. Colin Post, "Shining Path Ambush Kills 10 on Eve of Peru's Election," *Peru Reports,* April 12, 2016; Anatoly Kurmanaev and Mitra Taj, "Peru Massacre Revives Trauma of Maoist Violence Ahead of Polarized Vote," *New York Times,* May 24, 2021.

24. Marco Aquino, "Peru Probes Whether Police Killed People to Earn Promotions, Rewards," *Reuters,* August 1, 2016.

25. Ibid.; Aviles, "Despite Insurgency"; Barnett S. Koven, "The Second Image Sometimes Reversed: Competing Interests in Drug Policy," *E-International Relations,* March 8, 2016; Maria Godoy, "The Women of Peru Are Suffering from a 'Shadow Pandemic,'" NPR, September 10, 2020.

26. Toyin Falola, *The History of Nigeria* (Westport: Greenwood, 1999); "Freedom in the World: Nigeria," Freedom House, 2021.

27. Felix Onuah, "Nigeria Says Has Pushed Boko Haram out of All but Three Areas," *Reuters,* March 17, 2015.

28. John Campbell and Nolan Quinn, "What's Behind Growing Separatism in Nigeria?" Council on Foreign Relations, August 3, 2021; "Countries with the Highest Number of Deaths by Terrorism in 2019, by Percentage of Total Deaths," Statista, 2021; "Sixth Time Unlucky: Abubakar Shekau, Boko Haram's Vicious Leader, Is Said to Be Dead," *The Economist,* May 29, 2021; Jacob Kurtzer, Judd Devermont, and Kelly Moss, "Boko Haram's Leader Is Dead: What Are the Humanitarian and Security Implications?" Center for Strategic and International Studies, June 15, 2021.

29. Kurtzer, Devermont, and Moss, "Boko Haram's Leader Is Dead"; Ruth Maclean, "Leader of West African Terrorist Group Is Dead, Nigerian Army Says," *New York Times,* October 15, 2021; Vanda Felbab-Brown, "As Conflict Intensifies in Nigeria's North East, So Too Does a Reliance on Troubled Militias," Brookings Institution, April 21, 2020; "Sixth Time Unlucky: Abubakar Shekau, Boko Haram's Vicious Leader, Is Said to Be Dead," *The Economist.*

30. "Nigeria Bomb Toll Rises as Government Admits It Was Warned," *Reuters,* October 2, 2010; Tife Owolabi, "Military Sweep in Nigeria's Delta Risks Fuelling More Dissent," *Reuters,* June 10, 2016; Dionne Searcey, "Nigeria Finds a National Crisis in Every Direction It Turns," *New York Times,* July 17, 2016.

31. Adam Nossiter, "Poverty Could Imperil the Amnesty in Niger Delta," *New York Times,* November 27, 2009; Alex Perry, "In Nigeria, an Ailing President and Peace Process," *Time,* December 21, 2009; Chris Ewokor, "The Niger Delta Avengers: Nigeria's Newest Militants," BBC Africa, June 2, 2016; Max Siollun, "Nigeria's Military Is Part of the Problem. It's Also the Solution," *Foreign Policy* (June 7, 2021).

32. John Campbell and Nolan Quinn, "What's Behind Growing Separatism in Nigeria?" Council on Foreign Relations, August 3, 2021; Searcey, "Nigeria Finds a National Crisis in Every Direction It Turns."

33. "Curbing Violence in Nigeria (III): Revisiting the Niger Delta," Africa Report no. 231, International Crisis Group, September 29, 2015; Maggie Fick, "Nigeria: Running on Empty," *Financial Times,* May 30, 2016; Ruth Maclean and Ismail Alfa, "Nigerian President Ousts Military Chiefs Who Failed to Quell Violence," *New York Times,* January 27, 2021.

34. Siollun, "Nigeria's Military Is Part of the Problem."

35. Ngwabi Bhebe and Terence Ranger, "Volume Introduction: Society in Zimbabwe's Liberation War," in *Society in Zimbabwe's Liberation War,* ed. Ngwabi Bhebe and Terence Ranger (Oxford: Currey, 1996).

36. From this point on, ZANU became known as ZANU-PF—with PF indicating "Patriotic Front."

37. Dickson A. Mungazi, *Colonial Policy and Conflict in Zimbabwe* (New York: Crane Russak, 1992).

38. Richard P. Werbner, "In Memory: A Heritage of War in Southwestern Zimbabwe," in Bhebe and Ranger, *Society in Zimbabwe's Liberation War.*

39. "Out in the Cold," *The Economist,* June 11, 2005.

40. MacDonald Dzirutwe, "No 'Arab Spring' in Zimbabwe, Mugabe Warns Protesters," *Reuters,* August 27, 2016.

41. Celia W. Dugger, "Diamond Find Could Aid Zimbabwe, and Mugabe," *New York Times,* June 21, 2010; Celia W. Dugger, "Zimbabwe's Diamond Fields Enrich Ruling Party, Report Says," *New York Times,* June 26, 2009.

42. Dugger, "Diamond Find Could Aid Zimbabwe, and Mugabe"; "Zimbabwe Aims to More Than Triple Diamond Production by 2023," *Reuters,* October 14, 2019.

43. Dumisani Muleya, "Mugabe Versus the Military," *Zimbabwe Independent,* June 17, 2016.

44. Amnesty International, "Zimbabwe 2020," 2021; Human Rights Watch, "Zimbabwe: Events of 2020," Human Rights Watch World Report, 2021.

45. Tarek Osman, *Egypt on the Brink: From Nasser to Mubarak* (New Haven: Yale University Press, 2010).

46. "Egypt's Brazen Crackdown on Critics," *New York Times,* November 9, 2015; Paul R. Pillar, "Trouble Brewing in Egypt," *Washington Report on Middle East Affairs* 35, no. 4 (June–July 2016), pp. 37–39.

47. Barbara Zoller, "Surviving Repression: How Egypt's Muslim Brotherhood Has Carried On," Malcolm H. Kerr Carnegie Middle East Center, March 11, 2019.

48. Jeremy M. Sharp, "Egypt: Background and US Relations," *Congressional Research Service: Report,* February 5, 2016.

49. Tahrir Institute for Middle East Policy, "Egypt's Rising Security Threat," November 15, 2015; Lisa Blaydes, "Challenges to Stability in Egypt," Hoover Institute, April 22, 2019; Stratfor Analysis, "For Egypt, Islamic State One Threat Among Many," July 2015.

50. US Department of State, "Egypt Country Security Report," OSAC: Bureau of Diplomatic Security, July 29, 2021.

51. Ibid.; Wilson Center, "Sinai Province: Egypt's ISIS Affiliate," May 19, 2016.

52. Thomas Chenesseau and Chantal Azzam, "Egypt," *Counter Terrorist Trends and Analysis* 7, no. 1 (January–February 2015).

53. Council on Foreign Relations, "Instability in Egypt," August 24, 2021; Wilson Center, "Sinai Province"; "Croatian Hostage 'Killed by IS in Egypt,'" *BBC News,* August 12, 2015; US Department of State, "Egypt Country Security Report."

54. Stratfor Analysis, "For Egypt, Islamic State"; Sharp, "Egypt: Background and US Relations"; US Department of State, "Egypt Country Security Report."

55. Sharp, "Egypt: Background and US Relations"; Kareem Fahim, "'Systematic' Killings in Egypt Are Tied to Leader, Group Says," *New York Times,* August 11, 2014; Council on Foreign Relations, "Instability in Egypt."

56. Sharp, "Egypt: Background and US Relations"; Stratfor Analysis, "For Egypt, Islamic State."

57. Emad El-Din Shahin, "Egypt's Revolution Turned on Its Head," *Current History,* December 2015; Zoller, "Surviving Repression"; Nathan J. Brown, "Egypt 2021: The Muslim Brotherhood," Wilson Center, March 17, 2021.

58. Saeid Golkar and Kasra Aarabi, "Iran's Revolutionary Guard Is Radicalizing Young Men Across the Middle East. The U.S. Needs a Counterinsurgency Strategy," *Time,* February 10, 2021.

59. Mark J. Roberts, *Khomeini's Incorporation of the Iranian Military* (Washington, DC: Institute for National Strategic Studies, National Defense University, 1996).
60. Ibid.
61. "Profile: Iran's Revolutionary Guards," *BBC News,* January 3, 2020.
62. Alex Vatanka, "Iran's IRGC Has Long Kept Khamenei in Power," *Foreign Policy* (October 29, 2019).
63. Saeid Golkar and Kasra Aarabi, "Iran's Revolutionary Guard Is Radicalizing Young Men Across the Middle East"; Elliot Hen-Tov and Nathan Gonzalez, "The Militarization of Post-Khomeini Iran: Praetorianism 2.0," *Washington Quarterly* 34, no. 1 (2011); "Profile: Iran's Revolutionary Guards," *BBC News,* January 3, 2020.
64. "Profile: Iran's Revolutionary Guards," *BBC News.*
65. Kasra Jani, "Iran's Revolutionary Guards Take Lead on Foreign Affairs," *BBC News,* January 29, 2015.
66. Arash Azizi, "Why Is Iran Kidnapping and Executing Dissidents?" *New York Times,* January 12, 2021. The 2019 US State Department Country Report on Iran highlighted the arrest or expulsion of Iranian government officials implicated in various terrorist plots in their respective territories, noting Denmark's decision to recall its ambassador from Tehran after evidence of an Iran-backed plot to assassinate an Iranian dissident in Denmark emerged. See US Department of State, "Country Reports on Terrorism 2019: Iran," 2019.
67. Barbara Demick, "Uncovering the Cultural Revolution's Awful Truths," *The Atlantic,* January–February 2021.
68. Charlie Campbell, "How Beijing Is Redefining What It Means to Be Chinese, from Xinjiang to Inner Mongolia," *Time,* July 12, 2021.
69. Ibid.
70. "China-Taiwan Tensions: Xi Jinping Says 'Reunification' Must Be Fulfilled," *BBC News,* October 9, 2021.
71. James Char, "What a Change in China's Officer Rank and Grade System Tells Us About PLA Reform," *The Diplomat,* March 31, 2021.
72. David E. Sanger and William J. Broad, "As China Speeds Up Nuclear Arms Race, the U.S. Wants to Talk," *New York Times,* November 28, 2021.
73. Ibid.
74. Helene Cooper, "China Could Have 1,000 Nuclear Warheads by 2030, Pentagon Says," *New York Times,* November 3, 2021.
75. Bill Chappell, "In South China Sea Islands, Anti-Aircraft and Radar Systems Emerge in Full Color," NPR, December 15, 2016; John Feng, "China Militarizing South China Sea with Warships and Militia: Manila," *Newsweek,* April 14, 2021.
76. Natalie Sambhi, "Generals Gaining Ground: Civil-Military Relations and Democracy in Indonesia," Brookings Institution, January 22, 2021.
77. Karlis Salnaa and Yudith Ho, "Jokowi Taps Ex-General amid Terrorism Threat, China Tensions," *Bloomberg,* July 27, 2016.
78. Richard C. Paddock and Muktita Suhartono, "Indonesian President Is Sworn in amid High Security and Protest Ban," *New York Times,* October 20, 2019; "Wiranto: Indonesia Security Minister Stabbed by 'IS Radical,'" *BBC News,* October 10, 2019.
79. Natalie Sambhi, "Generals Gaining Ground: Civil-Military Relations and Democracy in Indonesia," Brookings Institution, January 22, 2021.
80. "'Our Suffering Is Complete': Promotions for Ex–Tim Mawar Members Adds Insult to Injury for Kidnapped Activists' Families," *Jakarta Post,* September 29, 2020.
81. Richard C. Paddock, "Indonesian Defense Chief, Accused of Rights Abuses, Will Visit Pentagon," *New York Times,* October 14, 2020.
82. Natalie Sambhi, "Generals Gaining Ground."
83. Ardila Syakriah, "Indonesian Military Deployed for Coronavirus Fight," *Jakarta Post,* September 21, 2020.
84. Natalie Sambhi, "Generals Gaining Ground"; Zacharias Szumer, "Coronavirus Spreads Anti-Chinese Feeling in Southeast Asia, but the Prejudice Goes Back Centuries," *South China Morning Post,* April 29, 2020.

85. Richard C. Paddock, "Indonesia Governor's Loss Shows Increasing Power of Islamists," *New York Times,* May 6, 2017; Erwida Maulia, "Fears Grow over Indonesia's Terrorism Threat After Recent Attacks," *Nikkei Asia,* April 9, 2021.

86. "The Guantánamo Docket," *New York Times,* May 21, 2021; "Hunt for Hambali—the Osama of the Far East," *The Telegraph* (London), October 16, 2002; James Vicini, "Guantanamo Prisoner Known as Hambali Seeks Release," *Reuters,* March 11, 2010.

87. Louisa Loveluck, "High-Profile Guantanamo Prisoner Makes His First Appearance Before a Review Board," *Washington Post,* August 18, 2016.

88. Carol Rosenberg, "Three Guantánamo Detainees Charged in 2002 Bali Bombing," *New York Times,* August 31, 2021.

89. "Indonesian Flashpoints: Papua," *BBC News,* October 22, 2010.

90. Johnny Blades, "West Papua: The Issue That Won't Go Away for Melanesia," Lowy Institute, May 1, 2020; "Protests Flare in Papua as Students Demand Independence Referendum," *The Guardian,* September 29, 2020.

91. Richard C. Paddock and Muktita Suhartono, "Indonesian General Is Killed in Rebel Ambush, Sparking Fears of Retaliation," *New York Times,* April 27, 2021.

12

Democracy: Reform, Reconfiguration, or Disintegration?

> If the 20th century was the story of slow, uneven progress toward the victory of liberal democracy over other ideologies—communism, fascism, virulent nationalism—the 21st century is, so far, a story of the reverse.
>
> —*Anne Applebaum, historian and journalist*[1]

There was a time—not all that long ago—when it appeared that we were living in the so-called "democratic age." In the mid-1990s through the early aughts, even in the most unexpected places freedom was making great strides, and DEMOCRACY in its many variations seemed to have become the standard form of government. Yet, in 2021, for a fifteenth consecutive year, analysts have observed declines in the measure of global freedom.[2] Between 2005 and 2016 this trend was treated by most analysts as "worrying but not threatening." But since then there has been a precipitous decline in support for democracy across countries (including the United States) that gives us stronger reasons for pessimism.[3]

The message has only become more urgent over time. As Freedom House and others report, democracies aren't just wavering; democracy has been in retreat. Why is this happening? One of the most common explanations is that it is due to diminishing satisfaction with the way that democracy works in practice. Poor governance, or democracy's inability to live up to its promises, is due to overlapping structural and institutional challenges, both political and economic, external and internal that are going nowhere anytime soon. This includes democracies' lack of state capacity, their inability to deliver basic public goods or guarantee the RULE OF LAW. Citizens in established and emerging democracies alike are disgusted with continuing public corruption and the lack of accountability. Impatient with democracy (and blaming much of this on foreign forces out of their control, or globalization), many people are turning to illiberal democracies, putting their faith in strong leaders over legislatures, and believing that they need a savior who can get things done. The rise of populist leaders only heightens political polarization, undermines checks and balances, and can create a vacuum that these strongmen can exploit, resulting in electoral autocracies.[4]

You won't be surprised to hear that some blame this on Trump. But analysts say that although democratic erosion accelerated during his presidency, the trend predates it. Others look to Russia and China, which, as authoritarian "role models," delight in pointing out the failures of democracy. President Biden joins many others in predicting that the fundamental struggle in the post-PANDEMIC era will be democracies versus autocracies.[5] But others say that the change is driven by declining faith in democracy itself. American-style governance isn't delivering on the promise of prosperity or freedom and therefore it isn't as appealing as it once was.[6]

Democracy nearly everywhere—including weak and fragile, as well as robust or mature democracies—shows signs of decay. In all regions, democracy has clearly lost ground to authoritarianism. In 2021, the number of countries that experienced declines in freedom outnumbered those with improvements by the largest margin recorded since the negative trend began in 2006. And as we will discuss later, Covid only hastened the shifting international balance in favor of tyranny as incumbents on the right and left are, in the name of public health, using the Covid crisis to justify delaying elections and extending their time in office, weaken oversight of their actions, and crush their opponents. According to those who track these trends, the democratic recession is only deepening, with no end in sight.[7]

As you read in Chapters 5 and 6, much of the progress that had been made in promoting growth and development in the global south has been lost due to Covid. Recovery from the pandemic recession is two-track, determined by each country's access to vaccines. And in Chapter 10, you read about how violent conflicts and the military's tendency to assume political power can be set off (or justified) by economic troubles. Austerity certainly has an effect on political performance and the prospects for democracy in all of the regions we discuss. Ethnic and religious strife and other divisions are aggravated by struggles over resources and create very real problems for both democratic and nondemocratic governments, as well as some countries that seem to fall in between these extremes, what some have termed "THE MESSY MIDDLE"—hybrid forms of government that appear to be democratic (or not), yet defy simple regime type. In the most difficult cases, even SOVEREIGNTY, the STATE'S right to exist, is contested. As in the cases of Israel and Ethiopia, for example, there are often profound differences over who should be part of a political community or what should be its territorial boundaries. In a democracy, citizens agree that the government can make legitimate claims to their obedience. However, if the military or another powerful group of people does not accept these demands as legitimate, this poses serious problems for the viability of the government. Until such claims are resolved, democracy is imperiled, if not impossible.

What Is Democracy?

But before we can talk about how difficult it is to sustain, we should first ask ourselves, what is democracy? What makes a country democratic? Let us first say that there is wide disagreement over what should be emphasized when defining democracy. There is no single archetype for democracy, no single, unique set of institutions that are characteristic of democracy. In this chapter we will limit ourselves to a discussion of political democracy, as opposed to social or economic conceptions of democracy. As you will soon see, within political democracy there are different kinds of constitutional systems, and democracies vary widely in levels of citizen participation, access to power, checks and balances, governmental responsiveness to popular demands, party strength, and political pluralism. Therefore, in defining democracy we need to be as general as possible to allow for the many systems that are differently democratic.[8]

However, for all its variations, certain minimal criteria must be met for a political system to be considered democratic. Although governments satisfy these criteria to different degrees (and none of them perfectly), three conditions are commonly named as essential to any democracy: the existence of competition, participation, and respect for civil liberties. With the identification of these common denominators we can begin to define democracy. Democracy is one type of political system. As opposed to systems of AUTHORITARIANISM, in which decisionmaking power is concentrated in the hands of a few and authority is unchallengeable, democracies are based in the decentralization of authority. In democracies citizens take part in making the decisions of government. Put more simply, democracy is a system of governance in which citizens hold their leaders accountable for their public actions. ACCOUNTABILITY is ensured through open competition for office. Democracy institutionalizes competition for power through elections that are free, fair, and held on a regular basis.[9]

But another important part of competition is inclusiveness, which demands a high level of political participation in the selection of leaders and policies. Where government makes room for people to add their voices, the political process has been opened up to promote effective political participation.[10] In a democracy, citizens should be able to influence public policy. At its core, democratization entails the accommodation of a wide range of opinions. For a country to be considered a democracy, there must be room for a lively and vibrant CIVIL SOCIETY, with active parties, trade unions, and religious and cultural groups that operate independently of the regime. Of course, it is also expected that people will be free to organize and express themselves without worry of harassment or imprisonment. This is necessary to satisfy the democratic requirements of both participation and competition.

Therefore, participation is expressed as the right of all citizens to take part in the democratic process. "Taking part" can mean any number of things, but it must at the very least include the right to political equality. In democracies there should be very few restrictions on the citizen's right to vote or run for office. No one should be excluded because of gender, ethnicity, religion, CLASS, or sexual orientation, etc. Neither should there be a property or literacy requirement for citizens to participate in the process. The greater the number of people who are denied citizenship and whose opportunities are hurt by such denial, the more unlikely states will be able to achieve a CONSOLIDATION of democracy, or make it durable. Democratic governments will take pains to be inclusive, to ensure collective as well as individual rights, to ensure that minority and traditionally oppressed groups have equal representation, and to ensure that the votes of all citizens are weighted equally (one person, one vote).[11]

The term "free" is often used synonymously with the term "democratic." As mentioned earlier, according to the human rights organization Freedom House, the number of countries defined as "free" nearly doubled from 69 in 1989 to 120 in 2000. But then it fell significantly, to 82 by 2020, continuing the longest downward trend in freedom since Freedom House began the report nearly five decades ago.[12] The organization offers Venezuela, Ethiopia, Algeria, and Hong Kong as examples of places that not long ago seemed poised for democratic gains, but have made the dangerous turn to authoritarianism. And it wasn't just the newer or proto-democracies that lost ground. India, the world's most populous democracy (with a population of over 1.3 billion), and one of the oldest democracies in the global south, fell in the Freedom House rankings from "free" to "partly free" in 2020 due to a crackdown on dissent and several years in which the Hindu nationalist government has imposed discriminatory policies against Muslims.[13]

Another way to conceptualize the decline of democracy is that just a few years ago 50 percent of the world's population lived in countries ranked as free. Yet, as of 2021, fewer than 20 percent lived in a "free" country (mostly due to India's decline). In terms of regions, democracies in all regions showed strain, but the Middle East is the least free, followed closely by sub-Saharan Africa where over thirty-nine countries experienced declines as well. Was there any good news? Sure. Examples include Malawi, which had a successful rerun of flawed elections. Taiwan and South Korea, both of which were authoritarian a few decades ago, are now considered full and resilient democracies.[14]

So, back to defining terms. What does "freedom" mean? Countries, or to be more precise, political systems, that are termed "free" generally allow for a high degree of political and civil freedoms, but they do so to varying degrees. Some people offer up the sheer number of elections held in the late twentieth century as evidence that a democratic revolution has taken place. They identify elections as the watershed event marking the DEMOCRATIC TRANSITION and treat democracy as an event rather than a process. This is problematic for a variety of reasons. Elections can sometimes result in a setback for democracy, especially if antidemocratic candidates are elected or if divides are deep and elections are perceived as win-or-lose events. This is why democracy must be rooted in a POLITICAL CULTURE that promotes popular participation, one that tolerates differences and accepts the consensus.[15]

Although there have been significant setbacks over the past few years, it is remarkable that between 1990 and 2005, forty-four of forty-eight countries in sub-Saharan Africa held multiparty elections, compared to only four African countries in 1990.[16] In East Asia in the 1980s, only Japan was considered democratic. Nearly forty years later, there were three "full democracies" in the region: Japan, South Korea, and Taiwan; four more states in that region held multiparty elections: Indonesia, Papua New Guinea, Mongolia, and Malaysia.[17] That's an important step, but elections alone do not make a democracy. Rather, democracies have electoral and nonelectoral dimensions. Be careful not to fall for the FALLACY OF ELECTORALISM, or the tendency to focus on elections while ignoring other political realities. Many countries have gone through the motions of elections, yet real power remains in the hands of an oligarchy or the military. Or there are civilian leaders but without broad, unconditional, mass support for democracy or a clear disavowal of authoritarianism.[18]

As we will see, individual countries have made significant progress in some areas of political and civil rights, but there are still other crucial reforms that these countries need to address. Sure, how rulers come to power is important, but just as important is the strength of democratic institutions and whether they can hold elected leaders accountable for their actions. In determining the success of a democratic transition, it is more important to ask whether the RULE OF LAW prevails and whether an independent, impartial judiciary guarantees the protection of political and civil rights, rather than simply relying on the "litmus test" of elections. As of 2020, 115 out of 193 states were classified as electoral democracies (democracies in the most minimal sense, many of which are only "partly free").[19]

On the other hand, democracies that pass a more comprehensive test are commonly known as LIBERAL DEMOCRACIES. As opposed to the minimal framework of electoral democracies, liberal democracies are based on a deeper institutional structure that offers extensive protections for civil and political rights—individual and group liberties such as freedom of thought and expression, freedom of the press, and the right to form and join assemblies or organizations, including political parties and interest groups. Where civil rights are protected, people feel that they have the freedom to participate in the political process. Democratizing societies will encourage civil society to flourish, and encourage political parties and interest groups to organize without constraint. Again, there are no perfect democracies. No country completely lives up to all the standards listed here. And what can start as a major political transformation can turn out in a variety of ways.

For example, transitions frequently become sidelined by disputes between democrats over the meaning of freedom, the best constitutional and electoral system, or whether to organize as a unitary or federal state. All democracies, even the most established ones, must continuously work to improve their democratic practices. For example, the economic inequality that exists in the United States (and in every democracy to some degree) has the effect of skewing political power. Despite claims of political equality, the affluent are "more equal than others," because they can use their resources to exert disproportionate influence over policy.[20]

Because of problems with democratic practice, often the line between democratic and nondemocratic regimes is unclear. Several countries are hard to place because they may satisfy some requirements of democracy but not others. Governments that are characterized as "free" or "democratic" commonly experience isolated violations of civil liberties or occasional electoral malpractice such as voter suppression (when the state creates barriers that make it hard for qualified voters to exercise their constitutional right to cast a ballot).[21]

Beyond certain fundamentals, democracies differ markedly from one another, with varying strengths and weaknesses. In the years following the "third wave" of democratization that began in 1974, more than eighty countries made significant progress toward democracy. However, contrary to popular belief, there is no end point at which a country can be said to have "attained" democracy, and many of these have lost ground. It should be expected that it will take some time for appropriate political systems to be created, and that they will evolve at least partly in response to political failures. Around the world, many in the wave of countries that made a democratic transition have reversed themselves. For example, Mexico had been ranked as "free" for several years after its FOUNDING ELECTIONS in 2000, but in 2010 Freedom House dropped its rating to "partly free," largely because of deficits in the rule of law and its ongoing drug wars—a decline that continues through 2021.[22]

Therefore, democratization is something that should be understood as an ongoing, dynamic process instead of a singular achievement. Just as we recognize that some countries may come closer to fitting the democratic ideal than others, we must recognize that a similar continuum exists for their less-than-democratic counterparts. In the end, most governments fall somewhere in between the two poles of democracy and TOTALITARIANISM, an extreme form of authoritarianism. Many governments allow for more freedoms than do rigidly totalitarian regimes, but these freedoms are so few that such governments cannot adequately qualify as democracies. As you will see in the next chapter, there is an unusually large array of names for those systems that fall in the "messy middle": somewhere in between.[23] For example, many global south governments, including those of Nigeria and Iran (at the opposite ends of this range), can be viewed as DELEGATIVE DEMOCRACIES: they are neither liberal democracies nor quite full-blown dictatorships. Delegative democracies are sometimes called democratic because they have an outward appearance similar to that of their more democratic counterparts. However, delegative democracies are led by ELITES whose commitment to democracy is contingent and instrumental, not routinized, internalized, and principled.[24] Delegative democracies are a peculiar form of democracy; through competitive elections a majority empowers someone to become the embodiment and interpreter of the nation's interests. No, this doesn't sound very democratic, but as Guillermo O'Donnell contends, delegative democracies can sometimes be more democratic than they are authoritarian. What is important to remember is that even though some governments are doing a better job of promoting certain aspects of democracy than are others, the success is relative and the work is ongoing. A similar concern is raised by the in-between examples, what some have called pseudo-democracies or electoral authoritarian

Figure 12.1 Respect for Political and Civil Rights: How Our Cases Rate

Freedom House is a highly respected nongovernmental organization that monitors democratization and human rights worldwide. As part of its work, the organization rates virtually every country based on its respect for political rights and civil liberties. Here's how our cases rated in 2021:

Mexico:	Partly Free	Egypt:	Not Free
Peru:	Partly Free	Iran:	Not Free
Nigeria:	Partly Free	China:	Not Free
Zimbabwe:	Not Free	Indonesia:	Partly Free

Source: Freedom House, *Freedom in the World 2021.*

regimes: there are a variety of complex processes involved in governing, and labels can sometimes gloss over achievements (as well as detriments).[25]

Background to the Transition

As mentioned earlier, starting in the 1970s and accelerating through the 1990s, a number of what were sometimes characterized as stunning political changes occurred throughout the world, including the global south. The winding down of the COLD WAR (from the end of World War II until 1989, a period during which both the United States and Soviet Union backed dictators throughout the global south) coincided with a period of what some called a global democratic revolution. A "third wave" of pro-democracy movements rose up not only in Europe, but also in sub-Saharan Africa, Asia, Latin America, and to a lesser extent the Middle East (the Middle East and North Africa's third wave mostly came later, with the "Arab Spring" of 2010–2012, but the only one of these countries to sustain a democratic transition was Tunisia, and by 2021 that democracy was in doubt, the president ruling by decree).[26]

Some analysts have characterized the 1970s–1990s as a critical historical moment, "the greatest period of democratic ferment in the history of modern civilization."[27] Much of this commotion grew out of an *ABERTURA*, or a political opening, associated with a mix of reforms. Countries undertaking such reforms are often described as experiencing a POLITICAL LIBERALIZATION. Periods of political liberalization are generally associated with a variety of changes such as greater press freedoms, greater freedom of assembly, and the introduction of legal safeguards for individuals. People living in countries experiencing a political liberalization witness the release of most political prisoners, the return of exiles, and perhaps most important, a growing tolerance of dissent.

At the end of 2021, about half of the world's population was living in countries that could claim to be broadly democratic, with only 8 percent living in countries considered fully democratic and more than one-third living in countries characterized as "not free" (many of them living in China).[28] However, not all governments that can be described as "broadly democratic" are necessarily headed toward democracy. As O'Donnell has noted, not all processes culminate in the same result. For example, at times over the past decade and a half, China and Iran have been said to have liberalized politically, but this does not mean that they are democratizing or are in the process of a democratic transition. Let's be clear: China and Iran do not appear to be on their way toward adopting the kind of political system that the West usually considers democratic. And in both countries, even as gains are made, they can be (and have been) quickly retracted. On the other hand, what was remarkable about the "third wave" was not only the sheer number of countries that made political reforms, but also the number that began a democratic transition of one kind or another. In understanding how so many countries arrived at this point, it is important to recognize that each country's situation is unique; its citizens are responding to a particular set of historical challenges and socioeconomic problems. Consequently, no single set of determinants can satisfactorily explain the origins and evolution of democratic transitions throughout the world.[29]

As you will recall from Chapter 8, some analysts emphasize the significance of internal factors in understanding change. Their interest is in the roles played by civil society or domestic actors, whether elites or masses, in the dramatic political events we've been describing. The preceding chapters have demonstrated how people around the world are mobilized by a variety of pressures. Citizens have demanded the opening of political space in which a variety of new relationships can be crafted. Not all of these groups are mobilized by democratic interests, yet whatever their goals, new forms of social mobilization and patterns of state-society relations are emerging in which relationships of power and accountability are redefined. Yet often it has been political elites who have played crucial roles in the political transition. Frustrated over their inability to govern effectively or faced with a crisis of LEGITIMACY, civilian and military leaders have on occasion stood aside to allow for democratic change. Once the transition is under way, elite commitment to democracy (or the lack of such commitment) has often played a large role in its success or failure. Egypt is a good example of this. Its Arab Spring uprising in 2011 ushered out a long-standing dictatorship and ushered in Egypt's very first democratically elected government. But in a second rebellion in 2013 the protesters turned against constitutional government, rejecting the new president, Mohamed Morsi of the Muslim Brotherhood. The result was a military takeover and a dictatorship worse than ever.[30]

Other analysts emphasize the role played by economic forces in promoting political change. They contend, for example, that the industrialization and economic success of South Korea and Taiwan created in these countries an environment conducive to democratization. There and elsewhere, as the middle class has grown, these citizens have become more politically conscious and vocal in demanding political and civil rights. However, around the world it is more common to find that political change has occurred as people have struggled to cope with devastating economic crises. There are cases from all four regions we study in which the hardship associated with austerity incited popular protests that nearly brought down governments, democratic and nondemocratic. In the immediate post–Cold War period (and since), such demonstrations often persuaded authoritarians to initiate political reform—or at least the appearance of reform.

Although the political liberalization of some countries predated the end of the Cold War, external pressures associated with its demise (such as the withdrawal of superpower support for authoritarians) are recognized as another factor driving reform. Yet even now the governments of many countries in the global south continue to be highly extroverted; their survival depends on foreign patronage. As discussed in Chapter 6, since the 1970s, in return for aid, international organizations such as the INTERNATIONAL MONETARY FUND (IMF) have directed developing countries to impose economic reforms on their increasingly disgruntled populations. However, after the Cold War ended, donor countries began to insist that governments throughout the global south initiate political reforms aimed at promoting "good governance"—increasing the accountability and TRANSPARENCY of government.[31]

This is the "all good things go together" argument: proponents of NEOLIBERALISM tend to assume that economic GROWTH and democratization complement each other and are mutually reinforcing (although there is still disagreement about which comes first). However, the developed countries have never been consistent in their demands for political liberalization; the vigor with which such calls were made varied depending on the target of reform (e.g., for strategic and economic reasons, most Middle Eastern countries were largely exempt from donor attention).

A variety of other external factors have also been used to explain the recent political changes experienced in so much of the world. Some analysts credit the dramatic events of the late twentieth century to a zeitgeist (or "spirit of the times"), unique to the immediate post–Cold War era, because at that moment in history democracy appeared to be breaking out all over the world and democratic IDEOLOGY had no serious contenders. This zeitgeist is believed by some to have contributed to a snowballing or demonstration effect as authoritarian governments toppled like dominos. Analysts interested in this facet of change argue that among states closely linked by culture, geography, or some other shared experience, the more successful a transition in any one country in the group, the more likely we are to see similar political change among the other members of that group.[32]

This effect has been magnified by the revolution in communications such as satellite television, which allows outsiders to watch events literally as they unfold. For better or worse, the intriguing role that this technology (especially social media) plays in political change is only one part of an "international diffusion effect" (what some call the "Twitter effect"), which can change expectations, affect crowd behavior, and even alter the balance of power almost overnight. Such an effect has often been associated with military coups (illegal attempts to take power through force). In recent years, it has grown with authoritarians' exploitation of digital tools to censor and manipulate information to gain or maintain control over domestic (and foreign) populations. In many countries, communications technologies have been associated with piecemeal democratic backsliding, decline, and collapse. In the global south and north leaders have come to office through elections and then undermined norms and institutions to remove any restraints on their power. Yet, during the past three decades the information revolution has also worked to support a resurgence of democracy, even if its use is sometimes confined to more secular, affluent, and often bilingual elite, as we observed in the Arab Spring, for example.[33] Leaders in China, North Korea, Iran, and even Nigeria recognize its power to foment change, and have banned Twitter and similar platforms. In the global south—and global north—Twitter has blocked, deleted the accounts of, and/or permanently suspended heads of state from the site for using it to incite violence.[34]

After the Transition: Consolidating and Deepening Democracy

One way to understand the resurgence of democracy is to think of it as occurring in phases. Some have taken just the very first (often tentative) step. There are certainly more recent examples, but this one is notable for its audacity: in late 2016, after twenty-two years of repressive rule, Gambia's "elected" dictator Yahya Jammeh (who said he was ready to rule for "a billion years, if God wills it") finally allowed himself to lose elections—but when the time came, resisted

Figure 12.2 When Islamists Win Elections

Algeria's experience, as well as that of the Palestinians and Egypt's, has been a lesson for many people seeking change in predominantly Muslim North Africa and the Middle East. Under a variety of pressures for political liberalization, Algeria's authoritarian government allowed democratic elections in 1991. A number of parties organized to participate in these elections, among them the Islamic Salvation Front (FIS), an umbrella party representing many smaller Islamist groups. When the FIS was poised to win a strong majority of seats in a second round of parliamentary elections in 1992, the Algerian government (with the tacit backing of France and the United States) voided the elections, declared the FIS illegal, and set out on a campaign to portray all Islamist contenders for power as a threat to democracy in Algeria and to the West. Supporters of this policy argued that Islamists were totalitarians in disguise, adopting the rhetoric of democracy only to gain power. What happened in Algeria confirmed views of the West as hypocritically supporting democracy only when in its own interests.

In 2006, after the Palestinian movement Hamas won a surprise landslide victory in parliamentary elections, the United States led a group of Western states that immediately set out to isolate and undermine the new democratically elected government (designated by the United States as a terrorist organization because of its attacks on Israel). Similarly, the West was criticized as slow to support Arab Spring uprisings in 2011, including in Egypt, as it feared the Islamist Muslim Brotherhood would move into the vacuum created by President Hosni Mubarak's departure. The Brotherhood did move into that vacuum. Its candidate, Mohamed Morsi, was the first democratically elected president of Egypt and the party won more seats in parliament than any other political party. But Egypt's divisions only deepened during its year in power. When the military stepped in to put an end to this experiment in democracy, the Barack Obama administration, which insisted it wasn't taking sides, voiced its deep concern and called for a return to democratic rule. But the United States was also careful not to call it a coup—so as not to imperil US military and economic assistance to Egypt, and Egypt's peace with Israel.[a] The United States has fully resumed its partnership with Egypt, which (under former general Abdel Fattah al-Sisi) has resumed its dictatorship.

While such a response may seem reasonable to some, this perceived ambivalence about democracy is problematic—particularly in the Middle East. Whether the United States likes it or not, the Islamist appeal has grown and exists in all Arab countries, and this may be as much due to sympathy for Islamist programs as it is based in resentment of corrupt government and Western hypocrisy.[b]

Notes: a. Dan Roberts, "US in Bind over Egypt After Supporting Morsi but Encouraging Protesters," *The Guardian,* July 3, 2013.

b. Emmanuel Sivan, "Illusions of Change," *Journal of Democracy* 11, no. 3 (July 2000); Laith Kubba, "The Awakening of Civil Society," *Journal of Democracy* 11, no. 3 (July 2000).

handing over power to the winner. He eventually did step down, but only after stealing millions and sparking an international crisis.[35]

Of the political systems that are democratizing, most made the transition from authoritarian rule and begun to establish democratic regimes with less drama. While they vary in terms of the quality of democracy, many countries, including South Africa and Ghana, South Korea and Taiwan, and much of Latin America and the Caribbean are well into a second phase of democratization, known as consolidation. When is a democratic transition complete? According to analysts Juan Linz and Alfred Stepan, it is complete when there is sufficient agreement about the political procedures to produce an elected government. It is complete when a government comes to power as the direct result of a free and popular vote, and when this government has the authority to generate new policies. Finally, a democratic transition is complete when we can be sure that the executive, legislative, and judicial power generated by the new democracy is not subservient to other bodies such as the military. Most important perhaps, all politically significant groups agree to abide by the procedural rules of the game. In effect, a democracy has progressed from transition to consolidation when no significant political groups are seriously trying to overthrow the democratic regime or secede from the state.[36] These are the democratic rules and procedures that must be established before one can begin to speak of consolidation.

Even when a transition can be described as complete, there are still many tasks that must be accomplished, conditions that must be established, and culture (attitudes and habits) that must be developed before democracy can be considered durable, or consolidated. How do we know when a democracy has been consolidated? Analysts admit that it is easier to recognize consolidation by its absence. Unconsolidated regimes are fragile, unstable, and plagued by signs of disloyalty. Beyond this it is hard to define consolidation, because no single indicator other than general stability serves as its marker. We know that the road to consolidation is a long and complicated one. Perhaps the simplest way of telling if consolidation exists is if democracy has become "the only game in town." The majority of people believe that the system is a good one, and that it is the most appropriate way of governing collective life.[37] When this is the case, the regime enjoys broad and deep levels of popular legitimacy.

When a democracy is consolidated, the issue for government is no longer how to avoid democratic breakdown. You know you have a consolidated democracy when, even in the face of extreme economic or political hardship, the overwhelming majority of people believe that any political change must occur through the democratic system. All political actors have become accustomed to the idea that political conflict will be resolved according to the established rules, and convinced that violations of these rules will be ineffective and costly. In other words, when it is consolidated, democracy becomes a habit; it is routinized and widely accepted. This takes years of practice—some political scientists argue that two generations of uninterrupted democratic rule must pass, allowing the rules of the game to be refined, tested, and strengthened. However, even when elections are free and fair, and electoral commissions and courts do their jobs, we have seen the result rejected by the incumbent and his followers in some of the oldest, most long-standing democracies, as the January 6, 2021, insurrectionist attack at the US Capitol illustrates. This spectacle was a shock for many in the United States and worldwide. The United States didn't change in status from "free" to "partly free," but it is, according to Freedom House, one of the twenty-five countries to see the steepest declines in freedoms over the past ten years.[38]

How do we ensure that democracy lasts? Democratic stability is promoted when the leaders and citizens uphold the norms that make democracies succeed. Among these is the belief that the rights of the political opposition and minorities are safeguarded. That may sound counterproductive, especially where divisions are deep, but analysts tell us that conflict becomes less intense as it is contained within institutional channels. Most important, over time there is a change in the political culture of elites and masses, as commitment to the democratic framework is no longer simply instrumental but rather a commitment based in principle. As democracies consolidate, we gradually see within them the development of what some analysts call a "civic culture." Although mutual trust between potential opponents, willingness to compromise, and cooperation between political competitors are all identified as key components of civic culture, the particulars of any democratic political culture will vary by country.[39] In general, though, as consolidation proceeds, political elites and the masses gradually internalize democratic values and develop habits of tolerance and moderation. Rights become realities and there is an agreed standard of fairness. Of course, this balanced political culture is only likely to occur where inequalities are relatively low and people can afford not to care too much about politics—and such circumstances do not yet exist in most new democracies. As one analyst put it, "The trick, then, is for democracies to survive long enough—and function well enough—for this process to occur."[40]

In other words, consolidation is another breakthrough of sorts. It is fostered through a combination of institutional, policy, and behavioral changes and is an important achievement for any budding democracy. Yet just because a regime is consolidated does not mean that it is immune to future breakdown. Any number of crises could occur to make a nondemocratic alternative attractive and undo even a consolidated regime. One way of avoiding such a breakdown is by recognizing the intimate connection between consolidation and the deepening of democracy. This qualitative shift is sometimes described as a third phase of democratization. Democracies are deepened as they improve, by promoting equality and extending to more citizens the opportunity for participation in political life. By this definition, even older, more established democracies may still become more democratic. All democracies can be improved—that is, made more responsive and representative.[41]

At this stage countries often find themselves in a Catch-22 situation. In what is sometimes called "the democratic dilemma," democracies need to be deepened in order to fully consolidate. However, the deepening of democracy can undermine the prospects of consolidation. Deepening democracy means addressing social and economic inequalities, and this is likely to threaten elite interests and provoke an authoritarian reaction. Consequently, in the short term at least, the most stable democracies are also often the most superficial ones—the ones that forestall necessary changes to minimize the risk of coup. Ironically, because they are defective, "shells of what they could be," these democracies ultimately fail.[42] Incapable or unwilling to deal with the problems of massive inequality, they are vulnerable to "reverse waves" or democratic breakdowns. Such democratic breakdowns should be expected, just as they followed the first and second waves of democratization earlier in the twentieth century. These reverse waves have been traumatic times for human rights and international peace; they gave rise to fascist and communist regimes in the period between World Wars I and II, as well as military dictatorships in the 1960s and 1970s.[43]

Is there any indication that the world is headed in this direction again? Nearly two decades into the twenty-first century there were troubling signs that support for democracy in some developing countries was eroding.[44] The expected reverse wave appeared to be hitting all regions, even Latin America, the region furthest along in its transition. For example, a 2018 survey of everyday people conducted by the highly respected polling organization Latinobarómetro found a continued decline in satisfaction with the level of democratic performance in their country—to an all-time low: 75 percent of those polled expressed a negative judgment about political life in their country. For the first time in twenty-five years, since Latinobarómetro began asking the question, fewer than 50 percent of citizens expressed full support for democracy as a form of government. Moreover, the proportion of people who described themselves as having no preference between authoritarian and democratic regimes reached its highest point ever: 28 percent (this number has doubled since 1997). Interestingly, women and young people were consistently most likely to express dissatisfaction with democracy as a system. The main drivers identified with satisfaction with the political system (and predictors of political system resilience) were levels of satisfaction with the functioning of the economy. In a vicious circle, as satisfaction with the system declined, so did support for it.[45]

According to this study, in 2018, the Latin American countries predicted to have the greatest democratic resilience were Costa Rica, Uruguay, and Argentina. The countries believed to have the lowest democratic resilience were Bolivia, Peru, and Mexico. Popular support for democracy was strongest in "not free" Venezuela (75 percent: people who don't have democracy want it) as well as "free," full democracies that perform relatively well: Costa Rica (63 percent), and Uruguay (61 percent). In a virtuous circle, we see rising support for democracy in democracies that perform well. On the other hand, support for democracy was lowest in two countries that are "not free": Guatemala and El Salvador, each with 28 percent.[46] It will be interesting to see if support for democracy in Guatemala and El Salvador increases when people see that abandoning freedom doesn't necessarily mean better performance, as we have seen support for democracy highest in "not free" states that fail to perform.[47]

Similar global surveys of ordinary people over the last decade suggest that regime performance is very important in explaining the changes in support for democracy in most countries in all regions. According to an Afrobarometer report, across the eighteen African countries surveyed in 2019–2020, two-thirds of citizens were increasingly pessimistic, saying that their countries were going in the wrong direction, politically and economically. However, more than two-thirds (68 percent) of respondents expressed a preference for democracy over any other political system. Even larger proportions rejected presidential dictatorship (81 percent), one-party rule (76 percent), and military rule (73 percent). A large but declining majority believes that elections are the best way to select leaders.[48]

On the other hand, Latin America is the region that has suffered the most glaring drop in support for democracy and the most backsliding toward authoritarianism. Interestingly, in East Asia, satisfaction with "democracy" is higher (72 percent) in strong-performing hybrid regimes and one-party nondemocracies (such as Singapore and China) than in democracies, such as South Korea, Taiwan, and Mongolia, where the satisfaction level is modest, averaging 61 percent. Analysts explain that in these relatively new democracies, young people have unusually high standards for judging their countries' democratic systems whereas "baby boomers" are often nostalgic for their authoritarian past. In a

2016 survey, 25, 28, and 37 percent of respondents in South Korea, Taiwan, and Mongolia, respectively, embraced the view that "Under some circumstances, an authoritarian government can be preferable to a democratic one."[49]

Such views hardly provide the best foundation for a successful democracy, and there are very real risks that if democracies don't improve their performance, populations will turn against them and more democracies will slide toward authoritarianism, into "the messy middle." What is the messy middle? Since the end of the Cold War, leaders in the global south have been faced with donor pressure to democratize (in addition to juggling myriad preexisting and new social, economic, and political crises). These pressures and crises have been managed in a variety of ways. The result, however loosely defined, is a fascinating array of variations on democracy. Catherine Boone identifies the most common manifestations of this crisis management as REFORM, RECONFIGURATION, and DISINTEGRATION. Here and continuing into the next chapter we will describe these forms of crisis management as practiced throughout the global south. However, the particulars vary by country, and whether a political system has reformed, reconfigured, or disintegrated can also at least in part be explained by the structural differences among states. Individual decisions must be factored in, as people worldwide make choices and take actions in response to the unique predicaments they face. In other words, just as the extent of the crisis each country faces is a function of the relative weakness of the regime and the strength of the pressures bearing on it, so too is the outcome.[50]

Reform

To review the fundamentals, for a political system to be considered a democracy it must be based in certain principles such as participation, representation, accountability, and respect for human rights. No government has a perfect record in this regard; however, some countries have made more progress in certain areas than in others. Long-standing, well-established democracies exist in India, Costa Rica, Botswana, Mauritius, and a handful of other global south countries. Given the diversity of these countries, it should come as no surprise that no single set of institutions, practices, and values embodies democracy. Similarly, various mixes of these components produce different types of constitutional systems. However, most democracies operate under some variant of the PARLIAMENTARY SYSTEM or the PRESIDENTIAL SYSTEM. Although US citizens are most familiar with the presidential system, which is also found in much of Latin America and scattered throughout Africa and Asia, the largest democracy in the world, India, has a parliamentary system, and parliamentary systems are common in Europe.

The choice of constitutional design and electoral system is significant because it may impact the quality and stability of democracy. There are pros and cons to each constitutional system, and each system involves some trade-offs. Analysts disagree about which is best for developing countries. One group, led by Juan Linz, argues that although the presidential system has worked well for the United States, its record in low-income countries is more problematic. The presidential system tends to concentrate power in the executive branch, perhaps making the president too strong and (where there is little commitment to democratic values or practices) facilitating the abuse of power. In Peru, Zimbabwe, South Korea, and elsewhere, presidential systems have been associated with executive coups (self-coups) and executive strikes against democracy.

This is one of "the perils of presidentialism," based in the tendency for executives in presidential systems to view themselves as having authority independent of the other branches of government. Even when they have won by the slimmest of margins, presidents are more likely than prime ministers to find opposition in the legislative branch irritating and to consider it an interference with their mission. Not all presidential systems suffer from this problem, but where presidentialism exists, whoever is elected president believes he or she has a mandate, or the right to govern as he or she sees fit. Under such circumstances, the executive is constrained only by the "hard facts of existing power relations" and the constitutionally limited term of office.[51]

It might appear that such an approach does not build a strong basis for the development of democratic institutions. Not only does presidentialism adversely affect the quality of democracy, but it is also commonly viewed as a major factor contributing to democratic breakdowns. Part of the reason for this is lack of capacity: while a strong executive is capable of making rapid decisions, it is often less proficient at coping with crises. In relatively democratic governments, where there is presidentialism, gridlock (resulting from the mix of a domineering president and a newly assertive legislature) is more likely. And some analysts contend governments with strong executives tend to be more rigid and are less likely to avail themselves of the creative approaches demanded by most crises.[52]

Fearful that mounting problems will overwhelm a weak or inexperienced government, voters tend to create presidentialist regimes, as they frequently flock to candidates who promise to save the country. Such leaders appear to be strong, courageous, and above partisan interests. This image is very seductive, especially for people who have lived through difficult or uncertain times. Consequently, we should not be shocked by the frequency of presidentialism. It is important to remember that democratic elections are not an end unto themselves. Newly democratizing countries can be expected to continue on in a transition that is not necessarily linear in its progression. There is rarely a simple trajectory from authoritarian to democratic rule; transitions are often longer and more complex. This is in part because the values and beliefs of officials are embedded in a network of inherited power relations and do not change overnight. This helps to explain why elections in newly democratizing countries can be such emotional and high-stakes events. Often the candidates compete for a chance to rule virtually free of all constraints. After the elections, voters are expected to become passive cheerleaders for all of the president's policies.[53]

For these reasons, parliamentary systems are described by Linz as better suited for most countries. According to Linz, parliamentary systems are more stable and more representative than presidential systems. In parliamentary regimes the only democratically legitimate institution is parliament. The executive's authority is completely dependent upon parliamentary confidence. As opposed to presidential systems (in which the executive is usually selected through direct popular elections), in parliamentary systems there is no worry about executives reaching out to appeal to people over the heads of their representatives.[54]

However, Donald Horowitz argues that parliamentary systems can actually end up more polarized and coalitions can end up more unstable than they are in presidential systems, and that this can impede the business of governance. Unlike presidential systems, parliamentary governments risk periodic crises (known as votes of "no confidence") that can result in the ousting of executives and the disruption caused by new elections. On the other hand, Linz argues that what appears to be instability in parliamentary governments can actually be a benefit: since parliamentary systems are more flexible, they are self-correcting. Parties under parliamentary systems often find themselves forced to cooperate and make coalitions to appoint a prime minister and move legislation through. Moreover, Linz contends that fragmentation is not a problem unique to parliamentary systems. Because there are fewer incentives to make coalitions in a presidential system, gridlock is a persistent problem and the legislative and executive branches end up competing against each other rather than working together. Although coalitions and power-sharing are possible under such systems, more often the institutional rivalry associated with the separation of powers in a presidential system can be extremely destabilizing, especially for unconsolidated democracies.[55]

The tendency of presidential systems toward majoritarianism (in which majorities govern and minorities oppose) makes politics a winner-take-all ZERO-SUM GAME. Because it creates a sharp divide between the government and the opposition, majoritarianism aggravates divisiveness in countries where it is already a problem. What one wins, the other loses. However, the zero-sum nature of majoritarian politics is also associated with parliamentary systems such as those of Britain, India, and Jamaica. In parliaments dominated by a single majority party, this party controls both the executive and legislative branches. Consequently, the prime minister may end up having more effective power than that of the typical president.[56]

Still, not all parliamentary systems are majoritarian. Some forms of parliamentary government tend to be multiparty and to create governments built on what is called a consensus model. As opposed to the sharp divides of majoritarianism, the consensus model found in most of continental Europe as well as Pacific Island states such as Fiji and Tuvalu attempt to share, disperse, and restrain power in a variety of ways. For example, under the consensus model a parliamentary government can promote power-sharing with the creation of broad coalition cabinets and an executive-legislative balance of power. According to Linz, in such parliamentary systems the executive is more accountable before the legislature. This is important, since in deeply divided societies it is crucial that particular groups not be excluded. In the consensus model, government must work to build agreement. It gives everyone a stake in the system by encouraging coalitions. Yet, believe it or not, gridlock is not always the rule in presidential systems and conciliatory practices are not unheard of. Some analysts argue that the mode of election (such as single member versus proportional representation) is actually more important in fostering conciliation and consensus building than whether the constitutional system is parliamentary or presidential.[57]

An additional factor considered in these debates concerns another aspect of rigidity versus flexibility. The proponents of presidential systems argue that the rigidity of fixed presidential terms is an advantage as opposed to the uncertainty and instability that are characteristic of parliamentary politics. However, there are also disadvantages to the inflexibility of presidential systems. Not only is reelection possible only on a fixed term, but it is also very difficult to impeach or remove a president from power before his or her term is over. As a result, the country may be stuck with a "lame duck" government that has lost public confidence and support. Or, because of fixed terms and limits on reelection, experienced and capable leaders must step down at the end of their terms.[58]

Conversely, advocates of parliamentary systems say that such systems are advantaged by their greater flexibility and adaptability. With a vote of "no confidence," in which the majority of members of parliament vote to "censure" the prime minister, the legislative branch can force new elections to be called at any time to turn out an executive who has lost popular support—without regime crisis. And popular, effective executives can be retained indefinitely, whereas a president may be required to retire just as he or she is becoming an adept leader. Moreover, because in presidential systems the executive is both head of government and head of state, there is no constitutional monarch or ceremonial president who serves as a moderating influence on the executive (as there is in parliamentary systems). Although it is increasingly the case in parliamentary systems as well, presidential systems tend to place a heavy reliance on the personal qualities of a single political leader. Again, Linz argues that this is risky, especially in countries where there is an authoritarian tradition.[59]

In the end, consideration of a country's history and culture is crucial in the selection of a constitutional system, since the issue of "fit" is so important. Lack of fit between a country and its constitutional system can greatly undermine popular support for democracy. Some countries have switched from one type of constitutional system to another in an effort to get it right: Nigeria has tried parliamentary and presidential systems (it is currently a federal republic using the presidential system) while many Latin American countries suffering from presidentialist politics have considered adoption of parliamentary forms of government. Chileans voted overwhelmingly in 2020 to rewrite their constitution, which could make theirs the first Latin American country to (among other things) install a parliamentary system. Still, some analysts argue that the constitutional system matters little, since the differences between the two types of systems are exaggerated—both systems have succumbed to military coup and single-party rule. They add that perhaps other factors, such as political culture or the economy, are more important than institutional choice in promoting durable democracies. The one thing these political scientists seem to agree on is that any system involves some trade-offs.[60]

As you will see in the sections that follow, no matter if it is presidential or parliamentary, democratization must be based on certain bedrock principles: democratic institutionalization, political competition, and various forms of horizontal and vertical accountability. Beyond this, there is room for an enormous variety of formal and informal rules and institutions within what we broadly recognize as democracy.[61]

Democratic Institutionalization

Political systems are classified as democratic as long as they have made or are making observable progress toward what is often referred to as DEMOCRATIC

INSTITUTIONALIZATION. In order for democratic systems to be long-lasting and meaningful, democratic institutions must be crafted, nurtured, and developed.[62] When democratic institutions are strong, the processes of government are established and less vulnerable to nondemocratic intrusions (for example, military takeovers). Under such circumstances, citizens and leaders alike can develop reasonable expectations about the rules and procedures of government, which are "above" the whims of individuals or groups. In other words, the rules should be stable and formalized—they should not vary dramatically based on which particular leader is in office. This development of regularized processes is often referred to as institutionalization. Through their various functions, institutions ensure participation, representation, accountability, and respect for human rights.

Democratic institutions are often thought of as the formal, concrete organizations (such as the executive, legislative, and judicial branches of government, as well as political parties and civil society) that are the principal means through which citizens select and monitor democratic government. Yet other democratic institutions are more procedural, such as regularized patterns of interaction that are widely accepted and practiced, like electoral rules, the checks and balances of presidential systems, or the rules governing the transfer of power. Whatever their form, democratic institutions promote (in one way or another) the individual's right to participate in the political life of the community. In their particular capacities, each institution in a democracy serves a critical function.[63]

Political Competition

Political competition is a procedural part of democratic institutionalization. It involves much more than the right to form parties or to take part in elections. For example, in order for parties and candidates to freely compete for political office, they need access to the media, just as citizens need independent sources of information. Individuals and parties seeking power know that positive press and advertising are crucial to any campaign. Media-savvy parties enlist public relations firms to create commercials full of slick images. They hire spin-doctors to manipulate sound bites so as to put their candidate in the best light. However, they also run extremely negative campaigns, including internet smear campaigns.

Beyond access to the media, political competition is based in the principle that political parties must be free to organize, present candidates for office, express ideas, and compete in fair elections. Even in democracies, political parties vary enormously in the way in which they select the candidates they put forward; some (such as Nigeria's People's Democratic Party) are the product of insider wheeling and dealing. To help safeguard the process from undue influence of elites, more democracies are developing rules concerning campaign finance, including ceilings on how much money private individuals and groups can contribute to political parties and candidates. Strict enforcement of limits on donations and other aspects of party financing is a necessity. In Mexico, it is the law that parties must rely on public funding for most of their campaign financing. In reality, donors buy influence and campaign financing limits are not respected. Dark money (clandestine donations) has factored into Mexican elections for decades. In a recent example from Mexico, a businessman linked to a massive scandal involving Brazilian construction giant Odebrecht testified it had channeled millions of dollars to the presidential campaign of former president Enrique Peña Nieto.[64]

Campaign finance reform is just one aspect of a number of procedural elements meant to safeguard democracy. Although governments vary widely in terms of these procedural elements (such as when elections are to be held), in democracies the procedures for holding governments accountable are well established and respected. Regular, free, and fair elections are taken for granted in democracies. While elections are often upheld as an indicator of freedom, and they can be an important part of a democracy, in and of themselves they hardly guarantee that a country is democratic. Remember the electoral fallacy: even nondemocratic states may hold elections.

Whether it is the first election or the fiftieth, the orchestration of free and fair elections is a complicated undertaking. This can be quite difficult in a country without reliable transportation and communication facilities, or with an enormous population (India has over 900 million eligible voters). The investment of a great deal of time, money, and effort is necessary long before election day to lay the basis for a legitimate result. Free and fair elections require the creation of an independent electoral commission as well as neutral poll workers and multiple international and domestic observers. Too often electoral commissions (even in

Figure 12.3 Elections in China

While it should be clear that elections are an extremely important component of democracy, the existence of competitive elections alone is not sufficient evidence of the stirrings of a democratic transition. In the People's Republic of China, for example, truly competitive elections at the local level have taken place since the mid-1980s, although these have been confined to villages and county-level people's congresses. (A few townships have also experimented with elections, although these moves have been "discouraged" by Beijing). At the village level, citizens now elect members of "villagers' committees" every three years. These committees are officially nongovernmental organizations, since villages are not a formal level of government. They manage public affairs and social welfare, help maintain public order, and promote economic development, primarily job creation. Hundreds of millions of Chinese have participated in this grassroots-level exercise, sending 3 million officials to office with some level of popular, albeit limited, mandates.[a] International observers, many under the auspices of the Carter Center, have followed the election campaigns and have consistently noted a level of competition and campaigning previously unknown in China. Political parties other than the Chinese Communist Party are not allowed, but candidates are able to run as independents, though the nomination of candidates is tightly controlled.

Observers have noted concerns about voter privacy: People routinely mark their ballots from their seats, rather than using private booths. As this is common practice, people who would attempt to use the more private polling booths might raise suspicion among their fellow villagers. Most analysts believe that these elections have been implemented less to promote democratic sentiment and more to facilitate control over unruly agents in the countryside. Talks about expanding the polls to higher levels of governance (i.e., townships) have stalled. Giving peasants the opportunity to vote out corrupt Communist Party officials is believed by the government to be enough, for now—particularly if it helps citizens view the government as more legitimate.

Note: a. Kerry Brown, *Ballot Box China: Grassroots Democracy in the Final Major One-Party State* (New York: Zed, 2011).

transitioning democracies) are nominated and funded by the executive branch. Yet the reputation of such a commission must be beyond reproach as it undertakes the tedious and painstaking work that is critical to the honesty of any vote.

Part of that painstaking work involves the registration of voters, and where there is no recent or reliable census, that can be an enormous task. It sounds so mundane, but conducting a census can be an expensive and massive logistical undertaking—not to mention a political landmine. Fears that a census will lead to the redrawing of the political map (and redistribution of wealth and power) have resulted in mass rioting in more than one country. Because they have so much potential to be used toward political purposes, censuses are highly contested events that have set off violent confrontations and worsened divisions. As a result, Nigeria went fifteen years without a headcount, from 1991 to 2006. Although the 2006 census did not use modern methods and was considered by many to be unreliable, the next census wasn't planned until 2022.[65]

So, instead of simplifying things, technology has sometimes created more problems. For over a decade, one of the greatest electoral challenges has been cybersecurity. Both new and mature democracies suffer from vulnerabilities in the electoral process that can undermine its integrity. Cyber risks and threats vary, but even countries without any form of electronic voting need to invest in defending their elections against digital threats. These threats include unauthorized access to election-related infrastructure as well as disinformation campaigns designed to shape the political debate. As we know in the United States, there have been cyberattacks against political parties, candidates, and the media. Even just the rumor of such an attack can undermine the credibility of elections and democratic institutions.[66]

Electoral commissions across the global south use state-of-the-art technologies to uphold the integrity of the elections process. For example, Mexico's National Electoral Institute (INE) supervises elections and enforces regulations on campaign financing and the content of political advertising, However, although the 2018 elections in Mexico were generally considered free and fair the INE struggled to address problems such as misuse of public funds, vote buying, and ballot stealing. In addition, hackers spread disinformation about the electoral process with a variety of rumors meant to undercut trust in the system. Steps by MORENA, President López Obrador's party, to cut the INE's budget have raised concerns that the administration seeks to reduce electoral oversight and give itself an advantage in future elections.[67]

Electoral commissions such as the INE serve other functions as well. In 2019, nearly 2 billion people in more than fifty countries headed to the polls, the largest number ever. In 90 percent of the world, citizens must be at least eighteen to vote, although sixteen-year-olds are eligible to vote in seven countries, including Brazil, Argentina, and Cuba. Where citizens have had little or no experience participating in free and fair elections, voter education is a necessity. Beyond ensuring that they have access to the information required to make an informed decision, voters must understand the ballot and be able to indicate their choices. Sometimes this requires designing a ballot in more than one language and/or using symbols or photographs of the candidates as well as the written word.[68]

Furthermore, there are a number of practices that democracies use to help minimize irregularities at the polls or with the count and build credibility. In 2000, Brazil was the first country in the world to use 100 percent electronic ballots, and it's largely considered a success, as it cut down on invalid votes and greatly sped up the counting process so that the results are known in a few hours. Nearly 25 countries, including India, the Philippines, and Singapore, also use electronic ballots. However, voting in most of the world is low-tech; in most cases paper ballots are marked by hand or with fingerprints. Some countries, such as Ghana, Zimbabwe, and Iraq, have used a biometric identification process, in which the voter places a finger on a biometric verification device, to register and verify voters. But the system hasn't proven reliable due to technical problems, which has only raised questions about the integrity of the process. Elsewhere, much simpler measures (such as voting using fingerprints) helps to cut down on fraud, since the ink stains the skin for a few days and helps identify anyone who might wish to vote twice.[69]

Beyond efforts to guarantee privacy, local and international election observers must also be trained and posted in sufficient numbers to help ensure the fairness of the process. A large part of this involves things like making sure that the process is orderly, that there is no intimidation at the polls, and that no one who is registered to vote is turned away. People often have to travel and wait for hours to vote in mile-long lines—and they do. Turnout for elections is much higher in many countries in the global south than it is in the United States, where it is not unusual for fewer than 60 percent of registered voters to cast their ballots—even in presidential elections. In addition, the electoral commission must ensure that there are enough ballots at the polls, collect and tabulate the vote accurately (done by hand in most countries), and report the results in a timely manner (as delays tend to draw suspicion and raise tensions).

Taken together, these procedures help to ensure that an authentic democratic transition is under way. For countries experiencing their first democratic elections, or FOUNDING ELECTIONS, these are historic events. They often symbolize a departure from authoritarianism and dramatically demonstrate the power of a mobilized citizenry. In many ways the 2000 presidential vote in Mexico symbolized such an event. Virtually everyone agreed that it was Mexico's freest and fairest vote ever. And most importantly, the result served as an indicator of the authenticity of Mexico's democratic transition: the governing party allowed itself to lose the elections. This was a surprise for many as it put an end to over seventy years of uninterrupted one-party rule. There was similar jubilation when democratic elections were held in Nigeria in 1999 after fifteen years of military dictatorship. Likewise, the parliamentary elections in Indonesia in 1999 were celebrated as the freest since 1955, and 2004 was another watershed year when Indonesians directly elected their president for the first time.

While founding elections mark an important watershed event, most analysts agree that it is the second round of elections that is a more vital step toward consolidation, especially if they result in an orderly transfer (or alternation) of power from one party to another. Ghana, which transitioned to democracy from a long-standing dictatorship, is an example of a success story in this regard.

Between 2000 and 2020 it had six presidential elections including three alternations in power in which the incumbent party lost and the opposition peacefully assumed the presidency.[70] Unfortunately, this track record is unusual for newer democracies, as the transfer of power can be a tense period associated with heightened political violence.

However, if electoral management bodies are above reproach, the alternation in power can serve to decrease the tensions between electoral winners and losers. In the long run, this is key to getting buy-in to the system. Many Nigerians were concerned that their second experience with elections, in 2003, would pose the greatest challenge for their new democracy. To their relief, it went relatively smoothly, compared to their experience a decade earlier, when the presiding dictator, who was unhappy with an election's result, quickly ended a democratic experiment. However, the real test—of a transfer of power from one political party to another—didn't come until the 2015 elections in Nigeria, when Progressive Democratic Party nominee, incumbent President Goodluck Jonathan, was defeated by General Muhammadu Buhari of the All Progressives Congress by 55 percent to 45 percent.[71] Thus, establishing a precedent for the peaceful transfer of power is a watershed event. Maintaining norms (i.e., that electoral losers must accept their defeat with grace) takes a sustained effort.

Although there are "dominant-party democracies," such as in Botswana, in which there has never been a transfer of power because one party has always won elections, these countries are also widely regarded as democracies. For as long as the possibility of change through election exists, the system is democratic. Still, for most countries the transfer of power from one party to another is a crucial part of the transition to democracy.

Beyond these procedural elements and general principles, there are a number of other qualities we expect to see in countries making democratic reform. Some analysts focus on the recruitment of candidates and argue that a democratizing country must allow for the people's representatives to be drawn from an "open" political elite. Candidates for office in democracies are often sensitive to accusations of being part of an "old boys' club" and portray themselves as part of a new "breed" of leaders, capable of making real change. For example, Indonesia's Joko "Jokowi" Widodo, elected president in 2014, is the first Indonesian president without connections to the military or political elite. Originally viewed as "Indonesia's Obama," the progressive former furniture maker had a meteoric rise to power, starting first as a small-town mayor. He won over many with a vision of a diverse and democratic Indonesia, his grassroots style, and his willingness to break with authoritarian traditions and political elites. "Outsider" candidates such as Jokowi appeal to voters because they offer the prospect of change. However, many who were counting on this have been hugely disappointed, as the president later changed gears to ally with hard-line Islamists and those who served the dictatorships. In the end, Jokowi became an insider, and has sidelined both political reforms and anti-corruption efforts.[72]

Whereas the idea of any elite dominating politics is perhaps antithetical to the democratic ideal, the fact remains that the economically rich have a disproportionate hold on power in both democratic and nondemocratic governments. Yet, it is hoped at least that democratic systems will be more accessible to newcomers, more concerned with the interests of the general public, and more likely to work for the interests of the majority. At the very least, because in democratic systems the political elite can be held accountable to the voters, we can assume that those who are elected will try harder to make good on their promises than those who don't have to answer to the people.

Horizontal Accountability

Another element that we would expect to see in democracies is horizontal accountability: the imperative for various political actors from the different branches of government to work together. The idea here is that no branch should overstep its boundaries and seek to dominate the others. In reality, maintaining (or establishing) horizontal accountability is usually about the legislative and judicial branches seeking to limit executive power. This is not quite as true for parliamentary systems, which have a fusion of powers: voters select the legislators (the members of parliament), who then select (or create) the executive (the prime minister). On the other hand, presidential systems are distinguished by a separation of powers in which each branch of government is independent of the others. Voters in presidential systems directly select the executive as well as the legislators, which can result in divided government. As mentioned earlier, the democratic process (a separation of powers with checks and balances) can result in potential gridlock.

From the executive point of view, any number of obstacles can interfere with a leader's ability to make good on his or her promises. In Nigeria, presidents have been constantly at odds with the fractious national assembly, even when it has been their own parties that controlled both houses. Then president Obasanjo was known to refer derisively to the young, ambitious lawmakers dominating that body as "children" who were causing him no end of trouble. A frosty relationship has continued through successive administrations (including that led by President Buhari) as legislators of his own All Progressives Congress party defected to the opposition, depriving the party of its majority. The result is deadlock over budgets and policy paralysis; disbursements have been put on hold and salaries unpaid. Halfway into his first term it was said that President Buhari's biggest achievement was just getting elected. In democracies worldwide, it is hard to get anything done during the second half of a president's term—once election season starts. Unfortunately, executive-legislative conflict can take a toll on governance. It can lead to citizen frustration with democracy. It can also lead to executive overreach and a decline into authoritarianism (unfortunately, Tunisia is a good example of this).[73]

Of course, the social and economic crises that the Tunisian, Nigerian, and other governments have inherited from their authoritarian predecessors make everything more difficult, as they reinforce certain practices and ideas about the proper exercise of political authority. Moreover, dominant political cultures may value decisive leadership over institutional checks and balances. As mentioned earlier, presidentialism is likely to develop where a state of constant crisis has generated a strong sense of urgency. As a parentlike figure, the president (and sometimes the prime minister) tends to become the embodiment of the nation—benevolent guardian and defender of its interests. Because of their stature, presidents may come to see other institutions such as the legislature and courts as nuisances that interfere with the full authority delegated to them.[74] Situations like this explain why we're in the situation we are—with democracy in decline worldwide.

Vertical Accountability

So, how do we hold off rising authoritarianism? Well, one of the cardinal rules of democracy is "you can't stay in power by doing nothing." No democracy is likely to be consolidated (or last) without high levels of support offered by legitimacy, and no democracy will garner high legitimacy rates without some degree of effective governance. As mentioned earlier, one of the most commonly understood components of good governance is accountability. But there are two kinds of accountability: horizontal and vertical accountability. By vertical accountability, we refer to a government's relationship with its citizens. The more responsive a government is to popular demands, the more satisfied people will be with the way government works and the more they will support it through hard times. In other words, the better the government is at promoting the general welfare, the more that people will trust it, believe the system to be a good one, and remain committed to it.[75] Initiatives associated with vertical accountability include capacity building, establishing the rule of law, reconciling group conflict, and maintaining civilian control over the military.

Capacity building. The ability to strategize, prioritize, and carry out state functions to improve people's lives, or capacity building, is a crucial test for most new democracies. One measure of a government's capacity is its ability to deliver public services. Yet, although people commonly cite effectiveness as a highly valued attribute of governments, democracies don't necessarily make for the most efficient of administrations. And decisive action is even more difficult for democracies under economic strain. As discussed in Chapters 5 and 6, undemocratic governments have sometimes proven to be quite capable of delivering not only services, but also economic growth. It could be argued that when it comes to capacity building, democracies are actually disadvantaged in that, by definition in this type of political system, a variety of actors must be consulted in decisionmaking. Consequently, democracy tends to be a messy and slow business. New democracies certainly face many challenges, and one of the first things their leaders must learn is to restrain expectations. New democracies are often expected not only to stabilize economies and promote economic DEVELOPMENT, but also to make good on promises of political freedoms and representativeness. They are to be accountable to their citizens, establish order, and promote the rule of law.[76]

Beyond that, there are more mundane expectations of new democracies as well. The problem is that often these governments do not inherit usable bureaucracies and therefore lack the administrative capacity to make progress in providing services, implementing policy, and so on. Elected government should at the very least be capable of performing what are commonly regarded as ESSENTIAL FUNCTIONS: collecting taxes, providing a sense of security throughout the country, and enforcing the law, as well as designing and implementing policies responsive to the majority. Some analysts expand the definition of essential functions to include concern with the population's economic and social well-being. This typically includes the supply of public goods (such as the rehabilitation of communications and transportation systems, or the provision of water, sanitation, and electrification). Unless democracy can provide these things, it is unlikely to be viewed favorably for long. But for economic reasons if nothing else, this is out of reach for many governments.[77]

Newly elected governments not only face economic shortfalls, but also often find it extremely difficult to pick up the pieces after years of mismanagement and abuse. It is hard to increase governmental capacity when the infrastructure has decayed beyond the point of viability. People become bitter waiting in long lines for gasoline (especially in countries that are major exporters of oil), or where the electricity and mobile phone service are unreliable. Fledgling democratic governments know that they don't have much time to prove themselves. Where citizens have spent years under wasteful authoritarian rule, many expect to see a DEMOCRACY DIVIDEND, a general improvement in quality of life and standard of living in just a few years' time. Yet turning around an economy often takes longer, and although some populations have demonstrated impressive patience, sooner or later they are likely to become frustrated if the benefits of change don't materialize. Under such pressures to perform, communication with the masses is of the utmost importance, and leaders who lose touch with their constituencies soon find themselves out of work. In much of the world, the appeal of POPULIST authoritarians (e.g., AMLO in Mexico, Jair Bolsonaro in Brazil, or Trump in the United States) has grown as more people are disappointed by the political establishment and sense that democracy isn't meeting their expectations.[78]

Covid, capacity, and governance. Different countries have been challenged in different ways, but few countries had developed the institutional capacity to deal with Covid. As you will recall, at one point or another, the virus overwhelmed the capacity of most of the world. In richer countries and poorer ones, health care systems struggled (and in some cases collapsed). Healthcare workers couldn't access basics, like personal protective equipment. People even in major cities suffocated needlessly from lack of oxygen. For many, one of the most frightening things about that time was the government's stunning lack of capacity. The pandemic accelerated a preexisting democratic decline, exposing the weakness and corruption of many governments. Countries that responded the least effectively to the disease early on (Brazil, the United States) had populations that were skeptical of their governments—and leaders who had ridden to power on that sentiment.[79] The countries whose political leaders downplayed the pandemic and minimized the threat caused by the disease suffered some of the worst outbreaks in the world—and the highest death tolls. For example, in Brazil former health ministers testified that the Bolsonaro government's initial strategy was to first downplay the disease, then pursue herd immunity and promote the use of hydroxychloroquine, an antimalarial drug shown to be ineffective against Covid. Meanwhile, Pfizer says that the Bolsonaro government ignored multiple offers to sell Brazil vaccines (as of late 2021 Brazil's death toll from the coronavirus was the second highest in the world). Consequently, a Senate committee that investigated President Bolosaro's response to Covid called for him to face criminal charges for (among other things) charlatanism, inciting crime, and crimes against humanity.[80]

On the other hand, according to Chu et al., many of those countries that were able (at least initially) to weather and contain the disease were ones where the citizenry was norm-conforming and prioritized collective welfare over individual freedoms for the sake of social well-being. In the consolidated democracies of Taiwan and South Korea, citizens accepted government restrictions as necessary to get outbreaks under control. These governments, particularly Taiwan (given its experience with SARS in 2002–2004), had universal, easily accessible, affordable, efficient, and responsive healthcare services. As a result, in these countries there was also a reservoir of popular trust in public authorities that proved helpful in the crisis, so that government instructions to self-quarantine, social distance, and wear masks weren't resisted. Many of these countries (at least after the initial jolt) fared much better than countries in the global north. They were more prepared for such a crisis and had developed the capacity to cope with challenges (natural disasters or disease) better than many others.[81]

But some, namely China, the Philippines, and Vietnam, went much farther, and operated from preexisting, strict structures of social control. For example, structures that were normally used to control dissent were used to control epidemics. These governments gave repressive security forces usually focused on controlling government critics additional, arbitrary powers in the fight against Covid.[82] Facing one of Southeast Asia's worst outbreaks, then president Rodrigo Duterte of the Philippines threatened to jail any citizen who refused the vaccine. Duterte, known for his tough persona, ordered local officials to search for those avoiding the shot—despite the fact that under Philippine law, even in a state of emergency, the president can't make such an order without legislation.[83]

What was called the "zero Covid" approach largely worked to contain the outbreak and provide stability in China, which avoided being blamed for concealing and exacerbating the epidemic. Initially, China was able to switch the narrative, turning its handling of Covid into an opportunity to showcase the advantages of its system, compare itself favorably to the ways that democracies were handling it, and expand its influence.[84] However, few countries are afforded this much control, certainly not democratic ones. In many places, actions that would normally be considered authoritarian were billed as lifesaving. In states already on the downward slope, the coronavirus may have accelerated a preexisting democratic decline. Some leaders in "the messy middle" between democracy and authoritarianism used the threat of Covid to consolidate their power over distracted and traumatized populations. They put out misleading information and claimed emergency powers, using the crisis to shut down protests (Guyana, Algeria) or to justify postponing elections (Ethiopia, Haiti, Sri Lanka, and Bolivia). Many others, such as India, imposed lockdowns that displaced millions of migrant workers. India's Hindu nationalist government sought to distract from its own failures by encouraging the scapegoating of Muslims, who were blamed for the spread of the virus.[85]

Untold numbers of governments have used Covid as an opening to siphon off resources for personal gain. By declaring a state of emergency, several countries suspended regulations governing public contracts. This has created ideal conditions for schemes misusing millions in public funds. In one unusually egregious example of how the crisis was exploited, with deaths from the coronavirus surging, health officials in Ecuador awarded a criminal ring a contract to sell body bags to hospitals at thirteen times the real price.[86] Such actions, whether a shift in norms or the creation of coercive controls, are likely to be difficult to reverse and have negative long-term political and economic consequences.

On the other hand, the global south did offer role models for leadership during the pandemic as well. In consolidated democracies such as Uruguay and Costa Rica, leaders have boosted trust in the government by operating transparently and efficiently. Many countries, including richer ones, should replicate the strategy of countries that had learned valuable lessons from previous outbreaks and did better than expected (for example, Liberia and Ebola or Taiwan and SARS). However, the pandemic plunged most of the world into the deepest recession unlike anything most of us have ever experienced. Leaders had to grapple with the fact that the decision to impose lockdowns could lead to more deaths from deprivation than from Covid. Of course, poverty made everything to do with fighting the virus more difficult; just accessing adequate water for handwashing was a challenge for many in the global south. Many countries provided emergency assistance to citizens. Meanwhile, some governments, such as Mexico's and Pakistan's, left the poor to rely on charity rather than state assistance.[87]

Covid certainly made everything more difficult, but the idea that democratic transitions are greatly affected by economic factors is nothing new. Certainly other factors come into play, but several consecutive years of negative economic growth lessen the chance of survival for a democratic regime (or a nondemocratic regime, for that matter). Poverty and economic inequality are key obstacles to democratization, and many countries that have experienced economic misery have fallen to what is called "the totalitarian temptation" in the search for alternatives. However, poverty does not guarantee failure. Some low-income countries such as Uruguay have completed their transitions and consolidated their democracies despite hardship. The oldest global south democracy (and the world's most populous democracy), India, is often characterized as a puzzle in that it retains democratic governance against all odds—poverty, entrenched caste and religious divisions, and other problems. Certainly such hardship makes these democracies more prone to risk, but a few cases show that it is possible for democracies to survive. To a great extent the ability to survive depends on whom the population blames for the economic problems, and the perceived desirability of political alternatives. Even where democratic government appears to be getting off to a slow start, as long as most people believe that democracy is the best political system for them, it can survive even under difficult economic conditions. If, however, people and their leaders believe democracy itself is compounding the problem, or that it is incapable of remedying the situation, democratic breakdown is likely.[88]

One of the first initiatives of many new leaders (democratic or not) is to attempt to bond with the masses by blaming the country's problems on the previous administration. It is common for candidates to be elected based on their promises to fight CORRUPTION—the abuse of power for private gain. Corruption is a problem shared by all forms of government in virtually every country in the world, including the oldest democracies. It is especially difficult to combat because some of the most corrupt people in any country are the most powerful. As of 1995, thanks to the example set by long-standing dictators, Indonesia was ranked as dead last (180th out of 180 countries on the list)—the most corrupt country in the world. By 2019, however, Indonesia's scores were much improved, to 89th out of 180. It got there in part due to the efforts of democratically elected

Indonesian President Susilo Bambang Yudhoyono. In 2002, Yudhoyono, known as "Mr. Clean," strengthened the Corruption Eradication Commission (known as the KPK), giving it the power to investigate and prosecute any public official for any type of corruption. Although his successor, Joko Widodo, has not proven to be as committed to this effort, the KPK seeks to convince the population otherwise by sentencing more than 1,000 public officials for corruption. Now, some do look askance at the KPK's 100 percent conviction rate. But due to the KPK's extraordinary powers (it can wiretap without a warrant) and willingness to go after targets across the political spectrum, Indonesia has continued to improve its score for fighting corruption, although it remains a serious problem.[89]

It is not unusual to hear of governments accused of using anti-corruption campaigns as witch hunts to target their political opponents. Nigeria's President Buhari promised to clean up corruption. He won praise for freezing the bank accounts of a former first lady, and in 2020 recovered over $300 million in funds reportedly stolen by late president Sani Abacha (1993–1998). However, some cried foul when former officials affiliated with the main opposition party—which dominated the government for sixteen years, until Buhari's election—faced criminal charges. Make no mistake about it: corruption is still a massive problem in Nigeria, yet it has shown some relative improvement over the years. In 2003 Nigeria was identified by Transparency International, the international watchdog group, as the most corrupt country in the world (Somalia has taken that title and held it for several years). As of 2020, Nigeria ranked 149th out of 179 countries.[90]

Progress is slow, but fighting corruption by promoting accountability and transparency is crucial if democracies are to progress. In old and new democracies alike, pervasive official misconduct can contribute to democratic breakdown. Bribery, extortion, influence peddling, and other scandals can greatly damage political legitimacy and disillusion people, alienating them from the political process. Clearly, the most stable countries of the world are the least corrupt (and vice versa); in 2020–2021, six out of the ten most corrupt countries in the world ranked among the top ten least peaceful places as well.[91]

How can corruption be reduced? Most experts recommend a broad strategy based around the idea of increasing TRANSPARENCY, which can be understood in a number of interrelated ways. In one crucial sense, transparency means openness, particularly in terms of spending and budgetary matters. During Mexico's political liberalization, the government began declassifying information and publishing the federal budget in full (something that had traditionally been cloaked in secrecy). A number of countries, including Brazil, have laws requiring budgetary disclosure, but a variety of long-standing practices prevent citizen oversight, including a lack of complete or specific information or standardization that makes it possible to compare different offices or track expenditures.[92]

Accountability is the goal, but fighting corruption is not only about punishing wrongdoers. It is also about reducing the incentive to steal. Many countries trying to stem corrupt impulses work to increase the wages of civil servants—although not every country can pay their leading executive as much as Singapore's Prime Minister Lee Hsien Loong, who earns $1.6 million annually (the US presidential salary is $400,000/year).[93] Another approach is raising the risks and costs associated with corruption. It means that from top to bottom, from high-ranking officials who treat the state treasury as a private source of wealth, down to police and petty officials who supplement their meager incomes with *una mordida* (a bite) or *bakshish* (a gift), government actors must no longer be allowed to violate the law with impunity, and will be prosecuted if they do. Governments must improve the ability to detect extortion and other abuses so as to better expose, punish, and disgrace those guilty of misconduct. However, the problem in many countries is all-pervasive; too often, graft is understood as the only platform for attaining dreams of wealth and success. Those who are making their way up the ladder find that "fear of the unknown" fuels corruption; they are determined to take their cut before they lose their footing on that ladder.[94]

The police are the government actors most likely to demand bribes; daily petty extortions from them and other civil servants hit the poorest the hardest. Corruption exists everywhere, but as we have seen in Transparency International's rankings, it is worse in some places than others. In Latin America and the Caribbean, Africa, and the Middle East, the police are reportedly the most bribery-prone of public services, although political parties were identified as by far the most corrupt institution. More than 20 percent of respondents said they paid a bribe to a law enforcement officer in the previous year. And the lockdowns, roadblocks, and quarantines associated with Covid have only opened up more opportunities for police and soldiers on the take. In much of Asia and Africa, it is a common practice not only to bribe but to use personal connections to speed up government bureaucracies or obtain services such as healthcare or education. How much one can increase the speed or quality of the service depends on how much one can pay, reinforcing inequality. For institutions to be perceived in this way poses a real threat to democracy, since corruption is said to impact the psyche of a nation, breaking trust and creating cynicism. If people don't expect much from elected government, this will limit democracy's life expectancy.[95]

Establishing the rule of law. There are important distinctions between rule of law and rule by law. Rule by law is commonly employed by authoritarian regimes to repress populations—to crack down on "enemies of the state." On the other hand, the rule of law is one of the core functions of a high-quality democracy. Though not easy to define because it comprises several elements (and there is disagreement over what these elements are and how they should be prioritized), at its most basic the rule of law provides the foundation for the enjoyment of political rights and civil liberties. It means that no one is above the law. The government is ruled by law and subject to it. Certainly, the rule of law can be compromised and there can be gaps or flaws in its operation (in the laws themselves, in the application of the law, in access to the judiciary and a fair process). Like so many other things, it is probably best to conceptualize rule of law as existing on a continuum, in that some democracies have made more progress than others in establishing it.[96]

The rule of law means several things, including that legal systems in democracies should be able to guarantee predictable and impartial treatment from governmental agents, including the police, the military, and judges. This poses a major challenge for many governments, especially where these public servants have long traditions of acting with impunity. In Egypt, under both the Mubarak and al-Sisi regimes, the security forces were and are given broad powers to arrest people without charge and detain them indefinitely. There and elsewhere, officers see themselves as enforcers for the government, not public servants. They were above the law, rarely punished for abuses.[97] Human rights groups in Nigeria and other transitioning democracies report similar problems, with security forces involved in sexual brutality, disappearances, and extrajudicial killings. One way of promoting public security is for democracies to curb the power of ministries of the interior, the agencies whose role it is to police the police, which have often earned the nickname "Ministry of Fear." People need to be able to trust the police as public servants and they need to have confidence in the administration of justice.

A strong, efficient, and independent judiciary is another decentralizing institution crucial to the success of both parliamentary and presidential systems. Transitioning democracies must improve performance when it comes to ensuring not only personal security, but also that disputes are settled quickly and fairly. Citizens should not have to fear arbitrary arrest or being left to rot in overcrowded prisons while awaiting charge. A powerful judiciary—professional, depoliticized, and largely free from executive or other partisan interference—can be the greatest protector of a democratic constitution and source of democratic legitimacy. It is the ultimate guarantor of the rule of law.[98] Yet analysts recognize the judicial branch to be one of the democratic institutions that take the longest to create, and progress is probably most accurately measured by degree.

For example, the arrest and imprisonment of former president Jacob Zuma in 2021 was a victory for the rule of law in South Africa. There and elsewhere, executives (especially heroes of liberation movements) have rarely been held accountable, and the imprisonment of Zuma was for many unthinkable. But after Zuma refused to appear before the courts as part of a major corruption investigation, he was found guilty of contempt of court. Despite the massive unrest that followed his arrest and threats against the court, the judges were unfazed, upholding the principle that all are equal before the law.[99]

Therefore, there are several different elements that work together in the rule of law. Whether that means making it safe for people to walk around their neighborhoods at night or a policy of zero tolerance for official corruption, strengthening the rule of law is a tremendous challenge for many democratizing regimes. Twenty years into Mexico's democracy, two-thirds of adults say they feel unsafe where they live. The good news is that that number is down slightly from recent years. Although the homicide rate in Mexico has increased annually since 2014, with 24.8 intentional homicides per 100,000 inhabitants, its homicide rate is still much lower than that of El Salvador, where it is more than twice as high: 61.8 homicides per 100,000 inhabitants. But concerns about security in Mexico are real. More than half of respondents say they witnessed a robbery or assault in the first quarter of 2021, and almost 40 percent said that they frequently hear gunshots. Yet few Mexicans bother to report crime, perhaps because an estimated nine out of ten murders in the country are never solved.[100]

Although analysts disagree about whether crime rates have actually risen since the transition to democracy in several Latin American countries, they confirm that the fear of crime has definitely increased. In Argentina, Uruguay, and Mexico, fear of crime has become a major election issue. In Mexico, tens of thousands have marched and gone on strike to protest the lack of public security and femicide in particular, as an average of ten women are killed in Mexico every day.[101] Around the world, public frustration with democratic governments' inability to impose the rule of law has also led to vigilantism. In some places this amounts to community-based policing, necessary where the government has in effect ceded significant powers to local communities. For example, as violence (and especially kidnappings) continued to rise in Mexico, citizens took matters into their own hands and formed clandestine vigilante groups to fight off drug traffickers and gangs—a development that may make citizens feel safe, but, human rights groups fear, may only be worsening the violence.[102]

According to the *Rule of Law Index* (a publication of the World Justice Project), the overall quality of rule of law continues a global downward slide, especially in measures of constraints on government powers.[103] For example, even though in 2020, Indonesia's formal score slightly improved (its first noted gain in five years), significant weaknesses remain (including regulatory enforcement and fundamental rights, especially for citizens who cannot afford an attorney).[104]

These are just a few of the challenges for democracies seeking to impress citizens with a sense of vertical accountability. As mentioned earlier, 2021 marked the fifteenth consecutive year of decline in global freedom and those that had declining scores outnumbered those with improvements by the largest margin recorded since the negative trend began in 2006. Some of the most significant declines in freedom between 2015 and 2020 were related to rule of law: in the areas of fundamental rights (fifty-four countries declined, twenty-nine improved), constraints on government powers (fifty-two declined, twenty-eight improved), and absence of corruption (fifty-one declined, twenty-six improved). Although countries in every region lost ground overall in the rule of law over the five-year period, the countries that showed the most significant declines in the rule of law were Egypt, Venezuela, Cambodia, Cameroon, and the Philippines. On the other hand, Nepal, Namibia, Uruguay, and the United Arab Emirates led their regions with best overall scores for the rule of law.[105]

Reconciling group conflict. As Robert Dahl famously noted, at its base the exercise of democracy is the institutionalization of conflict.[106] Unlike autocrats, democratic leaders, because they are accountable to the people, must spend a great deal of their time at least appearing to be responsive to the interests of groups with conflicting interests. States are not independent of ethnicity, class, gender, and other interests, but the legitimacy of democratic governments is partly derived from their ability to appear to be independent of these interests, to modify conflict, and to build consensus. Yet democracy has an inherent paradox: it requires both representativeness and conflict, but not too much of either. Democracy must allow for competition, but only within carefully defined and accepted boundaries. Reconciling group conflict is at the heart of democratic politics, but the ability to do this doesn't happen overnight. New democracies must work to promote understanding and contain conflicts so that CLEAVAGES don't tear their countries apart. As mentioned earlier, democracy is institutionalized competition for power. However, if that competition is too intense, the system can break down entirely. It is therefore crucial that new democracies find mechanisms to mitigate conflict and promote consensus. They must do this in a way that works successfully to pull together all the core principles of democracy: participation, representation, accountability, and respect for human rights.[107]

Cleavages are found in every country in the world. They tend to run along lines of class, ethnicity, religion, region, and party. Ethnicity, because it is wrapped up in issues of IDENTITY, is often seen as the most difficult type of cleavage for a democracy to manage. In MULTINATIONAL STATES, compromise is difficult, and in deeply divided plural societies, ethnicity is often thought to predetermine access to power and resources. What one group wins, another group fears it will lose—and fear of exclusion is not an unreasonable concern, given the experience of many countries. Elections become a desperate struggle between parties, as well as ethnic groups, regions, even religions. The rules matter little, since to lose political power is to lose access to virtually everything that is important. Under these circumstances the potential for polarization is such a real threat that some analysts hold out little hope for democracy where divisions are deep and identity has been politicized.[108]

Democratic governments must therefore attempt to manage or soften this conflict in a variety of ways. As described in more detail in Chapter 10, they can attempt to generate crosscutting cleavages—to find common ground between groups—as well as work to moderate political views and promote tolerance and cooperation. Another way of mediating these pressures is through institutional designs that encourage the decentralization of power. Federal systems of government may be crucial to the survival of democracy where cleavages are deep, since they allow for more autonomy and responsiveness at the local level. They also diminish the winner-take-all character of politics by facilitating greater representation of minorities and other marginalized groups. Conflict may be reduced and interethnic accommodation promoted through other efforts to reconcile historical differences. The protection of minority rights may go a long way toward managing deep divides—for instance, through the recognition of more than one official language, respect for a variety of legal codes, and toleration of parties representing different communities.

A number of countries, such as South Africa, have been relatively successful in managing tensions between dominant and non-dominant groups by promoting inclusion and skillfully crafting democracies that take into account the particular mix of cultures and identities contained within their territory. Some analysts suggest designing coalitions that allow for sharing or rotating power. More commonly such efforts have the goal of ensuring that all people have equal rights to citizenship, and protecting the rights of minorities to retain their own culture, religion, and language. But coalitions are hard to build; the divisions are very real (and very small minority groups, as well as groups that hold alternative identities beyond ethnonationalist divides are often totally excluded from this power-sharing). Yet, institutional design is one of the best ways to accommodate dominant and non-dominant groups. It is important, because those who are allowed to share power are much more likely to view a democracy as legitimate.[109]

However, unfortunately (and often tragically), in a ploy to win elections, some politicians actually encourage "tribalism" and manipulate issues of ethnicity to their own political advantage. It may not be possible to dissipate tribalism by generating crosscutting cleavages (so that the identity and interests of one ethnic or religious group are spread among different classes or regions). For example, in Nigeria, cleavages often coincide, and people are divided by region, ethnicity, and religion.[110] As a result, reconciling group conflict often poses a nearly impossible task for many newly elected governments.

In addition to political cleavages concerning ethnicity and religion, there are also often deep divides over matters concerning women's equality. As countries democratize, political space has gradually opened to women. Of course, simply allowing previously disenfranchised groups the right to participate in elections as candidates and voters is not enough to result in a true *abertura* or political liberalization. For example, affirmative action to guarantee women's representation in political bodies may be one way of prodding such an opening. But such actions, which include quotas, vary widely and can be controversial. Political parties can adopt quotas. However, often they come in the form of reserved seats in legislatures or legislated numerical targets that stipulate either the number or percentage of seats to be allocated to women. Some argue that quotas are the only way to press toward gender parity in political representation: of the twenty-three countries where 40 percent or more of the parliamentarians are women, more than two-thirds opened space for women's political participation with gender quotas.[111]

Yet even when such rules exist (as they do in some form or another in eighty-one countries), they often go unenforced. More women than ever are running for office worldwide, and the proportion of women in parliamentary seats has reached an all-time high, but the average proportion of female members of parliament (MPs) worldwide is just over 25 percent. All regions have to varying degrees moved toward equal representation since 1995, when women held only an average of 11 percent of seats in parliament. But men still outnumber women by nearly four to one in most legislatures around the world and as the number of women seeking political office has grown, so has the backlash against them.[112]

Whenever underrepresented groups are perceived as gaining political power and threatening the status quo, their risk of facing politically motivated attacks increases. Even women who merely seek to exercise their right to vote are nearly four times more likely than men to fall victim to violence. Often these women are threatened with gender-based forms of violence, such as public stripping and rape. The Inter-Parliamentary Union estimates that even though more women than ever are taking these risks to participate in politics, at the current rate, it will take fifty years before the number of women in parliaments worldwide approaches parity.[113]

Whether gender quotas are successful or not depends on a number of factors, including the nature of the political system, the type of quota and voting system, as well as cultural attitudes about the role of women in politics. As of 2021, four countries had reached or surpassed gender parity. Rwanda (61 percent), Cuba (51 percent), Bolivia (53 percent), and the UAE (50 percent) were the countries with the largest proportions of women serving in parliament.[114] Rwanda, where only 4 percent of MPs were female in 1995, has quotas and continues to hold the distinction as the country with the highest proportion of women ever recorded by a parliamentary chamber. In 2021, the United States ranked sixty-seventh, with 27 percent of the members of its

House of Representatives being female. This was a record for the United States, the highest percentage in US history.[115] Reforms in the United Arab Emirates and Tunisia have added some women to the political ranks, but in much of the Middle East, North Africa, and Oceania (except New Zealand), women's representation has grown but remains very low. Micronesia, Papua New Guinea, and Vanuatu have zero women in parliament. Zero female representation is rare; rather, countries without quota laws are electing women, but more slowly and less steadily than those with quotas.[116]

Yet, for all the talk of "progress," increasing the formal representation of women doesn't guarantee that the distribution of political resources will change. Yes, research shows that gender diversity (and diversity in general) correlates with better governance. Women are more likely than men to advocate for laws supporting child and social welfare. Women's political participation is associated with a lower risk of civil war and lower incidence of state-sanctioned violence. On the other hand, although women are often thought to be less corrupt and more connected to the people, this is not necessarily so. Moreover, women politicians (who often see themselves as needing to conform to succeed) are not usually in a good position to challenge the existing system, which is resistant to change. Democratic and nondemocratic governments commonly include a ministry or department specifically established to deal with "women's issues." However, it is rare for such offices to hold much power; in most cases they are marginalized. The women heading them are mere tokens in otherwise overwhelmingly male cabinets. Although it could be argued that women's status has generally improved in most regions, progress has come very slowly. There continues to be great unevenness in women's experience of gender equality, both between and within countries, based on regional, class, ethnic, and other divides.[117]

As you can see in Figure 12.4, the United Nations Development Programme (UNDP) has developed a composite measure to examine the opportunities that are made available to women in countries around the world. This index, called the Gender Inequality Index (GII), provides a detailed look at the prospects females face in terms of health and educational well-being, as well as economic and political participation and decisionmaking. An examination of the GII rankings for more than a hundred countries shows that overall, prior to Covid, the world was doing a better job at narrowing inequalities in healthcare and education than it was regarding economic and political participation. However, since 2020, thanks to Covid, the world has lost ground toward gender parity—at the current rate of progress, closing the gender gap will take 135 years. Of course, this varies by country and within countries, but interestingly, not all countries in the global north are more equal than those in the global south. According to the World Economic Forum's Global Gender Gap study, in 2021 the United States ranked 30th out of 156 countries, behind several developing countries, including Namibia (6th) and Rwanda (7th). Iceland, Finland, and Norway earned the top rankings, while Afghanistan came in last, with the largest gender gap in the world (and this was before the Taliban retook the country).[118]

Sonia Alvarez points out that states are slowest to work on particular types of issues defined as private, outside the "proper" realm of politics. As of 2018, twelve countries and territories still had laws exempting perpetrators from pros-

Figure 12.4 Measuring Gender Inequality, 2020

	Gender Inequality Index Rank	Share of Seats in Parliament (% held by women)	Female Labor Force Participation (% age 15 & older)	Female Population w/Some Secondary Education (% age 25 & older)
China	39	24.9	60.5	76.0
Mexico	71	48.4	44.2	62.2
Peru	87	30.0	70.3	58.9
Egypt	108	14.9	21.9	73.5
Iran	113	5.9	17.5	67.4
Indonesia	121	17.4	53.1	46.8
Zimbabwe	129	34.6	78.1	59.8
Nigeria	NR	4.1	47.9	NR

Source: United Nations Development Programme (UNDP), *Human Development Report 2020,* tab. 5: "Gender Inequality Index."

ecution for rape if they were married to—or were willing to marry—the victim. After years of campaigning led by women from these countries, in 2017 Jordan, Tunisia, and Lebanon repealed or reformed laws on the books that compelled women to marry their rapists. However, around the world, even where laws recognize rape in marriage as a crime, the perpetrator is rarely charged.[119]

Many states fail to recognize or even collect data on the violence perpetrated against transgender and gender-nonconforming people. In 2019, 82 percent of the homicides of trans people (mostly trans women) were in Central and South America (43 percent of the total in Brazil alone). Many governments in the region have taken steps to protect LGBTQIA rights and to address the challenges that non-heterosexual, trans, and gender-nonconforming people face, but there has also been a backlash against such efforts.[120] It is only in the past five decades that well-established liberal democracies have begun to deal with spousal rape, sexual harassment, and other forms of gender-based violence. In many democracies (newly established or not) hate crimes against all these groups are pervasive and perpetrators operate with impunity. Therefore, while the *abertura* that comes with a democratic transition offers a range of possibilities perhaps once unheard of in terms of human rights, the window of opportunity has only partially opened. Interestingly, sometimes it is the less-than-democratic regimes (like Rwanda) that can push through policies promoting gender equality. Ironically, in democracies, through a process that is supposed to foster inclusion and consensus building, the promotion of human rights, especially women's and LGBTQIA rights, may be set aside in the interests of "unity."

Civil control over the military. As discussed in Chapter 10, in the face of growing instability, civilian leaders have often sent in the police and even the military to restore order among unruly crowds. Unless they find some other way of building legitimacy, these leaders become heavily dependent on the support of the security forces. However, the military often views itself as the supreme arbiter of the national interest. Its concern over civilian inability to impose calm in the midst of a political or economic crisis has on occasion prompted the military to take matters into its own hands.

Of course, any government that must continually look over its shoulder out of fear of an army takeover is in an extremely precarious situation. Many new democracies find themselves coexisting with powerful militaries and must take care not to challenge their prerogatives. Ideally, freely elected democracies would not be constrained or compelled to share power with other actors, including the military. Democratically elected governments should have unquestioned and full authority to generate new policies or carry out their core functions. Therefore, it is crucial that militaries be removed from politics and firmly subordinated to civilian control. MILITARY PROFESSIONALISM, or the military's depoliticization and recognition of civilian supremacy, is absolutely critical to the survival of democracy. The military must view itself as serving the civilian government, not as the definer and guardian of the national interest. For example, Mali's parliamentary elections in March 2020 were broadly free and fair, but a few months later, the military, frustrated by the government's lack of progress against insurgents, nullified the elections with a coup.[121] On the other hand, military professionalism can be achieved: Senegal's military is not considered a threat to civilian control. Some countries, such as Namibia, Botswana, and South Africa, have never had a coup.

Unfortunately, few countries experiencing a democratic transition can rest fully assured that the military accepts this subordinate role. Where the transition was preceded by a military regime (or a military-dominated regime), unless it is eliminated by foreign intervention or by revolution, the security forces will still hold a powerful place in government during and after the transition. The military is a crucial part of the government that the new democracy must attempt to manage. Many new regimes have made efforts to establish civilian supremacy, with varying degrees of success.

Although ultimately the goal is for military decisionmaking to be subject to civilian control, leaders must consider the military's power in determining when and how far to push reform. As Nigeria began its democratic transition in 1999, analysts agreed on the need to reduce military prerogatives. However, many Nigerians suspect that their democratically elected presidents have been backed by military financiers. Two of the four presidents were generals who earlier in their careers ruled Nigeria as military dictators. Not one has so far made significant reforms in civil-military relations.

Under every administration since Nigeria's transition to democracy, soldiers committed massacres without worry of prosecution, in part because the president didn't want to provoke a coup. And the military has refrained from intervening in several crises. For example, many worried about a coup when then president Yar'Adua died in office and the acting president broke his promise not to run for office. Perhaps this is a sign that Nigeria's democracy is consolidating, since experts warn that if these scenarios had played out ten years earlier, it would have almost certainly led to coup. But it could be argued that the military doesn't have to take center stage because it has so much influence from the wings. In

Nigeria as in many other democracies, getting (and keeping) the military out of power is a formidable task.[122] In the end, persuading the military to stay out of politics may sometimes necessitate AMNESTY deals that excuse its members from ever facing punishment for their abuses of human rights. This can truly amount to a deal with the devil, as it so often leads to a culture of impunity (among other problems) later on, greatly limiting the possibilities for consolidation.[123] Consequently, until the possibility of a coup d'état becomes remote, no system can be considered durably democratized.

Conclusions: When the Transition Turns Out to Be the Easy Part

Where democratic experiments have been attempted and failed, it is impossible to identify a singular cause for their failure. The lesson is that we cannot assume there will be a simple, unilinear advance to democracy in the global south, given the heterogeneities and inequalities that exist there. As we've seen in more than one country, the last few years have been devastating. Democracy has suffered serious setbacks. But over time, democracies have shown themselves to be adaptable and resilient, capable of recovery. It is important to remember that even in the worst of years, successful elections were held across the global south, in countries at all income levels. Judicial bodies displayed independence; they provided checks on the executive branch and held leaders to account for abuses of power. Journalists and ordinary people bravely spoke out against even the most repressive governments and demanded better, calling for change.[124] So, despite fifteen years of continuous democratic decline and rising authoritarianism it is important to celebrate the countries that managed to continue on their democratic transition. Given the large number that exist in the messy middle, somewhere between "free" and "not free," perhaps our interest should be the substance of their institutions, at least as much as their sustainability. And, as we have seen with the complex processes required in both the transition and especially in the consolidation of democratic rule, there can be great variety in experience. It's not a matter of black and white/democracies or dictatorships, but often, some sort of gray, in-between phase (that can itself become consolidated). As one political analyst points out, "When confronted with an existential threat, countries that did not already have deep democratic systems are choosing tactics that help leaders consolidate their power."[125] It is crucial then, that we find ways to reverse the global shift to authoritarianism and to support the deepening of democracy. At the very least we need to do all that we can to avoid undermining democracies. The pandemic may mark just the beginning of a long wave of unrest and authoritarianism breaking out all over.[126] As the events of January 6, 2021, remind us, no democracy—not even one of the world's oldest—can be complacent in the face of such forces.

Notes

1. Anne Applebaum, "The Bad Guys Are Winning," *The Atlantic,* November 15, 2021.
2. Arch Puddington and Tyler Roylance, "Anxious Dictators, Wavering Democrats," Freedom House, Washington, DC, 2016.
3. Yun-han Chu, Kai-Ping Huang, Marta Lagos, and Robert Mattes, "A Lost Decade for Third-Wave Democracies?" *Journal of Democracy* 31, no. 2 (April 2020).

4. Sarah Repucci and Amy Slipowitz, "Democracy Under Siege," Freedom House, Washington, DC, 2021.

5. Max Fisher, "US Allies Drive Much of World's Democratic Decline, Data Shows," *New York Times,* November 16, 2021; David E. Sanger and Mark Landler, "Biden Urges G7 to Act to Limit Reach of China," *New York Times,* June 13, 2021.

6. Fisher, "US Allies Drive Much of World's Democratic Decline."

7. Anatoly Kurmanaev, "Latin America Is Facing a 'Decline of Democracy' Under the Pandemic," *New York Times,* July 29, 2020; Repucci and Slipowitz, "Democracy Under Siege."

8. Philippe C. Schmitter and Terry Lynn Karl, "What Democracy Is . . . and Is Not," in *The Global Resurgence of Democracy,* ed. Larry Diamond and Marc F. Plattner (Baltimore: Johns Hopkins University Press, 1993).

9. Ibid.

10. Ibid.; Juan J. Linz and Alfred Stepan, *Problems of Democratic Transition and Consolidation* (Baltimore: Johns Hopkins University Press, 1996); Larry Diamond, Juan J. Linz, and Seymour Martin Lipset, "Introduction: What Makes for Democracy?" in *Politics in Developing Countries: Comparing Experiences with Democracy,* ed. Larry Diamond, Juan J. Linz, and Seymour Martin Lipset (Boulder: Lynne Rienner, 1995).

11. Schmitter and Karl, "What Democracy Is . . . and Is Not."

12. Repucci and Slipowitz, "Democracy Under Siege."

13. "Global Democracy Had a Very Bad Year," *The Economist,* February 2, 2021.

14. Ibid.; Repucci and Slipowitz, "Democracy Under Siege."

15. Adebayo Adedeji, "Popular Participation, Democracy, and Development: Is There a Dialectical Linkage?" in *Nigeria: Renewal from the Roots? The Struggle for Democratic Development,* ed. Adebayo Adedeji, Onigu Otite, Kunle Amuwo et al. (London: Zed Books, 1997).

16. Freedom House, *Freedom in the World 2010.*

17. Freedom House, *Freedom in the World 2021.*

18. Doh Chull Shin and Jason Wells, "Is Democracy the Only Game in Town?" *Journal of Democracy* 16, no. 2 (April 2005).

19. Larry Diamond, "Introduction: In Search of Consolidation," in *Consolidating Third Wave Democracies,* ed. Larry Diamond, Marc F. Plattner, Yun-han Chu, and Hung-mao Tien (Baltimore: Johns Hopkins University Press, 1997); Diamond, Linz, and Lipset, "Introduction: What Makes for Democracy?"; Schmitter and Karl, "What Democracy Is . . . and Is Not"; Freedom House, *Freedom in the World: 2021.*

20. Diamond, Linz, and Lipset, "Introduction: What Makes for Democracy?"

21. Shin and Wells, "Is Democracy the Only Game in Town?"

22. Ibid.; Jeffrey Herbst, "Understanding Ambiguity During Democratization in Africa," in *Pathways to Democracy: The Political Economy of Democratic Transitions,* ed. James F. Hollifield and Calvin Jillson (New York: Routledge, 2000); Freedom House, *Freedom in the World 2021.*

23. Andrea Kendall-Taylor, Natasha Lindstaedt, Erica Frantz, *Democracies and Authoritarian Regimes* (New York: Oxford University Press, 2019).

24. Larry Diamond, "Is the Third Wave Over?" *Journal of Democracy* 7, no. 3 (July 1996); Guillermo O'Donnell, "Delegative Democracy," *Journal of Democracy* 5, no. 1 (January 1994); and Larry Diamond and Marc F. Plattner, "Introduction," in *The Global Resurgence of Democracy.*

25. O'Donnell, "Delegative Democracy"; Larry Diamond, *Developing Democracy: Toward Consolidation* (Baltimore: Johns Hopkins University Press, 1999); Steven Levitsky and Lucan A. Way, *Competitive Authoritarianism: Hybrid Regimes After the Cold War* (New York: Cambridge University Press, 2010).

26. Vivian Yee, "As Tunisia's President Cements One-Man Rule, Opposition Grows," *New York Times,* September 27, 2021.

27. Diamond and Plattner, "Introduction"; Linz and Stepan, *Problems of Democratic Transition and Consolidation.*

28. "Democracy Index 2020: In Sickness and in Health?" *The Economist Intelligence Unit,* 2021.
29. Merilee Grindle, *Challenging the State: Crisis and Innovation in Latin America and Africa* (Cambridge: Cambridge University Press, 1996).
30. Noah Feldman, *The Arab Winter: A Tragedy* (Princeton: Princeton University Press, 2020).
31. Seymour Martin Lipset, *Political Man* (Garden City, NY: Doubleday, 1959); Linz and Stepan, *Problems of Democratic Transition and Consolidation.*
32. Laith Kubba, "The Awakening of Civil Society," *Journal of Democracy* 11, no. 3 (July 2000).
33. Amanda Taub, "It Wasn't Strictly a Coup Attempt, but It's Not Over, Either," *New York Times,* January 7, 2021; Thomas B. Edsall, "Trumpism Without Borders," *New York Times,* June 16, 2021.
34. Joe Walsh, "Nigeria Has Banned Twitter—Along with These Other Countries," *Forbes,* June 5, 2021.
35. "Gambia's Yahya Jammeh Ready for 'Billion-Year' Rule," *BBC News,* December 12, 2011; Kelsey Lilley, "The Gambia Votes: A Rare Victory for Democracy in Africa?" Atlantic Council, December 2, 2016.
36. Linz and Stepan, *Problems of Democratic Transition and Consolidation;* Diamond, "Introduction: In Search of Consolidation."
37. Ibid., Schmitter and Karl, "What Democracy Is . . . and Is Not."
38. "Global Democracy Has a Very Bad Year," *The Economist;* Kehinde A. Togun, "Why Ghana Does Disputed Elections Better Than the United States," *Foreign Policy,* January 7, 2021; Repucci and Slipowitz, "Democracy Under Siege."
39. Schmitter and Karl, "What Democracy Is . . . and Is Not."
40. Larry Diamond, "Three Paradoxes of Democracy."
41. Diamond and Plattner, "Introduction"; Diamond, "Introduction: In Search of Consolidation"; Linz and Stepan, *Problems of Democratic Transition and Consolidation.*
42. Jorge G. Castañeda, *Utopia Unarmed: The Latin American Left After the Cold War* (New York: Knopf, 1993).
43. Diamond, "Introduction: In Search of Consolidation."
44. Ruchir Sharma, "When Borders Close," *New York Times,* November 12, 2016.
45. Emanuele Sapienza, "Public Perceptions of Politics and Implications for COVID-19 Responses in Latin America and the Caribbean," *UNDP in Latin America and the Caribbean Blog,* August 10, 2020; "Attitudes Towards Politics in Latin America: A Review of Regional Perception Data," United Nations Development Programme, 2020; Daniel Zovato, "Latin American Democracy Faces Its Midlife Crisis," International Institute for Democracy and Electoral Assistance, November 21, 2018.
46. Sapienza, "Public Perceptions of Politics and Implications for COVID-19 Responses in Latin America and the Caribbean"; United Nations Development Programme, "Attitudes Towards Politics in Latin America: A Review of Regional Perception Data"; Zovato, "Latin American Democracy Faces Its Midlife Crisis."
47. United Nations Development Programme, "Attitudes Towards Politics in Latin America"; Zovato, "Latin American Democracy Faces Its Midlife Crisis"; Chu et al., "A Lost Decade for Third-Wave Democracies?"
48. Carolyn Logan and E. Gyimah-Boadi, "African Citizens Expect More from Their Lives—and Their Governments, Afrobarometer Survey Finds," *Washington Post,* October 23, 2020.
49. Chu et al., "A Lost Decade for Third-Wave Democracies?"
50. Catherine Boone, "'Empirical Statehood' and Reconfigurations of Political Order," in *The African State at a Critical Juncture,* ed. Leonardo A. Villalon and Phillip A. Huxtable (Boulder: Lynne Rienner, 1998).
51. Juan J. Linz, "The Perils of Presidentialism," in *The Global Resurgence of Democracy.*
52. O'Donnell, "Delegative Democracy"; Grindle, *Challenging the State.*

53. O'Donnell, "Delegative Democracy."
54. Linz, "The Perils of Presidentialism."
55. Donald L. Horowitz, "Comparing Democratic Systems," in *The Global Resurgence of Democracy.*
56. Ibid.
57. Arend Lijphart, *Patterns of Democracy: Government Forms and Performance in Thirty-Six Countries* (New Haven, CT: Yale University Press, 1999); Linz, "The Perils of Presidentialism"; Horowitz, "Comparing Democratic Systems."
58. Horowitz, "Comparing Democratic Systems."
59. Linz, "The Perils of Presidentialism."
60. Ibid.; Linz and Stepan, *Problems of Democratic Transition and Consolidation;* María Jaraquemada, "Chile Can't Wait Longer for a New Constitution," *Americas Quarterly,* October 7, 2020.
61. Linz and Stepan, *Problems of Democratic Transition and Consolidation;* Diamond and Plattner, "Introduction."
62. Linz and Stepan, *Problems of Democratic Transition and Consolidation.*
63. Ibid.
64. Christine Murray and Stefanie Eschenbacher, "Anti-Corruption Watchdogs Wonder: 'Who Is Funding Mexico's Presidential Candidates?'" *Reuters,* June 29, 2018.
65. Dino Mahtani, "Nigeria on Alert as Census Takers Begin Mammoth Task," *Financial Times* (London), March 22, 2006; Nkechi Onyedika-Ugoeze, "NPC Targets 2022 for National Census," *The Guardian* (Nigeria), July 9, 2021.
66. Sam van der Staak and Peter Wolf, "Cybersecurity in Elections: Models of Interagency Collaboration," International Institute for Democracy and Electoral Assistance, 2019.
67. van der Staak and Wolf, "Cybersecurity in Elections"; Freedom House, *Freedom in the World: Mexico,* 2021.
68. Mohammed Haddad, Alia Chughtai, and Kali Robinson, "How the World Votes," *Al Jazeera,* 2019; Shannon Schumaker and Aidan Connaughton, "This Is How Different Countries Vote in Their Elections," World Economic Forum, November 3, 2020.
69. Abdur Rahman Alfa Shaban, "Ghana's Voting Process—Ballot Papers, Biometric Verification and Secret Ballot," *Africa News,* June 12, 2016; Cristina Tardáguila, "Electronic Ballots Are Effective, Fast and Used All over the World—So Why Aren't They Used in the U.S.?" *Poynter,* July 12, 2021.
70. Togun, "Why Ghana Does Disputed Elections Better Than the United States."
71. Rubin Ruiz-Rufino and Sarah Birch, "The Effect of Alternation in Power on Electoral Intimidation in Democratizing Regimes," *Journal of Peace Research,* January 6, 2020.
72. Richard Javad Heydarian, "A Revolution Betrayed: The Tragedy of Indonesia's Jokowi," *Al Jazeera,* November 24, 2019.
73. Rasheed Obasekore Garuba and Ibrahim O. Salawu, "Adversarial Executive-Legislative Relations on Governance in Nigeria: Insights from Buhari's Presidency (2015–2019)," *KIU Journal of Social Humanities* 5, no. 2 (2020).
74. O'Donnell, "Delegative Democracy"; Schmidt, "Delegative Democracy in Peru?"
75. Diamond and Plattner, "Introduction"; Adedeji, "Popular Participation, Democracy, and Development."
76. Ibid.
77. Linz and Stepan, *Problems of Democratic Transition and Consolidation.*
78. Anatoly Kurmanaev, "Latin America Is Facing a 'Decline of Democracy' Under the Pandemic," *New York Times,* July 29, 2020.
79. Ibid.; Matthew Desmond, "Can America's Middle Class Be Saved from a New Depression?" *New York Times,* May 26, 2020.
80. "Brazil's President Jair Bolsonaro Is Under Siege," *The Economist,* May 29, 2021; "Brazil Senate Report Urges Charging Bolsonaro with Crimes over the Pandemic," *Associated Press,* October 20, 2021.

81. Yun-han Chu, Michael Valkiotis, Mosharraf Zaidi, and Catherine Putz, "The State of Democracy in Asia," *Global Barometer Surveys,* November 2, 2020; Desmond, "Can America's Middle Class Be Saved from a New Depression?"

82. Desmond, "Can America's Middle Class Be Saved from a New Depression?"; Bill Hayton and Tro Ly Ngheo, "Vietnam's Coronavirus Success Is Built on Repression," *Foreign Policy,* May 12, 2020; Yuan, "In a Topsy-Turvy Pandemic World, China Offers Its Version of Freedom"; Kurmanaev, "Latin America Is Facing a 'Decline of Democracy' Under the Pandemic."

83. Jason Gutierrez, "In the Philippines, Rodrigo Duterte Threatens to Jail Those Who Refuse Shots," *New York Times,* June 22, 2021.

84. Desmond, "Can America's Middle Class Be Saved from a New Depression?"; Hayton and Tro Ngheo, "Vietnam's Coronavirus Success Is Built on Repression"; Li Yuan, "In a Topsy-Turvy Pandemic World, China Offers Its Version of Freedom," *New York Times,* January 4, 2021; Repucci and Slipowitz, "Democracy Under Siege."

85. Repucci and Slipowitz, "Democracy Under Siege."

86. Natalie Kitroeff and Mitra Taj, "Latin America Also Confronts Graft Epidemic," *New York Times,* June 21, 2020.

87. Colm Quinn, "Do Poor Countries Face a Greater Risk from Coronavirus?" *Foreign Policy,* May 21, 2020.

88. Linz and Stepan, *Problems of Democratic Transition and Consolidation.*

89. Wawan Heru Suyatmiko, "The Importance of Political Integrity in Eradicating Corruption in Indonesia," *Transparency International Blog,* February 7, 2020; Jonah Blank, "How the (Once) Most Corrupt Country in the World Got Clean(er)," *The Atlantic,* May 2, 2019.

90. "Nigeria Anti-Graft Agency Rejects Ex-First Lady's 'Witch-Hunt' Accusation," *Reuters,* October 4, 2017; Transparency International, "Corruption Perception Index 2020."

91. Diamond and Plattner, "Introduction"; Institute for Economics and Peace, "Global Peace Index 2021," 2021; Transparency International, "Corruption Perception Index 2020."

92. Gisele Craveiro, "Brazil," Global Information Society Watch, 2012.

93. Mike Monteiro, "Here Are 20 of the Highest Paid World Leaders—Trump Makes the List, Who Else?" *USA Today,* April 21, 2019.

94. Larry Diamond, "The Uncivic Society and the Descent into Praetorianism," in *Politics in Developing Countries;* Olumide Taiwo, "Challenges and Possibilities for Progress in Nigeria," Brookings, May 17, 2010.

95. Transparency International, "Police Corruption Is Becoming a Pandemic Too," September 23, 2020; Transparency International, "Fix the Police," June 5, 2020; Transparency International, "Bribery or Personal Connections?" November 24, 2020.

96. Guillermo O'Donnell, "Why the Rule of Law Matters," in *Assessing the Quality of Democracy,* ed. Larry Diamond and Leonardo Morlino (Baltimore: Johns Hopkins University Press, 2005).

97. Freedom House, *Freedom in the World: Egypt,* 2021.

98. Robert I. Rotberg, "Nigeria: Elections and Continuing Challenges," Council on Foreign Relations, CSR No. 27, April 2007; Diamond, Linz, and Lipset, "Introduction: What Makes for Democracy?"

99. Eusebius McKaiser, "Zuma's Arrest Was a Victory for Rule of Law," *Foreign Policy,* Fall 2021.

100. "66% Feel Unsafe Where They Live, Down from 68% in December," *Mexico News Daily,* April 20, 2021; Ioan Grillo, "How Mexico's Drug Cartels Are Profiting from the Pandemic," *New York Times,* July 7, 2020; "How Dangerous Is Mexico?" *BBC News,* February 18, 2020.

101. Benjamin N. Gedan and Nicolás Saldiás, "What Recession? Argentina's Tough-on-Crime Minister Changes the Pre-Election Debate," *Americas Quarterly,* January 15, 2019; Carrie Kahn, "Mexico Is Holding Its Largest Elections Ever. They're Also One of Its

Deadliest," National Public Radio, June 4, 2021; Paulina Villegas, "In Mexico, Women Go on Strike Nationwide to Protest Violence," *New York Times,* March 9, 2020.

102. Council on Foreign Relations, "Mexico's Long War: Drugs, Crime, and the Cartels," February 26, 2021.

103. World Justice Project, "WJP Rule of Law Index 2020," 2021.

104. "Legal Experts Scoff at Indonesia's Improved Rule of Law Ranking," *Jakarta Post,* March 20, 2021.

105. World Justice Project, "WJP Rule of Law Index 2020."

106. Robert Dahl, *Democracy and Its Critics* (New Haven, CT: Yale University Press, 1989).

107. Howard J. Wiarda and Harvey F. Kline, *An Introduction to Latin American Politics and Development* (Boulder: Westview Press, 2001); Sonia E. Alvarez, *Engendering Democracy in Brazil: Women's Movements in Transition Politics* (Princeton: Princeton University Press, 1990).

108. Diamond, "The Uncivic Society."

109. Timofey Agarin and Allison McCullough, "How Power-Sharing Includes and Excludes Non-Dominant Communities: Introduction to the Special Issue," *International Political Science Review,* October 24, 2019.

110. Diamond, Linz, and Lipset, "Introduction: What Makes for Democracy?"

111. Drude Dahlerup, Zeina Hilal, Nana Kalandadze, and Rumbidzai Kandawasvika-Nhundu, "Atlas of Electoral Gender Quotas," Inter-Parliamentary Union, June 20, 2014; "Facts and Figures: Women's Leadership and Political Participation," UN Women, January 15, 2021.

112. Alvarez, *Engendering Democracy in Brazil;* "Proportion of Women Parliamentarians Worldwide Reaches 'All-Time High,'" *UN News,* March 5, 2021.

113. Jamille Bigio and Rachel Vogelstein, "Women Under Attack: The Backlash Against Female Politicians," *Foreign Affairs,* January/February 2020, pp. 131–138; Inter-Parliamentary Union, "Women in Parliament, 1995–2020," 2020.

114. Joy McCann, "Electoral Quotas for Women: An International Overview," Parliament of Australia, November 14, 2013; Carrie Blazina and Drew Desilver, "A Record Number of Women Are Serving in the 117th Congress," Pew Research Center, January 15, 2021.

115. Niall McCarthy, "The Countries with the Most Women in National Parliament," Statista, March 8, 2021.

116. "Proportion of Women Parliamentarians," *UN News;* Inter-Parliamentary Union, "Women in Parliament, 1995–2020."

117. Jane S. Jaquette, "Regional Differences and Contrasting Views," *Journal of Democracy* 12, no. 3 (July 2001).

118. World Economic Forum, "Global Gender Gap Report 2021," March 2021.

119. Alvarez, *Engendering Democracy in Brazil;* UN Women, "Progress of the World's Women 2019–2020," 2019.

120. Joseph Rojas Jr., "Protecting the World's Trans Population Requires Political Representation," Atlantic Council, March 23, 2021.

121. "Global Democracy Has a Very Bad Year," The Economist.

122. Gilbert da Costa,"Nigerians Wonder: Could a Military Coup Help Us?"; Richard Joseph, "Economic Transformation and Developmental Governance in Nigeria: The Promise of the Obama Era," Brookings, June 24, 2010.

123. Linz and Stepan, *Problems of Democratic Transition and Consolidation.*

124. Repucci and Slipowitz, "Democracy Under Siege."

125. Kurmanaev, "Latin America Is Facing a 'Decline of Democracy.'"

126. Ibid.

13

Authoritarianism's Appeal: Why Now?

The public's eyes are blind, their ears are deaf, and their mouths have no words.

—*Reporter in China who had been detained for investigating officials*[1]

Rouba mas faz (He steals but he gets things done). —*Brazilian saying*

According to Pulitzer Prize–winning historian Anne Applebaum, "Something else is going on right now, something that is affecting very different democracies, with very different economics and very different demographics, all over the world." What has been going on, which the PANDEMIC only accelerated, is the erosion of democratic norms and the spread of AUTHORITARIANISM, hobbling and in some cases taking down democracies (new and old) across the world, including the United States.[2] Given the difficulties associated with the DEMOCRATIC TRANSITIONS described in the preceding chapter, it is important to recognize that transitions can be tough, protracted, and inconclusive. Many countries inhabit what is called "THE MESSY MIDDLE": they exist somewhere in the middle of the continuum between "free" and "not free." How did they get there? Some set out on a process of POLITICAL LIBERALIZATION and have already reversed and returned to authoritarianism, while others hang on precariously and DEMOCRACY is under serious threat. It has long been recognized that the so-called transitions we see in many countries may be more virtual than real. We discussed in previous chapters how some political leaders are exploiting the crisis to clamp down on their critics. The consequences of Covid could reverberate into the future, with long-term damage to progress made over the past two decades. It is the same story with politics, as the PANDEMIC (along with economic strain, fear of terrorism, and immigration) has added gas to long-simmering conflicts. Feelings of resentment, a belief that "the system" is unfair—plus a disenchantment with democracy—are being used by POPULISTS to win elections and strongmen to consolidate power, accelerating the trend toward authoritarianism. As we have seen, democratic transitions can be co-opted, controlled, or aborted.[3] Mature and newer democracies have wavered, or worse, been discarded. According to Larry Diamond, populations worldwide have experienced an authoritarian resurgence as antidemocratic leaders like Russia and China used "sharp power" (information warfare and political penetration) to distort the political environment and erode the integrity of civic institutions in democratic societies. Diamond shows how Russia and China have been able to compromise vulnerable countries and strengthen their influence by pointing to the United States' need to repair its own democracy—and to democracy's decline as proof of its inherent inferiority.[4]

According to analysts, the malign influence of external actors has only emboldened local antidemocratic forces seeking to consolidate power. As we will see in this chapter, although we often think about democracy's demise being marked by something sudden and dramatic, like a coup, Steven Levitsky and Daniel Ziblatt say that democracy "no longer ends with a bang," but with a whimper. It's usually a slow death, brought on by the weakening of critical institutions such as the judiciary and press, and the gradual erosion of long-standing norms.[5]

Sometimes, it may be hard to tell when the end has come, as it is not unusual for authoritarian governments to seek to legitimize their rule through elections. As we have seen in cases across the world, such leaders are not above affecting the appearance of reform and will go to any lengths to hold on to power. Just as there are many different varieties of democracy, there are even more varieties of authoritarianism.[6] However, with some important exceptions, authoritarians have tended to perform poorly. In Somalia and a handful of other cases, years of authoritarian rule have aggravated various divides to such an extent that government has disintegrated or collapsed. As we will see, more than a few states today are at risk of imploding or failing.

Reconfiguration

So, let's turn to the story of how less-than-democratic leaders have scrambled to hold off pressures for real change by simply appearing to be more democratic. According to Catherine Boone, this scramble can be described as a RECONFIGURATION, which can play out in any number of ways.[7] Reconfigurations are not in themselves necessarily bad things or nonevents. Even the most incremental steps or alterations can accumulate into substantial reform, if not transformative change. Simply the fact that regimes are squirming to renovate or reconfigure is evidence that the pressures upon them offer the potential for more substantive change. Reconfiguring systems are capable of change; they may become more democratic or more authoritarian. Again, the outcomes will vary because they are shaped by the choices made by individuals and groups operating under the set of constraints unique to each country.[8]

Just as tyrants, for all their differences, share certain commonalities, so do authoritarian governments. They are rarely wedded to any particular IDEOLOGY besides nationalism, self-enrichment, and staying in power. They may claim to be right-wing and conservative, seeking to maintain the status quo or even turn back the clock to an idealized time, or they can be left-wing and radical, promising a brave new world and transformative change. THEOCRACIES and communist dictatorships, like Iran and Venezuela, tend to be treated by the West as pariahs and dismiss the West as imperialistic. But most NATIONALIST or populist dictatorships are dependent on aid from the West and interested in at least effecting the appearance of reform. They are what analysts call "reconfiguring regimes."[9]

One common type of reconfiguring regime is an illiberal or DELEGATIVE DEMOCRACY. Executives in illiberal or delegative democracies are strongmen. They dominate the other branches of government, institutions erode, and they subvert the entire democratic process. However, they may not appear quite as repressive as old-style authoritarians—except to minorities and other marginalized groups. Most citizens may continue to enjoy personal rights; the levels of repression today may not rank equally in terms of severity and magnitude with what occurred during the height of the COLD WAR. Still, in reconfiguring systems, there can be significant restrictions on participation, competition, and civil liberties. They may have elections, but they are patently unfair. For example, governments in Venezuela, Nicaragua, Guyana, Bolivia, and Haiti either claimed victory in "highly problematic elections" or simply refused to leave office after a loss in a free and fair vote.[10] In Côte d'Ivoire, one of the incumbent's campaign slogans in 2010 was actually "We win or we win," and this was one promise he made good on, refusing to give up power after more Ivoirians voted for his opponent than for him.[11]

Reconfiguring regimes ban parties at will, and restrict most political organization and competition. Egypt's former president Hosni Mubarak (known as "the last pharaoh") won landslide elections—it helped that the main opposition party had been banned and his challengers imprisoned. Egypt's Abdel Fattah al-Sisi government continues that tradition and, as other reconfiguring regimes, is repressive of civil and political freedoms. Like Mubarak and al-Sisi, such leaders may go through the motions to appear democratic, but they strenuously avoid any real political reforms—sometimes until it is too late, as Mubarak and some of his neighbors have learned.[12]

The leaders of these countries are frequently quite unabashed about their behavior. They often make EXCEPTIONALIST claims that the rules don't apply to them. President Robert Mugabe, who was for many years the world's oldest serving head of state, declared that he would rule Zimbabwe until he was 100. He signed into law a constitutional amendment that allowed him to choose a successor should he ever decide to retire, but was forced out before he got the chance, at age ninety-three.[13] Although these leaders deny the impact international pressure has on them, many are sensitive to their image overseas and few can face down the threat of sanctions. In effect, what many leaders have created is what has come to be known as "donor democracy." To keep the flow of Western aid open, these "democratic authoritarians" try to at least look like they're making some progress at "getting politics right."

Until recently, most Middle Eastern governments have not had to bother reconfiguring, because of their oil and because they are relatively pro-Western. Out of fear that democracy might produce governments that are not so compliant (witness the Muslim Brotherhood's short-lived control of the presidency in post-Mubarak Egypt), the West has done little to pressure Saudi Arabia and other Middle Eastern states to democratize. To varying degrees, these governments are

Figure 13.1 The Unusual Cases of China and Iran

"Getting politics right" may actually mean putting stability first, especially where experiments in democracy have been associated with corruption, inefficiency, instability, and economic chaos. This is the government's point of view in China, which along with Iran is one of a handful of countries that need not much concern themselves with appearances. In fact, Iran and China claim to be pursuing their own versions of democracy. In China's case, it is a socialist democracy "with Chinese characteristics." In Iran's case (at least until its handling of the widespread protests against the disputed election results in 2009), the theocracy could arguably be more outwardly democratic than the governments of many of its neighbors in the Middle East. Leaders of Iran and China insist that their countries are exceptional and will not follow the path of other countries. They continue to buck trends toward democratization, writing off Western democracy as "a great lie" or "bourgeois liberalization" that they hope to keep far from their borders. Chinese leaders have extended their attempts to ward off Western influence by cracking down on universities, international prep schools, and high schools where, the regime contends, "hostile" forces attempt to spread their "subversive" ideas. Iran behaves similarly, vigilant against "vaguely defined national security charges."[a]

Yet, only a handful of countries have been able to ignore or contain Western pressures for reform. Because of its size and perceived power, China can scorn Western advice on good governance and still rest assured of the continuation of benefits such as normalized trade relations and membership in the World Trade Organization. The Iranian economy has been hurt badly by US sanctions, but it has evaded Western pressures for democratization (and it has apparently "handled" pressures for change from within, at least for now).

Note: a. Simon Denyer, "China's President Takes Campaign for Ideological Purity into Universities, Schools," *Washington Post,* December 12, 2016; "Iran: Bloody Crackdown on Dissent," Human Rights Watch, January 14, 2020.

corrupt and unpopular—but the Arab Spring failed and they have held off internal pressures for change. Oil-rich regimes still find that they can co-opt the opposition with pork barrel items. They also try to create new friends, mobilize old ones, and find new ways to channel and control participation. Often this results in only the most superficial of changes.

For all the political diversity that exists in the global south, we find that what those in the messy middle are doing is in effect crisis management. Sure, some fall back on the old strategy of mass repression. But other authoritarians must come up with new survival strategies as the old ones become less viable due to Western donor pressures for good governance. Of course, each regime varies in the degree to which it uses these strategies, reflecting a unique historical context, as well as donor interests and response. It is this combination of factors that explains the variation in results we see across the world.[14]

Despite the fact that they can come in many different shapes and sizes, there are certain fundamental qualities associated with reconfiguring regimes. For example, reconfiguring regimes centralize power in the hands of one or a few. They are personally appropriated states, in which the leader (and his pals) becomes interchangeable with the government. With little or no ACCOUNTABILITY, such governments easily fall prey to the temptations of CORRUPTION. To ensure that they retain their position and maintain the appearance of LEGITIMACY, they may practice what we characterize as "low-intensity democracy." When they can't win elections fairly, they are not above drawing from a bag of tricks—or even resorting to various means of repression. The following sections describe what's in this bag of tricks, practices that may keep reconfiguring regimes in power in the short term, but ultimately leave these shape-shifters vulnerable to collapse.

Centralization of Power

Ironically, authoritarians justify their centralization of power as a way to secure their countries from collapse. The leader argues that the country is in crisis, and therefore every institution that might interfere with the effective exercise of power must be controlled. For example, during the Cold War, dictatorships kept judiciaries weak and submissive—so as not to be distracted with questions of constitutionality. However, some courts appear to be taking all this talk about democracy seriously, rendering decisions that proclaim that they cannot be bought or repressed into submission. In virtual democracies, this is often a thankless task. Historically, Zimbabwean courts have at times attempted to demonstrate their independence by ruling against the government in sensitive cases. But this is rare, such rulings have not always been respected, and under both Mugabe's and Mnangagwa's governments, judges have been pressured to support the president's policies and protect the interests of the ruling party. Some judges have been physically harassed and many independent judges in Zimbabwe have (in one way or another) been forced to resign.[15] In Iran, the Supreme Leader appoints the head of the judiciary, who appoints senior judges. Frequently, trials are closed, confessions are coerced, and the accused are denied access to legal counsel. In the aftermath of the Green Movement in 2009, hundreds were convicted in a televised series of mass show trials, none of which met international standards for justice.[16]

Authoritarians typically demonstrate a similar predilection toward forcing the legislative branch of government into line. For years, the parliaments and congresses serving such regimes have in one manner or another become rubber stamps for executive initiatives. For example, there is a dual track of power in Iran and China. In both countries, there is a government hierarchy of executive power. But running parallel to most institutions and often trumping the government is the true locus of power in each country. In Iran, the clergy and its institutions are supreme. In China, the parallel hierarchy is the branches (and "small groups") of the Chinese Communist Party.

Occasionally, however, governments playing at democracy have made the mistake of allowing their hold over the legislature to get away from them. In the 2008 elections in Zimbabwe, Mugabe's party for the first time lost its majority in the parliament and he also nearly lost the presidential elections that year (winning only because the opposition candidate pulled out of the race to protest the government's use of election violence).[17] What happens in such cases in reconfiguring regimes is that things change because either the executive has deluded himself into vainly believing that popular support would continue his party's domination at the polls, or he has simply proven unable to control the outcome in the way he could in the past.

Low-Intensity Democracy

Yet, despite these failures, reconfiguring regimes are hard to overthrow. Their leaders operate under what Phillip Huxtable calls "the universal law of politics":

those in power strive to stay in power.[18] Few authoritarians willingly relinquish the reins of government to anyone but a handpicked successor. Instead of caving in to Western pressures, the "reform" they seek to initiate is entirely on their own terms, with their own timetables, and within the constraints they impose.[19] One common sleight of hand is to rush elections through before the opposition can organize or unify quickly enough to compete against the incumbent. The result is what we call "low-intensity democracy," in which there may be great fanfare about the coming democratic reforms. A new constitution may be created, opposition parties may be legalized, and elections may be held—but the reform process itself is hijacked. Elections are carefully calculated to produce the victory of the incumbent, who can then resist further change by claiming the popular mandate.[20]

And it works. Authoritarians who allow a vote generally last longer than those who don't. There are a variety of ways of manipulating elections: vote buying, voter fraud, stealing or stuffing ballot boxes, gerrymandering, repressing opponents, election hacking, media manipulation and spreading false information, or voter suppression—adding burdens making it harder for certain voters to cast their ballots. Examples include purging voter rolls, imposing strict voter ID laws, and erecting barriers that hinder people from registering to vote or voting. [21]

Thus, the quality of elections varies enormously worldwide. Moreover, the national electoral organizations established to guard the integrity of the process are often funded by (and working for) incumbents. The highest-quality elections are transparent; international and domestic election observers watch elections to report rule violations and interference with the democratic process, including intimidation and violence at the polls, irregularities in vote counting and tallying, and lack of objectivity at polling stations (i.e., who gets to vote without proper documentation). For example, Brazil's president Jair Bolsonaro, who was trailing in the polls in 2021, set the stage to reject the upcoming 2022 elections saying that he may not accept the result and turn over power unless Brazil replaces the computers currently used to record votes with the printed ballots that he favors. In many countries, the collection of ballots can only be described as chaotic, as computer systems have been said to break down for hours or even days, resulting in highly suspicious delays in the count. However, Bolsonaro offered no evidence to support his claims that the electoral system is vulnerable to fraud. But the damage may be done and could further undermine the already teetering Brazilian democracy.[22]

Control of the Media

Often, governments seek to hang on to power by controlling the media. Social media, which has long been recognized as a disruptive technology, is being used by parties, candidates, and CIVIL SOCIETY to either strengthen or undermine governments.[23] When Nigeria's president Muhammadu Buhari was a young military dictator, he decreed that those who published anything that brought the government "ridicule or disrepute" were "guilty of an offence" for which they could be imprisoned. Forty years later, this "converted democrat," duly elected to the presidency, suspended the local operations of Twitter (yes, he did use Twitter to announce the ban). Why? He sought to control social media, which he blamed for setting off protests against police brutality in 2020. In addition, Twitter had irked the president by removing one of his own tweets in which he ominously referenced Nigeria's devastating Biafran civil war and said that those "misbehaving" would be dealt with in "the language they understand." Such language violates the platform's rules against threatening violence. Meanwhile, while Nigeria is sliding into authoritarianism, Nigerians are finding ways around the ban—and the government has threatened to prosecute those who tweet.[24]

In much of the world, it is not uncommon for journalists and bloggers to be arrested, imprisoned, and tortured, often in the name of "state security." Such "preventive measures" have commonly been used against any who oppose the government. The world had already been experiencing a downward trend in press freedom in the years just prior to the pandemic, but since then there has been dramatic deterioration in people's access to information, with 2020 having the dubious distinction of shattering the record for number of journalists imprisoned globally: 273—the highest number since the Committee to Protect Journalists began tracking arrests in the early 1990s.[25] According to Reporters Without Borders, Eritrea and North Korea were ranked as the most repressive places in the world for journalists and netizens. China, Turkmenistan, and Djibouti joined them to round out the bottom five.[26]

Personally Appropriated States

As you will recall from the first chapters of this book, most (but not all) global south countries have long histories of authoritarian government that go at least as far back as the colonial period. The result is now a tradition of arbitrary and unchecked power operating in civilian single-party states and military dictatorships. Whether headed by a civilian or military leader or leaders, such governments can best be described as PERSONALIST REGIMES or "personally appropriated states." By this, we mean that there is such a consolidation of power in the hands of one individual that this leader comes to personify the nation. Sure, as often as not these leaders are backed by a kleptocratic, powerful network of cronies who control money, security, and the media.[27] But there's always a front man—and they hold on to power for a long time; the leaders of Uganda, Equatorial Guinea, Cameroon, and Cambodia have ruled for thirty years or more.

Of course, the willingness to rely on repression is key to each of these leaders' longevity in office, but personality is (often, but not always) a big part of being able to pull this off. Personalist, populist leaders, such as Uganda's Yoweri Museveni, tend to be exceptionally charismatic, or at least have a talent for making people believe that they have a near-mystical ability to know what is good for the country. In richer countries as in poorer ones, charismatic populists rely on a politics of affect. They discredit the facts from public debate and, instead, seek to draw from their followers an emotional reaction. Museveni, who came to power in 1986 as a guerrilla freedom fighter after overthrowing a horrendous dictatorship, has made the most of his reputation as a liberator. Attempts by political ELITES to appear to be populist, "regular guys," may be all about winning trust in government (which isn't as crucial for authoritarians as it is in democracies, but it doesn't hurt). It is certainly easier to do when one can manipulate the media with censorship. Often it takes a combination of carrots and sticks, which includes neutering the opposition. This has worked in Uganda, where for three-quarters of the population, Museveni is the only president they have ever known.[28]

During the Cold War, many of these leaders literally appointed themselves "president for life." Or, as in the case of the previous rulers of Iraq and Syria, they groomed their sons to succeed them in "hereditary republics." For years, then president Mubarak was believed to be preparing his son, Gamal, to eventually inherit Egypt's presidency. But Gamal had a reputation as a playboy and no military credentials. The generals said no and Mubarak backed off the idea. The al-Assad family, which has ruled Syria since 1971, has so far more successfully (ruthlessly) constructed a system that guarantees their personal control (and wealth) into perpetuity.[29]

Corruption

During the Cold War, what sustained such long-standing regimes (besides superpower support) was often a combination of co-optation and repression. Now as then in these PATRIMONIAL regimes, the leader plays the role of the benevolent but stern father. Under the continuation of a very old tradition in much of the world, PATRON-CLIENT RELATIONSHIPS are based on reciprocity. The patron allocates resources and in return the client owes the patron his or her political loyalty. Although President Mugabe's replacement, Emmerson Mnangagwa, promised political and economic reforms, Mugabe was the new president's mentor and it turns out that little has changed—and some say it is even worse. At the very least, the old patronage-based system, which serves the new president and his cronies' interests (i.e., access to the country's rich diamond fields), continues unabated. So too did using patron-client relations at the polls. In the 2018 election, there were reports of misdeeds by other parties as well, but mainly the ZANU-PF coerced citizens by reminding them of violence during past elections and by allocating food aid in exchange for political support.[30]

Another example of how this patron-client system works is illustrated by the relationship between potentially politically relevant interest groups (e.g., trade unions or peasant organizations) and the government. CORPORATISM is most associated with fascism in Nazi Germany, but it has existed all over the world. Whatever its variant, corporatism describes the behind-the-scenes relationship between a governing party (or state) and various organized interests or sectors. It is built around a relationship of reciprocity in which the party seeks to control interest groups by recruiting, partially including, or co-opting them. The interest groups affiliated with the state, in turn, get recognition as "official" organizations, the only ones with the right to speak on behalf of specific groups. Although the state defines the powers of these organizations, the organizations do attain some of their objectives, and the state gains a new base of support. Part of the deal is that the interest group will aggregate and deliver the vote to swing elections. Some groups argue that they are being pragmatic in embracing such relationships—since the only alternative may expose them to massive government repression. Those who place a premium on stability and maintenance of order view corporatism as a benefit; however, under corporatism the MASSES are left out, and change, if it comes at all, is likely to be slow. Worse, these patronage networks also often result in gross governmental excess and a distortion of priorities. In the worst cases, they amount to kleptocracies, in which leaders and their cronies help themselves to the nation's treasury and resources.[31]

Another form of corruption involves the sweetheart deals and kickbacks struck between political elites and MULTINATIONAL CORPORATIONS. In Afghanistan, for example, more than $1 trillion in untapped minerals, such as gold, copper, iron, and lithium, promise to make it one of the most important mining centers in the world. Corruption has long been endemic there: in 2009, Afghanistan's minister of mines was convicted of accepting a $30 million bribe in return for awarding China the rights to a copper mine. Efforts to reduce corruption have been ongoing, but according to a 2019 survey by the Asia Foundation, 81.5 percent of respondents said that corruption is a major problem in Afghanistan. In a similar survey, more than one in four Afghans reported personally experiencing corruption in just the previous twelve months. The problem is so bad that the United States even describes the government it supported as "largely lawless, weak and dysfunctional."[32] The graft was so epic that it was said to have provided the Taliban with their primary recruiting tool. Greed in large part explained the government's swift collapse after the US withdrawal in 2021.[33]

Of course, no government in the world is completely honest. In many countries, the corruption can be characterized as the "politics of the belly," in reference to grossly underpaid civil servants who moonlight or take bribes to make ends meet. Elsewhere, there may be a long tradition of gift-giving or nepotism, but the government still manages to function. However, in the most predatory states, corruption is so pervasive that the system is rotten. Ultracorrupt states (some of the worst today are said to be Somalia, South Sudan, and Syria) are often notorious not only for their private use of public resources, but also for their lack of capacity and incompetence.[34] For example, South Sudan has some oil wealth, but few have seen any benefit from it. The country is so under-developed that it is said that a South Sudanese girl is more likely to die in childbirth than to complete secondary school. Humanitarian aid workers say that their view of the "murderous, larcenous" South Sudanese government veers between despair and disgust.[35]

Mobilization Through Repression

Another trick employed by reconfiguring regimes under stress is to make the most of a divided and polarized citizenry. In a climate of economic hardship, incumbents can successfully portray democratic politics as a ZERO-SUM GAME and play up fears, accentuating divisions along ethnic, religious, and other lines to mobilize the public. Often reconfiguring regimes fall back on their long-established networks of support. Despite the fact that they too have been affected by budget cuts, systems of patronage are often more institutionalized and, therefore, slower to break apart. For example, because poverty is often most pronounced in rural areas, the people living there fear losing what little state support they receive. As a result, rural areas are often major bastions of support for governments attempting to reconfigure.[36]

Besides manipulating rural-urban divides, reconfiguring governments may encourage a resurgence of ethnoregional or religious ideologies to mobilize populations and divert attention from the government's failures. As a result, communal conflict often worsens under authoritarian rule. NATIONALISM may also be used to divert attention from the government's failings by identifying scapegoats as the source of the country's problems. For example, leaders may exaggerate the threat by certain out-groups, either foreign or domestic, or hold them responsible for the country's problems. In the lead-up to the fiercely contested 2021 election in Uganda, President Yoweri Museveni claimed the opposition was receiving support from "outsiders," "terrorists," and "homosexuals" seeking to destabilize the country. Museveni's principal opponent was placed under house arrest, opposition leaders were harassed, hundreds of Ugandans were imprisoned, and dozens were killed. Calling the poll "the most cheating free" in the history of the country, Museveni won his sixth term (he has been president since 1986).[37]

In terms of enemies at home, it is not uncommon for minorities, women, immigrants, or LGBTQIA folx to be blamed for economic hardship, political instability, or a "decline in values." To legitimate their rule, reconfiguring regimes lash out at all kinds of enemies—real or invented. In an effort to appeal to conservative traditional and religious elements, authoritarian leaders commonly call for a reassertion of IDENTITY. Egypt's dictatorship, led by al-Sisi, persecutes gays, lesbians, and gender-nonconforming people to distract from the country's multiple problems, inciting moral panic about foreign threats to Egyptian culture. This secular state is also seeking to build legitimacy with its citizenry by appearing "more Islamic than Islamists," partnering with the media to broadcast humiliating public raids and arresting people for vague crimes such as "debauchery" and "insulting public morals," which can result in three- to eleven-year imprisonments.[38]

In another example of the use of this strategy to build legitimacy, authoritarians are notorious for manipulating "family values" and reinforcing traditional conceptions of women's proper role. Whether it is the imposition of "protective legislation" that denies women access to employment, or reproductive controls that refuse them access to contraception or abortion, what reconfiguring leaders are doing is building political alliances, more specifically partnerships with traditional and conservative elements. Whereas some women are mobilized by conservative appeals to their "innate" commitment to the family and morality and have even supported military coups against democratic governments, those women who do not or cannot conform to "traditional" roles are designated as traitors. In countries around the world women and LGBTQIA folx are stigmatized and even attacked for their inability or unwillingness to stay within the boundaries set for them by the patriarchal order.[39]

Hard States

As states weaken and cleavages resurface, the possibility of state collapse grows. Where leaders stubbornly refuse to stand down, the ensuing instability is used as a justification for a more repressive authoritarianism. The late Kim Jong-Il and his son, Kim Jong-Un, who have literally starved North Koreans into submission, are classic examples (the Pyongyang government arguably stands alone as the most repressive in the world today). When Zimbabwe's president Mugabe lost the first electoral round in a head-to-head race against his opponent in 2009, he unleashed such an onslaught of violence on opposition supporters (more than 200 were killed and thousands tortured) that their candidate, Morgan Tsvangirai, decided to withdraw before the runoff. Although

Tsvangirai would likely have won the elections if they had continued (and been the least bit free and fair), he withdrew to save his supporters, fearing that Mugabe might order another massacre like the one he ordered that killed tens of thousands of people in Matabeleland in the 1980s.[40]

Governments that commit such atrocities are described as "hard states." In such cases, authoritarianism itself risks becoming the cause of state collapse. Not to be confused with strong states, hard states such as North Korea, Eritrea, and Myanmar become totally dependent on the military for their survival. In many of these countries, the government may have a civilian façade, but the military has an overwhelming influence—it is the only thing propping the government up.

As we have seen in the preceding chapters, the civil and military spheres in much of the world are not as distinct as they are in consolidated democracies. Howard Wiarda and Harvey Kline argue that such a separation is not traditional in much of Latin America, where an alternation in power between military and civilian rule was for many years the norm. Even today, it is not uncommon for constitutions in Latin America to assign militaries the right, even the obligation, to intervene in the political process under certain circumstances. If not constitutional, then certainly by custom, militaries view themselves as the saviors of the nation. In still relatively democratic Peru in 2021, after the right-wing presidential candidate lost the elections and declared fraud, a group of retired military leaders called on the armed forces not to recognize an "illegitimate" president—in effect blowing a dog whistle for a coup.[41]

Post-TOTALITARIAN regimes (especially communist ones, such as China's) have more longevity and even more resources at their disposal to resist democratization than merely authoritarian regimes. For example, Seymour Martin Lipset's theory, one of the most influential (and controversial) in social science, suggests that economic DEVELOPMENT and democratization go hand in hand.[42] Yet, as we see in China, if there are any democratizing effects of development, they have been blunted and/or even neutralized. Few interpret the number of antigovernment demonstrations in China as a sign that the government will soon collapse or democratize. Rather, since Xi Jinping rose to power as a strongman, China has reverted to neo-Stalinist rule. After decades of economic GROWTH and development, the government has become more repressive at home.[43]

Development may create pressures for liberalization, but instead of liberalizing, it is more likely that demonstrations in China will prod the government to make just the reforms necessary to survive. Instead of being a sign of a STATE'S declining power, such modifications may actually work to enhance administrative efficiency, further entrenching the government's rule—as we have seen with villagers' committees' elections. In post-totalitarian authoritarian states like China's (as well as run-of-the mill authoritarians), even in the face of mass discontent, such regimes can continue to consolidate power as long as the core leadership can avoid factional struggles and keep the support of the military and police.[44] However, under these and similar circumstances, it is not unheard of for mere authoritarians to lose this crucial source of support. The security forces step in to fill the political vacuum and to establish order—if nothing else.

While it is common for military leaders in merely authoritarian regimes to promise a transition to democracy, most coups should be viewed as nothing

Figure 13.2 Xinjiang: China's "Dystopian Hellscape"

As we discussed in Chapter 10, since 2017 the Chinese government has faced serious allegations of crimes against humanity involving members of its ethnic and religious minorities—including the Uighurs and Kazakhs. Since the establishment of the People's Republic of China in 1949, authorities have kept a close eye on organized religious communities, with this recent campaign mostly targeting adherents of Islam. Muslims constitute approximately 1.8 percent of China's population (roughly 22 million people), with ten predominantly Muslim ethnic groups (of which the Uighurs, a Turkic ethnic minority, are one).[a] Approximately 12 million Uighurs live in Xinjiang, China's largest province (where they constitute less than half of the population).[b] For years, it has been clear that traditional Uighur culture is under attack, evidenced by a substantial surveillance system (fueled by advanced artificial intelligence tools), in addition to the impact of the mass migration of other ethnic groups (most notably the majority Han) to the region.[c] Cameras monitor every street (relaying footage to the police), residential compounds have facial recognition systems, and citizens are encouraged to openly snitch on anyone perceived to threaten "social stability."[d] Beyond that, the evidence of a network of prison camps is vast. The incarceration of as many as 1 million Uighurs is not disputed by Chinese authorities (although they deny that any of the evidence constitutes human rights abuses).[e] The cultural erasure and human rights violations are part of a "dystopian landscape on a staggering scale," according to Amnesty International's secretary general.[f] Beijing insists that actions have been taken to "de-radicalize" members of the population and that the prisons are "re-education" camps lawfully established to respond to separatism and Islamist militancy. Additionally, reports of systematic rape, the widespread use of forced labor, as well as involuntary sterilization and insertion of contraceptive devices have been documented by former detainees.[g]

Notes: a. Eleanor Albert and Lindsay Maizland, "Backgrounder: Religion in China," Council on Foreign Relations, September 25, 2020.

b. "Who Are the Uyghurs and Why Is China Being Accused of Genocide?" *BBC News,* June 21, 2021.

c. Drew Harwell and Eva Dou, "Huwaei Worked on Several Surveillance Systems Promoted to Identify Ethnicity, Documents Show," *Washington Post,* December 13, 2020.

d. Alice Su, "'Will They Let Us Live?' Inside Xinjiang, Survivors of China's Internment Camps Speak," *Los Angeles Times,* December 17, 2020.

e. In 2019, the *New York Times* published analysis of more than 400 pages of internal Chinese documents that detail the systematic organization of this mass detention effort and the endorsement of this campaign by officials at the highest levels of the Chinese government. See Austin Ramzy and Chris Buckley, "'Absolutely No Mercy': Leaked Files Expose How China Organized Mass Detentions of Muslims," *New York Times,* November 16, 2019.

f. Amnesty International, "China: Draconian Repression of Muslims in Xinjiang Amounts to Crimes Against Humanity," June 10, 2021.

g. Brenda Brockman Smith, "China's Use of Forced Labor in Xinjiang—a Wake-Up Call Heard Round the World?" Council on Foreign Relations, August 26, 2021; "China Forcing Birth Control on Uighurs to Suppress Population, Report Says," *BBC News,* June 29, 2020.

more than yet another reconfiguration. There are some cases, such as Nigeria, where (at least for a while) it appeared that the promised transition might finally take place. As mentioned in Chapter 11, some are skeptical about Nigeria's democracy. Although the military godfathers act mostly in a covert fashion, many doubt that the military will ever truly turn over power to civilians. Too often we see that transitions are delayed, incomplete, or temporary. Increasingly, coups are unnecessary; sometimes, military leaders simply reconfigure themselves as civilian candidates for president, hold staged elections, limit the ability of the opposition to compete, and (if all else fails) rig the results. More often, as is feared in Nigeria, now led by a democratically elected former dictator, the military just continues to govern from the wings.[45] When this is the case, it should fool no one. It amounts to merely another manifestation of virtual democracy.

Disintegration

When the reconfiguration gets out of control, when the government will not budge in the face of overwhelming opposition and divisions within the military render it unable or unwilling to prevent a breakup, the result is a crisis of governance or (in its most dramatic form) a DISINTEGRATION. It happens, and it is more likely as climate stressors add up, but in the years just before the pandemic, at least, outright disintegration has been the least frequent outcome associated with reconfiguring regimes. It is much more common to find countries on the cusp of failure, characterized as "weak" or "failing" states. In the 2021 Fragile States Index, ten states were identified as at "high alert" or "very high alert" for failing. Most, but not all of them, are in sub-Saharan Africa. Of our cases, Zimbabwe and Nigeria just missed the cutoff and were categorized as on "alert."[46]

The countries at greatest risk of failing are vulnerable because of a mix of factors: a high degree of income inequality, rising ethnic tensions, and low levels of public trust in institutions (to name just a few). But there were some new entries on the list. Although it is categorized as "more stable," the heavy-handed state reaction to large protests in response to police violence, efforts to delegitimize the election process, political polarization, congressional gridlock, rampant misinformation, and a failed early response to Covid—as well as the steepest contraction in GDP in sixty years—all contributed to the United States being the country whose total score worsened more than any other in the world in 2020.[47]

What differentiates a weak state from a failed state? According to Stuart E. Eizenstat, John Edward Porter, and Jeremy M. Weinstein, the difference isn't so much about poverty per se as it is about lapses in three critical functions of government: (1) the provision of security (and preserving SOVEREIGNTY over the territory); (2) the provision of basic services; and (3) the protection of civil freedoms. Weak states are deficient in one of these areas, while failed states are not capable of fulfilling any of the three.[48] Under what Applebaum calls "the Maduro model" (after Venezuelan dictator Nicolás Maduro), some leaders (e.g., Bashar al-Assad in Syria) are willing to accept economic collapse, isolation, and mass poverty. They are even willing to risk having their country become a failed state—if that's what it takes to stay in power. And it's not hard to go off that cliff. Facing internal and external demands for substantive change, weak states can quickly erode, becoming failed states. But failed states are at risk of DISINTEGRATION. In 2021, analysts again identified Somalia, along with Yemen and Syria, as in the process of decay and on a long slide toward disintegration.[49]

What is disintegration? According to I. William Zartman, disintegration is best conceptualized as a long-term degenerative disease. Countries in decay are in varying stages of decline, but what they have in common is state paralysis: they can no longer perform the functions that make them states. Under such circumstances government retracts and the countryside is left on its own. The state becomes a shell; there is no sovereign authority. Power is up for grabs and warlord politics, or rival power centers, play increasingly larger roles in people's lives. There is a breakdown of law and order and organized violence becomes generalized. The effect is societal collapse. People retreat into ethnic nationalisms or religious affiliations as a residual source of identity and organization, and no single institution can claim to receive the support of or exercise control over the people living there.[50] Under such circumstances, even the firmness of national borders becomes vulnerable, and the fracturing or breakup of states becomes even more likely. Certain states in Nigeria fit this bill. Analysts tell us what we are seeing now is not unique—except perhaps in its magnitude: previous waves of democratization have been followed by reverse waves of democratic breakdown.[51]

But the degenerative disease that so many states are experiencing does not always prove fatal. A cure, or more likely a remission, is possible. Some states may survive political turbulence of the kind described, exist on the brink of collapse, and still emerge with new vigor. And more analysts are arguing that given the arbitrary boundaries demarcating states, perhaps in some instances fragmentation is not a bad thing. Juan Linz and Alfred Stepan make the interesting point that to have a democratic regime, there must first be a viable state.[52] While we must never forget the human tragedy so often associated with disintegration, for some countries disintegration is increasingly being thought of as a necessary first step—before democratization can even be considered. Given the foundation of a more viable state, democratic forces may then regroup and substantive REFORMS can begin. Although external actors need to be kept in mind for the considerable role they play in shaping outcomes in weak states, what may prove to be more crucial to their recovery is the ability of civil society to rebound. Even a collapsed state can come back from the dead. To some degree, Rwanda after the 1994 genocide was at this crossroads. The inhabitants of a territory must come together to establish a democracy. However, if the pieces do not come back together, authoritarianism or warlord politics is a likely fate. Still, nothing is preordained. Even weak states evolve differently and no outcome is inevitable.[53] The one thing we can bet on is that unless something changes, this is a scenario we are likely to see more of in the future.

Conclusions: Coping with Reversals and Fragility

Looking back on the dramatic political changes of the past thirty to forty years, most leaders have acceded to internal and external demands for political liberalization not only in a variety of ways, but also to varying degrees, depending on the intensity of the pressures they face. Some leaders have been willing to make the reforms necessary to build the base for a still-fragile democratic system. And while a strong economy is an asset, even democracies in some of the poorest countries, against all odds, have proven to be impressively resilient. Elsewhere both new and old democracies have lost ground as leaders have made only partial changes, or reconfigured the political system in such a way as to maintain their own economic interests and power bases. Meanwhile, to varying degrees, authoritarians of diverse stripes have put on only the appearance of change. Some don't even go through the motions. During this period of democratic decline and authoritarian resurgence, some states appear to be explicitly bucking the liberal democratic trend. In the case of China, for example, one specialist characterizes efforts by pro-democracy activists as the "lessons of failure."[54] Lipset's theory has not held up for China, and after decades the West has realized that its assumption (that the growth of a middle class in China will lead it toward democracy) was misplaced.

Still other political systems have disintegrated (or may yet disintegrate) under the cumulative effect of the pressures already described. Because they are so fragile, some democracies will struggle and eventually fail. Does this sound like the situation in any of our case studies? A firestorm was created in 2009 when a US Joint Forces Command report listed Mexico as at risk of rapid and sudden collapse. Yet, more than ten years later it is the cartels, not the government, that control wide swathes of the country.[55] The coronavirus served as yet another driver of fragility worldwide, and increased the number of countries expected to experience instability (and the likelihood of war) to thirty-five in 2020—its highest number over the past thirty years. Of our cases, these thirty-five included Mexico, Egypt, and Nigeria, which were already experiencing what could be considered civil wars. Peru and Zimbabwe weren't much better off; they were identified as at increased risk of war. In any of these countries, if already challenged and rapidly delegitimized democracies continue to find themselves unable to deal with factionalized elites, to address group grievances and uneven DEVELOPMENT, it could mean the end of civilian rule—whether through military coup or civil war.[56]

Ironically, given the current climate, it is the reconfiguring regimes (like Egypt, perhaps) that are more likely to survive, at least in the short term. Despite donor talk about the importance of good governance, it is the virtual democracies that are best placed to enforce the economic reforms the donor countries so desire. Yet, perhaps the worst thing for democracy is for developed countries to accept an incumbent's portrayal of political reform as destabilizing and dangerous. Unwilling to budge on neoliberal economic reforms or fearful of political vacuums, too often donors lower the threshold for their political expectations. They back off from demands for reforms, such as respect for civil rights, arguing that we need to stop foreign interventions and endless wars, in effect agreeing with authoritarians that perhaps the people "aren't ready yet" for democracy.

Yet, in the case of authoritarians, we know from history that the more repressive a government is, the more likely it will threaten its neighbors, as well as its own people. As the United States and NATO pull out after their twenty-year war, it is also important not to forget the lessons of Afghanistan—states left to fail can pose a world of problems for all of us. As Larry Diamond and Marc Plattner observe, it is in our interests to do everything we can to nurture and support fragile democracies.[57] Yet, does that mean staying there forever? There is nothing inevitable about the triumph or persistence of democracy. Even consolidated democracies can decay if there is a long period of incompetent leadership. In the end, it is important to remember that there are a wide variety of possible outcomes to the transformations under way.

International pressure alone did not create the third wave of democratization, but if international support for it should continue to wane, the viability of already frail democracies will be further diminished. President Joe Biden has called on democratic allies to unite and defend against authoritarianism's rise by fighting corruption and promoting human rights worldwide. As many have pointed out, these are not just foreign policy issues for the United States. The United States has work to do at home, fighting corruption and promoting human rights, to strengthen its own democratic credentials—and it will face resistance in trying to do so. However, it is crucial that the international community and regional actors assist fledgling democracies in their deepening and CONSOLIDATION.[58] If the past few years have taught us anything, it is that the flexibility and adaptability of democracies can be severely tested by the resilience of authoritarians.

Notes

1. Quoted in Javier C. Hernández, "'We're Almost Extinct': China's Investigative Journalists Are Silenced Under Xi," *New York Times,* July 12, 2019.
2. Anne Applebaum, *Twilight of Democracy: The Seductive Lure of Authoritarianism* (New York: Doubleday, 2020).
3. Ibid.; Larry Diamond and Marc F. Plattner, "Introduction," in *The Global Resurgence of Democracy,* ed. Larry Diamond and Marc F. Plattner (Baltimore: Johns Hopkins University Press, 1993).
4. *Freedom in the World 2016,* Freedom House, 2016; Sarah Repucci and Amy Slipowitz, "Democracy Under Siege," Freedom House, 2021; Larry Diamond, "Democracy Demotion: How the Freedom Agenda Fell Apart," *Foreign Affairs* 98, no. 4 (July–August 2019), pp. 17–25.
5. Steven Levitsky and Daniel Ziblatt, *How Democracies Die* (New York: Crown, 2018).
6. Andrew J. Nathan, "Authoritarian Impermanence," *Journal of Democracy* 20, no. 3 (July 2009).
7. Catherine Boone, "'Empirical Statehood' and Reconfigurations of Political Order," in *The African State at a Critical Juncture,* ed. Leonardo A. Villalon and Phillip A. Huxtable (Boulder: Lynne Rienner, 1998).
8. Merilee Grindle, *Challenging the State: Crisis and Innovation in Latin America and Africa* (Cambridge: Cambridge University Press, 1996); Leonardo A. Villalon, "The African State at the End of the Twentieth Century: Parameters of the Critical Juncture," in *The African State at a Critical Juncture,* ed. Leonardo A. Villalon and Phillip A. Huxtable (Boulder: Lynne Rienner, 1998).
9. Villalon, "The African State at the End of the Twentieth Century"; Anne Applebaum, "The Bad Guys Are Winning," *The Atlantic,* November 13, 2021.
10. Anatoly Kurmanaev, "Latin America Is Facing a 'Decline of Democracy' Under the Pandemic," *New York Times,* July 29, 2020.
11. Adam Nossiter, "Ensconced in the Presidency: With No Budging in Ivory Coast," *New York Times,* December 26, 2010.
12. *Freedom in the World 2021,* Freedom House, 2021; "Egypt's Opposition Protests, Challenging Legislative Vote," *AP,* December 12, 2010.
13. Conor Gaffey, "Zimbabwe's Mugabe Plans to Live to 100 and Won't Retire," *Newsweek,* March 4, 2016; "Mugabe Signs in a Successor Law," *BBC News,* November 1, 2007.
14. Grindle, *Challenging the State;* Boone, "'Empirical Statehood'"; Larry Diamond, Juan J. Linz, and Seymour Martin Lipset, "Introduction: What Makes for Democracy?" *Politics in Developing Countries: Comparing Experiences with Democracy,* ed. Larry Diamond, Juan J. Linz, and Seymour Martin Lipset (Boulder: Lynne Rienner, 1995).
15. *Freedom in the World: Zimbabwe,* Freedom House, 2021.
16. *Freedom in the World 2010,* Freedom House, 2010.
17. "Zimbabwe Election: Mugabe's Zanu-PF 'Wins Majority,'" *BBC News,* August 2, 2013.

18. Phillip A. Huxtable, "The African State Toward the Twenty-First Century: Legacies of the Critical Juncture," in *The African State at a Critical Juncture,* ed. Leonardo A. Villalon and Phillip A. Huxtable (Boulder: Lynne Rienner, 1998).

19. Boone, "'Empirical Statehood.'"

20. Grindle, *Challenging the State.*

21. Nic Cheeseman and Bryan Klaas, *How to Rig an Election* (New Haven: Yale University Press, 2019); "Block the Vote: How Politicians Are Trying to Block Voters from the Ballot Box," *ACLU,* August 18, 2021.

22. "Brazil's Bolsonaro Says He May Not Accept 2022 Election Under Current Voting System," *Reuters,* July 7, 2021.

23. Nic Cheeseman, Jonathan Fisher, Idayat Hassan, and Jamie Hitchen, "Nigeria's WhatsApp Politics," *Journal of Democracy* 31, no. 3 (July 2020).

24. "Nigeria's Twitter Ban Prompts Ridicule—and Fear," *The Economist,* June 12, 2021; Rachel Vanderhill, *Autocracy and Resistance in the Internet Age* (Boulder: Lynne Rienner, 2020).

25. "Record Number of Journalists Imprisoned in 2020—Report," *Reuters,* December 15, 2020.

26. Reporters Without Borders, "World Press Freedom Index," 2021.

27. Anne Applebaum, "The Bad Guys Are Winning," *The Atlantic,* November 15, 2021.

28. Boris Muñoz, "Hola, President Biden. Latin America Has a Message for You," *New York Times,* January 23, 2021; Patience Atuhaire, "Uganda's Yoweri Museveni: How an Ex-Rebel Has Stayed in Power for 35 Years," *BBC News,* May 10, 2021.

29. "Succession Gives Army a Stiff Test in Egypt," *New York Times,* September 12, 2010; Tom Allinson, "Stealth Wealth: How Assad's Family and Others Have Filled Their European Coffers," *Deutsche Welle,* April 29, 2020.

30. "Zimbabwe: Lack of Reform Risks Credible Elections," Human Rights Watch, June 7, 2018; Patrick Kingsley and Jeffrey Moyo, "A Coup Offered Hope to Zimbabwe. Has Its New President Delivered?" *New York Times,* August 10, 2019.

31. Douglas A. Chalmers, "Corporatism and Comparative Politics," in *New Directions in Comparative Politics,* ed. Howard J. Wiarda (Boulder: Westview, 1985); Roy C. Macridis and Steven R. Burg, *Introduction to Comparative Politics* (New York: HarperCollins, 1991).

32. Asia Foundation, "A Survey of the Afghan People: Afghanistan in 2019," 2019; United Nations Office on Drugs and Crime, "Despite Progress, Afghanistan's Total Corruption Cost Increases to $3.9 Billion," February 7, 2013; "Why Afghanistan's Government Is Losing the War with the Taliban," *The Economist,* May 18, 2019; Integrity Watch, "National Corruption Survey 2018: Afghans' Perceptions and Experiences of Corruption," 2018.

33. James Risen, "US Identifies Vast Mineral Riches in Afghanistan," *New York Times,* June 13, 2010; United Nations Office on Drugs and Crime, "Corruption Widespread in Afghanistan, UNODC Survey Says," January 19, 2010; "Why Afghanistan's Government Is Losing the War with the Taliban," *The Economist,* May 18, 2019.

34. Christopher Walker and Sanja Tatic, "Corruption's Drag on Democratic States," *Christian Science Monitor,* August 2, 2006; "Corruption Perceptions Index 2015," Transparency International (January 27, 2016).

35. "South Sudan's Second Decade May Be as Troubled as Its First," *The Economist,* July 10, 2021.

36. Boone, "Empirical Statehood."

37. Abdi Latif Dahir, "'Tell Us if He's Dead': Abductions and Torture Rattle Uganda," *New York Times,* April 11, 2021; "Uganda's Long-Time Leader Yoweri Museveni Declared Election Winner," *BBC News,* January 17, 2021.

38. Human Rights Watch, "Egypt: Security Forces Abuse, Torture LGBT People," October 1, 2020.

39. Valentine M. Moghadam, *Globalizing Women* (Baltimore: Johns Hopkins University Press, 2005).

40. *Freedom in the World 2010,* Freedom House.

41. Howard J. Wiarda and Harvey F. Kline, *An Introduction to Latin American Politics and Development* (Boulder: Westview, 2001); "The Clash in Peru over the Election Result Continues," *The Economist,* July 10, 2021.

42. Seymour Martin Lipset, "Some Social Requisites of Democracy: Economic Development and Political Legitimacy," *American Political Science Review* 53, no. 1 (March 1959).

43. Minxin Pei, "China: Totalitarianism's Long Shadow," *Journal of Democracy* 32, no. 2 (April 2021).

44. Andrew F. Nathan, "Present at the Stagnation," *Foreign Affairs* 85, no. 4 (July/August 2006).

45. Wole Soyinka, "Lessons from Nigeria's Militarized Democratic Experiment," *New York Times,* October 9, 2019.

46. Fund for Peace, "Fragile States Index 2021," 2021.

47. Ibid.

48. Stuart Eizenstat, John Edward Porter, and Jeremy Weinstein, "Rebuilding Weak States," *Foreign Affairs* 84, no. 1 (January/February 2005).

49. Applebaum, "The Bad Guys Are Winning"; Fund for Peace, "Fragile States Index 2021."

50. I. William Zartman, "Introduction: Posing the Problem of State Collapse," in *Collapsed States: The Disintegration and Restoration of Legitimate Authority,* ed. I. William Zartman (Boulder: Lynne Rienner, 1995).

51. Larry Diamond, "Is the Third Wave Over?" *Journal of Democracy* 7, no. 3 (July 1996); Guillermo O'Donnell, "Delegative Democracy," *Journal of Democracy* 5, no. 1 (January 1994); Diamond and Plattner, "Introduction."

52. Juan J. Linz and Alfred Stepan, *Problems of Democratic Transition and Consolidation: Southern Europe, South America, and Post-Communist Europe* (Baltimore: Johns Hopkins University Press, 1996).

53. Monte Palmer, *Comparative Politics: Political Economy, Political Culture, and Political Independence* (Itasca, IL: F. E. Peacock, 1997); Zartman, "Introduction: Posing the Problem of State Collapse."

54. Andrew J. Nathan, *China's Transition* (New York: Columbia University Press, 1997).

55. Bernd Debusmann, "Among Top US Fears: A Failed Mexican State," *New York Times,* January 9, 2009.

56. Jonathan P. Moyer and Oliver Kaplan, "Will the Coronavirus Fuel Conflict?" *Foreign Policy* (July 6, 2020).

57. Diamond and Plattner, "Introduction."

58. Applebaum, "The Bad Guys Are Winning"; Diamond, Linz, and Lipset, "Introduction: What Makes for Democracy?"; Villalon, "The African State at the End of the Twentieth Century"; Julius E. Nyang'oro and Timothy M. Shaw, "The African State in the Global Economic Context," in *The African State at a Critical Juncture,* ed. Leonardo A. Villalon and Phillip A. Huxtable (Boulder: Lynne Rienner, 1998).

14

Linking Concepts and Cases

Great variation exists among our eight case studies in terms of history, economy, and society. In the following pages we will briefly review each country's recent political history, using examples to illustrate some of the concepts discussed in the preceding two chapters. As you read these case studies, look for the major similarities and differences of experience—especially with regard to their REFORM, RECONFIGURATION, or DISINTEGRATION. Keep in mind that because of the dynamic nature of politics, it is likely that some things have changed since this book was published, so further research may be needed to answer some of the questions posed here.

Where, and why, would you locate each case on the continuum from consolidated LIBERAL DEMOCRACY to AUTHORITARIAN regime? Why do you think some countries are taking the reformist route, while others reconfigure? What are some of the ways in which government leaders attempt to hold on to power? To what extent have the military, the economy, and the existence of pluralism complicated transitions, or CONSOLIDATION?

In which cases have we seen the most democratic decline? Where has the population appeared to choose the order provided by authoritarianism over the instability associated with democracy? Of those that have made the most progress toward democracy, how have they achieved their success? What are the major supports and constraints for democracy in each country? Where have the constraints become crises, and which are the most prone to disintegration? Which of these countries have made progress toward deepening democracy? In what ways are they accomplishing this?

Case Study: Mexico

Over the past few decades, Mexico has been engaged in one of the world's longest and most dramatic DEMOCRATIC TRANSITIONS. Until 2000, Mexicans had lived for seventy-one years under a government controlled by the Institutional Revolutionary Party (PRI). Politics in Mexico was for generations a ZERO-SUM

GAME in which all formal power was centralized under the control of this one party. Although this was no democracy, many Mexicans appreciated the relative stability their country enjoyed under the PRI.

Still, by the mid-1990s it had become clear to many Mexicans that the relative stability provided by one-party rule could not make up for the excesses that came with it. Mexico was experiencing a series of crises, most notably associated with an economic collapse in 1994 and a civil war in the south. In addition, Mexicans were rocked by a number of major scandals, pervasive CORRUPTION, and a growing lawlessness in the country, much of it linked to Mexico's newly prominent position in the international drug trade. Moreover, Mexico's economic difficulties and growing inequalities were contributing to a situation in which stability could no longer be ensured. In the end, a combination of internal and external pressures convinced PRI to move forward with a "silent revolution," or gradual democratization of Mexico.

It was President Ernesto Zedillo's dramatic break with the tradition of the *dedazo* (or "the tap of the finger," in which the outgoing president handpicked his successor) that opened up the political space for Mexicans to take part in truly democratic elections in 2000.[1] There were some irregularities, but in many ways this election amounted to Mexico's second revolution—after seven decades of uninterrupted rule, the PRI lost and actually allowed itself to be removed from power.

The personality dominating this "electoral revolution" was Vicente Fox of the conservative National Action Party (PAN). Just as surprising as the result of the vote was that the transfer of power was remarkably smooth. However, with a term limit of six years, Fox had precious little time to demonstrate to Mexicans that he could make good on his grand promises.[2] Ironically, part of the reason that President Fox failed to meet the people's high expectations was because Mexico's democracy was working—since 2000 it has become stronger, more accountable, and more transparent.

Still, the presidential election of 2006 was extremely divisive and a test for the new democracy. For months up until the election it looked as if Mexicans would choose by a landslide their first leftist president, the Party of Democratic Revolution's (PRD) Andrés Manuel López Obrador, a POPULIST former mayor of Mexico City. However, when the PAN candidate, conservative, Harvard-educated Felipe Calderón, came from behind to win, López Obrador, known as AMLO, called foul and demanded a recount, claiming that the election had been stolen from him by a conspiracy of government and business ELITES. Mexico's federal electoral tribunal came to the unanimous decision that Calderón was the rightful winner—by less than one percentage point. But in this country with a long history of fraudulent elections, López Obrador and his supporters refused to accept defeat. It was not uncommon to hear Mexicans question whether they had a democracy at all.[3]

This lack of legitimacy is dangerous for any new democracy. The new president's term was plagued by difficulties. Meanwhile, as the second PAN administration struggled, PRI revived and rebranded itself.[4] Rested and ready, PRI was building momentum and, by 2012, people were ready for a change. Enrique Peña Nieto, a telegenic young PRI candidate beat AMLO and a field of candidates. Perhaps most notably, that year Mexico's democracy passed a crucial litmus test with a successful alternation in power. The party that replaced the dictatorship passed the torch to the democratically elected winner: the party that was the dictatorship.

Sure enough, the PRI's comeback was a failure as Peña Nieto's government was unable to make headway on two of the most important issues for Mexicans: corruption and security (he and his wife were caught up in their own corruption scandals). By the time of the 2018 elections, Mexicans were again ready for something new. On his third try, AMLO, now with the National Regeneration Movement (MORENA), swept into power in a landslide, winning the presidency with 53 percent of the vote—and a MORENA-led coalition majority of seats in Congress.[5]

AMLO's election signaled a repudiation of the outgoing PRI government and a fundamental departure from the NEOLIBERALS who had ruled Mexico since the democratic transition. Instead, he promised Mexico an ambitious "fourth transformation" (much like its war for independence and revolution) by fighting corruption, crime, and poverty to create a more egalitarian country. AMLO's government has increased pensions and supported apprenticeships for young people. But the president has also centralized power, attacked the press for "fake news," and tested the independence of institutions such as the Supreme Court and the National Electoral Institute while increasingly relying on the army for building public works, controlling migration, and so forth. In fact, the rising influence of the military and erosion of checks on the presidency have concerned many observers. In the 2021 midterm elections, Morena lost the congressional seats necessary to change the constitution or push through the president's agenda. However, nearly halfway through his term, which ends in 2024, AMLO continued to be personally popular with two-thirds of the population, despite the broad disapproval of his handling of the PANDEMIC, the economy, and the cartels.[6]

Case Study: Peru

Peru, which experienced eight military coups in the twentieth century, is hardly unique in Latin America for having more experience with authoritarianism than democracy. It, like many countries in the region, set out on a POLITICAL LIBERALIZATION back in the early 1980s, but it hasn't been a steady transition to democracy—in Peru or in most of Latin America. Many Peruvians view the system as deeply flawed and they have no hope that elections will make a difference. Analysts predict that under such circumstances, antisystem populists and authoritarian leaders will rise. This is a real threat in Peru, which has swung back and forth between authoritarian and democratic rule so often that it has come to be known as an "intermittent democracy."[7]

Thirty years ago, facing a double threat of guerrilla insurrections and hyperinflation, Alberto Fujimori, the democratically elected president of Peru, determined that democratic dialogue was inefficient. Frustrated with the limitations placed on him by the checks and balances of Peru's democratic institutions, in 1992 Fujimori assumed for himself the powers of a military dictator. By 1995 he had vanquished a terrorist group, turned the economy around—and was reelected by a landslide. Why were Peruvians willing to surrender their hard-earned, but still somewhat restricted, democratic liberties to Fujimori? Even his enemies admit that the president was able to provide Peruvians with a sense of stability relatively unknown in the Andean region.[8]

While some were appreciative of the order he provided, by the late 1990s Fujimori was second only to Fidel Castro as the longest-sitting head of state in Latin America.[9] To stay in power, the president pulled out all the stops and won in 2000 what is widely agreed to be the dirtiest campaign and election in the country's history. Eventually, a corruption scandal brought him down.[10]

Since Fujimori's ouster in 2000 and Peru's return to democracy, Peruvian leaders have been challenged to deal with several problems at once.[11] Today, Peruvians do enjoy more political and civil liberties. The RULE OF LAW has been strengthened, and Peru's institutions are more accountable. Until Covid hit in 2020, the country had experienced relatively impressive economic GROWTH.[12] But even in the good years, Peru has continued to have problems with inequality, corruption, controlling the military, and restoring Peruvians' faith in politics.[13]

Reflective of this crisis of legitimacy, Peruvian voters have proven fickle, too, choosing presidents from the center-right, swinging to the left, and back to the center-right again.[14] Parties exist, but few are identified by IDEOLOGY. Instead, it is more common to find candidate-centered movements closely identified with a single personality or "flash parties," because they are disposable and vanish almost as quickly as they appear. One recent president (Pedro Pablo Kuczynski) ran under different party labels in 2006, 2011, and 2016.[15]

But many Peruvian voters have proven loyal to personalities, and it is not at all uncommon for once-disgraced politicians to make comebacks. Some fear it, others applaud it, but in some ways even Fujimori is getting a second act. In this case, it is his daughter, Keiko Fujimori, who served as his first lady and who has made her own runs for the presidency. On the right wing of the spectrum, the younger Fujimori appealed to many fearful of Peru's growing crime rate. She is widely viewed as the toughest on national security and her supporters are nostalgic for her father's iron-fisted record.[16]

However, Keiko was just one of many Peruvian politicians, including four former presidents, who have been caught up in a multiyear political crisis. Known as the Odebrecht scandal, the Brazilian engineering firm Odebrecht was accused of paying $800 million to politicians in a dozen countries.[17] By 2020, disgust over corruption revelations—along with an astonishing death rate from Covid and an economic contraction that caused millions to lose their jobs—sent Peru into a political crisis and the largest demonstrations seen in decades. After clashes between the executive and legislative branches, a spiral of political crises resulted in one resignation after another. Incredibly, in a single week in November 2020, the country was led by three different presidents.[18]

The highly polarized 2021 elections eventually came down to a contest of "the princess or the peasant." Keiko Fujimori, who was being investigated for corruption, faced off against left-wing but social conservative Pedro Castillo. Castillo supported redistribution of wealth, but not LGBTQIA rights or abortion whereas Keiko ran warning about "the radical left" turning the country into a Cuba or Venezuela. Pro-business, she garnered support from white, coastal elites.[19] Castillo, a mestizo outsider with little political experience but a populist touch, was backed by mostly rural and Indigenous supporters disgusted with corruption and demanding change. In the end, Castillo just squeaked by to win (some say because he was viewed by many Peruvians as the "least bad" choice).[20]

As has occurred elsewhere when the result was close, Keiko at first refused to accept defeat and there were fears of a coup. But after 200 years of independence, Peru experienced its fifth consecutive, peaceful transfer of power. This was a record for the country. Still, the upheaval was likely to continue as Castillo had a weak mandate and Keiko led a conservative-majority Congress with a habit of impeaching presidents. Just a few months in, forecasters were predicting that Castillo wouldn't last the first year of his term.[21] If the turmoil of 2020 is to be a sign of what is to come, Peru may at best be an intermittent democracy, after all.

Case Study: Nigeria

Since the country's independence in 1960, two government leaders have been assassinated and there have been six successful coups, with many more failed ones. Until 1999 the military had spent more time in power than had civilians, and when civilians have ruled, it has mostly been at the discretion of the armed forces.[22] Even in Nigeria's twenty-year-old democracy, there are concerns that the military considers itself above all other institutions.

Nigeria has come through a nightmare to begin its democratic transition. Earlier experiments with democracy failed in the midst of intense political crises, polarization, and a lack of economic DEVELOPMENT. Nigerians have endured incompetent and corrupt civilian governments; they suffered worse through a civil war and through coup after coup, but the country hit bottom during the five years it spent under the dictatorship of Sani Abacha (1993–1998).

It is difficult to briefly relate just how venal this government was. Those with political power amassed enormous fortunes from the country's oil wealth. Under both civilian and military rule, the vast majority of Nigerians have been permanent outsiders.[23] Yet, in what has been described by many Nigerians as divine intervention, in June 1998 Sani Abacha suddenly dropped dead. And by that time, the military had tired of the exercise of government and was willing to give civilians another shot. To create what would become known as the Fourth Republic, Nigerians poured into the voting booths in February 1999. They elected representatives at all levels of government. A former dictator and retired general Olusegun Obasanjo won, the military remained in the wings, and Nigeria began its fourth go at democracy.

Since then, there has been growing public dissatisfaction with the government. The country's progress on civil and political rights has been pretty stagnant.[24] Between 2000 and 2020, Nigerians' trust in their president fell from 77 to 40 percent, and their satisfaction with democracy fell from 84 to 36 percent. However, in 2020, 74 percent of Nigerians still said that democracy is preferable to any other form of government.[25] As this book went to print, Nigeria had managed to survive without a coup and without breaking apart. But the country's democracy, for a variety of reasons, was not consolidating.

What is going on? Nigeria is said to be experiencing a "trapped" transition, a democracy that fails to thrive, or to improve in quality or results. The democratic consolidation has been slow, which is in part due to a variety of factors. These include election crises, but also weakened democratic institutions and a political class that has hijacked the system to promote their own self-interests.[26] However, some remarkable things have happened. In 2007, for the first time in Nigeria's history, one democratically elected leader transferred power to another democratically elected leader. But both presidents were from the same party, the People's Democratic Party (PDP), and Obasanjo (a Christian Yoruba from the South West) had a lot to do with choosing Yar'Adua (a northern Fulani Muslim) as the party's candidate. So, the outcome was not quite the triumph for democracy that many hoped for: it amounted to one member of the governing party merely handing power over to another. In fact, Nigeria for a while became known as a dominant-party democracy (until 2015, both houses of parliament and most of the governorships had been PDP).

To his merit, President Yar'Adua did initiate reforms to the electoral process. However, he died while in office, nearly creating a crisis of state. His vice president and successor, Goodluck Jonathan (a Pentecostal Ijaw from the south) was sworn in as president. At first he appeared to abide by the unwritten deal made by Nigeria's political elites. This deal is known as "zoning" and the understanding is that the two-term presidency will rotate between regions.[27] Jonathan serving out Yar'Adua's term and then stepping down was important since, as far as many people were concerned, northern Muslims hadn't finished their turn at the presidency. However, the system of rotation was the practice, but not the law; in the end Jonathan ran as the PDP candidate, violating the unwritten deal—one that is (arguably) responsible for sustaining the longest period of civilian rule since independence. In 2011 tensions were high and the election was ugly; at least 800 people were killed in postelection violence.[28] Many feared that Jonathan's win could bring on a coup, but he managed to serve out his term and even try for another.

Yet, despite the advantages of incumbency (access to revenues and patronage networks, influence over the administration of the elections and ballot counting), Jonathan was unable to secure a second term due to a split in the PDP. Defectors joined with smaller opposition parties to form the All Progressives Congress coalition and Muhammadu Buhari, another retired general and former dictator (1983–1985)—who had run for president in all four democratic elections since 1999—was finally victorious in 2015.[29] This was a watershed event for Nigeria: until then, no democratically elected Nigerian president had ever before handed power over to another democratically elected leader—from another party.

With support even outside his traditional base in the north, Buhari (who is known for being tough) promised to vanquish corruption and Boko Haram—and with the savings produced, turn the economy around. Those would prove to be hard promises to keep, especially since there were already signs of trouble between him and the National Assembly.[30] It also didn't help that Buhari has suffered from a mysterious illness that kept him in London for more than 200 days since he took office in 2015. Buhari managed to win a second term in 2019, but was a lame duck: two years in, both the All Progressives Congress (APC) and PDP were already talking about zoning, whether the power should shift once more to the south—and whether it was time for generational change.[31]

Case Study: Zimbabwe

Since the overthrow of white minority rule in 1979 until 2017, Robert Mugabe and his party, the Zimbabwe African National Union–Patriotic Front (ZANU-PF), effectively dominated the country's politics. It should be pointed out that when he was first elected, this hero of the war for liberation inherited from colonial Rhodesia a highly centralized state and powerful security force. Over time, the president established a state and security force that continues on—in many ways, just as centralized and powerful as the one he once fought. For years Mugabe and now his successor, Emmerson Mnangagwa, have claimed that the country is "democratic," yet have made a determined effort to undermine Zimbabwe's democratic institutions since the mid-1980s. Through alternating policies of co-optation and repression, first Mugabe and now Mnangagwa have so far been largely successful at controlling their opponents.[32]

Until about two decades ago, Mugabe could count on the full cooperation of the legislature in this effort, since ZANU-PF party loyalists held virtually all the seats in the House of Assembly. However, by the late 1990s, internal and external pressures forced the president to undertake a reconfiguration. Vain and desperate for foreign aid, Mugabe very much needed the prestige of legitimacy, and believed he could obtain this with the pretense of democracy. The parliamentary elections due to be held in 2000 had to at least appear to be democratic, but a new opposition group, the Movement for Democratic Change (MDC), was making headway in the cities.[33]

Recognizing these realities, Mugabe met these expectations partway. He did not outlaw opposition parties, but did not intervene to stop the preelection violence aimed against them. If the right to campaign is as important as the right to vote, then clearly the 2000 elections were marred from the start. Yet, here again is evidence of a reconfiguration: Mugabe permitted the opposition a partial success. Perhaps, it was just part of the democratic façade erected to assuage donors, but for the first time in two decades, ZANU-PF actually lost its two-thirds majority.[34]

For years to follow, the Mugabe government attempted to reconfigure while also attempting to crush any checks on its authority. MDC party leader Morgan Tsvangirai was tried for treason, a crime punishable by death (he was acquitted). In the 2008 elections, when Mugabe came in second place to Tsvangirai in the first round of the vote, the president and his party reverted to old tactics. The lead-up to the runoff elections was so bloody that Tsvangirai pulled out to save his supporters, and Mugabe, in a one-man race, celebrated victory with 85 percent of the vote.[35]

After months of pressure from Zimbabwe's neighbors, the country's three main parties agreed in February 2009 to form a unity government. Despite grave reservations, Tsvangirai entered into the pact, as he put it, "to change the fronts on which we wage the struggle."[36] However, it was clear before long that Mugabe held the reins (leaving Tsvangirai with responsibility, but no power).[37] "Power-sharing" proved to be a rocky road, as it became increasingly clear that the MDC was being played. As a result, the MDC's energies dissipated; outmaneuvered it became even more divided and drained of resources. The presidential and parliamentary elections in 2013 amounted to a devastating loss for the

MDC. That put an end to the power-sharing charade and left Mugabe and ZANU-PF back solidly in charge, where they remained until 2017.[38]

But by then, an unusually public divide had formed within ZANU-PF's Politburo, its supreme decisionmaking body. The schism was based in regional and clan rivalries, as well as ego and good old power politics—but not ideology (there were no democratic reformers left: all the moderates had been purged). After a tussle for power to determine who would succeed Mugabe, the ambitious, hard-line contender Vice President Emmerson Mnangagwa, known as "the crocodile" (and head of the faction known as Team Lacoste) beat out Mugabe's wife Grace and another faction, Generation 40 (G-40).[39] Mnangagwa isn't just known as the crocodile for his preppy style, but as a hero because he fought for liberation and was tortured by Rhodesians. Mnangagwa later became a spymaster and was associated with some of the worst atrocities committed by the Zimbabwean government against its opposition. Mnangagwa was also supported by the war veterans who had been Mugabe's staunchest defenders for decades, but who eventually broke with the president, blaming him for corruption and the economic crisis.[40]

In the end, when President Mugabe, frail and falling asleep at public events, sought to keep power in the family and dismissed Mnangagwa from his post, he made the mistake of antagonizing his generals. After nearly forty years in power, it was suddenly the president who was forced to resign in a palace coup. Mugabe was provided a "dignified exit" with a lavish retirement package, and he died at age ninety-five in Singapore, two years later.[41]

Although many analysts predicted that his departure would mean the end of an era, it actually wasn't so much. Yes, the world's oldest head of state was out of the picture, but his party, ZANU-PF, decided to retrench into a hard-line dictatorship rather than put up a candidate who could actually win votes in a democratic election. Yes, Mnangagwa promised reforms, and he won the 2018 presidential election. But observers warned about the conduct and integrity of the vote, including delays and vote-tallying irregularities. All signs suggest that the new government is now a fully fledged military dictatorship that has actually stepped up repression to consolidate its authority. As a result, Freedom House in 2021 changed Zimbabwe's status from "partly free" to "not free."[42] Not too long ago it was hard to imagine anything worse than Mugabe, but Mnangagwa has outdone himself—and in a fraction of the time.

Case Study: Egypt

Is Egypt destined to live under dictatorship? There appear to be just enough people (inside it and out) who prefer it that way. Perhaps it is out of a sense of nostalgia. Compared to many other Arab dictators, Hosni Mubarak ran a "soft" dictatorship: he ruled under a state of emergency and heavy policing. He was an autocrat, like his predecessors Gamal Abdel Nasser and Anwar Sadat, and all three were military men who ruled with the support of a small elite, through patronage.[43] Mubarak used some of the trappings of democracy to maintain his hold on government. But Mubarak, who assumed power in 1981, was "like the guest at a party who refused to leave."[44] As old dictators tend to do, thirty years on Mubarak insisted that he had to stay, as he was the only alternative to chaos.[45]

But Mubarak's "win" of a fifth term in 2005, followed by rumors that if Mubarak ever did step down, his playboy son was the heir apparent, breathed new life into the opposition. In late 2010, the long-standing dictator of Tunisia was overthrown through popular protests, and what would become known as the Arab Spring began to sweep the region. Given a deteriorating economic situation and a lack of economic prospects, Egyptians (especially the young) were ripe for revolution. Those under age forty (nearly 75 percent of the population) had only ever lived under two presidents.[46] In more than one way, the social contract had fractured. There had long been an understanding between the government and citizens that those who kept their heads down, who "walk by the wall," could avoid trouble from the security forces. Yet, Facebook was disseminating graphic evidence showing that no one was safe in Egypt anymore.[47]

All of these feelings were amplified by social media, which helped mobilize and organize an uprising. Young men and women of all political stripes, including some who usually avoided politics, convened in Cairo's Tahrir Square on January 25, 2011. They came initially to demand police reform. But before long, protesters were calling for Mubarak's resignation and were joined by tens of thousands more (including Muslim Brotherhood members) in what would become Egypt's largest demonstrations in fifty years.[48]

So, for a brief, awe-inspiring eighteen days, reformists and revolutionaries, secular and religious people from across the political spectrum came together in a coordinated fashion to demand political freedoms and economic justice. The protests spread across the country, despite repeated police crackdowns that resulted in the deaths of approximately 850 (mostly young) people. In the face of government violence, with few exceptions the protesters maintained a nonviolent stance and refused to back down.[49]

Faced with a standoff, the military, the most powerful and admired political institution in the country, was finally persuaded that Mubarak had to go. But the military had only sacrificed Mubarak to protect their own interests. It is part of what was known as the Deep State—the core of military, security, political, and business interests that has run the country behind the scenes since 1952 (this was a few years before some Americans began using the term in reference to their own government, by the way).[50] What happened after Tahrir was a quiet coup; Mubarak was moved aside, which allowed the military to openly take control of the transition—and, in time, the country. But first the Muslim Brotherhood, the only group that had the money and organization to run a nationwide campaign, (briefly) prevailed in relatively free and fair 2012 elections in which it won control of parliament and its presidential candidate, Mohamed Morsi, was elected with 51 percent of the vote.[51]

Yet, it was only a matter of time before the Tahrir protesters turned on each other. Although the Brotherhood had long claimed to defend individual rights and a civil state, many were skeptical of its democratic credentials. Morsi was blamed for adopting a winner-take-all swagger and displaying (what his critics called) the Brotherhood's true authoritarian streak. Morsi and his supporters argued that his government was only wresting control of the political transition from foreign enemies and the Deep State. In the end, the military found it impossible to tolerate such assertiveness from a civilian president and accomplished what it probably had in mind all along: a reconquest. Ironically, it was assisted by hundreds of thousands of young Egyptian demonstrators who went back out in the streets to protest that the revolution had been hijacked. On July 3, 2013, Tahrir's secularists, liberals, and nationalists finally united—to applaud the overthrow of Egypt's first democratically elected government, after just one year in power.[52]

Fatigued, many Egyptians welcomed the military's return to power, which was followed by rigged elections in 2014 that brought to power a then little-known retired general, Abdel Fattah al-Sisi. This new president, who won a second term in what observers agree were sham elections in 2018, could be confident of the support of not only state institutions and economic elites but also many Egyptians who feel that he has provided stability and saved them from Islamist extremists and civil war. The state (with the military playing a leading role) seems to have learned the lesson that if you allow the people too much freedom, they might overthrow you. As a result, the thin-skinned authoritarian government tightly controls politics. Al-Sisi has filled parliament with his corrupt toadies.[53]

Meanwhile, Egypt is known as the world's third biggest jailer of journalists. Al-Sisi's overcrowded jails are in abysmal conditions, said to hold tens of thousands of political prisoners (including healthcare workers who criticized the government's Covid response). The opposition is punished and weakened. Dissidents (and sometimes their family members) are forcibly disappeared, arbitrarily arrested, and tortured. Some say that it is as if Tahrir had never happened.[54] All the preexisting problems in Egypt remained unresolved. But the promise of Tahrir shows that the world doesn't always evolve slowly; sometimes it has a capacity for surprise and makes staggering leaps. In the Tahrir protests, Egyptians made the leap in that they conquered their fear and learned that they can topple a government.[55] Even though in Egypt under al-Sisi, change in terms of meaningful citizenship and dignity appears unattainable, Tahrir was more than just a moment. The capacity for change is there; it is just out of reach, at least for now.

Case Study: Iran

Iran is a country gripped by competing visions of its revolutionary legacies that has undergone cyclical changes. The 1979 revolution that overthrew Shah Mohammad Reza Pahlavi sought to erase "Westernization" and establish an Indigenous Islamic Republic. Former president Ali Akbar Hashemi Rafsanjani is often credited with maneuvering Iran through a decade of economic struggles and international isolation, and concurrently launching the country in an *ABERTURA*-type direction. This helped promote a reform movement embodying limited pluralism that gained prominence during Mohammad Khatami's presidency from 1997 to 2005. Yet, this movement activated a powerful conservative reaction, from leaders and citizens, preparing the foundation for the populist presidency of Mahmoud Ahmadinejad (2005–2013). Initially welcomed for his humble beginnings, Ahmadinejad is now viewed as one of the most divisive presidents of Iran who oversaw a "disaster" that isolated the regime.[56] His successor, Hassan Rouhani (2013–2021), a cleric, former nuclear negotiator, and academic, was viewed as the leader of the "Coalition of Hope" that included reformists, centrists, and pragmatic conservatives who supported Iran's easing of tensions with the West. This coalition, though, received less support outside of urban Tehran, and Rouhani faced a delicate balancing act, especially after the Joint Comprehensive Plan of Action (JCPOA) unraveled and many sanctions were reinstated. Rouhani's perceived failures catalyzed a swing toward conservatism, as the "stage-managed" election, with the lowest turnout since Iran's foundation, propelled Ebrahim Raisi to the fore.[57] This election was about more than the presidency—for the first time, people were openly discussing what the regime may look like beyond the reign of Khamenei. Raisi, notorious as a brutal firing squad executioner in the early days of the Islamic Republic, is Khamenei's hand-picked successor.[58]

Power in the Islamic Republic has long been concentrated in a small group of leaders unaccountable to democratic procedures: the elected president, for example, is "head of government," but the more powerful position is "chief of state," held by the Supreme Leader. Former president Rouhani even publicly lamented his status, rhetorically asking, "What do you want from someone who has no power?"[59] Yet, elections in Iran can be competitive, participatory, and raucous. The Iranian executive branch is the only one in the world with an elected president that must then be approved by an unelected group of individuals.[60] Candidates are first vetted by the Council of Guardians, established in 1979 to ensure legislation's conformity with the sacred law of Islam. This twelve-person group, whose members are appointed (six by the Supreme Leader), approves all laws before they are enacted, as well as all candidates before they withstand any public votes. In the 2016 and 2020 parliamentary elections, the Council disqualified nearly 50 percent of intended candidates, with more than 12,000 candidates applying to run in each election (for approximately 290 seats)—sometimes even eliminating current lawmakers.[61] The Council also rejected former president Ahmadinejad's comeback attempt in 2017.[62] All new members of parliament (as opposed to incumbents) are also now required to hold an advanced degree (at least at the master's level), a law passed in response to the steady decline in the number of clerics in parliament.[63]

Iran has no horizontal ACCOUNTABILITY. The Supreme Leader is answerable only to the Assembly of Experts, an eighty-eight-member body that is elected every eight years (and selects the Supreme Leader). Both the president and elected members of parliament are subordinate to the Supreme Leader. Major organizations, including public security, military, and broadcasting units, are not accountable to the executive or legislature. Within the judiciary, there is no attempt to feign autonomy. Judges brandish political and religious qualifications. Religious judgments (*FATWAS*) cannot be repealed by civil courts. The Supreme Leader, however, may veto actions. For example, Iran's Supreme National Security Council voted in favor of improved relations with the United States in 2000, but Ali Sayyid Khamenei vetoed the motion.[64]

Modern Iran provides a clear example of the electoral fallacy. The disputed 2009 elections signaled a defining blow to the already weak façade of any meaningful form of procedural democracy. The 2021 election has been labeled the most boring (rigged from the start) and the most consequential (setting up the Supreme Leader's successor) election in Iran's history.[65] Yet, Iran also helps us understand the functions that elections may serve in nondemocratic contexts, from providing a safety valve for citizens to express frustrations, to allowing regime leaders to signal their popularity to rivals.[66]

Political parties in Iran are banned (in favor of informally allied associations).[67] Reformist goals are often blocked by clerical leadership. Be careful, though, not to assume that all religious leaders and activists hold the same view. Many deeply religious individuals within the Islamic Republic are opposed to the actions of the Council of Guardians or the Supreme Leader. Iranian clergy have served as both supporters and opponents of social and political movements, with a long tradition of clerical involvement in popular freedom movements.[68] Iranian seminarians are not immune to social media, and Supreme Leader Khamenei has cautioned young religious scholars from adopting versions of "American Islam," or even so-called Merciful Islam that prioritizes individual free will over the more traditionalist interpretations of senior regime ayatollahs.[69] Debates—even if officially muted—about the proper relationship between governing and governed, as well as the most appropriate role(s) for religious teachings within the public sphere, have long marked life in Iran. As the Islamic Republic moves toward the half-century mark, it comfortably sits within the ranks of countries strengthening the appeal of authoritarianism.

Case Study: China

Until 2013 or 2014, one could state that life for ordinary citizens in China was, in many ways, freer than it has ever been since the commencement of the People's Republic. Yet, under the leadership of Xi Jinping freedoms have considerably retracted. The so-called Imperial President[70] has launched coordinated campaigns to limit the (already severely restricted) liberties gained in the 1990s and 2000s. Arrests, surveillance, and harassment are becoming commonplace for perceived troublemakers; lawyers, journalists, and labor activists have fared the worst. As one observer put it, "Any rights activist can be a target at any time."[71] The People's Republic of China (PRC) has consolidated a modern, technology-infused authoritarian regime.

Chinese elite politics have long been dominated by strong personalities. People commonly refer to generations of leaders: Mao Zedong led the first generation, Deng Xiaoping the second, Jiang Zemin the third, Hu Jintao the fourth, and now Xi Jinping is at the helm of the fifth. Leaders are handpicked years in advance to help avoid ugly power struggles that could endanger the party's sense of legitimacy among the population. And now, after changes adopted in 2018, Xi faces no term limits on his leadership. As this book goes to press, Xi is heading toward a tradition-breaking third term as general secretary of the Chinese Communist Party (CCP) to begin in late 2022. In preparation, Xi's legacy was formally enshrined in CCP documents, noted for his achievements, including "the tremendous transformation from standing up and growing prosperous to becoming strong."[72] Only two prior CCP leaders—Mao Zedong (leader from 1949 to 1976) and Deng Xiaoping (1978–1989)—have had their legacies written into major party documents in such a manner. Some suggest the move was to "fireproof" Xi against challenges ahead.[73]

The CCP of the 2020s looks much like the zealous CCP of the 1960s, focused on loyalty and struggle—emphases that marked the leadership of PRC founder Mao. In a message to the CCP faithful, mapping out a post-Covid future for the Party, Xi contended, "Our party has relied on struggle up to this day, and must rely on struggle to win the future."[74] Early in his rule, anti-corruption was the mantra. More recently, Xi has turned attention to China's wealthy entrepreneurs, including Alibaba's Jack Ma and others—ostensibly to close the gap between the rich and the poor. Some of China's biggest names (and wealthiest individuals) have been accused of tax avoidance, sexual misconduct, and other improprieties, in what many view as concocted "crimes" that support an ideological tightening around Xi's notion of "common prosperity."[75] Again echoing political campaigns of the PRC's earlier decades, individuals who used to be publicly praised and emulated have been framed as villains, evil capitalists, and "bloodsucking ghosts."[76]

Since at least 2018, China has been named the world's leader in political prisoners, issuing sentences for political dissidents that are harsher even than Leonid Brezhnev's Soviet era.[77] From the prominent individuals, including Nobel Peace Prize recipient Liu Xiaobo, to the mass imprisonment camps rounding up Uighurs and Kazakhs, to the lesser known individuals—including ones punished for posting on social media sites that few Chinese are even able to access due to censorship controls in the country—CCP officials prescribe harsh and swift sentences for dissent.[78] Only North Korea and Eritrea rank lower than the PRC for the treatment of journalists, as critics bold enough to openly express their disagreement with the Party pay the price—dearly.[79] One journalist who was well known for her daring reports about police brutality and environmental disasters lamented that, as independent-minded journalists, "we're almost extinct."[80]

The Chinese surveillance state is massive, with a facial recognition database that includes nearly every one of China's 1.4 billion citizens.[81] This technology permits officials to profile members of particular groups, singling them out for "tracking, mistreatment and detention."[82] Even if it remains incomplete, gains in harvesting, analyzing, and acting upon the findings of big data are part of Beijing's goals (announced in 2014) of creating a nationwide "social credit system." This effort aims to fuse financial creditworthiness and matters of routine life (parking tickets, and, more recently, compliance with Covid guidelines) to decisions related to not only government self-discipline (among officials), but also individual citizen behaviors as well—social credit scores may impact an individual's ability to book flights or purchase optimum broadband packages, for example.[83] Even matters of perceived convenience become sources of information that may be used for nefarious purposes; take cashless financial transactions, an area in which Beijing is a leading global player. In 2021, the PRC became the first country to create its own digital national currency. While making purchases easier to complete, this development, which is trying to rival the numerous commercial digital payment systems that are already popular in China, gives CCP leaders the capacity to track individual financial transactions.[84]

The implementation of the National Security Law in Hong Kong in 2020 cast a huge pall on the limited freedoms that existed in the Special Administrative Region of Hong Kong, which—according to the agreement signed between the United Kingdom and China in 1984—is supposed to maintain political autonomy until the 2040s. For all intents and purposes, the "One Country, Two Systems" arrangement for Hong Kong's "autonomy" ended in 2020.[85] This could have profound impact on the future of Taiwan, for which the One Country, Two Systems formula was originally crafted. With the widespread crackdown on dissent and religious expression within mainland China, the undermining of legally guaranteed freedoms within Hong Kong, and the growing reach of the Chinese surveillance state, the status of freedom in China—at least for the foreseeable future—is dark.

Case Study: Indonesia

The politics of transition in Indonesia began with a bang: following the resignation of President Suharto in May 1998, the country embarked on an uncertain path of reform. The post-Suharto leadership inherited a series of grave problems, headlined by hopelessness that followed economic collapse. The degree of challenge was so high that *The Economist* stated that, following Suharto's fall after his thirty-two-year reign, "the very integrity of the country seemed in doubt."[86] Indonesians have marked many key turning points since their transition from authoritarianism. They needed to clean out a political system infested with corruption, tame a military accustomed to wielding considerable influence, and manage a complicated economic recovery. Reforms in the early 2000s motivated Freedom House to upgrade Indonesia's 2006 rating to "free" status, a rating it lost in 2014 and has yet to regain.

Indonesia has had a series of significant presidential elections: 1999 was the first election after the fall of the authoritarian system, and 2004 was important because it was the first direct election of the chief executive. Turnout (almost 80 percent) was impressive, and polls were conducted without violence. *Time* contended that the elections in 2009 "silenced skeptics who doubted whether Indonesia—with its diversity of islands, religions and ethnicities" was fit for democracy.[87] The election of Jokowi Widodo in 2014 was another pivotal election, as he became the first elected president without significant ties to the political or military elite.

Campaigning as the "people's president," the former mayor of a city the size of Cleveland (who has a well-known taste for heavy metal music) raised the hopes of ordinary Indonesians. As a tradesman with small business experience, he faced formidable tasks, including dissent within his own party, the Indonesian Democratic Party–Struggle (PDI-P). After he was reelected in 2019 (with 55.5 percent of the vote), he named his challenger, former general and special forces commander Prabowo Subianto, as defense minister. For his second term, he also selected a new running mate, Ma'ruf Amin, a well-known cleric whose presence on the ticket attracted Muslim support while giving pause to the president's secular supporters.[88] Observers noted a stark contrast between Jokowi's first term (2014–2019), during which he promoted moderate Islam and safeguards for Christians, and his second (2019–2024), when the country began to embrace more political Islam, including Saudi Arabian–influenced Wahhabism that challenges the Indigenous, syncretic forms of Islam that had dominated

Indonesian POLITICAL CULTURE.[89] As a worrying sign of insecurity, protests were banned during Jokowi's second inaugural in 2019.[90]

Indonesia is an example of a transitional state that has established key institutions necessary for democracy, but democratic norms have either stagnated or, more concerning, regressed.[91] Democracy in Indonesia has clearly not consolidated. Some call it a "medium capacity" electoral democracy that exhibited democratic decline even prior to Covid.[92] Illiberalism lurks. Crises provide ample cover for elites to "protect" democracy (or stability).[93] Analysts express concern with religious expression, including the politicization of defamation and blasphemy laws, and the lack of formidable protections to minorities, including sexual minorities.[94] Women and girls continue to face a harsh climate throughout the country, with more than 300 discriminatory local regulations, including "virginity tests" and regulations permitting employees within the Ministry of Defense to take on a second wife if their first spouse is "unable to bear children."[95]

Corruption is rampant. Citizens distrust the police and the judiciary, while they view the military as a legitimate actor in politics, even if it is still viewed with disdain.[96] To date, no senior military leaders have ever been convicted for their prior abuses of power. As a candidate, Jokowi created great hope that this deeply dark time in Indonesian political history would be thoroughly examined, including matters related to the deadly anticommunist massacre after the 1965 coup (in which the death toll ranged from 500,000 to up to 3 million people).[97] Coming to terms with the violence of this period, in which ordinary people, official security forces, and major Muslim organizations were all known to take part, is complicated by many factors, including the sense among some participants that reconciliation is unnecessary.[98] Adding to the challenges, recently declassified State Department files highlight the knowledge and, in some cases, the complicity of US officials, reflecting the Cold War concern that Southeast Asia would become a hotbed of communism (the Indonesian Communist Party was once the second-largest communist party in the world).[99]

The consolidation of democracy can be more difficult and complex than the genesis of democratic change, and struggles surrounding IDENTITY and inclusion mar this lengthy process. Perhaps, it is not surprising that some refer to Indonesia as an "unfinished nation."[100] Citizens have struggled through a tremendously difficult path following the collapse of the authoritarian system, and may now be experiencing authoritarian nostalgia, or, at the very least, "democracy fatigue."[101] Increasingly, observers note uncertainty over Indonesia's future direction, with growing intolerance and hypernationalism.[102] Viewed as "an important bellwether for the state of democracy in the era of Covid,"[103] Indonesia's ability to rise to the multifaceted challenges it faces will likely have consequences beyond its borders.

Now It's Your Turn

After considering the problems of democratization described in this chapter, how do you think democracy can be made more sustainable? In your view, what are the most important factors in determining the overall success or failure of a democracy? Given what you know of these cases, do you find the Western model of democracy's divisiveness appropriate here? Could this model be applicable for much of the global south? What would you think are the challenges of having a democratic system during a crisis situation? What would be its benefits? Do you think it likely that political liberalization alone can address the needs of countries experiencing great economic and political instability? Are there any circumstances in which you believe disintegration might be a better outcome? Why?

Notes

1. Daniel C. Levy and Kathleen Bruhn, "Mexico: Sustained Civilian Rule Without Democracy," in *Politics in Developing Countries: Comparing Experiences with Democracy,* ed. Larry Diamond, Juan J. Linz, and Seymour Martin Lipset (Boulder: Lynne Rienner, 1995).

2. John Rice, "Mexico's Fox Admits Efforts Have Fallen Short," *AP,* September 4, 2003.

3. Jorge G. Castañeda, "A Way to Peace in Mexico," *New York Times,* September 6, 2006; Enrique Krauze, "Furthering Democracy in Mexico," *Foreign Affairs* 85, no. 1 (January–February 2006).

4. Krauze, "Furthering Democracy in Mexico"; Luis Rubio and Jeffrey Davidow, "Mexico's Disputed Election," *Foreign Affairs* 85, no. 5 (September–October 2006); Marla Dickerson, "A Free Market Man for Mexico," *Los Angeles Times,* July 16, 2006; Elisabeth Malkin, "In Mexican Vote, Nostalgia for Past Corruption," *New York Times,* July 6, 2009.

5. Mariana Campero and Ryan C. Berg, "Mexico's Midterm Elections Matter to the United States," Center for Strategic and International Studies, June 2, 2021.

6. "AMLO's Weak Spots: The Mexican Economy Has Been Battered by the Pandemic," *The Economist,* April 10, 2021; Campero and Berg, "Mexico's Midterm Elections Matter to the United States"; "Mexico's False Messiah: Voters Should Curb Mexico's Power-Hungry President," *The Economist,* May 29, 2021; Anatoly Kurmanaev and Oscar Lopez, "Mexico President's Grip on Congress Slips, Showing Limits of Mandate," *New York Times,* June 7, 2021.

7. "Peru's Presidential Election: The Known Against the Unknown," *The Economist,* June 3, 2006.

8. "Deconstructing Democracy: Peru Under Alberto Fujimori," Washington Office on Latin America, February 2000.

9. Ibid.

10. Cynthia McClintock and Abraham Lowenthal, foreword, *The Peruvian Labyrinth: Polity, Society, Economy,* ed. Maxwell A. Cameron and Philip Mauceri (University Park: Pennsylvania State University Press, 1997).

11. Gonzalo Ruiz Tovar, "Toledo's Biggest Achievement Was Survival as Peru's Leader," *Deutsche Presse-Agentur,* July 27, 2006.

12. Ibid.

13. A Murky Democratic Dawn in Post-Fujimori Peru," *The Economist,* April 7, 2001; David Gonzalez, "New Chance for Peru's Chief to Take Reins," *New York Times,* January 13, 2002; "Peru's New Government: Teething Troubles," *The Economist,* December 8, 2001; Steven Levitsky and Cynthia Sanborn, "A Hard Choice in Peru," *New York Times,* May 9, 2001; Ernesto García Calderón, "Peru's Decade of Living Dangerously," *Journal of Democracy* 12, no. 2 (April 2001).

14. Simon Romero, "Leading Again, Peru's President Still Unpopular," *New York Times,* August 27, 2010.

15. Patricio Navia, "Peru's Problem Is Bigger Than Not Having a President," *Americas Quarterly,* November 16, 2020.

16. *Freedom in the World 2020,* Freedom House, 2020.

17. Ibid.

18. Andrea Zarate and Nicholas Casey, "Pedro Kuczynski Holds Thin Lead over Keiko Fujimori in Peru Presidential Election," *New York Times,* June 6, 2016; Manuel Rueda and Franklin Briceno, "AP Explains: The Arrest of Peru Powerbroker Keiko Fujimori," *AP,* January 29, 2020.

19. "Peru Election: Pedro Castillo to Face Keiko Fujimori in Run-off," *BBC News,* April 14, 2021.

20. Dan Collyns, "Leftist Teacher Takes on Dictator's Daughter as Peru Picks New President," *The Guardian,* June 3, 2021; "Two Extremists Vie in a Run-off for Peru's Presidency," *The Economist,* April 17, 2021.

21. "The Man with the Straw Hat: Pedro Castillo Is on the Verge of Becoming Peru's President," *The Economist,* June 12, 2021; Simeon Tegel, "Can Pedro Castillo Save His Presidency?" *Foreign Policy* (October 15, 2021).

22. Peter M. Lewis and Pearl T. Robinson, *Stabilizing Nigeria* (New York: Century Foundation, 1998).

23. Larry Diamond, "The Uncivic Society and the Descent into Praetorianism," in Diamond, Linz, and Lipset, *Politics in Developing Countries.*

24. *Freedom in the World 2016,* Freedom House, 2016.

25. Craig Timberg, "Support for Democracy Seen Falling in Africa," *Washington Post,* May 25, 2006; "Afrobarometer Round 8: Summary of Results for Nigeria," Afrobarometer, 2020.

26. J. Shola Omotola, "Trapped in Transition? Nigeria's First Democratic Decade and Beyond," *Taiwan Journal of Democracy* 9, no. 2 (December 2013).

27. Olumide Taiwo, "Challenges and Possibilities for Progress in Nigeria," Brookings Institution, June 24, 2010; Richard Joseph and Alexandra Gillies, "Nigeria's Season of Uncertainty," *Current History,* May 2010; Gilbert da Costa, "Is Goodluck Jonathan the Answer to Nigeria's Woes?" *Time,* February 13, 2010.

28. Kathleen Caulderwood, "Nigeria Election 2015: Struggling Economy Poses Problems for Jonathan or Buhari," *International Business Times,* March 26, 2015; John Campbell, "Good Luck, Jonathan: The Problem with Democracy in Nigeria," *Foreign Affairs* (January 27, 2015).

29. Brandon Kendhammer, "Nigeria's New Democratic Dawn?" *Current History,* May 2015.

30. Campbell, "Good Luck, Jonathan"; Kendhammer, "Nigeria's New Democratic Dawn?"

31. Kabir Yusuf, "Timeline: Buhari Has Spent 200 Days in UK for Treatment Since Assuming Office," *Premium Times,* August 4, 2021; Akin Irede, "Buhari's Bothersome Baton: Nigeria's Power Rotation Controversy Causes Gridlock for Atiku, Tinubu," *Financial Times,* April 9, 2021; John Campbell, "Nigeria's Election Disappoints," Council on Foreign Relations, March 18, 2019.

32. Michael Bratton, *Power Politics in Zimbabwe* (Boulder: Lynne Rienner, 2014).

33. Robert I. Rotberg, "Africa's Mess, Mugabe's Mayhem," *Foreign Affairs,* (September–October 2000).

34. "Zimbabwe at the Abyss," *The Economist,* June 29, 2000.

35. Celia W. Dugger and Barry Bearak, "Mugabe Sworn to Sixth Term After Victory in One-Candidate Runoff," *New York Times,* June 20, 2008.

36. Celia W. Dugger, "Opposition Party to Join Zimbabwe's Government," *New York Times,* January 31, 2009.

37. "Zimbabwe: Power-Sharing for Bankrupt Beginners," *Africa Confidential* 50, no. 3 (February 6, 2009); Celia W. Dugger, "Rift Endangers Power-Sharing Deal in Zimbabwe," *New York Times,* October 10, 2010.

38. "Crime and Amnesty," *Africa Confidential* 50, no. 10 (May 15, 2009); Celia W. Dugger, "Fears Growing of an Iron Grip over Zimbabwe," *New York Times,* December 26, 2010; International Crisis Group, "Zimbabwe: Stranded in Stasis," February 26, 2016.

39. Mabasa Sasa, "No Imminent Elections," *New African* 493 (March 2010).

40. "Mugabe Calls War Vets Dissidents, Threatens Another Gukurahundi," *New Zimbabwe,* September 6, 2016; Stephen Chan, "Looking Beyond Mugabe," *New York Times,*

October 26, 2015; "Emmerson Mnangagwa: The 'Crocodile' Who Snapped Back," *BBC News,* August 3, 2018.

41. Hopewell Chin'ono and Norimitsu Onishi, "In Zimbabwe, Mugabe's Birthday Is Rife with Political Jockeying," *New York Times,* February 29, 2016; "Robert Mugabe, Zimbabwe's Strongman Ex-president, Dies Aged 95," *BBC News,* September 6, 2019.

42. Martin Meredith, "Mugabe's Misrule: And How It Will Hold Zimbabwe Back," *Current History,* March–April 2018; *Freedom in the World: Zimbabwe,* Freedom House, 2021; Abigael Ajuma, "Prospects for Peace and Security in Zimbabwe," Brookings Institution, July 28, 2021; Jeffrey Moyo and Patrick Kingsley, "Zimbabwe Locks Down Capital, Thwarting Planned Protests," *New York Times,* July 31, 2020.

43. Thanassis Cambanis, *Once upon a Revolution: An Egyptian Story* (New York: Simon and Schuster, 2015).

44. Ashraf Khalil, *Liberation Square: Inside the Egyptian Revolution and the Rebirth of a Nation* (New York: St. Martin's, 2011).

45. Cambanis, *Once upon a Revolution.*

46. Scott Anderson, "Fractured Lands: How the Arab World Came Apart," *New York Times,* August 14, 2016.

47. Cambanis, *Once upon a Revolution.*

48. Khalil, *Liberation Square.*

49. Ibid.; Cambanis, *Once upon a Revolution;* "Tahrir Square's Place in History," *BBC News,* November 22, 2011.

50. Cambanis, *Once upon a Revolution;* Emad El-Din Shahin, "Egypt's Revolution Turned on Its Head," *Current History,* December 2015.

51. Cambanis, *Once upon a Revolution.*

52. Ibid.

53. Human Rights Watch, "Egypt: Events of 2020," 2021; "No Contest: Another Sham Election Highlights Egypt's Problems," *The Economist,* October 24, 2020; Tamara Cofman Wittes, "Egypt: Trends, Politics, and Human Rights," Brookings Institution, September 9, 2020.

54. Ibid.

55. Cambanis, *Once upon a Revolution;* Alaa Al Aswany, "Sisi's Choices: Good and Bad," *New York Times,* June 15, 2014.

56. Ali M. Ansari, *Iran Under Ahmadinejad: The Politics of Confrontation* (New York: Routledge, 2007); Scott Peterson, "After 8 Defiant Years, Ahmadinejad Leaves Iran Isolated and Cash-Strapped," *Christian Science Monitor,* August 2, 2013.

57. Reuel Marc Gerecht, "In Ebrahim Raisi, Iran's Clerics Have Groomed and Promoted Their Ruthless Enforcer," *Washington Post,* June 25, 2021.

58. Alex Vatanka, "Iran's IRGC Has Long Kept Khamenei in Power," *Foreign Policy* (October 29, 2019).

59. Ibid.

60. Albert B. Wolf, "The 2021 Iranian Presidential Election: A Preliminary Assessment," Policy Note 97, Washington Institute for Near East Policy, February 2021.

61. The unicameral Consultative Assembly consists of 290 representatives; 285 members are directly elected, and 1 seat each is reserved for Zoroastrians, Jews, Assyrian and Chaldean Christians, northern Armenians, and southern Armenians. Arash Azizi, "Factbox: Iran's 2020 Parliamentary Elections," IranSource, Atlantic Council, February 14, 2020; Emma Borden and Suzanne Maloney, "Iran's Guardians' Council Has Approved a Record-Low Percentage of Candidates. What Will That Mean for the Upcoming Vote?" Brookings Institution, February 24, 2016; Nasser Karimi, "Iran Disqualifies Thousands from Running for Parliament," *AP,* January 14, 2020.

62. Wolf, "The 2021 Iranian Presidential Election," p. 5.

63. Borden and Maloney, "Iran's Guardians' Council Has Approved a Record-Low Percentage of Candidates."

64. Scott Peterson, "Iran Opens Door—a Little—to US," *Christian Science Monitor,* February 25, 2000.

65. Reuel Marc Gerecht, "In Ebrahim Raisi, Iran's Clerics Have Groomed and Promoted Their Ruthless Enforcer," *Washington Post,* June 25, 2021.
66. Wolf, "The 2021 Iranian Presidential Election," pp. 2–3.
67. Ibid., p. 3.
68. Ladan Boroumand, "Iranians Turn Away from the Islamic Republic," *Journal of Democracy* 31, no. 1 (January 2020), pp. 173–175; Mehrangiz Kar, "Reformist Islam Versus Radical Islam in Iran," Working Paper no. 4, Brookings Project on US Relations with the Islamic World, November 2010, p. 1.
69. Boroumand, "Iranians Turn Away," pp. 175–176.
70. Elizabeth Economy, "China's Imperial President: Xi Jinping Tightens His Grip," *Foreign Affairs* (November–December 2014).
71. "Why China Arrested, Then Released, Five Feminists," *The Economist,* April 27, 2015.
72. Chris Buckley, Steven Lee Myers, Liu Yi, and Claire Fu, "Eyeing His Future, Xi Jinping Rewrites the Past," *New York Times,* November 11, 2021.
73. Ibid.
74. Chris Buckley, "'The East Is Rising': Xi Maps Out China's Post-Covid Ascent," *New York Times,* March 3, 2021.
75. Chris Buckley, "Incendiary Essay Ignites Guessing over Xi's Plans for China," *New York Times,* September 9, 2021.
76. Li Yuan, "Why China Turned Against Jack Ma," *New York Times,* December 24, 2020.
77. Arch Puddington, "China: The Global Leader in Political Prisoners," Freedom House, July 26, 2018.
78. Chun Han Wong, "China Is Now Sending Twitter Users to Prison for Posts Most Chinese Can't See," *Wall Street Journal,* January 29, 2021.
79. Andy Meek, "It's Official: China Treats Journalists Worse Than Almost Every Other Country," *Forbes,* April 28, 2021.
80. Javier C. Hernández, "'We're Almost Extinct': China's Investigative Journalists Are Silenced Under Xi," *New York Times,* July 12, 2019.
81. Amanda Lentino, "This Chinese Facial Recognition Start-Up Can Identify a Person in Seconds," CNBC, May 16, 2019.
82. Jianli Yang and Doklun Isa, "China's Attempt to Spy on Uyghurs at Home and Abroad," *Newsweek,* April 27, 2021.
83. Alexandra Ma and Katie Canales, "China's 'Social Credit' System Ranks Citizens and Punishes Them with Throttled Internet Speeds and Flight Bans if the Communist Party Deems Them Untrustworthy," *Business Insider,* May 9, 2021; Jessica Reilly, Muyao Lyu, and Megan Robertson, "China's Social Credit System: Speculation vs. Reality," *The Diplomat,* March 30, 2021.
84. James T. Areddy, "Chinese Consumers Resist Digital Version of the Yuan," *Wall Street Journal,* December 3, 2021.
85. "The End of One Country, Two Systems in Hong Kong," *Financial Times,* July 1, 2020.
86. "Indonesia's Future: A Golden Opportunity," *The Economist,* September 10, 2009.
87. Hannah Beech, "Indonesia Elections: A Win for Democracy," *Time,* July 8, 2009.
88. Richard C. Paddock and Muktita Suhartono, "Indonesian President Is Sworn in amid High Security and Protest Ban," *New York Times,* October 20, 2019.
89. Hannah Beech and Muktita Suhartono, "Faith Politics on the Rise as Indonesian Islam Takes a Hard-Line Path," *New York Times*, April 15, 2019.
90. Paddock and Suhartono, "Indonesian President Is Sworn In."
91. Natalie Sambhi, "Generals Gaining Ground: Civil-Military Relations and Democracy in Indonesia," Brookings Institution, January 22, 2021.
92. Marcus Mietzner, "Economic Capacity, Regime Type, or Policy Decisions? Indonesia's Struggle with COVID-19," *Taiwan Journal of Democracy* 16, no. 2 (December 2020), p. 3.

93. Thomas Pepinsky, "COVID-19 and Democracy in Indonesia: Short-Term Stability and Long-Term Threats," Brookings Institution, January 26, 2021.
94. *Freedom in the World 2021: Indonesia,* Freedom House, 2021.
95. Human Rights Watch, "Indonesia: Events of 2015," 2016.
96. Natalie Sambhi, "Generals Gaining Ground: Civil-Military Relations and Democracy in Indonesia," Brookings Institution, January 22, 2021.
97. Marguerite Afra Sapiie and Ghina Ghaliya, "Jokowi Vows to Settle Past Human Rights Abuses Cases. But Which Ones?" *Jakarta Post,* December 11, 2019; "Looking into the Massacres of Indonesia's Past," *BBC News,* June 2, 2016.
98. "Looking into the Massacres of Indonesia's Past," *BBC News.*
99. Hannah Beech, "U.S. Stood By as Indonesia Killed a Half-Million People, Papers Show," *New York Times,* October 18, 2017.
100. Max Lane, *Unfinished Nation: Indonesia Before and After Suharto* (New York: Verso, 2008).
101. Richard Javad Heydarian, quoted in Hannah Beech, "Myanmar Coup Puts the Seal on Autocracy's Rise in Southeast Asia," *New York Times,* April 12, 2021.
102. Miki Hamada, "Comment on 'Making Economic Policy in a Democratic Indonesia: The First Two Decades,'" *Asian Economic Policy Review* 15 (2020), pp. 235–236; Thomas Paterson, "Indonesian Cyberspace Expansion: A Double-Edged Sword," *Journal of Cyber Policy* 4, no. 2 (2019), p. 217.
103. Pepinsky, "COVID-19 and Democracy in Indonesia."

Part 4
International Affairs

Given the events of recent years, it is likely that we have all given more thought to being part of a larger global structure than perhaps many of us had imagined. The geographical lines dividing governments and people are at once both less and more apparent than in decades past. This reality has profound effects on the issues that face us all, as well as on the institutions through which we respond to many of these challenges. In the chapters that follow, we examine some of the issues that are decidedly multinational if not global in scope, and discuss some of the institutions, regional and global, that have developed in response.

15

Sovereignty and the Role of International Organizations

> We the peoples of the United Nations, determined to save succeeding generations from the scourge of war . . . and to reaffirm faith in fundamental human rights, in the dignity and worth of the human person, in the equal rights of men and women and of nations large and small, and to establish conditions under which justice and respect for the obligations arising from treaties and other sources of international law can be maintained, and to promote social progress and better standards of life in larger freedom . . . have resolved to combine our efforts to accomplish these aims. —*Charter of the United Nations*

Among many developments in past decades, few parallel that of the increased interconnectedness of the world's STATES and of issues that affect citizens of the globe. We begin this chapter with a discussion of the role of states, acting not alone but rather in regional and global organizations, with special attention to the UNITED NATIONS. What are some of the issues that these organizations have tackled? Have they achieved much success? We conclude by discussing the other major types of organizations that operate on the international level, those that have organized independently of governments, known as NONGOVERNMENTAL ORGANIZATIONS.

The rise of groups outside of the traditional NATION-STATE, in part, has led to a rethinking of the idea of national SOVEREIGNTY, commonly understood as government's autonomy or independence to act, especially within its own borders. The legitimate authority over any given territory, usually viewed as the entitlement of the state, includes the right to self-defense and the determination of its own destiny. The principle of sovereignty implies a degree of NONINTERVENTION in one's affairs. Yet, some have argued that state sovereignty may be limited when countries are unable (or unwilling) to protect their citizens from crimes against humanity, which include ethnic cleansing, mass rape, and genocide (or the systematic decimation of people). This approach, known as the RESPONSIBILITY TO PROTECT (R2P), promotes awareness of the state's need to shield its citizens from harm. This principle, endorsed by member states at the 2005 World Summit, is a prime example of a concept rife with implementation difficulties. It calls on the international community to support the United Nations and other organizations in establishing an early warning capacity to help prevent such atrocities in the first place. How can the international community respond to systematic injustices perpetrated against groups of people within regions or countries, or the systematic rape and torture of vulnerable groups? How should other countries respond? These are not new questions in international relations. Rather, they are reminders that the quandaries surrounding our past inaction in the face of mass violence, especially the Holocaust, have not all been answered, and that the controversy over how and when to intervene in others' affairs still haunts our world.

Many of the global and regional institutions that we discuss in this unit have their genesis in the ashes of World War II, after which influential voices emphatically stated that "never again" would citizens of the world permit such inhumane treatment to occur. Yet, systematic torture and the murder of targeted groups of people continue to take place today. And, we continue to struggle with how to adequately respond. Does sovereignty mean that government leaders can violate the human rights of individuals and groups within their borders? As we discuss below, some argue that humanitarian needs in countries or regions permit (or even require) the response of other countries, including a military response. A central tension remains: Do problems that cross national borders demand an international response? What if the issue is confined within a single state? Are other countries justified to take action, in the name of promoting human rights? How should this response be coordinated, implemented, and monitored? This approach poses many other questions: What degree of suffering warrants a response from others? Under what conditions is international action justified? Who has the LEGITIMACY to carry out such actions? How are the objectives of intervention determined? Is unilateral action, undertaken by a single state or group, justified as long as it is in the name of humanitarian needs? Does a multilateral approach, involving the coordinated effort of multiple governments, necessarily make an action more legitimate? The answers to these questions have the capacity to dramatically change the way in which nation-states and the governments that lead them view themselves and their roles. But as you have likely guessed, the questions are much easier to raise than to answer.

To this point in the book, much of our discussion has centered on the role of state actors. Yet, recognizing the principle of INTERDEPENDENCE, supranational organizations that go beyond single nation-states have taken a more active role in international affairs. Some of this action is taken by groups of governments who willingly forgo some degree of their independent sovereignty to accomplish particular goals. Other action is taken by nongovernmental actors who organize not around their governmental IDENTITY, but rather around a particular cause or interest. Both types of organizations are increasingly prominent on the world stage.

International Governmental Organizations

INTERNATIONAL GOVERNMENTAL ORGANIZATIONS comprise official representatives of states who gather to discuss responses to issues and conflicts that affect the world community. We have already discussed two prominent IGOs, the INTERNATIONAL MONETARY FUND and the WORLD BANK, which were both established at the 1944 Bretton Woods conference. In this section, we discuss the role of IGOs and other multilateral institutions in resolving global issues. We focus on regional and global IGOs as a tool of fostering cooperation among governments. One important feature of IGOs is that their memberships comprise official governmental representatives, and their goals are to calibrate the policies of like-minded states as well as to solve contentious issues that arise between conflicting state policies and goals. These goals are different from those of the other major type of organization discussed in this chapter, the nongovernmental organizations.

Each of these organization types poses different challenges for the global south. Often, less powerful countries are excluded from decisionmaking structures within these organizations, either explicitly or implicitly. This contradiction of universal membership is most stark with respect to the United Nations, in which each state is guaranteed a relatively equal voice in some chambers, most notably the UNITED NATIONS GENERAL ASSEMBLY, but not others, including the much more powerful UNITED NATIONS SECURITY COUNCIL. The lack of TRANSPARENCY—clear, publicly available decisionmaking processes—challenges the participation of many states and groups, as well as the perception that actions taken by these organizations are positive. Many of these organizations are undergoing reform to fix these drawbacks, but formidable obstacles remain.

Regional Organizations

Over the past several decades there has been a proliferation of regional economic blocs, free trade areas, CUSTOMS UNIONS, and COMMON MARKETS. Since the late 1970s, the impetus for this growth has come from the desire to form regional trade organizations, as well as a defensive response to GLOBALIZATION. Regionalism is a framework of cooperation, with an indefinite duration, intended to include multiple issues, most often economic- or security-related in nature.[1] The latter part of this explanation captures the transition that has touched many organizations in the global south; quite a few began with an initial focus on economics and trade within a defined (although not absolute) geographical space, and are now adopting other complementary agendas as well.[2]

A few observations on regional alliances focus our attention on some of the unexpected aspects of these organizations. Sometimes, former enemies (or countries with continuing hostilities) seek alliances as a way to formally move beyond their conflict. In Latin America, for example, Peru is a member of many regional organizations to which countries it has had past disputes with also belong, including Ecuador and Bolivia. The Association of Southeast Asian Nations (ASEAN) began largely in response to the regional perception of the growing communist threat in Southeast Asia. ASEAN's predecessor, the Southeast Asia Treaty Organization (SEATO), was distinctly strategic in focus. Member states within this organization continue to hold competing views on a variety of issues, including economic growth, the environment, and threats to security.

Another regional organization that originally brought together states in the larger interest of promoting stability and a common defense is the Southern African Development Community (SADC). The SADC was established in 1980 to provide political and economic protection against the apartheid regime in South Africa (which itself joined the SADC after its independence in 1994). From the start, members recognized the gains to be had through consultation and cooperation. The SADC has been praised for its realistic priorities for regional planning.[3] Leaders have promoted small-scale irrigation over grandiose dams, as well as the use of appropriate technology, including attempts to combat widespread deforestation by developing more fuel-efficient stoves and alternative energy sources for cooking pots. As we find in other regional organizations, members have benefited from functionalist arrangements on technical matters, including efforts to sustain tropical forests, curtail the illegal trade in ivory and diamonds, promote the repatriation of refugees, and manage the distribution of limited natural resources, including through oil and natural gas pipelines. The sixteen SADC member states are working to build deeper INTEGRATION, including the promotion of a free trade area, a customs union, and a common market, in addition to responding to the ongoing challenges of peace and security, energy, and human capital that plague countries individually and as a community.[4]

Increased interaction and contact can have many unintended consequences. Just as regional organizations developed to promote greater economic integration or cooperation in security matters, less formalized interaction has helped to promote regional solidarity through personal and cultural exchanges. For example, South American member states of Mercosur, also known as the Common Market of the South, promote leadership and cultural exchanges to complement the economic imperative of its founding. Mercosur formed in the absence of developed economic linkages among states and, as it increased trade among member states tenfold in its early years, it now constitutes one of the world's largest economic blocs. However, Mercosur continues to struggle on both the economic and political front. Formed with high ambitions of fusing a customs union with a political side, some refer to it as "South America's Fractious Trace Bloc."[5]

Two other prominent regional actors, ASEAN and the Organization of American States (OAS), had their genesis during the COLD WAR, forming as alliances to combat the rise of communist governments. Both organizations have moved beyond this ideological focus in the post–Cold War era, with ASEAN welcoming its former nemesis, China, on a consultative basis. Current member states of ASEAN, formed in 1967, include Brunei, Cambodia, Indonesia, Laos, Malaysia, Myanmar, the Philippines, Singapore, Thailand, and Vietnam, with consultative status held by the "dialogue partners": Australia, Canada, China, the European Union, India, Japan, New Zealand, the Republic of Korea, Russia, and the United States. The China-ASEAN Free Trade Area was established in January 2010 to further increase regional integration, prompting some fears about international competition among Indonesian farmers.

With the commencement of the ASEAN Regional Forum (ARF) in the mid-1990s, the noneconomic aspect of the organization has again been highlighted. This component of ASEAN was developed to promote peace and security in the Asia Pacific region. Greater participation by China will be needed to bring more power to the association, and, in recent years, conflicting maritime claims have dominated much of the forum's discussion. The ARF has become a high-profile forum for discussing security issues across the region. With the goal of consensus, the emphasis within the ARF is much more on dialogue than decisionmaking.

The OAS, the preeminent organization for the Western Hemisphere, began with an agreement among member states in 1948, and the organization was launched three years later. All thirty-five countries in the region are official members, although Cuba's participation has been curtailed, largely at the demand of the United States. US dominance of the OAS during the Cold War meant that the organization focused on isolating Marxist governments and fighting against leftist rebels. Since the end of the Cold War, the emphasis has shifted greatly. The priorities of the OAS today are to preserve and strengthen DEMOCRACY through the promotion of social justice, human rights, and good governance, and to provide solutions to the debt crises many member states face. It often sends observer delegations to watch elections in member states—as it did for the first time in the United States in 2016—and has expanded to include elections throughout the region.[6] The regional organization received the ire of some of its members when its permanent council condemned the leadership of Nicaragua for imprisoning presidential candidates and restricting the role of independent media.[7]

Despite the presence of many regional economic organizations in Latin America, the OAS has also helped promote microenterprise and telecommunications trade, while shining attention on abuses of labor rights and the need to promote SUSTAINABLE DEVELOPMENT throughout the region. The OAS has been a major diplomatic player and peacemaker in the region as well. It also was a leading regional voice in challenging Alberto Fujimori's hijacking of Peru's presidential elections in 2000 (and rejected his daughter Keiko's allegations of fraud in the 2021 race). The organization suspended Honduras after a constitutional crisis in 2009, when, for the first time in the organization's history, the OAS invoked the part of its charter that calls for the suspension of a member for an "interruption of democratic order."[8] This focus on democracy was not as prominent, though, as OAS states lifted the ban (in place since 1962) on Cuba's membership in June 2009 (an invitation that Havana promptly rejected, and continues to do so).

In Africa, the premier regional organization is the African Union (AU), which succeeded the Organization of African Unity (OAU) in 2002. Few mourned the loss of the OAU, scorned by many as the "dictators' club" for its failures to protect citizens against tyrannical leaders.[9] With the same members and many of the same problems as its precursor organization, the African Union has a stronger charter (but not yet larger funds) to promote integration between member states. The AU covers the whole continent and several island states (in 2017, Morocco rejoined after a thirty-three-year absence). AU architects hope that it will one day operate along the lines of the European Union, with a pan-African parliament (launched in 2004), a central bank (with the goal of developing a common currency), and an AU Court of Justice (which merged with another judicial body to create the African Court on Human and Peoples' Rights in 2004).

The African Union's mission is to promote peace and prosperity in a united continent. Reflecting on past weaknesses of the AU and similar multilateral institutions, by design the African Union is attempting to limit the gross abuse of power in the name of state sovereignty. The OAU operated under the principle of noninterference, meaning that member states should stay out of each other's business, which resulted in the failure to act to stop atrocities. Taking this criticism into account, the AU shifted to a policy of indifference. The organization established its right to intervene against genocide or gross human rights abuses in any member state, but its impact in this regard has been limited. It suspended Guinea, a founding member, after its 2021 coup, but took little action to decrease violence in Ethiopia, where the OAU had originally been based. Peacekeeping forces under AU command (authorized by the fifteen-member AU Peace and Security Council) have served in several countries, including Somalia, Burundi, and Sudan. A rapid response unit, the African Standby Force, has been in planning for decades, but has yet to be formally activated.[10]

Based in the belief that one can't have peace without prosperity, the other major focus of the AU is the improvement of living standards for citizens across the continent. In this light, the New Partnership for African Development (NEPAD) was formed in 2001. It is an ambitious recovery and antipoverty program that ties good governance (which involves transparency, ACCOUNTABILITY, and similar reforms) to increasing aid and investment from high-income countries. Through voluntary, independent "peer reviews" of performance, African governments encourage each other to follow a program of agreed standards aimed at remedying institutional deficiencies and promoting sustainable development. For example, some members have been suspended over coups, and are readmitted only once constitutional rule is resumed. In their 2020 annual report, they highlighted the challenges of resources and coordination, emphasizing the need for further infrastructure development, as well as improving upon the organization's technical expertise.[11] It's a work in progress, and one that will take time, resources, and determination to implement.

Other IGOs bring together states across multiple geographic regions to highlight a common identity or cause. One of the largest IGOs in the world today is the Organization of the Islamic Conference (OIC), which encompasses fifty-seven states across four continents and includes nearly one-third of the members of the United Nations—from Albania and Nigeria to Guyana and Indonesia. (Despite the presence of approximately 175 million Muslims in India, its membership has been blocked by Pakistan.) The goals of the OIC, founded in 1969 after an arson attack against Al-Aqsa Mosque in Jerusalem, are to promote cooperation among members, safeguard Islamic holy sites, and eliminate racial discrimination and colonialism. Trying to coordinate such a diverse group of states, even though unified by religious identity, has proven quite difficult, and while the OIC has carved out an important role as a facilitator of discussion among states, it has also lacked the teeth to implement decisions made within its chambers. In part because of its broad reach, the organization has suffered some famous disputes among members, and has been unable to unite even on some key proposals, including following up on promises for aid in the aftermath of natural disasters and implementing a coordinated economic policy toward the state of Israel.

How can membership in a multilateral organization, with either a regional or a global scope, change conduct within a country? Turkey's decades-long attempt to join the European Union provides a possible test case. Turkish leaders submitted their formal application for full membership in 1987, but the EU did not accept Turkey as a candidate until December 1999. Formal accession negotiations did not begin until 2005, and the completion of this process appears indefinitely delayed.[12] This is due to a number of problems, including its continued sparring over the divided status of Cyprus, Turkey's human rights abuses, as well as the erosion of democracy and the rule of law within the republic. In an effort to acquire EU membership, Turkey's parliament enacted some reforms that could have favorable outcomes for the respect of human rights: military judges have been removed from civilian courts, longer prison terms have been established for those guilty of torture, and the use of capital punishment is banned during peacetime. However, many within Turkey are growing weary of the demands for change coming from the European Union, and believe that the republic will likely be permanently excluded from EU membership because of the Union's status as a "Christian Club," as elaborated by former EU Commission president Jacques Delors. Opinion polls within Turkey show that support for EU membership is waning. Turkey may provide a good study of how some domestic decisions are influenced by the desire to acquire membership in broader associations, as well as the difficulties in expansion and absorption of new members from the perspective of multilateral organizations.

The United Nations

Among the myriad international organizations that exist in the twenty-first century, the United Nations, founded in the immediate aftermath of World War II, stands alone as the most universally recognized. Its goal, as stated in the UN Charter, is intricately tied to the period from which it grew: to "save succeeding generations from the scourge of war." Its predecessor, the League of Nations, a product of World War I, was largely unsuccessful in reaching this goal, as World War II broke out within two decades of its establishment. While the causes of the League's failures are still hotly debated, many have identified one of its key weaknesses as the granting of equal voice to every member state. This, some argue, failed to accurately reflect differences in power and influence. Today's United Nations comprises 193 member states, following the admission of South Sudan in 2011, and its organizational structure gives greater influence to some countries than others—an issue we will return to later. The main headquarters of the UN is in New York City, with principal offices in Geneva (headquarters of offices for human rights and disarmament), Vienna (headquarters of offices for drug-abuse monitoring, criminal justice, peaceful uses of outer space, and trade law), and Nairobi (headquarters of offices on human settlements and environmental programs). Through its committees, agencies, assemblies, and related organizations, the United Nations gathers leaders to debate and define policy goals, set standards, and monitor compliance with internationally agreed programs in pursuit of its overarching goal—to promote the peaceful resolution of conflict throughout the world.

The UN Charter, signed in 1945, outlines the principles of COLLECTIVE SECURITY, state sovereignty, and the equal rights of SELF-DETERMINATION of all peoples. Collective security embodies the concept that states can impede an aggressor state by binding together in a cooperative framework. The goal of such action is to prevent conflict, but if conflict does occur, aggression is met with a united force of collaborators. It is a tactic that combines the pooled resources and power of united countries, seemingly indicative of "world opinion," with the threat to use force if security and peace are threatened.

During the Cold War, collective security took a back seat to the old power politics the UN was designed to replace; the one collective security action was that taken in Korea from 1950 to 1953, made possible only because the Soviet Union boycotted the Security Council to protest the exclusion of the People's Republic of China from the United Nations. The force was commanded by a US general whose orders came from Washington rather than the United Nations per se. The operation of collective security was more evident in action taken following Iraq's invasion of Kuwait in 1990, when the powerful, veto-wielding, permanent members of the Council all acquiesced in agreement to challenge the invasion.

Again, though, this action must be viewed only as a limited example of collective security, especially given the commanding role of the United States during the war. The doctrine of self-determination, although incompletely applied, has been an important force for non-Western peoples within the United Nations. In a nutshell, the concept embodies the belief that all peoples of the world have the right to rule themselves, rather than being ruled by external, colonial powers. The processes of decolonization, spearheaded by African and Asian representatives to the UN, led to the peaceful independence of many states, especially in the 1950s and 1960s. However, as discussed in Chapter 3, the remnants of colonialism, including the vestiges of imperial governments, continued well into the twentieth century.

Chapter XI of the UN Charter establishes a pivotal role for member states regarding "non-self-governing territories." Members of the United Nations have a responsibility to assist in the establishment of self-government where it does not yet exist. The independence of Namibia in 1990 is one of the most unusual cases of UN-supervised decolonization. Formerly known as South West Africa, the territory was placed under the responsibility of the United Nations, rather than being given status as a member state, in 1950, after South Africa refused to administer the territory as it previously had under the League of Nations system. More recently, this aspect of the Charter has enabled the United Nations to assist in the development of newly self-governing states, such as East Timor (now known as Timor-Leste), which achieved its independence from Indonesia in 2002. Currently, fewer than twenty non-self-governing territories remain under the tutelage of a United Nations member state (down from seventy-two in 1946), with the United Kingdom and the United States as the dominant administering authorities.

One of the most important resolutions passed in the United Nations General Assembly is the 1948 UNIVERSAL DECLARATION OF HUMAN RIGHTS (UDHR). The development and acceptance of this document have helped to promote a wide-ranging body of human rights law, including treaties that recognize economic, social, cultural, political, and civil rights. Articles 1 and 2 of the Universal Declaration state that "all human beings are born equal in dignity and rights" and are entitled to rights "without distinction of any kind such as race, color, sex, language, religion, political or other opinion, national or social origin, property, birth or other status." Through its committee structure, fact-finding missions, international conferences, and advocacy, the UN attempts to promote these ideals in all of its work.

Organization of the United Nations. The main structures within the United Nations include the General Assembly, the Security Council, the Economic and

Social Council (ECOSOC), and the International Court of Justice (ICJ), the principal judicial organ. The General Assembly, in which each member state is represented, makes recommendations in the form of nonbinding resolutions. Some committees of the UN write reports analyzing the implementation of standards and solutions, or propose new organizations to monitor situations. The main aim of the UN is to promote consensus, and this work is achieved through the laborious and detailed processes of drafting resolutions that have the support of a plurality of state representatives. Although all nonbudgetary resolutions in the General Assembly are nonbinding, they highlight steps that governments should take to resolve conflict and promote peace and prosperity, and elements of resolutions are often incorporated into the national laws of the supporting countries. The General Assembly is the most procedurally democratic arm of the United Nations, since each state gets one vote, irrespective of size, power, or prestige. From the speeches and debates within the General Assembly, we can ascertain a great deal about the voices of world opinion.

One of the most visible agencies of the UN is the Security Council, which can initiate binding action, including final approval of the General Assembly's choice of UNITED NATIONS SECRETARY-GENERAL, the chief administrative officer of the UN. Additionally, the Security Council recommends states for membership to the General Assembly. The Secretary-General, referred to by some as the "punchbag in chief,"[13] is appointed by the General Assembly on the recommendation of the Security Council for a five-year, renewable term. Since 1946, half of the Secretaries-General have come from countries in the global south: U Thant, of Burma, who served from 1961 to 1971; Javier Pérez de Cuéllar, of Peru, from 1982 to 1991; Boutros Boutros-Ghali, of Egypt, from 1992 to 1996; and Kofi Annan, of Ghana, who led the organization from 1997 to 2006. Ban Ki-moon, a former South Korean minister of foreign affairs and trade, served as the eighth Secretary-General of the United Nations from 2007 until the end of 2016, the second man from Asia to hold this post. He was replaced by António Guterres, of Portugal, on January 1, 2017, who was appointed for a second term running through 2026. A former prime minister of Portugal (1995–2002) and president of the Socialist International (1999–2005), he was elevated to the post of Secretary-General largely due to his experience as the United Nations High Commissioner for Refugees (UNHCR) from 2005 to 2015. During his tenure at UNHCR, Guterres expanded the emergency response of the organization and led the agency, one of the world's largest humanitarian organizations, throughout the worst human displacement crisis since World War II, as we discuss in Chapter 16. His candidacy marked the first time that Secretary-General candidates had to present their platform in public hearings at the UN General Assembly—where he emerged as a surprising choice, in part because many believed it was time for a woman to be the world's top diplomat.[14] In the end, though, with surprisingly quick agreement by the major members of the UN Security Council, and welcomed transparency in the early nomination process, he was elected in a rare show of unity.[15] (Guterres was reelected, as the only endorsed candidate, for the 2022–2027 term as well.)[16] In addition to the ongoing migrant crises, Secretary-General Guterres has been at the helm attempting to champion climate action, digital cooperation, and access to Covid vaccines.

As the name implies, the Security Council is designed to deal with threats to peace and security. It convenes a meeting at the call of any member state that feels threatened or violated, and it often summons representatives of conflicting sides to present their case to the chamber. Representatives on the Security Council are frequently required to make very rapid decisions that carry great weight. In circumstances determined to constitute "threats to the peace, breaches of the peace, or acts of aggression," as defined by CHAPTER VII of the UN Charter, the Security Council can order binding action, including economic sanctions or the use of armed force. In the post–Cold War era, the Security Council has been especially active in peacekeeping and humanitarian responses to conflict.

There are two sets of countries that sit in the Security Council. Reflective of their strength, the five post–World War II powers—the United States, the Soviet Union, the United Kingdom, France, and China—were given permanent, veto-power seats in the Security Council.[17] These countries are known as the permanent five members (P-5). This privileged position was given to the powerful countries of the mid-1940s to recognize their importance at the time of the UN's birth, a lesson taken from the experiment with the League of Nations. Granting these countries a veto over substantive (not procedural) matters bestows on them a tremendous amount of power; a single no vote by any of these five countries will halt any action taken by the Security Council. Members' use of their veto power has fluctuated across time, with vetoes being used much more frequently to block action during the Cold War than since the 1990s. The most frequent invoker of the veto has been Russia (formerly the Soviet Union); the United States ranks second. France has used the veto least, and China, which used to use the veto only sparingly, has cast its veto seventeen times since 1992.[18] Notably, Russia, sometimes joined by China, has exercised its veto power nearly twenty times to block resolutions critical of the Bashar al-Assad regime in Syria. Yet, even if the veto is rarely used, the threat of its action can certainly change policy proposals and influence the topics that are brought to the Security Council for discussion. It is a powerful tool that the vast majority of member states do not have, nor are they likely to have in the future.

The second group within the Security Council consists of ten other states, elected by the General Assembly on a temporary, two-year rotating basis, without veto power. Some voices, within the global south as well as the global north, argue that this structure is outdated and needs to be modified, to more accurately reflect the balance of power in today's world and to be more representative of modern power dynamics. Structurally, the body remains nearly unchanged since its founding in 1946. Developed countries dominate its membership. Most glaringly, no Muslim-majority country has a lasting seat within this powerful chamber—Turkey and Indonesia are consistently raised as the most likely claimant of the so-called Muslim seat on the Security Council. Former Secretary-General Kofi Annan, among others, frequently called for increasing the size of the Security Council to give it more diversity and a stronger voice for developing nations. According to the proposals, an enlarged Security Council could include a permanent seat from each region of the developing world, including, for example, permanent (nonveto) positions for Africa, Asia, and Latin America to be rotated among states in these regions. Currently, there is a regional focus to the election of nonpermanent members; five are elected from Africa and Asia combined, one from Eastern Europe, two from Latin America, and two from Western Europe and other areas. Another proposal for a larger Security Council could include permanent states irrespective of regions. Brazil, Germany, and Japan are the states most often cited, because of their realized or potential economic strength, although former US president Barack Obama expressed his support for India's permanent representation on the Security Council during his visit to India in November 2010 (much to the surprise of many). Germany and Japan also argue that they contribute more financially to the UN than Russia, China, Great Britain, and France, making them deserving of a more permanent voice in the UN's chamber of power, according to many. In 2013, Saudi Arabia surprised everyone when it declined a rotating seat on the Security Council, announcing that, in the absence of meaningful institutional reform, it would not take up a seat on the belabored chamber.[19] The challenge is crafting a Council that is "large enough to be representative, but small enough to do business."[20]

Any change in the makeup of the Security Council will require an amendment to the UN Charter (which has happened only twice since 1945), and is likely to take a long time. Gaining the approval of the current P-5 is only the first step, to be followed by approval and ratification by two-thirds of all UN member states. In addition to P-5 concerns, opposition to Security Council enlargement also comes from less powerful states that are not currently represented in the Security Council, but that fear the power such a change could give to their adversaries. Pakistan, for example, opposes any proposal that might give India a role. Iran favors an increase in geographic representation, but wants to limit the exercise of veto power. Argentina, Bangladesh, Malaysia, and Egypt oppose any new members to the Security Council—often because they do not favor particular candidates for this new membership. The number of competing reform proposals and the fierceness of both support and opposition for these plans demonstrate the power of the Security Council as well as widespread distrust of a group that increasingly operates behind closed doors. At best, today's Security Council represents the world power structure as it was in the late 1940s, heavily favoring the victors of World War II in an institution designed to give equal voice to all states. At worst, it is an enduring legacy of big-power politics that operates without systematic input from the majority of people whom it is designed to serve.

Both supporters and critics commonly discuss the need for UN reform. Within the UN system, advocates point to the need to modify structures and operating procedures to accommodate the increased membership, mandate, and visibility of the services the organization provides. In just over seventy years, membership mushroomed from 50 original member states to 193, with few fundamental changes in between. Trying to create a unified, efficient, and streamlined approach to the wide variety of crises (political, humanitarian, environmental, and others) to which the United Nations responds proves difficult, as each situation has unique needs and vulnerabilities. A former assistant secretary-general for field support, who left office only after he published a scathing op-ed of failures of the organization that he firmly believes in and wants to succeed, argued that the UN is "a Remington typewriter in a smartphone world."[21]

After a series of high-profile blunders, including an "oil for food" scandal that reached all the way to former Secretary-General Annan, all agree that stricter financial management within the organization is necessary. The problems associated with being a consensus-driven body can also impede the work of the organization, as was seen in the Geneva-based Commission on Human Rights, which was replaced by a smaller Human Rights Council in 2006. The new council includes a process for reviewing the human rights situation in all countries that are members of the General Assembly, and selects its members through a simple-majority vote of all Assembly members rather than by approving regional slates as in the past. These changes were designed to help minimize the presence of human rights violators on the council and counter their ability to avoid criticism by gaining a seat. The new council also meets throughout the year—rather than the six-week session of the old Human Rights Commission—as a way to respond to crises and highlight the continuous importance of human rights protection.

Another area of controversy within the United Nations surrounds its expanding mandate to take action in countries in the name of humanitarian relief or R2P, which was formally adopted by the General Assembly in 2005. One of the fundamental questions plaguing UN strategies is the hot topic of intervention: When and how should a global body respond to crises in another state's affairs? Since the end of the Cold War, the United Nations has increased its activism, first in military opposition to the Iraqi invasion of Kuwait, and later with involvement in internal conflicts in the former Yugoslavia, Somalia, Cambodia, El Salvador, the Democratic Republic of Congo, and East Timor, among others. The fundamental right to sovereignty of all states—the almost sacred principle upon which the United Nations is based—is enshrined in the UN Charter. State leaders who resist UN action in their countries predictably invoke this principle, which helps explain why there has been no UN response to humanitarian crises in Tibet and Xinjiang (due to China's objection) or Chechnya, Ukraine, or Syria (because of Russia's opposition). A narrow interpretation of R2P, endorsed by former Secretary-General Ban, limits its enforcement. This rendered the Security Council impotent in its ability to respond to crises in Ukraine, Syria, and elsewhere.

As a large, global body consisting of representatives from almost every country of the world, what can the United Nations realistically accomplish, in addition to providing a forum for discussion and diplomatic solutions to problems? The primary modes of influence available to UN actors include censure, economic sanctions, and intervention, either with or without military backing. These actions are permissible under Chapter VII of the UN Charter, which authorizes the Security Council to take enforcement measures to either maintain or restore international peace and security. During the Cold War, Chapter VII provisions were invoked twice: to impose economic sanctions on the white minority regime in southern Rhodesia in 1965, and to impose an arms embargo against the South African apartheid regime in 1977. The latter set of sanctions is now viewed as the most comprehensive package implemented under Chapter VII provisions. They were lifted with the end of apartheid in 1994.

Sanctions imposed under Chapter VII authority have become a much more common tool in recent years. They have been invoked against Iran, Iraq, the former Yugoslavia, Libya, Haiti, Côte d'Ivoire, Liberia, Rwanda, Somalia, Angola, Sudan, and Sierra Leone, with consideration of sanctions in many other cases. Sanctions can be either mandatory (all member states face risk of punishment if they do not comply) or voluntary. Their imposition is nearly always controversial, because they risk harming ordinary citizens more than powerful leaders. In their favoritism of one group over another, they can prolong and deepen existing conflict. In Bosnia, for example, economic sanctions tied the hands of the Bosnian Muslims, while the Bosnian Serbs were being rearmed by Serbia. Sanctions can also worsen already difficult situations faced by civilian populations. In part due to the widespread recognition of the human toll of sanctions against Iraq from August 1990 to March 2003, the Security Council approaches sanctions and their utility with great caution. Since the mid-1990s the United Nations has applied more selective or targeted sanctions, such as banning financial transactions, travel, or arms trade in an attempt to bring countries in line with the desires of the international community. These are sometimes referred to as "smart sanctions" or "restrictive measures," and focus on not only states but also individuals and nonstate actors (e.g., terrorist organizations).[22]

While recognizing that sanctions are preferable to the use of force, the pragmatic impact of sanctions on changed behavior remains in question. North Korea's ability to evade Security Council sanctions on its weapons' programs is a solid example, as Pyongyang finds illicit ways to exceed caps on sanctioned imports and exports.[23] Given the difficulties crafting consensus—especially among the P-5 members—increasingly some countries develop their own unilateral sanctions first, which then become the starting point for more wide-reaching Security Council sanctions.[24] While most contend that multilateral approaches are more successful than action taken by a single (or small group) of actors, the unilateral impulse is unlikely to fade.

Peacekeeping operations. The term "United Nations" often conjures an image of the so-called peacekeepers—the people who wear the famous "blue hats." Yet, the processes of "keeping the peace" in areas marred by conflict have fundamentally changed. As the plan was originally designed in the late 1940s, soldiers participating in PEACEKEEPING OPERATIONS (PKOs) were supposed to keep warring parties separated, provide monitors between former combatants, or guarantee a cease-fire, as they did in the first UN peacekeeping mission, designed to observe the Arab-Israeli truce in 1948. (Peacekeeping is a much more elaborate process than peacemaking, which is viewed as bringing the warring parties to agreement. Ideally, but not always, peacekeeping forces pick up where the peacemakers leave off.) Peacekeeping troops can fight only if attacked, and they can remain only as long as all warring parties agree to their presence.

Before we discuss their tasks, let's clarify who the peacekeepers are. The UN Department of Peacekeeping Operations coordinates the work of approximately 88,000 uniformed personnel globally, serving in twelve operations as of mid-2021, with 121 countries contributing uniformed personnel.[25] Countries with the highest number of personnel serving in operations are Bangladesh, India, Ethiopia, Nepal, and Rwanda.[26] PKO forces are also often drawn from regional groups, in the attempt to avoid aggravating conflict by inviting "outsiders" into local conflicts. (It is important to note that regional organizations also organize and deploy peacekeeping missions, the largest being the AU's PKO to Somalia, which involves nearly 20,000 personnel.)[27] Some have proposed increasing the contingency of so-called regional cops, which are funded internationally but sanctioned by the United Nations to enforce Security Council mandates. They could provide the legitimacy of the international community, but place the onus on self-interested, local agents.

The United Nations has supported seventy-one peacekeeping operations since 1948, with prominent PKO missions responding in Haiti, Sudan, the Democratic Republic of Congo, East Timor, and Cyprus. Peacekeepers have also been involved in the coordination of administrations in Kosovo (where they operate parallel to the North Atlantic Treaty Organization [NATO], which handles military matters). Responsibilities placed on the individuals who don the blue helmets of the United Nations, a color explicitly chosen because it is not worn in combat, are likely to increase in the future.

Yet, peacekeeping has become a dangerous business, especially in immediate postconflict situations, when the presence of peacekeepers is largely unwelcome. For example, following the 1999 election in East Timor, a UN-sponsored relief office in West Timor was stormed by angry crowds, and the bodies of three UN workers (from the United States, Croatia, and Ethiopia) were burned in the streets. The United Nations and international diplomats expressed disappointment in the outcome of the trials for these deaths, as the accused were tried for "mob violence resulting in death" rather than manslaughter. This was particularly disturbing after the defendants openly admitted complicity in the aid workers' deaths, expressing national pride rather than remorse.[28] In the Central African Republic in 2014, forces including soldiers from France, the Democratic Republic of Congo, and the Republic of Congo were alleged to have engaged in a "persistent pattern" of rape and abuse—of precisely the people (including children) whom they were sent to protect. Even after a UN official sent a report on child sexual abuse to the UN Human Rights Commission and UNICEF, neither took action.[29]

In addition to the danger, peacekeepers often have a limited mandate. In 1995, Dutch peacekeepers stood helplessly by in Srebrenica, Bosnia, as Serbs murdered thousands of Muslim men and boys. And the mostly Belgian UN force pulled out of Rwanda at the start of the genocide in 1994, after a number of their own were killed. The same mistake was repeated in Mali in early 2013, when 10,000 soldiers and police officers were sent to respond to a terrorist outbreak without sufficient training. PKO missions are limited by severe financial constraints. Many states demonstrate a tremendous lack of commitment, especially financial, refusing to pay even when they vote to authorize a mission. The United States shoulders much of the blame in this regard: even though it has long been the single largest financial contributor to the UN, it has also racked up a large debt of past dues to PKOs, owing more than $1 billion that accrued from 2016 to 2020.[30]

Another common problem is that the presence of peacekeepers can give citizens a false sense of security, while the forces themselves lack the real power to intervene (or even bring new problems with them). As a devastating outbreak of cholera ravaged crisis-weary Haiti in mid-2010, serious allegations—initially rebuffed by the UN—charged Nepali PKO forces as responsible for the disease.

There was an active outbreak of cholera in Nepal at the time, and the allegations state that forces did not adequately separate their waste, allowing it to infect canals and water sources. It took the UN until 2016 to admit that their operations may have played a role in the initial outbreak of the cholera epidemic in Haiti, which eventually killed at least 10,000 and sickened hundreds of thousands more, yet UN leaders contend that their legal responsibilities are limited.[31] Former Secretary-General Ban acknowledged that the matter "forever destroyed" respect for UN actions in Haiti.[32]

An even darker side of PKOs implicates troops for sexual exploitation, rape, human trafficking, and abuse. UN officials call the sexual violence in Congo the worst in the world.[33] PKOs are impotent at best, complicit at worst: "Despite more than 10 years of experience (in Congo) and billions of dollars, the peacekeeping force still seems to be failing at its most elemental task: protecting civilians."[34] Unfortunately, the debacle involving the impotence of UN forces in Congo (during which women in their eighties were repeatedly gang-raped while peacekeepers were deployed nearby) seems to reflect a pattern of neglect repeated elsewhere. Human Rights Watch contends that PKOs have a sexual abuse problem stretching from Haiti to Somalia, and the DRC to Uruguay.[35] One UN official termed the problem of sexual abuse by peacekeepers "rampant," highlighting the troubling combination of extreme vulnerability and impunity that allows this scourge to fester.[36]

These challenges within peacekeeping operations are related to UN interventions more generally. The UN and related agencies need better staffing and processes to collect information and respond to, even potentially prevent, outbursts of violence that require international action. Following the crisis in Rwanda in 1994, former Secretary-General Annan (who was at the time of the genocide the head of the UN's peacekeeping office) repeatedly argued for the need for better intelligence-gathering. While increased intelligence capacity might be necessary, many view this assertion by Annan (which Bill Clinton supported) to be a halfhearted attempt to excuse the explicit decision not to take action in Rwanda even after evidence of the coming genocide was made available to the Secretary-General. If peacekeeping missions need anything, critics argue, it is better equipment, common training for interoperability, and updated maps: UN troops got into trouble when they became lost in Sierra Leone's countryside and their radios did not work. Yet, decades after the horror, many contend, including Special Adviser to the UN Secretary-General on the Prevention of Genocide Alice Awirimu Nderitu, that little has changed since Rwanda, and that accountability remains difficult but crucial for justice and prevention.[37] The inability of the United Nations to take action against any P-5 states (due to their veto power in the Security Council) also constrains the organization's response. In Xinjiang, for example, even though a UN human rights committee announced that it had "credible reports" that China was holding up to a million people in what it called "counter-extremism" centers, the UN was impotent to respond.[38]

One comprehensive strategy, suggested by Francis Deng, who formerly served in the special adviser role, comprises three phases: monitoring developments to draw early attention to an impending crisis; interceding in time to avert the crisis through diplomatic initiatives; and mobilizing international action when necessary. Ideally, problems should be addressed and solved within domestic frameworks, with international involvement only after the failure of internal efforts. In some cases, where the consequences of delay are grave, the international community may need to act earlier. But crisis-induced reactions are often more symbolic than effective in addressing the causes of conflict. External intervention is a major intrusion. Although some will welcome it because of the promise of tangible benefits, we should expect peacekeepers to encounter resistance on grounds of national sovereignty or pride, so the justification for intervention must be reliably persuasive, if not beyond reproach. Deng says that the difference between success and failure is the degree of spontaneous acceptance or rejection by the local population.[39]

Another struggle in responding to crises is the lack of a streamlined process that allows for quick and efficient action. Currently, only after the Security Council has authorized an intervention, and only after the host country has agreed to that intervention, can the Secretary-General and General Assembly begin assembling a collection of troops from countries that volunteer them. The requirement for host country authorization is at least partly to blame for Sudan's long-standing refusal to allow African Union troops to be replaced by UN peacekeeping forces, even though hybrid forces were also proposed for consideration.

Many have highlighted the need for a trained army ready for emergency intervention. One proposal calls for a rapid reaction force that would be composed of up to 15,000 personnel, including military, police, medics, and conflict transformation specialists, and could be ready to deploy within forty-eight hours of Security Council authorization. Standby units have long been discussed within the United Nations (and formally debated since the mid-1990s), but their actualization remains fraught with difficulty, and plagued by concerns surrounding the creation, maintenance, and potential misuse of such a force.

The need for a coordinated international intervention arises, according to one point of view, because powerful nations do not have direct interests at stake, and are therefore unwilling to get involved. There is often a delay, during which time rebel forces may try to "finish the job" before "outsiders" arrive. Humanitarian intervention, especially, requires distinguishing between the "good guys" and the "bad guys," and it is not always clear which side is the most deserving of support. Sometimes intervention can strengthen the weaker side, giving it little incentive to compromise and prolonging the conflict that troops were sent to end. As we have seen in many cases, noble intentions can lead to disastrous consequences, especially if they are not backed up with sufficient international determination, including military force, finances, and the willingness to stay until the problem, sometimes intractable, is solved.

Most of the problems with PKOs are exacerbated by the fact that we ask peacekeepers today to do much more than their original mandate—they are called on to clear landmines, monitor elections, seize weapons, enforce international law, contain violence, protect civilians, supervise postwar reconstruction, and arrest war criminals.[40] Peacekeepers have been placed in charge of disarmament operations as well, a mix of policing and military operations that is untenable at best. Where is the line between keeping the peace and quelling unrest? Increasingly, peacekeepers are forced to walk this dangerous line. The accumulation of tasks by PKO forces has been challenged by both the financiers of the missions, but more importantly by the recipients of the action, who often have little if any say in operations in their own country. The other view is that humanitarian interventions smack of imperial control because of the particularistic politics that are involved in each case. "Humanitarian" may sound well and good, but these interventions are also designed to achieve political objectives.[41] Such actions for the international community are taken in uncharted territory, and often have unintended effects. As we have seen, peacekeeping and humanitarian intervention can clearly make a bad situation worse.

Some interventions have exacerbated or prolonged crises, since they diffuse the specific interests that foreign powers, such as France or the United States, seek to project or protect. While participants ostensibly need to be impartial, the longer multinational forces stay, the greater the danger of loss of impartiality and, therefore, effectiveness in carrying out their mandate. Mission mandates need to be clear and achievable: an imprecise mandate is a recipe for confusion and a worsening of the crisis. Often the immediate purpose of humanitarian interventions is to deliver relief. But to have a lasting impact, such missions must move beyond Band-Aids to promote more substantive change, which can be a massive undertaking.

Lasting peacekeeping also includes state reconstruction, a focus that was ignored in Rwanda after efforts failed so miserably in Somalia. In a sense, peacekeepers are asked to engage in a complex process of engineering, including the preventive work that could be done by other agencies within the UN. Societies torn apart by strife need a comprehensive approach that pays more attention to the conditions that led to the crisis in the first place. Also, peacekeeping efforts especially need to encourage the rebuilding of CIVIL SOCIETY, which, as discussed in Chapter 8, emerges rather than being created. The processes of peacekeeping need to provide protections for minority groups and individuals, as well as reassure people that it is acceptable to express opinions without fear of reprisal. The RULE OF LAW, or the impartial and universal application of legal norms, must gradually prevail. A lesson we have learned from mistakes in past operations is that we cannot rush to elections: nascent parties need time to consolidate, form platforms, and present them to voters. In addition, there is a huge need to defuse armed movements, which is a controversial undertaking and difficult to implement. When major portions of the society feel unsafe, they are unlikely to surrender their sometimes only means of defense to outside intruders in the name of "making the peace." Otherwise, it will be easy for disenchanted groups to reject election results, with or without violent means, and voters will have little choice but to vote on the basis of ethnic or religious identity. Elections held under the wrong conditions can be a real setback for democratization.[42]

The United Nations and social development. In recent years, the crisis-response aspect of the United Nations has received much of the limelight. The UN and its agencies have also been at the forefront of attempts to promote international law and universal principles. Since its inception in 1945, a key aspect of the United Nations has been its promotion of peace through programs designed to enhance the well-being and development of the world's population.

One aspect of social development it has attempted to tackle is child neglect and abuse. Many children are forced to forgo daytime educational opportunities to make money on city streets, shining shoes, washing cars, or collecting recyclables. Educational programs under the auspices of UNICEF allow these street children to receive an education in the evenings. As discussed earlier in the book, child labor is a huge (and complex) problem in the global south.

The Convention on the Rights of the Child (CRC), adopted in 1989, is the most broadly signed convention in the world (after Somalia ratified the CRC in 2015, the United States became the only country in the world that has not ratified the CRC).[43] Establishing the standards that all civilized countries should attempt to meet in caring for their children, the CRC is comprehensive in scope, promoting four core principles: nondiscrimination; devotion to the best interests of the child; the right to life, survival, and development; and respect for the views of the child.

Among other things, the CRC calls for the protection of children from abuse and abandonment, as well as the provision of basic needs, including prenatal healthcare. Although the convention does not directly address the issue of abortion, it can be read to challenge the use of prenatal sex selection, a practice in which parents choose to abort female fetuses and carry male fetuses to full term, which is especially evident in China and India. In China, where traditional preferences and low-tech means have been accelerated by its population planning policies and cheap, accessible ultrasounds, preferential sex selection (before and after pregnancy) has distorted the gender ratio in the country.

The United Nations has also been a pivotal IGO in promoting the rights of women. As one example, in the 1940s, women's rights were viewed as something separate from the universal human rights of all people. Largely due to efforts of the UN and related agencies, this status changed by the 1990s to completely incorporate, in theory at least, women's rights within the notion of universally applicable human rights.[44] One of the most important documents attempting to institutionalize these ideas is the 1979 Convention on the Elimination of All Forms of Discrimination Against Women (CEDAW).

The convention, which has the force of international law, has been ratified or acceded to by 189 state parties and is considered to be the most wide-ranging attempt to eliminate discriminatory acts against women. Many refer to it as the "International Bill of Rights of Women" in that it establishes minimum standards for combating prejudice based on gender. It is also the only human rights treaty that affirms the reproductive rights of women. The convention recognizes that socially defined gender roles require provisions against discrimination and abuse that go beyond equal treatment of men and women. CEDAW asserts the inhumanity of torture and cruel and degrading treatment, and stresses that intimate violence is no less severe than violence committed by the state. It also focuses on the need to combat military sexual slavery, workplace abuse, and violence in the family. CEDAW condemns the use of rape as a tool to humiliate women and their communities. Of the countries on which we focus, seven have ratified the document: China (1980), Mexico (1981), Egypt (1981), Peru (1982), Indonesia (1984), Nigeria (1985), and Zimbabwe (1991). The United States joins Iran, Sudan, Somalia, Palau, and Tonga in not yet having ratified the treaty, and is the only industrialized country in the world to hold this dubious honor. This document served as the springboard for the commencement of global conferences on women, held in Mexico City (1975), Copenhagen (1980), Nairobi (1985), and Beijing (1995). Each of these events, and meetings held to monitor the implementation of proposals from each conference, sparked a related increase in the number of women-related NGOs and networks of organizations designed to investigate and resolve issues, including marriage and reproductive rights, healthcare and educational inequities, and physical, sexual, and psychological abuse, in times of peace and conflict, faced by women.[45] In fact, at each UN-sponsored world conference on women, a meeting in conjunction with NGO representatives was held as a way to complement the work of the conference and increase networking opportunities made available to all participants.

Activists in each country have used the force of CEDAW to accomplish varying aims. Many signatory states have altered their constitutions and national laws to enter into compliance with the treaty. In Nepal, CEDAW has empowered women to push for stiffer penalties for rape, as well as legislation that, for the first time, codifies women's right to inherit property. In Botswana, CEDAW was used to challenge citizenship laws under which children of a woman married to a foreigner were not considered citizens of the state (even though children of a man married to a foreigner were granted all the rights of citizenship). After US forces toppled the Taliban in Afghanistan in 2001, legislation to eliminate violence against women was based on CEDAW components, notably making rape a crime for the first time in the country's history.[46] Once the Taliban regained power in 2021, leading voices within the human rights community urgently called on Afghan leaders to abide by their expressed commitment, as a state party to CEDAW, to guarantee the human rights of women, including their role in political and public life.[47] This did little to change the retraction of freedoms from women in what some contend is more about tactics than ideology.[48]

In 1994, a special rapporteur on violence against women was appointed. This momentous achievement enabled more direct investigation and advocacy on behalf of the rights enshrined in CEDAW. For example, the rapporteur conducts field visits to countries that have ratified CEDAW to investigate claims of breaches of the human rights of women and girls, acting as an advocate and working to ensure proper punishment. Additionally, since an optional protocol took effect in December 2000, women may bypass their national governments and complain directly to the United Nations. The most prominent case to use this legal tool, which has been ratified by 114 countries, is the inquiry into the murders of nearly 300 women in Ciudad Juárez, Mexico (whose deaths still remain a mystery). CEDAW has also been raised as a tool for nudging the government of South Africa to do more to respond to domestic violence.[49]

The United Nations and justice: Tribunals, truth commissions, and courts. The United Nations and other IGOs have been integral in dealing with violent legacies of states in transition and international crimes against humanity. This work demonstrates the enabling role that international organizations can play in assisting countries during transitional periods. There are two primary types of institutions designed with this type of mandate: war crimes tribunals and TRUTH COMMISSIONS.

Criminal tribunals are established nationally (and sometimes internationally), often following the breakup of a regime or the end of a war or other act of aggression. Two of the most famous such tribunals were the Nuremberg and Tokyo trials following World War II. Yet, these initial tribunals, though international in name, were largely controlled by the victorious Allied powers to prosecute aggressors from the defeated Axis states.[50] War tribunals are based on the Geneva Conventions, and attempt to locate and prosecute "persons responsible for serious violations of international humanitarian law." Ad hoc international criminal tribunals have been established to investigate the war in the former Yugoslavia (which operated from 1993 to 2017) and the genocide in Rwanda (whose mandate lasted from 1997 to 2015).

In March 2003, the United Nations established an international criminal tribunal to prosecute former Khmer Rouge leaders in Cambodia. Justice has been particularly slow going in the investigations of the more than 1.7 million deaths during the 1975–1979 Khmer Rouge period. In fact, it wasn't until mid-2010 that the first senior member of the Khmer Rouge regime was sentenced (Kang Guek Eav, also known as "Duch"). He was the only one of five defendants to acknowledge guilt, admitting to overseeing the torture and killing of more than 14,000 people in the so-called killing fields. According to the journalists who interviewed him shortly before he was arrested, Duch had decided to confess to prove that the notorious prison he had overseen had really existed, to rebut claims by Khmer Rouge leader Pol Pot that it had only been a work of propaganda.[51] Duch, who was sixty-seven years old at the time of his sentencing (he died in mid-2020), was convicted of war crimes and crimes against humanity. As many of the likely defendants enter their twilight years (and some of the most brutal Khmer Rouge leaders have already died), many fear the time for achieving any sort of justice is running out.

Tribunals are quite concrete—their goal is to investigate claims of human rights violations and atrocities, to hold trials, and to punish responsible individuals. A major part of the investigation of such tribunals includes the perusal of murder sites and purported mass graves in which aggressors attempted to conceal the evidence of their crimes. One of the difficulties faced by the International Criminal Tribunal for Rwanda (ICTR), based in Arusha, Tanzania, was the sheer number of accomplices and perpetrators of the crimes.

The tribunal has been criticized for being slow and expensive, its total cost over two decades of operation was over $2 billion. By its close in late 2015, the Rwandan tribunal had indicted ninety-three individuals and sentenced two-thirds of them. This ad hoc tribunal, created as a temporary body to rule on atrocities committed during the 1994 genocide in Rwanda, rendered the first genocide convictions under international law, including one against Jean Kambanda, the prime minister at the time of the carnage. Another important precedent set by the ICTR is that it was the first to convict for rape as a war crime. However, another criticism of the tribunal is that it did not include much attention to abuses committed by the Tutsi forces nor did it provide compensation for the victims or survivors.[52]

For these tribunals to be established, governments must grant their approval, and oftentimes the logistics of a tribunal need to be approved by the affected national legislatures. While this can provide a lengthy hindrance to the commencement of tribunals, an opening is usually found after a change of regime or the death of an authoritarian leader. For example, Indonesia repeatedly rejected calls to establish a tribunal for East Timor that would investigate the human rights abuses that occurred in the territory during the 1975–1999 Indonesian occupation. Former president Abdurrahman Wahid once stated that even if former general Wiranto, who is widely blamed for either ordering or failing to stop the militia violence, were convicted, he would be pardoned in the interest of maintaining national harmony. (Years later, President Jokowi appointed Wiranto as a security minister, in a move decried by many.)[53] In response to widespread pressure to bring the responsible parties to justice, Indonesia established an ad hoc human rights tribunal, which has been largely dismissed as a meaningless façade. The United Nations established a Serious Crimes Investigation Unit to hear trials concerning alleged crimes against humanity in Dili, the capital of Timor-Leste, but Jakarta has virtually blocked action in this regard by refusing to extradite the accused. Although the investigatory unit processed more than eighty cases, it is unable to prosecute Indonesian military figures. Finally, in 2002, the Commission for Reception, Truth, and Reconciliation in East Timor was founded. Under pressure to promote reconciliation rather than justice, as of 2021 it prosecuted fewer than ten cases, which were all acquitted on appeal.[54]

The initiative to establish the INTERNATIONAL CRIMINAL COURT (ICC) began in 1948 to address a need to replace ad hoc, conflict-specific tribunals with a permanent war crimes tribunal. The ICC, which entered into force July 1, 2002, does not replace national courts, but rather serves as a court of last resort when they are unwilling or unable to handle cases. The idea of such a court was tabled by superpower politics during the Cold War, but was resurrected in the early 1990s. In 1998, 160 states signed an agreement to create this permanent court (with the conspicuous exception of the United States, which has expressed concern that politically motivated cases will be brought against it). The ICC, which deals only with crimes committed after its establishment, is located in The Hague, with the International Court of Justice. (The ICJ is empowered to hear cases waged between governments, while the ICC allows individuals and groups to prosecute individuals for genocide, war crimes, and crimes against humanity. Additionally, the ICJ is a civil court, while the ICC prosecutes criminal cases.)

At the ICC, a panel of eighteen judges hears cases—with the maximum allowable penalty of life imprisonment. The ICC is designed to investigate and prosecute the most notorious human rights abusers. So far, nearly all of those indicted are African. This fact has won the body scorn from many African heads of state, who accuse it of neocolonial bias. Some, including Burundi, South Africa, and Gambia have registered their intention to withdraw from the body and others are likely to follow, given the support for the idea of a mass withdrawal at the African Union. Supporters of the court point out that the chief prosecutor, Fatou Bensouda, is from Gambia and that the ICC is conducting investigations and may bring forward cases from Colombia, Afghanistan, and the UK in Iraq. But it will take a conviction of a leader from outside of Africa to win over skeptics.[55] A multiyear investigation against former Philippine president Rodrigo Duterte's war on drugs may produce a conviction, but it is hampered by the leader's insistence that ICC representatives will be blocked from entering the country, shortly after Duterte pulled his country out of the Rome Statute in defiance of their investigation.[56]

Somewhat similar to international tribunals, truth commissions are designed to air grievances about past wrongs committed by individuals or groups as a way to prevent future crimes against humanity, to restore a semblance of "normalcy" after periods of unrest, and to promote a human rights culture. Yet, truth commissions are different from war crimes tribunals in a few important ways. Trials are designed to punish, and may deprive individuals of life, liberty, or property. Truth commissions vary in their aims; they often seek to promote individual and structural healing, piece together past reality, and establish a historical memory so that it can never be denied. Because they are separate from courts of law, truth commissions do not usually have the right of subpoena; they are less bound by concerns of DUE PROCESS, and may admit hearsay and other forms of evidence that would be unacceptable in a war crimes tribunal.[57]

The most widely known truth commission is the Truth and Reconciliation Commission of South Africa. However, other truth commissions (some dating back to the 1970s) have been established in many countries, including Haiti, Guatemala, Nigeria, Uganda, Bolivia, Argentina, Peru, Uruguay, Chile, and the Philippines. Not all truth commissions are the same, and few follow the model established in South Africa, which granted widespread amnesty to participants in exchange for their role in the investigation. Some of these commissions, such as the ones in Guatemala and El Salvador, are established under UN auspices, while others are domestic initiatives alone. Some, but not most, allow amnesties. A few truth commissions are established for the primary purpose of honoring those hurt by abuse and promoting closure, while others gather information and pass it on to courts for prosecution.

Truth commissions are generally established after a civil war, or after an authoritarian government steps aside, as part of a DEMOCRATIC TRANSITION. Timor-Leste fits this description. Its truth commission, known as the Commission for Truth and Friendship, makes creative use of local customs. Those who are accused of the most serious crimes will be brought before courts, but because there are too many people to handle, the approximately 10,000 East Timorese who participated in lesser crimes with Indonesian-backed militias will come before the truth commission. Many of these people are hiding out in West Timor, afraid they might be lynched if they return home. For those who want to come home, the truth commission will bring them before local village councils. If they admit their crimes and apologize, they will be sentenced to community service. According to local custom, they will then be safe from acts of revenge.

Some critics of truth commissions characterize them as "some-of-the-truth commissions" or "Kleenex commissions" that do more harm than good. Many people resist the idea of granting amnesties to individuals who admit to committing atrocities, in return for their cooperation with the commission. The trade-off is viewed as necessary to allow a more complete airing of misdeeds, including public testimony that often allows victims (or their families) to confront the perpetrators of the crime. Several truth commissions have televised their proceedings. They vary over whether they provide the names of those who come forward. Despite their differences, the goal of truth commissions is to make sure that the acts of injustice cannot be ignored, even if, in the end, the commissions breach justice by "letting some people off the hook."[58] For a variety of reasons, truth commissions often face powerful resistance and need money, a broad mandate, and high-level backing if they are to succeed. South Africa's Archbishop Desmond Tutu, in his justification for amnesties in the South African trials of apartheid leaders, argued that criminal justice can be sacrificed if it leads to a greater sense of social justice.

* * *

As you can see, the tasks before the United Nations are enormous, and some may say nearly impossible to achieve. Many around the world, including leaders within the organization itself, are increasingly questioning the relevance of the United Nations, especially as powers beyond the formerly dominant United States and European states assert their role, making compromise more difficult. Many question whether the most well-known IGO is "at the center of global responses" to the big problems facing the world as it moves toward "mini-lateral cooperation" of smaller coalitions of big countries instead. As one analyst put it, the UN is no longer "the only game in town."[59] Organizations such as the GROUP OF 20, with more manageable memberships and less pomp, may actually provide more latitude for discussion and negotiation among world leaders.

As one historian (who also served as an informal adviser for former Secretary-General Ban) stated, "The U.N. is not the sun of the international solar system; everything doesn't revolve around it. But it is the final reference point on most issues, which have to come to the U.N. for legitimacy."[60]

It should be clear that international governmental organizations have played a pivotal role in the world community, sometimes fostering cooperation among governments, and other times taking action against governments that are perceived to be violating universal norms of conduct. All organizations have their limitations, and generally IGOs are constrained by the fact that they are established by governments to act in the interest of governments. This means that they are beholden to the interests and concerns of powerful elite groups, and that political agendas, as we have seen, tend to predominate over the humanitarian interests that they profess to promote. And despite the talk of inclusion and equal voting privileges for small states as well as big states, weaker governments of the global south can get caught in big-power agendas that limit their voice and ability to take action. In the end, while states participating in IGOs give up some degree of sovereignty to work in concert with others, that power can be snatched back when considered necessary. We now turn to another type of collaborative organization—groups of people who organize outside state authority to promote particular agendas in the global community.

International Nongovernmental Organizations

In Part 2 of this book, we discussed the influence of some NGOs, namely MULTINATIONAL CORPORATIONS. International NGOs are private, transnational associations of individuals or groups that organize around a shared interest or understanding, and have strong ties to civil society. NGOs are extremely diverse, in their size, organizational structure, and range of interests. Their numbers have exploded since the 1980s, to the point that many countries have thousands, if not tens of thousands, of NGOs or affiliates. Even though scarce resources for programming and advocacy present formidable obstacles to groups in the global south, NGOs have a strong presence. They include universities, civic organizations, churches, and other religious institutions.

You are probably aware of many such organizations, even if you do not identify them as NGOs per se: Habitat for Humanity, the International Federation of Red Cross and Red Crescent Societies, the International Planned Parenthood Federation, Greenpeace, Oxfam, WarChild, Amnesty International, Catholic Relief Services, Lutheran World Relief, Bread for the World, Save the Children, and Goodwill Industries International are just some of the most widely recognized. These organizations are powerful in that they help countries incorporate ideas into national (and international) policies and programs. They are also vital in shaping and conveying public opinion to large gatherings of policymakers. They may be national or international in scope. NGOs are often able to open previously closed discussions or bring attention to taboo topics, including violence against women and child labor. NGOs rarely work alone. Rather, they work together with other organizations and with governments to promote their causes, often by hosting international meetings in conjunction with other associational conferences, such as those of the United Nations, a presence that has increased dramatically since the early 1970s.

What can NGOs accomplish that national governments cannot? NGOs like Amnesty International have been especially critical in exposing human rights abuses and educating citizens about their rights, with less of the government interference that mars the work of peacekeeping missions. NGOs work in dangerous circumstances and under many rules, and they are often subject to retaliation. Often, these organizations voice impatience with the slow action of government-based organizations. Nongovernmental organizations are less beholden to bureaucratic and electoral interests, and they have power that IGOs like the UN, which is bound to act only on the expressed interests of its members through the Security Council, do not. Even though they are made up of individuals and interest groups, their target audience is most often the governments of countries or world opinion. Many of the issues that we have discussed throughout this book have NGOs associated with them.

One of the best-known associations of NGOs dedicated to the promotion of human rights is Amnesty International. Its success, in part, is due to a wide-reaching network of local (often university-based), national, and international offices. One of the key areas that Amnesty International focuses on is advocacy for individual political prisoners and prisoners of conscience—people who suffer persecution for their beliefs. Amnesty International has been particularly effective in targeting governments to reveal violations of universal standards of human rights. Additionally, its members coordinate campaigns for the release of political prisoners throughout the world, and spearhead an international campaign against the use of capital punishment. One of this organization's greatest strengths is its work in raising the awareness of particular issues by publicly turning the spotlight on countries that abuse human rights.

Another NGO that campaigns for humanitarian issues and also works "on the ground" is the International Federation of Red Cross and Red Crescent Societies (IFRC), part of the larger International Red Cross and Red Crescent Movement, which also includes the International Committee of the Red Cross (ICRC) and the more than 190 national Red Cross and Red Crescent Societies around the world. This is a highly acclaimed and almost universally accepted set of organizations that works largely independently of governments so that it can remain impartial in handling humanitarian crises during times of peace and war. Because the IFRC is not tied to any official government, or even to the United Nations, it can accomplish tasks or change its mandate without needing to muster the will of the international community or the consensus of multiple nation-states. Unlike the campaigning organizations discussed above, the IFRC attempts not to change opinion, but rather to take action, promoting the most universal perspective of humanity—protection and humane treatment of all individuals, even combatants wearing enemy uniforms.

The International Red Cross and Red Crescent Movement's record of humanitarian interventions is quite impressive. The complexities facing refugees, particularly related to legally defined "genuine refugees" versus "DISPLACED PERSONS," serve as a case in point. The ICRC has successfully procured legal exemptions to allow its representatives to come to the aid of displaced persons in conflict-ridden areas, where other international organizations, notably those affiliated with the UN, lack jurisdiction to respond.[61] It has also been quite active in repatriating prisoners of war, including 10,000 Iraqi prisoners held in Iran.

The ICRC, based in Geneva, has been absolutely pivotal in promoting global cultural values, especially related to times of war. In fact, as an NGO it was a key player in the drafting and signing of the first Geneva Convention in 1864, also known as the "Red Cross Convention," which when combined with follow-up conventions provides the universally acknowledged rules of warfare. The ICRC stressed that states need to protect the worth and dignity of individuals "even when this is most difficult and costly for states."[62] It has also been instrumental in advocating the need for quality medical care, even during times of strife, and especially for the protection of medical care providers who identify themselves in war-torn areas with the recognizable symbol of either the red cross or the red crescent.

Yet, not all NGOs attempt to maintain the neutrality of the International Red Cross and Red Crescent Movement. Two NGOs that attempt to promote advocacy within particular substantive topics—medicine and journalism—irrespective of geopolitical borders, are the Paris-based associations Doctors Without Borders (MSF) and Reporters Without Borders (RSF). MSF was founded in 1971—in the aftermath of the Biafran war in Nigeria—to publicly challenge the neutrality of the IFRC. The organization unites medical professionals around the world to provide medical training and emergency assistance, especially in areas of conflict. In 1999, MSF won the Nobel Peace Prize for its humanitarian work with victims of wars, famine, and other disasters. MSF has also been active in refugee issues, particularly in camps and temporary settlements. MSF is famous for its fierce independence, but it does not attempt to appear neutral in the face of conflict.

The goal of Reporters Without Borders, founded in 1985, is to publicize threats to the free flow of information in an increasing number of forums, especially by highlighting the arrest and torture of journalists who suffer because of their profession. It publishes an annual report of press freedoms in countries around the world, highlighting the arrests, kidnappings, imprisonment, torture, and murder of journalists. Not surprisingly, many reporters suffer these fates when they investigate and attempt to report on CORRUPTION, abuse of power, or drug trafficking, especially if they highlight the complicity of politicians. More than half the member states of the United Nations impose limits on freedom of the press—RSF and similar organizations call out the worst violators.

A new direction in press freedom that RSF and other NGOs are pressing is the free flow of information on the internet. Increasingly, many global south countries are imposing restrictions on communication via this channel, by installing filters that block access to websites, forcing computer users to register, or sharply limiting access for all citizens. RSF publishes annual lists of "Enemies of the Internet," which detail access restrictions as well as punitive efforts taken against individuals who use this medium to express their views. In 2020, RSF began compiling a list of "digital predators" (companies and government agencies that use digital technology to spy on and harass journalists). Of our cases, Mexico, Iran, China, and Egypt made the inaugural list of twenty, for harassment and state censorship.[63]

Other NGOs promote environmental causes. The better-known environmental NGOs include the Nature Conservancy, Greenpeace, and the World Wildlife Fund. These are huge, multinational organizations with large budgets to accomplish advocacy, education, and mobilization around environmental issues. These NGOs, even more than others, have linked arms with similar-minded organizations in networks to accomplish great feats. Greenpeace, for example, states that one of its primary goals is to stop the "chemicalization" of the planet, especially by ending the threat of nuclear weapons and nuclear power as well as other forms of "dirty" technology, and to limit ozone depletion caused by the production and use of greenhouse gases. It has also been highly critical of genetically modified organisms and crops. Yet, Greenpeace is also linked with other human rights and environmental organizations that promote responsive government and biodiversity.

Churches and religious institutions are other examples of NGOs that have crossed over into multiple issue areas to promote human welfare. The Catholic Church, for example, is a widely recognized NGO with a high degree of activism in the global south, directly and through its many institutions. One of these is Caritas, which attempts to promote Christian ideals of social justice and charity by working with and for impoverished peoples. Like many NGOs, Caritas is part of an international-level umbrella organization, but most of its work is increasingly being conducted at the regional, even the state, level. Another religiously affiliated NGO is the International Association for Religious Freedom (IARF), which, having been established in 1900, predates many other NGOs. The goal of the IARF, which is one of many NGOs affiliated with the United Nations, is to promote the universal right of freedom of religion. The IARF includes persons of many faiths, including Buddhists, Hindus, Humanists, Sikhs, Universalists, Christians, and Indigenous peoples, in its advocacy and operation.

NGOs have become increasingly prominent within state networks of global power and influence in recent decades. They serve a particularly prominent role within the United Nations, where they increasingly work in a consultative capacity.[64] Although NGOs are currently confined to ECOSOC committees, without any formal access to the General Assembly and its committees, there is much pressure to change this. Within the United Nations, NGOs cannot vote, because they do not represent a state, but they are welcomed as participants in most UN debates because of their grassroots experience and data, which states may not be able to gather or have the desire to do so. As interest groups, they actively lobby delegates and provide connections between grassroots citizenry and international diplomatic channels that otherwise do not exist. Additionally, NGOs work with UN agencies in the field, taking on massive grassroots tasks that the overburdened and overly bureaucratized UN agencies would be less able to accomplish. For example, over 500 NGOs work with the United Nations High Commissioner for Refugees to intervene in crisis situations where refugees are involved.[65]

We have discussed a wide array of organizations, national and international in scope, with differing levels of expertise and involvement. Increasingly, many question whether these organizations are necessary, or even relevant. To be sure, they have both strengths and weaknesses. Perhaps, though, the increasing push from many countries, especially those within the global south, to join and become active members in these organizations, is a sign of some level of vitality. Taking the United Nations, for example, nearly every state that is eligible for membership has sought a seat in this world body—the only countries that lack membership are the Vatican (which holds observer status) and several "microstates" with extremely small populations.[66] Including more voices makes things messier, but perhaps more inclusive as well. The struggle to balance representation, efficiency, and productivity takes on more urgency as the global community faces ever more complex challenges—especially since Covid.

Notes

1. This perspective is based largely on the views on "new regionalism" expressed by Sheila Page in her book *Regionalism Among Developing Countries* (New York: St. Martin's, 2000), pp. 5–6.

2. Michael Hirsh, "Calling All Regio-Cops: Peacekeeping's Hybrid Future," *Foreign Affairs* 79, no. 6 (November–December 2000).

3. Carol B. Thompson, "Beyond the Nation-State? Democracy in Regional Economic Context," in *Democracy and Socialism in Africa,* ed. Robin Cohen and Harry Goulbourne (Boulder: Westview, 1991).

4. Kizito Sikuka, "Year SACD Showed Resilience, Solidarity, Courage in Face of Adversity," *The Herald* (Zimbabwe), December 23, 2020.

5. Claire Felter, Danielle Renwick, and Andrew Chatzky, "Mercosur: South America's Fractious Trade Bloc," Council on Foreign Relations, July 10, 2019.

6. Brian Naylor, "Another Election Day First: OAS Will Observe U.S. Voting," NPR, September 13, 2016.

7. "OAS Condemns Nicaragua's Jailing of Potential Presidential Rivals," *Reuters,* June 15, 2021.

8. Mary Beth Sheridan, "For U.S. and OAS, New Challenges to Latin American Democracy," *Washington Post,* July 6, 2009.

9. Paul Reynolds, "African Union Replaces Dictators' Club," *BBC News,* July 8, 2002.

10. Ndubuisi Christian Ani, "Is the African Standby Force Any Closer to Being Deployed?" Institute for Security Studies, November 2, 2018.

11. African Development Bank, *New Partnership for Africa's Development (NEPAD) Infrastructure Program: 2020 Annual Report,* May 2021.

12. Robin Emmott, "EU Says Turkey Still 'Backsliding' on Reforms, Gloomy on Membership Chances," *Reuters,* October 19, 2021.

13. Rob Watson, "What Makes a Good UN Secretary General?" *BBC News,* October 2, 2006.

14. Arora Akanksha, a native of India and Canadian citizen who currently works as an auditor coordinator for the UN Development Programme, formally submitted her letter of application for the 2022–2027 term of the UN Secretary-General. Although she received the backing of no countries, her self-financed campaign helped give voice to those who remain concerned about the transparency and accessibility of the world's top diplomatic post. For a profile of Arora, see Rick Gladstone, "Who Is Arora Akanksha, the 34-Year-Old Running for U.N. Secretary General?" *New York Times,* February 26, 2021.

15. Julian Borger, "António Guterres to Be Next UN Secretary General," *The Guardian,* October 5, 2016.

16. Rick Gladstone, "U.N. Security Council Recommends António Guterres for a Second Term," *New York Times,* June 8, 2021.

17. Because much of the world did not recognize the Communist Party's leadership of the People's Republic of China on the mainland, the "China seat" was occupied by the Nationalist Party, which operated from Taiwan after its loss to the CCP in 1949. The Taiwanese government of the Republic of China occupied this position until 1971, when the PRC first joined the United Nations.

18. Ranking is based on data from the "Security Council—Veto List" compiled by the Dag Hammarskjöld Library. Also, it is important to note that Russia and China both vetoed five Security Council resolutions (each related to the Syrian crisis), between 2011 and 2016.

19. "Statement by Saudi Foreign Ministry on UN Security Council Membership," press release, Embassy of the Kingdom of Saudi Arabia, October 18, 2013.

20. "Thinking the Unthinkable," *The Economist,* November 13, 2010.

21. Anthony Banbury, "I Love the U.N., but It Is Failing," *New York Times,* March 18, 2016.

22. Nadeshda Jayakody, "Refining United Nations Security Council Targeted Sanctions: 'Proportionality' as a Way Forward for Human Rights Protection," *Security and Human Rights* 29 (2018), pp. 90–119.

23. Sang-min Kim, "North Korea Keeps Evading UN Sanctions," *Arms Control Today,* May 2021, p. 33.

24. Richard Nephew, "A Price of Success, or Buyer's Remorse? The Tension Between the United Nations Sanctions and the United States' Unilateral Approach," *Georgetown Journal of International Affairs* 21 (Fall 2020), pp. 96–104.

25. "Fact Sheet: United Nations Peacekeeping," United Nations Department of Peacekeeping Operations, September 30, 2021.

26. "Troop and Police Contributions," United Nations Department of Peacekeeping Operations, July 13, 2021.

27. Niall McCarthy, "The Biggest Contributors to UN Peacekeeping Missions," *Forbes,* May 28, 2021.

28. Irwan Firdaus, "Three E. Timorese Sentenced in Deaths of Aid Workers," *AP,* May 5, 2001.

29. Anthony Banbury, "I Love the U.N.," p. SR5; Kambiz Foorohar, "The UN Peacekeepers Rape Scandal Gets Worse," *Bloomberg,* June 16, 2016.

30. Madeleine K. Albright, John D. Negroponte, and Thomas Pickering, "The United States Must Pay the United Nations What It Owes," *Foreign Policy* (March 29, 2021).

31. Jonathan M. Katz, "U.N. Admits Role in Cholera Epidemic in Haiti," *New York Times,* August 17, 2016.
32. Rick Gladstone, "Cholera 'Forever Destroyed' U.N.'s Image in Haiti, Ban Ki-moon Says," *New York Times,* June 6, 2021; Rick Gladstone, "After Bringing Cholera to Haiti, U.N. Can't Raise Money to Fight It," *New York Times,* March 19, 2017.
33. Jeffrey Gettleman, "Frenzy of Rape in Congo Reveals U.N. Weakness," *New York Times,* October 3, 2010.
34. Ibid.
35. Skye Wheeler, "UN Peacekeeping Has a Sexual Abuse Problem," Human Rights Watch, January 11, 2020.
36. Zack Baddorf, "Ordered to Catch a Warlord, Ugandan Troops Are Accused of Hunting Girls," *New York Times,* May 14, 2017.
37. Nasra Bishumba, "Genocide: The World Is Yet to Learn from Rwanda's Experience—Experts," *New York Times,* April 29, 2021.
38. "Who Are the Uyghurs and Why Is China Being Accused of Genocide?" *BBC News,* June 21, 2021.
39. Francis Mading Deng, "State Collapse: The Humanitarian Challenge to the UN," in *Collapsed States: The Disintegration and Restoration of Legitimate Authority,* ed. I. William Zartman (Boulder: Lynne Rienner, 1995).
40. Mary Kaldor, "Humanitarian Intervention: A Forum," *The Nation,* May 8, 2000. In this piece, Kaldor argues that "a genuine humanitarian intervention is much more like policing than warfighting or traditional peacekeeping." See also Mary Kaldor's book, *New and Old Wars: Organized Violence in a Global Era* (Stanford: Stanford University Press, 1999).
41. These two opposing views are expressed by Mahmood Mamdani in "Humanitarian Intervention: A Forum," *The Nation,* May 8, 2000.
42. Ibrahim A. Gambari, "The Role of Foreign Intervention in African Reconstruction," in *Collapsed States: The Disintegration and Restoration of Legitimate Authority,* ed. I. William Zartman (Boulder: Lynne Rienner, 1995).
43. Jo Becker, "America Should Not Lag Behind on Protecting Children," Human Rights Watch, November 18, 2019.
44. Karen A. Mingst and Margaret P. Karns, *The United Nations in the 21st Century,* 3rd ed. (Boulder: Westview, 2007).
45. Nitza Berkovitch, "The Emergence and Transformation of the International Women's Movement," in *Constructing World Culture: International Nongovernmental Organizations Since 1875,* ed. John Boli and George M. Thomas (Stanford: Stanford University Press, 1999).
46. Waxhma Frogh, "CEDAW Ratification Would Be a Triumph for Afghan Women," *The Hill,* November 17, 2010. Frogh, an Afghani activist, provided testimony before the US Senate Judiciary subcommittee hearing on CEDAW ratification, stating, "The U.S. failure to ratify CEDAW is of huge international significance."
47. Melissa Upreti et al., "Statement by United Nations Human Rights Experts," Office of the High Commissioner for Human Rights, September 15, 2021.
48. Amanda Taub, "Why the Taliban's Repression of Women May Be More Tactical Than Ideological," *New York Times,* October 4, 2021.
49. Human Rights Watch, "Submission to the Committee on the Elimination of Discrimination Against Women Review of South Africa," September 29, 2021.
50. Richard J. Goldstone, "Bringing War Criminals to Justice During an Ongoing War," in *Hard Choices: Moral Dilemmas in Humanitarian Intervention,* ed. Jonathan Moore (Lanham: Rowman and Littlefield, 1998).
51. Seth Mydans, "Duch, Prison Chief Who Slaughtered for the Khmer Rouge, Dies at 77," *New York Times,* September 1, 2020.
52. Alastair Leithead, "Rwanda Genocide: International Criminal Tribunal Closes," *BBC News,* December 14, 2015.
53. "Jokowi Urged to Reverse Wiranto's Appointment," *Jakarta Post,* July 28, 2016.

54. Galuh Wandita, "Ah Khu and Ana: How Many More Will Be Lost While ASEAN Looks the Other Way?" *Jakarta Post,* April 5, 2021.

55. Karen Allen, "Is This the End for the International Criminal Court?" *BBC News,* October 24, 2016.

56. Jason Gutierrez, "Philippines Is Defiant as Hague Court Announces Full Drug War Inquiry," *New York Times,* September 16, 2021; Felipe Villamor, "Philippines Plans to Withdraw from International Criminal Court," *New York Times,* March 14, 2018.

57. Robert I. Rotberg and Dennis Thompson, eds., *Truth v. Justice: The Morality of Truth Commissions* (Princeton: Princeton University Press, 2000).

58. This is a dominant perspective expressed by many, although not all, of the contributors to the Rotberg and Thompson collection on truth commissions: Rotberg and Thompson, *Truth v. Justice;* Priscilla B. Hayner, *Unspeakable Truths: Confronting State Terror and Atrocity* (New York: Routledge, 2001).

59. Interview with Stewart M. Patrick, "Crisis of Relevance at the UN," Council on Foreign Relations, September 20, 2010.

60. Colum Lynch, "U.N. Struggles to Prove Its Relevance," *Washington Post,* September 19, 2010.

61. "When Is a Refugee Not a Refugee?" *The Economist,* March 3, 2001.

62. Martha Finnemore, "Rules of War and Wars of Rules: The International Red Cross and the Restraint of State Violence," in *Constructing World Culture: International Nongovernmental Organizations Since 1875,* ed. John Boli and George M. Thomas (Stanford: Stanford University Press, 1999).

63. Reporters Without Borders, "RSF Unveils 20/2020 List of Press Freedom's Digital Predators," March 10, 2020.

64. On the role of NGOs in the United Nations, see Karen A. Mingst and Margaret P. Karns, *The United Nations in the Post–Cold War Era* (Boulder: Westview, 1995), p. 77.

65. "When Is a Refugee Not a Refugee?" *The Economist.*

66. Courtney B. Smith, *Politics and Process at the United Nations: The Global Dance* (Boulder: Lynne Rienner, 2006), p. 278.

16

Confronting Global Challenges

These people fall through the cracks. It's hard for countries to come to a consensus on something like this. —*Erol Yayboke, a development expert at the Center for Strategic and International Studies, referring to the growing numbers of climate migrants around the world*[1]

Last year, if you had told somebody that we have over 1,000 deaths a day—and the real number might be five times that—they would have said that is completely unacceptable. This year, people are as if "It's just 1,000 deaths a day. It's fine. We can manage with that." —*Ramanan Laxminarayan, director of the Center for Disease Dynamics, Economics and Policy, referring to the toll from Covid in India*[2]

There was a time, not that long ago, when many spoke of a "borderless world." Changes in transportation, information communication technology, and economics all seemed to make state boundaries less important. Physical borders became more permeable; trade, travel, and other interactions became quicker; and many recognized both the advantages and disadvantages of interdependence. The Covid pandemic, of course, brought this reality to the surface even more intimately. Never before in our lifetimes have most of us encountered the day-to-day reality of our lives being genuinely impacted by events that started far beyond our homes. Remember the conversations about supply chain issues, including of fundamental supplies like antibiotics, personal protective equipment, and ventilators? In facing large-scale, border-busting issues, what are the best ways to respond? How do we respond to disparities in the capacity to respond? These questions become more challenging when there is a recognized gulf between those responsible for the problem and those most impacted by the challenge. To examine these phenomena, we take a brief look at three of the key global issues in our world today—environmental degradation, human migration, and public health. Because of the scope and breadth of these issues, many believe that durable solutions to these problems can be achieved only with a multilateral response, meaning the conduct of activities by three or more states or transnational actors. The challenges, and responses to them, both affirm and question the notion of our world's borderless character.

Many of these global challenges illustrate examples of the so-called free-rider problem, which shows that individuals (or groups) can benefit from attempts to solve a problem without contributing to its cause. Similarly, people can attempt to skirt limits or constraints without being caught. This provides individuals and groups little incentive to put forth the effort or the resources to solve problems, which is the main reason why many contend that these issues need larger, sometimes global responses to successfully combat further decay. Exacerbating this free-rider problem is the long-term view on change: we may not see the lasting effects of changes made today for many years to come. This delay in results often limits people's sense of urgency for taking action, and underscores the need for regional or global organizations and specialized institutions that can reach large audiences to take the lead.

Environmental Degradation: Science and Global Politics

Many view the natural environment as the clearest example of the interconnectivity of this planet's residents, human and nonhuman as well. Pollution, whether in the form of air, water, land, or otherwise, does not stop at border control. Fish swim in shared waters, moving between the sovereign areas of states. Air damaged in one region often worsens as it travels to another. Changes in the natural environment are often experienced firsthand by people who are not responsible for the problem in the first place. These challenges are then exacerbated by population pressures. Population centers in the global south, already strained by limited resources and increasing urbanization, will face greater pressures in the coming decades as today's world population of nearly 8 billion people swells to more than 9.8 billion by 2050, with nearly all of that increase projected to be in developing countries.[3]

What are some of the consequences of the population explosion in many parts of the world? In Mexico City, once tagged the world's most polluted city, air quality is dangerous throughout much of the year, caused by industrial waste and widespread forest fires resulting from excessive heat and drought. Widespread logging (often coordinated by criminal groups), quickens the loss of habitats critical for biodiversity; Indonesia, Mexico, and Brazil have some of the worst records in this regard. In the first months of 2020, for example, forest loss in Indonesia increased by 50 percent, despite travel restrictions and lockdowns associated with the Covid pandemic.[4] Researchers connected smoke from fires in Mexico and Central America to tornado outbreaks in the United States.[5] China's economic boom, based on the use of coal and fuel-inefficient technologies, has created pollution problems of unparalleled magnitude. China, India, the United States, and Russia are now the world's top polluters, with China alone accounting for approximately one-third of global carbon dioxide emissions.[6] The World Health Organization estimates that air pollution is responsible for approximately 7 million deaths every year, with more than 90 percent of air pollution–related deaths occurring in low- and middle-income countries, mostly in Asia and Africa.[7] In a blunt statement, the World Economic Forum nailed it: "The poor breathe dirtier air."[8] This reality has very real consequences on health and well-being.

An overwhelming majority of scientists agree that modern environmental problems are initiated and worsened by human activity. Industrial emissions trap heat close to Earth's atmosphere, leading to an increase in average temperatures across the planet. These phenomena are not natural—they are consequences of human consumption patterns. Although the actual degree of increase is debated (and based on future models), there is widespread agreement that the average global temperature is increasing, and that Earth is hotter today than at any other time in at least 1,000 years, possibly longer.[9] We observe the effects everywhere: glaciers and ice sheets are shrinking, crops mature earlier, animals move toward higher elevations, and weather has grown more extreme. Flash floods, droughts, heat waves, and wildfires destroy livelihoods, disrupt food supply chains, and claim lives. According to a recent international report, eight of the ten countries that have been hardest hit by extreme weather events since 2000 are economically poorer states, with less capacity to prepare for and respond to natural crises.[10] For decades, scientists have been clamoring for aggressive policies to curtail the impact of human behavior on the natural environment, especially as the differential impacts across countries become clearer.

What responsibility do wealthier countries and international organizations have to decrease devastation, including loss of life, in climate-vulnerable countries? As one analyst put it, "No other narrative envelopes all of humanity in quite the same way, forcing answers about the ethics of food, of oil, of technology, of economic security, of democratic republics and command capitalism, of colonialism and indigenous peoples, of who in the world is rich and who in the world is poor."[11] The divide between cause and impact runs counter to the notion that "we're all in this together" and points to another way of viewing an extremely unequal world. Some have captured this dynamic by contrasting the free-riders (countries that are top emitters, yet mostly immune to the impact) and the "forced-riders" (countries that have low emission rates yet are extremely vulnerable to rising sea levels and other impacts of climate change).[12] In addition to individual countries, the International Monetary Fund, World Bank, and other donor agencies have come under increasing pressure to be more environmentally responsive, and have allocated larger staffs to address the issue. Environmental targets fare prominently in the Sustainable Development Goals (SDGs), for example. There is more funding for environmental projects, and environmental impact statements for development projects are now mandatory.

Water is at the center of this crisis: some places have too much of it (from floods and rising sea levels), while others face prolonged droughts or lack access to potable water that is safe to drink or use for food preparation. The UN estimates that 2.2 billion people, or roughly one in three, live without access to safe water.[13] The World Resources Institute found that across Africa, Southeast Asia, and South America, the number of urban residents lacking access to water piped to their residence has increased by more than 200 million people since

1990.[14] On the other extreme, many parts of the world are finding themselves suddenly inundated by water, as extreme weather is leading to flooding in crowded urban areas that are often ill-equipped to deal with an onslaught by the elements, even if leaders (belatedly) worked to expand green space and make other efforts to help mitigate the effects of natural disasters. One of the world's largest insurance providers warns that the effects of climate change "can be expected to shave 11 percent to 14 percent off global economic output by 2050," amounting to as much as $23 trillion in decreased global economic output, as crops fail, diseases spread, and coastal cities become inundated by water.[15]

What can be done? Much of it goes back to the free- and forced-rider designations we discussed earlier. Since the early 1970s, multiple international conferences have been held to discuss sources of the problems and debate potential solutions. As you can imagine, the cause and effect exchange has animated much of the debate, especially as some note that wealthier countries may actually benefit from increased global temperatures, while economic growth has been shown to decrease in poorer countries.[16] After meetings in Montreal in 1987, governments committed to reducing all substances, but especially human-made materials that deplete the world's ozone layer. At the Rio de Janeiro meetings in 1992, greater cooperation was forged between developed and less developed states, promoting "common but differentiated" responsibilities for the environment. The expressed goal is to foster all countries' right to development, while chipping away at a growing problem at the same time. The spirit of Rio was widely adopted as a workable solution to environmental issues and, with the adoption of the Framework Convention on Climate Change in 1994, the United Nations formally recognized, for the first time, the explicit dangers of climate change.

Further negotiations led to a comprehensive first set of actions that was approved at the Kyoto conference in 1997. Signatories agreed to reductions in fossil fuel combustion, differentiated by their economic status. The lion's share of responsibility was placed on developed countries, from which the largest portions of harmful emissions originate. The allowance of different emission rates, based on level of development, ultimately led to Kyoto's undoing, especially with China, India, and Brazil exempt from targets (one of the main reasons why the United States failed to ratify it). Some have argued that Kyoto's emphasis on defensive reductions rather than proactive developments of alternatives was the crux of the challenge.[17] When the Kyoto protocols expired in 2012, the prospects of a meaningful global agreement on curbing greenhouse gas emissions looked dim.

It was in this context that the world's leaders again gathered in an attempt to strike a balance: how to get countries to work together to help mitigate future challenges without permitting significant shirking of responsibility. In December 2015, world leaders established a legally binding and universal agreement on climate change. Even though many believe that the stated goal, that of keeping the mean global temperature increase well below 2 degrees Celsius, was less than what is actually needed, supporters hailed the Paris Agreement as the "turning point in the climate crisis."[18] Despite many setbacks to the Paris Agreement, including the withdrawal (under President Donald Trump) and later rejoining (under President Joe Biden) by the United States, as well as disputes from China and India surrounding the phasing-out of coal power, scientists, governmental leaders, and activists recognize the imperfect agreement is an attempt at collective action for which the cost of failure may be too great to imagine. Nevertheless, at one of the meetings of the G-20, months ahead of a major international gathering to discuss progress since Paris, climate activists tagged the deliverables as "pollution, poverty and paralysis."[19]

In another case of broken promises, leaders of the less developed countries group at the international gathering of signatories to the United Nations Framework Convention on Climate Change accused the richer countries in the world of not following through on their promises to provide significant financing for poorer countries to help them mitigate emissions and cope with climate change, a failure many see as evidence of the lack of good faith. The chair of the Africa group of negotiators pointed out, "In 2009 and 2015, they promised to deliver climate finance by 2020. Yet this is still to be met, and we don't have a clear plan to achieve it."[20]

Migrants

One of the greatest crises facing the world community is the widespread displacement of the world's people, whether that relocation is external (across international borders) or within one's home country (internal displacement). When we speak of forcibly displaced individuals, we include refugees, asylum seekers, internally displaced people (IDP), as well as stateless people who seek protection from persecution. In the aftermath of the Covid pandemic, ongoing wars, and continued instability in many parts of the world, migration has become the focus of domestic and international policies, especially as migrants experience severe hardships and endure great dangers attempting to relocate away from their homes.

Since its establishment in 1951, the Office of the United Nations High Commissioner for Refugees (UNHCR), which twice received the Nobel Peace Prize (1954 and 1981), has been the main international agency relegated to assist people in these processes. One of the major responsibilities of the UNHCR is to find "durable solutions" for the world's refugees. This includes searching out possibilities for repatriation, through voluntary return to their homeland, integration into another country via the granting of asylum, or resettlement in a third country. Unfortunately, the complex tasks facing this agency, and others related to the handling of refugees, continue to increase in manifold ways, and, similar to the other global challenges, a coordinated response to the burgeoning migration crisis remains elusive.

Lately, migration figures have shattered records multiple years in a row, with nearly 4 percent of the world's population being displaced from their homes. This upward trend, which began in 2010, seems unlikely to reverse itself anytime soon—in fact, the global number of forcibly displaced people doubled between 2010 and 2020. Despite an initial decrease in numbers in 2020, largely due to mobility restrictions imposed during the Covid pandemic, migration pressures resulting from persecution, conflict, violence, and human rights violations continue to soar. At the end of 2020, the UNHCR reported that there were 82.4 million forcibly displaced persons in the world (this number includes 48 million IDP).[21] Two aspects of this trend are alarming. One is the increase in refugees

Figure 16.1 Climate Migrants

The challenges we discuss here are vexing, in part, because none of them are confined to a particular geographic region or entity; each demonstrates the challenging aspects of interdependence. Compounding the matter, though, these areas are rarely discrete, meaning they are rarely stand-alone issues. For example, the effects of climate change are adding to the number of people on the move, leading to a new group of migrants, referred to as climate migrants, or sometimes climate refugees. While political unrest or government programs force some people to leave their homes, in the case of these individuals, it is nature. In 2018, the World Bank estimated that three regions alone (Latin America, sub-Saharan Africa, and South Asia) will generate 143 million additional climate migrants (some will stay within their country's borders) by 2050, and the UNHCR believes that extreme weather events are already causing an average of more than 20 million people each year to leave their homes.[a] Nevertheless, they lack formal legal recognition, and some refer to this growing group of displaced individuals as "the refugees the world barely pays attention to,"[b] even if many forecast that the looming changes may result in "the greatest wave of global migration the world has seen," as the land seems to turn against the people living and working on it.[c]

Severe desertification is forcing families from their land, ruining the livelihoods of families who have tended to pastures for centuries. A "sea of sand" envelopes the land, swallowing precious grasslands that are necessary for the herds of sheep and other animals to survive.[d] "Unprecedented storms" are now becoming commonplace.[e] After two hurricanes hit Honduras in a nearly back to back fashion, impacting more than 4 million people (nearly half of the population), an aid worker put it bluntly: "People aren't migrating; they're fleeing."[f] In Bangladesh, up to 70 percent of the 5 million people living in the slums of Dhaka were displaced from their homes by environmental problems.[g] In addition to extreme weather events, slow-onset changes resulting from water diversion projects, droughts, and climate change are fundamentally changing the landscape, as in the disappearance of Lake Poopó in Bolivia and Lake Chad in West Africa. Citizens of low-lying island states facing existential threats due to rising sea levels have no legal precedent to relocate to another country.

In addition to the rising numbers of migrants and the humanitarian needs they carry, a legal framework to provide these individuals protection is needed, especially as there are no legally binding agreements obliging countries to receive or support them (despite formal recommendations from the 2015 Paris Agreement and related international mechanisms).[h] Adding to the legal limbo, migrants who flee as a result of the onset of weather hazards, sudden or not, do not receive formal refugee status under the UNHCR, although, in 2020, the agency issued guidance stating that some people may have a valid claim for refugee status if the adverse effects of climate change are combined with armed conflict and violence near their homes.[i]

Notes: a. Kantha Kumari Rigaud, Alex de Sherbinin, Bryan Jones, and Jonas Bergmann, *Groundswell: Preparing for Internal Climate Migration* (World Bank, 2018), p. 2; "Climate Change and Disaster Displacement," United Nations High Commission for Refugees (UNHCR), n.d.

b. Tim McDonnell, "The Refugees the World Barely Pays Attention To," NPR, June 20, 2018.

c. Abrahm Lustgarten, "The Great Climate Migration," *New York Times,* July 23, 2020.

d. Maxim Babenko, "Surviving in Isolation, Where the Steppe Has Turned to Sand," *New York Times,* May 10, 2021.

e. John Podesta, "The Climate Crisis, Migration, and Refugees," *Brookings Report,* July 25, 2019.

f. César Ramos, of the Mennonite Social Action Commission, quoted in Natalie Kitroeff, "'We Are Doomed': Devastation from Storms Fuels Migration in Honduras," *New York Times,* April 6, 2021.

g. McDonnell, "The Refugees the World Barely Pays Attention To."

h. Podesta, "The Climate Crisis, Migration, and Refugees."

i. Ibid.; "Climate Change and Disaster Displacement," UNHCR.

under the age of eighteen: UNHCR reports that 42 percent of the forcibly displaced population in 2020 were children, including almost 1 million children who were born as refugees between 2018 and 2020.[22] The other is the growing number of migrants at least partially resulting from climate change, which the UNHCR refers to as the "defining crisis of our time."[23] The UNHCR estimates that extreme weather events and the breakdown of environmental conditions lead to an average of 20 million people each year leaving their homes.[24] (Please see Figure 16.1 for more discussion.)

According to UNHCR, the key source countries of external human displacement include Syria, Venezuela, Afghanistan, South Sudan, and Myanmar; these five states constitute the country of origin for 68 percent of all refugees.[25] Where do international migrants go? Many assume that displaced persons are exclusively crowding the borders of the developed states. Statistics, however, tell a very different story. Turkey has become a gatekeeper of sorts in recent years for migrants traveling from the global south to Europe. The other major refugee-hosting countries in 2020 were Colombia, Germany, Pakistan, and Uganda, with nearly 90 percent of the world's refugees hosted in already overstretched low- and middle-income countries.[26]

Although millions of migrants are estimated to have illegally entered developed countries, the majority of migrants from low-income countries do not cross international boundaries. Rather, they are setting up residence in São Paulo, Mumbai, Shanghai, and Manila, adding to the legions of individuals living in these already overcrowded cities. As you can imagine, their living conditions are often wretched and dangerous, especially to newcomers who may be ill-prepared for urban life. The growth of cities is especially stark in the global south, and the UN forecasts that 96 percent of future urban growth will be found in the less developed regions of East Asia, South Asia, and Africa, with three states (India, China, and Nigeria) making up 35 percent of the increase in urban population between now and 2050.[27] Internally, the flight from rural areas to urban centers has had a number of consequences, including over-urbanization and the rapid creation of megacities, or cities with populations over 10 million (currently there are thirty-four megacities, with this figure projected to increase).[28] The crush of bodies contributes to overcrowding and a number of health problems. It also raises a number of serious political, economic, and social dilemmas; in Cairo, Egypt, for example, it is estimated that nearly half of the population of 21 million lives in slums.[29]

The two biggest sources of internal displacement are conflict- and weather-related disasters—and often, the two forces converge. The International Displacement Monitoring Center reports that, in 2020, the number of people living in internal displacement (48 million) is the highest figure on record, and the greatest increase from year to year in more than a decade.[30] Challenges throughout Africa led to a huge increase in numbers of IDP, especially as civil war in Ethiopia, Africa's second most populous country, launched a surge in displacement.[31] Remember that this was all happening in the midst of the global Covid pandemic. Simmering conflicts and weather-related events in Yemen, Mozambique, Burkina Faso, Syria, Bangladesh, and Afghanistan also contribute to this trend, with many people displaced for a second or third time, adding to their already vulnerable status.[32]

The dangers of migration have always been steep, but they are, in this era of unprecedented displacement, increasing. Migrant passage is unsafe, relying on unmonitored border crossings (often patrolled by gangs or cartels), which can include dangerous waterways and illegal channel crossings. You may remember the tragedy captured in a photograph of a Turkish police officer gently carrying the lifeless body of a three-year-old Syrian boy of Kurdish background, who died, along with his five-year-old brother and mother, attempting to cross the Mediterranean and travel to the Greek Island of Kos, in 2015. At least twelve people died in this singular journey alone, which cost families thousands of dollars to attempt. The International Organization for Migration reports thousands of deaths on migration routes annually, with more than 32,000 migrant deaths being charted since they began tracking deaths in 2014.[33] The US Department of State contends that one northern border territory of Mexico, Tamaulipas, is as dangerous as Syria, Yemen, or Afghanistan—riddled with shootouts, bodies hanging from bridges, even piles of charred bodies and severed heads.[34]

People seeking passage often find human smugglers, sometimes referred to as "coyotes," to facilitate their journey (usually paying between $7,000 and $15,000 for this "service"). This is a lucrative, sometimes comprehensive business that thrives on the risks some people will take in the hope of a better life. Smugglers take advantage of the absence of government controls, have little incentive to invest in seaworthy or roadworthy vessels, and go to great lengths to avoid detection. The result is that inflatable rafts overloaded with thousands of people venture out onto the high seas, people are left to die in the desert, SUVs crash, and vulnerable individuals are raped or sold into sexual slavery. In Reynosa, Mexico, the federal government disbanded the municipal police force, surrendering to the organized criminals who had famously collaborated with police, leaving people "only the protection of God."[35]

For the most part, conflict within each one of these regions is confined to single countries; they are wars within, rather than between, NATION-STATES. The internal nature of these conflicts, over which states can claim SOVEREIGNTY, makes a response by the outside community more difficult, because aggressors (and their supporters) may frame it as an unwelcome invasion into internal matters. World leaders struggle to cope with these changes and with these forms of violence. In the case of international refugees, it is illegal under international law to force "genuine" refugees to return to the country from which they fled, even though the United States and other countries have done so. But how should international organizations respond?

Much attention within the United States has been focused on migration from Latin America, especially Mexico. Even at the height of the Covid pandemic, illegal crossings by migrants without documents reached new extremes, noting a fivefold increase in March 2021 as compared to March 2020, with an alarming increase in unaccompanied minors as well.[36] Interestingly, this increased outmigration comes at a time when the United States and other developed countries attempted to build higher physical barriers and to militarize the borders to cut down on illegal migration. Former president Trump's effort to fortify the southern US border with the "Great Wall of Mexico" was one of many such attempts. The Spanish government, for example, erected a ten-foot-high fence around

Melilla, a contested territory off the coast of northern Africa, that has become a major crossing point for migrants. Israel put up a razor wire–lined "smart fence" along its border with Egypt, designed to stop illegal migration from Africa with not only its physical barrier but also a vast network of high-tech sensors that can launch a robotic six-wheeled car at intruders, complete with turret-mounted machine guns.[37] These actions have only forced people to find ever more difficult and dangerous routes.

Terminological debates about "types" of refugees capture the emerging problem: while a technical definition exists, based in the 1951 UN Convention Relating to the Status of Refugees, many feel it is far too narrow and that it fails to provide an accurate picture of modern migration. This difficulty is only compounded by the complex reasons that people flee: some, although they are believed to be a minority, seek better economic opportunities. Of course, it is often difficult to untangle individuals' motivations, and economic rationales can be as much about "pure survival" as they are political. Others fear political persecution and violence. In fact, many flee violence for a safe, but poverty-filled, future. The reasons people pack up may be diverse, but their situation as displaced people tends to be uniformly dangerous. Many trade one set of insecurities for another when they seek asylum in countries experiencing conflict. The Convention Relating to the Status of Refugees confines the status of "refugee" to "a person who, owing to a well-founded fear of being persecuted for reasons of race, religion, nationality, or membership of a particular social group or political opinion is outside the country of his nationality and unable, or, owing to such fear, is unwilling to avail himself of the protection of that country." In 2020, refugees made up approximately 12 percent of all international migrants (an increase from 9.5 percent in 2000).[38]

Refugee camps are hardly the "safe havens" that you might expect. Officially, displaced people are the responsibility of their home governments, which in many cases are the source of their persecution in the first place. While gang violence, sexual mutilation, and organized crime are documented and well-known realities of life in the camps, one story from a camp within Syria highlighted the tensions that pervade everyday life. After a six-year-old girl choked to death while feverishly eating a meal, it was revealed that she had often been shackled in her family's makeshift tent by her father, who had been otherwise unable to keep her from wandering around the camp.[39]

Children, who make up nearly half of the world's refugee population around the world (a statistic that more than doubled between 2005 and 2019), are often forced to educate themselves, or put up with woefully inadequate makeshift schools.[40] Some end up finding other ways to spend their time, including adopting various survival tactics such as the illicit distribution of drugs, weapons, and sexual favors. Refugees and displaced persons are common targets for exploitation and harassment by soldiers, militia members, and even refugee camp officials. A spokesman for the international NGO Save the Children reported that suicides among refugee children and teenagers are on the rise, stating instances of children eleven years old or younger who have completely given up on life.[41]

In other areas, internal refugees are holed up in internment camps, ostensibly for their own safety, but in reality, to prevent them from aiding the opposition groups that purportedly threaten government or other powerful forces. Whole families have been murdered while they slept in such camps. Refugees are being "warehoused," or confined to camps or segregated settlements for five years or more, oftentimes while being denied basic rights enshrined in the Convention Relating to the Status of Refugees. Refugees in a protracted situation without any lasting end in sight have the right to employment, freedom of movement, and education, although these privileges, including noninterference in personal affairs, are rarely afforded them. Entire generations have grown up as refugees—the average length of time of displacement ranges between ten and twenty-six years; the vast majority of refugees spend an average of seventeen years either in a camp or informally in an urban area with scant access to international aid.[42] Ad hoc creations to help people in crisis become new settlements. People already facing tremendous dislocation and vulnerabilities get lost in the shuffle as attention moves beyond their prolonged plight.

Not only do these uprooted people need assistance in the short term, including food, shelter, clothing, and security, but they face daunting long-term needs as well. The vast majority of refugees desire repatriation in their home country, or asylum in a country of choice that would allow them to start their lives relatively anew. Attempting repatriation in the midst of the Covid pandemic has been especially challenging, increasing vulnerabilities, exploitation, and trafficking possibilities within an already vulnerable population. As a result of increased challenges, hardening attitudes on behalf of potential host countries, and Covid, resettlement rates sunk to the lowest levels in at least two decades (despite increasing numbers of forced displacement).[43]

When it comes down to it, few migrants truly want to leave their home. As one expert at the UN's International Organization for Migration put it, "They would rather stay where they are. But they need the *means* to stay where they are."[44] Responding to those complex needs has remained an elusive achievement.

Disease and Public Health

Throughout this book, we have highlighted the deep and lasting impacts that Covid has had around the world, and most especially throughout the global south. Predating the Covid pandemic, economic malaise, corruption, violence, and war have led to the weakening, and, in some cases, complete failure, of public health systems. Some contend that gaps in the global public health system are reflections of power imbalances traced back to colonial legacies.[45] Even philanthropic programs, such as the creation of a telehealth option to assist pregnant women in Ghana and India, are designed as much to promote opportunities for untapped markets (referred to in some circles as "philanthro-capitalism") as they are to promote positive health outcomes.[46]

Despite the justified prominence of the Covid pandemic, if we examine global public health from a broader perspective, we find that, consistently, the leading causes of death around the world include heart disease, respiratory infections, HIV, diarrhea, tuberculosis, and malaria. One of the biggest puzzles in public health in the twenty-first century is that, despite a wealth of resources, knowledge, and treatments, people continue to die of treatable diseases or con-

Figure 16.2 Human Trafficking

Another dark side of migration can be found in human trafficking. One of the fastest-growing criminal enterprises and a multibillion-dollar industry, trafficking in humans is second only to the illicit smuggling of drugs (and the two often intersect). Human trafficking touches nearly every country in the world today, with Asia and sub-Saharan Africa being the primary sources for trafficked individuals. Traffickers thrive on vulnerabilities and unstable situations, using false promises, misinformation, and threats to prey on people who are economically or socially vulnerable. Trafficked persons are then forcibly engaged in domestic work, as mail-order brides, in illicit adoptions, and in street-begging and commercial sex enterprises. The United Nations Office on Drugs and Crime reports that approximately 50 percent of known victims are trafficked for sexual exploitation. Although trafficking in persons includes both male and female victims, it is estimated that the majority are female victims; for every ten persons trafficked globally, approximately five were adult women and two were girls, with approximately one-third of all known trafficked individuals being under the age of eighteen.[a] Children are viewed as a desirable commodity in this abhorrent industry fueled by misconceptions. Popular myths that children are free of AIDS and that sex with a virgin can cure disease have greatly contributed to the growth of this form of child labor in nearly every corner of the world.

The Covid pandemic exacerbated vulnerabilities and challenges, as it essentially created conditions under which traffickers thrive: exploitation was also aided by the increased amount of time children and adults were spending on the internet and traffickers were able to go further and deeper underground.[b] At the height of the pandemic, Indian officials reported a 95 percent increase in online searches for material that sexually exploited minors, an increase that was noted in other countries—including the United States as well.[c] In some situations, traffickers capitalized on families' loss of income to convince parents to sell their girls into marriage as legitimate sources of income dried up.[d] Not only did the pandemic produce greater numbers of vulnerabilities upon which traffickers could capitalize, but the public health challenges and lockdowns also made it more difficult for persons who were trafficked to escape or return home. Lockdowns, which the United Nations Educational, Scientific and Cultural Organization estimates affected 90 percent of the world's students at pre-primary, primary, secondary, and tertiary levels, also cut individuals off from schools, which often serve as the primary point for positive interventions of all types.[e] The high numbers of children orphaned by the Covid pandemic also significantly increase individuals' risks, especially in states like India, where trafficking of children is rampant, and where Covid exacted an excruciating toll.[f]

Notes: a. United Nations Office on Drugs and Crime (UNODC), *Global Report on Trafficking in Persons: 2020* (New York: United Nations, 2020), p. 9.

b. UNODC, *The Effects of the COVID-19 Pandemic on Trafficking in Persons and Responses to the Challenges: A Global Study of Emerging Evidence* (New York: United Nations, 2020), p. 8.

c. Lara Jakes, "Pandemic Lockdowns Aided Predators Worldwide, Especially Online, U.S. Says," *New York Times,* July 1, 2021.

d. Ibid.

e. "The Evolution of Human Trafficking During the COVID-19 Pandemic," Council on Foreign Relations, August 13, 2020.

f. Suhasini Raj, "'Mother, When Will You Come?': The Covid Orphans of India," *New York Times,* July 10, 2021.

ditions. Yet, there is great apathy among citizens of the developed world about developing world health problems like diarrhea, even though globally it is the third leading cause of death in children (behind pneumonia and preterm birth complications).[47] Preventing deaths from diarrhea does not require complex deals between global drug companies or fistfuls of pills but, rather, oral rehydration therapy and basic sanitation. Even though high-profile rock stars aren't

Figure 16.3 Weapons Proliferation: Light Weapons, WMD, and Cyber Weapons in the Global South

When we discuss the spread of weapons around the world, attention is nearly always centered on the buildup of nuclear weapons, which is understandable, given the threat that they pose. Yet, small, portable weapons (including machine guns, assault rifles, and hand grenades) are responsible for most of the deaths from conflict around the world. The United Nations under-secretary-general and high representative for disarmament affairs notes that there are 1 billion small arms in circulation worldwide, with lethal consequences.[a] The flow of these light weapons adds to the misery of human displacement, unsustainable development, and gender inequality. In addition to these weapons, indiscriminately placed landmines, prepared and laid for conflicts sometimes decades ago, continue their destruction in many parts of the world; more than 5,500 people were injured or killed by landmines in 2019 alone, with civilians comprising approximately 80 percent of these deaths.[b] Conflicts in many parts of the world are exacerbated by landmines, including Afghanistan, Colombia, Iraq, Mali, Nigeria, Ukraine, Yemen, and Myanmar.[c]

Nevertheless, the presence of nuclear, radiological, biological, and chemical weapons, often referred to as weapons of mass destruction, looms large in the global south, as the arms race has moved away from being exclusively in the domain of the major dominant powers in the world. In this so-called second nuclear age, the risk of escalating conflict emanating from smaller, so-called secondary nuclear powers, such as India, Pakistan, and North Korea, presents a different type of proliferation challenge.[d] For decades after the United States detonated the first atomic bomb in 1945 (followed by the Soviet Union in 1949), deterrence was ensured by the notion that "mutual assured destruction" held both sides in check. Given developments in Russia (including the development of the "doomsday device" known as Perimeter, believed to be able to fire nearly all Russian intercontinental ballistic missiles at America in the case of an attack), as well as stealth bombers and cyber-warfare, in addition to China's foray into the major powers' arms race (China has had nuclear weapons capability since 1964), prior calculations about deterrence hold less water. The arrival of other, smaller states to the table of WMD holders also threatens this uneasy balance.

Since the late 1990s, membership in the elite "nuclear club" has expanded, with India, Pakistan, Iran, and North Korea acquiring the capability to produce (and potentially deploy across great distances) nuclear weapons. Syria is also suspected of having pursued a covert nuclear program, widely believed to be assisted by North Korea. In recent years, attention has focused on Iran and North Korea, as both states enhanced their weapons capabilities, including advanced delivery systems, making them states of immediate proliferation concern. Prior to the negotiation of the Joint Comprehensive Plan of Action in 2015, scientists within the Islamic Republic of Iran pursued a uranium enrichment program capable of producing bomb-grade fissile materials for nuclear weapons. While the JCPOA eventually restricted this development, Tehran formally resumed nuclear activities after the United States withdrew from the deal and re-imposed sanctions in 2018. Afterward, Iran began exceeding prior limits to its stockpile of low-enriched uranium, as well as developing new centrifuges to increase uranium enrichment to levels that are necessary only for weapons development. Efforts in late 2021 to try to bring them back to an agreement along the lines of the JCPOA were stalled by competing visions of how best to accommodate all sides' needs.

North Korea's nuclear gains in recent years have been even more alarming, in speed, scope, and context. By the time the Democratic Republic of North Korea, as it is formally known, withdrew from the Nuclear Non-Proliferation Treaty in 2003, Pyongyang had already restarted its major nuclear reactor at Yongbyon, and it proceeded in a dizzying pace to develop its capabilities, conducting its first nuclear test in 2006. Six-party talks hosted by China (which also included the United States, South Korea, Russia, and Japan, and later expanded to include Germany) decreased tensions, but failed to produce any measurable change. After Kim Jong-Un gained power upon his father's death in late 2011, the pace again picked up and by 2018 US intelligence officials estimated that the North had enough fissile material for sixty-five weapons, as well as capabilities to produce additional weapons each year, with multiple tests demon-

continues

Figure 16.3 Continued

strating their capacity with missile delivery systems as well.[e] By 2018, it became clear that the world was going to "learn to live with North Korea's ability to target the United States with nuclear weapons," according to one analyst.[f] After the landmark summit between Kim and President Donald Trump in Singapore in June 2018 (the first-ever meeting between sitting US and North Korean leaders), Kim appeared only more emboldened, despite pledges to work toward de-escalation. Following the collapsed summit in Hanoi in 2019, where Kim and Trump were at odds over sanctions relief and the meaning of denuclearization, Pyongyang resumed its testing activities, pledging to expand its arsenal, including nuclear, ballistic, and chemical weapons.

In addition to these worrisome developments, the People's Republic of China is expanding its nuclear and missile holdings at a seemingly alarming pace, not only with the expansion of its nuclear armaments and missiles, but also with the testing of a new hypersonic weapon that could potentially evade prior missile defense systems. The latter development was termed as "very close" to a Sputnik moment by General Mark Milley, chairman of the Joint Chiefs of Staff, referencing the sense of shock among the United States and its allies after the Soviet launch of its space satellite in 1957.[g] A combination of political will, economic resources, and advances in technology are creating a situation in which it is entirely conceivable that, absent major changes, China will surpass Russia and the United States in terms of military power.[h]

The other major potential for disruption emanates from a completely different type of weapon, that which attacks or attempts to damage information and computer networks within corporations or companies. Individuals and groups, often aided by governments, are able to launch powerful cyberattacks using malware and other digital tools to cause disruption (and extort high sums of money). Examples include viruses, phishing, and computer worms that disable critical infrastructure (including water, transportation, and communication systems), that are dependent upon the reliable communication through digital channels. Cyber-warfare also includes the powerful distributed denial-of-service (DDoS) attacks that prevent legitimate users from being able to access computer networks of devices.

Hackers in China, Iran, Russia, and North Korea, among other states, have engaged in unsettling computer-based attacks on major electronic information systems, impacting financial, medical, and operational data. In most cases, operations are led (or at least coordinated) by high-level government organizations and, in the case of North Korea at least, the bounty is used to fund weapons programs.[i] Cyber weapons and cyberattacks are neither new nor exclusively a tool of smaller states, but they are powerful instruments in the hand of smaller states and groups as they "level the battlefield" for disruption: they can inflict great damage without achieving perfection or building an expensive conventional weapons system.[j] Cyberattacks are successful not only because of the chaos they sow, but also because their attribution is easy to hide; clever perpetrators can easily mask their identity as an adversary. Unlike traditional terrorist attacks, few groups claim responsibility after the use of a cyber weapon.[k] As sophistication and central coordination increase, especially within intelligence units of countries, some forecast an "arms race in cyber" to develop over the coming years.[l]

Notes: a. "Half of All Violent Deaths Involve Small Arms and Light Weapons," *UN News*, February 5, 2020.

b. Elizabeth Landau, "How Glowing Bacteria in the Dirt May One Day Save Lives," *New York Times*, June 21, 2021.

c. "Landmine Monitor 2020: Major Findings," International Campaign to Ban Landmines and Convention on Cluster Munitions, November 12, 2020.

d. Paul Bracken, *The Second Nuclear Age: Strategy, Danger, and the New Power Politics* (New York: Times Books, 2012).

e. Eleanor Albert, "North Korea's Military Capabilities," *Council on Foreign Relations Backgrounder*, November 16, 2020.

f. Ibid.

g. Robert Burns, "Pentagon Rattled by China's Military Push," *AP*, November 5, 2021.

h. Ibid.

i. Ed Caesar, "The Incredible Rise of North Korea's Hacking Army," *The New Yorker*, April 19, 2021.

j. Sue Halpern, "Should the U.S. Expect an Iranian Cyberattack?" *The New Yorker*, January 6, 2020.

k. Ibid.; Caesar, "The Incredible Rise of North Korea's Hacking Army."

l. Nicole Perlroth, "How China Transformed into a Prime Cyber Threat to the U.S.," *New York Times*, July 19, 2021.

likely to devote a world tour to building more toilets around the world, the construction of simple latrine systems could go a long way toward curbing unnecessary deaths from dehydration, as well as cholera and typhoid fever. The United Nations reports that 4.2 billion people, more than half of the world's population, live without access to safely managed sanitation, such as septic systems and waste treatment plants.[48]

Health crises, acute as well as on-going, demonstrate the world's deepening interdependence in at least two very stark ways: first, diseases cross increasingly porous borders without consideration of economic, political, or other status, even if the impact of diseases may vary according to income level or other factors. Second, because health concerns are rarely isolated phenomena, sustainable responses to disease and public health challenges require the coordinated response of multiple actors, including state and nonstate alike.

For example, the dramatic global increase in the incidence of dengue fever in recent decades is due to not only explosive outbreaks of the disease, but also its spread into new areas. Half of the world's population is now at risk of this disease, which is spread by mosquitoes. Its spread and treatment have, like so many other issues, been complicated by the Covid pandemic, especially since dengue fever symptoms are quite similar to Covid. Surges of dengue fever in Sri Lanka and Bangladesh overwhelmed their overburdened hospital systems, and dengue remains endemic in India, Nepal, and Pakistan, as well as much of Latin and South America, including Brazil, Venezuela, Peru, and Mexico.[49]

In a vicious circle, these are diseases of poverty and causes of poverty; the UN and others have long drawn an explicit link between financial well-being and health. For example, economic and environmental pressures are contributing to the emergence of resistant strains of malaria, as well as to the surfacing of new diseases such as the West Nile virus and Ebola. Austerity has contributed to rapid urbanization, which means that health workers must deal with a host of public health nightmares—just as the budget cuts often necessitated by austerity have left them profoundly ill-equipped to deal with these problems. Total healthcare spending per capita in the Democratic Republic of Congo in 2018 was $18. In Nepal, it was $58. Of our case studies, Mexico, at $520 per capita, had the highest healthcare expenditure in 2018, while China spent $501, Egypt spent $126, and Nigeria allotted $84, the lowest per capita among our cases.[50]

While Covid has justifiably grabbed the lion's share of our recent attention, the world has faced other major public health threats. In addition to coronavirus, there have been the AIDS (acquired immunodeficiency syndrome) pandemic, severe acute respiratory syndrome (SARS), Middle East respiratory syndrome (MERS), Ebola, avian influenza, and swine flu. For many decades, we have known of the potential for these events to significantly disrupt life in every country of the world. And scientists have long warned of the potential for diseases to transform from epidemic potential—that is, one that spreads rapidly to a large population—to pandemic disease, in which an infectious disease impacts a high percentage of the population across a significant portion of the planet.

The AIDS pandemic continues to exact an enormous toll around the globe, and has especially hit the global south. The world has been living with AIDS and the virus that causes it, HIV, since 1981. AIDS has claimed at least 36 million lives (with an additional approximately 38 million people currently living with the disease). These data include approximately 1.8 million children under the age of fifteen.[51] Even prior to the public health setbacks of Covid, the AIDS pandemic was expanding in Eastern Europe, Central Asia, the Middle East, and North Africa.[52] The United Nations created an agency devoted entirely to the problem, and in 2000, the Security Council formally labeled AIDS a threat to international peace and security. Progress has been made, though, as the numbers of new HIV infections and deaths from AIDS are falling globally, down significantly since the peak of the epidemic in 2004.[53] The emphasis in AIDS eradication by 2030, one of the targets included within the Sustainable Development Goals, requires a redoubling of efforts, especially in light of the disruptions caused by Covid. The UN General Assembly framed AIDS as an "epidemic of inequalities," highlighting its eradication as a "prerequisite and a result of implementing the SDGs.[54] To accomplish this critical task, significant gains must be made in access to medicines and prevention.

Even though there remains no cure for AIDS, prevention strategies, antiretroviral treatments, and pre-exposure prophylaxis medications have prolonged the lives of those living with the disease and also provided protection against contracting HIV among vulnerable populations. Yet, the limited availability of affordable medicines and lack of access to testing and treatment remain barriers. For example, even though 26 million people around the world receive lifesaving antiretroviral treatments, at one point less than 1 percent of people living with HIV in lower- and middle-income countries had access.[55]

We of course didn't realize it at the time but, in 2003, the outbreak of SARS became an early test of global plans that were developed to respond to an infectious pandemic disease. This mystery illness, which presented as a flulike condition, was first discovered in Vietnam, and was caused by a coronavirus similar to that which causes Covid. Within two weeks of the initial diagnosis following the death of a Toronto man, the World Health Organization issued a global alert. The outbreak had actually begun two months earlier in one of China's southern provinces, and the epicenter of the disease was one of Hong Kong's major hotels where a Chinese doctor who had treated some of the earlier cases fell ill. Because of the port city's status as a major transit point in Asia, and the rapidity with which cases spread from Asia to North America, the response by the WHO and governments was swift—regulating air travel, monitoring healthcare workers, and quarantining anyone believed to be a carrier of the virus. In pictures that would foreshadow the Covid pandemic nearly twenty years later, global media reports and social media were filled with stark images of people across multiple continents with ventilated masks covering their mouths and noses. In the end, these efforts to control the global transmission of SARS were successful. DNA analysis quickly uncovered the genetic code of the disease, and its spread was limited—even though it claimed approximately 770 lives globally before the respiratory disease was contained by late 2004.

The proximity of human and animal populations is of particular concern to the spread of disease among human populations, as well as the mutation of dangerous strains of illnesses. One of the many strains of the influenza virus includes "bird flu," which was directly transmitted from birds to humans in

Hong Kong in 1997, spreading throughout Asia. In just two years, human infections multiplied, hitting Vietnam, Cambodia, Thailand, Indonesia, Turkey, Azerbaijan, Egypt, and Djibouti, with outbreaks among poultry populations in many other countries. Concerns about this particular virus, scientifically known as H5N1 for the combination of two specific proteins appearing on its surface, surround its reach within the poultry population (it had already caused the largest poultry outbreak on record, devastating many local economies) and its ability to mutate and become more virulent. H5N1 has long been feared to be a strain with pandemic potential because of the virus's ability to adapt and become contagious among humans, who lack any natural immunity to the disease. The H1N1 (also known as "swine flu") pandemic in 2009 reignited this debate, even if, in the end, that particular strain did not become the crisis many feared.

In 2014, the Ebola virus provided many painful lessons in the need for disease surveillance, clearer communication, better understanding of cultural practices (especially burial practices), and coordinated responses. The disease spiraled out of control—raging especially in Guinea, Liberia, and Sierra Leone—not because of accumulated flaws in the global health system, but because of the absence of "a system at all," according to one observer.[56] The outbreak—which hit the healthcare worker and first responder communities especially hard, revealed glaring gaps between the aspirations of global health officials and the realities of controlling infectious diseases.[57] One official described the response as "using a pea shooter against a raging elephant."[58] More than 10,000 lives were lost; even as 3,000 US military personnel were sent to West Africa to assist with hospital construction and treatment, terrible flaws in emergency response were evident.

A mosquito-borne virus was the world's next test. The Zika virus, which was first detected in Africa in the late 1940s and for which there remains no cure, led to an outbreak of babies born with severely under-developed brains. As the WHO forecast Zika's likely spread across nearly all of the Americas, the capacity of regional and global response systems to deal with rapidly changing health epidemics was tested. But by the end of 2016, the international public health emergency was declared over, with the UN and affiliated agencies calling for sustained efforts to continue to address the disease. Nevertheless, there was serious discussion about delaying or relocating the Rio Olympic Games, despite the WHO's assurances of safety (some delegations from wealthier countries, including South Korea, sported specially made suits enhanced with natural mosquito repellant).

Each of these disease outbreaks demonstrates the classic struggle between haves and have-nots. Similar to many of the issues that we have examined in this book, there are few simple solutions. Although many efforts have been undertaken at the global level, most have not yet been effectively implemented on the ground. For example, a global program launched in 1988 to completely eradicate polio through a wide-reaching oral vaccination plan cosponsored by the WHO has been stalled by paucity of medical professionals in needed areas, lack of political will to implement national programs, and Covid. Part of the challenge is related to a basic public health weakness: the absence of reliable forms of waste management. Earlier versions of the live polio virus, used in the oral vaccine, can be shed through the feces and replicate. Complicating matters further is that most children born after 2016 have no immunity to this strain because it was believed to be on the verge of elimination and no longer was included in the main oral vaccine they would have received.[59] During Covid, vaccination campaigns were halted in most places as part of lockdown requirements, perhaps leaving as many as 80 million children unprotected.[60] And, as the Taliban increased their presence in Afghanistan and Pakistan, even prior to Covid they barred door-to-door vaccination drives, leading to an increase in cases in Taliban-controlled regions of Afghanistan and Pakistan. These vaccination bans, among some of the least-served populations within the countries, impede vaccination against other diseases, such as measles and pneumonia.

Each disease outbreak, whether localized, epidemic, or pandemic in nature, reveals difficult truths about public health and the differentiated capacity of countries and regions to respond. We know that valid, reliable testing for infection is key. Once treatments, medicines, and proactive vaccines are available, the challenges of distribution mount. The inequitable allocation of Covid vaccines showed, in the starkest of terms, inequity in public health access. COVID-19 Vaccines Global Access (COVAX) was created as a joint venture between the WHO, the Center for Epidemic Preparedness and Innovation, the Global Alliance for Vaccines and Immunization (GAVI), and UNICEF. Established in April 2020, nearly nine months before vaccines to counter Covid became available, the goals of COVAX were to accelerate the development and manufacturing of Covid vaccines, and to set up a structure to prepurchase and globally distribute vaccines in the most equitable way possible. Despite pledges of solidarity and lessons learned, the vast majority of vaccines administered at the height of the pandemic went to wealthy states, with low-income countries receiving only 0.2 percent of vaccine doses.[61] COVAX struggled to meet organizers' stated promise of having at least 20 percent of everyone in the world vaccinated against Covid, with wealthy states having purchased large portions of the vaccine (even as leaders in some of these countries struggled to convince their own populations to accept it).[62] Perhaps, a clearer way to visualize the discrepancy is this: in the spring of 2021, in high-income countries, almost 1 in 4 people received a vaccine. In low-income countries, it was 1 in more than 500.[63] This produces a new form of stratification, which some term "immunity inequality," in which the wealthiest people have access to vaccines that the rest of the world lacks.[64] In a pointed play on President Joe Biden's catch phrase "build back better," the director of the International Labour Organization quipped, "We are building back worse at least as looked at from the perspective of the developing world."[65]

Many of the struggles the world witnessed during the Covid pandemic were challenges that had been clearly identified before. These include testing (especially problematic in the cases of asymptomatic carriers, as well as diseases with accompanying social taboos), overcoming disinformation, as well as socioeconomic barriers to education, treatment, and awareness. For example, if state leaders and NGOs are indeed committed to providing treatment to all who need it, a commitment that is questionable at best, another pitfall emerges: How will governments of the developing world provide for those so-called medical pensioners whose life is prolonged by the regular delivery of drugs and support facilities? In many cases, a health infrastructure must be built where none exists. In the worst cases, as we discussed with the resurgence of polio, the absence of water projects, reliable sanitation systems, and even the most basic institutions, including schools and clinics, makes simple tasks gargantuan. Expensive laboratory work must be done on a continual basis to monitor this complicated regimen of drugs. Otherwise, it is feared that drug-resistant strains will develop, as they have for malaria and tuberculosis.

The availability of supplies for treatment and prevention becomes a huge challenge. Medical oxygen, perceived as a staple in most healthcare facilities around the world, became a hot commodity during the Covid pandemic, even though it is a natural element that makes up 21 percent of the world's atmosphere. Lethal shortages of medical-grade oxygen, captured, purified, and prepared for bulk delivery, broke out all around the world, including in the United States, but were most potent in Brazil, Mexico, and India, where it was estimated that half of the unmet need could be found, even though India is a major producer of compressed oxygen.[66] In a single hospital in the capital, New Delhi, on one night alone, more than twenty people died because the hospital's supply of oxygen had been depleted.[67] The global shortage of ventilators, machinery that helps pump oxygen into the lungs of individuals with compromised respiratory systems, was but one critical weakness observed in the early stages of the Covid pandemic. Even though ten African countries lacked ventilators at the beginning of Covid in early 2020, possible chronic shortages in supplies including soap, clean water, masks, and medical oxygen were likely far more consequential: it is estimated that only 15 percent of sub-Saharan Africans had access to basic handwashing facilities in 2015, with some countries experiencing far worse shortages.[68] Political crises, such as the Taliban's takeover of Afghanistan or the instability in Myanmar after the coup, exacerbate these challenges. Shortly after the military took over governance in Myanmar in 2021, cases exploded, raising the possibility that the state could become a superspreader of Covid in the midst of one of the worst-affected regions of the world.[69]

Even when affordable, accessible treatments exist, cures remain elusive. And they do nothing to prevent transmission of the disease. Prevention and education remain critical in this process, despite their expense, in direct and indirect financial terms. But the failure to treat the disease will lead to even higher costs that we cannot even begin to tabulate. The first step to treatment and prevention is awareness of one's infection, which is why some of the most successful public health programs have promoted simple, confidential testing—to encourage quick treatment and also to decrease the likelihood of infecting others. To prevent spread, we know it is crucial to begin testing before individuals become symptomatic. None of this is simple. When the Covid pandemic began, only two of Africa's fifty-four states had laboratories to test for the disease, and even though this increased quickly, distribution has been extremely uneven, with a few countries carrying out the lion's share of reliable testing, which requires molecular testing capacity for accurate diagnoses.[70] In Peru, which at one point had the highest per capita death toll from Covid in the world, the lack of sufficient testing made treatment and accurate death toll reporting nearly impossible.[71] But we need to be careful about making generalizations, as the capacity and response varied greatly. During the first summer of the Covid pandemic, Rwanda set an example of how to prevent and contain the outbreak, employing testing, quarantine, and contact tracing lessons learned from their response to HIV, even using human-sized robots to take patients' temperatures and deliver supplies. As one news source provocatively claimed, Rwanda, clearly categorized as a low-income country, handled Covid "better than Ohio," stating that other countries should emulate its experience.[72]

Clearly, none of these issues can be understood in isolation. Health is a multifaceted aspect of daily living, directly impacted by socioeconomic status, opportunities for education and employment, and interconnected social and political realities, among other factors. Scientists tell us that many of the factors related to environmental challenges (especially deforestation and human encroachment on wildlife habitats) are making diseases worse, especially by increasing the opportunity for viruses to jump from animal to human populations.[73]

Should we be surprised that it took a global pandemic, claiming millions of lives and disrupting daily life around the world, to again realize the porous nature of borders and the difficulty individual countries have in coming to grips with an infectious disease? In the case of AIDS, many argued that it was only after scientists emphasized the security and political implications of the continued spread of disease—rather than "simply" a humanitarian catastrophe—that political leaders took notice.[74] National security requires health security. And, as we have discussed, the broader aim of human security requires attention to the root causes of challenges, including poverty, political disenfranchisement, and corruption. As much as we can look back on our prior disease outbreaks and say, with the advantages of hindsight, that we should have seen something like Covid coming, we also need to accept the fact that this will not be the last pandemic, perhaps even in our lifetimes. Are we better prepared to respond to the next one? What can (and will) we do differently?

Conclusions: Global Capacity for Response

What are the advantages of responses by global or regional actors? Multilateral responses can give less powerful countries a stronger voice because they can find strength in numbers. In the United Nations, for example, two-thirds of all member states are developing countries. Although there are limits to what individual countries can achieve, as we have seen, the sheer number of developing countries represented in the UN provides a channel for diplomatic influence that they cannot find elsewhere. Multilateral efforts can also compel action when individual states either will not or cannot comply, due largely to financial constraints. Multilateralism can also promote an internationally acceptable setting in which nations can more freely negotiate in an atmosphere of compromise and diplomacy, which would be more difficult to achieve with individual states.

Yet, an "international community" seems to exist more in symbol than reality, and, as the Secretary-General himself has stated, we seem more divided than ever, moving in the wrong direction on key issues like climate change and other longer-term challenges that are being ignored in favor of shorter-term gain by a few.[75] Contrary to the exasperated claims of some, we do not have a world government, nor are we close to achieving one. The coordinated response of major powers is about as close as we have come to a singular community in action, and this response has been limited. Much of the world, especially the powerful countries, continues to frame matters in terms of major powers and large countries, as has been evidenced in more than one of the issues discussed in this chapter.

What differences exist between regional and global responses? Because of the limited scope and number of actors, it may be easier to build consensus for action within a regional context, although this is not always the case. For global responses, consensus (or at least verification of the absence of opposition) takes more time to craft. For some regions, assembling an intervening force would be difficult, because of historical or contemporary problems that make no one trustworthy. The larger organizations bring more economies of scale and more people to the table, but they are also more bureaucratically cumbersome—a common criticism of the United Nations—and it is easier in the larger global organizations to leave out voices of the disenfranchised and less powerful. Or, even if the opportunity to speak and participate is present, many of the global south countries feel they still have no teeth in these institutions. Regional organizations and specialized NGOs overcome some of these problems of size, but they can also lack influence and might. Yet, even international organizations such as the United Nations do not have compelling force; more powerful countries can bypass the UN if they feel their sovereignty would be impeded. One example of such diversion was the action of the North Atlantic Treaty Organization in Kosovo taken on behalf of the Albanian Serbs: the US-led coalition bypassed the Security Council because China and Russia would have vetoed the measure as an unwanted and unwarranted intrusion of state sovereignty, though the UN did later take on a role, providing a Security Council resolution and sanctioning a peacekeeping force.

Yet, an overarching concern for the global south, in the face of much multilateral activity, is the responsiveness of such forces to the needs and concerns of the less powerful. Organizations, large and small, make decisions affecting individuals, who have little or no impact on the process. The need to include disparate, less powerful voices is especially magnified at higher levels. While the problems inherent in this enterprise have been brought to our attention through street demonstrations against the World Bank and the International Monetary Fund, the same is true with the United Nations and nongovernmental organizations that take action in the name of the people. How to make such organizations more representative and more accountable will remain a huge task for the future. If these institutions are perceived to be overtly partisan, they will lose their legitimacy and ability to act. Multilateral institutions are favored, because they seemingly prevent (or at least limit) the impulse for self-interest or self-delusion. But they are problematic because, in the search for consensus, they can sit idly by while massacres, such as those in Darfur, take place. Faced with changing conceptions of sovereignty and global action, many speak of a forthcoming "borderless world." Yet, from the global south it appears that some borders are stronger than ever.

Notes

1. Quoted in Tim McDonnell, "The Refugees the World Barely Pays Attention To," NPR, June 20, 2018.

2. "Quotation of the Day: Village Fought Off Virus, but Neighbors Didn't. It's a Bad Sign for India," *New York Times,* July 11, 2021.

3. United Nations, "World Population Projected to Reach 9.8 Billion in 2050, and 11.2 Billion in 2100—Says UN," United Nations Department of Public Information, June 21, 2021.

4. Vanda Felbab-Brown and Elisa Norio, "Global Warming, Fires, and Crime in Mexico and Beyond," Brookings Institution, September 28, 2020.

5. Gwen Aviles and Mary Murray, "Mexico City's Residents Are Engulfed in a Thick Haze of Air Pollution," *NBC News,* May 14, 2019.

6. "Fact-Checking the US and China on Climate and Environment," *BBC News,* November 13, 2020.

7. "9 out of 10 People Worldwide Breathe Polluted Air, but More Countries Are Taking Action," World Health Organization, May 2, 2018.

8. World Economic Forum, "Will Clean Air Become a New Global Currency?" July 28, 2021.

9. Julia Rosen, "The Science of Climate Change Explained: Facts, Evidence and Proof," *New York Times,* May 12, 2021. Rosen, who holds a PhD in geology, asserts that more than 90 percent of climate scientists (and 97 percent of those scientists who are actively publishing), as well as major scientific associations, from NASA to the World Meteorological Organization, "agree that the planet is warming and that humans are the primary cause."

10. "Climate Change Hit Poorest Countries Hardest in 2019," *Deutsche Welle,* January 25, 2021.

11. Robinson Meyer, "Is Hope Possible After the Paris Agreement?" *The Atlantic,* December 12, 2015.

12. Justin Worland, "How Climate Change Unfairly Burdens Poorer Countries," *Time,* February 5, 2016.

13. United Nations, "World Water Day 2021," n.d.

14. Tim McDonnell, "Report: There's a Growing Water Crisis in the Global South," NPR, August 13, 2019.

15. Christopher Flavelle, "Climate Change Could Cut World Economy by $23 Trillion in 2050, Insurance Giant Warns," *New York Times,* April 22, 2021.

16. Somini Sengupta, "Global Wealth Gap Would Be Smaller Today Without Climate Change, Study Finds," *New York Times,* April 22, 2019.

17. Damian Kahya, "Global Warming Talks Just Hot Air?" *BBC News,* December 3, 2010.

18. Meyer, "Is Hope Possible After the Paris Agreement?"

19. Climate activist network Avaaz, spoofing the official tagline of the Naples meeting of the G-20, which was "People, Planet, Prosperity." Quoted in Gavin Jones, "G20 Fails to Agree on Climate Goals in Communique," *Reuters,* July 23, 2021.

20. Tanguy Gahouma-Bekale of Gabon, quoted in Fiona Harvey, "Move Faster to Cut Emissions, Developing World Tells Rich Nations," *The Guardian,* July 15, 2021.

21. Sean Fleming, "This Is the Global Refugee Situation, in Numbers," World Economic Forum, June 18, 2021.

22. "UNHCR: World Leaders Must Act to Reverse the Trend of Soaring Displacement," UN High Commission for Refugees (UNHCR), June 18, 2021.

23. "Climate Change and Disaster Displacement," UNHCR, n.d.

24. Ibid.

25. UNHCR, "Refugee Data Finder," June 18, 2021.

26. UNHCR, *Global Trends in Forced Displacement: 2020,* 2021; "UNHCR: World Leaders Must Act," UNHCR. In 2020, Turkey hosted 3.7 million displaced people; the next highest host country was Colombia, with 1.7 million; "UN Refugee Agency Releases 2022 Resettlement Needs," UNHCR, June 23, 2021.

27. *World Cities Report 2020: The Value of Sustainable Urbanization,* United Nations Human Settlements Programme (UN-Habitat), 2021.

28. "The Age of Megacities," *National Geographic,* April 27, 2021.

29. Ibid.

30. *GRID 2021 (Global Report on Internal Displacement),* International Displacement Monitoring Center, 2021, p. 11; Somini Sengupta, "Even amid a Pandemic, More Than 40 Million People Fled Their Homes," *New York Times,* May 20, 2021.

31. Fleming, "This Is the Global Refugee Situation, in Numbers."

32. *GRID 2021,* p. 6.

33. "Missing Migrants Project," International Organization for Migration, n.d.

34. Seth Harp, "The Coyote Cartel," *Rolling Stone,* June 14, 2021.

35. Ibid.

36. Ibid.

37. Sébastien Roblin, "Israel Is Sending Robots with Machine Guns to the Gaza Border," *The Daily Beast,* June 25, 2021.

38. "Growth of International Migration Slowed by 27%, or 2 Million Migrants, Due to COVID-19, Says UN," United Nations Department of Economic and Social Affairs, January 15, 2021.

39. Hwaida Saad, "A 6-Year-Old Was Chained and Hungry in a Syrian Camp. Then She Died," *New York Times,* May 30, 2021.

40. "Worldwide, Nearly 33 Million Children Have Been Forcibly Displaced at the End of 2019," UNICEF, April 2021.

41. Saad, "A 6-Year-Old Was Chained and Hungry in a Syrian Camp."

42. Elizabeth Ferris, "When Refugee Displacement Drags On, Is Self-Reliance the Answer?" Brookings Institution, June 19, 2018; Serena Parekh, "Reframing the Refugee Crisis from Rescue to Interconnection," *Ethics and Global Politics* 13 (February 2020), pp. 21–32.

43. "UN Refugee Agency Releases 2022 Resettlement Needs," UNHCR, June 23, 2021.

44. Mariam Traore Chazalnoel, a climate expert at the UN International Organization for Migration, quoted in McDonnell, "The Refugees the World Barely Pays Attention To."

45. Adia Benton, "COVID-19 in Ebola's Wake: Safe Haven in Sierra Leone?" *Current History* 120, no. 826 (May 2021), pp. 167–171; Abraar Karan, "Opinion: It's Time to End the Colonial Mindset in Global Health," NPR, December 30, 2019; Eugene T. Richardson, *Epidemic Illusions: On the Coloniality of Global Public Health* (Cambridge: MIT Press, 2020).

46. Marine Al Dahdah, "From Ghana to India, Saving the Global South's Mothers with a Digital Solution," *Global Policy* 12, no. 6 (July 2021), p. 52.

47. "This Is How We Can Prevent One of the Biggest Killers of Children Worldwide," World Economic Forum, August 22, 2019.

48. Dave Davies, "Is it Possible to 'Transform the Toilet'?" NPR, June 30, 2021.

49. Melinda Wenner Moyer, "'A Fearless Virus Hunter' Tackles a Coronavirus Mystery in Children," *New York Times,* September 9, 2020; Aayna Wipulasena and Saif Hasnat, "A Surge in Dengue Cases Adds to the Hospital Burden in Covid-Racked South Asia," *New York Times,* August 10, 2021.

50. World Bank, "Health Expenditure per Capita," 2021. Average spending globally was $1,111, and the United States spent $10,623.

51. "The Global HIV/AIDS Epidemic," Fact Sheet: Global Health Policy, Kaiser Family Foundation, March 2, 2021.

52. Chris Beyrer, "A Pandemic Anniversary: 40 Years of HIV/AIDS," *The Lancet,* June 1, 2021.

53. "Step Up HIV Fight, to End AIDS 'Epidemic of Inequalities' by 2030," *UN News,* June 8, 2021; "Fact Sheet 2021," Joint United Nations Programme on HIV/AIDS (UNAIDS), n.d.

54. "Step Up HIV Fight," *UN News.*

55. "Lessons from Experience with HIV Invaluable for Response to COVID-19, Deputy Secretary-General Says, at Opening of High-Level Meeting," UN press release, June 8, 2021.

56. Olsa Khazan, "How to Prevent the Next Ebola," *The Atlantic,* March 18, 2015.

57. Lena Sun, Brady Dennis, Lenny Bernstein, and Joel Achenbach, "Out of Control: How the World's Health Organizations Failed to Stop the Ebola Disaster," *Washington Post,* October 4, 2014.

58. Ibid.

59. Jason Beaubien, "The Campaign to Wipe Out Polio Was Going Really Well . . . Until It Wasn't," NPR, October 30, 2020.

60. Ibid.

61. "Low-Income Countries Have Received Just 0.2 per Cent of All COVID-19 Shots Given," *UN News,* April 9, 2021.

62. Jason Beaubien, "What Is This COVAX Program That the U.S. Is Pouring Millions of Vaccines Into?" NPR, May 19, 2021.

63. "Low-Income Countries Have Received Just 0.2 per Cent," *UN News.*

64. Bill and Melinda Gates, "The Year Global Health Went Local," *Gates Notes,* January 27, 2021.

65. Nick Cuming-Bruce, "Unequal Vaccine Access Is Widening the Global Economic Gap, a U.N. Agency Says," *New York Times,* October 27, 2021.

66. Richard Pérez-Peña, "Why Some Hospitals Lack the Oxygen to Keep Patients Alive," *New York Times,* May 4, 2021; Jeffrey Gettleman, Emily Schmall, Suhasini Raj, and Hari Kumar, "The Night the Oxygen Ran Out," *New York Times,* June 28, 2021.

67. Gettleman et al., "The Night the Oxygen Ran Out."

68. Ruth Maclean and Simon Marks, "10 African Countries Have No Ventilators. That's Only Part of the Problem," *New York Times,* April 18, 2020.

69. Jaclyn Diaz, "Southeast Asian Countries Struggle to Contain a Devastating Third Wave of COVID-19," NPR, July 19, 2021.

70. Carley Petesch, "Increased Testing Needed as Africa Sees Rise in Virus Cases," *AP News,* December 31, 2020.

71. Jaclyn Diaz, "Peruvian Officials More Than Double COVID Death Toll, Saying They Undercounted," NPR, June 1, 2021.

72. "Why Rwanda Is Doing Better Than Ohio When It Comes to Controlling COVID-19," NPR, July 15, 2020.

73. Victoria Gill, "Coronavirus: This Is Not the Last Pandemic," *BBC News,* June 6, 2020.

74. Geoffrey Cowley, "The Life of a Virus Hunter," *Newsweek,* May 15, 2006, p. 63.

75. "UN Chief: World Is at 'Pivotal Moment' and Must Avert Crises," *PBS Newshour,* September 11, 2021.

17

The Global South and the United States: Friends or Foes?

> Today, the world doesn't care about "America First" or "America is Back." If rationality prevails in the minds of the decision-makers, they have to realize that nations' perseverance is stronger than the power of the superpowers.
>
> —*Iranian president Ebrahim Raisi, in his first speech to the UN General Assembly, September 2021*[1]

> Events showed that the US has no moral right to punish another nation under the guise of upholding democracy.
>
> —*Zimbabwean president Emmerson Mnangagwa, reflecting on the January 2021 siege of the US Capitol*[2]

Leaders are noticed. As the leading military, economic, and political power in the world, the United States possesses great influence and great responsibility. In responding to global problems, the role of the United States is critical, but certainly not benign. Many American students are surprised to hear that the United States is viewed with both respect and contempt beyond its borders. Some have a difficult time seeing that actions of the United States are viewed as threatening to many, because Americans tend to believe that their country's actions are taken in the name of some larger, more noble cause. Yet, it is important to remember that others take actions, some of which we deem irresponsible or even reprehensible, with seemingly good motivations as well.

After the collapse of the Soviet Union and the end of the Cold War, the United States stood as the world's strongest country, the world's lone (and, some people believed, last) superpower. Some labeled the United States a "hyperpower"—"dominant or predominant in all categories."[3] Now, many are openly questioning the durability of this status, tested by economic changes, military interventions abroad, recent protectionist tendencies, as well as the Covid PANDEMIC.

Whether or not it is technically accurate, many view the United States as an empire—willing and able to exert influence and project power beyond its borders.

Sometimes, this happens in the pursuit of a worthy goal. Other times, US actionshave been less noble. For decades now as multilateralism waned and the United States increasingly justified its need to be treated differently, Washington's power projection and execution of economic, political, and military power lent evidence to this title. The pursuit of the so-called forever wars[4]—most overtly in Afghanistan and Iraq—as well as US dominance in economic matters, mimicked the imperial overstretch observed long ago, in the eyes of many.

Take weapons, for example. While the United States champions hard-won arms accords aimed at promoting DETERRENCE, Washington has a record of leaving (or breaking) agreements when they no longer fit its needs. This is not a recent development. US leaders rejected international protocols on germ warfare and demanded amendments to an accord on the illegal sale of small arms. President Bill Clinton, facing pressure from the Pentagon, refused to sign the Ottawa Treaty outlawing landmines (ostensibly because an exception for the Korean peninsula was not granted). In 1999, the US Senate rejected the Nuclear Test Ban Treaty because—even though US leaders have made clear that they would like the rest of the world to halt weapons development—they don't want to have their own hands tied. President George W. Bush discarded the 1972 Biological Weapons Draft Protocol (which 143 countries, including the United States, had ratified), and opposed international efforts to limit the trade in small arms. US withdrawal from the landmark 1972 Anti-Ballistic Missile (ABM) Treaty in 2002, as well as its withdrawal from the Intermediate-Range Nuclear Forces Treaty in 2019, in the eyes of many, ended the United States' ability to legitimately speak about reducing the spread of dangerous weapons. Despite assurances from the International Atomic Energy Agency that Iran remained in compliance with the JCPOA, Donald Trump abandoned the 2015 agreement, restoring harsh unilateral sanctions. "Ever since the end of the Cold War, the United States as the world's most powerful state has frequently sought one-sided advantages."[5] It is more difficult to lead by example if one keeps breaking the rules that others are obliged to follow.

Many perceive some US actions as bullying. One case in point would be US-Cuban ties. The US embargo against Cuba, in place since 1962, has been the most enduring trade limitation in modern history. The embargo has become even more biting as Cuba's digital civil society and online engagement explode in the 2020s—citizens are blocked from cloud services, social media managers, video calling, and more, not due to the communist government's censorship, but because of the "boomerang" effect of US laws that restrict product use in Cuba.[6] Every year since 1992, the UNITED NATIONS GENERAL ASSEMBLY has overwhelmingly passed a nonbinding resolution condemning the embargo, with few countries siding with the United States. During the 2021 vote, when delegates crafted a humanitarian appeal in the midst of the Covid pandemic, Israel was the only state to vote with the United States, with 184 countries voting for the repeal (Brazil, Colombia, and Ukraine abstained).[7] The US perspective has been that the United States will trade with Cuba after it shows signs of political reform. Even after former president Barack Obama signed an executive order lifting many of the trade limits on Cuba (as part of the normalization of US-Cuban ties that began in 2014), restrictions remained in place. Former president Trump took a tough line toward Havana, returning many sanctions that had been lifted by Obama and, in his final days in office, again listed Cuba as a sponsor of state terrorism, reinstating some prior sanctions, which President Joe Biden has yet to remove. As an editorial in *Newsweek* argued, "The embargo is the perfect example used by anti-Americans everywhere to expose the hypocrisy of a superpower that punishes a small island while cozying to dictators elsewhere."[8]

The Limits of Strength

The perspective beyond US borders, though, is that the United States does not have the authority to tell other countries with whom they should be conducting business. US sanctions against Iran for the nuclear weapons program, originally intended to strengthen global sanctions enacted by the UNITED NATIONS SECURITY COUNCIL in 2010, received mixed responses. Even after the UN lifted sanctions against Iran in January 2016, US sanctions continued, to the consternation of many around the world (including allies in the global north).[9] Sanctions, as a form of economic coercion, have become the favored tool of recent US administrations, deployed as a powerful way of enforcing Washington's priorities. It's one thing for Washington to decide to use an economic tool to enforce a policy or value preference with regard to a country—as it has done with Cuba, Russia, North Korea, Venezuela, and Zimbabwe, among others. But for many of these economic levers, which analysts contend are increasingly unsuccessful at achieving their policy aim, "secondary sanctions" are applied against other sovereign countries (and companies) that trade with US-sanctioned countries.[10] These—and other—actions invite claims from countries that the United States is invoking EXTRATERRITORIALITY, or the attempt to impose one's rules and laws outside of one's own sovereign territory.

The criticism expands well beyond US trade interests. A prison camp built more than twenty years ago on contested US territory in Cuba (Guantánamo Bay Naval Base) has evoked similar calls. It began housing alleged terrorists in 2002, riling human rights activists around the world and propelling many of those held into legal limbo. The names and nationalities of the detainees were not released until 2006, after a Freedom of Information Act request was filed by media outlets. It was five years after the camp opened, when the US Supreme Court branded the detention unconstitutional, that the George W. Bush administration even afforded Geneva Convention protections to detainees (which, as you may remember from Chapter 15, define the rights of wartime prisoners). Obama's record on Guantánamo was not much better. Despite the executive order (issued on his second day in office) to shut down the detention camp within one year, he left office in 2017 with seventy-six prisoners in legal limbo as they were unable to be returned home and barred (by Congress) from being taken to the United States for trial. Then, as a candidate, Trump vowed to expand the facility and load it up "with bad dudes," possibly even detaining American citizens accused of terrorism (even though such a move would violate US law).[11] To many outside of the United States, these pledges sounded like forms of vigilante justice. As of late 2021, the United States continues to hold thirty-nine detainees, twelve of whom have been cleared for release, pending security agreements.[12] Accounts of torture by CIA agents and operatives at

Guantánamo Bay, as well as in secretive "black sites" (clandestine interrogation sites) around the world have created "a stain on the moral fiber of America," according to a US Navy captain who led a jury in a war crimes court.[13]

These actions lead some to perceive the United States as a government that abides by laws only when it is useful, while attempting to force others to follow US laws and policies. In this sense, many countries of the world believe that the United States holds an EXCEPTIONALIST view of its place in the world. The examples are plentiful and stretch across all recent presidential administrations. The United States condemned the Iraqi invasion of Kuwait in 1990, yet the same US leaders had ordered the invasion of Panama in 1989 to capture President Manuel Noriega and try him for criminal drug operations in the United States. The United States long produced the most greenhouse emissions of any other country in the world (surpassed by China in 2006), yet US presidents have sought exceptions from international environmental treaties designed to combat these ills. The lack of US support for the INTERNATIONAL CRIMINAL COURT, including the demand that US military personnel be exempt from its jurisdiction, is yet another case in point. Out of concern that US service personnel would be targeted by the ICC, the US Congress passed the American Service-Members' Protection Act that requires the US government to cut off financial assistance to countries that refuse to commit to not surrender US personnel to the ICC. As the ICC continues to probe potential war crimes during the twenty-year war in Afghanistan, its leader announced, in September 2021, that US personnel would be excluded from their investigation and prosecution.[14] Even if these policies do not convey a growing sense of exceptionalism or even isolationism, as some claim, there has been a clear increase in US unilateralism—long before the "America First" policies of Trump.

The United States also faces criticism for failing to provide support to international movements promoting the same rights and privileges that Americans espouse the world over, including women's rights and the rights of persons with disabilities. In 2012, the US Senate failed (by six votes) to ratify the Convention on the Rights of Persons with Disabilities, which has been in effect since 2008, even though it was modeled after the Americans with Disabilities Act and enjoyed largely bipartisan support.[15] Also, as discussed in Chapter 15, the United States is the only country to have signed, but not ratified, the Convention on the Elimination of All Forms of Discrimination Against Women. Ratification of the convention, which the US delegation helped draft in 1979, has been caught up in domestic politics and concern by some critics that UN committee members would have authority over private decisions and US laws (which they would not, due to the principle of SOVEREIGNTY). The US Senate Foreign Relations Committee even supported ratification of the convention in 2002, but the measure, which is vehemently opposed by the pro-life lobby, was never introduced to the full Senate for a vote. This not only has harmed the credibility of the United States in some circles, but it has been used by others to deny women's rights in their countries as well. As one Afghani activist testified before the US Senate Judiciary Committee, "Even in Afghanistan . . . conservative elements use this [US failure to ratify] to attack women's rights defenders. They say that if the United States believes in women's rights as a universal right, why haven't they signed on to CEDAW?"[16]

Additionally, the United States often withholds support for international organizations that conduct work seen as being in opposition to the policy goals of some interest groups in the country—even if the action is perfectly legal in other societies of the world. One example of this is the US condemnation of organizations that provide family planning or abortion services. US presidents Ronald Reagan, George H. W. Bush, George W. Bush, and Donald Trump each denied funding to any agency that viewed abortion as a policy option, describing themselves as taking a moral stance on "right to life" issues. Meanwhile, the same leaders sided with businesses to oppose international efforts to eliminate child labor. The United States refuses to sign treaties prohibiting the use of child soldiers and, until the US Supreme Court ruled the practice unconstitutional in 2005, remained one of the few countries in the world that executed juveniles. In 2018, the United States walked away from its elected seat on the Human Rights Council of the United Nations (to which it returned in 2022).[17] Months into the Covid pandemic, President Trump withdrew the United States from the World Health Organization, stopping funding and pulling US government technical advisers, accusing the WHO of being too "China-centric."[18] To many, the contradictions between US rhetoric and action are glaring.

As the world's leading power, the United States faces a paradox: it is often expected to respond, even when its leaders and citizens do not want to. In part, this is due to a history of involvement (sometimes welcomed; other times not), and, in part, this is due to the role of being perceived as the leading voice on core issues (a reality often embraced by US leaders and citizens). A paradox of power is that the lack of response—as we have seen in the muted engagement with many of the Arab Spring transitions, for example—can sometimes speak more loudly than coordinated engagement. In this view, Obama's attempts to decrease the US footprint in the Middle East after 2012 can be perceived as being as problematic as Bush's unilateral moves after September 11. Some derisively framed the "Obama Doctrine"—especially after the formal withdrawal of US forces in Iraq—as the "American retreat."[19] Even as formal US forces departed—from Iraq under Obama, from Afghanistan under Biden—the US remained a player on the scene. As one observer put it, the "notion of neutrality, for a country as powerful as the United States, is illusory."[20]

From "America First" to "America's Back"?

Since 1945, the United States has been a driving force behind many of the changes on the world stage—from the creation of the major institutions of the international financial system, to hosting the international headquarters of the United Nations, to crafting most multinational agreements on pressing global issues. Changes in its role have been long in coming (dating to the shift toward unipolar status in the early 1990s), and uneven. US leaders have attempted, in rhetoric and in action, differing visions of this role. Few will forgive Bush for the preemptive war in Iraq (2003–2011), ostensibly launched to find weapons of mass destruction (WMD) as part of the president's "war on terrorism," and belatedly framed as an effort in democracy promotion, perceived throughout much of the global south as a reinvented form of imperialism.[21] While the Bush Doctrine focused on the war on terrorism ("you're either with us or you're with the terrorists"), an Obama Doctrine, to the extent one was ever articulated, communicated a more comfortable engagement with allies and multilateral responses, but embodied a heavy dose of skepticism toward interventionism.

Human rights seemed to fall by the wayside, especially when the United States failed to characterize the Egyptian military's overthrow of democratically elected President Mohamed Morsi as a coup in 2013. Even after Human Rights Watch called it the "worst mass killing in modern Egyptian history," President Obama (and Congress) continued to provide substantial military aid to Cairo, despite the legal obligation to suspend such aid in the event of a coup.[22] He was also faulted for failing to respond after Syria violated the so-called red line and used sarin gas against its own population in 2018.[23] Asked once to define his approach, President Obama stated that the United States "remains the most powerful, wealthiest nation on Earth, but we're only one nation, and that problems that we confront, whether it's drug cartels, climate change, terrorist, you name it, can't be solved just by one country."[24]

If each US president crafts their own approach to the role of the United States in global affairs, few have been clearer than Trump. Trump grounded his foreign policies in his solid objection to the perceived multilateralism of his predecessors, pledging that he will "no longer surrender this country or its people to the false song of globalism."[25] Trump lambasted prior US foreign policies for promoting "raw deals," criticizing allies and foes alike.[26] He insulted large swaths of the global south with demeaning characterizations and travel bans. He insisted that climate change was a hoax and, early in his term announced his intention to leave the Paris Agreement on Climate Change, a move that required a year-long waiting period and did not actually take effect until November 2020.[27] He delivered on his promises to craft a new, narrower role for the United States in the world—putting domestic priorities visibly ahead of international goals—and was emulated by some of the most notorious human rights abusers in the world.[28] The initial US response to the Covid pandemic heightened this sense of America being out for itself. In what was perceived as an overt move toward isolationism, the state that rescued Europe after World War II by crafting the Marshall Plan skipped the first major teleconference of global leaders pledging contributions for coronavirus vaccines.[29] Lack of confidence in President Trump became a global phenomenon, with the highest negative sentiment coming from Mexico (89 percent "no confidence") although 58 percent of Nigerians expressed confidence in him.[30]

As Joe Biden returned to the world stage, many expected a dramatic change of approach from the former vice president (2008–2016) who was also a long-term member of the US Senate Committee on Foreign Relations (including serving multiple years as chair). In both posts, he racked up a lengthy resume of global engagement, and by the time he was elected president in 2020, he was either on a first name basis or had previously developed a successful working relationship with many world leaders. He wasted no time, for example, by restoring US membership in the WHO and signing a letter of intent to rejoin the Paris Agreement on Climate Change—on his first day in office.[31] The "return" of the United States to a more multilateral approach, though, was met with some caution and urging for humility, as the world had "gone on" once the United States abdicated prior leadership, in the words of the executive director of Greenpeace International.[32] While Biden took strong steps, including dramatically increasing the number of refugees permitted to enter the country annually, the view—spread from the global north to the global south—is concern that the United States is not reliable. Some have even suggested that perhaps the American political system is "broken," complicating alliances even in the face of perceived mutual challenges—including the degree to which China should be confronted or accommodated.[33] As this book goes to press, Biden has served as president for just over a year, and any "doctrine," if one is to be formed, is still nascent. While he has clearly staked out a major role for collaboration with allies and, at least rhetorically, is poised to challenge China, some, including Richard Haass, president of the Council on Foreign Relations, contend that President Biden is continuing Trump's "America First" policies—just in a different guise.[34] It is perhaps too soon to evaluate the degree to which this is true (and the war in Ukraine may change this even more),[35] but, from the perspective of the global south, some of the Biden administration's actions feel more familiar than not. A journalist in Cuba, reflecting on the continuation of US sanctions under Biden, lamented, "Biden hasn't shown himself to be any different from Trump. . . . What's needed is action and deeds."[36]

Post-Americanism?

Shortly after the terrorist attacks of September 11, 2001, journalist Fareed Zakaria asserted that we are moving into a "post-American world." It was his contention that, for the first time many can remember, the charge is not being led by the United States, and that the world was experiencing "tectonic power shifts" as new powers rise.[37] While the United States may maintain its dominance in the areas of military and politics, power is shifting in other dimensions, including industrial, financial, social, and cultural power. Pundits commenting on the strengths of the United States point to its status as a flexible society, open to competing views and welcoming of other peoples and cultures.[38] As crises mount—from migration to climate change, pandemic and epidemic diseases, and more—some are turning inward, believing less, rather than more, engagement is the best response. For decades, some (across the political spectrum) have argued that the United States should take care of its own, unencumbered by messy commitments and diversions on the world stage. They contend that the United States should be "out of the world order business" and that it is high time to behave like a "normal" nation, rather than an "abnormally unselfish" nation that sometimes works to the benefit of others more than itself.[39]

Supporters of this view believe that the "comforting story" of the United States as the sole superpower is an "outdated myth," and that only with its relative decline can we begin to create something akin to a truly international order, rather than one reliant on the leadership of a single country.[40] Yet, others decry the decline of US leadership, believing that this path makes the United States (and other countries) more vulnerable to problems, even if they take time to fester. America has long been divided between those who are excited by that prospect and those who are frightened by it. Meanwhile, the world, including the global south, is watching this unfold with—as we have discussed throughout the book—some painful conclusions. The hyperpower status that the United States experienced since the 1990s has ended. Current affairs, in the view of some, expose the "flaws and mediocrities [that] have been sustained and amplified because of that unprecedented power."[41]

As we have discussed, the United States is sometimes labeled—both positively and negatively—as an exceptionalist country. Former US secretary of state Madeleine Albright long espoused the notion of this country as "indispensable"—which, in her mind, does not imply going it alone.[42] History has shown tremendous achievements as well as tremendous disasters that have emanated from US decisionmaking, from the wars in Vietnam, Iraq, and Afghanistan to illicit interventions in Africa, Latin America, Southeast Asia, and the Middle East.[43] There has been blowback from US support of dictators and notorious human rights abusers who were favored by Washington for their strategic importance, especially in the ideological battles between liberalism and communism. People don't forget when the powerful are on the wrong side of history. Take, for instance, the sentiment expressed by someone who runs an Indonesian nongovernmental organization for survivors of the Cold War battles that claimed approximately 1 million lives from 1965 to 1966. When asked why he believes America "won" the twentieth-century Cold War, he retorted, "You killed us."[44] Declassified documents from Indonesia, Guatemala, Iraq, Chile, and elsewhere provide evidence of similar culpability on the part of the United States, in what may be viewed as the "darker side of hegemony" that exists alongside the record of positive achievements promoted by this country as well.[45] The skepticism, criticism, and lack of trust that many in the global south express about the United States today are grounded in decades of engagement that includes both selfless and self-serving behaviors. Understanding the fullness of the impact this country has had—good *and* bad—opens the door for a more complete understanding of how and why others approach the United States with mixed sentiment.

Notes

1. "Raisi Tells UN: Nuclear Talks Useful Only if They Lead to Lifting All Oppressive Sanctions on Iran," *Tehran Times,* September 21, 2021.

2. "US Capitol Storming: Autocracies Gloat, Allies Fret," *Financial Times,* January 7, 2021.

3. Richard Wike, "From Hyperpower to Declining Power: Changing Global Perceptions of the U.S. in the Post–Sept. 11 Era," Pew Research Center, September 7, 2011; "To Paris, U.S. Looks Like a 'Hyperpower,'" *New York Times,* February 5, 1999.

4. Asma Khalid, "Biden Says He's Ended the 'Forever Wars,' but Some Say They've Just Shrunk," NPR, September 3, 2021.

5. George Perkovich and Pranay Vaddi, "Arms Control and Disarmament," Carnegie Endowment for International Peace, February 21, 2021.

6. Vera Bergengruen, "'Give Us a Break!' Cuban Activists Say U.S. Sanctions Are Blocking Them from Online Services," *Time,* November 19, 2021.

7. "Adopting Annual Resolution, Delegates in General Assembly Urge Immediate Repeal of Embargo on Cuba, Especially amid Global Efforts to Combat COVID-19 Pandemic," United Nations press release, June 23, 2021. In 2016, the United States abstained

Figure 17.1 Is China a "Superpower"?

As history has shown, a single country cannot remain the preeminent power forever. Empires based in Greece, Rome, Turkey, and China once ruled large regions of the world, seemingly unchallenged. Increasingly, it looks as though the next major power could come from the global south. Many point to the People's Republic of China as the likely superpower for the twenty-first century.

To many, China's outsized role in world affairs is unsurprising. China's self-perception and role started to shift in 2008, and gained momentum as it came through the Great Recession relatively unscathed. Economically, militarily, and, to a lesser extent, diplomatically, Beijing is making its case. China's economic strengths are vast, as it rivals not only the size of the US economy, but even the dominance of the US dollar. No longer is China keeping a low profile; in fact, its core leader has proclaimed a "new era" during which China "should take center stage in the world."[a] Its economic presence is vast: more states have China as their leading trade partner than the United States.[b] On the security front, Xi Jinping has been clear: China plans to achieve military parity with the United States by 2027 and become the world's leading power by 2050.[c] Even top military leaders admit that the United States is behind China (and Russia) in hypersonic capability for disrupting missile defense systems.[d] Its Belt and Road Initiative, a significant source of offshore investment and loans for many, is likely to serve as a starting point for expanded bases and influence abroad. Beijing's first overseas military base, a naval base in Djibouti, has been operational since 2017, and it is likely to be followed by other expansions.

Diplomatically, Chinese leaders have been increasing their presence abroad—through the BRI, as well as increasing the numbers of diplomatic posts (surpassing the United States in 2019).[e] Yet, quantity is never the same as quality, and Beijing's wariness of collective security agreements and alliances demonstrates that it would be a different type of superpower.[f] If indeed China is successful in its reemergence as a global superpower, it would be the first nation in history to have gone into decline after a period of greatness, only to recover its former glory.[g] While we should be leery of deterministic assumptions, and cautious not to overlook the many weaknesses within the PRC, Beijing continues to exert influence and project power in ways that set it apart from other states of the global south.

India, with its impressive economic growth, diplomatic influence, and dominant regional presence, is likely to have a significantly larger role in the future—perhaps as a hedge between the United States and China. For example, India is a member of the US-led Quadrilateral Security Dialogue that includes Japan and Australia. India is also the largest recipient of funding from the Chinese-led Asian Infrastructure Investment Bank, as well as a full member of the Shanghai Cooperation Organization, which is led by China and Russia. South Asia's giant is projected to be the world's second largest economy (surpassing the United States) by 2050. "Superpower" or not, it seems clear that power in the twenty-first-century world is becoming dispersed, rather than concentrated in one country, region, or worldview. History has shown that analysts are rarely successful forecasting the rise (or even collapse) of great powers. Nevertheless, it seems clear that the United States' "unipolar" moment has passed. The frame for what will follow remains under construction.

Notes: a. "Xi Jinping: 'Time for China to Take Centre Stage,'" *BBC News,* October 18, 2017.

b. Joseph Nye, "Cold War with China Is Avoidable," *Wall Street Journal,* December 31, 2020, p. A15.

c. John A. Tirpak, "DIA Says China's Weapon Technology Advancing Fast While Russia Falls Behind," *Air Force Magazine,* April 30, 2021.

d. Paul Mcleary and Alexander Ward, "U.S. 'Not as Advanced' as China and Russia on Hypersonic Tech, Space Force General Warns," *Politico,* November 20, 2021.

e. Ben Westcott, "China Has Overtaken US as World's Largest Diplomatic Power, Think Tank Says," CNN, November 26, 2019.

f. Gideon Rachman, "China Is Still a Long Way from Being a Superpower," *Financial Times,* July 19, 2021.

g. See Geoffrey Murray, *China: The Next Superpower—Dilemmas in Change and Continuity* (New York: St. Martin's, 1998).

from the UN vote condemning the embargo (Israel joined as the only other abstention), to great applause from the world body. See Somini Sengupta and Rick Gladstone, "U.S. Abstains in U.N. Vote Condemning Cuba Embargo," *New York Times,* October 26, 2016.

8. Moises Naim, "The Havana Obsession: Why All Eyes Are on a Bankrupt Island," *Newsweek,* June 12, 2009.

9. Michelle Nichols, "Thirteen of 15-Member U.N. Security Council Oppose U.S. Push for Iran Sanctions," *Reuters,* August 21, 2020.

10. Daniel Drezner, "The United States of Sanctions," *Foreign Affairs* (September–October 2021).

11. Connie Bruck, "Why Obama Has Failed to Close Guantánamo," *The New Yorker,* August 1, 2016; David Welna, "Trump Has Vowed to Fill Guantanamo with 'Some Bad Dudes'—but Who?" *All Things Considered,* NPR, November 14, 2016.

12. Carol Rosenberg, "Detention of an Afghan at Guantánamo Bay Is Ruled Unlawful," *New York Times,* October 20, 2021.

13. Ibid.

14. Anthony Deutsch and Stephanie van den Berg, "War Crimes Prosecutor Would Not Focus on U.S. Forces in New Afghanistan Probe," *Reuters,* September 27, 2021.

15. Brian Montopoli, "U.N. Treaty on Disabilities Falls Short in Senate," *CBS News,* December 4, 2012.

16. Quoted in Waxhma Frogh, "CEDAW Ratification Would Be a Triumph for Afghan Women," *The Hill,* November 17, 2010. (Afghanistan ratified CEDAW in 2003, Qatar in 2009, and South Sudan in 2015.)

17. Rick Gladstone, "U.S. Regains Seat at U.N. Human Rights Council, 3 Years After Quitting," *New York Times,* October 14, 2021.

18. As we discuss below, the United States rejoined the WHO on Joe Biden's first day in office. Donald G. McNeil Jr., "Trump Administration Will Redirect $62 Million Owed to the W.H.O.," *New York Times,* September 2, 2020.

19. Frederick W. Kagan and Kimberly Kagan, "Retreating with Our Heads Held High," *Weekly Standard,* October 21, 2011.

20. Shadi Hamid, "Islamism, the Arab Spring, and the Failure of America's Do-Nothing Policy in the Middle East," *The Atlantic,* October 9, 2015.

21. Irfan Ahmad, "How the West De-Democratised the Middle East," *Al Jazeera,* March 30, 2012. These attempts, and negative responses to them, did not begin with the George W. Bush administration, either. For historical context and discussion of such perceptions, see John Judis, *What George W. Bush Could Learn from Theodore Roosevelt and Woodrow Wilson* (New York: Scribner, 2004).

22. Hamid, "Islamism, the Arab Spring, and the Failure."

23. Jeffrey Goldberg, "The Obama Doctrine," *The Atlantic,* April 2016.

24. Stephen F. Hayes, "Thoughts on an 'Obama Doctrine,'" *Weekly Standard,* December 10, 2009.

25. "The New Nationalism," *The Economist,* November 19, 2016.

26. Max Boot, "Trump's 'America First' Is the Twilight of American Exceptionalism," *Foreign Policy* (November 22, 2016).

27. Rebecca Hersher, "U.S. Officially Leaving Paris Climate Agreement," NPR, November 3, 2020; David Jackson, "Donald Trump Takes His 'America First' Agenda to a World War I Commemoration," *USA Today,* November 9, 2018.

28. Michael Gerson, "Trump Is Delighting Dictators Everywhere," *Washington Post,* August 22, 2017.

29. Matina Stevis-Gridneff and Lara Jakes, "World Leaders Join to Pledge $8 Billion for Vaccine as U.S. Goes It Alone," *New York Times,* May 4, 2020.

30. Scott Neuman, "Much of the World Doesn't Trust President Trump, Pew Survey Finds," NPR, January 8, 2020.

31. Christina Morales, "Biden Restores Ties with the World Health Organization That Were Cut by Trump," *New York Times,* January 20, 2021.

32. Matt McGrath, "US Rejoins Paris Accord: Biden's First Act Sets Tone for Ambitious Approach," *BBC News,* February 19, 2021.

33. Robin Wright, "The World Likes Biden but Doubts the U.S. Can Reclaim Global Leadership," *The New Yorker,* February 5, 2021.

34. Anne-Marie Slaughter, "It's Time to Get Honest About the Biden Doctrine," *New York Times,* November 12, 2021.

35. Damien Cave, "The War in Ukraine Holds a Warning for the World Order," *New York Times,* March 4, 2022.

36. Portia Siegelbaum, "Why Cubans See Biden as No 'Different from Trump,'" *CBS News,* June 24, 2021.

37. Fareed Zakaria, "Why Do They Hate Us? The Politics of Rage," *Newsweek,* October 15, 2001.

38. See Fareed Zakaria, *The Post-American World* (New York: Norton, 2008), especially chap. 15; James Fallows, *Postcards from Tomorrow Square* (New York: Vintage, 2008), especially chap. 7.

39. Robert Kagan, "Trump Marks the End of America as World's 'Indispensable Nation,'" *Financial Times,* November 19, 2016.

40. Suzy Hansen, "The End of the End of American Exceptionalism," *New York Magazine,* July 2, 2021; Zachary Karabell, "The Upside of a 'De-Americanized' World," *The Atlantic,* October 17, 2013.

41. Hansen, "The End of the End of American Exceptionalism."

42. David Marchese, "Madeleine Albright Thinks It's Good When America Gets Involved," *New York Times,* April 25, 2020.

43. Ibid.

44. Vincent Bevins, "The 'Liberal World Order' Was Built with Blood," *New York Times,* May 29, 2020.

45. Ibid.

18

Linking Concepts and Cases

In the preceding chapter, we discussed how countries throughout the global south have attempted to deal with the United States as a superpower. We focused on how the actions of various presidential administrations have been received by the global south. Has the Joe Biden administration's approach to, and interactions with, the global south been significantly different from that of his predecessors? What are some of the long-lasting impacts of former president Donald Trump's "America First" approach? What is the likely future trajectory for bilateral ties with these countries? Which issues are more or less likely to be important in the next five to ten years?

Case Study: Mexico

"Poor Mexico. Poor United States. So far from God. So near to each other."[1] This expresses the ambivalence many Mexicans have about living next door to the United States, known throughout Latin America as "the colossus of the north." This sense only grew during the 2016 US presidential election, as many Mexicans were alarmed by the characterization of Mexicans by the Republican nominee, Trump. As you may recall, building a wall (and making Mexico pay for it) was a hallmark of the Trump campaign. Former Mexican president Vicente Fox punched back, saying that Trump epitomized the ugly American, the gringo hated around the world.[2] Certainly, Trump's claims stirred Mexican nationalism. But Mexico's love-hate relationship with the United States is nothing new. As one analyst put it, this proximity means that Mexico and the United States are prisoners of each other's problems.[3]

Yes, the Mexican-US relationship is one of INTERDEPENDENCE. Yet, it is not and has never been one of equal dependence. Since the North American Free Trade Agreement was instituted in 1994, cross-border trade between Mexico and the world's largest economy has boomed.[4] In 2019, Mexico surpassed China to become the largest US trading partner. Mexico depends on its neighbor to buy 80 percent of its exports, and the United States invests more there than any other country. Two-way trade between the two countries amounted to a whopping $677 billion in 2019.[5]

Americans' grievances regarding the loss of manufacturing jobs as corporations relocate to Mexico to pay lower wages aided Trump's election. Still, American workers benefit from trade with Mexico as well: in 2017, nearly 5 million jobs in the United States depended on sales to Mexican consumers.[6]

Another source of contention between the two countries is that too often the United States has treated Mexico as a source of its problems and never considered how it might be contributing to troubles in Mexico. As at least one president has pointed out, Mexico has the misfortune of living next door to the world's biggest drug addict. Americans, who comprise 4 percent of the world's population, constitute much of the world's demand for illegal drugs—and spend an estimated $150 billion a year on them.[7] The United States has partnered with Mexico, providing it with billions of dollars to help in Mexico's drug war.[8] But the disbursement of these funds has come slowly and the United States has largely failed to curtail the shipment of weapons from the United States to Mexico. According to the US Department of Justice, approximately 70 percent of the guns used by Mexican traffickers originate in the United States.[9]

Another tie that binds the two is migration. As of 2017, an estimated 10.5 million undocumented immigrants lived in the United States and many entered the country through Mexico.[10] As a candidate for president, Trump insulted Mexicans when he attributed the loss of jobs and rising crime rates to illegal immigrants coming across the United States' southern border. Mexican leaders have been concerned about the increasing dangers faced by Mexicans in the United States. US leaders have been talking about immigration reform for decades now, but the issue remains extremely divisive. President Barack Obama took executive actions to protect "Dreamers," people brought to the United States illegally as children, but he also deported record numbers of people—so many that he became known as "the deporter-in-chief."[11]

As you will recall, President Trump took a harder line on Mexico. His administration became known for separating families at the border and deporting unaccompanied minors. After the United States threatened to impose tariffs on Mexico if it did not cooperate, AMLO's government assisted in detaining and deporting Central American migrants headed north. Mexico also bowed to US pressure by requiring those seeking asylum to "remain in Mexico" in border cities while their cases were processed—despite the dangers this entailed.[12]

Many expected a reversal of Trump's policy under President Biden. Biden has allowed unaccompanied minors to pursue asylum claims. He also suspended construction of Trump's wall and emphasized cooperation with Mexico on migration, trade, and climate change. The Biden administration is investing in DEVELOPMENT in Mexico and Central America as a way to address the root causes of migration. But the current administration is also using Trump's public health rules to turn people back and it (reluctantly) resumed Trump's "Remain in Mexico" policy.[13]

Biden, who called the policy inhumane, only did so to comply with a court order. He has promised to speed up the processing of asylum applications and to provide basic services for those waiting in Mexico. But critics point out that in many ways, Biden's immigration policy is just a "lite" version of Trump's.[14] This is a challenge for Mexico as well. People are coming from all over the world to Mexico, which now receives as well as sends migrants. The United States has a long history of interference in Mexico, and it will be impossible to make progress in curtailing drug violence without also dealing with trade and immigration. Mexico's president cannot appear to be a "yes man" to the United States. This complicates the task, but, from Mexico's perspective, the United States must accept and understand this.[15]

Case Study: Peru

The Peruvian-US relationship has had its ups and downs, and at times that relationship has been strained. Since the mid-nineteenth-century guano boom, the United States has had significant economic interests in Peru. Trade between the two countries has increased from $9.1 billion in 2009 to $15.8 billion in 2019. However, China replaced the United States as Peru's top trading partner in 2014, and Peru is one of China's most important Latin American partners. China is a major investor in Peru, and is a leading importer of Peruvian copper. Meanwhile, the US role in Peru has been diminished. China's growing role in Latin America has concerned the United States, and the Biden administration has taken steps to balance growing Chinese influence in the region.[16]

The United States and Peru are strong allies and work cooperatively in a variety of areas, most notably counter-narcotics. For decades, the Andes have become a major battlefield in the US war on drugs, as Peru is one of the world's largest suppliers of coca, the plant from which cocaine is derived. The United States has supported crop eradication, crop substitution, and "alternative development," with the view that drug eradication was a development issue. However, more effort has been put into the US "Andean strategy," which aimed to cut off the cocaine trade at its source of supply using a military approach. US forces have worked with the Peruvian military and police at drug interdiction, and Peru has been a major recipient of US military assistance. For several years, it appeared that this strategy was working, as coca cultivation in Peru plummeted in the late 1990s.[17]

Convinced that counter-narcotics operations in the region could not continue without Alberto Fujimori's support, the United States overlooked the growing authoritarianism of his government in the 1990s. Humanitarian and drug-fighting assistance continued as the democracy eroded because the United States feared that the instability associated with the drug war in Colombia could spread to Peru. Although US military assistance was appropriated only to fight the drug war, some of this money was diverted by Peru for use in its war against the Shining Path (Sendero Luminoso) GUERRILLAS, under the argument that the terrorists were playing a central part in the drug trade. Consequently, the United States became an important ally for the Peruvian government in its civil war.[18]

Even though they're not always recognized as such, drug cartels are criminal terrorist groups. And the war on terrorism and the war on drugs are a lot alike. In neither case is the United States likely ever to win a final victory, but the consequences of not dealing with these problems could be even worse than waging a war without end.[19] Remember from Chapter 11, *plomo o plata* in Mexico?

This is the offer (lead or silver, that is, take a bullet or take the cash) that many police find they can't resist. In Peru, because *plata* always works, *plomo* isn't needed. Peru's cartels are relatively peaceful, compared to Mexico's. There isn't anywhere near the kind of bloodletting that we've seen in Mexico, in part because the government hasn't gone after kingpins or adopted a Calderón-style war on drugs. In fact, Peruvian presidents pardoned hundreds of drug traffickers. But between the drug business, illegal gold-mining, human trafficking, and the trade in other illicit goods, there is a great deal of money to be made (most estimate \$5–\$7 billion a year).[20] It can't help but fuel corruption, which weakens democracy.

You won't be surprised to hear that as of 2021, Peru is no longer winning its war on drugs. In response to lower prices for alternative crops such as coffee, Peruvian farmers have returned to coca production. During the PANDEMIC, quarantines meant that eradication efforts were put on hold for months; meanwhile, coca and cocaine production in Peru reached record levels.[21] However, supply outpaced demand during the pandemic, as drug trafficking routes shrank due to Covid shutdowns. Just as it did with toilet paper, the lockdowns associated with Covid interrupted supply chains for illicit drug producers in Peru, who also struggled to source the precursor chemicals to make methamphetamines, fentanyl, and even cocaine.[22]

Although the United States views Peru as an ally in the war on drugs, Peru's leaders are caught between two constituencies: the United States and many of their own citizens. Some Peruvian presidents have been concerned that forced eradication, which is highly controversial in Peru, would aggravate social unrest in the regions where coca is produced, because economies are dependent on it. Coca farmers have violently resisted eradication efforts precisely in the remote areas of the country where the Shining Path has held on. From the perspective of many Peruvians, who remember the bloody civil war not too long ago, this is a concern. So, when trying to understand why foreign leaders adopt seemingly erratic policies, it is important to keep this in mind: domestic considerations are paramount for democratically elected governments, which are accountable to their people. Particularly when it comes to counter-narcotics policy in Peru, the United States needs to remember that it is not dealing with a dictatorship anymore and rethink its strategy and adopt an approach with that in mind.[23]

Case Study: Nigeria

Frankly, despite its enormous significance and potential, US presidents have generally shown little interest in Nigeria—or in Africa for that matter. Bill Clinton was the first US president to visit Nigeria since Jimmy Carter's trip in 1977 and Barack Obama never visited Nigeria as president. President Trump, who famously referred to African nations as "sh—hole countries," included Nigeria in a travel ban, seeking to sharply curtail immigration (surprisingly, Trump's popularity ratings were high in Nigeria "because he says it like it is").[24]

Yet, Nigeria matters. Only South Africa rivals it as a regional superpower. Described as Africa's equivalent to Brazil, India, or Indonesia, Nigeria is vital to US interests for several reasons. As of 2021, it was Africa's largest oil exporter, and, although it has declined in importance in recent years, Nigeria was still a major supplier of oil to the United States.[25] In addition, with a rapidly growing population of approximately 219 million, it is not only the region's most populous country, but also the largest market in sub-Saharan Africa, full of tremendous trade potential. Nigeria's population is expected to double by 2050, and by the end of the century, it is projected to be the third most populous country in the world. And present-day Nigeria is part of the region that was home to the ancestors of most African Americans. Although Nigeria has historically been more closely tied to Britain (its former colonizer), Nigerian-US ties have grown closer as the United States seeks strategic partners in Africa.[26]

However, until recently, the US approach to Nigeria was described as paradoxical, alternating between close diplomacy and benign neglect.[27] Since its democratic transition in 1999, US-Nigerian economic ties have grown. Not only did the United States support the debt relief described in Chapter 6, but US companies like Chevron and Exxon-Mobil are two of Nigeria's largest investors. Nigerian goods such as groundnuts and sorghum have duty-free access to US markets until 2025, under an extension of the African Growth and Opportunity Act (AGOA).[28] For many years, the United States needed to diversify its oil dependence away from the Middle East, and its relationship with Nigeria and other African oil and gas producers grew. In 2010, for example, 40 percent of Nigeria's oil exports went to the United States. However, for the past ten years, growing US oil production meant significantly reduced dependence on foreign oil, including US imports from Nigeria.[29]

Although Nigeria is less important to the United States now when it comes to oil, something that makes the US-Nigerian relationship more important than ever is security cooperation. Nigeria is West Africa's unrivaled military power. The United States wants a moderate ally in the region and recognizes that Nigeria is a regional powerhouse essential to any international effort to stabilize not only West Africa, but the continent. Since the debacle in Somalia in 1993, the slogan "African solutions for African problems" has been popular in the West. There are certain problems in Africa that the United States cannot ignore, and one convenient compromise is to promote Nigeria's role as a regional peacekeeper, since it is cheaper to train and equip Nigerian troops than it is to send US forces.[30]

The United States provides military assistance and training to African governments and in return (through the Trans-Sahara Counterterrorism Partnership) seeks cooperation in the global war on terror. Nigeria is a member of this partnership, which has been criticized by some who predict that it will be used by unpopular regimes against political opponents they choose to characterize as terrorists.[31]

Although Boko Haram and ISWAP are widely recognized as terrorist groups, Nigerian presidents can be accused of mischaracterizing the government's opponents in the Niger Delta as such. President Muhammadu Buhari has repeatedly asked the United States to send not only military advisers but also combat soldiers, perhaps Special Forces troops, to fight militant jihadists in Africa. Buhari is so frustrated with his military's inability to prevail against jihadists and separatists that he even requested that the United States move its headquarters that oversees Africa to Africa from Germany. More recently, Buhari has also called for the United States and Western allies to provide more development aid to invest in Nigeria, recognizing that the government cannot win the war against terrorism without addressing its root causes.[32]

The United States has trained and equipped Nigerian soldiers, but closer cooperation between Nigeria and the United States has been limited because the United States had very real concerns about abuses committed by Nigerian security forces.[33] The United States blocked the sale of American-made helicopters to Nigeria for several years due to these concerns, and for a while bypassed Nigeria to work directly with neighboring Cameroon, Chad, and Niger. However, Trump, who was said to have "zero interest in Africa," reversed this policy, ignoring human rights abuses and pushing on with the arms deal.[34]

What can we expect from President Biden? Biden says that "America is back" and promised a values-based foreign policy. As of 2021, that remains to be seen. He criticized Buhari's crackdown on those protesting police terror, and he reversed Trump's travel ban on Nigerians. Biden is concerned about the ground China gained in Nigeria and throughout the continent in recent years. As elsewhere in the global south, if the United States is going to compete with China, it will have to make up for lost ground economically while being unafraid to distinguish itself from China. US presidents must send their counterparts in Nigeria the message that, with all due respect, Nigeria needs to do better.[35] What happens in Nigeria does affect US interests—and it is one country that Americans are likely to hear much more of in future years.

Case Study: Zimbabwe

It could be argued that the United States has been on the wrong side of history in much of southern Africa. During the Cold War, the United States at various times directly and indirectly supported white racist governments in the region, for economic as well as strategic reasons. US paranoia that Africans were procommunist became a self-fulfilling prophecy, as Black nationalists had nowhere but the Soviet Union and China to turn. This did not make for an auspicious start to relations between the United States and the new government of Zimbabwe. Although the United States welcomed Zimbabwe's independence in 1980 with a significant aid package, relations between the two countries cooled quickly. This difficult relationship fell to its lowest point in the mid-1980s and again at the turn of the twenty-first century. At times, the Zimbabwe-US relationship has been marked by outright hostility.[36]

At independence, Zimbabwe was eager to assert itself in international forums. As an aspiring leader of the "third world" in the NON-ALIGNED MOVEMENT (NAM) and as one of the frontline states opposed to the apartheid government in South Africa, Zimbabwe was determined to shape its own policy. The government had taken an outspoken stance in criticizing US support for apartheid South Africa and apartheid-backed rebels in Angola, Mozambique, and elsewhere. In the 1980s, when Zimbabwe indicated that it would vote its own conscience at the UNITED NATIONS on issues important to the United States, the United States slashed foreign aid to Zimbabwe. In response and swearing that Zimbabwe would be no one's puppet, Robert Mugabe famously proclaimed that Zimbabwe "would rather be poor, eat grass, and be sovereign."[37]

Although relations gradually improved and aid resumed in the years that followed, by 2001 the relationship was again at a low point. In response to then US secretary of state Colin Powell's condemnation of Mugabe's "totalitarian methods," Mugabe told the United States to leave Zimbabwe alone and mind its own business. Instead, the US Senate passed the Zimbabwe Democracy and Economic Recovery Act of 2001 (then senator Biden cosponsored the legislation). Instead of general trade sanctions, which have been criticized as hurting the poor, these were targeted, personal sanctions against those who were responsible for the corruption and violence in Zimbabwe. Much like the European Union, the United States imposed an arms embargo, as well as travel and economic sanctions against Mugabe, his family, his associates, and other senior government officials. These sanctions, which now target Emmerson Mnangagwa, his family, and associates, have been renewed every year since.[38]

President Obama's approach to Zimbabwe was a continuation of the George W. Bush policy of isolation, and Mugabe continued to view the United States with hostility. Over the years, the Mugabe government has described its efforts as a continuation of the liberation struggle and reminded the world that Zimbabwe is nobody's colony. According to Mugabe, not only was the United States to blame for the suffering of millions of Zimbabweans, it was promoting regime change. Despite this friction, the United States has provided significant assistance annually ($318 million in 2019) mostly for health programs and other development and humanitarian assistance, and mainly through civil society groups.[39] On the other hand, US law required that for the US to support financial assistance to Zimbabwe (e.g., the clearance of debt arrears or the opportunity to benefit from market access to the United States), the US president must certify that several conditions have been met, including the restoration of the rule of law in Zimbabwe, land reform, and a freer environment for holding elections. Those conditions have not yet been met. Zimbabweans are still waiting.[40]

Interestingly, Mugabe enthusiastically celebrated the election of Trump, whom he described as a fellow populist that has shaken up the establishment and been unfairly attacked by the media. Mugabe was looking for a reset of relations, but given Trump's stated views of Africa, his disinclination to push human rights, and the fact that the United States has relatively few economic interests in Zimbabwe, under his administration the United States directed little of its attention to the country—which suited Mugabe just as well.[41]

Although Mugabe's successor, Mnangagwa, hasn't changed things much in terms of domestic policy, he has made clear his intent to reengage and normalize relations with the West. As opposed to Mugabe's anti-imperialism, the new president has spoken often of his commitment to human rights. In doing so, he is seeking not only to secure the removal of sanctions but, by declaring that Zimbabwe is "open for business," to encourage investment. However, Mnangagwa's acts (his repressive policies and human rights abuses) have undercut those words. Despite their poor track record in Zimbabwe (and the fact that studies across the globe show that unilateral sanctions haven't been especially effective at inducing regime change), President Biden has long believed in their potential. Although critics call for the United States to try something else, Biden renewed sanctions in Zimbabwe, pressed for democracy, and condemned the government.

For his part, President Mnangagwa shot back after the January 6 riots at the US Capitol, saying that the United States is hardly a democratic role model.[42]

In the meantime, in what some call the new Cold War, China—which could care less about Zimbabwe's human rights record—had supported Mugabe since he was a liberation fighter in 1979. The relationship deepened with the "Look East" policy Zimbabwe adopted to offset the effect of US sanctions. It has only grown with China's BELT AND ROAD INITIATIVE, as things continue to be chummy with Mnangagwa. The new patron is more than happy to import Zimbabwe's resources, sell Zimbabwe its manufactured goods (including arms), and invest in the country. China now has massive investments in Zimbabwean agriculture, infrastructure, and mining—it invests more there than any other country. Yet, the relationship has become strained in recent years, as Zimbabwe's dependence on China grows. More Zimbabweans are beginning to see the superpower as a self-interested new colonizer. Meanwhile, China becomes increasingly impatient with Zimbabwe's inability to pay on its debt to China.[43] It's up to the United States and the West to decide if they want to watch this play out, or try to influence the trajectory of this relationship.

Case Study: Egypt

For decades, Egypt was the closest Arab ally of the United States. The two are still important to each other, but the relationship (which was always transactional) has altered in recent years. The fundamentals haven't changed, but it is not what it once was.[44] Each can be accused of having a wandering eye: Egypt is looking for new partners to make up for what it isn't getting from the United States and the United States is more interested in Iran's nuclear program and the continuing Palestinian-Israeli conflict. The two have grown apart and clearly each would say that the other has not lived up to expectations.[45]

Historically, due to its geography and diplomacy, Egypt has been crucial to US national security interests. It is home to the Suez Canal, and, since 1979 when Egypt became the first Arab state to sign a peace deal with Israel, its former foe, the United States has rewarded Egypt, making it the second largest recipient of American aid for many years (by 2019 it ranked fourth, behind Afghanistan, Israel, and Jordan). In total, Egypt has received from the United States more than $50 billion in military and economic assistance combined since 1978, ranging from $1 billion to $2 billion a year.[46] Their close partnership is also a strategic benefit to the United States, as it allows the United States to project power in the region. In sum, it has for decades been a foundation of US policy in the Middle East.

This relationship continued and expanded in the twenty-first century to include cooperation in the war on terror. However, recognizing that US support for dictatorships might actually be fueling terrorism, President George W. Bush briefly pressed Egypt for democratic reforms. After some resistance, Mubarak did allow for freer, though still limited, elections in 2005. But when the Muslim Brotherhood won nearly 20 percent of the seats, the United States backed off and Mubarak rolled back the reforms.[47]

Out of fear of the alternative, US presidents, Democrat and Republican alike, put stability above democracy in Egypt and stood steadfastly by its dictators. The

Obama administration was surprised by the events of 2011 and slow to warm to the Tahrir uprising.[48] Fearful of the greater conflagration to come if Mubarak insisted on staying, the United States broke with past policy and publicly called for an orderly transition of power.[49] When President Mohamed Morsi was removed from office in a coup in 2013, the Obama administration condemned the military's removal of a democratically elected government, but chose not to call it a coup because to do so would have meant (under US law) immediately cutting off aid to Egypt—and a likely end to Egypt's peace deal with Israel. After the military resumed power, the Obama administration declared that the US-Egyptian relationship could not return to "business as usual," but in effect it did.[50]

What threat to national security could justify the resumption of aid to a dictatorship that overthrew a democratically elected government? The Islamic State in Iraq and al-Sham (ISIS)—and its presence in the Sinai. The counterterrorist imperative ushered in a strengthening of the strategic relationship.[51] And yes, that confirmed US hypocrisy in the eyes of many, who found the continuity in policy between the Bush and Obama administrations striking. There were some differences of nuance, but both interpreted US national interests—broadly defined—in the same way. This trumped everything else.[52]

President Trump continued this tradition—and took it to new heights. Trump made it clear that he had no interest in lecturing others on human rights abuses. He had no problem working with autocrats and much preferred the stability they offer to the alternative. In fact, Abdel Fattah al-Sisi helped to manage relations between Israel and Hamas and lobbied other Arab states to recognize Israel, which Trump claimed as one of his greatest foreign policy achievements. Trump described al-Sisi, who is even more repressive than Mubarak was, as "a fantastic guy," "his favorite dictator"—which had the effect of strengthening the regime.[53]

At least in his first year in office, President Biden appeared less willing to cozy up to dictators, specifically al-Sisi. Biden, who campaigned promising a reengagement with the international community with "America's Back," reengaged Egypt on democracy and human rights and vowed "no more blank checks" for President al-Sisi. In 2021, the Biden administration threatened to withhold $130 million (of the $1.3 billion in annual military aid) to Egypt, making its release conditional on the release of sixteen political prisoners (a tiny fraction of the total number imprisoned in Egypt) as well as "sustained and effective" progress in human rights and democracy. This is far less than the $300 million Congress sought to withhold until the al-Sisi government improves its behavior, and prominent human rights groups were disappointed. But Biden's policy is at least a partial break with that of past administrations, which waived such conditions on national security grounds. Biden may not yet be ready to break it off with al-Sisi because there are no obvious and reliable alternatives. But the message that the United States is willing and able to push back against resurgent authoritarianism is important—and not just in Egypt.[54]

Case Study: Iran

With the more recent history of strained ties between Iranian leaders and the United States (the BBC once called the relationship "one of the most antagonistic in the world"),[55] it may be tempting to discount their relations prior to the Islamic Revolution. Such an omission would be a mistake. In fact, the coziness of the Shah with Western leaders is a major source of mistrust. Many Iranians viewed the West, especially the United States, as double-talking supporters of a corrupt and antidemocratic regime.

Iran long considered the United States its archenemy, and fierce animosity reigned on both sides, especially after 1979 when hostages were held at the US embassy in Tehran for 444 days (today, the former embassy serves as a militia training center and museum of the "den of spies").[56] Yet, neither can ignore the other, as Iran's access to the Persian Gulf solidifies its status as a central player in the Middle East. Since 1980, the two sides have lacked diplomatic ties; Pakistan represents Iranian interests in Washington, and Switzerland represents US interests in Tehran. This distance is complicated further by the fact that the current Iranian president, Ebrahim Raisi (inaugurated in August 2021), stands accused of "grave human rights violations" dating back to the 1979 revolution, and is formally blacklisted by the United States.[57] Even when they are in close proximity (the same hotel in Vienna) discussing high-level matters (e.g., the attempts to revive the 2015 nuclear deal), principals for both sides pass notes through European intermediaries.[58] Within the Islamic Republic, the weekly jeers of "death to America" continue. Supreme Leader Sayyid Ali Khamenei often references the "global arrogance" of the United States.[59] Of the Joint Comprehensive Plan of Action, Khamenei contends, "I said from the first day: don't trust America."[60]

Almost all commercial transactions between the United States and Iran were banned from 1995 until 2016, under a 1995 executive order that was reinforced with the 1996 Iran-Libya Sanctions Act (which has been extended until at least 2026).[61] This US law imposes penalties on foreign firms that invest in either Iran or Libya, accused by the United States of supporting terrorism.[62] Even after the nuclear-related sanctions were lifted in 2016, others (focused on Iran's support of terrorism, human rights abuses, and its ballistic missile program) remained, and many US sanctions were reimposed in 2018 by the Trump administration.

Iran was designated by the US State Department as a state sponsor of terrorism in 1984, and the United States ranked the Islamic Republic as the "world's worst state sponsor of terrorism," branding their threat as "truly global" in nature.[63] The United States alleges Iranian complicity in the bombing of Marine headquarters in Beirut (1983), and in the 1996 Khobar (Saudi Arabia) bombing of US military barracks, which killed nineteen members of the US Air Force. Since 2019, the United States has designated the Islamic Revolutionary Guard Corps a foreign terrorist organization, responsible for brutality in Iraq, Syria, and elsewhere. The United States contends that the Islamic Republic is involved in multiple activities designed to destabilize the region, through its alliance with Hezbollah and others.

Iran's concerns with the United States are also deep-rooted. Iran views the United States as the source of most of its problems. There is remaining anti-American sentiment tied to the Central Intelligence Agency–engineered coup that toppled the popular government of Prime Minister Mohammad Mossadeq in 1953, as well as to US support for the Shah. The decision to permit the ailing leader to enter the United States was viewed by many ordinary Iranians as part of a Western conspiracy to restore a dynasty. Iranian animosity only increased after President Ronald Reagan supported Saddam Hussein during the 1980–1988 Iran-Iraq War, and continued while the United States expanded its influence in the region. Iranian leaders were also upset that the international community took little action against Iraq, which had killed tens of thousands of Iranians with chemical weapons. Iranian leaders believed they were snubbed at the conclusion of the Gulf War (in 1991), as they were excluded from postwar discussions, even though they tacitly assisted the effort to oust Saddam Hussein from Kuwait. Iranian leaders feel that they are adrift in a hostile international environment that has been largely created by the United States.

The JCPOA, crafted during the Obama administration, had the potential to link Iran economically with Europe (and to the United States, to a lesser extent) and move beyond much of its isolation. Yet, President Trump followed up on his promise to "tear up" the nuclear accord (the United States abandoned the agreement in 2018), reimposing sanctions and threatening to sanction countries and firms that buy Iranian oil.[64] After a US drone strike killed General Qasem Soleimani, one of Iran's top military commanders, Tehran vowed "severe revenge" and formally pulled back from the JCPOA, increasing its stockpile of highly enriched uranium and the equipment to manufacture it.[65] Attempts in late 2021 to prevent the total collapse of the agreement were fraught with difficulties as Iranian leaders insist the United States make the first move.[66] Despite many shared interests, the Islamic Republic of Iran and the United States have numerous (and sizable) conflicts and distrust. Under current circumstances, it remains difficult to perceive any major openings.

Case Study: China

"Completely dysfunctional."[67] That's the way UN Secretary-General António Guterres characterizes the relationship between the United States and China. Relations between these two powerhouses have the potential to significantly impact matters far beyond their own borders.

The United States opened a formal diplomatic relationship with the People's Republic of China during the 1970s, under the leadership of staunchly anticommunist president Richard M. Nixon. Previously the United States had supported the rival of the Chinese Communist Party, the Nationalist Party, which had been exiled to Taiwan after its defeat in 1949. Nixon's rationale for rapprochement with China viewed matters in a "strategic triangle" encompassing the United States, China, and the Soviet Union. Opening formal ties with China would exploit hostilities between the two communist giants and, ultimately, it was hoped, limit the influence of communism.

After the initial honeymoon period, China-US relations have had cycles of highs and lows, from Tiananmen Square (1989), to Bill Clinton's successful China tour (1998), to the bombing of the Chinese embassy in Belgrade (1999), and the collision of a Chinese jet with a US Navy surveillance plane (2001), which killed the Chinese pilot and resulted in China detaining the US crew for nineteen days. In the wake of the Great Recession (2008) and even the Covid pandemic, China has found more confident footing, shifting Sino-US relations toward uncharted territory as Beijing's influence rises.

Many within China frame US behavior as arrogant, self-interested, and imposing—characteristics of a HEGEMON. Leaders are especially critical of Washington's security alliances throughout Asia Pacific, US support of Taiwan, as well as the dominant US role in the world, which Beijing seeks to challenge as part of a "protracted war."[68] Following the initiation of the trilateral security pact between Australia, the UK, and the United States (AUKUS), Chinese foreign minister Wang Yi contended that the deal shifted the region toward "the brink of war."[69] Without naming Beijing explicitly, the impetus for AUKUS is clear: to counter China's growing presence in the Asia Pacific, especially its BRI investments, military buildup, and posture in disputed territories. In response, Chinese leaders term AUKUS "extremely irresponsible."[70]

Chinese citizens identify the United States as the main threat to the country, ranking higher than economic instability and terrorism. Data collected by the Carter Center show that a majority of Chinese (62 percent) have a negative view of the United States.[71] This compares to 73 percent of US respondents holding negative views on China—the highest percentage since Pew started tracking this attitude in 2005 (when it measured 35 percent).[72] A popular Chinese foreign policy blogger who attended graduate school in the United States highlights Chinese disillusionment with American democracy, pointing to US criticism of China's role in Hong Kong, tariffs on Chinese exports, and other issues that he says have increased Chinese patriotism in response to US pressure.[73]

China's economic power is the focal point of most of its bilateral ties, including with the United States. China holds approximately $1.1 trillion of US debt as of 2021, down from the peak of $1.32 trillion in 2013 (and ranking second to Japan in terms of foreign ownership of US debt).[74] Reverberations from the trade war between the two countries continue to echo loudly, especially as President Biden has largely maintained Trump's trade policies with Beijing, with minor modifications.[75]

The status of Taiwan is the most consequential bilateral issue. Let's be clear—from Beijing's point of view, this is a nonstarter: Taiwan is a renegade province that has been illegitimately separated from the Chinese mainland, and all Chinese on both sides of the Taiwan Straits need to work toward the eventual reunification. Beijing has long suspected that the United States harbored intentions of keeping Taiwan and mainland China separate. This belief is based on US efforts to defend Taiwan and is bolstered by US weapons sales to the island—a staple since the 1980s—despite the absence of formal ties. As we discussed in Chapter 10, some are concerned that China's patience on this matter is wearing thin, possibly leading to a shifting calculus that would most definitely involve the United States.

Sino-US ties during the Trump administration were tempestuous and inconsistent, vacillating from his labeling of Beijing as a "currency manipulator," to referring to Xi Jinping as a "very, very good friend," to threats of decoupling.[76] Trump's framing Covid as the "China virus," including his suggestion that Beijing should pay $10 trillion in compensation for "the death and destruction they have caused," led to accusations from Beijing that Trump was scapegoating the country to deflect attention away from US domestic problems.[77]

President Biden is adopting a slightly different approach, attempting to forge a coalition of democracies to counter Beijing's presence. The first face-to-face meeting between US and Chinese diplomats was rocky, filled with "verbal jousting" and belligerent "grandstanding," demonstrating that President Biden would be dealing with a more confident, assertive China than he had encountered during his prior interactions with Chinese leaders as vice president.[78] Biden's decision to include Taiwan in the US-hosted "Summit for Democracy" in late 2021, along with the "diplomatic boycott" of the Beijing 2022 Winter Olympic Games, increased tension even more. As China deepens its investment in the BRI, and expands its overseas military bases and embassies abroad, it is clear that an "overt competition for global leadership" exists.[79] In spite of their differences, there's one important commonality between China and the United States: they each define the other as their greatest threat.

Case Study: Indonesia

Indonesia's ties with the Western world have long been strained. Some of this derives from Indonesia's experience with the Dutch, and its prolonged fight for acceptance as an independent state. As a founder of the Non-Aligned Movement in the 1960s, Indonesia positioned itself to be largely independent of the West, and indeed sometimes in opposition to it. The latter part of the Sukarno era was very anti-Western and, specifically, anti-American. After the 1965 anticommunist coup, in a period of US history that remains under scrutiny, the United States cultivated a close relationship with Suharto's Indonesia, viewing it as a regional stronghold against communism.[80] Yet, Western powers maintained a cozy relationship with Suharto at great cost, ignoring human rights atrocities and propping up a military regime, all in the name of regional stability. The United States trained Indonesian military leaders: former president Susilo Bambang Yudhoyono (SBY) received formal instruction in the United States in the 1970s and 1980s. Since Indonesia's democratic transitions, the inconsistencies of the Indonesia-US relationship have become more visible.

The events of September 11, 2001, put Indonesian leaders in a tight spot, especially with US leaders. As president, Megawati Sukarnoputri's support of Washington rankled some Indonesian citizens; many viewed her initially unqualified support of US efforts to be blasphemous against Muslims. As the war on terrorism waged further, this perception grew stronger. In 2004, a respected Indonesian survey institute found that 55 percent of Indonesian citizens believed that the United States was at war with Muslim countries, rather than with terrorists who happen to be Muslim.[81] When George W. Bush made a six-hour stop in Indonesia in 2006, for example, some demonstrators chanted, "We hope Bush dies."[82]

In part because of his childhood connections to Indonesia, many expected President Obama to extend a closer US relationship to this major Southeast Asian state. (Obama lived outside of Jakarta for four years as a young boy, attending Catholic and public schools; one of the elementary schools he attended erected a statue of him on its grounds.) After having twice postponed his first official state visit, he returned to Jakarta in November 2010 to cheering and jeering crowds, praising Indonesia as a model of pluralism and democracy. In a deeply personal speech in Jakarta, Obama stated (in both English and

Indonesian), "Indonesia is part of me."[83] Yet, many Indonesians responded with skepticism. According to a Pew Research Center report, since 2000 Indonesians' views of the United States have fluctuated quite a bit, with favorable views of the United States bouncing between a high of 63 percent in 2009 (during Obama's first term), to a low of 15 percent in 2003 (shortly after the US-led invasion of Iraq), and 42 percent in 2019 (during the Trump administration).[84] It was only in 2020 (after he had been named defense minister) that the United States dropped its ban on Prabowo Subianto's entrance to the country, a long-standing US foreign policy decision reflecting Prabowo's involvement in human rights atrocities in East Timor, Jakarta, and West Papua.[85] In response to Trump's fiery anti-Muslim rhetoric, Indonesians (citizens and leaders alike) were especially concerned that his emphasis on limiting support to crucial allies in the region (especially Japan) would ignite a regional arms race, that his protectionist economic priorities would cut into Indonesian exports, and, in general, that shifting American priorities in Asia would be accompanied by harmful instability.[86] The former Indonesian ambassador to the United States, Dino Patti Djalal, contended that the US-Indonesian relationship had "lost its soul."[87]

Indonesia has long viewed itself as sandwiched between the world's major powers, which today places it in the middle of the United States and China. Jakarta's leaders realize Indonesia's key geopolitical position, and recognize that there may be some benefits to being caught in the middle of two powers, especially as they seek investment (and assurances from both).[88] Many have observed a "double hedging" strategy from Jakarta, with Indonesia pursuing a pragmatic economic policy (benefiting from China's Belt and Road Initiatives) while seeking security support from the United States (especially in the face of China's increased assertiveness in the South China Sea). Yet, Indonesian leaders still hold firmly to the country's heritage as a founder of the NON-ALIGNED MOVEMENT, by not becoming too closely aligned with either the United States or China.

Indonesia's relations with the Western world, dominated by its ties with the United States, are most definitely changing from the days when Jakarta orchestrated the global movement to chart an independent path. Today, Jakarta attempts to balance (and leverage) its relations with both the United States (which emphasizes Jakarta's credentials as the world's third largest democracy and as a model of democracy in an Islamic country) and China (which emphasizes its economic ties with the world's fourth most populous state). In some ways, Indonesia has come full circle. In the 1950s, it was caught between the superpowers of the United States and the Soviet Union. More than half a century after claiming the mantle of nonalignment by hosting the Bandung Conference in 1995, today it again finds itself straddling two large powers with conflicting (and competing) worldviews. The degree to which Jakarta's leaders will be successful promoting their "independent and active" foreign policy is likely to have lasting consequences on regional and even global dynamics for many years to come.

Now It's Your Turn

How do recent events complement or challenge the material presented in the case studies? If you had to brief a US government delegation on the perceptions of a particular bilateral relationship between the United States and the global south, what issues and perspectives would you highlight? Do you believe that many Americans understand or can agree with some of the concerns expressed by people in the countries we have studied? Why or why not? How would you explain the animosity expressed in some corners of the world toward the United States? If you had to outline a policy plan for future US relations with one of the countries studied here, what would it entail? How would this proposal be different if you were to chart it from the perspective of a country in the global south?

Notes

1. Arlos Fuentes, *The Crystal Frontier* (New York: Farrar, Straus and Giroux, 1997), p. 266.

2. Kirk Semple, "Mexico Prepares to Counter 'the Trump Emergency,'" *New York Times,* May 22, 2016; Eli Watkins, "Ex-Mexican President Vicente Fox Knocks Trump, Sanders," *CNN Politics,* May 10, 2016.

3. Roderic Ai Camp, *Politics in Mexico: The Decline of Authoritarianism* (New York: Oxford University Press, 1999).

4. NAFTA was renegotiated and replaced by the US-Mexico-Canada Agreement (USMCA) in 2020.

5. "Mexico," Office of the US Trade Representative, 2019.

6. "New Study: International Trade Supports Nearly 39 Million American Jobs," Business Roundtable, March 18, 2019; Ana Swanson, "Panel Find 'Serious Concerns' with Mexican Labor Reforms," *New York Times,* December 15, 2020.

7. Mario Berlanga, "A Victimless Crime?" *New York Times,* September 27, 2016; Beau Kilmer, "Americans' Spending on Illicit Drugs Nears $150 Billion Annually; Appears to Rival What Is Spent on Alcohol," Rand Corporation, August 20, 2019.

8. "Mexico's Long War: Drugs, Crime, and the Cartels," Council on Foreign Relations, February 26, 2021.

9. US Government Accountability Office, "Firearms Trafficking: U.S. Efforts to Disrupt Gun Smuggling into Mexico Would Benefit from Additional Data and Analysis," March 24, 2021.

10. Abby Budiman, "Key Findings About U.S. Immigrants," Pew Research Center, August 20, 2020.

11. "Barack Obama: Deporter-in-Chief," *The Economist,* February 8, 2014.

12. "Mexico's Long War," Council on Foreign Relations; Lizbeth Diaz and Laura Gottesdiener, "Immigration Raids Sweep Mexico as Central American Exit Grows Under Biden," *Reuters,* March 15, 2021.

13. Michael Shifter, "President Biden Should Not Underestimate Challenges in Latin America," *New York Times,* February 10, 2021; "US Will Resume 'Remain in Mexico' Policy for Asylum Seekers," *AP,* December 2, 2021.

14. Boris Munoz, "Hola, President Biden. Latin America Has a Message for You," *New York Times,* January 23, 2021; Anita Kumar, "Biden Mulls 'Lite' Version of Trump's 'Remain in Mexico' Policy," *Politico,* September 6, 2021; Aída Chávez, "Biden's Immigration Policy Picks Up Where Trump Left Off," *The Nation,* September 30, 2021.

15. Enrique Krauze, "Mexico's President May Be Just Months Away from Gaining Total Control," *New York Times,* March 15, 2021; "With 'Remain in Mexico' Program, U.S. and Mexico Grapple with Similar Challenge," NPR, December 4, 2021; Gary Martin, "It's Not All Smiles as Leaders Meet," *San Antonio Express-News,* November 10, 2006.

16. US Department of State, "US Relations with Peru," July 30, 2021; Maria Cervantes, "Peru and U.S. Close to Signing Deal to Counter Chinese Influence in Region: Diplomat," *Reuters,* December 5, 2019; Marco Aquino, "Peru's New Leftist President Prioritizes China Ties During Early Days in Office," *Reuters,* August 5, 2021; Juan Pablo Cardenal, "Sharp Power: Rising Authoritarian Influence," National Endowment for Democracy, December 2017.

17. Simon Romero, "Coca Production Makes a Comeback in Peru," *New York Times,* June 13, 2010.

18. David Scott Palmer, "Peru, the Drug Business and Shining Path: Between Scylla and Charybdis?" *Journal of Interamerican Studies and World Affairs* 34, no. 3 (Autumn 1992), pp. 65–88.

19. Cited in Dennis Jett, "Remember the Drug War?" *Washington Post,* January 13, 2002.

20. Robert Muggah and Jeremy McDermott, "A Massive Drug Trade, and No Violence," *The Atlantic,* April 24, 2013; "Peru Profile," *Insight Crime,* April 6, 2018.

21. White House, "Update: ONDCP Releases Data on Coca Cultivation and Potential Cocaine Production in the Andean Region," July 16, 2021.

22. Thomas Grisaffi and Linda Farthing, "Cocaine: Falling Coffee Prices Force Peru's Farmers to Cultivate Coca," *The Conversation,* February 8, 2021; Robert Muggah, "The Pandemic Has Triggered Dramatic Shifts in the Global Criminal Underworld," *Foreign Policy* (May 8, 2020); Anthony Faiola and Lucien Chauvin, "The Coronavirus Has Gutted the Price of Coca. It Could Reshape the Cocaine Trade," *Washington Post,* June 9, 2020.

23. Barnett S. Koven, "The Second Image Sometimes Reversed: Competing Interests in Drug Policy," E-International Relations, March 8, 2016; Maureen Taft-Morales, "Peru in Brief: Political and Economic Conditions and Relations with the United States," Congressional Research Service, June 7, 2013.

24. Adaobi Tricia Nwaubani, "Trump Trashes Nigeria and Bans Its Immigrants. Nigerians Love Him for It," *Washington Post,* February 7, 2020; Emmanuel Akinwotu, "'He Just Says It as It Is': Why Many Nigerians Support Donald Trump," *The Guardian,* October 31, 2020.

25. Grace Goodrich, "Top 10: Africa's Leading Oil Producers in 2021," Energy Capital and Power, June 16, 2021.

26. CIA, "Nigeria," *CIA World Factbook,* 2021; John Campbell, *Nigeria and the Nation-State* (Washington, DC: Rowman and Littlefield, 2020).

27. Stephen Wright, *Nigeria: Struggle for Stability and Status* (Boulder: Westview, 1998).

28. Office of the US Trade Representative, "Nigeria," 2020.

29. US Energy Information Administration, "Frequently Asked Questions," March 8, 2016; US Energy Information Administration, "Nigeria," June 25, 2020.

30. US Department of State, "U.S. Security Cooperation with Nigeria: Fact Sheet," March 29, 2021.

31. Doyinsola Oladipo and Mike Stone, "Proposed U.S. Arms Sale to Nigeria on 'Hold' over Human Rights Concerns," *Reuters,* July 30, 2021.

32. Neanda Salvaterra and Drew Hindshaw, "Nigerian President Goodluck Jonathan Wants US Troops to Fight Boko Haram," *Wall Street Journal,* February 13, 2015; Sa'eed Husaini, "Nigeria Is in Disarray. So Its President Banned Twitter," *New York Times,* June 8, 2021; John Campbell, "Nigeria's President Buhari Argues 'Africa's Fight Against Terror Is the World's Fight,'" Council on Foreign Relations, August 24, 2021.

33. Campbell, "Nigeria's President Buhari Argues."

34. Judd Devermont, "Learning from #EndSARS—a New U.S. Policy Toward Nigeria," Center for International and Strategic Studies, November 10, 2020.

35. Helene Cooper and Dionne Searcey, "After Years of Distrust, U.S. Military Reconciles with Nigeria to Fight Boko Haram," *New York Times,* May 15, 2016; Zainab Usman, "How Biden Can Build U.S.-Africa Relations Back Better," Carnegie Endowment for International Peace, April 27, 2021.

36. Bernard Gwertzman, "Aid to Zimbabwe Suspended by U.S.," *New York Times,* July 10, 1986; Gregory Elich, "The Battle over Zimbabwe's Future," Pan-African News Wire, April 13, 2007.

37. Quoted in Mike Nizza, "Mugabe Loses Honorary Degree from U Mass," *New York Times,* June 13, 2008.

38. Dewa Mavhinga, "What Should Biden's Election Mean for Zimbabwe?" Human Rights Watch, November 13, 2020; White House, "A Letter on the Continuation of the National Emergency with Respect to Zimbabwe," March 3, 2021.

39. US Department of State, "US Relations with Zimbabwe," January 17, 2020.
40. George F. Ward, "Political Instability in Zimbabwe," Council on Foreign Relations, March 2015.
41. Lynsey Chutel, "With Donald Trump in the White House, Robert Mugabe Wants to Restore Ties with the U.S.," *Huffington Post,* November 16, 2016.
42. Henning Melber and Roger Southall, "Zimbabwe's Foreign Policy Under Mnangagwa," *Journal of Asian and African Affairs* 56, no. 2 (January 2021); Zack Budryk, "Zimbabwean President: Capitol Riots Show US Has No Right to Punish Other Nations 'Under the Guise of Upholding Democracy,'" *The Hill,* January 7, 2021; Steve Coll, "Will Biden's Sanctions Help Restore Democracy in Myanmar?" *The New Yorker,* February 24, 2021.
43. Henning Melber and Roger Southall, "Zimbabwe's Foreign Policy Under Mnangagwa," *Journal of Asian and African Studies* (January 12, 2021); Alex Vines, "What Is the Extent of China's Influence in Zimbabwe?" *BBC News,* November 20, 2017; "Zimbabwe—China Relations on Solid Foundation—Mnangagwa," *Africanews,* January 14, 2020.
44. Scott Anderson, "Fractured Lands: How the Arab World Came Apart," *New York Times,* August 14, 2016.
45. Tamara Cofman Wittes, "Egypt: Trends, Politics, and Human Rights," Brookings Institution, September 9, 2020.
46. US Department of State, "US Relations with Egypt," January 5, 2021; Katharina Buchholz, "Where US Foreign Aid Is Going," Statista, December 23, 2020.
47. Ashraf Khalil, *Liberation Square: Inside the Egyptian Revolution and the Rebirth of a Nation* (New York: St. Martin's, 2011); Barbara Ann Reiffer-Flanagan, "Democratic Dreams Neglected in the Land of the Pharaohs: US Democracy Assistance in Egypt," *Human Rights Review* 15 (2014), pp. 433–454.
48. "Egypt's Brazen Crackdown on Critics," *New York Times,* November 9, 2015.
49. David E. Sanger, "As Mubarak Digs In, U.S. Policy in Egypt Is Complicated," *New York Times,* February 5, 2011; Khalil, *Liberation Square.*
50. Rieffer-Flanagan, "Democratic Dreams Neglected"; Michael Wahid Hanna, "Getting over Egypt: Time to Rethink Relations," *Foreign Affairs* (November–December 2015).
51. Elissa Miller, "Five Years On: Egypt's International Relations," Atlantic Council, January 25, 2016.
52. Peter Baker, "Obama Removes Weapons Freeze Against Egypt," *New York Times,* March 21, 2013.
53. Cristiano Lima, "Trump Praises Egypt's al-Sisi: 'He's a Fantastic Guy,'" *Politico,* September 22, 2016; Larry Diamond, "Democracy Demotion: How the Freedom Agenda Fell Apart," *Foreign Affairs* (July–August 2019).
54. "What We Learned from Mubarak," *New York Times,* February 15, 2021; Michael Wahid Hanna, "Biden Says No More Coddling Dictators. OK, Here's Where to Start," *New York Times,* December 7, 2020; "Opinion: Biden Has Put More Pressure on Egypt's Repressive Regime. Will It Be Enough to Bring Results?" *Washington Post,* September 19, 2021.
55. "Iraq: What Iran and Syria Want," *BBC News,* November 13, 2006.
56. Thomas Erdbrink, "Former American Embassy in Iran Attracts Pride and Dust," *New York Times,* October 31, 2013.
57. Farnaz Fassihi, "A Roadblock for Iran's President-Elect: He's on the U.S. Sanctions List," *New York Times,* June 19, 2021.
58. Steven Erlanger and David E. Sanger, "U.S. and Iran Want to Restore the Nuclear Deal. They Disagree Deeply on What That Means," *New York Times,* May 9, 2021. Other Western powers, however, have normalized their political relations with Tehran (in 1999, the United Kingdom, the last EU country without a diplomatic emissary to Iran, exchanged ambassadors with Tehran). UK-Iranian relations were downgraded by Iran after new sanctions were implemented in November 2011, related to Iran's nuclear program. After the UK embassy compound in Tehran was stormed by hundreds of Iranian students, the UK closed the embassy and ordered the Iranian embassy in London also closed; British interests in Iran were maintained by the Swedish embassy in Tehran, while Iranian interests in the UK were maintained by the Omani embassy in London.

Both Iran and the UK announced they would restore diplomatic relations after progress in nuclear talks, and the embassies were reopened in August of 2015. See "British Embassy in Tehran Reopens Four Years After Closure," *BBC News,* August 23, 2015.

59. Karim Sadjadpour, "The Sources of Soviet Iranian Conduct," *Foreign Policy* (November 2010).

60. "Iran: How Ayatollah Khamenei Became Its Most Powerful Man," *BBC News,* March 9, 2020.

61. Patricia Zengerle, "Extension of Iran Sanctions Act Passes U.S. Congress," *Reuters,* December 1, 2016.

62. It is not only the clerics in Tehran who are bothered by these actions: India, Russia, and European governments, including Germany and France, have expressed their displeasure at this perceived US meddling in their financial affairs.

63. "U.S. State Department: Iran Remains 'World's Worst State Sponsor of Terrorism,'" Radio Free Europe/Radio Liberty, November 1, 2019; Ryan Browne, "State Department Report Finds Iran Is Top State Sponsor of Terror," CNN, June 2, 2016.

64. "US-Iranian Relations: A Brief History," *BBC News,* January 6, 2020.

65. Erlanger and Sanger, "U.S. and Iran Want to Restore the Nuclear Deal"; "US-Iranian Relations," *BBC News.*

66. "US and Iran Seek to Break Impasse at Talks on Reviving Nuclear Deal," *BBC News,* November 29, 2021.

67. Edith M. Lederer, "The AP Interview: UN Chief Warns China, US to Avoid Cold War," *AP,* September 20, 2021.

68. Statement from Chen Yixin, a security official close to Xi Jinping, speaking to CCP officials in January 2021. Quoted in Chris Buckley, "'The East Is Rising': Xi Maps Out China's Post-Covid Ascent," *New York Times,* March 3, 2021.

69. "China Warns Against AUKUS, to Make Meetings Routine with Pacific Island Countries, Enhancing [*sic*] Ties to Higher Level," *Global Times,* October 21, 2021.

70. "Aukus: UK, US and Australia Launch Pact to Counter China," *BBC News,* September 16, 2021.

71. Carter Center, "Chinese Perceptions of the US and China's Image Abroad," *U.S.-China Perception Monitor,* January 11, 2021.

72. Emily Geng, "As U.S. Views of China Grow More Negative, Chinese Support for Their Government Rises," NPR, September 23, 2020.

73. Ibid.

74. Karen Brettell and Karen Pierog, "China Unlikely to Wield U.S. Bond Weapon as Tensions Stay High," *Reuters,* April 1, 2021.

75. Asma Khalid, "Biden Is Keeping Key Parts of Trump's China Trade Policy. Here's Why." NPR, October 4, 2021.

76. Elizabeth Economy and Adam Segal, "Time to Defriend China," *Foreign Policy* (May 24, 2010); Edward Wong and Michael Crowley, "The Biggest Obstacle to China Policy: President Trump," *New York Times,* June 18, 2020.

77. John Feng, "China Hits Back at Donald Trump's Demand They Pay $10 Trillion for Causing Pandemic," *Newsweek,* June 8, 2021.

78. Lara Jakes, "In First Talks, Dueling Accusations Set Testy Tone for U.S.-China Diplomacy," *New York Times,* March 18, 2021. Joe Biden had extensive personal contacts with Chinese leaders, including Xi Jinping as well as his predecessors, both as vice president (when he had multiple meetings with Xi, even prior to his promotion to CCP general secretary) and as chair of the Senate Foreign Relations Committee (when he helped pave the way for China's entry into the World Trade Organization). See Edward Wong, Michael Crowley, and Ana Swanson, "Joe Biden's China Journey," *New York Times,* September 6, 2020.

79. Bob Davis and Lingling Wei, "Biden Plans to Build a Grand Alliance to Counter China," *Wall Street Journal,* January 6, 2021.

80. As more documents from the Cold War era are declassified, the historical record reveals much US awareness and even complicity in violent acts against Indonesian civilians, especially during the anticommunist coup from 1965 to 1966, during which time

at least 500,000 Indonesians were killed. See, for example, Hannah Beech, "U.S. Stood By as Indonesia Killed a Half-Million People, Papers Show," *New York Times,* October 18, 2017.

81. "Iraq a Key Point of Difference During Visit," *Jakarta Post,* November 20, 2006.

82. "Indonesians Protest US President's Visit," NPR, *Morning Edition,* November 20, 2006.

83. Quoted in Norimitsu Onishi, "In Jakarta Speech, Some Hear Cairo Redux," *New York Times,* November 10, 2010.

84. "Opinion of the United States," Pew Research Center, 2021; Richard Wike, "Indonesia: The Obama Effect," Pew Research Center, March 17, 2010.

85. The US State Department refused to grant Prabowo a visa to attend his son's graduation from Boston University, for example. While he stands accused of masterminding human rights abuses in many times and regions, he has been most vilified for his support in abducting student activists during the 1998 anti-Suharto demonstrations; thirteen of whom remain missing. See Phil Stewart and Idrees Ali, "Pentagon Prepares to Welcome Once-Banned Indonesian Minister, Despite Rights Concerns," *Reuters,* October 15, 2020.

86. Jon Emont, "Indonesia Savored Its Ties to Obama. Now It Prepares to Say Goodbye," *Washington Post,* December 6, 2016.

87. Noto Suoneto, "The Five Strategic Challenges Facing US-Indonesia Relations," *The Diplomat,* October 7, 2020.

88. Aaron Walayat, "Stuck in the Middle with You: Indonesia in US-China Relations," *US-China Perception Monitor,* April 11, 2016.

Part 5
Conclusion

19

Looking Forward: Responses to Interdependence

You must be the change you want to see in the world. —*Mahatma Gandhi, Indian political and spiritual leader (1869–1948)*

It is the populations of advanced countries coming to the recognition that this is a serious issue that is causing the needle to move. . . . It is that kind of domestic political pressure from ordinary people that is going to save the world in my view. —*Mia Motley, prime minister of Barbados, on climate change*[1]

These past few years have brought home the reality of being in a world in which our lives are affected by happenings perhaps far away from us. The Covid pandemic has shown us, among many other things, the mutual vulnerability of interdependence. A microscopic virus nearly literally shut down the world.[2] Despite our many differences, our interconnectedness became a reality that virtually all the world shared in common.

So where do we go from here? Some have said that the Covid pandemic will be the defining event for this generation, similar to the way in which World War II impacted prior generations. Others contend that while great-power rivalries ended up shaping recent history over the past century, our current era will instead be defined by global challenges, most notably climate change and economic inequalities, alongside our ability—and will—to address them or ignore them.[3] Once again, we humbly realize that, even if we pay close attention, tectonic shifts are rarely forecastable, and we are almost never able to foresee the far-reaching impacts that events may have. On the cusp of big changes, it is common to miss the shifts, even if, in retrospect, it seems easy to explain them away. Yet, as we send this book to press, it seems that we find ourselves again on the edge of another far-reaching, perhaps even transformational, moment.

Our world of the early twenty-first century is rife with potential conflicts as well as potential new alignments. Interactions between the governments, societies, cultures, and economies of the world may very well chart whether this future follows a path of peace and prosperity, or stagnation and decline. If there is one lesson that we have highlighted throughout this book, though, it is that it will take an increased recognition of all of the world's peoples to craft any meaningful, lasting solutions to the current challenges we face, and to those that we do not yet envision.

In recent years, we've had a lot of conversation about the ways in which the world is changing. With some distance now from some major global events—September 11, 2001, the Great Recession, the Arab Spring, and others—we have the chance to discern lessons learned and opportunities missed. In the wake of the September 11 attacks, for example, then UN Secretary-General Kofi Annan said that one of the lessons of that day that had not received much attention was that we can't ignore inhumane conditions in the rest of the world. The economic and social problems of others have a direct impact on security, within our own countries as well as around the world. Annan is joined by many others who highlight the many (often interrelated) challenges threatening world security. More than two decades ago, former Costa Rican president and Nobel laureate Óscar Arias cautioned that "terrorism is one of many challenges to humanity, but the basic threats to world peace are poverty, inequality, illiteracy, disease, and environmental degradation."[4] Currently, in the wake of a global pandemic, staring down the dangers of climate change, and facing a dangerously widening divide between the proverbial haves and have-nots, his words are striking in their simplicity and their truth. UN Secretary-General António Guterres now calls on the world to "wake up," as he highlights the "greatest cascade of crises in our lifetime."[5]

Some contend that perhaps we are living through "deglobalization," a decades-long trend that was launched years ago by the global recession, changes that may be hearkening the end of the so-called liberal world order. The more destructive aspects of globalization, including climate change, terrorism, and epidemics, have amplified opposition to these changes, in complex ways, especially with the resurgence of authoritarianism and populism, as we have discussed throughout this book.[6] Trade is more restricted, migrants are more encumbered. Identities, especially national and ethnic identities, seem more hardened, especially as part of the wave of populism that is sweeping many parts of the globe—north and south alike. Many of the economic challenges in the global south—income disparity, for example—are increasingly recognized as scourges within developed countries as well, as gaps in income, education, and opportunity become more pronounced.

The world has picked up some lessons from the past few decades of experience trying to cope with, and improve, when possible, disparities in the human condition. Challenges are rarely (if ever) isolated events: therefore, we need a truly multipronged strategy for curbing the appeal of violence and extremism. Sickness, for example, is closely related to political instability; countries with high infant mortality rates are more likely to fall into civil wars. The absence of political voice or economic opportunity serves as an incubator for extremism. The lack of access to safe drinking water leads militaries to battle. Poverty worsens as economic stagnation deepens and assistance falters. We now have overwhelming data that point to long-term positive outcomes of educating girls, including decreasing infant mortality, improving health outcomes throughout society, raising economic standards within society, and decreasing the appeal of violence.

As we contemplate policy responses to the range of threats in the world today, it is clear that we need to move beyond the spread of weapons and threats from terrorism to the root causes of conflict and unrest. Without human security, peace will remain elusive. These are not new ideas. Many argue that we need to do whatever we can to reduce the number of fragile states around the world, since the combination of long-term grievances, masses of refugees, horribly uneven development, lack of human rights, and security challenges is known to produce human misery and political conflict. Over a decade ago, former US defense secretary Robert Gates argued that "dealing with such fractured or failing states is, in many ways, the main security challenge of our time."[7]

We've yet to learn the best way, as a world community of any sort of definition, to make this work. For example, even if a military response in Afghanistan seemed to make sense after 9/11, twenty years later President Joe Biden announced that not only was the United States withdrawing all troops but also that he was "ending an era of major military operations to remake other countries," even as he promised billions of dollars of additional aid to the government (that quickly collapsed).[8] In scenes woefully reminiscent of the US departure from Saigon in 1975, Afghan citizens fell to their deaths while clinging to the wheels of US military transport jets; the brutal difficulties of promoting development, security, and peace were laid bare for all to see. In a few short hours, an entire generation of Afghani lives were turned upside down; many felt abandoned, lost, and broken.[9] Yet, analysts and activists tell us, even if nation-building and military intervention are no longer seen as viable options, it would be an enormous mistake to write off countries, peoples, and the challenges they face. As we learn time and time again, security and well-being are inseparable; borders are permeable, and, like it or not, isolation is not a viable option.[10]

What is to be done? In recent years, we have witnessed an upsurge in collective action, including on the international scale, organizing around many interrelated themes, like climate justice, racial equity, and political liberty. As we discussed in Chapter 8, these mobilizations have been civil and uncivil in their orientation. No matter the rallying cry, it is important not to underestimate the power of individuals and groups to change the world: major global transformations—from the Renaissance to women's movements, LGBTQIA movements, environmental justice, Black Lives Matter, and beyond—started with ideas circulated among a group of like-minded individuals. Governments, as well as civil society organizations, can (and do) have impact.

The question can be raised in terms of foreign aid, which could be a much more effective instrument for change than it has been. Used in the proper way, foreign aid can be one of the best weapons against insecurities that may lead to violence. But even in the face of devastating consequences during the Covid pandemic, the world community failed to provide adequate responses to the spread of the coronavirus, as we saw with the uneven distribution of reliable vaccines, even after major world powers and pharmaceutical companies alike banded together to promise hoarding would not happen.[11]

Years ago, a *Wall Street Journal* op-ed jointly penned by Madeleine Albright and Colin Powell, two former US secretaries of state, highlighted the fundamental connection between richer and poorer countries and the imperative to maintain our awareness of interdependence: "Our country's economic health and security are inextricably linked to the prosperity and security of the rest of the world. . . . (Even in the midst of an economic crisis) pulling back from global engagement is not an option."[12] Yet, even prior to Covid, protectionist policies propped up by populist leaders were becoming the rage in many regions of the world.

The other major tool for influence, of course, is the military. Especially after the US military and diplomatic withdrawal from Afghanistan, there is little appetite, as we have discussed, for long-term military deployments. Yet, with the Marshall Plan, the large-scale US government–funded effort under President Harry S. Truman to rebuild Western Europe after World War II, we recognized how poverty bred instability and that promoting the development of other countries reinforced our national security. The Marshall Plan included both economic and military levers. Voices as diverse as the United Nations Conference on Trade and Development, former world leaders, and the American Enterprise Institute are calling for a similar—global—reconstruction effort to rebuild after Covid.[13] Any lasting action would need to include immediate relief (including debt forgiveness) as well as assistance with medium-term preparedness that would build capacity for medical testing, vaccine production, and other major public health needs. Recovery will require an infusion of significant aid and, to be lasting, will need to prepare as much for the next pandemic as it assists with overcoming the challenges of this one.

However, during the Cold War, US foreign aid was used to promote stability by propping up dictators—Washington's assistance to Indonesia's Suharto fits this mold precisely. The United States, and other states, need to remember the important role that aid can play in promoting stability, but they must be careful not to use it just to bribe authoritarians. There is a high price, we have learned, for such a policy: the United States is still paying for cozying up to the Iranian Shah for all those years. Nicaraguans, Indonesians, Egyptians, Chileans, and others fume at the role of Washington in supporting dictatorial leaders, or unseating popular leaders who seem opposed to US interests. Policies—if seen to be promoting security over human rights—risk similar blowback.

Joseph Nye's concept of "soft power," or the ability to influence others by attracting them to one's values, ideals, and norms, is increasingly tendered as a way to understand a country's (or organization's) appeal and leverage. The United States has benefited from soft power achieved through its widely recognized pop culture, universities, and political values. Nye has argued, "When Washington discounts the importance of its attractiveness abroad, it pays a steep price."[14] In a sense, soft power is about public diplomacy. It is something that, as of late, others have been aggressively promoting as well, especially China's investment and engagement across Africa, the Middle East, and South America, with its Belt and Road Initiative and its variants, including the "Digital Silk Road" and the "Health Silk Road."[15] Few have claimed that soft power is a zero-sum game, but China's offering up of an alternative to US policies is quite attractive to some countries that are frustrated with perceived US meddling, infringement, or absence. Even prior to the withdrawal from Afghanistan, when many claimed the United States was toppling from its pedestal of promoting soft power abroad, others lamented that "the

US has reserves of soft power that it has underused."[16] As analysts remind us, once soft power is lost, it is extremely difficult to get back.[17]

For many people around the world, including some of its closest allies in the West, the United States lost the moral high ground with its unilateral actions decades ago. This was most clear when the United States and Great Britain, with clear disapproval from a majority of their colleagues—friend and foe alike—within the United Nations, waged war against Iraq's Saddam Hussein and his purported weapons of mass destruction—which were never found. As much as many believed President Obama would bring a completely new approach and, by connection, new perceptions of the United States, few significant changes were realized, as we discussed in Chapter 17. For more than a decade now, under presidents from both major political parties, many around the world view the United States in retreat, or at least, they view the United States as less reliable than it used to be, a grim perception that predated and outlasted the Trump administration.[18] The matter is exacerbated by China's increasingly ominous presence. This is leading to rearmament as military spending is spiking in many regions of the world, with new hypersonic technology threatening to significantly change the traditional calculus of the arms races of the past—essentially undoing everything we've known about traditional deterrence. According to the Stockholm International Peace Research Institute (SIPRI), global spending on militaries rose to nearly $2 trillion in 2020, an increase of more than 2.6 percent over the year prior, and the highest total since it began tracking such rates in 1988.[19] It is a dangerous and ever-evolving exercise, with wide-ranging impacts. One nuclear analyst put it this way, "If big powers race to build up their arsenals, smaller powers will follow."[20]

But soft power is different from the traditional military and economic policy levers, which are wielded by states to demonstrate (and increase) their influence. While governments can manage and promote soft power, much of its appeal actually comes from citizens—from the observed interactions between leaders and the led, and from the projection of a sense of civic duty, commitment, and, often, philanthropy. This is why awareness, especially the appreciation of differences, and the ability to comprehend that others may not see the world from a singular perspective are so important. Especially in times of great uncertainty, many are comfortable focusing on local affairs, or perhaps on national issues alone. We're not sure it was ever entirely possible to understand matters in isolation, but these divisions seem more fabricated than ever.

Nevertheless, in the face of so much insecurity, once again we see leaders and citizens alike turning inward and viewing outsiders as threats to be contained and, quite literally at times, fenced in. At once, it seemed possible to celebrate the simultaneity of the digital global communications that allowed us to communicate in isolation, while also decrying international travel and commerce that had become the poster for globalization. Past challenges have shown the futility of trying to lock out the world; in light of Covid, one commentator warned of "biopolitical hypernationalism" and its ill effects.[21] Prior to 2020, antiglobalization was already a rallying cry for populist leaders around the world, fueled by slowing economic growth, rising inequality, and disaffection with traditional politics.[22] Xenophobia and isolationism are dangerously attractive in times of upheaval. They won't fix the problems we face, at least not in any enduring way. In a bipartisan letter to the Biden administration calling for the United States to assume the necessary international leadership to recover from Covid, advocates demanded a rejection of the "false dichotomy between domestic and global efforts."[23] In its place, leaders tell us, it is imperative for us to promote civic literacy, a deeper understanding of the many types of political, social, and economic processes around the world, and, concomitantly, the empathy to grasp the many different ways that cultures combine and societies function.

Prior editions of this book have highlighted the AIDS pandemic, the wars in Darfur and Syria, waves of the migration crises, and global economic recession. We have covered the perceived march toward—and then away from—liberal democratic freedoms. From the first edition (published in 2003), we have analyzed the threat of climate change around the world. The unifying frame of this fifth edition, provided by the unprecedented nature of the Covid pandemic, has only reinforced many of our prior concerns. The pandemic made interdependence concrete and personal. The "long arm" of Covid revealed strains and weaknesses in systems around the globe, leaving many societies—with various regime types, levels of income, and demographic features—in worse condition, highlighting racial, ethnic, and gender inequalities only made worse by a lethal pandemic.[24]

That's another call for our attention: for all of the importance of the pandemic, we cannot forget the progress reversed and other issues that continue (and, in many cases, have been made worse), as the world's attention has been focused on Covid—including gender violence, weapons proliferation, mass migration, and economic dislocation—just to name a few. Moving forward, what will be the so-called new normal when these trends converge? What balance of values and policies will follow? From where will the next major challenges to peace, security, and freedom emerge, and will our actions be more effective than before? Will we, in the words of the UN Secretary-General, "wake up"?

Notes

1. Somini Sengupta, "The COP26 Climate Talks Are Opening. Here's What to Expect," *New York Times,* October 30, 2021.

2. Human Rights Watch estimates that an unprecedented 1.4 billion students around the world faced closures and relocation of their educational institutions (from pre-primary through secondary levels) in more than 190 countries around the world; this accounts for approximately 90 percent of the world's school-aged children facing educational disruption in an effort to slow the spread of the coronavirus. See "Years Don't Wait for Them," Human Rights Watch, May 17, 2021. Distance learning was not an option for much of the world: 43 percent of homes globally, and 82 percent of households in Africa did not have a computer or access to the internet. See Rod Berger, "Global Literacy Efforts Aim to Reflect Readers and Their Representative Cultures," *Forbes,* June 24, 2021.

3. Richard Haas, "Deglobalization and Its Discontents," Council on Foreign Relations, May 12, 2020.

4. Quoted in Mike William, "Slow-Burning Problems Could Singe US," *Montreal Gazette,* February 14, 2002, p. A19.

5. Edith M. Lederer, "'The World Must Wake Up': Tasks Daunting as UN Meeting Opens," *AP,* September 22, 2021.

6. Ruchir Sharma, "When Borders Close," *New York Times,* November 13, 2016; Haas, "Deglobalization and Its Discontents."

7. Robert M. Gates, "Helping Others Defend Themselves: The Future of U.S. Security Assistance," *Foreign Affairs* (May–June 2010).

8. Steve Coll, "The Lessons of Defeat in Afghanistan," *The New Yorker,* September 5, 2021.

9. Ibid.

10. Haas, "Deglobalization and Its Discontents."

11. "A Dose of Reality: How Rich Countries and Pharmaceutical Corporations Are Breaking Their Vaccine Promises," Joint United Nations Programme on HIV and AIDS (UNAIDS), October 21, 2021.

12. Madeleine K. Albright and Colin L. Powell, "Don't Forget About Foreign Aid," *Wall Street Journal,* May 5, 2009. "Stability and prosperity go hand in hand, and neither is possible in the presence of widespread and extreme poverty."

13. Gordon Brown, "G20 Nations Must Devise a Global Plan for Growth Post-Covid," *Financial Times,* December 16, 2020; Mukhisa Kituyi, "Africa Needs a Marshall Plan to Ride Out Covid-19 Crisis; Prepare for Uncertain Times," United Nations Conference on Trade and Development (UNCTAD), April 16, 2020; Rizal Ramli, "The World Needs a New Marshall Plan," *The Diplomat,* August 4, 2021; Michael R. Strain, "A Marshall Plan for COVID-19," American Enterprise Institute, August 10, 2021; Ngaire Woods, "Brown's Blueprint for Softening the Blows of Globalisation," *Financial Times,* June 19, 2021.

14. Joseph S. Nye Jr., "The Decline of America's Soft Power: Why Washington Should Worry," *Foreign Affairs* 83, no. 3 (May–June 2004), p. 17.

15. Richard Ghiasy and Rajeshwari Krishnamurthy, "China's Digital Silk Road and the Global Digital Order," *The Diplomat,* April 13, 2021; Kristine Lee and Martijn Rasser, "China's Health Silk Road Is a Dead-End Street," *Foreign Policy* (June 16, 2020).

16. Carola McGiffert, ed., *Chinese Soft Power and Its Implications for the United States* (Washington, DC: Center for Strategic and International Studies, 2009), p. 126.

17. Aynne Kokas and Oriana Skylar Mastro, "The Soft War That America Is Losing," *Australian Financial Review,* January 15, 2021.

18. Steven Erlanger, "The Sharp U.S. Pivot to Asia Is Throwing Europe off Balance," *New York Times,* September 17, 2021; Uri Friedman, "America Is Alone in Its Cold War with China," *The Atlantic,* February 17, 2020; Stephen Kobrin, "How Globalization Became a Thing That Goes Bump in the Night," *Journal of International Business Policy* 3 (2020), pp. 280–286.

19. "Global Military Spending Rises 2.6% in 2020 Despite Pandemic Hit," *Reuters,* April 26, 2021; Aaron Mehta, "The World Spent Almost $2 Trillion on Defense in 2020," *Defense News,* April 26, 2021.

20. Steven Erlanger, "Are We Headed for Another Expensive Nuclear Arms Race? Could Be," *New York Times,* August 8, 2019.

21. Rob Ashghar, "Our Leaders Once Thought Globally; the Pandemic Has Made Them Parochial," *Forbes,* February 6, 2021.

22. M. Chatib Basri and Hal Hill, "The Southeast Asian Economies in the Age of Discontent," *Asian Economic Policy Review* 15 (2020), p. 185.

23. Aspen Economic Strategy Group, "AESG Member Statement: A Call for US Leadership on Global Vaccination Efforts," August 9, 2021.

24. Sarah Repucci and Amy Slipowitz, "Democracy Under Siege: Freedom in the World 2021," Freedom House, pp. 10–14, n.d.

Acronyms

AIIB	Asian Infrastructure Investment Bank
AMLO	Andrés Manuel López Obrador (Mexico)
APC	All Progressives Congress (Nigeria)
ARF	ASEAN Regional Forum
ASEAN	Association of Southeast Asian Nations
AU	African Union
AUKUS	Australia, United Kingdom, and US trilateral security pact
BRI	Belt and Road Initiative
CCP	Chinese Communist Party
CEDAW	Convention on the Elimination of All Forms of Discrimination Against Women
CIA	Central Intelligence Agency (United States)
COVAX	COVID-19 Vaccines Global Access
CRC	Convention on the Rights of the Child
CWC	Chemical Weapons Convention
DDoS	distributed denial-of-service
ECFs	extended-credit facilities
ECOSOC	Economic and Social Council (UN)
EPZ	export processing zone
ESN	Eastern Security Network (Nigeria)
EU	European Union
FIFA	International Federation of Association Football
FIS	Islamic Salvation Front (Algeria)
G-20	Group of 20
G-40	Generation 40
GAVI	Global Alliance for Vaccines and Immunization
GDI	Gender-Related Development Index
GII	Gender Inequality Index
GNI	gross national income
GNP	gross national product
HDI	Human Development Index
HIC	high-income country

HIPC	highly indebted poor country
HMIC	higher-middle-income country
IAEA	International Atomic Energy Agency
IARF	International Association for Religious Freedom
IBRD	International Bank for Reconstruction and Development (World Bank)
ICBL	International Campaign to Ban Landmines
ICBM	intercontinental ballistic missiles
ICC	International Criminal Court
ICJ	International Court of Justice
ICRC	International Committee of the Red Cross
ICTR	International Criminal Tribunal for Rwanda
IDP	internally displaced people
IFI	international financial institution
IFRC	International Federation of Red Cross and Red Crescent Societies
IGO	international governmental organization
ILO	International Labour Organization
IMF	International Monetary Fund
INE	National Electoral Institute (Mexico)
IPCC	Intergovernmental Panel on Climate Change
IPE	international political economy
IPOB	Indigenous People of Biafra
IRGC	Islamic Revolutionary Guard Corps
ISIS	Islamic State in Iraq and al-Sham
ISIS-SP	Islamic State in Iraq and al-Sham–Sinai Province (Egypt)
IS-K	Islamic State Khorasan
ISWAP	Islamic State West Africa Province (Nigeria)
ITU	International Telecommunication Union
JCPOA	Joint Comprehensive Plan of Action
JEI	Jamaat-e-Islami (Pakistan)
JI	Jemaah Islamiah (Islamic Organization)
KMT	Nationalist Party (China)
KPK	Corruption Eradication Commission
LDC	less developed country
LGBTQIA	lesbian, gay, bisexual, transgender, queer/questioning, intersex, and asexual/aromantic/agender
LIC	low-income country
LLDC	least–less developed country
LMIC	low- and lower-middle-income countries
LRA	Lord's Resistance Army (Uganda)
MDC	Movement for Democratic Change (Zimbabwe)
MDRI	Multilateral Debt Relief Initiative
Mercosur	Common Market of the South (also known as Mercosul)
MERS	Middle East respiratory syndrome
MNC	multinational corporation
MORENA	Movement of National Regeneration

MSF	Doctors Without Borders
NAFTA	North American Free Trade Agreement
NAM	Non-Aligned Movement
NATO	North Atlantic Treaty Organization
NGO	nongovernmental organization
NPT	Nuclear Non-Proliferation Treaty
OAS	Organization of American States
OAU	Organization of African Unity
OECD	Organisation for Economic Co-operation and Development
OIC	Organization of the Islamic Conference
OPEC	Organization of the Petroleum Exporting Countries
P-5	permanent five members of the UN Security Council
PAN	National Action Party (Mexico)
PAP	People's Armed Police (China)
PDI-P	Indonesian Democratic Party–Struggle
PDP	People's Democratic Party (Nigeria)
PHDI	Planetary pressures–adjusted Human Development Index
PKI	Communist Party of Indonesia
PKK	Kurdistan Workers Party (Turkey)
PKO	peacekeeping operation
PLA	People's Liberation Army (China)
PRC	People's Republic of China
PRD	Party of Democratic Revolution (Mexico)
PRI	Institutional Revolutionary Party (Mexico)
RSF	Reporters Without Borders
R2P	responsibility to protect
RUF	Revolutionary United Front (Sierra Leone)
SADC	Southern African Development Community
SAP	structural adjustment program
SARS	severe acute respiratory syndrome
SARS	Special Anti-Robbery Squad (Nigeria)
SBY	Susilo Bambang Yudhoyono (Indonesia)
SDGs	Sustainable Development Goals
SEATO	Southeast Asia Treaty Organization
SIPRI	Stockholm International Peace Research Institute
SOE	state-owned enterprise
UAE	United Arab Emirates
UDHR	Universal Declaration of Human Rights
UDI	Unilateral Declaration of Independence (Rhodesia)
UNCTAD	United Nations Conference on Trade and Development
UNDP	United Nations Development Programme
UNEP	United Nations Environment Programme
UNHCR	United Nations High Commission(er) for Refugees
UNICEF	United Nations Children's Fund
UNIFEM	United Nations Development Fund for Women
UNODC	United Nations Office on Drugs and Crime
USMCA	US-Mexico-Canada Agreement

VPN	virtual private network
WHO	World Health Organization
WMD	weapon of mass destruction
WTO	World Trade Organization
ZANU	Zimbabwe African National Union
ZANU-PF	Zimbabwe African National Union–Patriotic Front

Glossary

abertura A Portuguese term borrowed from the Brazilian experience, describing a political opening that may or may not lead to democratization. *See* **political liberalization**.

absolute poverty The term used by the United Nations to describe dire material hardship, a standard of living beneath human dignity. It is a crushing poverty in which people lack access to the basic necessities of life such as food, clean water, shelter, and healthcare.

accountability A characteristic of democracy existing when government is held responsible for its actions. Governments that are promoting accountability seek to control corruption not only by reducing the incentive to steal, but also by raising the costs and risks of official misconduct and demonstrating to the population that no one can violate the law with impunity.

acephalous society A "headless society" or "stateless society" in which there is no full-time executive; rather, groups of people are governed by committee or consensus.

amnesty A pardon granted by governments to individuals and even groups of offenders as a gesture of reconciliation, often during a transition or change of regime.

anti-vaxxers Those opposed to vaccination. Extreme vaccine skeptics galvanized by, but not limited to, the vaccines against Covid-19. Known for its aggressive messaging, the anti-vaccine movement predates Covid, is based more on disinformation and conspiracy theories than science, and appeals to populations inclined to distrust government.

aspiration gap Disparity between what is desired or hoped for and what can be attained. This concept helps us understand the consequences of unmet expectations.

austerity plan Another name for structural adjustment, denoting the hardship associated with implementing such measures. *See* **structural adjustment programs and extended-credit facilities**.

authoritarianism A nondemocratic political system in which the ruler depends on coercion rather than popular legitimacy to remain in power. Such systems are characterized by their abuse of human rights. Power is concentrated in the executive branch of government, and executives act with little if any interference from legislatures or judiciaries.

Belt and Road Initiative A major foreign policy initiative launched by Xi Jinping in 2013, the Belt and Road Initiative (BRI) represents a commitment by the Chinese government to invest in countries throughout Asia and even in Europe. The BRI is more of a collection of bilateral agreements than it is a coherent singular plan. Pragmatically, the BRI, once referred to as the "One Belt, One Road" initiative, demonstrates the might of the Chinese economy. Strategically, it embodies Beijing's aspirations for greater regional and global influence. Although it has been compared to the US Marshall Plan after World War II, the amount of investment (pledged and realized) dwarfs the Marshall Plan. Additionally, the focus on loans (often with opaque repayment terms) rather than grants, negative environmental impacts, and preference for Chinese corporations and labor in many overseas projects have subjected the BRI to criticism.

bottom-up approach An approach to change or development in which policies or projects are initiated and directed from the grassroots or masses. *See also* **top-down approach**.

bourgeoisie Originally from the French word *bourg* for "market town," this became a prominent term of analysis in Marxist socialism, separating the working class (known as the proletariat) from the landowning merchant classes and capitalist entrepreneurs (known as the bourgeoisie). In the Marxist framework, it is the bourgeoisie who will be eliminated by class struggle to produce a classless, communist society. *See also* **proletariat**.

Bush Doctrine President George W. Bush's foreign policy approach following the terrorist attacks of September 11, 2001. He conceptually divided the world community into two categories—those who support terrorists versus those who fight terrorists. The doctrine may be summed up in his statement that "either you are with us, or you are with the terrorists." In many parts of the world, this simplification was rejected as self-serving and unreflective of the complexities of the twenty-first century.

cadre party A type of political party dominated by personality-driven cliques and factional groupings that depend on local notables to choose and groom candidates. Cadre parties are recognized for their limited recruitment and are often found in states with limited voting rights. The term "cadre" has also been used to refer to the most dedicated members of a political party.

case study A detailed examination of a particular phenomenon or institution (in this context, a state). A method that seeks to find and demonstrate causal connections by tracing them through a series of cases, which are then compared.

caudillo A political strongman, often a member of the military.

Chapter VII The section of the UN Charter that permits the Security Council to "order binding action, including economic sanctions and the use of armed force." It sets enforcement mechanisms to prevent or deter threats to international peace. So-called Chapter VII authority has been used often since the end of the Cold War to justify intervention in conflict or unstable circumstances.

civil society Generally refers to voluntary social interactions between individuals that are independent of the government. Civil society organizations are commonly recognized as intermediaries between the government and the family. As a concept, civil society (also known as public space) includes nongovernmental organizations, social movements, and professional associations.

class (social) A number of people or things grouped together. A group of people who are linked together because of certain things held in common, such as occupation, social status, or economic background.

cleavage A socially supported division between groups in society who are significant enough to have forms of expression. Cleavages are often based on ethnicity, socioeconomic factors, or gender. Scholars have highlighted two dominant patterns of such divisions. Coinciding cleavages are clear and distinct, in which multiple competing viewpoints or points of division line up in clearly divided categories, presenting a situation that is more ripe for conflict. Crosscutting cleavages are mixed between and among various groups, producing an outcome in which cleavages are dispersed throughout society; therefore, those seeking support from the population must appeal to a wider variety of groups.

Cold War The period of intense US-Soviet rivalry that ran from World War II until the dissolution of the Soviet Union in 1991. Although this antagonism was played out in many different ways across every part of the world, it is known as being "cold" because, fearing nuclear catastrophe, the two parties never engaged in direct military confrontations.

collective security The principle that aggression against one state is taken as an aggression against all. Agreement to collectively resist aggression against another is a founding idea of the United Nations. Collective security arrangements are pursued by states in the hope of deterring threatening action.

common market Allows for the free circulation of goods, services, and capital between member states.

comparative advantage Liberal principle that holds that efficiency is maximized through specialization in production.

comparative studies This approach seeks to comprehend the complexity of human experience by adopting an eclectic, multidisciplinary approach. It utilizes the comparative method to produce generalizations that describe, identify, and explain trends—and even predict human behavior. This approach identifies relationships and interactions between actors, as well as patterns of behavior, by making comparisons (of two or more countries or of one country over time) to find similarities and differences in experience.

comprador The Indigenous elite who dominate the economies and politics of many non-Western countries. They often enter into sweetheart deals with foreign interests—at great cost to the local majority.

consolidation Said to exist when democracy has put down deep roots and is durable—when democracy "is the only game in town." Democracies become consolidated by becoming more inclusive, by respecting human rights, and by guaranteeing equal representation to minorities and other marginalized groups. Stability, citizen loyalty, and a widespread belief that the system is good are all signs of consolidation.

convergence Said to be attained when less developed countries "catch up" with developed countries.

corporatism Terminology describing relations between groups and political authority; government restricts the development and operation of independent organizations. In corporatist systems, society is divided by functions (e.g., unions, professional associations), and government attempts to coordinate society by balancing groups that must negotiate with government for legal or economic benefits.

corruption Official misconduct or the abuse of power for private gain. A problem in developed and less developed countries that has contributed to the breakdown of military and civilian governments as populations call for accountability and transparency.

cross-national analysis A study comparing two or more countries to make larger generalizations.

cultural relativism The view that worldwide there is no commonly held morality. Rather, human rights and other ethical issues vary depending on the group, and, consequently, the promotion of any set of moral codes as somehow universal is misplaced and imperialistic.

Cultural Revolution Formally called the Great Proletarian Cultural Revolution, a chaotic period in modern Chinese history, officially from 1966 to 1969, when Chairman Mao Zedong directed the Red Guards to attack officials to prevent the spread of capitalism and materialism. Many individuals (especially businesspeople and intellectuals) were sent to the Chinese countryside to "learn from the peasants," while others were sent to "reeducation" camps to have their problems rectified. Most analysts today argue that the chaos of the Cultural Revolution did not truly end until Mao's death in 1976.

customs union A form of economic integration in which states agree to promote trade among members by eliminating tariffs and nontariff barriers, and to cooperate to protect their producers by setting a common tariff against nonmember states.

Debt Service Suspension Initiative (DSSI) Group of 20 donors, aiming to stave off a debt crisis offered partial, temporary debt postponement to seventy-seven of the poorest developing countries so that these nations could concentrate on the pandemic.

delegative democracy A political system that has an outward appearance of being democratic, and is more democratic than authoritarian. However, such systems are led by elites whose commitment to democracy is said to have limits. In delegative democracies, the executive claims to personify the nation's interests and, therefore, has the exclusive right to interpret them.

democracy (political) "Government by the people," existing in several variations and operating through different kinds of constitutional systems. A type of government or political system that is based on a decentralization of power and built on the principle of popular sovereignty: in democracies people choose their representatives, who compete for political office through free and fair elections held on a regular basis. Consequently, citizen participation and respect for civil liberties are integral to democracy, as citizens must have the freedom to hold political leaders accountable for their actions.

democracy dividend Popular expectation that after years of abuse, the transition to democracy will bring an economic expansion, an end to corruption, and an improved quality of life. There is usually much goodwill created by a democratic transition; however, this honeymoon is often short-lived and the resulting disillusionment is dangerous for fragile new democracies.

democratic institutionalization The process of crafting, nurturing, and developing democratic institutions to ensure participation, representation, accountability, respect for human rights, and so on. Institutionalization refers to the development of regularized processes; as democratic institutionalization occurs, "the rules of the game" become stabilized and formalized.

democratic transition A phase of political liberalization in which a political system is democratizing (opportunities for political participation and competition are expanded, free and fair elections are scheduled, and so on). Not every political liberalization results in a democratic transition, and not all democratic transitions result in democracy—they can turn out many different ways.

deterrence Defense policy in which a country attempts to prevent attack by threatening credible retaliation. The logic of deterrence is that an initiating action will cause mutual suicide. The greatest deterrents are considered to be nuclear weapons—the mere possession of nuclear weapons is believed sufficient to deter an enemy, because unless a country's entire nuclear arsenal could be wiped out by a first strike, the destruction caused by the inevitable retaliation would be too great a price to pay.

development There is little agreement on how best to describe development. The UN defines political development as "the achievement of a stable democracy that promotes the economic well-being of its citizens in an equitable, humane, and environmentally concerned manner." Some identify it as a process associated with increasing humans' choices and opportunities. Development is now widely recognized as promoting material and nonmaterial forms of well-being; it is associated with improved living standards, although it rests on political participation and human security and is concerned with the distribution of and access to resources. Often confused with "growth," development should be understood as both a process and an end.

devotee party Type of political party that is dominated by a charismatic leader.

disintegration When political reconfiguration spirals out of control. Divides are aggravated by internal and external demands for change, the military's unwillingness or inability to prevent a breakup, and the state's inability to meet demands for change. Weak states are said to "implode"—to decay and collapse from within.

displaced persons People who are forced to flee their homes, but who have not crossed internationally recognized borders. The numbers of internally displaced people are often higher than official counts of refugees, and are considered to be more reflective of the magnitude of human suffering.

divide and conquer A common means of colonial conquest in which a usurping power sets two parties against each other, aggravates tensions to the point that the parties bleed each other dry, and then moves into the vacuum. Also known as divide and rule.

due process The expectation that certain procedures must always be followed in making policy; guarantees of fair legal procedures designed to protect the rights and liberties of individuals.

economic liberalization Neoliberal economic reforms that dismantle government controls and promote opening up economies to foreign trade and investment. Also known as market reforms.

economic nationalism An ideology that is highly skeptical of neoliberalism and globalization. Also known as economic patriotism or economic populism, it includes left- and right-wing variants that disagree on almost everything except the need to protect domestic producers from foreign competition (what they consider to be unfair trade).

efficacy An attitude about one's competence to effect change; a perception of ability or the sense that one's participation can make a difference. A sense of efficacy is an important factor in the decision to be engaged in public affairs—people with a strong sense of efficacy are more likely to be active in civic life than those who believe their actions would be worthless. The antonym of efficacy in this sense would be *alienation.*

elite revolution Special type of revolution that is rapid and swift, with minimal participation by those outside of the initiating core and with limited violence. Also known as revolution from above.

elites Those who hold more power than others, whether cultural, political, economic, social, or otherwise. According to elite theory, elites are always outnumbered by those ostensibly holding less power, often referred to as the masses. Elites possess certain advantages, of wealth, privilege, education, training, status, political power, and the like.

empire The largest, most complex form of state organization, distinguished from a chiefdom by the size of the territories and the populations it controls. Empires are usually vast and impose a centralized government or single sovereign over a collection of different communities or nations. Empires often dominate regional and international trade; known for their large militaries, they frequently amass great riches through conquest and demands for tribute.

essential functions The most basic duties expected of elected governments, such as collecting taxes, enforcing laws, designing policies, and being responsive to the majority.

exceptionalist A belief or behavior that demonstrates the view that one's group is different from the norm, and therefore above the rules by which others are supposed to abide. An exceptionalist view of a group or event emphasizes the singular, unique qualities of whatever is being examined—making it seem that any particular circumstance is difficult to compare to another.

export processing zone (EPZ) A special trade area established by less developed countries to attract foreign investment. In the hope of creating jobs, obtaining technology transfers, and gaining other benefits, EPZs offer low or no taxes and guarantee cheap, "docile" labor and minimal government regulation or interference with regard to health or environmental codes or the repatriation of profits.

extended-credit facilities (ECFs) Said to be "kinder and gentler" than structural adjustment programs (SAPs), this austerity plan allows for more input from the countries they target and treats them more like stakeholders. ECFs often include fewer conditions and more emphasis on poverty reduction (as opposed to a singular emphasis on growth). But critics contend that the difference between them is mostly window-dressing.

extraterritoriality Imposing one's rules and laws outside of one's own sovereign territory. Extraterritoriality was invoked during the colonial period; now, many developing countries view the United States as attempting to return to this state of affairs by insisting that foreign countries abide by US laws or policies.

fallacy of electoralism The mistake of focusing on elections as "proof" of democracy and ignoring other political realities.

fatwa A religious judgment issued by Muslim clerics.

formal sector The "above-ground" part of the economy (as opposed to the informal sector), calculated into gross domestic product.

founding elections The first elections marking a democratic transition, symbolizing a departure from authoritarianism.

Four Tigers Hong Kong, Singapore, South Korea, and Taiwan—distinguished by their record of strong growth rates and their shared reliance on state capitalism.

globalization Describes the world's increasing interconnectedness, particularly with regard to communications, economies, and cultures, and associated with faster and greater international flows of trade, investment, and finance as well as migration, cultural diffusion, and communication—more specifically, a process describing the spread of capitalism and "modernization" worldwide. Alternatively viewed as a positive force that promotes development and brings the world closer together, or as a negative phenomenon contributing to worsening under-development and the homogenization of the world's cultures.

grassroots-based approach An approach that is designed, implemented, and controlled by local communities. Often lauded for being not only more democratic in principle but also more effective in operation. *See* **bottom-up approach**.

Group of 20 (G-20) Founded in 1999, the G-20 is a forum that brings together finance ministers and central bank governors from the leading industrialized and emerging market economies in a regular dialogue to discuss a range of key issues in regard to the global economy. Together the partners constitute 90 percent of the world's gross national product, 80 percent of world trade, and two-thirds of the world's population.

growth A summation of economic performance referring to an increase in the volume of trade or economic output of a country, measured by gross domestic product (GDP), gross national income (GNI), or gross national product (GNP). Growth is usually a key indicator of a healthy economy, measured against the previous performance of each national economy, not a single worldwide standard (e.g., a 10 percent growth rate in a small economy, albeit impressive, actually indicates a smaller amount of absolute economic activity than a single-digit growth rate in a larger economy).

guerrilla From the Spanish, literally "little war." Guerrillas are loosely organized, nonuniformed combatants, often small in number. Guerrilla tactics are mobile and swift, incorporating the element of surprise with sabotage, hit and run, and ambush, all in violation of conventional laws of warfare.

hegemon A strong, controlling force that attempts to impose its preferences on others. Used in discussions of international affairs to describe the dominance of a specific country. If the nineteenth century was the period of British hegemony, the post–Cold War era is one of US hegemony, with the United States being the sole remaining superpower.

highly indebted poor country (HIPC) A country falling into this category is eligible for a program of debt relief if it makes the required neoliberal economic reforms.

human security Defined as the absence of structural violence, which is understood as widespread poverty and other forms of economic, social, and environmental degradation. Human security is a new, but increasingly recognized, understanding of security that goes far beyond issues of armaments and territorial security. It addresses individual and collective perceptions of present and potential threats to physical and psychological well-being.

identity The collective aspect or characteristics by which a person or group is known. Humans have multiple identities that they choose to emphasize, depending on context. Common identities uniting people in action include race, class, gender, and region.

ideology The belief systems of individuals and groups; a linked set of ideas that describe the world, help people understand their role within society, and arouse them to take action, whether to change or preserve the existing situation.

import substitution industrialization A development strategy especially popular in the mid-twentieth century that seeks to diversify economies and lessen the dependence of less developed countries (LDCs) on foreign imports of manufactured goods. It encourages industrialization headquartered within LDCs by subsidizing and protecting local producers from foreign competition.

informal sector Also known as the informal economy. A shadow economy comprising semilegal or illegal activities that are unreported, unregulated, and untaxed—and therefore not included in the calculation of a country's gross domestic product. Because it is so often the case that their opportunities in the formal economy are limited, women compose a large number of informal-sector workers.

integration A process that increases the quantity and quality of interconnectedness between countries through small or large steps; promotes cooperation between countries based on common security or economic concerns. For example, the European Union began in the 1950s (as the European Economic Community) as an agreement on coal and steel and, over the years, has moved increasingly toward the creation of a single market—the world's largest.

interdependence A political and economic relationship based on mutual vulnerability between two countries, each of which is sensitive to what happens in the other. The term implies that even developed countries are bound to less developed countries by interdependence, as opposed to those who characterize the relationship as one of dependence—largely the dependence of less developed countries on developed countries.

International Criminal Court (ICC) The world's first permanent international criminal court, the ICC was established by the Rome Statute in 1998 and entered into force in 2002. More than a hundred states have ratified the Rome Statute in recognition of the court's authority. The court resides in The Hague, where this independent entity serves as a mechanism for trying individuals accused of committing the world's most serious crimes: war crimes, crimes against humanity, and genocide.

international economic system The network of world trade, which is based on the remains of what was known as the Bretton Woods system. Formed in the post–World War II period, this international economic system has been dominated by developed countries under US leadership. Bretton Woods gave lip service to liberal economic policies, such as open economies and free trade. However, even its most ardent advocates routinely practiced protectionist policies that have hamstrung the development of less developed countries. Consequently, critics of this system argue that it is structured to benefit the already rich, to the detriment of the poor.

international financial institution (IFI) An organization that governs fiscal matters within and between states. Most IFIs (e.g., the International Monetary Fund and the World Bank) promote the neoliberal agenda and are run by developed countries—with little input from the less developed countries over which they have tremendous influence.

international governmental organization (IGO) An organization with two or more member states that may serve as a forum for discussion to promote cooperation on either regional or functional (issue-oriented) matters. The largest IGO is the United Nations; however, IGOs can be limited in scope and membership also.

International Monetary Fund (IMF) Central to the world financial system, this international organization is dedicated to promoting market economics. Established soon after the 1944 Bretton Woods conference, the IMF is a global lending agency originally created to aid in the postwar recovery of Europe and

Japan. Rich countries continue to dominate the IMF, which operates under a weighted voting system based on the amount of money members donate to the organization. The IMF is charged with several responsibilities, including stabilization of exchange rates and promotion of fiscal conservatism. One of its most important roles is to assist with balance of payments problems, and in this capacity it serves as an international credit bureau—for countries. Just as is the case with individuals, countries are assigned credit ratings. If the IMF blackballs a country, it will have a difficult time obtaining credit—from the IMF or from any international financial institution, for that matter. On the other hand, to remain in good stead with the IMF, countries must accept conditionality, or demonstrate their willingness to submit to neoliberal economic reforms, such as those promoted through extended-credit facilities.

international political economy The study of the relationship between politics and economics at the international and transnational levels; examines how international politics affects the world's economies and how economics affects international political relationships. Advocates of this approach contend that an understanding of international political economy is necessary, since economic factors shape most areas of political life. International political economy focuses on issues such as world markets, global financial institutions, and multinational corporations.

intifada From the Arabic, meaning "shivering" or "shaking off." The term was first applied to the Palestinian uprising against Israeli occupation from 1987 to 1993, in protest of killings near a Palestinian settlement. A "Second Intifada" began in October 2000, triggered by frustration over the failure of the Israeli-Palestinian peace process.

irredentist war A form of violent interstate conflict stemming from a nation's efforts to redraw political boundaries to include territory considered its homeland or to unite with its people living on the other side of a border.

jihad From the Arabic, signifying "struggle." Although it has recently been taken to narrowly mean a "holy war," its more accurate meaning encompasses the internal struggle that faithful Muslims undergo in their attempts to contend with the challenges facing them. Jihad also encompasses the requirements for a permissible and legitimate war, similar to other faith traditions' teachings on justifiable combat.

legitimacy The popular perception on the part of large numbers of people that the government, its leaders, and its policies are valid, right, just, and worthy of support. A legitimate regime is not necessarily the same as a legal regime, nor does it mean that a regime is democratic. A political regime is legitimate when it is accepted by the majority of its citizens as right and proper enough to be obeyed in most instances. Legitimacy can be achieved through all sorts of means, including propaganda, clientelism, and coercion.

legitimate trade The trade of raw materials in Africa, which Europeans began to pursue more ardently to serve the needs of industry. For a variety of reasons, by the early nineteenth century the "legitimate trade" had displaced the "illegitimate trade" (the term abolitionists had used for the slave trade) along the African coast.

liberal democracy A political system that has undertaken (and continues to undertake) comprehensive political reform in which democratic institutions are routinized and internalized and civil and political rights are protected—so much so that democracy is said to be "consolidated."

liberation theology A movement that started within the Catholic Church in Latin America and has spread to other Christian churches and regions of the world; an action-oriented ideology that promotes social justice through local activism. Liberation theology teaches that the cause of poverty is capitalism, and that the Church should lead a revolution to establish governing systems that will redistribute wealth, end all forms of imperialism, and promote democracy. It was especially popular throughout the 1980s, but has faced opposition because of its use of Marxist revolutionary ideals.

mandatory system The system for administering the territories taken from Germany and its allies after World War I, under Article 22 of the Charter of the League of Nations. The League appointed states such as Britain, France, and South Africa to help prepare the mandates for their eventual independence, yet in many cases the mandatory system was considered no more than "a fig leaf for colonialism." Later, when the mandates became trust territories administered by the United Nations, the mandatory powers were held somewhat more accountable for their actions.

maquiladora A subsidiary of a multinational corporation that assembles imported parts and exports manufactured goods; originally the assembly plants that have proliferated along the US-Mexican border since the implementation of the North American Free Trade Agreement (NAFTA). However, the term is now sometimes used to describe such enterprises wherever they exist in the global south.

mass party A type of political party that attempts to be as inclusionary as possible, often attempting to incorporate less politically engaged individuals and groups into the political process. Mass parties are marked by a formal nationwide structure, and are used to mobilize large groups of voters.

masses Relative to the elites, the masses are those who lack power and influence and who always outnumber the elites; the vast majority of the population in a country tend to be lumped into the category of the "masses" or the "common people."

mercantilism A precapitalist stage of development marked by accumulation of capital and accomplished through trade and plunder on a worldwide scale. This aggressive economic policy was the guiding force behind the conquest of many areas; it provided the capital base for Europe's industrialization. In its more contemporary form, mercantilism describes the situation when a power seeks commercial expansion to achieve a surplus in its balance of trade.

the messy middle Hybrid forms of government that may appear to be democratic (or not) yet defy simple regime type. Neither liberal democracies nor quite full-blown dictatorships, they may have an outward appearance like that of their more democratic counterparts but are led by elites whose commitment to democracy is contingent and instrumental.

military professionalism Critical to the survival of democracies, this term refers to the military's depoliticization. Where it exists, coups d'état are unthinkable, as the military recognizes the supremacy of civilian rule and views itself as serving civilian government.

mother country Another name for a colonizing country; its use denotes the exclusive ties that bound the colonies to the mother country much like an umbilical cord. Also refers to the parental role the colonizers portrayed themselves as playing in the non-Western world.

Multilateral Debt Relief Initiative (MDRI) An enhancement of the highly indebted poor countries (HIPC) initiative, the MDRI cancels the eligible debt of the poorest countries that have "graduated" or completed their HIPC requirements. Under this program, monies saved from the cancellation of this debt are to be used to meet a variety of development goals.

multinational corporation (MNC) A business enterprise headquartered in one country (usually a developed country) with activities abroad stemming from direct foreign investment located in several countries. As MNCs conglomerate and form near-monopolies, international trade is increasingly dominated by a handful of corporations. Enormously powerful because they are so flexible, they can readily move capital, goods, and technology to fit market conditions.

multinational state A political unit of organization that includes two or more ethnic or national groups. Largely due to colonialism's arbitrary boundaries, a nation may or may not reside within the political boundary of a state, thereby producing a multinational state.

nationalism A set of political beliefs that center around the shared sense of characteristics attributable to a group of people known to each other as a nation. Nationalism has been used to promote the interests and needs of a particular group of people, and has been a particularly strong rallying force, both uniting and dividing groups.

nation-state A term that combines the ideals of two concepts. A nation is considered to be a group of people who recognize a similarity among themselves because of common culture, language, or history. Nations often, but do not always, coincide with political boundaries of states, thereby producing multinational states. A state is considered to be a political entity with legal jurisdiction and physical control—an internationally recognized government.

neocolonialism A term used to describe the condition from which many non-Western states today suffer, as they continue to be indirectly controlled by their former colonizers or other developed countries; said to exist because less developed countries operate under so many of the constraints of colonialism that they are considered independent only in name.

neoliberalism The contemporary version of pro-capitalist liberal economic strategy, which holds that all benefit from an open economy and free trade, or the unencumbered movement of goods and services between states. It is the dominant view held by the governments of developed countries and most international financial institutions, such as the World Bank and the International Monetary Fund. Neoliberals fervently believe that globalization is a positive force and that the current international economic system based on free competition can work for all if countries will just embrace it. Most global south countries then must adopt the proper reforms, promote openness, and prepare for a period of austerity to get their economic houses in order.

Non-Aligned Movement (NAM) Formed in 1961 in opposition to the polarizing tendencies of the Cold War, the NAM is an alliance of over a hundred countries that shunned military alliances and coalitions with other states—especially the dominant powers during the Cold War, during which time the NAM advocated the neutrality of its members. Prime Minister Jawaharlal Nehru of India, President Josip Broz Tito of Yugoslavia, and President Gamal Abdul Nasser of Egypt founded the movement as a vehicle for nonaligned countries to come together to solve mutual problems without benefit of military alliance. A summit is held every three years.

nongovernmental organization (NGO) A private association of voluntary membership that works together to accomplish set goals. The numbers of NGOs in the world exploded throughout the 1980s, and continue to swell. General examples of NGOs include universities, churches, and civic and professional associations. Increasingly, at the global level, the "on the ground" competency of NGOs is being recognized in policymaking and decisionmaking. One of the foremost examples of the partnership between NGOs and international organizations was the Ottawa Treaty process, which was born of the efforts of the International Campaign to Ban Landmines.

nonintervention Not interfering in the internal affairs of other countries; associated with sovereignty, nonintervention is an international principle traditionally thought to promote international stability.

pandemic A global disease outbreak; the spread of an infectious disease that impacts a substantial number of people across a large region, usually multiple continents or worldwide. Pandemics are differentiated from epidemics—the rapid spread of an infectious disease to many people—by the wider geographic reach of a pandemic.

parliamentary system A democratic constitutional system in which citizens select members of parliament, and executive authority is dependent on parliamentary confidence. Variously characterized as flexible and unstable, gridlock is much less likely in a parliamentary than in a presidential system. Since the majority party in parliament selects the executive, the prime minister can usually be confident that his or her initiatives will be warmly received by the legislature. In a parliamentary system, new elections are called by the prime minister, and can be called at any time (within a certain time frame). As opposed to presidential systems, effective executives can be kept in power indefinitely. However, the system is self-correcting for executive abuse, since the legislative branch can censure and rid itself of an errant executive with much more ease than the painstaking process of impeachment necessary in a presidential system.

party system Referencing the collection of political parties in a given state or region—analysts often distinguish between single-party systems and multiparty systems, based on the number of active and viable parties in the regime. For example, a one-party-dominant system is one in which there are political alternatives, but in which a single party exercises a near-monopoly on power, either due to the lack of alternatives or because of the overwhelming support of citizens. A multiparty system is one in which there are two or more major contenders for power.

patrimonial A form of governance that exists when the ruler treats the state as his or her own personal property. Appointments to government office are assigned on the basis of loyalty to the ruler, who plays the role of a benevolent but stern parent, often through a mixture of co-optation and repression.

patron-client relationship A method of co-optation based on a relationship of reciprocity in which the powerful patron (a leader, party, agency, or government) allocates resources to his or her clients (the people) with the expectation that the clients will pledge to the patron their political loyalty.

peacekeeping operation (PKO) A noncombat military operation mandated by the UN Security Council and sent into conflict areas in an attempt to promote a peaceful transition. PKOs consist of outside forces acting on the consent of all major belligerent parties. Their tasks range from keeping apart hostile parties to helping them work together peacefully. PKOs have monitored cease-fires, created buffer zones, and helped to create and sustain nascent political institutions. PKO forces are often distinguished by their famous "blue helmets."

personalist regime Also known as a personally appropriated state—an authoritarian style of government. This regime exists when a single, highly charismatic individual, who represents himself or herself as the personification of the nation, holds unchecked power. It may exist under civilian or military rule, when the leader seeks to guarantee his or her personal control in perpetuity, as "president for life" or through a hereditary republic.

Planetary pressures–adjusted Human Development Index (PHDI) Like the Human Development Index, PHDI is a composite measure of "development that meets the needs of the present without compromising the ability of future generations to meet their own needs." To arrive at the PHDI, HDI is adjusted to account for greenhouse gas emissions, the social costs of carbon, and for natural wealth. PHDI encourages choices that advance human development without contributing further to planetary pressures. This updated measure recognizes the connections between development and climate change. *See* **sustainable development**.

political culture The context out of which political action is taken, recognizing the importance of systems of values and beliefs. While few people would deny that culture impacts people's views on politics and government, it has been difficult to articulate the precise connections between these variables and political outcomes. In 1959, Gabriel Almond and Sidney Verba identified three root (or "civic") cultures in the countries they studied: participant, subject, and parochial.

political liberalization A process of political reform based on the extension of civil and political rights, and the promotion of a more open political system. Signs that a system is liberalizing politically include a variety of changes, such as an increasing tolerance of dissent and the release of political prisoners. Although they are often associated with democratization, not all political liberalizations will result in democracy. Also known as an ***abertura***.

political spectrum Conceptual map used to compare and contrast political ideologies. Along a horizontal line, ideologies are listed according to their views on change, the role of government in economic matters, and the relationship between religious institutions and their place in politics. The modern convention of the "left-right" political spectrum derives from legislative arrangements in the National Assembly of France, when those who supported the monarch and the Catholic Church sat on the right of the monarch, and those who favored democracy and revolution sat on the left.

populist An agenda, political party, campaign, or image designed to appeal to the "common people" rather than to the minority elite, rallying them around a shared sense of belonging and promising many things. The term was originally used to describe political movements in Europe at the end of the nineteenth century that appealed to the rural poor. The term is now used to describe mass political movements or party platforms that purport to represent sentiment akin to the collective voice of ordinary people on social and economic issues. On the political spectrum, they can lean left or right.

praetorianism Military supremacy in politics; a type of increased involvement by soldiers in politics when military officers threaten or use force to influence political decisions and outcomes. The term derives from the praetorian guards of the Roman Empire, who were established as a unit to protect the emperor, but who abused their power to overthrow and select the emperor themselves.

presidential system A type of democratic constitutional system in which citizens directly select their legislators and their executive. Because the executive and legislative branches are elected separately, it is not uncommon for one party to hold the presidency and another to dominate the legislature. As a result, gridlock is much more likely in a presidential than in a parliamentary system. Although there are checks and balances between the various branches of government, the executive is relatively independent of the legislature, and power tends to concentrate in the executive. The rigidity of a fixed presidential term means that it is harder to remove an errant executive from power, and effective executives are constitutionally prohibited from serving beyond the prescribed term.

proletariat The socioeconomic group (or class) identified in Marxist socialism, defined by their relationship to the means of production. The proletarians are the workers who will unite together in revolutionary zeal to overcome the more powerful and entrenched bourgeoisie. Karl Marx argued that most workers own nothing but their labor (unlike artisans, who may own their machinery or tools). The proletariat is commonly called the working class.

proxy war A type of warfare undertaken by the superpowers during the Cold War. In an attempt to avoid the massive casualties associated with mutual assured destruction, the superpowers took sides in conflicts around the world, choosing intermediaries and supplying and arming them to play out the East-West rivalry with less risk of escalation to nuclear war.

reconfiguration A form of crisis management in which governments take very small steps or effect the appearance of reform while maintaining significant restrictions on civil liberties, political participation, and competition. Analysts maintain that reconfiguration is not necessarily antidemocratic in nature—even incremental steps may add up to more substantive reforms, which may in turn contribute to democratization.

relative deprivation A comparative statement that reveals the sense that individuals or groups are not doing as well as other groups.

relative poverty Denotes a trend in terms of the gap between rich and poor countries. While some countries have made progress in eliminating absolute poverty, rising incomes during the economic boom of the 1990s have actually contributed to widening inequality overall. Consequently, while absolute poverty is said to have declined, for many less developed countries relative poverty has increased.

rescue package An assortment of loans, credits, and other forms of aid offered by the International Monetary Fund and other international financial institutions to countries suffering from massive economic dislocation (e.g., much of Asia during the "Asian flu" of the late 1990s). Aimed at stabilizing these economies, such packages are offered, however, only to countries willing to accept certain conditions, such as a neoliberal series of economic reforms.

resource mobilization A conceptual approach to collective behavior and social movements that emphasizes the resources necessary for success, taking into account the material and the nonmaterial needs of participants in collective action.

responsibility to protect (R2P) An evolving international norm establishing the right of humanitarian intervention. In response to then UN Secretary-General Kofi Annan's 2000 call to establish a global consensus on when such interventions should occur, UN member states adopted R2P as a key principle of international affairs at the 2005 World Summit. The principle emphasizes the responsibilities of sovereignty, which include protecting their populations from coordinated acts of violence, especially war crimes, crimes against humanity, and genocide. Under R2P, if a government is unable or unwilling to guard the safety of its citizens, the international community has a responsibility to help or intervene, using diplomatic channels and even military force as a last resort.

revolution Meaning "to turn around," a revolution is the attempt (often sudden) to promote fundamental change in political and social institutions of society, often accompanied by violence and economic and cultural upheaval.

revolution of rising expectations The recognition that improvement (often in the economy, but also in life choices and options) is often not as great as predicted or promised. Leaders frequently deliver inflated promises to their people, and rapid change can often increase hopes and desires for the future. The concept of "rising expectations" is used to distinguish from the "revolution of falling expectations," in which people anticipate a bad future and the future turns out to be even worse than expected.

rule of law A situation in which the power of individuals is limited by a supreme set of rules that prevent arbitrary and unfair actions by governmental officials. A reliance on written rules to govern and operate, rather than on the vice and virtue of rulers.

secession The act of withdrawing or breaking away from some organized entity, such as a nation, as when Bangladesh seceded from Pakistan in 1971.

secularism The separation of civil or educational institutions from ecclesiastical control; the act of de-emphasizing spiritual or religious perspectives in political, cultural, or social life.

self-determination The right of a people who share cultural ties and live in a given territory to choose their own political institutions and government. A central international political concept of the twentieth century associated with nationalism and anticolonial movements.

sharia Sometimes known as *shariat,* from the Arabic, meaning "way" or "road." Sharia is Muslim religious (or canonical) law based on rules for moral conduct developed over the first few centuries after the death of the Prophet Muhammad. Sharia governs the individual and social lives of believers, and provides followers with a basis for judging actions as good or evil. Despite debates over the degree of observance and the role of authorities for enforcement, most agree that a common understanding of sharia unites most Muslims around the world.

social movement Human beings with a common purpose engaged in discussion and action designed to bring about change. Social movements are responses to a perceived state of affairs and often identify specific groups in society as the source of the problem to be rectified. Often, collective actions stimulate a countermovement in response.

sovereignty Freedom from foreign control; a principle widely accepted in international law that speaks to a state's right to do as it wishes in its own territory; a doctrine that holds that states are the principal actors in international relations and the state is subject to no higher political authority. Also refers to widespread international acceptance of a particular country's control of territory.

state An organized political entity that occupies a specific territory, has a permanent population, is controlled by a government, and is regarded as sovereign. Currently, there are approximately 190 recognized states worldwide. *See* **nation-state**.

state capitalism An economic system that mixes capitalism with government planning; private enterprise accounts for most of the country's economic activity, but the government intervenes on the side of business with subsidies and other supports aimed at promoting domestic producers' competitiveness on the world market.

state society A centralized form of political organization; an outgrowth of the sedentarization of human populations, the intensification of agricultural production, and population booms. State societies are distinguished by increasing social stratification as classes emerge and power is centralized in the hands of full-time political leaders. This broad category includes many different forms of political organization, from simple, small states to immense empires.

stateless nation A group of people (with a shared identity based on language, ethnicity, religion, or common heritage) who consider themselves to have no country to call their own; people without citizenship in any state.

stateless society A smaller, decentralized grouping of the type in which the earliest humans lived. It is relatively democratic in that power is shared and there are no full-time political leaders. Also known as **acephalous society**.

state-owned enterprise (SOE) A business that is owned and operated wholly or partially by the government. In many countries, SOEs have been concentrated in sectors thought vital to the national economy. They were built from nationalized properties, as an attempt to reclaim a country's resources from foreign domination or to promote import substitution industrialization. Throughout much of the world, SOEs have been large employers. However, they have been criticized as notoriously inefficient drains on state budgets. Also known as state-owned industry.

state-sponsored terrorism (or state terror) Violent methods used by government forces or vigilante groups acting with at least the tacit approval of state officials to intimidate and coerce people, often the state's own citizens.

structural adjustment program (SAP) The neoliberal prescription offered by international financial institutions to indebted countries. As a condition for international assistance (*see* **rescue package**), countries must commit to an SAP, usually a three- to five-year program that includes a variety of reforms associated with economic liberalization (e.g., privatization, devaluation of currency, cutting social spending, raising taxes, welcoming foreign investment). *See also* **extended-credit facilities**.

structuralism A school of thought that includes a range of opinion from radical to reformist. Structuralists share the view that the current international economic system works to the benefit of the already rich and that globalization is inherently disadvantageous to poor countries. Structuralists are highly critical of neoliberal programs, which they see as dooming much of the world to under-development.

sustainable development An approach that considers the long-term impact on the environment and resources of current development strategies. *See* **Planetary pressures–adjusted Human Development Index**.

sweatshop A place of labor, usually a factory. The term is used derisively to describe a business establishment profiting from inhumane working conditions.

terrorism The use of violence or the threat of violence and intimidation to achieve aims and spread a message. Terrorists aim for symbolic targets to manipulate adversaries and to achieve political, religious, or ideological objectives.

theocracy From the Greek, meaning "government of God"—a system of rule based on religion and dominated by clergy. Rules are often inspired by some form of holy book.

top-down approach As opposed to a bottom-up approach, top-down policies are ostensibly aimed at benefiting the majority and are initiated by elites.

totalitarianism A full-blown dictatorship, marked by the severity and magnitude of the state's interference in the lives of its citizens. In totalitarian systems the state, guided by an overarching ideology, attempts to exercise absolute control over virtually every aspect of citizens' lives. Power is concentrated in the hands of the leader or party and dissent is not tolerated. There is no right of political competition or participation, leaders are not accountable for their actions, and the state violates civil and human rights with impunity. Classic examples of totalitarian states include fascist regimes such as Nazi Germany, as well as Communist Party–dominated states such as Joseph Stalin's Russia and Mao Zedong's China.

transparency A policy promoted to reduce corruption; exists when the government is open about its spending and budgetary matters, and people are encouraged to report misconduct.

truth commission An official mechanism launched usually during periods of political transition to investigate wrongs of the recent past, especially human rights abuses. Truth commissions represent attempts to deal with the past by promoting the public acknowledgment of wrongdoing, sometimes as an alternative to criminal prosecution. There are multiple models of truth commissions, which vary in the scope of crimes examined, mandate and investigation, and the types of justice employed. Most truth commissions are established to achieve an accurate historical description of what took place, to promote reconciliation, and to help promote more durable democracies by creating a culture of human rights. Truth commissions are viewed by many as but one part of the complex healing process after periods of trauma, but much disagreement about their long-term impact remains.

United Nations Preceded by the League of Nations, the UN was founded in 1945 as an international governmental organization that now includes almost all of the world's states. It provides a forum at which complaints are heard and conflicts are discussed and sometimes resolved. The UN is also involved in promoting human development through the work of its specialized agencies, which promote standards for world heath, education, and the environment in addition to commonly accepted terms for trade and commerce.

United Nations General Assembly An organ of the United Nations in which each member state is represented; it is primarily a deliberative organization centered around debate and discussion. Some matters, including those on peace and security and the admission of new members, require a two-thirds majority; others are adopted by a simple majority. Decisions of the General Assembly have no legally binding force on governments, but they represent the weight of world opinion.

United Nations Secretary-General The chief administrative officer of the United Nations. The Secretary-General is nominated by the Security Council and elected by a two-thirds majority in the General Assembly for a five-year renewable term. In addition to presiding over the United Nations, the Secretary-General has become increasingly more visible in mediating and responding to global issues outside UN organizations. António Guterres's first term began in 2017. The Portuguese diplomat was appointed to a second term, which runs through 2026.

United Nations Security Council The most powerful organ within the UN system. Its representatives include five permanent members (the P-5), which have veto power, and rotating members that do not have veto power. The ten nonpermanent members are elected to two-year terms by the General Assembly. Under the UN Charter, the Security Council possesses as its primary responsibility the maintenance of international peace and security. The Council works to achieve this through many means: mediation, cease-fire directives, and the use of peacekeeping forces, to name a few.

Universal Declaration of Human Rights (UDHR) The most comprehensive international statement on human rights. With over thirty articles pertaining to a wide array of political, civil, economic, social, and cultural rights, the UDHR was put forward in 1948 as a general resolution of the United Nations.

vanguard party Literally the "leading" party—Vladimir Lenin's term for the Communist Party, supposed to take a front role in the overthrow of capitalism and transition to communism. Lenin prescribed that a single, elite, highly disciplined party would be necessary to lead the revolution of the proletarians, or the workers. Lenin's idea of a vanguard party has been used by Marxist socialist states, such as China and North Korea, to argue against the creation of competing political parties, producing a monopoly of control with which other socialists disagree.

weapons of the weak Forms of confrontation that often go unnoticed because they tend to be concealed, disguised, or subtle—employed by the ostensibly powerless, including women, minorities, and peasants. Commonly used tactics include rumor, deception, hoarding, and suicide.

World Bank Also known as the International Bank for Reconstruction and Development (IBRD), the World Bank was formed as part of the Bretton Woods system in 1944, along with its counterpart organization the International Monetary Fund (IMF). Like the IMF, the World Bank is controlled by developed countries, as voting power is based on a country's financial contribution to the Bank. Its responsibilities are wide-ranging; although it was originally created to fund the reconstruction of postwar Europe and to promote a stable international economic system, it now focuses its efforts on long-term loans and projects in the non-Western world and, more recently, in Eastern Europe and the former Soviet republics.

World Trade Organization (WTO) Founded in 1995, the WTO is an institution designed to promote free trade and mediate trade disputes; an updated and expanded product of the General Agreement on Tariffs and Trade (GATT), which focused on manufactured goods. Compared to GATT, the WTO has much more extensive monitoring and enforcement powers, although some less developed countries fear that this international governmental organization is working primarily for the benefit of developed countries.

zero-sum game A situation in which there can be only one winner and all the rest are losers. One actor's gain is another's loss (as opposed to non-zero-sum game, in which all can be winners or all can be losers).

Selected Bibliography

Aarts, Paul, and Francesco Cavatorta, eds. *Civil Society in Syria and Iran: Activism in Authoritarian Contexts.* Boulder: Lynne Rienner, 2012.

Abbas, Megan Brankley. *Whose Islam? The Western University and Modern Islamic Thought in Indonesia.* Stanford: Stanford University Press, 2021.

Abedin, Mahan. *Iran Resurgent: The Rise and Rise of the Shia State.* New York: Oxford University Press, 2019.

Acemoglu, Daron, and James Robinson. *Why Nations Fail: The Origins of Power, Prosperity, and Poverty.* New York: Crown, 2013.

Afolayan, Funso. "Nigeria: A Political Entity and a Society." In *Dilemmas of Democracy in Nigeria,* edited by Paul A. Beckett and Crawford Young, 45–62. Rochester: University of Rochester Press, 1997.

Ai Camp, Roderic. *Politics in Mexico: The Decline of Authoritarianism.* New York: Oxford University Press, 1999.

Almond, Gabriel A., and Sidney Verba, eds. *Civic Culture: Political Attitudes and Democracy in Five Nations.* Princeton: Princeton University Press, 1963.

Alvarez, Sonia E. *Engendering Democracy in Brazil: Women's Movements in Transition Politics.* Princeton: Princeton University Press, 1990.

Applebaum, Anne. *Twilight of Democracy: The Seductive Lure of Authoritarianism.* New York: Doubleday, 2020.

Axworthy, Michael. *Revolutionary Iran: A History of the Islamic Republic.* New York: Oxford University Press, 2013.

Bailey, John. *The Politics of Crime in Mexico: Democratic Governance in a Security Trap.* Boulder: Lynne Rienner, 2014.

Bakewell, Peter. *A History of Latin America.* Malden, MA: Blackwell, 1997.

Banai, Hussein. *Hidden Liberalism: Burdened Visions of Progress in Modern Iran.* Cambridge: Cambridge University Press, 2021.

Barber, Benjamin R. *Jihad vs. McWorld.* New York: Times Books, 1995.

Berkovitch, Nitza. "The Emergence and Transformation of the International Women's Movement." In *Constructing World Culture: International Nongovernmental Organizations Since 1875,* edited by John Boli and George M. Thomas, 116–121. Stanford: Stanford University Press, 1999.

Bethell, Leslie, ed. *Ideas and Ideologies in Twentieth-Century Latin America.* Cambridge: Cambridge University Press, 1996.

Bhebe, Ngwabi, and Terence Ranger. "Volume Introduction: Society in Zimbabwe's Liberation War." In *Society in Zimbabwe's Liberation War,* edited by Ngwabi Bhebe and Terence Ranger, 6–34. Oxford: Currey, 1996.

Bizzozero, Lincoln. "Uruguayan Foreign Policies in the 1990s: Continuities and Changes with a View to Recent Regionalisms." In *National Perspectives on the New Regionalism in the South,* vol. 3, edited by Björn Hettne, András Inotai, and Osvaldo Sunkel, 177–197. New York: St. Martin's, 2000.

Blumi, Isa. *Foundations of Modernity: Human Agency and the Imperial State.* New York: Routledge, 2012.

Boahen, A. Adu. "Africa and the Colonial Challenge." In *UNESCO General History of Africa: Africa Under Colonial Domination, 1800–1935,* edited by A. Adu Boahen, 1–18. London: Heinemann, 1985.

———. "Colonialism in Africa: Its Impact and Significance." In *UNESCO General History of Africa: Africa Under Colonial Domination, 1800–1935,* edited by A. Adu Boahen, 782–809. London: Heinemann, 1985.

Bogle, Emory C. *The Modern Middle East: From Imperialism to Freedom, 1800–1958.* Upper Saddle River, NJ: Prentice Hall, 1996.

Boli, John, and George M. Thomas, eds. *Constructing World Culture: International Nongovernmental Organizations Since 1875.* Stanford: Stanford University Press, 1999.

Boone, Catherine. "'Empirical Statehood' and Reconfigurations of Political Order." In *The African State at a Critical Juncture,* edited by Leonardo A. Villalon and Phillip A. Huxtable, 129–142. Boulder: Lynne Rienner, 1998.

Bottaro, Jean. *Nationalism and Independence in India.* New York: Cambridge University Press, 2016.

Bracken, Paul. *Fire in the East: The Rise of Asian Military Power and the Second Nuclear Age.* New York: HarperCollins, 1999.

Bratton, Michael. *Power Politics in Zimbabwe.* Boulder: Lynne Rienner, 2014.

Bresnan, John, ed. *Indonesia: The Great Transition.* New York: Rowman and Littlefield, 2005.

Brewer, Douglas J., and Emily Teeter. *Egypt and the Egyptians.* Cambridge: Cambridge University Press, 2007.

Brumberg, Daniel, and Farhi Farideh. *Power and Change in Iran: Politics of Contention and Conciliation.* Bloomington: Indiana University Press, 2016.

Bueno de Mesquita, Bruce, and Alastair Smith. *The Dictator's Handbook: Why Bad Behavior Is Almost Always Good Politics.* New York: PublicAffairs, 2012.

Burbank, Jane, and Frederick Cooper. *Empires in World History: Power and the Politics of Difference.* Princeton: Princeton University Press, 2010.

Burkholder, Mark A., and Lyman L. Johnson. *Colonial Latin America.* New York: Oxford University Press, 1998.

Cambanis, Thanassis. *Once upon a Revolution: An Egyptian Story.* New York: Simon and Schuster, 2015.

Caraway, Teri L., and Michele Ford. *Labor and Politics in Indonesia.* Cambridge: Cambridge University Press, 2020.

Carmody, Pádraig. *Globalization in Africa: Recolonization or Renaissance?* Boulder: Lynne Rienner, 2010.

Carothers, Thomas, and Andrew O'Donohue, eds. *Democracies Divided: The Global Challenge of Political Polarization.* Washington, DC: Brookings Institution Press, 2019.

Castañeda, Jorge G. *Utopia Unarmed: The Latin American Left After the Cold War.* New York: Knopf, 1993.

Centeno, Miguel Angel. *Democracy Within Reason: Technocratic Revolution in Mexico.* University Park: Pennsylvania State University Press, 1997.

Chalmers, Douglas A. "Corporatism and Comparative Politics." In *New Directions in Comparative Politics,* edited by Howard J. Wiarda, 56–79. Boulder: Westview, 1985.

Chalmers, Douglas A., Maria do Carmo Campello de Souza, and Atilio A. Borón. *The Right and Democracy in Latin America.* New York: Praeger, 1992.

Chazan, Naomi, Peter Lewis, and Robert Mortimer. *Politics and Society in Contemporary Africa.* Boulder: Lynne Rienner, 1999.

Cheeseman, Nic. *Democracy in Africa: Successes, Failures, and the Struggle for Political Reform.* New York: Cambridge University Press, 2015.

Cheeseman, Nic, and Bryan Klaas. *How to Rig an Election.* New Haven: Yale University Press, 2019.

Chomsky, Noam. *On Anarchism.* New York: New Press, 2013.

———. *Pirates and Emperors: International Terrorism in the Real World.* New York: Claremont, 1986.

Cohen, Herman J. *US Policy Toward Africa: Eight Decades of Realpolitik.* Boulder: Lynne Rienner, 2020.

Collis, Maurice. *Cortés and Montezuma.* New York: New Directions, 1999.

Cortright, David, and George Lopez. *The Sanctions Decade: Assessing UN Strategies in the 1990s.* Boulder: Lynne Rienner, 2000.

Courtois, Stéphane, Nicolas Werth, Jean-Louis Panné, et al. *The Black Book of Communism: Crimes, Terror, and Repression,* edited by Mark Kramer. Translated by Jonathan Murphy. Cambridge: Harvard University Press, 1999.

Crenshaw, Martha, ed. *Terrorism in Context.* University Park: Pennsylvania State University Press, 1995.

Cribb, Robert, and Colin Brown. *Modern Indonesia: A History Since 1945.* New York: Longman, 1995.

Crowder, Michael. *The Story of Nigeria.* London: Faber and Faber, 1978.

Dahl, Robert. *Democracy and Its Critics.* New Haven: Yale University Press, 1989.

Daniel, Elton L. *The History of Iran.* Westport: Greenwood, 2001.

Danopoulos, Constantine P., and Cynthia Watson, eds. *The Political Role of the Military: An International Handbook.* Westport: Greenwood, 1996.

de Waal, Victor. *The Politics of Reconciliation: Zimbabwe's First Decade.* Trenton, NJ: Africa World Press, 1990.

Degregori, Carlos Ivan. "After the Fall of Abimael Guzmán: The Limits of Sendero Luminoso." In *The Peruvian Labyrinth,* edited by Maxwell A. Cameron and Philip Mauceri, 179–191. University Park: Pennsylvania State University Press, 1997.

Diamond, Jared. *Guns, Germs, and Steel: The Fate of Human Societies.* New York: Norton, 1997.

Diamond, Larry. "Introduction: In Search of Consolidation." In *Consolidating Third Wave Democracies,* edited by Larry Diamond, Marc F. Plattner, Yun-han Chu, and Hung-mao Tien, xv–xlix. Baltimore: Johns Hopkins University Press, 1997.

———. "Introduction: What Makes for Democracy?" In *Politics in Developing Countries: Comparing Experiences with Democracy,* edited by Larry Diamond, Juan J. Linz, and Seymour Martin Lipset, 1–66. Boulder: Lynne Rienner, 1995.

———. "Three Paradoxes of Democracy." In *The Global Resurgence of Democracy,* edited by Larry Diamond and Marc F. Plattner, 95–107. Baltimore: Johns Hopkins University Press, 1993.

———. "The Uncivic Society and the Descent into Praetorianism." In *Politics in Developing Countries: Comparing Experiences with Democracy,* edited by Larry Diamond, Juan J. Linz, and Seymour Martin Lipset, 417–492. Boulder: Lynne Rienner, 1995.

Dikőtter, Frank. *Mao's Great Famine: The History of China's Most Devastating Catastrophe, 1958–1962.* New York: Walker, 2010.

Doshi, Rush. *The Long Game: China's Grand Strategy to Displace American Order.* New York: Oxford University Press, 2021.

Duverger, Maurice. *Political Parties: Their Organization and Activity in the Modern State.* New York: Wiley, 1963.

Easterly, William. *The White Man's Burden: Why the West's Efforts to Aid the Rest Have Done So Much Ill and So Little Good.* New York: Penguin, 2007.

Eatwell, Roger. *Fascism: A History.* New York: Penguin, 1997.

Ebrey, Patricia Buckley. *The Cambridge Illustrated History of China.* New York: Cambridge University Press, 2010.

Economy, Elizabeth C., and Michael Levi. *By All Means Necessary: How China's Resource Quest Is Changing the World.* New York: Oxford University Press, 2014.

Ehteshami, Anoushiravan. *After Khomeini: The Iranian Second Republic.* New York: Routledge, 1995.

Ekiert, Grzegorz, Elizabeth J. Perry, and Xiaojun Yan, eds. *Ruling by Other Means: State-Mobilized Movements.* Cambridge: Cambridge University Press, 2020.

Elaigwu, J. Isawa. "Nation-Building and Changing Political Structures." In *UNESCO General History of Africa: Africa Since 1935,* edited by Ali A. Mazrui, 435–467. London: Heinemann, 1993.

Emmerson, Donald K. *Indonesia Beyond Suharto: Policy, Economy, Society, Transition.* Armonk, NY: Sharpe, 1999.

———. "Voting and Violence: Indonesia and East Timor in 1999." In *Indonesia Beyond Suharto,* edited by Donald K. Emmerson, 354–357. Armonk, NY: Sharpe, 1999.

Esty, Daniel C. "Environmental Protection During the Transition to a Market Economy." In *Economies in Transition: Comparing Asia and Eastern Europe,* edited by Wing Thye Woo, Stephen Parker, and Jeffrey Sachs, 357–385. Cambridge: MIT Press, 1997.

Euchner, Charles. *Extraordinary Politics: How Protest and Dissent Are Changing American Democracy.* Boulder: Westview, 1996.

Evans, Tony. *Human Rights in the Global Political Economy: Critical Processes.* Boulder: Lynne Rienner, 2010.

Fallows, James. *Postcards from Tomorrow Square.* New York: Vintage, 2008.

Falola, Toyin. *The History of Nigeria.* Westport: Greenwood, 1999.

Falola, Toyin, and Robin Law, eds. *Warfare and Diplomacy in Precolonial Nigeria.* Madison: University of Wisconsin–Madison Press, 1992.

Farmer, Edward L., Gavin R. G. Hambly, Byron K. Marshall, et al. *Comparative History of Civilizations in Asia.* Reading, MA: Addison-Wesley, 1977.

Ferguson, Niall. *Dead Aid: Why Aid Is Not Working and How There Is a Better Way for Africa.* Vancouver: Douglas and McIntyre, 2010.

Finnemore, Martha. "Rules of War and Wars of Rules: The International Red Cross and the Restraint of State Violence." In *Constructing World Culture: International Nongovernmental Organizations Since 1875,* edited by John Boli and George M. Thomas, 149–168. Stanford: Stanford University Press, 1999.

Frank, Andre Gunder. *Capitalism and Underdevelopment in Latin America.* New York: Monthly Review, 1967.

Freeman, Charles. *Egypt, Greece, & Rome: Civilizations of the Ancient Mediterranean.* Oxford: Oxford University Press, 2004.

Friedman, Thomas L. *The Lexus and the Olive Tree.* New York: Farrar, Straus and Giroux, 1999.

Fukuyama, Francis. *Identity: The Demand for Dignity and the Politics of Resentment.* London: Profile, 2018.

Fyle, Magbaily. *Introduction to the History of African Civilization.* Lanham: University Press of America, 1999.

Galeano, Eduardo. *Open Veins of Latin America.* New York: Monthly Review, 1973.

Gamer, Robert E. *Understanding Contemporary China.* Boulder: Lynne Rienner, 1999.

Gamson, William A. "The Social Psychology of Collective Action." In *Frontiers in Social Movement Theory,* edited by Aldon D. Morris and Carol McClurg Mueller, 53–76. New Haven: Yale University Press, 1992.

Garner, Roberta. *Contemporary Movements and Ideologies.* New York: McGraw-Hill, 1996.

Garrett, Laurie. *Betrayal of Trust: The Collapse of Global Public Health.* New York: Hyperion, 2000.

George, Susan. *The Debt Boomerang: How Third World Debt Harms Us All.* Boulder: Westview, 1992.

Gheissari, Ali, and Vali Nasr. *Democracy in Iran: History and the Quest for Liberty.* New York: Oxford University Press, 2006.

Ghonim, Wael. *Revolution 2.0: The Power of the People Is Greater Than the People in Power.* New York: Houghton Mifflin Harcourt, 2012.

Gilley, Bruce. *China's Democratic Future: How It Will Happen and Where It Will Lead.* New York: Columbia University Press, 2004.

Goldschmidt, Arthur, Jr. *Modern Egypt: The Formation of a Nation-State.* Boulder: Westview, 2004.

Goldstein, Joshua S. *International Relations.* 4th ed. New York: Longman, 2001.

Goldstone, Jack A. "The Outcome of Revolutions." In *Revolutions: Theoretical, Comparative, and Historical Studies,* 2nd ed., edited by Jack A. Goldstone, 194–195. New York: Harcourt Brace, 1994.

———. "Revolutions in World History." In *Revolutions: Theoretical, Comparative, and Historical Studies,* 2nd ed., edited by Jack A. Goldstone, 315–318. New York: Harcourt Brace, 1994.

Goldstone, Richard. "Bringing War Criminals to Justice During an Ongoing War." In *Hard Choices: Moral Dilemmas in Humanitarian Intervention,* edited by Jonathan Moore, 195–210. Lanham: Rowman and Littlefield, 1998.

Gould, Benina Berger. "Ritual as Resistance: Tibetan Women and Nonviolence." In *Frontline Feminisms: Women, War, and Resistance,* edited by Marguerite R. Waller and Jennifer Rycenga, 213–234. New York: Garland, 2000.

Graham, Richard. *Independence in Latin America.* New York: McGraw-Hill, 1994.

Green, Jerrold D. "Countermobilization in the Iranian Revolution." In *Revolutions: Theoretical, Comparative, and Historical Studies,* 2nd ed., edited by Jack A. Goldstone, 136–146. New York: Harcourt Brace, 1994.

Grindle, Merilee. *Challenging the State: Crisis and Innovation in Latin America and Africa.* Cambridge: Cambridge University Press, 1996.

Gurtov, Mel. *Superpower on Crusade: The Bush Doctrine and US Foreign Policy.* Boulder: Lynne Rienner, 2006.

Hacker, Frederick J. *Crusaders, Criminals, Crazies: Terror and Terrorism in Our Time.* New York: Norton, 1976.

Han Han. *This Generation: Dispatches from China's Most Popular Literary Star (and Race Car Driver).* Edited and translated by Allan H. Barr. New York: Simon and Schuster, 2012.

Hanke, Lewis, and Jane M. Rausch, eds. *People and Issues in Latin American History.* New York: Markus Wiener, 1993.

Hanlon, Joseph, Jeannette Manjengwa, and Teresa Smart. *Zimbabwe Takes Back Its Land.* Boulder: Lynne Rienner, 2012.

Harding, Robin. *Rural Democracy: Elections and Development in Africa.* Oxford: Oxford University Press, 2020.

Hayner, Priscilla B. *Unspeakable Truths: Confronting State Terror and Atrocity.* New York: Routledge, 2001.

Hemming, John. *The Conquest of the Incas.* Boston: Houghton Mifflin Harcourt, 2003.

Herz, Monica, and João Pontes Nogueir. *Ecuador vs. Peru: Peacemaking amid Rivalry.* Boulder: Lynne Rienner, 2002.

Heywood, Andrew. *Political Ideas and Concepts: An Introduction.* New York: St. Martin's, 1994.

Hirschman, Albert O. *Exit, Voice, and Loyalty: Responses to Decline in Firms, Organizations, and States.* Cambridge: Harvard University Press, 1970.

Hochschild, Adam. *King Leopold's Ghost.* Boston: Houghton Mifflin, 1998.

Hollifield, James F., and Calvin Jillson, eds. *Pathways to Democracy: The Political Economy of Democratic Transitions.* New York: Routledge, 2000.

Horowitz, Donald L. "Comparing Democratic Systems." In *The Global Resurgence of Democracy,* edited by Larry Diamond and Marc F. Plattner, 127–133. Baltimore: Johns Hopkins University Press, 1993.

Huntington, Samuel P. "Democracy's Third Wave." In *The Global Resurgence of Democracy,* edited by Larry Diamond and Marc F. Plattner, 3–25. Baltimore: Johns Hopkins University Press, 1993.

Huxtable, Phillip A. "The African State Toward the Twenty-First Century: Legacies of the Critical Juncture." In *The African State at a Critical Juncture,* edited by Leonardo A. Villalon and Phillip A. Huxtable, 279–294. Boulder: Lynne Rienner, 1998.

Ignatieff, Michael. *Human Rights as Politics and Idolatry.* Princeton: Princeton University Press, 2001.

Jaquette, Jane, ed. *The Women's Movement in Latin America: Participation and Democracy.* Boulder: Westview, 1994.

Jayawardena, Kumari. *Feminism and Nationalism in the Third World.* London: Zed, 1986.
Johnson, Paul. *The Civilization of Ancient Egypt.* New York: HarperCollins, 1999.
Joseph, Richard, and Alexandra Gillies, eds. *Smart Aid for African Development.* Boulder: Lynne Rienner, 2009.
Judt, Tony, and Denis Lacorne, eds. *With Us or Against Us: Studies in Global Anti-Americanism.* New York: Palgrave Macmillan, 2005.
July, Robert W. *A History of the African People.* Prospect Heights, IL: Waveland, 1992.
Kaldor, Mary. *New and Old Wars: Organized Violence in a Global Era.* Stanford: Stanford University Press, 1999.
Keen, Benjamin, and Keith Haynes. *A History of Latin America.* Boston: Houghton Mifflin, 2000.
Kemp, Geoffrey. *Forever Enemies? American Policy and the Islamic Republic of Iran.* Washington, DC: Carnegie Endowment, 1994.
Kendall-Taylor, Andrea, Natasha Lindstaedt, and Erica Frantz. *Democracies and Authoritarian Regimes.* New York: Oxford University Press, 2019.
Kesselman, Mark, Joel Krieger, and William A. Joseph. *Introduction to Comparative Politics: Political Challenges and Changing Agendas.* Boston: Houghton Mifflin, 2000.
Khalil, Ashraf. *Liberation Square: Inside the Egyptian Revolution and the Rebirth of a Nation.* New York: St. Martin's, 2011.
Kinsbruner, Jay. *Independence in Spanish America: Civil Wars, Revolutions, and Underdevelopment.* Albuquerque: University of New Mexico Press, 2000.
Klaren, Peter Flindell. *Peru: Society and Nationhood in the Andes.* New York: Oxford University Press, 2000.
Kohut, Andrew, and Bruce Stokes. *America Against the World: How We Are Different and Why We Are Disliked.* New York: Times Books, 2006.
Kurlantzick, Joshua. *Charm Offensive: How China's Soft Power Is Transforming the World.* New Haven: Yale University Press, 2007.
Kurniawan, Eka. *Man Tiger.* Translated by Labodalih Sembiring. New York: Verso, 2015.
Landes, David S. *The Wealth and Power of Nations: Why Some Are So Rich and Some So Poor.* New York: Norton, 1998.
Laqueur, Walter. *The New Terrorism: Fanaticism and the Arms of Mass Destruction.* New York: Oxford University Press, 1999.
Levitsky, Steven, and Lucan A. Way. *Competitive Authoritarianism: Hybrid Regimes After the Cold War.* New York: Cambridge University Press, 2010.
Levitsky, Steven, and Daniel Ziblatt. *How Democracies Die.* New York: Crown, 2018.
Levy, Daniel C., and Kathleen Bruhn. "Mexico: Sustained Civilian Rule Without Democracy." In *Politics in Developing Countries: Comparing Experiences with Democracy,* edited by Larry Diamond, Juan J. Linz, and Seymour Martin Lipset, 171–217. Boulder: Lynne Rienner, 1995.
Lewis, Peter M. "Nigeria: Cycles of Crisis, Sources of Resilience." In *Coping with Crisis in African States,* edited by Peter M. Lewis and John W. Harbeson, 147–170. Boulder: Lynne Rienner, 2016.
Leys, Colin. *Underdevelopment in Kenya: The Political Economy of Neo-Colonialism, 1964–1971.* London: Heinemann, 1975.
Lijphart, Arend. *Democracy in Plural Societies: A Comparative Exploration.* New Haven: Yale University Press, 1977.
———. *Patterns of Democracy: Government Forms and Performance in Thirty-Six Countries.* New Haven, CT: Yale University Press, 1999.
Linz, Juan J., and Alfred Stepan. "The Perils of Presidentialism." In *The Global Resurgence of Democracy,* edited by Larry Diamond and Marc F. Plattner, 108–126. Baltimore: Johns Hopkins University Press, 1993.
———. *Problems of Democratic Transition and Consolidation.* Baltimore: Johns Hopkins University Press, 1996.
Lipset, Seymour Martin. *Political Man.* Garden City, NY: Doubleday, 1959.
Lloyd, Alan B. *Ancient Egypt: State and Society.* New York: Oxford University Press, 2014.

Lynch, Marc. *The New Arab Wars: Uprisings and Anarchy in the Middle East.* New York: PublicAffairs, 2016.

Mackey, Sandra. *The Iranians: Persia, Islam, and the Soul of a Nation.* New York: Penguin, 1996.

———. *The Middle East.* 8th ed. Washington, DC: Congressional Quarterly, 1994.

Maier, Karl. *This House Has Fallen: Midnight in Nigeria.* New York: PublicAffairs, 2000.

Mamdani, Mahmood. *Citizen and Subject: Contemporary Africa and the Legacy of Late Colonialism.* Princeton: Princeton University Press, 1996.

Marsot, Afaf Lutfi al-Sayyid. *A History of Egypt: From the Arab Conquest to the Present.* Cambridge: Cambridge University Press, 2007.

Martin, Jacques. *When China Rules the World: The End of the Western World and the Birth of a New Global Order.* New York: Penguin, 2009.

Mazrui, Ali A., ed. *UNESCO General History of Africa: Africa Since 1935.* London: Heinemann, 1993.

McClintock, Cynthia. *Revolutionary Movements in Latin America.* Washington, DC: United States Institute of Peace Press, 1998.

Meyer, Milton W. *Asia: A Concise History.* Lanham: Rowman and Littlefield, 1997.

Mietzner, Marcus. *Democratic Deconsolidation in Southeast Asia.* Cambridge: Cambridge University Press, 2021.

Milanovic, Branko. *Global Inequality: A New Approach for the Age of Globalization.* Cambridge: Harvard University Press, 2016.

Moaveni, Azadeh. *Honeymoon in Tehran: Two Years of Love and Danger in Iran.* New York: Random House, 2009.

Moghadam, Valentine. *Gender and National Identity: Women and Politics in Muslim Societies.* London: Zed, 1994.

Moin, Bager. *Khomeini: Life of the Ayatollah.* New York: St. Martin's, 2000.

Monga, Célestin. *The Anthropology of Anger: Civil Society and Democracy in Africa.* Translated by Linda L. Fleck and Célestin Monga. Boulder: Lynne Rienner, 1996.

Morris, Stephen D. *Political Corruption in Mexico: The Impact of Democratization.* Boulder: Lynne Rienner, 2009.

Mungazi, Dickson A. *Colonial Policy and Conflict in Zimbabwe.* New York: Crane Russak, 1992.

Murphy, Ann Marie. "Indonesia and Globalization." In *East Asia and Globalization,* edited by Samuel S. Kim, 209–232. New York: Rowman and Littlefield, 2000.

Murray, Geoffrey. *China: The Next Superpower—Dilemmas in Change and Continuity.* New York: St. Martin's, 1998.

Nasr, Vali. *The Shia Revival: How Conflicts Within Islam Will Shape the Future.* New York: Norton, 2006.

Nathan, Andrew J. *China's Transition.* New York: Columbia University Press, 1997.

Needham, D. E., Elleck K. Mashingaidze, and Ngwabi Bhebe. *From Iron Age to Independence: A History of Central Africa.* London: Longman, 1985.

The 9/11 Commission Report: Final Report on the National Commission on Terrorist Attacks upon the United States. New York: Norton, 2004.

Nyang'oro, Julius E., and Timothy M. Shaw. "The African State in the Global Economic Context." In *The African State at a Critical Juncture: Between Disintegration and Reconfiguration,* edited by Julius E. Nyang'oro and Timothy M. Shaw, 27–44. Boulder: Lynne Rienner, 1998.

Nye, Joseph, Jr. *Soft Power: The Means to Success in World Politics.* New York: PublicAffairs, 2004.

O'Brien, Kevin J., and Lianjiang Li. *Rightful Resistance in Rural China.* New York: Cambridge University Press, 2006.

O'Gorman, Eleanor. "Writing Women's Wars: Foucaldian Strategies of Engagement." In *Women, Culture, and International Relations,* edited by Vivienne Jabri and Eleanor O'Gorman, 91–116. Boulder: Lynne Rienner, 1999.

Oliver, Roland. *The African Experience.* Boulder: Westview, 1999.

Osman, Tarek. *Egypt on the Brink: From Nasser to Mubarak.* New Haven: Yale University Press, 2010.

Page, Sheila. *Regionalism Among Developing Countries.* New York: St. Martin's, 2000.

Palmer, David Scott. "The Revolutionary Terrorism of Peru's Shining Path." In *Terrorism in Context,* edited by Martha Crenshaw, 249–308. University Park: Pennsylvania State University Press, 1995.

Palmer, Monte. *Comparative Politics: Political Economy, Political Culture, and Political Independence.* Itasca, IL: F. E. Peacock, 1997.

Payne, Leigh A. *Uncivil Movements: The Armed Right Wing and Democracy in Latin America.* Baltimore: Johns Hopkins University Press, 2000.

Paz, Octavio. "Latin America and Democracy." In *Democracy and Dictatorship in Latin America: A Special Publication Devoted Entirely to the Voice and Opinions of Writers from Latin America,* edited by Octavio Paz, Jorge Edwards, Carlos Franqui, et al., 5–17. New York: Foundation for the Independent Study of Social Ideas, 1982.

Peimani, Hooman. *Iran and the United States: The Rise of the West Asian Regional Grouping.* Westport: Praeger, 1999.

Pempel, T. J. "The Developmental Regime in a Changing World Economy." In *The Developmental State,* edited by Meredith Woo-Cumings, 137–181. Ithaca: Cornell University Press, 2001.

Pepinksy, Thomas, R. William Liddle, and Saiful Mujani. *Piety and Public Opinion: Understanding Indonesian Islam.* New York: Oxford University Press, 2018.

Pevehouse, Jon C., and Joshua S. Goldstein. *International Relations.* New York: Pearson, 2020.

Phimister, Ian. *An Economic and Social History of Zimbabwe, 1890–1948.* London: Longman, 1988.

Piketty, Thomas. *Time for Socialism: Dispatches from a World on Fire, 2016–2021.* New Haven: Yale University Press, 2021.

Pomfret, John. *The Beautiful Country and the Middle Kingdom: America and China, 1776 to the Present.* New York: Holt, 2016.

Pourmokhtari, Navid. *Iran's Green Movement: Everyday Resistance, Political Contestation and Social Mobilization.* New York: Routledge, 2021.

Purdey, Jemma, Antje Missbach, and Dave McRae. *Indonesia: State and Society in Transition.* Boulder: Lynne Rienner, 2020.

Pye, Lucian W. *China: An Introduction.* 3rd ed. Boston: Little, Brown, 1984.

Ranger, Terence. *Peasant Consciousness and Guerrilla War in Zimbabwe.* London: Currey, 1985.

Richardson, Eugene T. *Epidemic Illusions: On the Coloniality of Global Public Health.* Cambridge: MIT Press, 2020.

Roberts, Kenneth M. *Deepening Democracy? The Modern Left and Social Movements in Chile and Peru.* Stanford: Stanford University Press, 1998.

Roberts, Mark J. *Khomeini's Incorporation of the Iranian Military.* Washington, DC: Institute for National Strategic Studies, National Defense University, 1996.

Sachs, Jeffrey. *The End of Poverty: Economic Possibilities for Our Time.* New York: Penguin, 2006.

Sadri, Houman. "Iran." In *The Political Role of the Military: An International Handbook,* edited by Constantine P. Danopoulos and Cynthia Watson, 207–222. Westport: Greenwood, 1996.

Said, Edward W. *Reflections on Exile.* Cambridge: Harvard University Press, 2001.

Schelander, Björn, and Kirsten Brown. *Exploring Indonesia: Past and Present.* Honolulu: Center for Southeast Asian Studies, 2000.

Schell, Orville. "Letter from China." *New Yorker,* July 1994. Reprinted in *The China Reader: The Reform Era,* edited by Orville Schell and David Shambaugh, 246–256. New York: Vintage Books, 1999.

Schmitter, Philippe C., and Terry Lynn Karl. "What Democracy Is . . . and Is Not." In *The Global Resurgence of Democracy,* edited by Larry Diamond and Marc F. Plattner, 39–52. Baltimore: Johns Hopkins University Press, 1993.

Schneider, Thomas. *Ancient Egypt in 10 Questions and Answers.* Ithaca: Cornell University Press, 2013.
Shafer, Robert Jones. *A History of Latin America.* Lexington, MA: D. C. Heath, 1978.
Shahri, Sorayya. "Women in Command: A Successful Experience in the National Liberation Army of Iran." In *Frontline Feminisms: Women, War, and Resistance,* edited by Marguerite R. Waller and Jennifer Rycenga, 185–192. New York: Garland, 2000.
Shawcross, William. *Deliver Us from Evil.* New York: Simon and Schuster, 2000.
Siapno, Jacqueline. "Gender, Nationalism, and the Ambiguity of Female Agency in Aceh, Indonesia, and East Timor." In *Frontline Feminisms: Women, War, and Resistance,* edited by Marguerite R. Waller and Jennifer Rycenga, 275–296. New York: Garland, 2000.
Singer, P. W. *Children at War.* New York: Pantheon, 2005.
Skidmore, Thomas E., and Peter H. Smith. *Modern Latin America.* New York: Oxford University Press, 1992.
Skocpol, Theda. *States and Social Revolution: A Comparative Analysis of France, Russia, and China.* New York: Cambridge University Press, 1979.
Smith, Courtney B. *Politics and Process at the United Nations: The Global Dance.* Boulder: Lynne Rienner, 2006.
Smith, Mike. *Boko Haram: Inside Nigeria's Unholy War.* New York: Tauris, 2016.
Soled, Debra E., ed. *China: A Nation in Transition.* Washington, DC: Congressional Quarterly, 1995.
Stiglitz, Joseph E. *Globalization and Its Discontents.* New York: Norton, 2003.
———. *Making Globalization Work.* New York: Norton, 2007.
Stoez, David, Charles Guzzetta, and Mark Lusk. *International Development.* Boston: Allyn and Bacon, 1999.
Sweig, Julia E. *Friendly Fire: Losing Friends and Making Enemies in the Anti-American Century.* New York: PublicAffairs, 2006.
Takeyh, Ray. *Hidden Iran: Paradox and Power in the Islamic Republic.* New York: Time Books, 2006.
Tarrow, Sidney. *Power in Movement: Social Movements and Contentious Politics.* New York: Cambridge University Press, 1998.
Thompson, Carol B. "Beyond the Nation-State? Democracy in Regional Economic Context." In *Democracy and Socialism in Africa,* edited by Robin Cohen and Harry Goulbourne, 216–227. Boulder: Westview, 1991.
Tilly, Charles. "Reflections on the History of European Statemaking." In *The Formation of National States in Western Europe,* edited by Charles Tilly, 3–83. Princeton: Princeton University Press, 1975.
Ullman, Richard H. "Human Rights: Toward International Action." In *Enhancing Global Human Rights,* edited by Jorge I. Domínguez, Nigel S. Rodley, Bryce Wood, and Richard Falk, 1–20. New York: McGraw-Hill, 1979.
Valenzuela, Arturo. "External Actors in the Transitions to Democracy in Latin America." In *Pathways to Democracy: The Political Economy of Democratic Transitions,* edited by James F. Hollifield and Calvin Jillson, 116–129. New York: Routledge, 2000.
Vanderhill, Rachel. *Autocracy and Resistance in the Internet Age.* Boulder: Lynne Rienner, 2020.
Verba, Sidney. "Comparative Political Culture." In *Political Culture and Political Development,* edited by Sidney Verba and Lucian Pye, 512–560. Princeton: Princeton University Press, 1965.
Verba, Sidney, Victor H. Nie, and Jae-on Kim. *Participation and Political Equality: A Seven-Nation Comparison.* New York: Cambridge University Press, 1978.
Villalon, Leonardo A. "The African State at the End of the Twentieth Century: Parameters of the Critical Juncture." In *The African State at a Critical Juncture,* edited by Leonardo A. Villalon and Phillip A. Huxtable, 3–26. Boulder: Lynne Rienner, 1998.
Werbner, Richard P. "In Memory: A Heritage of War in Southwestern Zimbabwe." In *Society in Zimbabwe's Liberation War,* edited by Ngwabi Bhebe and Terence Ranger, 192–205. Oxford: Currey, 1996.

West, Guida, and Rhoda Lois Blumberg, eds. *Women and Social Protest.* New York: Oxford University Press, 1990.

Wiarda, Howard J., and Harvey F. Kline. *An Introduction to Latin American Politics and Development.* Boulder: Westview, 2001.

Wills, A. J. *An Introduction to the History of Central Africa: Zambia, Malawi, and Zimbabwe.* New York: Oxford University Press, 1985.

Wilson, Frank L. *Concepts and Issues in Comparative Politics: An Introduction to Comparative Analysis.* Upper Saddle River, NJ: Prentice Hall, 1996.

Woo, Wing Thye, Stephen Parker, and Jeffrey Sachs, eds. *Economies in Transition: Comparing Asia and Eastern Europe.* Cambridge: MIT Press, 1997.

Wright, David C. *The History of China.* Westport: Greenwood, 2001.

Wright, Stephen. *Nigeria: Struggle for Stability and Status.* Boulder: Westview, 1998.

Yu Kien-hong, Peter. "The Party and the Army in China: Figuring Out Their Relationship Once and for All." Working Paper no. 7. Singapore: East Asian Institute, 1998.

Zahedi, Dariush. *The Iranian Revolution Then and Now: Indicators of Regime Instability.* Boulder: Westview, 2000.

Zakaria, Fareed. *The Post-American World.* New York: Norton, 2008.

Zartman, I. William. "Introduction: Posing the Problem of State Collapse." In *Collapsed States: The Disintegration and Restoration of Legitimate Authority,* edited by I. William Zartman, 1–14. Boulder: Lynne Rienner, 1995.

Zenn, Jacob. *Unmasking Boko Haram: Exploring Global Jihad in Nigeria.* Boulder: Lynne Rienner, 2020.

Zhang, Maria Yue, and Bruce W. Stening. *China 2.0: The Transformation of an Emerging Superpower—and the New Opportunities.* Singapore: Wiley, 2010.

Index

About the Book

December Green and Laura Luehrmann show how history, economics, and politics converge to create the realities of life in the global south.

In this new edition, the authors continue to offer an innovative blend of theory and empirical material as they introduce the politics of what was once called the "third world." They consistently link theoretical concepts to a set of eight contemporary case studies: China, Egypt, Indonesia, Iran, Mexico, Nigeria, Peru, and Zimbabwe.

A central theme throughout the new edition is how the Covid-19 pandemic has worked as a hinge event—accelerating troubling trends and amplifying long-standing socioeconomic and political problems.

Other features of the fifth edition include

- Thoroughly revised chapters on economic and development issues
- An update on regime transitions and the rise of authoritarianism
- Analysis of the status of conflict, terrorist movements, and weapons proliferation
- An expanded discussion of populism and nationalism in both the economic and political spheres
- A comparison of the range of experiences and responses to the pandemic

The result is a text that has been successfully designed to challenge students' preconceptions, arouse their curiosity, and foster critical thinking.

December Green and **Laura Luehrmann** are professors of political science at Wright State University.